Traditions in Architecture

Africa, America, Asia, and Oceania

DORA P. CROUCH

JUNE G. JOHNSON

New York   Oxford
OXFORD UNIVERSITY PRESS
2001

Oxford University Press

Oxford   New York
Athens   Auckland   Bangkok   Bogotá   Buenos Aires   Calcutta
Cape Town   Chennai   Dar es Salaam   Delhi   Florence   Hong Kong   Istanbul
Karachi   Kuala Lumpur   Madrid   Melbourne   Mexico City   Mumbai
Nairobi   Paris   São Paulo   Singapore   Taipei   Tokyo   Toronto   Warsaw

and associated companies in
Berlin   Ibadan

Published by Oxford University Press, Inc.
198 Madison Avenue, New York, New York, 10016

Library of Congress Cataloging-in-Publication Data
Crouch, Dora P.
Traditions in architecture: Africa, America, Asia, and Oceania / Dora P. Crouch
and June G. Johnson.
p.   cm.
Includes bibliographical references and index.
ISBN   978-0-19-508891-5 (paper)

1. Vernacular architecture—Research—Africa.   2. Vernacular architecture—Asia
3. Vernacular architecture—Oceania.   4. Vernacular architecture—Research—America.
I. Johnson, June G.   II. Title.

NA208 .C76 2000
720'.9—dc21   99-039260

7 9 8

Printed in the United States of America on acid-free paper

To our students, from whom and for whom we have learned so much.

And to the University of California, Los Angeles, in gratitude for the education that prepared us to teach beginning courses in all fields of art history, so that we were eventually ready to write this book.

⊞ Contents

⊞ Preface

In the late 1980s, we met occasionally at conventions of the Society of Architectural Historians or the College Art Association. We talked of our experiences in teaching an introductory survey of architecture from outside the Euro-American tradition. We also commiserated with each other over the difficulties of teaching this material without a textbook and with only scattered resources in our college libraries. Available materials ranged in language and quantity from abundant materials in English for the architecture of India to scattered materials about the architecture of many peoples—but in languages that most American freshmen cannot read—to the total absence of material for the architectural history of Oceania. Remembering this problem, we have supplied not only a bibliography of all sources consulted at the end of the book, but a set of Suggested Readings at the end of each chapter, chosen because they are relatively easy reading, in English, and likely to be widely available.

We were not alone in finding the architecture of all the world as interesting as that of European and European-based American architecture. Increased respect for diversity in architecture, as in culture, has been characteristic of the 1990s. Ordinary people are now living in culturally diverse states, such as California, where no ethnic-racial group is a majority of the population, and they are traveling to Tahiti for honeymoons, to Africa on business, to Japan and the Middle East on religious quests. As soon as this book was announced, colleagues at many colleges and universities told us how eager they were to teach this material. Part of such professional interest is the dawning realization that other cultures may have architectural answers we lack or have asked architectural questions we have not even thought of.

The use and discussion of the materials presented here will, we think, broaden the readers' understanding and appreciation of the architectural accomplishments of all sorts of peoples. The book deals with nearly a hundred topics. Some units examine the same building from two different perspectives, as when the traditional Japanese house is considered first as a constructional problem and later as the container for a space—*the tokonoma*—of high aesthetic merit and some residual religious content.

Extended immersion in this material has made us realize that we still lack not only data but methods for handling it. For instance, little work has been done so far within or among cultures on the comparative costs of private and public buildings. The energetics method pioneered by Abrams and discussed in the last chapter has great potential, and we urge that detailed studies be done of all kinds of architecture by this method. The attentive reader will notice other gaps in knowledge. If these gaps are attended to and knowledge increases, in the next generation it may be possible to write not an introduction to world architecture, but a comparative and comprehensive study that will finally lay A. Bannister-Fletcher's tome to rest. Fortunately, we brought to this task years of travel and well-honed skills of investigation. Even more fortunately, we were assisted again and again by experts in many disciplines who provided material and illustrations, served as readers who reduced errors and pointed out improvements, and warned us against complacency or the use of out-of-date sources. From our resulting position "on the shoulders of giants" (Saint Alfred the Great), we offer sincere thanks. Special thanks are due to those who added to our knowledge and understanding of so many topics. We are especially grateful to Charles Ortloff, Lon Polk, C.B. Kristan-Graham, A.F. Aveni, L.A. Barba P., R. Bon, N. Alsayyad, G. Hirsh, C. Klein, E.C. Krupp, K. Correa, N. Nabokov and R. Easton, N. Neuerburg, S. Markel and J. Lipostad at LACMA, J. and M. Thapa, V.L. Scarborough, N.S. Steinhardt, R. Knowles, C. Asher, S. Blier, E. Cameron, E. Colson, D. Chakrabarti, H. Engel, W. Ferguson, O. Grabar, M. Harden, E. MacDougall, Ü. Ozis, J. P. Protzen, J. Reynolds, M. Robertson, F. Sahba, and Y. Watanabe and the reference librarians at the research library of UCLA. Later in the process, editorial suggestions of great value came from Cynthia Field, the anonymous reviewer for Oxford University Press, Rebecca Steffof, and our editor Joyce Berry. Joyce Berry and the staff at Oxford collaborated with us to offer to the public a useful book. Working with such professionals fulfills an author's dreams.

We are also grateful for the personal assistance of Robert Johnson and Daniel Crouch; the students' views of Jennifer Rainville and Marshall Crouch; the photographic assistance of Joseph Bevans; and, most of all, the creative cartography of Chase Langford, who turned rough sketches and indistinct photocopies into elegant illustrations.

⊞ Notes on the Text, Sources, and Appendix

We have used a minimum of diacritical marks. Standard spelling for other languages is often complicated by transliteration into French, German, or Spanish before a second transliteration into English. When several English possibilities exist, we followed our major sources but also give alternate spellings when they are well known. As unfamiliar technical words are introduced, they are defined; all of these words are presented in the Glossary. Words found in *Webster's Collegiate Dictionary* (1933 or later) are not defined unless we use a specialized meaning. Alternately, readers may consult their computer program's thesaurus.

We give measurements purely to provide a sense of the size and scale of structures. Measurements are in both English (inches, feet, or yards or miles, acres, or pounds) and in metric (meters, kilometers, hectares, or kilograms) terms, although we rounded many figures because feet and meters are incommensurable. Both the English and metric systems, being Eurocentric, have no connection with the units of measurement used by the various cultures we discuss.

Dates are labeled B.C.E. (Before the Common Era), C.E. (Common Era), or occasionally B.P. (Before the Present). Unlabeled terms, such as *seventeenth century,* refer to either B.C.E. or C.E. according to the context. We adopted this usage in the effort to be less Euro-American-centric. Dates for Islamic references are in the Common Era, rather than the religious dating of Islam (which equates 622 C.E. with the first year of the Islamic era).

Each section of a chapter has an abbreviated list of sources; each chapter has a short list of Suggested Readings that we think will be most useful to students and most easily available. A full Bibliography of all sources quoted, as well as background reading, is at the back of the book.

The Appendix has maps of Africa, North America, Central and northern South America, Asia, and Oceania, the Spread of Buddhism, and the Spread of Islam. Some chapters also contain maps. These maps do not include modern political boundaries; they include only the places we discuss.

The Appendix also has tables of materials.

⊞ Introduction

The outcome of any serious research [is] to make two questions grow
where only one grew before.

T. Veblen (1934)

All cultures use some sort of buildings. Our goal has been not only to illuminate the buildings of many of the world's peoples but to show the interaction between culture and architecture, for we agree with anthropologist Hauser-Schäublin, who wrote of New Guinea, "Building traditions are as much a specific cultural heritage of a group as is language and perhaps music."

Our observations of these interactions cannot be culture-free. Although we proceed with respect for what traditional theory and practice can teach us, acknowledging the importance of sacred and symbolic meaning in traditional societies, we expect intellectual and emotional conflict between traditional architectures and Western understanding. We have striven for accuracy but probably have not avoided all errors and misunderstandings. Yet the "so-called distortions of . . . observers and participants are more usefully taken as values than as errors. They represent the cultural forces at play," as Sahlins and Barrére remind us in their discussion of Hawaiian architecture.

We have selected and arranged examples of architecture to illustrate themes, noting the urgency and ubiquity of certain basic architectural solutions, such as housing, compared with later developments, such as the Friday mosque or the Chinese garden. Our examples, we believe, reflect tradition, human diversity, and creativity as expressed in architecture. But although we have adopted a thematic format, as historians we are a bit sorry that it precludes a chronological survey. In most cases, we use the "historical present" tense, sidestepping the thorny is-

sues of how much modernization has taken place in a traditional culture and when or whether modernism in architecture became dominant; those are questions for another book.

We make few deductive generalizations about culture. Rather, our approach has been to describe, detail by detail, how architecture forms the framework for people's lives. We have tried to give enough information about each topic to permit an understanding of the architecture, but this is not primarily a book of anthropology, sociology, or psychology. In many cases, we have not done the original research, but we have tried to indicate what is known and, when possible, the nature of current or potential research.

WHAT IS ARCHITECTURE?

Like *history*, the term *architecture* has both broad and strict meanings. In the widest sense, architecture is everything built or constructed or dug out for human occupation or use. A more restricted definition would emphasize the artistic and aesthetic aspects of construction. A third, and still more limited, definition would say that architecture is what specially trained architects do or make.

In this book, architecture includes three categories of built elements: professionally designed and built monuments; the houses and other structures erected by traditional building tradesmen; and structures, either fixed or movable, that ordinary people build for their own use, some of which attain the level of memorable art. We define architecture as "buildings that have been carefully

1

thought through before they were made."[1] We have broadened the concept of architecture to include residential spaces, such as houseboats, and natural objects that people use culturally, such as certain mountains.

Architectural history is local history. Unique combinations of local materials and methods, cultures and settings, clients and builders create a built environment that cannot be reduced to generalizations. In this sense, architectural history is like literature and unlike algebra. Mathematics evolves by adding one timeless and locationless truth to another, but literature and architecture have no such disembodied truths. New books and new buildings draw on "gene pools" of existing ideas, combining them in ways that are ever new yet related to tradition. Why is the architecture of one place different from that of somewhere else? Partly because of variations in climate, available building materials, and the like and partly because people in different cultures have different histories, beliefs, and ideas that fuse with their material resources and constraints to make a distinctive local architectural tradition.

Architecture is immensely diverse, as are the social arrangements that it serves. Nomads need movable homes. Kings need palaces. The religious need special structures . . . or they don't. Perhaps they simply contemplate a great natural feature like Mount Taylor in New Mexico (see Chapter 7), Mount Fuji in Japan, or Wu Tai Mountain in China to satisfy their religious impulses. The diversity of the built-unbuilt environment reflects an infinity of variations in human responses to constraints and possibilities.

Every society lives in the tension created by the intersection of the natural environment and human culture, and each develops its own architectural responses to that tension. D. G. Saile, an architect who studied the prehistoric pueblo architecture of the American Southwest, has shown that neither the simplicity nor the date of architecture limits its expressive quality. In its concentration on spatial organization and the communicative aspects of space, pueblo architecture reveals intangible qualities of the society that constructed it. Relationships among floor surfaces; changes in levels; walls; ceilings; columns; fixed elements, such as fireplaces and benches; and movable objects give the sensitive observer great insights into the conceptual, behavioral, and physical lives of the pueblo peoples. These architectural elements are both physical, or utilitarian and climate related, and protolinguistic, or connotative and associational. For example, the different sizes of the settlements Saile studied suggested a hierarchical organization of society, a standard anthropological assumption. But the same form can have more than one meaning. A space that is enclosed by a wall in such a way as to be easily defended is not the same as a space simply defined by a wall. Nor is the concept *wall* limited to walls that are parts of buildings, as we see when we look at the Great Wall of China.

The recent work of architect-sculptor J. Turrell shows us that there are ways of organizing reality other than the familiar Euro-American ways. Turrell began in the 1970s to dig at the "roots of perceptual reality" to make sculpture out of light, as C. Adcock explains. He crafted hard-edged templates and shone concentrated light through them. What the viewer perceived as a flat wall was actually an inner space; what seemed a protruding shape was made entirely of light. Carefully controlled light and background yielded images "composed of perception." Turrell's work distills and enhances architectural space; sculptor Robert Morris says of such rich austerity, "Simplicity of shape does not equate with simplicity of experience." As A. I. T. Chang points out in relating architecture to the Chinese worldview called the Tao (see Chapter 15), "the emptiness is in no way insufficient or meager." Turrell's perceptual and aesthetic exploration in the Arizona desert has stimulated our own examination of the variety of human solutions to architectural problems. His efforts to manipulate the landscape have precedents in other times and places.

The methods, needs, and ideas of people in Africa, Asia, Oceania, and Native America sometimes overlap with those handled in modern Euro-American architecture, but they often are quite different. These differences can make mutual understanding difficult. How and why are "they" different? What we think we know can prevent learning. As D. A. Freidel writes of Maya architecture, "The problem is that our empirical building blocks are often conceptual stumbling blocks." But differences can also highlight human potential that Euro-American solutions overlook, conceal, or trample. Certain baffling problems in our own societies may have solutions in the architectures of other peoples. We can no longer assume, as some people did in the nineteenth century, that "different" means "inferior."

TRADITION AND ARCHITECTURE

"What really is the nature of 'tradition' and what [may] the idea of tradition mean to southeast Asian peoples

---

[1]Our thanks to Patrick Quinn, architect and teacher of architecture at Rensselaer Polytechnic Institute, who first formulated this definition.

themselves?" asks R. Waterson in *The Living House*. For most of the peoples she has studied in Southeast Asia and the Pacific islands, it takes two generations for something to become traditional—although the word *tradition* seems to evoke an age-old custom, opposed conceptually to modernity and change. In its roots, however, tradition really means "handing down." It is the dynamic process by which knowledge passes from generation to generation, especially by word of mouth. Waterson argues:

> Tradition, like history, is something that is continually being recreated and remodeled in the present, even [though] it is represented as fixed and unchanging. . . . There is no architecture without inviolable rules of construction and interpretation that are formed in the course of history for every people by means of a more or less complex convergence and superposition of elements . . . and associations . . . [which lead to and act as] explanation of the world.

The Minangkabau people of West Sumatra, for example, are much given to discussion and analysis of their own *adat* (traditional customs) and social patterns. They describe their tradition as that which "neither rots in the rain nor cracks in the sun." Among them, man is considered mobile and woman sedentary, which ties in nicely with female ownership of houses. For several centuries, the Minangkabau have been Muslim, yet they have maintained matrilineal inheritance. Their tradition is always changing, and they are comfortable with its ambiguity.

Knowledge of architectural history varies as greatly in traditional as in modern cultures. Information may be oral, written, or printed. It may be generally known or closely guarded by an elite, hidden from foreigners or shared with neighbors and visiting scholars, as M. H. Nooter pointed out about Ndebele attitudes toward their own art (see Chapter 13). Indigenous or foreign researchers may be content with simple description as a first step or as an end in itself, or they may construct ambitious analytical or theoretical histories.

TOWARD A NEW ARCHITECTURAL HISTORY

We do not offer a comprehensive theory for the interdisciplinary study of architectural history—but we suggest that one is needed. The old Euro-American lens for architectural history, with its emphasis on the relations of form and content, is inadequate to the study of traditional architecture of the rest of the world. Like anthropologist

L. E. Talay and philosopher S. Harding, we question the utility of current Western models for interpreting the past and agree that alternative approaches may work better.

The classic questions of Euro-American architectural history take on new significance when we examine the architecture of the rest of the world. "Who" is not just the patron but also the builders and users. "Where" may be a whole region or a tiny site, a public or a private plot. "When" may be the brief length of a life, the reign of a dynasty, or even a whole era. "How" goes beyond the description of method to consider technical analysis and intellectual and historical influences. And "why" must add social processes and economic constraints to individual motives. "Why am I interested?" is not the same as "Why did they do it?"

When we were learning architectural history in the 1960s and 1970s, formal questions dominated the field. This was logical, for formal inquiries had been fruitful in art history studies of paintings and sculpture, especially in matters of period and style. In turn, information about period and style was useful in understanding and evaluating all kinds of art objects, including architecture.

Today architectural historians are still interested in the chronology of architectural development and in formal issues of style, but we also investigate a whole string of additional questions, as E. Kleinbauer's and D. Prezziosi's exemplary studies of architectural history, in 1971 and 1989, respectively, demonstrate. From the intellectual wars of the semioticists (who deal with signs and symbols) and the deconstructionists (who use critical analysis to expose unquestioned assumptions and inconsistencies) to the protechnological interests of the Historic American Engineering Record, architectural history has been part of the knowledge explosion of the past three decades.

Architecture, having multiple meanings, has required multiplicity in investigation. In this book, we view various examples through the lenses of archaeology, anthropology, sociology, geography, psychology, and engineering in addition to formal architectural and urban history. Often, when faced with anomalous information, we have been forced to find a new method, agreeing with I. Frazier that, "When reviewing experimental data, pay particular attention to the result not expected. The crazy data point might be the most important result, the breakthrough, the basis for a whole new invention."

We began with no preconceptions about what we should include, except that we wanted, as much as possible, to write about buildings and places that we had experienced in person. We have tried, however, to use new intellectual tools, when applicable. We would have liked to make greater use of energetics (see Chapter 17) as an analytic tool, but not enough site-specific research has been done. Another intellectual tool proved easier to wield: We have used gender to stand for the many issues of which architectural historians are becoming newly aware. The developing understanding of the women's viewpoint is here an intellectual, not a political, stance; we use it not to oppose other views but to enrich the discourse. But we cannot entirely set aside our own subjectivity in this matter or any other. Our opinions about how men and women do and should relate to each other have undoubtedly influenced our choice of examples and our selection of other analytical tools. Our answers cannot help being partial, in both senses of the word; we surmise that partiality is inevitable and inherent in every explication, gender related or not. We encourage the critical reader to note and ponder the less obvious examples of editorial bias that may have crept in despite our efforts to be both objective and respectful.

Our purposes in writing this book were to open doors for students and to suggest new research for scholars. We also wanted to share our fascination with and admiration for certain buildings, types, solutions, and builders. Our approach is a kind of democratic architectural history that incorporates both monumental and vernacular structures, both professional and amateur builders. By counterbalancing the usual Euro-American architectural history, we hope to stimulate new studies outside the Euro-American tradition. And we hope that another result will be an increased sense of world community, attained through recognition of the achievements of diverse cultures.

SOURCES: J. W. VOGT (1978); ADCOCK (1990); A. I. T. CHANG (1956); I. FRAZIER, QUOTING HIS FATHER, 1994: 361; FREIDEL (1983); HARDING (1991); HAUSER-SCHÄUBLIN (1990); KLEINBAUER (1971); NOOTER (1993); PREZZIOSI (1989); SAHLINS AND BARRÉRE (1992); SAILE (1978); TALAY (1994); J. W. VOGT (1978); R. WATERSON (1990).

SUGGESTED READINGS

Adcock, C. 1990. *James Turrell: The Art of Light and Space.* Berkeley: University of California Press. A beautifully written account of new ways of perceiving and exhibiting space and light by one of the most creative space handlers of our time.

Cordell, L. S., and F. Plog. 1979. "Escaping the Confines of Normative Thought." *American Antiquity* 44: 405–29. Philosophers examine the perceived necessity of accepting normative thought as the only "natural" way of thinking.

Crouch, D. 1984. *History of Architecture: Stonehenge to Skyscrapers.* New York: McGraw-Hill. See the last chapter, "Non-Western Architecture," for the first steps toward the present volume.

Fage, J. D. 1981. "The Development of African Historiography." In *General History of Africa: 1. Methodology and African Prehistory,* edited by J. Ki-Zerbo, 25–42. London: Heinemann Educational Books. African historiography resembles rapid-motion photography, so quickly is it changing.

Hodder, J., ed. 1978. *The Spatial Organization of Culture.* London: Duckworth. The seminal comparison of how different cultures organize their living spaces.

Kent, S. 1990. *Domestic Architecture and the Use of Space.* Cambridge, England: Cambridge University Press. Intellectual tools for analyzing the use of space developed rapidly between Hodder's 1978 book and this one of 1990, and the development continues.

Kostof, S. 1985. *History of Architecture.* New York: Oxford University Press. Probably the greatest of the 1980s texts on this topic, with much information and an overriding pro-urban framework. Written by one who had himself changed cultures—a Greek from Turkey who became an American.

Lee, D. 1966. "Lineal and Nonlineal Codifications of Reality." In *Explorations in Communication,* edited by E. Carpenter and M. McLuhan, 136–54. Boston: Beacon Press. Humans need to codify reality so they can act on a daily basis without having to think about every aspect of the world each time they encounter it. Anthropologist Lee studied African (specifically, Basarwa) society and contrasts African with Euro-American ideas.

Pratt, M. L. 1986. "Scratches on the Face of the Country; or what Mr. Barrow Saw in the Land of the Bushmen." In *"Race," Writing, and Difference,* edited by H. L. Gates, Jr., 138–63. Chicago: University of Chicago Press. An analysis of how an oblivious European recorded his mid-nineteenth-century visit to the Kalahari.

Talay, L. E. 1994. "Indiana Joans." *Archaeology.* (May–June): 60–63. Would archaeology be different if women's standards were the norm?

Vogt, J. W. 1978. "Sacred Space, Architectural Tradition, and the Contemporary Designer." In ERDA (Environmental Design Research Association) *Proceedings* 8:47–53. The questions that arise when a Euro-American designs for those outside his or her own tradition and some suggestions for solutions.

PART I

Multiplicity and Continuity in Tradition

Architectural historians use many investigative tools from the wider discipline of art history. With these tools, they define the forms of buildings, seek the origins of those forms, and relate them to both iconography—the symbolic representation of meanings—and iconology—the historical analysis and interpretive study of symbols in their contexts. For example, Chapter 1 explores the relations between form and content in the architecture of several Asian religious buildings. As often happens, people adapt forms that developed for one religion—for example, Hinduism—to serve other religions, including Buddhism. To complicate matters, Buddhism took many forms as it spread to countries far from its origin in Nepal. These variants of the religion were reflected in new architectural forms.

But the student of architecture must look beyond the surface of a building and ask how it came to take that particular form in that particular place. How did its builders acquire their knowledge of architectural forms and construction methods? In Europe, building is often the province of professional architects and engineers who work with artisans at many levels of skill and responsibility. In traditional societies outside the Euro-American tradition, however, construction activity was and is organized according to quite different customs, as is seen in Chapter 2. People in widely separated societies have developed ways of transferring building knowledge both through personal contact and through written materials, such as symbolic diagrams and construction manuals. (The Industrial Revolution and the subsequent modernist movement have greatly affected building practices in many traditional cultures; we focus, however, on traditional methods, rather than on the ways in which these methods have changed and continue to change.)

As we move into the world of traditional architecture—the great variety of forms, purposes, and methods reflected in the structures of Africa, America, Asia, and Oceania—we must avoid reading Euro-American theories or purposes into other architectures. Twentieth-century Europe and North America witnessed many arguments about the proper relationship between form and content in architecture, but we hesitate to ascribe that content to forms built by other societies. Because the purpose of construction affects both its form and its content, we try to be explicit about the purpose of each structure we examine.

1

Form and Content

Some of the oldest surviving structures in Asia are religious buildings. To the architectural historian, they are of interest in terms of form and in relation to their religious and cultural contexts.

EARLY SHRINES, INDIA

India's earliest temples served the prehistoric Vedic religion that we know in its late form as Brahmanism or Hinduism. The temples were made of ephemeral materials, and little has survived. Indian religious architecture achieved greater permanence around the sixth century B.C.E., when two new faiths arose: Jainism, which was an offshoot of Brahmanism, and Buddhism, which also shared some cultural and religious elements of Brahmanism, to which it is related in roughly the same way that Christianity and Islam are related to Judaism. Both Jains and Buddhists created religious structures of permanent materials, either faced with stone or carved into living rock. These structures linked the region's architectural past and its future: They suggest what the vanished earlier sanctuaries were like, and they influenced later Hindu builders.

Caves: Lomas Rishi, Barabar Hills, and Chaitya Hall, Karli

The earliest surviving religious shrines in India are in caves. Why? Since prehistoric times, people have sought protection from the elements and from enemies in caves. In India caves are a logical, permanent solution to the problem of shelter, offering relief from oppressive summer heat and torrential monsoon rains, and are protected places for spiritual purposes as well. Natural caves often resembled the freestanding, barrel-vaulted shrines of wood and thatch built earlier, from the second millennium to the seventh century B.C.E.

Other caves were man made to serve as temples. Among the best preserved of these caves is Lomas Rishi in the Barabar Hills of northeastern India (see Fig 1.1a; see also the map of Asia in the Appendix). The cave, carefully carved into a high cliff, was a locus of worship for the Ajivikas, an early group of Jain ascetics. Its most imposing feature is the entrance screen, a decorated arch surrounding the doorway that includes a curved eave with a procession of elephants in bas-relief approaching one of the sacred mounds called stupas. Elephants and stupas

7

Figure 1.1. a. *Entrance to Lomas Rishi Cave, India. The horseshoe arch of the stone cave, with details that imitate wood, preserves the form of prehistoric shrines made of perishable materials.*

alike figure largely in the sculpture of the region. As early as the Harappa civilization of the Indus Valley in the third and second millennia B.C.E., elephant motifs occurred on commemorative seals, and at the end of the first millennium C.E., the stupa occurs again at Borobudur in Java (see Chapter 5) among many other places.

The method used by the stonemasons at Lomas Rishi was repeated in scores of locations. Once the builders had selected the site of the sanctuary, they marked the shape of its entrance on the cliff. Working from the top, masons carved the vault downward, removing the rubble through the entrance, a method that required no scaffolding (compare with the rock-cut churches of Ethiopia, see Chapter 5).

Why dig a cave when India has many natural caves? Spaces cut by human effort into living rock serve religious

Figure 1.1. b. *Interior of one of several caves at Ellora, site of a monastery that was begun in the fifth century* C.E. *and climaxed in the eighth ceentury. A large statue of Buddha sits in front of a stupa that was cut from the living rock, as are the ribs of the vault.*

purposes at several levels. Like natural caves, they provide shelter, but they are also metaphors for the experience of religious growth. The effort of deliberately carving out a cave temple parallels the conscious effort of opening the mind to cosmic enlightenment as described in the Vedas:

> . . . the Supreme, hidden in the cave
> Where the universe assumes one single form . . .
> *Quoted by B. Bāumer (1991)*

Holy men of all faiths have lived—and still live—in caves. Many cultures view the cave in metaphysical terms as humanity's place of origin (see the discussions of Teotihuacán, Mexico, in Chapters 7 and 11). Mysterious and secret, caves can be seen as sources of infinite possibility, places where individuals may achieve enlightenment. The hollow void in the rock is the physical equivalent of the cave of the heart where Buddhist initiation takes place.

Man-made caves also served the needs of both pilgrims and resident monks. One example not far from Bombay is the Buddhist cave temple at Karli in the Western Ghats, the mountain edge of the Deccan plateau. Karli dates from the first century C.E. (see Fig. 1.2). Far more elaborate than the shrine at Lomas Rishi, it is the finest of the sculptured cave temples. Karli is large; its interior measures 124 feet long, 45 feet wide, and 45 feet high (38 by 14 by 14 meters). Of the pair of massive columns that once stood before the entrance. only one survives. Behind it, along the outer edge of the porch step, is a row of columns and then a vestibule with richly carved side walls. Sculptures of human figures, probably added to the walls later, include the seated Buddha, an image that would not have been considered appropriate when the facade was first built. The inner facade, visually similar to Lomas Rishi's screen wall, consists of three doorways in a lower wall topped by an upper gallery, with a horseshoe-shaped teak window above the gallery.

The main ritual space has a high central section and lower flanking aisles to accommodate processional rituals. Pillars of basalt, a hard volcanic rock that can occur naturally in angular columnar form, divide the nave from the aisles. Their capitals are carved with images of people and lions. Above, wooden ribs meet their stone replicas articulating the vault, one of the latest surviving examples in India of such a use of stone and wood together. In the apse or semicircular recess opposite the doorway, the ribs converge to a point over the ritual focus, a stupa almost 25 feet (7.6 meters) in diameter, cut from the living rock. Its umbrella-like finial is made of wood. (Compare with the interior of the cave at Ellora; see Fig. 1.1b.)

Cave temples were associated with Buddhist monasteries called *viharas*. Each vihara consisted of cells with a dining hall and an assembly hall, all arranged around a central courtyard. Viharas were sometimes freestanding, sometimes cut out of rock. Twenty-nine rock-cut monasteries, for example, were discovered in the limestone cliffs at Ajanta during the nineteenth century. They had been carved between the first century B.C.E and the seventh century C.E. Famous murals on their interior walls illuminate the lives and beliefs of the monks who once lived there.

The cave shrine was a continuing tradition in Indian religion. Indians carved cave temples until the thirteenth century C.E. or later, and such temples became a hallmark of Buddhism as it spread along trade routes into Central Asia and then China, where worshippers built cave temples and monasteries in cliffs. Because of their resemblance to long-vanished prototypes, these shrines now serve as texts for the study of early architecture in this region.

SOURCES: BAUMER (1991), ROWLAND (1977), SNODGRASS (1985).

The Stupa Form: Great Stupa, Sanchi

Certain architectural forms make intangible qualities of belief tangible; a structure can be the intellectual bridge between the visible and the invisible. When people copy and spread that structure's formal elements, they also spread the beliefs that informed it. The imposing domed form of the stupa (see Figs. 1.3, 1.4, and 1.5), with many variations in numerous Asian locations, correlates with the spread of Buddhism throughout Asia and beyond.

Buddhism originated with Siddhartha Gautama, the Buddha, or Enlightened One. Born in 563 B.C.E. at Lumbini in what is now southwestern Nepal, Gautama was an Indian prince born to the religion of Brahmanism. He renounced worldly life and its obligations—his wife, child, and throne—to devote his life to religious contemplation. At the age of thirty-five, he attained spiritual enlightenment while sitting under a banyan tree at Bodh Gaya. He soon promulgated a new religion based on his enlighten-

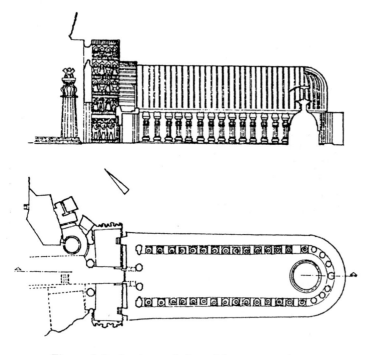

Figure 1.2. *Section and plan of the cave temple in Karli, India. The small stupa at the right end and the ribs of the vault are carved from the living rock. The vestibule and columns on the left are described in the text.*

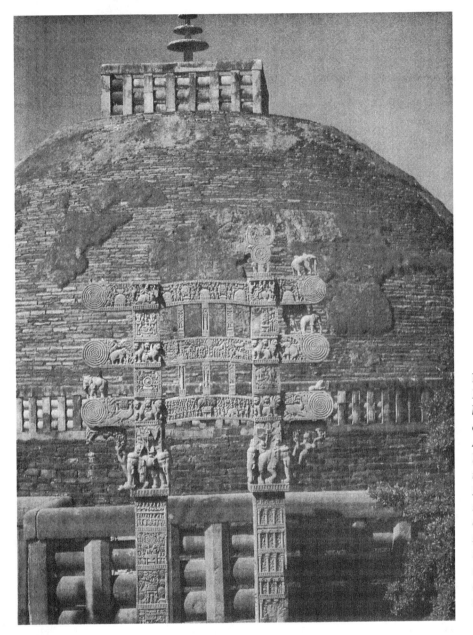

Figure 1.3. *Great Stupa, Sanchi, India. The stupa, an earth mound built over a relic of Buddha, was encased in stone by the Emperor Asoka in 237–32* B.C.E., *and enlarged with a stone casing during the next two or three centuries, Many auxiliary structures, such as stone fences and gates (seen here), embellished it, and both smaller stupas and monasteries were added to the precinct. Originally wooden, the gate was remade in stone, carved (according to an inscription) by workers in ivory and gold.*

ment. His disciples became the first Buddhist monks. The teachings of the Buddha, which emphasize moral conduct and spiritual concentration to achieve nirvana, or ultimate peace, attracted many people because they were more democratic and tolerant than Brahmanism. When the Buddha died in about 480 B.C.E. after a long life, his followers cremated him and deposited his relics in a traditional earthen mound called a stupa.

Until that time, stupas were reserved for the powerful, like similar mounds in many ancient civilizations. But after the sixth century, architects began to use the stupa as a metaphor for Buddha's person and teaching. A cubic base symbolizes his torso, the dome his head; these two elements together stand for the world of desire. The pinnacle or mast is like the symbolic protuberance on the Buddha's skull that indicated spiritual wisdom gained in

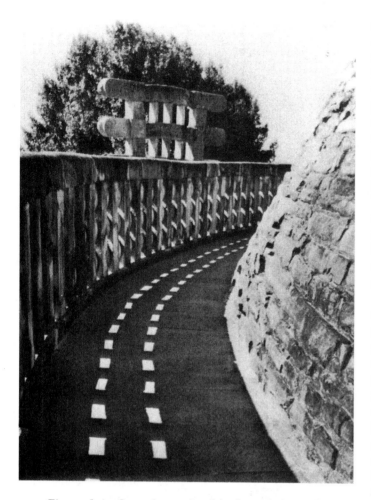

Figure 1.4. *Great Stupa, Sanchi. The ambulatory between the gate and the mound, clearly showing the stone casing of the mound.*

symbolic use of basic forms like the square, circle, cube, and sphere. All are solid forms, not hollow. These elements are also found in the Indian architectural tradition from which Buddhism emerged (see the discussion of Hindu and Jain Shrines). The three main types of stupas are the hemisphere (Sanchi), the terrace (Borobudur; see Chapter 5) or the stepped terrace/cosmic mountain (Angkor Wat; see Chapter 11), and the tower (pagodas; see Chapter 16). Because the stupa is where the visible and invisible meet, a believer sees it as enclosing a mountain or sees the tower as enclosed by an invisible stupa. The meshed forms refer to two aspects of reality, but only one is visible. The steps of the enclosed terrace-mountain and the roof lines of the pagoda tower refer to both the world-upon-world of Buddhist cosmology and to the levels of advancement as the believer attains Buddhahood.

The stupa and the later Indian temple share the architectural tradition of being three-dimensional developments of the mandala, a diagram that symbolizes the metaphysical structure of the cosmos (see Mandala Diagrams of India, Chapter 2). The elements of the stupa, like those of the mandala, combine to symbolize the cohesion and integrality of the cosmos: "The coordination of square and circle, the two most ancient symbols of earth and heaven, is indeed a practically universal sign of the transformation of matter into spirit, or death into life, of time into eternity," as Snodgrass reminds us. Like Indian astrology and the mandala that links astrology and architecture, the stupa form embodies the relationship of multiplicity to unity. To understand the building, we must try to understand the motivations of the builders and the intellectual and spiritual content of the form.

The stupa has four functions. First, it is a seed that proclaims the truth, beginning with the earliest stupas near the scenes of events in Gautama's life, fostering communication between worlds. Other cultures have also diagrammed their understanding of reality onto their local geography, such as embedding the pueblo village of Acoma in its desert landscape (see Chapter 7) or the Inca city Cuzco in its mountain-and-valley setting (see Chapter 8). Second, the stupa manifests the religious law and is analogous to the verbal law found in sacred texts. Third, it calms and gladdens the hearts of visitors. And fourth, it is the Buddha himself. Properly understood, the stupa is not merely an image or a reflection but reality itself, for the Buddha is wholly present in the architectural form.

It is easier for outsiders to grasp point three, the feel-

considering the world of form. The top disc of the stupa is the bridge to the formless void, and the tip of the spire stands for the void of neither consciousness nor unconsciousness. The world of desire, the world of form, the formless void, and the void of neither consciousness nor unconsciousness are the four steps of enlightenment in Buddhist doctrine, which sees the body as a microcosm of the universal reality.

The stupa, called in different languages *thupa, dogoba, chaitya, tope, chedi,* and *chorten*, gave rise to regional styles, the dialects of one architectural language. Yet all have certain elements in common: a defined center, an axis, orientation to the compass points, precise geometry, and the

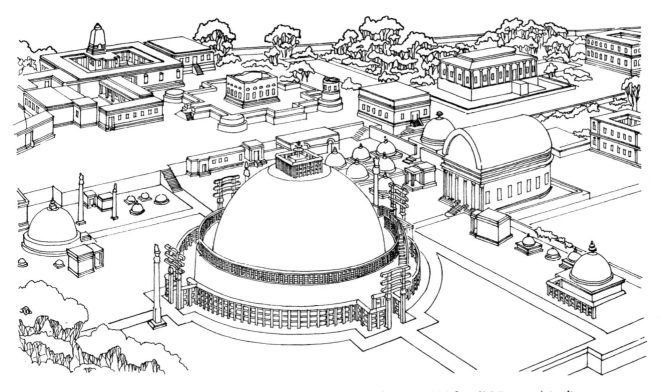

Figure 1.5. *Great Stupa, Sanchi, bird's-eye view. The earthen mound is some 120 feet (36.5 meters) in diameter and 54 feet (16.5 meter) high, standing on a square base. At its apex is a square form like a railing; rising vertically from it is a mast, or finial, that represents the world axis, with three horizontal, umbrella-like disks representing the worlds that must be traversed to reach Nirvana. The height from the ground to the top of the finial is about 70 feet (21 meters). Note that the gates are not oriented to the compass. Grouped around the stupa are smaller stupas, monastery buildings, and additional shrines.*

ing of calm gladness, than the other points; we must stretch beyond our accustomed notions and be willing to accept the previously inconceivable—not only for the stupa but for many other buildings discussed in this book.

One especially well-preserved example is the Great Stupa at Sanchi (see Figs. 1.3–1.5), built in the fifth century B.C.E. and enlarged and rededicated by the Emperor Asoka of India between 237 and 232. At the height of his powers, Asoka rejected conquest and Brahmanism, embracing nonviolence and Buddhism. He sent missionaries throughout India and to lands as far away as the Mediterranean Sea. He also built other stupas and set up memorial pillars, now called Asoka pillars, in many parts of India and Nepal, structures that embodied key concepts of the new faith, also expressed in myth, ritual, and doctrine.

In size, stupas range from the singular Bodnatha stupa at Kathmandu, Nepal, which is more than 300 feet (91

meters) in circumference, to the thousands of 2–5-foot (60–150-centimeter) stupas like sculptures dotted along streets and in courtyards all over Asia. Sanchi is a midsize stupa that stands on a base representing the earth. The 54-foot-high (16.5-meter) dome represents the Buddha's head but also the sky, womb, embryo, and egg—all symbols of change. At the apex of the dome is a square form like a railing; rising vertically from it is a 16-foot-high mast or finial with three horizontal, umbrella-like disks. The finial signifies an axis connecting heaven and earth and symbolizes the world-tree of a pre-Buddhist creation myth; it is grounded in the central core of the stupa that contains a relic of the Buddha (compare with the Horyu-ji temple in Fig. 1.9 and other pagodas in Chapter 16).

Later builders at Sanchi erected four gates, each consisting of two pillars joined by three lintels, around the stupa at the cardinal points (see Fig. 1.3). These gates copy in sandstone the wooden prototypes that had enclosed the stupa in the third century, which, in turn, had preserved the forms of second-millennium-B.C.E. wooden gateways. According to an inscription on the west pillar of the southern gate, ivory workers carved the gates, decorating them with reliefs of episodes from the Buddha's life and symbols associated with him, such as the wheel of the law (which stands for the recurrent patterns of human life) and the bodhi tree. The life Gautama had renounced is represented in these reliefs by lush vegetation, animals, and sensual female figures. In the final two centuries B.C.E., builders added two smaller stupas with their own gates, and over the following centuries the Sanchi complex acquired additional structures, such as monastery halls and memorial sculptures. Today the site attracts many visitors; it is especially appealing in the early spring, when it is uncrowded. At that season, visitors may perhaps feel a bit of what Sanchi's builders might have felt: calm gladness combined with profound seriousness.[2]

SOURCES: J. IRWIN (1980), J. MARSHALL AND FAUCHER (1940), OPIE (1970), SNODGRASS (1985).

HINDU AND JAIN SHRINES, INDIA

Dominating the art and architecture of the Indian subcontinent is the idea that the physical and spiritual aspects of life are united. Ideas of unity are especially marked in Nepal, where Buddhists and Hindus routinely worship together in the same temple (see Bhaktapur's Street Shrines, Nepal, in Chapter 7)—every religion interacts with all the others. Indira Gandhi, the former prime minister of India, once said that Westerners always insist on choices between A and B, but Indians do not see why one must choose.[3]

Some Hindu temples of India were man-made caves, like the Shiva temple complex at Elephanta, near Bombay, which dates from the sixth (to ninth?) century C.E. Others, built of stone, combine the symbolic aspects of the natural cave and the physical form of the manmade hall. Examples are the fine group of buildings at Khajuraho in the center of the Deccan Plateau.

Kandariya Mahadeva Temple, Khajuraho

The Chandella dynasty, which ruled central India from 950 to 1050 C.E., marshaled a huge labor force to make its capital Khajuraho one of India's largest cities. Chandella kings built at least eighty-five temples in the city. Isolated from the major trade and travel routes, the city and some of these temples survived the wrath of the invading Mughals who destroyed "idolatrous temples" in more accessible places (see Mughals in India in Chapter 8). Some twenty remain—Hindu temples west and Jain temples east of the modern village at the site.

The Hindu temples share certain patterns. They were made to look like mountains, appropriate as homes of the gods. Their exteriors consist of three increasingly higher towers, the highest rising above the sanctum. Although the lower towers are pyramidal, the tallest has a curved or bulging outline. The western group is placed in what was once a sacred lake, which may explain the high plinths that raise the temples. With one exception, the temples face east and are made of honey-colored sandstone. The exception, Chaunsath Yogni, an ancient temple made of granite, is dedicated to Kali, the malevolent mother goddess, and stands to the south, outside the group. Its design is much simpler than that of the other Hindu temples, probably because it is older.

The other temples are ornately carved with bands of fine sculpture outside and in, fully integrated with the architecture. These reliefs are famous for their many scenes of daily life and of gods, goddesses, warriors, musicians, real and mythological animals—but especially of women,

---

[2]In a formal, historical look at Indian cave temples and stupas, our investigative tools have been questions: Who built the temple and why? What earlier buildings were used as patterns? What were the ornaments, and from what tradition do they come? In the case of narrative carvings or paintings, what stories did the artists use? How were their treatments different from earlier versions? What do the techniques of carving and/or painting tell us about the artists or artisans who produced them? What chronology can we construct about the style and period using information from available documents and from the buildings and their decoration? Do documents give additional information about the patrons, builders, artists, periods, or social circumstances? If so, how can we correlate that information with what we have learned from the buildings themselves? The answers to these and similar questions are the basis for art-historical accounts of individual buildings, periods and period styles, and the relations of patrons to artists.

---

[3]Lecture at University of Michigan, ca. 1952, attended by Dora P. Crouch.

including dancing nymphs (asperses) and sensuously carved, erotic figures that shocked some early European visitors. A nineteenth-century guidebook said of the site, "Unfortunately it is obscene. Fortunately, it is difficult of access." R. Thapar points out that

> a great outburst of erotic poetry is characteristic of this period. . . . The cult of the erotic had come into its own, not only in poetry but also in temple sculpture and in Tantric ritual. . . . This was an age of abandon, with the lifting of the puritan impress of Buddhism which associated guilt with pleasure, which [sic] led to a more uninhibited reference to sexual behavior in both literature and the arts.

The Khajuraho temples were built while a late-tenth-century Tantric Shiva cult was gaining popularity at the Chandella court. This cult taught that creation, especially as embodied in sexual intercourse between men and women, was an offering to and a commingling with the divine; the divine gift in return was a child. Creation was nowhere more emphatically evident to humans than in the transports of sexual ecstasy. This spiritual path was open to everyone, and neither intellect nor moral superiority were prerequisites, although those qualities were expected to develop. Through the ritual use of sexual intercourse combined with yoga, the devotee came to transformation and union with the divine. It was therefore appropriate to depict such activity in the sculptures of the temples, which reflect the dynasty's intense spiritual and physical passions, according to Jordan. To get some sense of the fecundity celebrated at Khajuraho, note that the temple of Matangesvara, focused on a sacred lingam—a phallus, symbol of Shiva, the destroyer god—is perhaps the oldest shrine and still attracts worshipers.

Kandariya Mahadeva is the most artistically and architecturally perfect of the temples at Khajuraho. Built in the eleventh century, it is impressive in size and in the profusion of sculptural figures adorning its exterior and interior. The temple's profile resembles a mountain, and

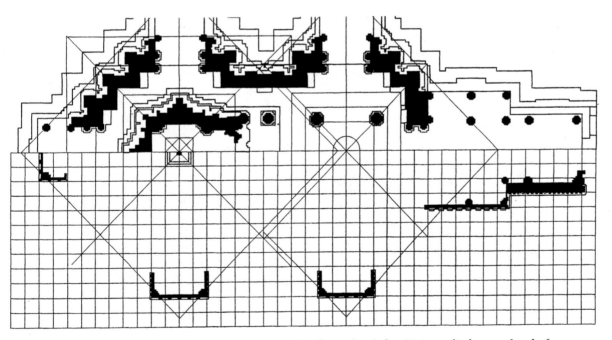

Figure 1.6. a. *Plan of the Kandariya Mahadeva Temple, Khajuraho, India. Visitors climb up to the platform by stairs that are off the plan to the right. From the small porch, they enter a vestibule and then the open hall, where they wait their turn to walk around the ambulatory that encircles the lingam at the center of the space at the left. The square units in the plan are those of the mandala that determined it. From full sunshine at right, one progresses to darkness in the main shrine at the left.*

the tower stands for the cosmic axis that connects this spot on earth with the unknown depths of earth and with the heavens above. Intersecting this cosmic axis at ground level is the ritual path followed by the ascending devotees.

The 872 voluptuous figures on the temple's three exterior friezes—each nearly a meter tall—are enjoying the ultimate in erotic activity (and thus approaching unity with the divine) or participating in wars, processions, lion hunts, elephant fights, music, dance, and mythological episodes. Visitors tear themselves away from the erotic reliefs, climb the stairs, penetrate the shrine through the finely carved gates of the entrance porch, and then go through a passage to enter the main hall. Passing through an interior vestibule, the pilgrims reach the inner sanctum, the "womb house," to circumambulate the lingam image, the pillar of the universe. (see Fig. 1.6b.)

Both the outer room and the inner sanctum are patterned on mandalas (Fig. 1.6a) Guardian figures stand at eight significant points around the sanctum. Of the many

Figure 1.6. b. *Section of Kandariya Mahadeva Temple. The stairs on the right lead to the platform. Going through the porch and hall, people enter the shrine, which is centered under the tallest tower. The upper levels are a series of compartments that support the towers.*

symbolic references in the temple's architecture, some are invisible in the thickness of the walls, but are known from study of the original mandala. Others are evident in the sculptures and the carefully modulated proportions of the plan. Orientalist D. Desai writes, "The Hindu temple in its developed stage represents man's efforts to symbolize cosmic order on earth. Its consecrated space, created by precise geometry and calculations, is designed to capture and regulate the cosmic powers in an orderly universe." Like the Buddhist stupa, the Hindu temple reconciles multiplicity with unity.

SOURCES: DAVENPORT (1981), DESAI (1992), JORDAN (1982), MICHELL (1988), THAPAR (1966).

Dilwara Temples, Rajputana, India

Like Hinduism, Jainism was an offshoot of Brahmanism. The semilegendary ascetic and teacher Mahavira ("great hero") Vardhamana Jinatiputra codified the religion in the sixth century B.C.E. Jainism, which survives today primarily among urban merchants and traders, values aestheticism and a sense of connectedness among all things.

Like the Hindu and Buddhist shrines, the earliest Jain shrines were in caves, such as Lomas Rishi. The most famous Jain shrines, however, are the three Dilwara Temples, located near the village of Mount Abu in the state of Rajputana (see Fig. 1.7). Noted for the unsurpassed beauty of their carved marble, the temples are dated from the eleventh, thirteenth, and nineteenth centuries. The earlier two are most noteworthy to the student of indigenous structures and traditions.

Vimala Vasahi is the oldest temple, built in 1031 by Vimal, a minister of the Gujarat court in northwest India, and dedicated to the first great Jain teacher, Adinath. Built in a northern Indian style, the temple is square in plan but appears cruciform owing to graduated projections at the center of each of the sides; the same pattern is seen in the Ananda temple in Pagan (discussed later). The tall central tower has a bulging curve upward. The courtyard shrine holds Adinath's image, with fifty-two identical images sitting cross-legged; these were repeated images of the twenty-four great religious figures of the Jain tradition, victors over the bondage of life and death, and analogous to saints in the Christian tradition. Forty-eight carved pillars guard the entrance. Opposite it, a second building, called the House of Elephants, seems to march toward the temple along the axis that unites them.

In 1230, two brothers, Tejpal and Vastupal, built the Tejpala temple to honor the twenty-second Jain teacher, Neminath. Like Vimal, the brothers were governmental ministers of the Gujarat state, which continued to favor Jainism. Tejpala is the most complete of the old Jain temples, noted for the intricacy and delicacy of its carved marble. Some detail is so exquisite that the marble appears almost transparent, especially the lotus flower hanging under the center of the dome (see Fig. 1.8). The profuse sculptural decoration of the temple is, however, subordinated to the architecture. Although Jain sculptures contain less overt sexuality than do the Hindu reliefs, they show equal enjoyment of the possibilities of the purely physical and homage to the sensuously beautiful.

In India, the common cultural impulse toward religion was stronger than any dogmatic ideas that required architectural differentiation. Families and individuals of all faiths honor the gods at whatever shrine they choose. Khajuraho's Tantric Hindu temples celebrate the fecundity of life, while its Jain temples are equally exuberant but with much less emphasis on the directly erotic.

SOURCES: HARLE (1988), THAPAR (1966).

BUDDHIST SHRINES, JAPAN, AND BURMA (MYANMAR)

After the second century B.C.E., Buddhism thrived outside India, in northern, eastern, and southeastern Asia. With the passage of time and the spread over an ever-widening territory, Buddhism's original simplicity of architectural form and unity of dogma both changed. Regional modifications in the stupa form accompanied changes in the religion that the form symbolized. Such variations as the simplicity of certain Japanese Buddhist temples and the abundantly decorated Tibetan Buddhist structures arose from the same set of religious insights but took on the ethos of the people they served. In Sri Lanka, for example, the stupa appeared not only in the original hemisphere form but in five other forms: the bubble, the rice-heap (like a sine-curve), the bell, the lotus, and the cogged wheel or tangerine shapes. Not the relics placed within the stupa but the stupa itself became the focus of worship, associated with a particular Buddha, for the historical Buddha came to be seen as one of a series of Enlightened Ones, a series that continues today in the persons of the Dalai Lama and other lamas.

Architectural variations within Buddhism are exemplified in two different temples, one in Japan and one in

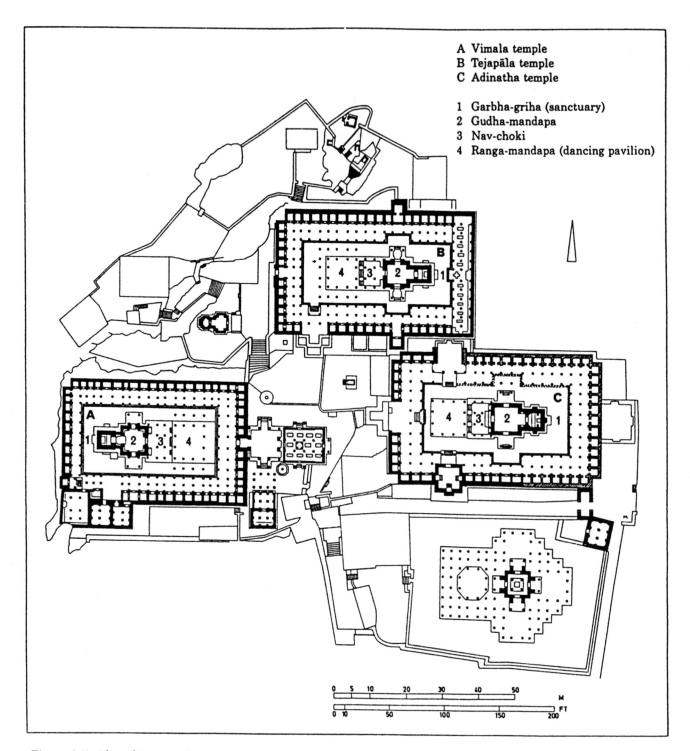

A Vimala temple
B Tejapāla temple
C Adinatha temple

1 Garbha-griha (sanctuary)
2 Gudha-mandapa
3 Nav-choki
4 Ranga-mandapa (dancing pavilion)

Figure 1.7. *Plan of Jain temples at Mount Abu near Dilwara, India,. A, B, and C are the historical temples discussed in the text, while the temple at lower right is from the nineteenth century. The scheme of a temple at the center of a courtyard is similar to Hindu temples, but the surrounding rows of small chambers are distinctive.*

Figure 1.8. *The waiting hall of a Jain temple at Dilwara, India. The exquisite marble carving in the waiting hall before the innermost shrine is justly famous for its elegant workmanship and profusion of beautiful details.*

Myanmar (formerly Burma). Buddhism reached Japan from China by way of Korea and Myanmar, by way of Sri Lanka and India. Both temples have statues of Buddha at their cores, enforcing the idea of the cosmic axis and its relationship to the concept of enlightenment. However, the temples differ in plan, elevation, material, and decoration because seventh-century Japan and eleventh-century Burma were different geographic and social settings.

a. View

b. Old   c. New

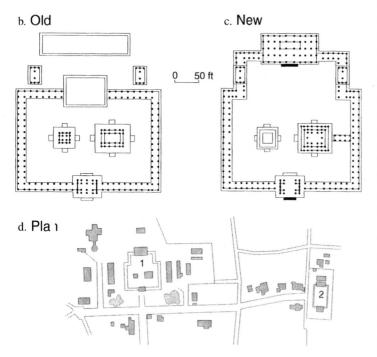

d. Plan

Figure 1.9. *Plan of the Horyuji Temple, Asuka, Japan.* **a.** *View of original complex.* **b.** *and* **c.** *Plans of the original (left) and present (right) buildings.* **d.** *Map of the area with the original complex at 1 and the palace of the founder with later additions to the monastery at 2.*

Horyu-ji Temple, Asuka, Japan

Southwest of present-day Nara in the village of Asuka stands the Buddhist temple of Horyu-ji, founded in the seventh century C.E. (Fig. 1.9) by Prince Skotoku, regent for the empress, who dedicated the temple to the memory of his father, the emperor. The temple was completed in 607 but burned to the ground in a lightning fire in 670. Builders reconstructed it in 676–700, shifting its location to the northwest but otherwise imitating and thus preserving the earlier style. The Horyu-ji complex contains the oldest surviving wooden buildings in Japan—in the world, some authorities believe.

The temple complex has two areas. Sai-in, on the west, includes the two-story Kondo (Golden Hall) and a five-story pagoda. To-in, on the east, includes the Hall of Dreams (Yumedono). By 711 both groups had acquired gallery-corridors, monks' quarters, and lecture halls. Today the monastery complex also has a dining hall, libraries, and outer gates (see Fig. 1.9a).

The Kondo resembles its prototypes, Buddhist image-halls (art galleries) in temples built by China's Tang dynasty in the seventh and eighth centuries C.E. The form is simple, double roofed with upcurved corners. Originally, the Kondo roofs protruded more than 13 feet (4 meters), and extra posts had to be added to support the corners. During the later Nara period, in the eighth century C.E., builders inserted an exterior corridor under the roof overhang; it is reached from the platform on which the temple sits. From the outside, the two levels of roof suggest additional levels of reality in the Buddhist cosmology and look as if they define two stories, but on the inside there is only one lofty space, partially confined by a coffered ceiling around the edges (see the additional discussion in Chapter 16, Stupas Become Pagodas).

The Kondo's wall paintings, severely damaged in a 1949 fire, were among the earliest temple murals known in Japan and resembled those painted in Korea in the sixth and seventh centuries. Surviving intact are fine bronze sculptures that represent a Buddha Sakyamuni (a name derived from the Sakkyas kingdom his father ruled) between two bodhisattvas (saints or enlightened persons) against a decorated backdrop. This group, dated 623 by inscription, is consonant in figural type with Wei dynasty (386–534 C.E.) examples in China—a style that was old-fashioned by the time it reached Japan. Thus, the Kondo incorporates images from both of its formal predecessors, the Korean and the Chinese, reflecting the route by which Buddhism entered Japan.

Next to the Kondo is a five-story pagoda, completed about 700 C.E. (see Fig. 1.10) and probably the original focus of the temple courtyard. Its style is that of a Tang dynasty or Korean structure of a later date than the sculptural works in the Kondo. Architectural details, such as brackets, capitals, and railings, are almost identical to those of the Kondo. The pagoda's function as a cosmic axis diminished as the images of Buddha and the Kondo became more important.

The pagoda retains the pattern of relic chamber and mast found in Indian stupas. Graceful in detail and contour, it measures some 107 feet (32.5 meters) to the base of the spire. A massive foundation stone set 10 feet (3 meters) into the ground has a hollow for holy relics. The sturdy central mast of the pagoda was originally set into this stone and penetrated all the levels above, which were tied to it for stability. Above the highest roof, the mast was finished with metal covers and symbolic ornaments, references to the path of enlightenment through a sequence of worlds. Later the mast was cut off above the ground-floor room, enlarging that room's usable space; apparently, the structural ties in the upper stories were sufficient to ensure the necessary stability. The ground-floor plan was a nine-by-nine-unit square grid (see Chapter 2, Fig. 2.10) patterned after what was considered a powerful mandala.

Each of the pagoda's five levels is smaller than the one below it, a feature more pronounced in early Japanese than in Chinese pagodas. Basic to Japanese structural design were the brackets supporting the projecting tile roofs. These brackets articulated the structure, being designed to absorb thrusts thorough their seemingly ornamental repetition of detail (see Chinese Construction Manuals, Chapter 2). An abundant supply of wood from Japan's forested mountains made it possible for Japanese architects to continue to use large, simple brackets longer than in China, where a vanishing forests forced builders to use smaller pieces in the bracketing.

The To-in area of the Horyu-ji Temple is some 400 feet (122 meters) east of the Sai-in (see Fig. 1.9 d). Prince Skotoku's palace once stood here. The hall where the prince lived while he annotated Buddhist scriptures came to be called Yumedono, or Hall of Dreams. In the group of buildings in this second area, the present octagonal chapel was built in 739 C.E. by Abbot Gyoshin and repaired in the ninth century by another monk, Dosan; the octagonal building contains handsome sculptures of bodhisattvas from the early Asuka era (seventh century C.E.),

as well as portrait statues of these men and a painted portrait of Prince Skotoku.

Source: Suzuki (1980).

Ananda Temple, Pagan, Burma (Myanmar)

The architecture of extended Buddhism took another form in a temple in Pagan, an early capital of Burma (Myanmar). This was long an important center of Buddhism, and there the stupa changed under the influence of local styles and customs.

Figure 1.10. *Asuka, Japan. Five-Story Pagoda, Horyuji.*

a.

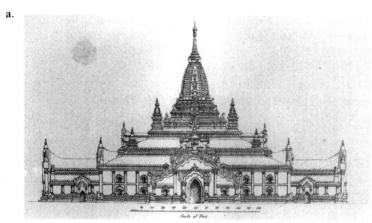

b.

ANANDA

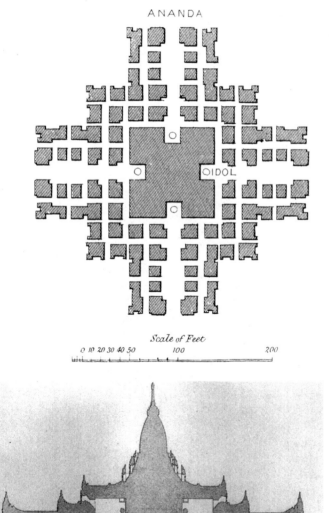

Scale of Feet

0 10 20 30 40 50   100   200

c.

The walled city of Pagan arose around 850 C.E. on one bank of the Irrawaddy River, financed by wealth from the trade routes that passed through the area and by spoils from military conquests (compare with the resource base of Angkor Wat, Chapter 11). From the eleventh to the thirteenth century, Pagan was the capital of a sizable region. Missionaries from Sri Lanka promoted their religion, a form of Buddhism (Theravada) that considers Buddha a moral example and teacher. Pagan's culture flourished until Mongols invaded in 1287. Although the Mongol conquest was temporary, it struck the city a blow from which it never recovered, although Burmese culture flourished in later cities like Rangoon.

The temples at Pagan incorporated formal elements from India's Pala dynasty (eighth to twelfth century C.E.), including a stupa, a high, terraced stone plinth with stairs, gates, small stupas, and pinnacles. The white stucco of the exterior, elaborated with terracotta moldings, can be read as an evocation of the snow-clad Himalayan holy mountains, visible on pilgrimages from Pagan to Buddha's birth-

Figure 1.11. *Ananda Temple, Pagan, Burma (Myanmar). Top to bottom: elevation, plan, and section, from 1858.* **a.** *(elevation) This shows gabled porticoes protruding from the center of each face, symmetrically organized. Pinnacles, spires, and small stupas rise above a blocky base, with a larger stupa at the center crowning the whole. The small arched openings in the ground story, with elaborate cornices of terra-cotta, are the windows in the outer walls, also evident in the section.* **b.** *(plan) The temple measures 175 feet (53 meters) on a side, with smaller rectangular halls extending outward in a form similar to a Greek cross, so that the overall width of the base is 300 feet (91 meters). In addition to three entrance passages in each protruding hall, there are two corridors around the central block. Within that core are four niches for Buddha statues (labeled IDOL on the plan). The function of this central core is to support the stupa that crowns the roof.* **c.** *(section) The temple is 35 feet (10.7 meters) high. Diagonal windows hidden behind the false fronts of the porticos (set between the second and third roof terraces in the gabled porticoes) focus light on the four recesses in the core, each containing a Buddha sculpture. Two of the four tall statues are shown here facing out from the central core, their heads rising higher than the vaults of the corridors. Small stupas, like pinnacles, edge the roofs and cluster around the base of the tall central stupa.*

place. Within were paintings of the life of Buddha and stucco decorations. Indian architects usually employed the corbelled arch, but the architects of Pagan's temples generally used the true radiating arch, either pointed or rounded. (The radiating arch, made of wedge-shaped stones, is found only rarely in pre-Islamic India, but it appears in the main structure of the Buddhist Mahabodi temple at Bodh Gaya in India, a structure that inspired several of Pagan's architects.)

One of many striking and elaborate structures at Pagan is the Ananda temple, just beyond the east gate (see Fig. 1.11a). Few temples at the site have remained in continuous use, but Ananda has been since King Kyanzittha or his chief queen, Apeyadana, founded it in 1091. The temple may have originally been called Anata Panna (endless wisdom), a name perhaps conflated popularly with Ananda (bliss), which was also the name of one of Gautama's two principal disciples.

The visitor or pilgrim to the temple enters, through one of four gates, a large courtyard surrounded by low walls that interrupt the thick tropical vegetation. The gates and four inner entrances to the temple align with the cardinal compass points. The plan of the 300-foot- (90-meter-) wide temple was a mandala based on a Greek cross form. Exterior walls of white stucco are articulated with two tiers of windows framed by pilasters and a string course. Many of these details are of terracotta, more durable in Pagan's hot, humid climate than stucco. The roof consists of two broad, sloping terraces surrounding four narrow, receding terraces that rise toward the center. Crowning the central core is a miter-shaped, truncated pyramid with bulging sides—a north Indian form similar to the towers of the Kandariya Mahadeva temple at Khajuraho. Atop this base sits the bell-shaped stupa, in turn topped with a tapering, ringed spire with a gilded metal finial—a typically Burmese compound of elements. The tall, gilded spire reaches a height of 180 feet (55 meters) above the ground. At the corners of the roofs and along the lowest terrace are miniature spires. The gables of the entrance porches repeat in large, projecting dormer windows that contribute to the dynamic lighting inside. Overall, the exterior gives an impression of soaring elegance, where a multitude of details come together in a compact, unified mass (see Fig. 1.11a).

The temple's interior is not a congregational meeting place, as one might assume from the size of the base, but a place where the individual worshipper can connect with the divine. Each of the exterior porches has three entrances into the high, vaulted, concentric double corridors that encircle the solid core of masonry supporting the tower (Fig. 1.11b). (Compare these corridors with the spiral path to the top of Borobudur, Chapter 5). The outer corridor is decorated with eighty-one stone reliefs of the life of Gautama Buddha; they are simple, animated, and graceful, finished in gilt and cinnabar (a vermilion pigment).

Niches set into the sides of the core are reached from the narrow inner corridor. In the western niche is a colossal sculpture of the historical Buddha; the other niches hold equally large sculptures of three Buddhas of the past and future (see Fig. 1.11c). One must stand very close and peer upward to see these sculptures, which are 40 feet (12.2 meters) tall. The sculptures are lit by narrow lancet openings in the dormer windows—a tour de force of illusionistic lighting that sends a wash of light down each figure's front. These niches at the center of the temple base remind us that Burmese temples are symbolic of caves as well as mountains.

The pagoda at Horyi-ji and the temple at Ananda are two different mountain images, but each manifests the intersection of the material and spiritual planes at a particular place. The two structures reiterate the essential components and meaning of the Sanchi stupa, focusing on the Buddha and his message. The form has changed, the worshippers are ethnically and culturally different, but the meaning and the devotion abide.

Sources: Davenport (1981); Hla (1978); Swaan (1966), pl. 29, 35, 36, 37, 40.

SUGGESTED READINGS

C. Alexander. 1977. *A Pattern Language*. New York: Oxford University Press. Alexander's thesis is that pleasing patterns of architecture are less culture dependent than people had thought.

Bäumer, B. 1991. "From Guha to Asoka: The Mystical Cave in the Vedic and Saiva Traditions." In *Concepts of Space Ancient and Modern*, 105–07, edited by K. Vatsyayan. New Delhi: Abhinav Publications. A good, brief summary.

Desai, D. 1992. "Man and Temple: Architectural and Sculptural Imagery of the Kandariya Mahadeva Temple of Khajuraho." In *Eastern Approaches: Essays on Asian Art and Archaeology,* 141 ff. edited by T. S. Maxwell. Delhi: Oxford University Press. This book is useful for anyone who wants to compare Eastern and Western approaches to architectural history and meaning.

Harle, B. 1988. *The Art and Architecture of India*. New York: Penguin Books. The Penguin books have a well-deserved reputation for being the basic sources for their respective areas.

Hla, U. K. (S. S. Ozhegov). 1978. "Traditional Town Planning in Burma." *Journal of the Society of Architectural Historians*. 37 (May): 92–104. An early analysis of Asian urban form using European methods, by a Russian who adopted a Burmese name.

Irwin, J. 1980. "The Axial Symbolism of the Early Stupa: An Exegesis." In *The Stupa—Its Religious, Historical and Architectural Significance*, 12–38, edited by A. L. Dallapiccola and S. Zingel-Avè Lallemant. Irwin is a noted scholar of Asian symbolic architecture. In the early tower-stupas, the axis symbol was more evident than the mountain symbol. This excellent collection of papers is a necessity for any serious student of the stupa.

Marshall, J., and A. Faucher. 1940. *The Monuments of Sanchi*, 3 vols. London: Probsthain. Many illustrations.

Panofsky, E. 1972. *Studies in Iconology*. New York: Harper & Row. An excellent display of art history "tools" in the hands of a master.

Roth, G. 1980. "Symbolism of the Buddhist Stupa. In *The Stupa—Its Religious, Historical and Architectural Significance*, 183–209, edited by A. L. Dallapiccola and S. Zingel-Avé Lallemant. A succinct account.

Snodgrass, A. 1985. *The Symbolism of the Stupa*. Ithaca, N.Y.: Institute of Southeast Asian Studies, Cornell University. Stimulating and indispensable, this book relates the content of Buddhism to the form of the stupa and to the alternate manifestation in pagoda form.

Suzuki, K. 1980. *Early Buddhist Architecture in Japan*. Tokyo: Kodansha. Essential reading, with good illustrations.

Swaan, W. 1966. "Pagan." In *Lost Cities of Asia*. New York: G. P. Putnam's Sons. See especially Pagan, 90–120, with photographs of Ananda.

Thapar, R. 1966. *A History of India*. Harmondsworth, England: Penguin Books. Old, but still interesting for those who want background.

2

Transfer of Traditional Architectural Knowledge

People in traditional cultures know how to make the buildings they need. Over the years, through trial, error, reflection, and new trials, building traditions have evolved that integrate materials, climate, other physical constraints, and cultural practice into architectural forms that meet the needs of individuals and groups. People in these cultures, although they have developed spoken and written means of codifying building traditions, also know how to transmit this knowledge from one generation to the next. They rely more often on spoken instruction and demonstration than on printed materials.

In considering oral tradition, we go beyond the scope of art history to wider inquiries that are based on regional studies and archaeological and anthropological investigations. The first two examples show the community as the source, transmitter, and receiver of building knowledge, as well as of labor supply. The next two examples also deal with the person-to-person transfer of knowledge, but they show more advanced levels of organization. Finally, we return to a standard art history approach to examine the written or printed documents that traditional societies use to transmit building knowledge.

More than one-third of the world's population lives in structures made from mud. Fewer, but still sizable numbers, live in tents. Almost half the world's people know how to build these kinds of dwellings and to pass their knowledge on to succeeding generations. The Hausa of Nigeria and the Native Americans of the Great Plains transfer skills from one generation to the next by word of mouth and by working together in construction.

PERSON-TO-PERSON TRANSFER

Case studies of the Nigerian Hausa and the Native Americans of the northern Great Plains show how communities, building together, transfer building knowledge and skills from one generation to the next. The responsibility for construction is allocated to men in the first instance and to women in the second, but each gender receives help from the other at crucial stages, and the community as a whole possesses the knowledge. In other traditional cultures, professional builders teach and learn their craft by word and example.

Community Case Studies

HAUSA FAMILY BUILDERS OF MUD HOUSES, NIGERIA

The building of Hausaland's traditional mud houses requires knowledge of the subtle relationships among climate, vegetation, earth, the forms and uses of structures, and the capabilities of a minimal tool kit. Ultimately, rain and high humidity, a range of temperatures, and gale-force winds define the local architecture.

During the wet season, the region receives 40 to 45 inches (100–115 centimeters) of rain, somewhat less in the north near the desert; the rest of the year is dry. Heat, however, is inescapable on most days of the year. Towns and villages are set between 1,000 and 2,000 feet (300–400 meters) above sea level (see Fig. 2.1), with favored locations in the heavily wooded river valleys or savannah parklands in the vicinity of inselbergs ("island mountains"— isolated hills that act as water reservoirs). Clay or mud houses that heat up slowly and cool off equally slowly have thermal advantages (see Hot and Dry, Chapter 4), and the Hausa build these houses where altitude results in a great contrast between hot days and cool nights.

Hausaland's cities, towns, and villages are intimately, even organically, connected with their setting, since they are built from the laterite (a mixture of sandy clay and clayey sand derived from decomposed basalts and other rocks) on which they stand, using local vegetation as a source of materials for roofs and fences. Their harmony with the environment is complete.

When Hausa builders decide to erect a house and have chosen the site, they begin by clearing the ground and marking the outline of the house. In 1910, an English official named A. J. N. Tremearne described the process:

> This may be done with sticks, or in the case of a round house, with string, and then the plan is drawn on the ground by the chief builder, who drags one foot along the marks so that they become wider and more distinct, hoes or shovels being used afterwards to deepen the impression thus made.

Traditionally, the builders are the father and his sons, although they may ask neighbors and relatives for help. Indeed, even strangers may be asked to help, for a Hausa

Figure 2.1. *A village in northern Nigeria. The houses have thatched roofs and walls of mud with surface patterns made by human hands. The walls of the compounds at the left and right edge the street.*

proverb says, "Though a naked man may be ignored on a feast day, he will be sought after when building is going on."

Building such a house does not require advanced technology. Over the centuries, the Hausa have learned to apply pottery techniques on a larger scale for building. Mud is free for the taking because the Hausa do not recognize the concept of exclusive ownership of land—only the right to use it, as regulated by the local chief. To make the building clay, the builders add water to the lateritic soil to achieve the proper consistency and workability. They may also add ashes, dung, or shells for increased malleability and impermeability. They knead the clay by foot in a pit and then leave it to mellow for a day or so. During this time, a chemical change takes place; the material is ready to harden into excellent and durable building material. Mud is impermanent, but the particular mud of Hausaland is more durable than most, as architect and planner J. C. Moughtin wrote:

> Earth or mud architecture is often described as impermanent and therefore as an inferior method of building. Yet unbaked earth has been used for many thousands of years, not only for housing, but for some of society's most prestigious developments: great ziggurats, pyramids, religious and public buildings have all been constructed from this material.

So ductile is the Hausa clay, so amenable to human manipulation, that the material contributes to the form but does not limit or define it. The clay is molded into rough cones or bowl-shaped "bricks" and then carefully built up in layers of cones or bricks, using the same clay for mortar. The builders place loose mud in the crevices between the bricks and square it off, leaving the wall surfaces smooth. For increased strength, the clay wall tapers upward from a base as much as 5 feet (1.5 meters) thick.

The pace of construction is adapted to the climate and to the nature of the material. Building generally occurs during the dry season, when agricultural demands are few and the mud is not too damp to bind properly. Builders raise the walls no more than 2 feet (60 centimeters) a day, to give the mud time to set, and when the sides are high enough, smooth them with another coat of mud. Then, when the clay has stiffened and is nearly dry, the workers cut out a doorway, commonly 5.5 feet by 2 feet (1.68 × .61 meters). Wall openings are few and small because they lead to erosion and increase heat gain. Where openings are needed, the Hausa have learned to thicken the wall surface at the edges of doors and windows, which are usu-

ally only ventilation slots, to compensate for the stress created by interruptions in the wall.

Wooden beams strengthen the walls and roofs of the houses. The most commonly used tree is the azara, a fibrous palm tree that is resistant to termites. The length of available tree trunks determines the sizes of the rooms. A common construction size is 6 feet long (2 meters). For a room of greater length (or width), mud columns and reinforced curved wood beams are used, giving the appearance of an arch (for a similar construction, see Figs. 16.5, 16.6). In some houses, pinnacles or buttresses may be added to the outer wall or the facades of the inner courtyards, symbolizing protection through visual association with the ancient shrines called "pillars of the dead" and with pinnacled mosques. Such elaborations, however, are more common on public architecture.

The material favored for the roofs is also mud—much better than other types of roofing at withstanding the region's gale-force winds, which may reach ninety miles an hour. All mud roofs require rain spouts and vertical wall channels to carry the water away. They also require frequent repair and maintenance—a Hausa proverb says, "The one who lives in the house knows where the roof leaks." Some roofs are flat, finished on the outside with thatch or waterproofed clay and on the inside with plaster. Others are curved, vaulted and reinforced with palm branches, or built of corbelled mud layers cantilevered inward as they rise to meet at the top of the "dome." Such roofs are thatched for protection. The Hausa also use a conical thatched roof, like a huge hat, which is especially convenient for the smaller round houses, in that it helps to protect the clay sides from erosion, although it may be used for larger ones. Women construct this roof on the ground. When they have finished, several men pick it up and set it on top of the standing walls.[4]

The interior of a mud house is plastered with mud. After the mud has dried thoroughly, it is coated—especially in sleeping rooms—with a mixture of mud and cow dung that repels insects. It may be whitewashed. The

---

[4]Close neighbors of the Hausa, the Bauchi of the Nigerian plateau build houses with complex roofs having double-shell domes to manage seasonal changes. The inner dome is made of mud. Pegs protrude from its exterior, and an outer shell of thatch rests on these pegs. The air space between the two roofs provides insulation during the heat of the day, and heat retained by the mud dome warms the interior on cool nights. The outer, thatched roof is well adapted to shed rain, keeping the inner roof dry.

floors are also clay, beaten as it sets to produce a hard surface. Sometimes floors have additional surface finishes, such as mosaics, aggregate, or cow dung, again mixed with ashes. The women of the family do much of this interior finishing work.

The exterior surfaces of mosques and expensive houses may be finished with a traditional Hausa waterproof cement, a silver-gray mixture of laterite and ash. If such a surface is repaired periodically, it remains waterproof for years. Even houses not waterproofed with this cement can last from two to twenty years, depending on local conditions, shelter by overhanging roofs, and the care they receive. Common wall finishes are dark purple and gray browns, colors obtained from natural clays. The final touch is surface decoration (see Fig. 2.2), with motifs, such as the magic square from Arab Muslim cultures to the north and northeast or indigenous patterns using the triangle, lozenge, circle, and line (see Fig. 13.7; compare with Ndebele decoration, Figs. 13.6 a and b.)

Urban or rural, a family house is a walled compound with irregular courtyards, as many freestanding mud-wall rooms as the inhabitants need, and a boundary wall (see Fig. 3.14). Because mud is readily available and free, the number of dwelling units and their internal arrangements can change as rapidly as do the extended families who live in them. It is easy and inexpensive to build or abandon a room, reusing materials as needed.

Figure 2.2. *Finger patterns on the wall of a merchant's house in Zaira, Nigeria, now in the Zaira House Museum. The same patterns were photographed on a building in the harem of the palace at Kano in 1904.*

The units are grouped under trees, around the court-yards—a sensible plan in a tropical climate where houses must provide both open and closed areas, shade and moving air for the humid part of the year, and protection from heat and wind for the dry months. Traditional mud houses are better suited to these annual climatic changes than are more modern houses with sheet metal-roofs. Until the 1960s, all the houses in Hausaland were made of mud. In contrast, even the least expensive commercial housing that has been built in Nigeria since 1965 far exceeds the budgets of working people—the cheapest house in a housing estate costs N 6082, while a messenger, for example, earns N 900 a year.

The aesthetic sense and architectural skills of the Hausa, together with the local materials, have created an extremely attractive built environment with distinctive character. The repetition of architectural patterns in constantly repeated structural forms produces an unusual unity of form and the meaning attached to it, so that, as Moughtin claims, Hausa building can be classified and studied as architecture. This built environment is the result of communities working together, sharing knowledge and many kinds of skill. The Hausa system of mud construction is based on an empirical knowledge of the strength of materials. In Euro-American terms, earthen materials are best in compression, and vegetable materials are best in tension. Without formal training, the Hausa builders have learned to bend earthen walls and curved wooden elements to compensate for the structural deficiencies of these materials. As anthropologist S. Denyer puts it, getting any building to stand up using limited materials requires skill, developed carefully over a long time. Construction skills were passed down from every member of one generation to every member of the next.

The person-to-person transfer of knowledge through words and shared actions gives architectural form to Hausa community life. As the builders erect a wall, layer a roof, and finish the surfaces, the older people talk to the younger ones about the way things have to be done to create a proper house. Through conversation and example, the older people transfer their acquired knowledge to their younger helpers.

SOURCES: MOUGHTIN (1985), PRUSSIN (1986), TREMEARNE (1910).

TIPIS AND GENDER ON THE AMERICAN GREAT PLAINS

Many people ascribe the tents called tipis (tepees) to all Native Americans, but the use of tipis was limited to the Blackfeet of the northern Plains, the central Cheyenne, the southern Comanche, the Sioux, and many of their neighbors living between the Mississippi River and the Rocky Mountains (see the map of North America in the Appendix). These groups lived in tipis while following the herds of buffalo (American bison) during the warm months and while camping in their home valleys during the long, cold winters (see Fig. 14.6). They lived by the buffalo and used all parts of their kill. Men did the hunting, everyone helped skin the carcasses with stone and bone tools, and the women cured the hides—some of which would become tipis.

Euro-Americans first saw tipis among the Sioux of the Missouri River area. Sergeant Pryor of the Lewis and Clark Expedition, who visited the Yankton Sioux in August 1804, described their dwellings in his journal. The camp

> was handsum made of Buffalow Skins Painted different Colour, all compact & handSomly arranged, their Camps formed of a Conic form Containing about 12 or 15 persons each and 40 in number.

When Meriwether Lewis decided in the spring of 1805 to buy a tipi for the next stage of the expedition, he wrote:

> This tent is in the Indian stile, formed of a number of dressed Buffaloe skins in such a manner that when foalded double it forms the quarter of a circle, and is left open at one side. Here it may be attached or loosened at pleasure by strings which are sewed to its sides for the purpose. To erect this tent, a parsel of ten or twelve poles are provided, fore or five of which are attached together at one end, they are then elivated and their lower extremities are spread in a circular manner to a width proportionate to the demention of the lodge; in the same position other poles are leant against those, and the leather is then thrown over them forming a conic figure.

This tipi was large enough for the expedition's two captains, two other men, and the Shoshone wife of one of them and her baby, as well as various materials that had to be sheltered from the weather.

Although the climate of the Great Plains is different from that of Hausaland and traditional Native Americans were nomads, rather than settled villagers, the dissemination of building knowledge is similar in both societies. The owner-designer-maker of housing carried on a construction tradition with the help of the community. Yet Native

American women, not men, were the owners and builders of their homes—as in several other societies around the world (see Access to Architecture, Chapter 6). Older women taught younger women housing construction, and the young women and girls assisted with every step of the process. Southern Plains women also developed tipi-sewing guilds.

A woman received her first tipi as a gift from her family at the time of her marriage. When the time came to create a new tipi, she called her female neighbors and relatives together, offering food in return for work—an event much like the quilting bees of the later Euro-American rural settlers. Each woman brought to the gathering several buffalo hides; twelve or so were necessary. On the first day, the women prepared many 2-foot (60-centimeter) lengths of sinew for thread, and on the next day, directed by an experienced older woman, they carefully cut the hides and sewed them to fit together tightly in a curved shape that was a degree or so more than half a circle. On the straight front edges, near the center of the cover, the workers added two flaps to cover the top opening and left an overlap for closure.

Once the cover was complete, it was ready to be placed on its frame and waterproofed. The frame consisted of three or four poles of lodgepole pine, spruce, or red cedar, tied together at the top with leather thongs in a special tipi knot (see Fig. 2.3). The frame was not a perfect cone; it was tilted forward, giving its outline a sharp angle in the rear but something closer to a right angle in the front, apparently to brace the structure against the wind. The ground plan was oval, with its wider side opposite the entrance. To place the cover on the frame, the women first lashed its center to another tall pole, raising the cover from the rear and drawing it toward the front of the frame. Once it was in position, they closed the flaps and waterproofed the cover by building a smoky fire with wet materials inside the tipi. The smoke both cured the skins and scented them with sagebrush. The finished tipi was supple, waterproof, and fragrant. Together, the frame and cover constituted a smooth, tight membrane. Figure 2.4 is Hungry Wolf's diagram of how to set up a tipi.

Access to the tipi was through a slit covered by a hide curtain. The opening, which widened to an oval with use, could be closed securely with sinew or rope laced around willow-stick pins. Where stones were available, people used them to secure the lower edges of the cover, but out on the stoneless Plains, they looped or tied the hem to hardwood stakes they carried with them. Two flaps at the top center controlled the amount of air entering through the upper opening, or smoke-hole. Depending upon wind and weather, people could adjust this opening with two long, exterior poles fastened through holes in the tops of the flaps; when it rained, for example, they folded the flaps over each other to close the opening. Ropes running from the bottom of each flap to sticks thrust into the ground near the doorway provided additional control. During a windstorm, the tent's occupants stabilized their dwelling by staking the dangling extension of the rope that tied the frame poles together at the top of the tent into the floor below.

The tipi was a marvel of functional economy, as well as a striking architectural form. Each was the design of one woman and, after the communal effort of initial construction, she was responsible for setting up and taking down her family's tent, with the help of her daughters. Most tipis could be set up in an hour or so, although Native American writer Hungry Wolf reports that when his grandmother was eighty-six years old and had slowed down, she could still erect her tipi in twenty minutes (see Fig. 14.7); by this time, the tipi may have been covered with canvas, lighter than buffalo skin and easier for one person to lift; by the third quarter of the nineteenth century, the buffalo had been nearly exterminated, and most tipi builders substituted canvas for hides.

The interior arrangement of the tipi varied. In some tribes, the woman-owner and her husband slept to the left of the entrance, and the children and other dependents slept on the right. In other groups, the owner and her husband slept at the rear, opposite the door, usually on the west side. Depending on local custom, the men might sit on the north side and the women on the south. Beds or couches for sleeping and sitting were piles of dry grass or twigs covered with soft buffalo hides. Individuals placed belongings between these couches to define their personal space. Backrests for day use consisted of trapezoidal frames of willow and thongs, pegged down at the head of a couch and sometimes at the foot as well, padded with additional skins.

For cooking and heating, a fire pit ringed with flat stones was set below the smoke hole, off-center toward the front of the tipi. These stones traveled with the family on the annual migration out onto the Plains, where they could not be replaced. Firewood, food, and cooking implements were stored near the doorway and close to the hearth. In a second, smaller pit toward the back of the tent, the inhabitants burned sweet grass and herbs in rituals. Ceremonial objects and trophies rested on the ground or hung from the poles near this pit.

Dakota or Sioux women Tanning and dressing skins   R.O.Sweeny. del 1852.

Figure 2.3. *A 1852 drawing of a Dakota tipi (Great Plains, United States). Left to right: Skin drying over a rack, possibly dyed, since the liquid is being caught in a shallow bowl below. A fire pit is being used to smoke skins suspended from a tree, to waterproof them. A woman is scraping a hide stretched on a frame. Two dogs: Dogs like these were the beasts of burden before runaway Spanish horses made the first great change in the nomadic lives of the peoples of the Great Plains. The tipi is made of regular pieces of skin. The metal pot, suspended from a tripod over a fire, was received in trade from the expanding United States.*

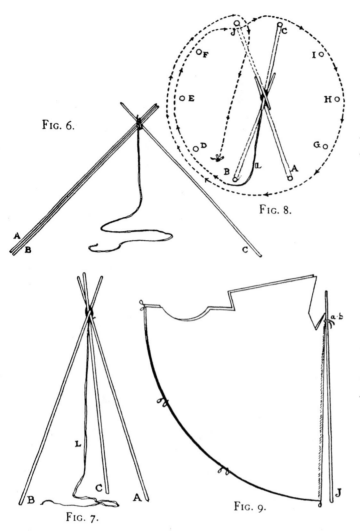

Fig. 6.

Fig. 8.

Fig. 7.

Fig. 9.

Figure 2.4. *Construction of a three-pole tipi. The directions reprinted here from Native American scholar Hungry Wolf (1972), refer to the late nineteenth–early twentieth century when canvas was the material used, but the method of erecting tipis had not basically changed from the days when the cover was made from buffalo skins:*

"Lay three poles on the ground . . . and bind firmly, two feet from the top. The poles are set up as a tripod (Fig. 7) for the skeleton frame. Poles A and B, in front and spread apart, will enclose the door.

Positions of the other seven poles of the frame are shown in the ground diagram, Fig. 8. A, B, and C are the three poles of the skeleton frame. Poles D, E, and F, on the left, and G, H, I, on the right, are raised in the order named. The rope or lariat L, Figs. 7 and 8, used for tying the skeleton frame, has been left hanging. This lariat is now drawn out through the door, between poles A and B, is carried quite around the frame, and is drawn [tight] about the tie.

The pole J in the rear of the tent is the last to be placed. On this pole the canvas cover is raised. Lay the cover on the ground, weather side up, and fold once over [making quarter circle]. Lay down pole J, and tie the cover to it by cord AB [attached to the upper edge of the fold], Fig. 9, two feet from the top. Pole J with the cover is then raised in place between C and F. Before the cover is drawn [around the framework to the front], the lariat L is carried to the rear of the tent, around pole J, back into the tent again between J and C, and anchored firmly to a pin [in the ground, between poles B and D].

The tent cover is now drawn around the frame and laced [up the front]. The door is hung over one of the lacing pins. The loops at the lower edge of the cover are secured to the ground by tent pins, driven in a slant.

Two poles are yet unused. They are raised and their upper ends are thrust into the pockets (or holes) of the smoke flaps."

The tipi was an efficient thermal envelope. Within the space outlined by the outer poles, six smaller poles, well smoothed to conduct moisture without spattering, were set in a circle leaning on the crossing point above, for the total of ten poles that Lewis mentioned. A liner about 5 feet (150 centimeters) wide was fastened inside these poles and hung down to the ground. Rain ran down the inner poles and, instead of falling onto the sleepers, continued down the outside of this liner. The humidity inside the tipi was higher than the dry outer air, adding to the inhabitants' comfort, and the air pocket between the liner and the outer cover acted as insulation, minimizing drafts and heat loss by conduction. This space was also used for storage, which increased its insulating properties. In cold weather, people stuffed the air pocket with grass and banked snow against the outside of the tipi for additional insulation. In warm weather, they lifted and tied the lower edge of the tipi, creating an opening around the bottom that drew in fresh air and pushed the hot interior air out through the smoke-hole. During daily life in her mother's dwelling, a young woman learned how to manage the tipi's inner environment, as well as how to make the tent and set it up.

After a year or more of use, holes were bound to develop in the leather covering of the tipi. Small holes were patched, but we have not found the seemingly practical custom of moving the central skins to the edges and adding new skins at the center, as is known among Bedouin tent dwellers (see Chapter 3, Portable Tents). When the tipi became too worn and tattered to be patched, the women recycled the leather; for instance, the softened, spongy part near the smoke flaps often became diapers.

The Plains dwellers needed movable dwellings because when following the buffalo, they had to travel long distances in the warmer months. Before the tribes had horses, a family transported its tipi on a travois dragged by a dog; this device consisted of two long poles tied together across the animal's back, with a frame between the poles near the ground to support the load. According to sixteenth-century Spanish travelers, a dog travois could carry a tipi made of "five to seven buffalo hides." After the tribes acquired horses, they began making larger tipis that used a dozen hides or more. A typical horse-pulled tipi was 14 feet (4.25 meters) in diameter and 10 feet (3 meters) tall, large enough for four beds. The Blackfeet, grown wealthy from the fur trade, made tipis of eighteen skins, and even larger ones were made for special people or circumstances. Some tipis from the mid-nineteenth century are known to have been as large as 20 feet (6 meters) in diameter, utilizing forty skins. One, requiring a forty-pole frame, had brass buttons from the Hudson's Bay Company fastening the back seam and traditional wooden pins in the front.

The history of the tipi is reflected in its structure—specifically, in the number of poles in its frame. The Sarsi, Blackfeet, Flat Head, Crow, Hidatsa, Mandan, Arikara, and Comanche typically used four support poles, while the Assiniboin, Lakota and Dakota (Sioux), Ponca, Omaha, Cheyenne, Pawnee, Arapaho, Kiowa, and Kiowa-Apache used three and the Nez Percé used either three or four. The variation is accounted for by T. J. Brasser's anthropological analysis of two traditions of tent building. For five thousand years, tent makers in the tundra of northern Canada have used four poles, and groups living in the northern part of the Great Plains followed this tradition. Perhaps the fourth pole provided extra strength against the vigorous northwesterly winds of winter. The four-pole tipi was also larger inside, offering more living space during long winters. The second tradition came to the Great Plains from the northeastern woodlands. Around 1600, the Cree introduced conical tents supported by three poles to the Great Plains. Three-pole tipis became more common in the southern region of the Plains, where the warmer climate allowed more outdoor living.

The adoption of white canvas as the basic tent material after the mid-nineteenth century led to greater regional variation in construction and appearance. In the north, the supporting poles were very long, with streamers or trophy scalps waving from them; in the south, the poles were shorter, and the poles of the smoke flap fitted into pockets sewn into the corners of the flaps. Eventually the northern tents had oval doorways tailored from the canvas, while the southern tents had a V-shaped doorway made by pulling back the two sides of the tent. (See Chapter 14, Overt Expressions of Status, for a discussion of tipi decorating.)

SOURCES: BRASSER (1976), FORDE (1934), GUIDONI (1975), HUNGRY WOLF (1972), LAUBIN AND LAUBIN (1957), MARRIOT (1945), NABOKOV AND EASTON (1989).

Professional Knowledge

Among the Hausa and the Native Americans of the Great Plains, owners and builders were the same persons. Other societies developed professional groups of builders and elaborate methods of organizing construction. When precision of construction was desirable for geographic or cultural reasons, people acquired and applied accurate geometric knowledge. One such method—an ancient one—involves the use of a gnomen to determine directions and angles based on sun shadows, and another is the use of cords and pegs to lay out building plans. Some written and drawn documents and numerous mason's marks on buildings survive to show us how ancient builders used these methods, which lie midway between the completely oral transmission of community building methods and the written diagram. The construction work of guild members in India is presented here as a link between folklore and professional knowledge of building. The group memory of the guild is a way to preserve the person-to-person transfer of knowledge and remains very much alive—a group of Tamil guild members from southern India built a Hindu temple in Malibu, Los Angeles, in the 1990s.

EARLY METHODS AND TOOLS: EGYPT AND CHINA

The Egyptians of 4,500 years ago used sophisticated methods and tools to lay out building plans. Their construction techniques may stand for other traditional systems that have left fewer records or have been studied less carefully. People in China, India, Nigeria, and Mexico still use methods similar to these to plan construction. Techniques for using these tools were passed on by word of mouth, since literacy was extremely rare in Egyptian society.

Builders working for the pharaonic governments of ancient Egypt used geometric, not numerical, methods of design and layout. The Egyptians were skilled geometers through necessity—they had to resurvey their fields each year after the Nile River flooded and had to know leveling procedures to construct irrigation systems.

A. Badawy, an Egyptologist trained as an architect, studied the ancient Egyptians' use of such geometric figures as isosceles triangles in the proportions 1:2, 1:4, 1:8, and 8:5 (the last of which closely approximates the ratio known to mathematicians, art historians, and architects as the golden section, in which the lesser of two sections of a line or figure is to the greater as the greater is to the whole). Badawy theorized that the Egyptians also based architectural proportions on the circle, square, double square, square in circle, right triangle in circle, inscribed and circumscribed triangles, and diagonals of a square or double square. The most frequently used figure, however, was the right triangle, with sides measuring three, four, and five units. By the Third Dynasty (ca. 2600 B.C.E.), builders knew how to construct such a triangle within a square (see Fig. 2.5, upper).

The builders' main measuring tools were the ruler—including extensions of it, such as measured ropes, rods, or chains—and the fixed post or peg. These tools gave their names to the cord-and-peg system of construction. Workers could easily lay out geometric figures in the field using pegs and a cord or rope knotted in twelve equal units (see Fig. 2.5, lower). This cord was such an important tool that the hieroglyph for the number 100 was a picture of a knotted rope wound up; the basic measuring unit, 100 cubits, was equal to 172 feet (52.5 meters).

The field measurements were keyed to studio drawings. We know of two kinds of working drawings from the design studios of Egyptian architects: construction diagrams and proportional diagrams. Selecting one element of the building to use as a module, the architect made freehand drawings on papyrus paper, carefully laying out the axis of symmetry and the dimensions so that the construction crews would be able to build to true dimension and scale. Proportional diagrams complemented the drawings by linking the plan and elevation, laid out on a square grid where the scale was given in modular form. The architects preferred whole-cubit dimensions that could most easily be presented on such a grid, but an analysis of the

monuments they built shows that they also used fractions and multiples of the cubit.

Building models also survive but seem to have represented, rather than guided, construction. The more common are the numerous models deposited in tombs from about 2258–2000 B.C.E. and later. They are of houses and farm buildings, complete with human figures. Rare and more precise are the demonstration models, frequently of temples, that were votive offerings in temples. Both kinds of models reveal construction information. We know that deliberate scale models for architecture are conceptually possible because we have found both scale models and scale drawings for sculptures.

A monument's site in Egypt was determined by orientation to the stars, especially those in the Great Bear (Ursa Major, or the Big Dipper), but the builders also had more immediate clues from the sun and shadows. For buildings oriented east–west, the changing pattern of shadows in a day served as a guide if the site was measured in the morning and afternoon of the same day. A tower or tall pole cast a shadow at the edge of a circle; the shadow pointed west in the morning and east in the afternoon. The surveyors made cross marks to indicate these east and west extremities and then bisected the line between them to find a true north–south line.

After the surveyors had gathered the necessary information about a building site, the workmen laid out the building using the knotted cord or rope, together with 4-cubit and 8-cubit rods. First, two men drove stakes into the ground with mallets (sledgehammers) and stretched a line between the stakes (see Fig. 2.5, lower). From this baseline, they could make right angles by starting at each end of the line and drawing two overlapping arcs (each with the same radius more than half the length of the baseline) that crossed the line; by connecting the intersections of the arcs, they located a second line perpendicular to the first. Then they prepared a network of knotted cords, with a knot at every important point on the drawn plan. Starting at the cross marks, they spread this net out on the site. At each knot they drove a peg, marking the basic points of the construction diagram. Thus, the prepared site became a one-to-one map of the proposed building.

For exactitude in planning and construction, the builders used leveling lines, setting marks to locate columns and pillars, and positioning marks to facilitate correct delivery positioning of stones. The precision of their measurements is shown in the levels of the north and south sides of Cheops' Pyramid, which differ by only 1 inch (2 centimeters), an achievement that would be hard

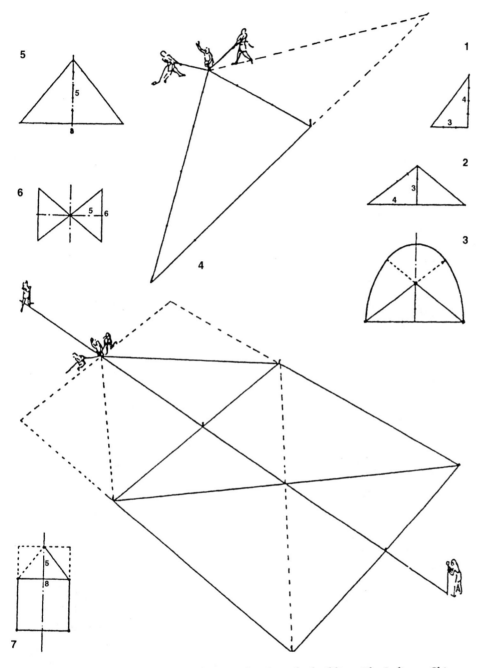

Figure 2.5. *Cords and pegs used to lay out the plan of a building. The Indians, Chinese, and ancient Egyptians used applied geometry in construction. In the lower part of the diagram, surveyors and workers plot the main axis. At the top, they work with a right triangle.*

to surpass with modern methods. In addition to the measuring ropes of 100 cubits and cubit rods of four or eight units, Egyptian builders used plumbs, squares, square levels, and grooved "bearing stones," the ancestors of pulleys; no maneuvering tools have survived, although they would have been necessary for using the bearing stones.

The Egyptians were not the only ancient people to position their buildings according to careful astronomical sightings. The Chinese also knew how to use a shaft called a gnomon—most familiar today as the raised, shadow-casting indicator of a sundial—to determine the sun's altitude or a location's latitude by the length of the shadow it cast. As early as the Shang dynasty (second millennium B.C.E.), the Chinese used the gnomon not only in astronomy, but in construction, to produce lines that were both straight and properly oriented (see Fig. 2.6). And like the Egyptian builders, they also used ropes, cords, and chains. By the late Chou dynasty (fourth century B.C.E.), they regularly used the drawing compass and square, plumb line, water level, and groma (a set of four plumb lines from the ends of two sticks attached at right angles like an open X) for laying out lines at right angles. They also possessed sighting tubes, the ancestors of azimuth bars that measure arcs in the landscape. So rapidly and widely did the art of measuring spread that by the third century C.E., Chinese generals and others who were neither professional astronomers nor builders routinely took measurements of mountains and other natural features wherever they camped.

Perhaps because Chinese culture was so strongly tied to the written word, we have documentary evidence from as early as the eighth century B.C.E. for the use of the plumb line and for the construction of tamped-earth walls in wooden forms. Documents also reveal that the two officials responsible for building a new palace and town were called the Master of the Works and Master of Lands. Architects of the Qin (Chin) and Early Han dynasties in the third century B.C.E. used much of the vocabulary of building construction as we now know it. Although this information has come down to us in documents, the Chinese construction process involved mainly person-to-person spoken directions. The printed construction manuals were written mainly for bureaucrats to control spending.

Like those of Egypt and China, construction methods of Central America and northwestern South America several thousand years ago included elegant engineering. Although there was no written language, the prehistoric hydraulic engineering of Peru and Bolivia (see Chapter 3) was so elegant and so precise that we were forced to realize that they had not only a viable engineering tradition but some way of thinking about the problems and trans-

mitting their answers that was different from but equal to our mathematical base for doing the same, according to engineer-archaeologist C. Ortloff (oral communication).

SOURCES: ARNOLD (1991), BADAWY (1965), ISLER (1989), NEEDHAM (1971), ORTLOFF.

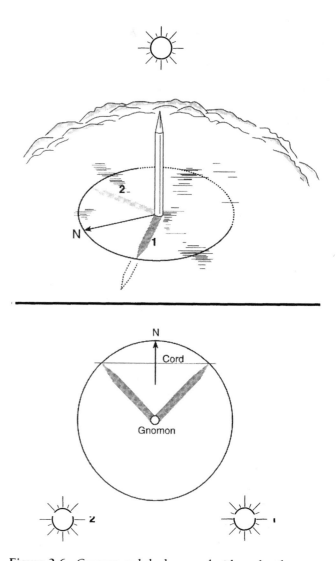

Figure 2.6. *Gnomon and shadows used with cord and pegs to locate the east–west axis of a building, as practiced in India and China. Above, a tall pole is set up in a circle, and a circle is drawn around it. In the early morning, its shadow reaches to the west; when the shadow touches the rim of the circle, the point is marked 1. In the afternoon of the same day, when the shadow reaches the eastern side of the circle, the second point is marked 2. A line between these two points lies east–west. Another line from the pole to the midpoint of the first line determines the direction of north.*

GUILD ORGANIZATION, INDIA

Professional builders in India belong to construction guilds that use person-to-person transfer of information. Each generation in a clan of builders passes its lore to the younger generation by verbal instruction and by working together. The guild system has been a prominent feature of Indian architectural practice since antiquity; ancient tales of the Buddha's previous births mention guilds. One of the first tasks of the guild apprentice who was engaged in temple building, for example, was to learn the rules of construction based on Indian cosmology (see the discussion of mandalas in the next section). Beginning in the fourth century C.E., these codified instructions for temple building were recorded in *sastras* (books about construction read by the priests who advised the builders) that were likely based on much earlier works.

Few recorded accounts of Indian guilds have survived, but one manuscript, written on a palm-leaf manuscript, describes the construction of the Surya temple at Konarak in Orissa in the thirteenth century. This illustrated manuscript shows the architect with a surveying tool and indicates that the height of the building was determined by the governing rules of the mandala diagram. It also lists the workmen's pay, the rules they followed, and other aspects of the building process. From it, we can determine the general procedure for constructing temples.

Guilds played a major role once a site had been selected and work was to begin. Historian G. Michell relates that the architect engaged artisans and workmen who were organized into several groups that acted as guilds (see Fig. 2.7). Contracts determined payments for architectural and sculptural services and set standards for workmanship and the rate of compensation for labor. They were also used to arbitrate disputes, maintain law and order at building sites, and regulate social behavior and stipulated the care of members' orphans and widows. The guilds usually consisted of extended family groups with hereditary membership. Each individual had a role in constructing temples. Men were craftsmen and builders; women kept the work area cleared and polished the stone sections. And just as in the guilds of medieval Europe, specialists' techniques were jealously protected monopolies. After a project was completed, guild workers and their families often migrated to other building sites where their skills were needed.

The chief architect and his superintendent of works were the most important individuals in the building process, along with the brahman priests who were present to ensure that religious tenets were adhered to and to give guidance in theoretical matters of artistic importance. Un-

der them were the head stonemason, also a guild member, and the overseer of the architectural and sculptural program—the two supervisors of craftsmen and apprentices. Together, they directed the work of the surveyors who plotted the axes of the building, stonemasons, artisans, sculptors, grinders, polishers, carvers, and painters.

Sculptors produced the abundant exterior decoration—one of the main characteristics of Hindu temples. Sculptors, highly skilled members of their guild, worked closely with the priests so that the images they carved would reflect orthodox beliefs. A sculptor was recognized only as a medium for executing the work, however, not as an artist with personal status. Status was obtained through membership in the guild, within the limits of the caste system, and by participation in large projects.

The chief patron of temple construction was the ruler of the state. Michell suggests that "temple building communicated [his] physical power . . . as it was an expression of his economic resources." However, individuals also made private donations, and inscriptions tell us that guilds often became wealthy enough to become patrons themselves.

With new methods and materials, India's guild system has changed over time, but it is still made up of family groups that carry out the work of construction (see Fig. 2.8). Fariburz Sahba, construction manager for the Baha'i House of Worship in New Delhi, India, summarizes the tasks of the guilds there. Women accompany their husbands to the temple site, carry loads of stone on their heads, clear the site, and carry concrete. As in the past, the techniques of specialists are guarded monopolies. Sahba cites an example in which builders needed thin, curved, concrete lotus-leaf shells for the main part of the temple. These shells were to be surfaced with marble sections fixed with stainless-steel anchors to the concrete, a system unusual for the Indian workers. Because the work demanded great precision, carpenters were better suited than masons to undertake it. It "took a lot of persuasion," Sahba relates, to convince the carpenters to make wooden panel molds that could then be replaced by marble slabs.

Although the guild system has maintained an important role in Hindu temple construction for hundreds of years and still flourishes in many areas, in modern times the craft tradition in India has been overshadowed by the advent of new materials, such as steel and concrete. Where foreign influences and shifts in the economy have affected the guild system, the skilled craftsmen needed to carve figures and ornamentation are in short supply.

SOURCES: MICHELL (1988), P. OLIVER (1987), ROWLAND (1977), SAHBA (PERSONAL COMMUNICATION), SLUSSER (1982).

Figure 2.7. *Red Fort at Agra, India. Painting depicting the construction of the water gate in the late sixteenth century. The Indian workers in turbans are supervised by Mughals. Materials arrive by boat and water buffalo. Near the top of the ramp, some women workers carry mortar in baskets.*

DOCUMENTED KNOWLEDGE

People use both person-to-person and impersonal methods of transmitting knowledge. Diagrams and written words can convey information across space and time without personal contact. Two documents that effectively communicated building knowledge in Asian societies are the Indian mandala and the Chinese construction manual.

The mandala diagram has an ancient history. Mandalas were the sole architectural documents in India until about the fifth century C.E. and still control how architecture is organized and what it means. Chinese culture, on the other hand, has been based on written language since early in its history. From their origin in the first millennium B.C.E., Chinese construction manuals reached their apogee in the seventeenth and eighteenth centuries.

Mandala Diagrams of India

Mandala is an ancient Sanskrit term for "circle," and a mandala is a symbolic diagram that imitates the metaphysical structure of the cosmos in a symmetrical pattern or geometric grid. Some mandalas depict theological understanding in paintings with bright colors and anthropomorphic forms (see Fig. 2.9). Others are geometric patterns that guide construction or represent a person's horoscope (see Fig. 2.10). A religious mandala has two purposes—as a schema of the cosmos and as a means to join human beings to the cosmos. It is thus both a map and a destination. Particularly in Hinduism, Jainism, and Tantric Buddhism—religions rooted in Brahmanism—the mandala is seen as protecting the learner and helping the learner to find his or her own center.

The vastu-purusha mandala presents a basic vision of creation, representing both the ordered world and the laws governing the world (see Fig. 2.10). Although the earth is known to be round, the comprehended world is diagrammed as square. The central squares of the grid represent the supreme but formless being called Brahman, later identified with the supreme god, Brahma; these squares also refer to the sacred mountain Meru, home of the gods. The diagram explains that Brahman expands to the four directions to find his real center. Grouped in a ring of squares around the center of the diagram are planetary deities and other gods. Then comes another ring, the realm of terrestrial phenomena. This is the world of humans, who can be in touch with Brahman only through the gods. Outside the human world is the region of

Figure 2.8. *Baha'i House of Worship, New Delhi, India. Guild members building the temple. Still organized in extended family groups, the guild members participate in the construction of both traditional and modern buildings. In this structure, erected in the 1990s, carpenters and concrete workers cooperated in an untraditional way to produce a special form.*

demons, goblins, and spirits, who have no contact with Brahman or the gods.

From this underlying theology, it is a short step to the use of a mandala as an organizing principle of architecture. By basing plans for temples and even entire cities on mandalas, the world could be brought closer to divine harmony (see Fig. 9.3). The Mayamata, a manual on ar-

Figure 2.9. *A mandala painting from Nepal, for religious contemplation. The gods Chakrasamvara and Vajravarahi embrace at the center, surrounded by symbols of the gods in the white circle and larger emblems of four goddesses in the corners of the square, followed by a ring with details of activities from the human world, while four more goddesses occupy the outer corners. The mandala is finished with a frieze of gods top and bottom, with a donor portrait in the lower right corner.*

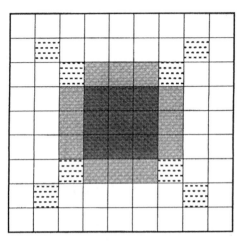

Figure 2.10. *Schematic plan of a mandala suitable for a Hindu temple, following the Brihatsamhita, of the Gupta period (320–540 C.E.). The center nine squares in dark gray represent Brahma, the creative force of the universe; they are surrounded by the realm of the planetary gods (light gray), followed by the world of humans (dotted squares), while demons are confined to the outer rows of squares (white).*

chitecture, states: "If the measurement of the temple is in every way perfect, there will be perfection in the universe as well." The squares of the mandala diagram were proportioned to reflect the perfection of the universe, and architects strove to achieve a similar effect by controlling the dimensions of the temple according to architectural texts. Each part of the design was calculated to conform mathematically to a specific proportional system based on an established unit.

Once a mandala was chosen to serve as the pattern for a building, the builders outlined it on the ground, oriented either to the cardinal points or as determined by astrology, the axis often conforming to the path of the sun. One advantage of the mandala was that because it was a drawing with no text, nonliterate individuals could understand and utilize it in construction work. The mandala also offered variety despite the underlying meaning common to all mandalas. For example, there are thirty-two ways to draw the vastu-purusha mandala, beginning with a square divided into 4, 9, 16, 25, 36, 49, 64, 81, or up to 1,024 equal squares. Of these possible combinations, the eight-by-eight and the nine-by-nine are considered the most powerful. One well-known nine-unit-by-nine-unit mandala has a human figure with the head in one corner, knees bent outward in the corner opposite the head, and

feet with soles placed together. The grid is suggested in an overlay. In other mandalas, the central four or eight squares are empty, and the others are filled with the names of deities and spirits.

Architecture in India was mainly an oral tradition until about a thousand years ago, when it became too complicated for oral transmission and texts began to appear. From the fourth century C.E., for example, we have only brief accounts of Hindu temple construction. Later compilations included artistic expressions, such as painting and sculpture, as well as data on the building arts. Priests set the themes of these documents, producing not a manual for construction but, as historian Michell states, "a collection of rules which attempt to facilitate the translation of theological concepts into architectural form." At a time when the Chinese were codifying and publishing the practical aspects of construction, Indian temple builders were concentrating on the meaning and experience of architecture.

The temple was to be a spiritual experience in itself. A visit to it was supposed to further the devotee's spiritual development. The mandala form of the temple and its axial pathway from the entrance through the inner spaces to the ultimate sanctuary link the monument to time in several ways. First, it takes time for the devotee to move from outside to the sanctuary, approaching and walking around it on the outer terrace and then around the inner corridors to the center. Second, the axial way both symbolizes and is the spiritual way, experienced not only during the visit to the temple but afterward throughout the devotee's life. Finally, the path and the sanctuary are the focus of rituals in the annual festival calendar.

The temple replicated in miniature the form of the created world. The square or rectangular temple platform enclosed by a railing was, like the mandala, a centered space with four or eight cardinal points (north, east, south, west, and perhaps the four intermediate points). Again, like the mandala, the temple form had several layers of meaning, all designed to connect the visitor to deeper reality. The visitor would understand the axis mundi as running from deep in the earth through the image at the center of the sanctuary to the top of the temple's tower and on to the heavens. The altar in front of the temple presented another image of this connection. Finally, the enclosure railing, like the edge of the mandala, embodied and contained the connected elements.

Monks and nuns who traveled throughout India and southeast Asia carried mandalas to ensure that temples were built in conformation with their cosmological plan.

For centuries, however, the meaning of the mandala was kept secret to guard against uninformed use of its power. Even now, the deeper meanings of the pattern are accessible only after diligent study. Since about 1970, scholars in India have been comparing newly discovered texts with the buildings to which they are related. As their study continues, we can expect to learn a great deal more about how people have used the mandala—as a mnemonic device and symbolic shorthand—to preserve architectural knowledge and pass it on.

SOURCES: G. HOUSTON (1976), MICHELL (1988), PAL (1985), ROWLAND (1977), SLUSSER (1982), VOLWAHSEN (1969).

Chinese Construction Manuals

As a tool for temple construction, the mandala was introduced to China along with Indian cosmology, but the Chinese had their own architectural tradition that included the codification of building standards in manuals. Unlike the mandala, which was concerned with a metaphysical plan, the Chinese construction manuals were designed to control building costs in a highly bureaucratic society. They covered the practicalities of costs, work units, materials required, construction details, and rules for carpentry. At the same time, however, craftsmen knew the general skills of carpentry, masonry, and other construction crafts needed to carry out the instructions—knowledge handed down through generations of builders who worked from tradition, rather than from written instructions.

Three kinds of Chinese texts set out architectural ideas. Treatises on the aesthetics of architecture were written by and for the wealthy and the cultivated (compare with Chapter 15). Books on the techniques and rituals of domestic building served the needs of carpenters, who worked from tradition, geomancers, and patrons and helped shape popular architecture; an example of this type of book is *Source of Building Techniques*. Published in the 1920s by the head of the carpenters' guild at Suzhou, it embodies traditions from the sixteenth century, including measurements, materials, and mnemonic lists.

The third type of architectural text was prepared for governmental officials and dealt with the techniques and organization of large imperial projects, covering such topics as financing and the standardization of parts. One of the earliest manuals of this kind was *Building Standards* (*Yingzao fashi*), published in 1103 by the Office of Building, a division of the Ministry of Public Works (see Fig. 2.11a). Six years earlier, Emperor Zhezong had asked for a revision of a previously unpublished manual as part of his overall governmental reform. The manual was intended to cut imperial costs for the construction of public buildings while allowing the architects and builders to produce imposing structures.

The revision was undertaken by Li Chieh (or Li Jie), who worked in the Department of Construction and had

a.

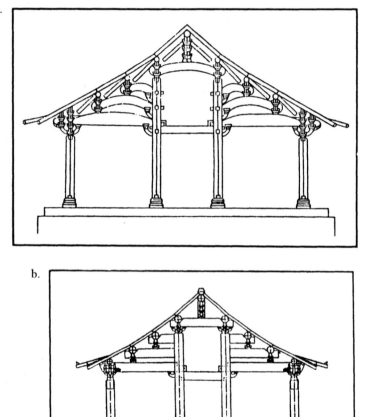

b.

Figure 2.11. **a.** *Cross-section of a building from the Yingzao fashi, a Chinese manual of building standards published in the Song dynasty (1103).* **b.** *Rendering of the section from Gongbu gongcheng zuofa zeli, a later (1734) Chinese engineering manual from the Qing dynasty. The horizontal members of the roof, shown as curved in the older drawing, are rectilinear in the newer one. The earlier brackets are drawn in more detail. Columns in the earlier version are set on bases. Both drawings from the 1925 edition of the Yingzo fashi.*

supervised a number of official building projects in northern China. Barbarian tribes invaded China in the 1120s, and as a result of the disturbances in those years, no published copies of Li's original text exist. But a second edition was printed in 1145. Many of those pages of the work have since been lost. The books that survive are, as historian E. Glahn states, "copies of copies of manuscript copies of the 1145 edition." In its final form, the manual consisted of 34 chapters and almost 2,000 pages of text, executed in wood-block engraving.

Li frequently cited sources that went back to 1000 B.C.E., according to modern scholars. The subject matter shows great attention to detail, a standardization that was intended to ensure no possibility of error or major deviations.

After the introduction, two chapters discuss fortynine architectural types, with quotations of a literary nature dating primarily to the Zhou Dynasty (1027–256 B.C.E.). The remaining thirty-two chapters form four unequal sections on construction methods involving structural elements; work units; the materials needed for various types of work; and the illustration of plans, details, and cross sections. Subdivisions discuss moats and fortifications, stone and brick masonry, carpentry, joinery, woodcarving, drilling, sawing, bamboo construction, plastering, painting, decorations, and the manufacture of tiles.

Since timber was the most commonly used material in Chinese construction, one of the most important features of the *Building Standards* was the rules for carpentry. These rules were set down according to modules for bracket sets, beams, columns, and curved roofs. One detail stands out: the bracket system. Brackets—structural elements that supported the weight of the roof eaves, rafters, and beams—were important features of Chinese construction. Used before the first millennium B.C.E., the system was common on many imperial buildings by the time of the Han dynasty (206 B.C.E.–220 C.E.). A bracket consisted of two main parts, the block (*dou*) and the arm (*gong*), which worked in conjunction with the tie beam and girder. At first, the brackets were purely functional. By the eighth century C.E. modifications had made them more elaborate until they formed complex ornamental clusters, often serving as status symbols. A description and illustration of a bracket roof support in the *Building Standards* (see Fig. 2.12) show a method of carrying the load of roof eaves, rafters, and beams while strengthening the connection between column and roof. The bracket system was especially effective in absorbing earthquake shocks. Whereas European architects used inert capitals, Chinese

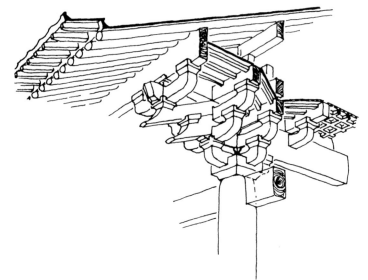

Figure 2.12. *Chinese bracketing system of the Song dynasty. Brackets carry roof eaves, rafters, and beams. The concave slope of the roof requires short rafters. The two main parts of the brackets, the block (dou) and the arm (gong) work in conjunction with the tie beam and girder; the weight of the roof pushes down on the block, which pushes the arm up, producing the springing quality of the eaves. Brackets are both practical and ornamental.*

architects discovered the dynamic strength of combined elements in balance.

The manual emphasized the standardization of materials. Most of its computations were accompanied by unit measures, of which the most basic were timber measurements. Glahn writes that public buildings were divided into eight categories by size, and the units of measurement were adjusted accordingly. For example, the dimensions of pieces for a lesser structure in Grade 8 would be about half those for a grander, Grade 1, building. In addition, various qualities of timber were designated for specific parts of buildings, such as pavilions or halls. For greater efficiency, timber sections were cut to the standard sizes and stored until needed.

The *Building Standards* regulated work as well as structure and materials. The workday was the unit for computing labor output. Its length varied by season; during the summer months, it was about 10 percent longer because of longer daylight hours than during the rest of the year. Until the time of the *Building Standards,* public works were built under a corvee system, in which authorities conscripted unpaid labor. Corvee servitude was replaced by the practice of collecting tax revenues to pay the craftsmen who worked on public projects. To curb excessive governmental spending, construction manuals, such as the *Building Standards,* listed strict classifications for payment in the building trades.

In 1734, the *Engineering Manual* for the Board of Works was published. Its purpose was the same as that of the earlier work: to expedite accounting procedures and improve the control of public works. Similar in format to that of the *Building Standards,* it consisted of seventy-four chapters that describe construction methods and measurements, fourteen chapters devoted to brackets for supporting roofs, and another fourteen chapters on labor. The early chapters discussed halls, city gates, residences, barns, and pavilions. Other chapters dealt with such elements as windows, screens, and doors and with building materials, such as stone, brick and earth. This manual was not illustrated, and despite its detailed procedural outlines, it did not appear to understand the system of standardization nor relate directly to the artisans, as Glahn surmises.

Both manuals generally lack floor plans, although a few were reproduced in the *Building Standards.* The reason may be, as historian S. Liang points out, that movable screens and partitions, not the floor plan, shaped a room for its particular function. Planning consisted not of designing rooms but of arranging individual buildings, usually around a courtyard (see Hollow Centers, Chapter 11).

The *Building Standards* fell into obscurity, and no serious historical study of Chinese building practices took place until the early twentieth century. In 1901, a group of Japanese architects focused attention on the subject by measuring and photographing the buildings of the Forbidden City of Beijing. It was not until 1919 that a Chinese official who was involved in restoration projects in the Forbidden City was shown a copy of the *Building Standards.* His eagerness to have a copy resulted in republication of the book, although it contained mistakes that were due to repeated copying by earlier scribes; for example, it contained examples of both Song and Qing dynasty illustrations (see Figs 2.11a and b). In the 1920s, people regarded Chinese architecture as static, but changes had, in fact, occurred between the Song and Qing dynasties so that proportions and methods were not identical. In 1929 a group of scholars who were devoted to the study of the *Building Standards* formed the Society for Research in Chinese Architecture. Since then, fieldwork has provided much new information, and scholars have published additional studies. We are still learning how the codification of standardized building instructions and governmental control of large projects shaped the Chinese built environment.

The mandala and the Chinese construction manual have a common purpose: to provide instructional guidelines for construction. Outlined on the ground, the mandala not only imitates the structure of the cosmos, but provides a plan that nonliterate builders can understand. In contrast, the Chinese construction manuals arose in a highly literate culture. Both transferred building knowledge, plans, or techniques. People have found many ways to transfer architectural know-how in permanent, impersonal media—didactic ornamentation in Islamic culture, for example, includes messages inscribed on architectural components (see Chapter 13).

Societies as different as the independent nomads of the Great Plains and the literate bureaucrats of imperial China have recognized the importance of safeguarding the techniques of construction and passing them down to younger persons. Builders may be organized into guilds, as in India; gender may determine roles, as with the Native Americans; religion may dominate the process, as in the use of the mandala as an architectural plan. In all these cases and more, people transfer construction technology to other people.

SOURCES: GLAHN (1981), S. LIANG (1984), STEINHARDT (1984).

SUGGESTED READINGS

Arnold, D. 1991. *Building in Egypt: Pharonic Stone Masonry.* New York: Oxford University Press. A simple and clear treatment, well illustrated.

Badawy, A. 1965. *Ancient Egyptian Architectural Design.* Berkeley: University of California Press. An architect who became an Egyptologist, Badawy has much to offer students, including the message of "learning by drawing."

Chandra, L. 1990. "Life, Space and Structures." In *Concepts of Space Ancient and Modern,* 211–18, edited by K. Vatsyayan. New Delhi: Abhinav Publications. A noted Indian scholar and politician meditates on the interconnected meaning of life and architecture.

Denyer, S. 1978. *African Traditional Arhcitecture.* New York: Africana. The basic reference work for African architecture, with many illustrations.

Forde, C. D. 1934. "The Blackfeet." In *Habitat, Economy, and Society: A Geographical Introduction to Ethnology,* 43–68. London: Methuen. Early but still sound. Forde is also useful for Chapter 3 (Portable Tents).

Glahn, E. 1981. "Chinese Building Standards in the 12th Century." *Scientific American* (May): 162–73. Directly applicable to the unit on construction manuals.

Glahn, E. 1984. "Unfolding The Chinese Building Standards: Research on the Yingzao Fashi." In *Chinese Traditional Architecture*, 48–57, edited by N. Steinhardt. New York: China House Gallery. Additional material on standards and manuals.

Houston, G. 1976. "Mandalas: Ritual and Functional." *Tibet Journal,* 2 (April–June): 47–58. An excellent short account of how mandalas are used.

Hungry Wolf, A. 1972. *Tipi Life.* Fort MacCloud, Alberta: Good Medicine Press. A little handbook by a member of the culture.

Isler, M. 1989. "An Ancient Method of Finding and Extending Direction." *Journal of the American Research Center in Egypt* 26: 191–206. Compares traditional Chinese and Indian methods of mensuration.

Laubin, R. and G. Laubin. 1977. *The Indian Tipi: Its History, Construction, and Use.* Norman: University of Oklahoma Press. More details about tipis, written by enthusiasts.

Meister, M. W. 1991. The Hindu Temple: Axis of Access. In *Concepts of Space Ancient and Modern*, pp. 269–80, edited by K. Vatsyayan. New Delhi: Abhinav Publications. Seeing the temple as a diagram of reality.

Michell, G. 1988. *The Hindu Temple: An Introduction to its Meaning and Forms.* Chicago: University of Chicago Press. Basic to current knowledge of architecture in India; material on guilds, pp. 49, 55–57.

Nabokov, P., and R. Easton. 1989. *Native American Architecture.* New York: Oxford University Press. An important book, well written and illustrated, by an anthropologist and an architect.

Needham, J. A. 1971. *Science and Civilisation in China.* Vol. 4, Part III: *Civil Engineering and Nautics,* 125ff. Cambridge, England: Cambridge University Press. Chinese engineering methods and accomplishments. Well illustrated, with citations of both Chinese and Western sources. See also for Chapters 2 (Early Methods and Tools), 3 (River Training), 8 (Great Wall), and 11 (Axial Arrangements, Beijng).

Pal, P. 1985. *Art of Nepal.* Los Angeles: Los Angeles County Museum of Art and University of California Press.

Rowland, B. 1953. *The Art and Architecture of India: Buddhist Hindu Jain.* Hammondsworth, England: Penguin Books. Excellent plans and sections, copious notes with a bibliography to date.

Steinhardt, N.S. 1984. "Bracketing System of the Song Dynasty." In *Chinese Imperial Architecture*, 122–25, edited by N. S. Steinhardt. New York: China House Gallery. A clear explanation of the structure and form of these support systems.

⊞ PART II

Practical Solutions

We can no longer afford to ignore what it takes to live in this world. Many architects in the United States today discuss and practice "sustainable architecture," with the goal of building economically and durably while making as little impact as possible on the environment. Yet traditional methods of architectural history are scarcely broad enough to take in all the necessary elements, since, as historian R. Macmullen writes of the ancient Greco-Roman world, "The general conditions of life . . . are either taken for granted . . . or they are ignored as unimportant, or they are not understood; for both writers and readers, belonging to the elite, were to some extent simply ignorant of how their more humble contemporaries lived and thought." We begin now to seek out other methodologies. The examples from traditional architecture that follow offer practical suggestions for managing water, providing shelter, facilitating food production and storage, coping with climate, and manipulating available resources—solutions that widen the discipline of architecture by incorporating knowledge and methods from other disciplines.

3

Survival: Water, Shelter, and Food

Water, shelter, and food are basic survival issues that may require architectural solutions. Since the beginning of formal architectural history in the late eighteenth-century era of the Enlightenment, architectural historians have often studied palaces and cathedrals as though ordinary buildings were invisible. We choose instead to examine some of the fundamental structures that support everyday life.

Built solutions for water management range in complexity from local urban water systems to regional irrigation schemes to a continental river-control system. Shelter includes not only movable and fixed dwellings, but the use of the ground itself for housing. Granaries and floating gardens are just two examples of construction that facilitates the food supply of urban areas.

WATER

Whether we wash with sand, as Bedouins do in the desert, or build elaborate irrigation works, as did the early Peruvians without benefit of bureaucratic overseers, we are re-
sponding culturally to water or to its absence. Built containers for water in a Nepalese city, a coastal valley in Peru, and a huge river basin in China suggest some of the many ways that people have managed water. Each increase in scale corresponds to an increase in the complexity of the problems for which these indigenous cultures developed sophisticated solutions.

In studying these works, we are unlikely to ask, "Is this the kind of art that I appreciate, or find useful, or even understand?"—a question that too often contaminates our study of the arts and the architectures of other peoples. Because most of us know little about water management in our own culture, we do not have strong opinions that may interfere with our appreciation of how it is done elsewhere. In this and other chapters, water management is a frictionless key that unlocks archives of data about the built environments of other cultures.

We can evaluate a water-management system for competence, serviceability, and longevity. Like other elements of the built environment, however, it can also rise above the purely utilitarian into the range of art. At the urban level in Kathmandu, it may be pleasantly surprising to find that the builders did not neglect the aesthetic aspect of construction, but in China, the scale of the work makes the aesthetic aspect difficult to perceive.

Municipal Water in Kathmandu, Nepal

The water system that serves Kathmandu, the capital of Nepal, and its nearby sister-cities Patan and Bhaktapur, dates from the seventeenth and eighteenth centuries but incorporates elements from at least as early as the fourth and fifth centuries C.E. It is a "system that responds well to the human values and the vast complexity of spiritual and psychological requirements of urban man," according to architect J. Nicolais.[5]

A mountainous country at the northern fringe of the monsoon weather belt, Nepal has ample snowpack resources for rural and urban water supplies, but the difficult terrain demands careful planning for the delivery of water. Water-system builders must begin with a survey of possible sources and then determine how best to develop each one, considering existing and potential rights to water. Other factors to consider include the efficient collection of the water and the protection of reservoirs from floods and contamination. Minimum flow in the dry season and maximum flow during the strongest monsoon storms determine the capacity and design of the pipeline and reservoir.

Water from the mountains surrounding cities in the Kathmandu Valley is brought by gravity-flow pipelines that use siphons, when necessary, to surmount hills. Water is delivered to a series of bath-fountains (dharas in the Newari language, hitties in Nepali—both languages still spoken in the valley) for public use, and the overflow is carried to a series of small, artificial lakes or large reservoirs called pokharas. Installations open to the sky were favored in both crowded neighborhoods and palaces.

Life, culture, and urbanity cluster around water. Bath-fountains are placed three or four blocks apart, so that no one has to walk far to reach one, unlike rural water users, who often must make a forty-five minute trip each way to obtain water. Channeling water to individual houses is uncommon, partly because people value the experiences of fetching water, bathing at a common source, chatting with other users, or resting in the warmth of the sun on benches incorporated into the design of the bath-fountains. As

Nicolais observes, the fountain and its environs are used for "laughter, prayer, conversation, argument, playing, washing clothes, sunning, bathing, picking lice," and much more. Porters rest near the fountains, grain is spread out after harvest, and dung patties are set to dry in the sun until they are ready to be burned as fuel. Venders sell single cigarettes or the graceful brass pots used for carrying water.

The bath-fountain, which has been used in Nepal since the fifth century C.E., perhaps earlier, is similar to the Indian stepwell (see Fig. 3.3) known since the seventh century. In Nepal, it is a roughly rectangular pit with a flat floor, with stairs leading down into the pit from the ground level on the south side. Waterspouts are placed in the northern retaining wall (see Fig. 3.3) and the other two walls are often terraced in several increments, depending on the depth. Small parapets serve as benches. This basic format varies in size and ornamentation from site to site. Builders can expand or reduce it, depending on the amount of water available, the size of the site, and the number of users. Ornamentation often includes religious reliefs or freestanding sculptures. and a shrine or temple may stand beside the fountain.

Bath-fountains are usually fronted by broad platforms with multiple spouts (see Figs. 3.2 and 3.3). Segregation of the sexes (for adults) occurs during bathing, usually by informal agreement; for example, men may bathe at one time of the day and women at another. Traditional modesty requires people to remain covered while bathing in public (a man retains his underpants and a woman her sari)—a technique that takes some practice. The water is cold (approximately 55 degrees F, 13 C) offering little inducement to linger under the spout. Ritual bathing can take place at a ghat, a wide set of steps descending to a river. The most notable ghat in Kathmandu is at the temple of Pashupatinath, one of the most holy places of the Hindu religion. People use this ghat for both ritual bathing and cremation.

Water for drinking is more important than water for bathing. Drilled or dug wells and tanks supplement the bath-fountains, but because running water is perceived as both ritually and physically purer than well or pond water, the fountains supply most of the drinking water.

Some fountains are designed to serve a large number of people at the same time. The Maruhitty and Sundharahitty are important fountains in central Kathmandu (see Figs. 3.2 and 3.3). Modest in architectural form, such a fountain not only supplies drinking and bathing water, but serves as a neighborhood center in a thickly popu-

---

[5]The following discussion draws heavily on the observations of J. Thapa and M. Thapa, environmental and civil engineers, and of D. P. Crouch, an expert on ancient water systems.

Figure 3.1. *Ambapur Stepwell, Gujarat, India. Stepwells like this, constructed in the late 1400s, may descend underground as much as 60 feet, to reach the fluctuating water table. At each level, reached by stairs, platforms on all sides of the shaft give access to water.*

Figure 3.2. *Sundharahitty bath-fountain, in Kathmandu. Bathers are at the central spout. Other spouts are available for collecting drinking water.*

Valley fosters the growth of algae, fungi, and microbes, and the fecal contributions of wandering cows, dogs, and young children make urban pollution a serious problem. In 1983, for example, the great fountain of the central square in Patan was draining freely down to its pavement because its drainage pipes had just been cleared out. One year later, however, the fountain was knee-deep in used water. Either the drains had already clogged or increased precipitation had raised the water table. Reservoir pollution is also a constant problem, as is providing pavement for laundry areas, since without pavement, the spillage produces mud that hampers efforts to keep the areas clean.

Another problem is the repair of damage. The Himalayas are a geologically unstable region where the Pacific and Asian plates grind together, causing the mountains to rise an average of 2.4 inches (6 centimeters) a century, a process accompanied by earthquakes and landslides that can break conduits. In Bhaktapur, for instance, a severe earthquake in 1934 severed most of the underground water and drainage lines—and for political reasons, these lines were not repaired for more than forty years. German assistance helped repair about half the city's supply and drainage pipes during the 1980s as part of a project to preserve the historic temples, palaces, and townhouses. Such repairs are not easy because perhaps to guard the water supply from danger during conflict, the water pipes of Kathmandu, Patan, and Bhaktapur are buried more deeply than concern for rare frost damage would require. The pipes run at 10, 15, or even 20 feet (3 to 6 meters) below the modern surface.

Patronage was key to the construction of the water-management system. The Hindu religion is preoccupied with ritual cleanliness, and devotees gain merit by building public bath-fountains. Individuals sometimes paid for the building of a fountain or tank and its supply and drainage pipes. In the Mangal Bazaar in Patan, this inscription was found:

> Now Bharavi built a water conduit as an object of fame for the enhancement of the virtues of his parents and of himself. To perpetuate his munificence he made a grant of land. . . . The date is Samvat 492 Vaisakha sukla diva 14 [late April–early May, 435 C.E.].
>
> *Inscription XLVII, quoted in D. R. Regmi*

lated part of the city. (See also the Manidhara at Patan, discussed in Chapter 12, and Fig. 12.5, No. 1.) In a palace courtyard, an especially handsome bath-fountain called a tushahitty can be the central focus. The tushahitty of the Mul-chok palace at Patan (see Fig. 12.5, No. 11), a small bath-fountain centered in the main courtyard, is notable for its elegant scale and fine sculptural ornament with religious themes.

The problem of water quality in the bath-fountain system has both engineering and religious components and has always been a challenge to administrators and builders. The humid tropical climate of the Kathmandu

The land grant was presumably an endowment for the conduit and reservoir. Traditionally, the yields from the lands granted with a fountain or other benefice were intended to repair and maintain it.

The water systems of Nepal's cities, like its palaces, were largely made of baked brick (*inta* in Nepali), with some use of finely cut stone, either sandstone, quartzite, or (most commonly) limestone. Long stone conduits lead to the spouts, the chief ornaments of the fountains. These spouts are fashioned of stone, gilded brass, or copper, carved in relief with fantastic animals that have symbolic meanings. The workmanship is excellent, and the designers' understanding of the use of simple line and mass as a foil to the exuberant carvings equals that of the finest modern architects. Nepal's fountains combine utility, flexibility, and beauty in an urbane form unsurpassed even by the famous fountains of Rome.

SOURCES: LIVINGSTON AND FORESTA (1991), NICOLAIS (1971), REGMI (1983).

Irrigation Systems in Peru

Providing water to an urban population presents one set of challenges. Creating a regional irrigation system in a desert presents another. Northwestern coastal Peru lies in a climatic zone where farming is possible only with irrigation—rain may fall but once in a century. To farm and live there, people had to manage river water, and the Lambayeque people of the Chicama River valley created an irrigation system during the first millennium C.E. that modern engineers and geologists have praised (see Fig. 3.4). The system's construction method is only slowly being recovered.

When the Chimu (900–1450 C.E.) conquered the Lambayeque, they took over the Lambayeques' water-management system. The Inka, in turn, conquered the Chimu sometime after the mid-fifteenth century, a generation before the Spanish conquest of Peru. All these peoples found that survival called for great ingenuity in the construction of irrigation systems. The valley walls form a gradually widening wedge, divided in two as the river descends toward the sea. To extend their farmlands onto riverine slopes, ancient engineers built canals that tapped the river high up, at the neck where it burst forth from the mountains. These canals formed artificial rivers along the higher contours on both sides of the river, dividing each half of the valley into narrower wedges. By watering more of the valley's fertile soil (see Figs. 3.4 and 3.5) and by allowing for differences in altitude, each long wedge gave its owners access to each local ecological zone and its various products, thus allowing greater integration of human life with the landscape.

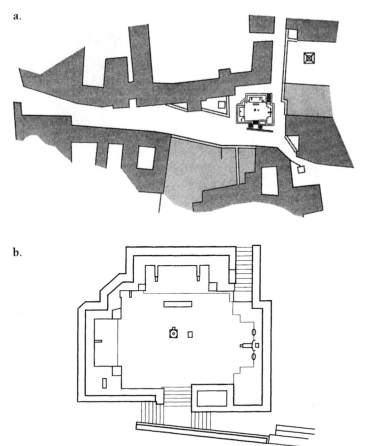

Figure 3.3. *Maruhitty (fountain), Kathmandu, Nepal (plan and detail).* **a.** *The large bath-fountain is set into an irregular T-intersection in central Kathmandu.* **b.** *The detailed plan shows five spouts for bathing and for collecting drinking water Around the edges are spaces for people to gather.*

The built elements of the system were terraces, dams, intakes (usually temporary weirs), canals, and sunken fields. In the mountains, the builders constructed elaborate terracing and storage tanks, but these elements were rare on the coast, and there were no large dams or reservoirs in the coastal valleys. The canals were cut out of rock or lined with stone or clay. Construction began at the edge of the mountains at an elevation of 640–960 feet (200–300 meters). Each canal watered the land downhill from it.

Some canals from high intakes on the river passed through upper terraces without watering them, carrying water to a down-valley area and ensuring that all fields,

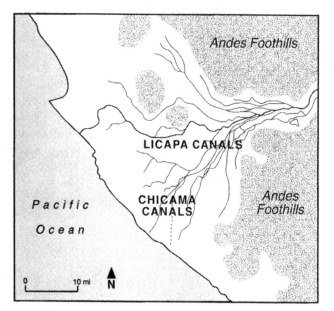

Figure 3.4. *Chicama River Valley, Peru. The river is the only line stretching from the ocean to the foothills. The other lines are canals that belonged to the sixteenth-century polities of Licapa and Chicama, made to divide the terraces into wedges that pierce several ecological zones. The dashed line is the trace of a disused canal.*

canal farthest from the intake at the neck of the valley annually cleaned and maintained not only the branch canal and ditches within their own section, but the main canal from their intake to the previous intake along the main canal. The next group cleaned its own branch canal and the main canal up to the next intake in the series, and so on. Ownership of land carried with it the obligation to repair and maintain the canal.

The wide diffusion of knowledge about irrigation technology, the segmentation of responsibility, and the hands-on management of local lords allowed people to

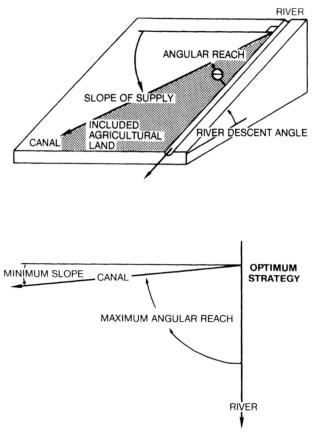

even those farthest from the intake point, received a fair share of water—a solution better engineered and more equitable than the later Spanish system of watering the higher fields first. If such a canal needed to pass over another, a wooden aqueduct carried it. Check-dams across gullies protected canals and their fields from mountain freshets. They also built weirs—small, temporary dams—of brush and stones to divert the river water through intakes into canals. Large building projects, such as inter-valley canals between river systems, delivered water in two valleys. One example is the Chicama-Moche Canal, probably built by the Chimu to water state lands in the Moche Valley.

The irrigation system fed two kinds of agricultural plots—the surface field completely supplied with water from canals and the sunken field. The latter was dug below the surface of the ground so that the crops' roots could reach the deep water table, but was also supplemented with water from the canals.

Although a regional set of canals had a unified design, local people built and maintained a section of each canal system. For instance, the users of the water of the

SLOPE, ANGLE, AND OPTIMUM STRATEGY

Figure 3.5. *Diagram of the slope, angle, and optimum strategy for an irrigation system on the north coast of Peru. As the river downcuts its bed, new intakes must be built higher and higher, until the mountain's wall is reached. Canals are located to irrigate the maximum amount of land per foot of canal length. As in Fig. 3.4, each canal mimics the river in dividing the land into wedges.*

solve both common problems and great crises efficiently and cooperatively. The lords provided necessary tools, food for the workers, and personal supervision; they were also responsible for allocating of the water and for carrying out the rituals considered necessary to bring rainfall in the mountains. Ordinary farmers provided the labor and materials. Currency never changed hands.

This cooperative system could contend with major problems, such as the damage caused by earthquakes or by the fearful rains that accompanied periodic storms caused by El Niño. Earthquakes are common along this coast, but rainfall is extremely rare. When it does occur, it is likely to be catastrophic, resulting in enormous floods. Such crises revealed the genius of the ancient water-management design.

Peru's irrigation culture functioned without a separate irrigation bureaucracy. Various groups worked together to repair the damage with minimal direction. Society was divided into moieties, or halves. The chief of the entire group functioned as head of the more important moiety and head of half that moiety (a quarter of the entire society). The number-two man was responsible for the other half of the population, land, and canals. Each of them had assistants who were responsible for a section of the canal system and the adjacent lands. This system of shared responsibility, easily expanded or contracted as circumstances warranted, coped with conditions that included spring planting, annual upkeep, and repair after a flood.

Although the political regime of Peru changed in the mid-sixteenth century with the Spanish conquest, the water-management system and the social architecture for managing the system changed little. Some canals fell into disuse, however, owing to depopulation caused by imported diseases or to tectonic uplift, which interfered with the slope of the canals. The indigenous design for water management was excellent, but nature was stronger.

The Spanish conquerors brought to Peru their own water tradition, which involved observing the local irrigation pattern and adopting as much of it as possible. They were usually content to leave in place a system that could produce one, two, or three crops a year, with a comfortable surplus for the ruling classes. Only the disasters of El Niño storms in 1578 and severe depopulation in the sixteenth and especially the seventeenth centuries forced the new masters to reorganize the irrigation system. Even then, they preserved many traditional Peruvian features.

Today the ancient system of water management can be seen in the remains of abandoned canals, in surviving agricultural fertility rituals, in conflict resolution, and in organization of the social group. Under a veneer of Christianity and modern political form, the age-old rituals of cleaning the canals are still carried on. The "lord"—today a politician—supervises the cleaning and conducts the ritual that manifests the group's understanding of its place in the cosmos and enforces social solidarity. Conflict that could affect that solidarity is resolved by the next-higher-level authority. There are still four sectors of the polity, all of which enjoy access to upvalley and downvalley resources, including rights to the littoral and the sea. Operating without a bureaucracy and with a high degree of decentralization, the irrigation and social systems mirror each other in their adaptive efficiency.

SOURCES: NETHERLY (1984, 1987), ORTLOFF ET AL. (1983).

River Training in China

On a continental scale, the management of the Yellow River Valley in China may be compared to the work of the Tennessee Valley Authority (TVA) in the southeastern United States—if the TVA controlled not only the Tennessee River watershed but the Ohio and lower Mississippi river basins. The TVA began in the 1930s, but the Chinese project began several thousand years ago.

Chinese water management developed during thousands of years of struggle against the Huang Ho (Yellow) and Chang Jiang (Yangtze) rivers, which drain immense portions of the country (see the map of Asia in the Appendix). Despite the construction of thousands of miles of dikes and canals and many reservoirs, these rivers have never been completely controlled. Still, management of the rivers led to the development of canals that improved water transportation, provided water for irrigation and municipal water systems, and contributed to defense efforts. The Chinese civil service system can be considered a direct outcome of these efforts, which required a complicated organization of managers at many places and many levels of administration. In China, water is political. The neglect of water management directly contributed to the overthrow of several dynasties and the founding of new governments.

About two thousand years ago, during the Han dynasty, the government saw the advantage of using teams of mathematicians, engineers, and administrators to control and conserve water. Experts in various disciplines could combine their knowledge and skills, debate problems, and come to the best solution. The Han Dynasty appointed the earliest water-conservation officials for each district. A water-conservation official, assisted by a chief hydraulic engineer, directed soldiers and corvee labor. The canal builders and river trainers that we call "engineers" graduated from an educational and civil service system that produced China's officials from 206 B.C.E. until 1905 C.E. After passing written examinations, successful candidates were assigned local positions. The more ambitious and capable could eventually become governors or court officials.

Chinese hydraulic engineers use the term *river training* to describe the process of managing China's major waterways. The principal goal of river training is to prevent the silting up of the lower part of the riverbed, which can lead to vast floods. The concept of river training is illustrated in the long history of the relationship between the Chinese people and the Huang Ho.

As it has for many generations, the Huang Ho combined blessing and curse for the 10 million people who lived in its valley in 1987 (see the map of Asia in the Appendix). The river is 2,890 miles (5,464 kilometers) long, but little more than a sixth of these miles is navigable (see the excellent map of this river in Needham's history of Chinese technology, Fig. 859.) With more than forty major tributaries, it drains an area of 750 million square miles, including more than 290 million square miles of loess—fine, wind-deposited soil, the source of troublesome silt.

The river's profile and its seasonal water flow have made it necessary for the Chinese to train it. In its upper section, the river drops 15,750 feet (4,800 meters), three-quarters of that in Mongolia alone. Swift and violent, the river plunges through a series of gorges in the middle section of its course, losing another 2920 feet (890 meters). High silt content and the combination of swift, violent flows with sudden rises and falls in the water level cause flooding in the lowest third of the river as it nears the sea.

In its 1,200-mile (2,000-kilometer) lowest section, the river descends only 262 feet (80 meters). Here, it runs slowly and deposits much sediment. Under natural conditions, silt deposits raise the bed of the river until it is higher than the plain it runs through. Thus, an elaborate system of dikes is essential to prevent disastrous flooding. In a hilly area near Jinan in Shandong province, the river is forced between dikes. There, silt that is pumped out of the water and is added to the dikes goes to strengthen them. In this area, therefore, the river is held to a steady bed level, but neglect of the levees sometimes has allowed the river to break out, disastrously.

Terrain problems are worsened by the pattern of four flood peaks a year, in January, April, July, and October. The latter two are four times greater than the April high. River management must thus accommodate vast deviations from the average flow. The river's total discharge has varied from as little as 7,000 to as much as 1,270,000 cubic feet (200 to 36,000 cubic meters per second; the maximum figure was recorded in the 1843 floods. In addition, the engineers must factor a load of at least 10 percent silt into their plans and expect that tributaries will add water carrying up to 68 percent silt.

The course of the Huang Ho changes frequently in the delta, but it also shifts in the upper sections. J. A. Needham reports eleven major beds of the river during historic times. At times, the river's mouth has been at the Pohai Sea and sometimes 210 miles (350 kilometers) away in the Chang Jiang river. In the four thousand years since the first recorded efforts to pacify the river, nearly two thousand breaks in the dikes have led to twenty-six major shifts in the riverbed. This river's fluid energy and wide range make training it essential—but extremely difficult.

As early as 2000 B.C.E., the Chinese began researching and recording the Huang Ho's habits, and by the eighth century B.C.E., they were using tanks and reservoirs to store surplus water. Floods in 602 B.C.E. stimulated them to build dike systems and dams to contain runoff. Since that time, there have been arguments about building dikes or forcing the river to scour its own bed that have never been resolved. As early as the fifth century B.C.E., the Chinese began building large-scale irrigation schemes, including canals to carry water from the river and its tributaries.

During the brief Chin Dynasty (221–207 B.C.E.), three important waterworks—the Chengkuo irrigation canal (Needham's Fig. 883), the Kuanhsien irrigation system, and the Ling Chhu transportation canal—were built. They supported the unification of the country under its first emperor. Two of the works are still functioning. Few civilizations can claim such longevity for their waterworks.

Although the most diligent civil servants paid close attention to the Huang Ho, disaster still occurred. In 11 C.E., a great flood afflicted half the population with disease and famine and resulted in forced migration and economic disruption. The Us and Tang dynasties (seventh to tenth centuries C.E.) saw twenty-one floods in 290 years. Under the Song Dynasty in 1060 C.E., the river—which had oscillated between its northern and eastern arms for a decade—cut a new channel to the northeast. Then, after a series of floods from broken dikes, it settled into the section of riverbed near Kaifung that it has occupied ever since. Further multiple breaches during the Jingo and Yuan dynasties (1127–1360) resulted in major changes in the river's middle section. Fortunately, an engineer named Jailu trained the river, dredging a flood bypass, damming the gaps, and generally strengthening the dikes until eventually he forced the river back into its old course.

Local catastrophe is well demonstrated in the tragic history of the city of T'an-ch'eng and its surroundings, located north of the river near the sea. The city was flooded again and again. Floods in 1649, 1651, and 1652 led to famine. In 1668 an earthquake struck a devastating blow, breaking dikes and causing widespread flooding. Sand-choked fields left by the floods prevented cultivation. Heavy rains in 1674 turned fields into lakes. These disasters, together with political instability, depopulated the region: In fifty years, the region lost 70 percent of its population, 60 percent of its cultivated land, 33 percent of its taxed land, and 63 of its 85 townships. To overcome the flooding problems in this area, engineers at the end of the century dredged the tributaries on the south bank of the river to divert excess flow southward, and on the north bank, they built hundreds of miles of dikes. One engineer, Pan Jixun, redeveloped in the eighteenth century a technique of washing away sediment with high-speed water, using the energy of the spring floods to remove the very silt that was exacerbating them.

Although the Chinese have built dikes since 5500 to 4000 B.C.E., they never succeeded in taming the rivers completely. When the dikes broke, people at first placed large bamboo trunks and stones across the breach in the levee. This was no small task: The earliest documents describe dikes 33 feet (10 meters) high, and a breach might be dozens of yards or meters wide. Workers began at each end of the breach, extending the remaining walls toward each other until at last they stopped the flow (Fig. 3.6a).

Great flood disasters later stimulated the development of a new technique, *shao* works, for filling gaps in dikes. Workers tied long reeds or branches together with bamboo, producing an enormous cylinder (see Fig. 3.6b) that required hundreds of men pulling on dozens of ropes to move it into place across a breach. Once in place, the cylinder was secured by piling earth and stone on it. Downriver and in later centuries, people more commonly used gabion (bamboo cages filled with stone). The cages were ferried by boat from both ends of the breach and then sunk—boats and all—to block the opening.

Under China's last dynasty, the Qing (1644–1911), engineers devised a new method of using the troublesome

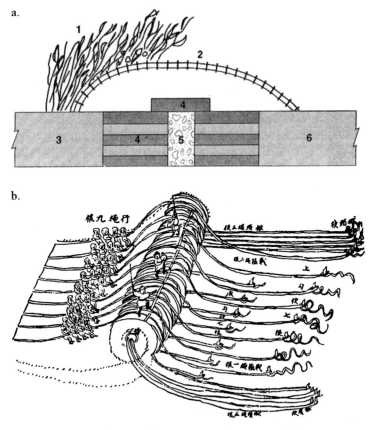

Figure 3.6. *Huang Ho (Yellow River), China.* **a.** *The earliest method of repairing a break in a dike. A pontoon bridge (2) of boats is placed in an arc upstream from the break. A series of shao (sao), or fascine bundles, are placed across the break, while additional poles and wood are sunk between the boats to slow the flow of the water.* **b.** *A giant fascine bundle being moved into place, On the left, the workers pull the bundle toward the water. Ropes running through the center of the bundle are played out slowly to act as brakes. Looped around each end of the bundle are another seven long cables that act as a safety "cage" in which the fascine bundle can roll. Eighteenth-century sketch.*

silt to strengthen the dikes: They built secondary canals paralleling the main canal (see Fig. 3.7). Water entered the secondary canal, where it flowed more slowly and deposited its silt, and then returned to the river. As silt filled the secondary canals, they were transformed into stronger and wider dikes. Even today, enormous projects using this principle are under way in China.

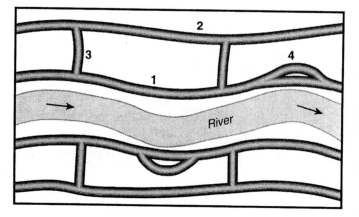

Figure 3.7. *River training in China. The modern method of building networks of dikes. Flood waters are released into the compartments between the dikes, where they slow and deposit their silt; the water is then returned to the river. Eventually, silt fills the compartments completely, and they become wide reinforcements for the levees.*

In 1995 a combination of torrential rains, an early thaw in the mountains, and deforestation of the eastern edges of the Himalayas combined to produce the worst flood in a century along the Chang Jiang, south of the Huang Ho. To generate electrical power and to help control such floods, Chinese engineers are now constructing a series of dams in the gorges of the Chang Jiang. These dams have been strongly criticized by environmentalists and some foreign engineers. On the Huang Ho, overdemand had, by early 1999, resulted in severe desiccation—a major share of the 22–33-billion-ton deficit of usable water for the whole country. Yet the empirical methods developed by ancient experts have worked well enough when supported by the political system. Chinese rivers are forceful and wily. Those who train them must apply stronger forces: human reason and social solidarity.

SOURCES: R. LIANG, ZHENG, AND HU (1987); NEEDHAM (1971): VOL. IV, PART III, 284–306; SPENCE (1978).

SHELTER

The two basic patterns of human life are sedentary and nomadic. Accordingly, people have learned to make both fixed and portable dwellings. Many aspects of community life—defense, worship, and the procurement and storage of food—are strongly affected by whether settlements are permanent or movable. There are many gradations be-

tween the two poles of fixed and movable dwellings. Between the nomad who lives in a tent and the farmer who lives in a brick house are the villagers who farm in summer and then move about to herd sheep and goats in the winter, as well as drovers who herd sheep and goats all year on the borders between settled farmland and wild pasture, patterns which ethnologist C. D. Forde understood as early as 1934.

Movable Dwellings

The brush shelters of the African Basarwa, which their occupiers hastily build and soon abandon, and the durable tents of the Bedouin, which their owners carry from place to place, are both temporary dwellings. But two kinds of "temporary" are clearly involved. In the first instance, only the fire that symbolizes the home is carried from place to place; in the second, beasts of burden allow people to transport the physical elements of their homes.

THE KALAHARI AS AN UNBUILT ENVIRONMENT

After two centuries of deliberate extermination by invading Europeans, the !Kung Basarwa (Bushmen)[6] of Africa and their culture survive only deep in the Kalahari desert (see the map of Africa in the Appendix). Until 150–200 years ago, the Basarwa lived throughout South Africa, and earlier, their range had extended to east and north Africa. Current research suggests that the Kalahari groups are not refugees from the Basarwa genocide that followed the European colonization of Africa, but have lived there, next to the Botswana swamp, for at least 20,000 to 30,000 years. Ten thousand years ago—recently, in geologic terms—the swamp was a large lake. Since that time, the people have evolved a notable tolerance for water scarcity as the land became desiccated.

Temperatures in the Kalahari reach 110–115 degrees Fahrenheit during summer days, with nights of 70–80 de-

[6]The Basarwa are perhaps the aborigines of Africa, according to L. L. Cavalli-Sforza (1994). They are short, with thin lips, hair tightly spiraled to form tufts, and yellowish-brown skin. They speak a language called Khoisan, which is full of clicks. In the 1,120-mile (1,800-kilometer) length of the Kalahari Desert, they have developed several major language groups with many sublanguages and dialects. Basarwa is their official modern name; in the past, they were called San. The !Kung are a specific local group.

grees F (43–45 and 21–25 C), but in winter, the temperature may drop to 30 degrees F (−1 C) and even to 10 degrees F (−12 C) at night. The Basarwa seem acclimated to the heat but suffer from the cold nights of winter. The severity of the climate demands that they move every few weeks or months to a new location for food and especially for water. They must carry everything they own because they have no beasts of burden, so they use their desert world as a storehouse, collecting new materials each time they build. Their dwellings are the most impermanent that we discuss, consisting only of a temporary shelter of brush in the form of a round enclosure with a fire in front, although in earlier times and in areas with different resources, the Basarwa built stone shelters.

Groups of five to sixteen households (twenty-five to sixty people) have traditionally divided the Kalahari into local territories of 300 to 400 square miles (115–155 square kilometers) each. During summer (November to July), increased rain allows individual families to gather in larger groups or camps. At these times, the families arrange trade and intermarriage. During the winter months, the shortage of water forces them to separate into much smaller, wide-ranging family groups. A viable camp-band has at least ten members, with a mean of nineteen over a ten-year period. This group of siblings, cousins, spouses, and spouses' relatives roams the territory in search of food and water for themselves, fodder where wild animals they hunt will gather, and trees for shade. The women gather wild foods within 5 miles (8 kilometers) of the camp and care for the children; the men hunt farther away.

The informal head of the group is the person with the most influence. Often an older man and a skilled hunter, his most important task is to plan how the group will use its food and water supply. He regulates the band's moves, working out the best annual path. Members of a band are free to join another band in which they have relatives or friends and frequently do so. Movement between bands reduces tensions and eases food shortages.

Because of their nomadic life and the need to hand-carry every item they own, the Basarwa tend to possess few objects. These few—beads, clothing, and blankets—are simple, well made, and well cared for. People do not accumulate artifacts as signs of wealth or status but share tools so that there will be less to carry. Rounds of gift-giving ensure that prized objects slowly circulate through the group. People stow the personal items they possess inside their shelters, hanging them from the branches of the inner framework.

Basarwa women build the family homes using ephemeral materials. Dry-season dwellings are mere wind-breaks of branches and grass that delimit an "inside" and an "outside" (Fig. 3.8a). These dwellings provide necessary shade, but little privacy. The !Kung people, however, do not expect Western-style privacy (compare these dwellings with Japanese houses, discussed later in this chapter and in Chapter 10, Japanese Floor-Level Living, and with iglus—Inuit for igloos—in Chapter 4.) "To seek solitude is regarded as a bizarre form of behavior. Even marital sex is carried on discreetly under a light blanket shared with younger children around the family fire. It is considered bad manners for others to look," writes anthropologist R. B. Lee.

The windbreak houses and their hearth areas are neither sex specific nor age specific. Children and adults of both sexes and all ages use the hearth area as a focus for their activities. In only a few groups the area of the shelter is allocated, the right side to the man and the left to the woman. In those groups, if the woman decides during the dry seasons not to build a hut, "she will occasionally place two sticks in the ground to symbolize the entrance to the shelter, so that the family can orient itself as to the appropriate side of the fire" to sit on, writes anthropologist S. Kent.

A woman can gather the materials for the dry-season shelter—6-foot (2-meter) branches, twigs, and grass—dig the necessary holes, insert the branches, weave them together at the top, tie them with a fiber cord, and thatch the outside with armloads of grass in an hour or less. Girls learn from their mothers how to build these shelters. Men also know how to build them and use them during hunting trips.

Rainy-season dwellings are more elaborate. They are domed shelters fashioned of branches interlaced with twigs, like baskets. Circular in shape, they are half- or three-quarter circles about 4 to 5 feet wide on the open side, 5 feet tall, and 3 to 4 feet deep (120–150 by 150 by 90–120 centimeters), thatched with grass or covered with mats to protect the inhabitants. It takes a woman up to fifteen hours to build the weather-resistant shelter, and she must spend about five minutes a day working to maintain it. Yet these shelters provide space only for storage and temporary escape from rain and heat, not living spaces. The open side of the shelter is usually placed away from the prevailing winds; the shelter is easy to move if the wind changes. The size of a dwelling relates less to the number of people who will occupy it and more to how long the people plan to stay at the location. Cultural fac-

a.

b.

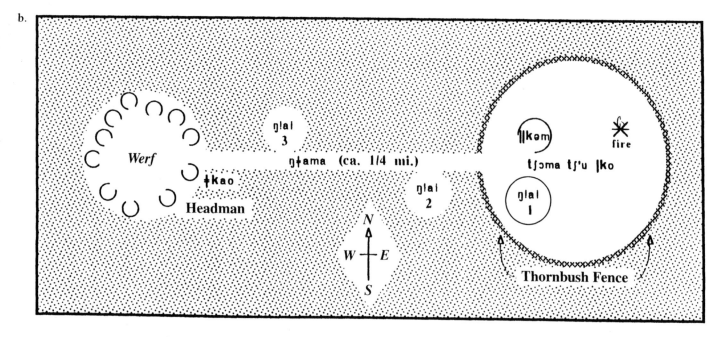

tors thus directly influence the use of space more than do the constraints of the physical environment (see Fig. 3.8).

The connotation "home" is attached not to the shelter but to the fire that each nuclear family builds in front of its dwelling. For protection against predators, the fires burn all night. From this base, the hunters and gatherers go out each day, carefully covering the fires with ashes before they leave. At night, they push away the ashes and fan the coals to restart the fires for cooking and security. If a new fire is necessary, they can use a fire drill or—more commonly, nowadays—a flint and steel.

Among some groups, the settlement has no fixed pattern except that the fires and shelters are close together. For example, L. Marshall, the first anthropologist to study the people of the Kalahari, noted eight family fires, with a total of thirty-two people, in an area 20 feet by 40 or 50 feet (6 by 12–15 meters), without a detectable pattern. Other groups may set up the camp in the form of a circle, possibly oriented to the east but centered on a fire or tree that is considered powerful (see Fig. 3.8b). Additional circles for dancing may be established. The plan of such a settlement has a physical reality on the ground, but the elevation is largely intangible, and hence metaphysical,[7] since, as Kent writes, "Conceptual boundaries create discrete activity areas as rigidly controlled as that created by physical walls or completely separate structures."

The Basarwa are careful not to place their settlements too near water holes for fear of disturbing the game. Even though the camp returns periodically to the same water hole, they never reuse the exact site, possibly for sanitary reasons. People shove household debris, such as inedible parts of plants and animals, to the edge of the living space and mix it with ashes from the fireplace. Defecation on the open ground outside the camp attracts flies, leading to infections, but this danger is lessened in summer by the

beneficial activities of dung beetles. Anthropologist G. Silberbauer reports, "Campsites are usually noticeably polluted within 10 days of occupation, and after 3 weeks pollution reaches the level of discomfort (judged by informants' standards)." Pollution of the campsite is another reason for moving five or more times a year.

These nomads of the Kalahari live in a materially simple way, as noted earlier. The Kalahari functions for them as an unbuilt storehouse, and their culture is highly evolved in response. All over central and south Africa, these original inhabitants have painted and engraved numerous caves with art, of which D. Lewis-Williams and T. Dowson made a detailed record. Early engraved rock art dates to 24,000 years B.C.E. at least, and the nomads were still creating cave paintings as late as a hundred years ago. When correlated with anthropological study, the ancient rock art of the Basarwa gives new insights into their lives and their beliefs, depicting events, ceremonies, and the visions of trance-dancers, illustrating beliefs and activities that the Basarwa of the Kalahari maintain to this day.

At a typical ceremony in a camp, the women, seated around a fire, sing and clap, while the men dance around them. Gradually, one person after another enters a trance, from which he or she can derive various powers: to cure others, make rain, or report on the struggles of the spirit world. The spirit world is as close as the edge of the dance circle; once they awake, the trance-dancers bring spirit messages to the group. At the home campfire or at the rock shelter, the danced trance interprets reality for the group and defends the group from dangerous aspects of that reality. Beliefs include the realization that God is angered by belittling or wasteful behavior, as well as by overharvesting that leaves no plants to grow again and replenish the store. Some important visions have been painted or chipped onto the surface of a rock shelter at a ceremonial center.

Architectural historians are particularly interested in two aspects of the rock art. First, the artists selected shal-

---

[7]Thanks to John Nichols for this suggestion.

Figure 3.8. *Basarwa camp, Kalahari desert, Botswana.* **a.** *A typical temporary shelter of the dry season. In the rainy season, a somewhat larger shelter is built.* **b.** *Plan of a Basarwa initiation camp. At the left are family windbreaks (shelters). A path leads past two dance circles into a second area enclosed within a thorn bush fence, set aside for the initiates. Ritual initiation is held in such a formal encampment every few years. 1, 2, and 3 are dance circles, and Ilkam is the shelter for the initiates. More commonly, the group of windbreaks may be centered on a special tree; rarely do they all open toward the center as here.*

low, domed space, so the rock shelter resembles a brush dwelling made large and translated into the permanent medium of stone. Both are places to be *at* more than *in*. Second, the shamanlike trance-dancer and the community conceive the spirit world to lie immediately behind the painted rock of the cave. The paintings are, in some sense, a transparent screen between the viewer, who is not in a trance, and the visionary world being reported. The curer-healer-painter pulls the spirit beings up to the surface for all to see.

Dancing, trances, and painting reveal the significance of the inhabited environment (see Fig. 3.8b). Like other hunter-gatherers, such as the aborigines of Australia, the Basarwa have had millennia to meditate on the meaning of their environment for their own lives. Their metaphysical world is rich and interesting.

The Basarwa also alter the desert landscape. For example, they build brush fences to control game during a chase. Hunting structures are surely of more use to them than are permanent houses. Some groups dig pits to trap game; others until recently, used existing *karst dolines* (natural funnels carved by water into stone) along a riverbed as giraffe traps that enable the lightly armed !Kung to capture these large and fleet animals for food.

Urban historian L. Mumford (1961) postulates that civilizations tend to make their necessities smaller and smaller, and the Basarwa, in both the domestic and religious uses of space, have dematerialized their culture to a marked degree. We shall return to this issue of the dematerialization of architectural form when we discuss Chinese architectural concepts (see Chapter 15, Being and Nonbeing in Chinese Architecture). Basarwa architecture and the following example of the Ruwala remind us that builders may not be male and may work for others than the elite of their society.

SOURCES: FORDE (1934), 309; KENT (1995); R. B. LEE (1979), 56; LEWIS-WILLIAMS AND DOWSON (1989); MUMFORD (1961); SILBERBAUER (1981), 285; TOBIAS (1978); VAN DER POST (1958).

PORTABLE TENTS OF THE BEDOUIN, ARABIA

The nomadic Bedouin of North Africa and Arabia live in portable tents that are precisely adapted to the circumstances of their wandering lives. Since camels carry the tents and other supplies, the Bedouin are able to live on a materially more complex level than are the Kalahari Basarwa, although this may mean only that their culture is different, not more evolved. There are many types of Bedouin tents; we focus on those of one tribe, the Ruwala of northwest Arabia.

The wealthy Ruwala Bedouin numbered some 3,500 households in 1930.[8] As they move about, seeking fodder for their animals and water for themselves and their animals, they keep within their tribal area; a family may possess rights to a certain part of that territory (see Fig. 3.9). These nomads spend the summer months near the Mediterranean Sea. In September they move eastward to the grasslands for water for their flocks, spending the winter camping near wells for periods ranging from a day to several weeks—as long as the pasturage and water hold out. In the spring, they turn south to the temporarily blooming desert and obtain water at oases. Finally, in the summer, they return to the coast to exchange surplus camels for grain, clothing, guns, and tent cloth.

To follow their herds of camels and sheep, the nomads have kept the items they carry to a minimum. Yet having pack animals allows them to accumulate many more possessions than the Basarwa. For the Bedouin, the desert is not a storehouse but a pasture. Camels are the main source of wealth. The Bedouin need one camel per person merely to carry the food grains necessary for the long weeks away from settlements. A powerful family may own fifty or more camels: some for the family to ride, others to carry food (grain, dates, salt, coffee), and a few for guests. Camels also give milk and are sacrificed occasionally for meat. The food supply from the herd is supplemented with some hunting and gathering and by purchased grain.

The Bedouin way of life has persisted at least since the camel was domesticated around 1600 B.C.E. Thanks to the camel, about 10 percent of the Arabs of the Middle East and Africa are nomadic pastoralists, who maintain local traditions and ways of life. In the past they controlled the long-distance trade of the area, both overland and seagoing. They traded across the northern half of Africa, as well as throughout the Middle East and Southeast Asia, achieving wealth and status through their monopoly of the African carrying trade in gold, ivory, and slaves, which were exchanged for salt. Now, however, the Bedouins mostly raise sheep and camels.

Many Bedouin groups set up their tents in a circle into which they drive the animals at night, but the Ruwala

---

[8]C. D. Forde (1934), based on the studies of A. Musil (1928), a Czech explorer who lived for several years with the Ruwala, from 1928 on.

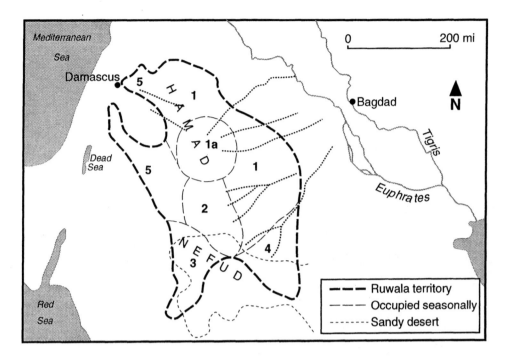

Figure 3.9. *Map of Ruwala Bedouin territory, in the northern Arabian Desert, between the eastern edge of Mediterranean Sea and the two rivers of Mesopotamia. Pastures are designated by numbers: (1) winter, with (1a) the richest pastures; (2) spring; (3) alternate winter pastures, when the rains are good or the pastures fail in the central (1a) Hamad area; (4) alternate, used when pastures to the north and west fail; and (5) oasis settlements visited in the summer. The top of the map marks the end of the desert and the beginning of the northern steppe lands of higher rainfall, suitable for horse breeding.*

Arabs disdain such precautions, arranging their tents in two parallel rows. Each family group has at least one tent. Divorce is easy, but former wives with their children, widows, and other dependents are still part of the group and have their tents with those of visitors in the tent rows. Sometimes tents are attached to one another to enlarge the interior space, so that an entire commercial enterprise may be housed in one tent, as the late nineteenth-century traveler C. M. Doughty saw in a temporary marketplace for the pilgrims to Mecca.

A tribe's tents provide not only protection but camaraderie. The tent of the sheik, or chief, is the largest. It has a spacious guest area with a small hearth for making coffee, where the men gather to talk, eat, and smoke. In front of this seating area, the tent is left open facing whatever direction is most convenient at that campsite and for the current weather.

Because both Islam and Arab customs emphasize hospitality, each tent (not just the chief's) is arranged for the ceremonial feeding of visitors. Cooking takes place on a larger hearth in the women's part of the tent or just outside it. For visitors, hosts place platters of whole roasted mutton, surrounded by boiled rice, pine nuts, and other tidbits, in the center of a rug. Such festive food contrasts with the daily ration of camel milk, grain, and dates. Treasured ceramic or metal bowls and platters for food are among the most important Bedouin possessions and are often of fine workmanship.

The tents are notably efficient tensile structures: lightweight, portable, and requiring little in the way of material resources (see Fig. 3.10 a and b). (Further illustrations of different membrane constructions from various nomadic peoples of Africa may be found in L. Prussin, 1986 and 1995.) Their occupants can set them up and

a.

Figure 3.10. *Bedouin tent, Tunisia.* **a.** *The tent is made of narrow strips of wool, their white selvages creating a pattern against the black. Supporting poles and stay lines control the height, shape, and tension of the roof.* **b.** *The tent as membrane construction. Guy ropes pull outward, while poles push upward, and the fabric of the tent stretches between. All can quickly be dismounted, rolled, and transported to the next camp.*

b.

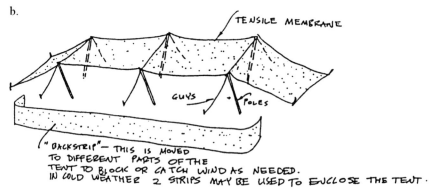

take them down quickly. All the work of erection and dismantling is done by the women, who also design and make the tents—and are their owners. Yet when a marriage takes place, the groom is said to "build a tent over his wife." Thus, certain symbolic as well as practical meanings are attached to the tents, the nomadic dwelling taking on community symbolism.

The tents are made of 2-foot-wide (60-centimeter) strips of woven or felted hair or wool sewn together. The women may weave the strips from sheep's wool, goat's hair, or camel hair or they may obtain the cloth by trade in the towns. Sometimes the tent fabric or the dividing curtains are specially woven in striped patterns, but usually they are black or dark gray with white cotton selvages.

Although "the black color of the goat hair might be expected to absorb the sun's rays and make the tent uncomfortably hot, the dark hue means that the cover casts a dense shade and insulates against radiant heat," according to anthropologist P. Oliver. Tent strips, 10–40 yards long (11–44 meters) are sewn together along the edges; a tent of normal size requires four strips, 10 yards long. The cloth lasts twenty years or so, eventually wearing soft and thin, giving less and less protection against the elements.

The process of setting up a Bedouin tent (see Fig. 3.10 b) is this: Lay the six to eight poles that make up the frame on the ground in their proper pattern. Over them stretch the material of the tent roof flat on the ground, with cords running out from each point of attachment at the edge of the tent. Attach a pair of stakes to every pair of cords, except at the center of the tent, where each pair has three stakes. Raise the poles and pound the stakes into the ground. A larger tent has the same pattern, but uses taller poles and more cords-plus-stakes.

The design resists even strong blasts of wind if the tent is set up firmly. Long panels of cloth pinned with wooden skewers to a narrow strip along the edge of the roof provide side walls that can easily be moved to block or admit the wind; they may be doubled in severe weather. Within the tent, a breast- or neck-high cloth, hung between the waist poles, divides the space into two main areas.

In some groups, the eastern section is allocated to the men and the western section to the women. Visitors are entertained in the smaller but higher-status men's space. The larger space is where the children sleep while the women and slaves work together, perhaps cooking or weaving. This area is also used to store supplies. Bedouins practice floor-level living, like the Japanese (see Chapter 10), the Basarwa, and others. The basic furnishings inside the tent are rugs for the floor. A few backrests may be present, with saddlebags serving as armrests. There are also quilts and cushions. Next to each tent is the family's outdoor area, where activities, such as caring for animals, take place.

Other nomad groups exhibit much diversity in the sizes and shapes of their tents, but the framing method and size tend to remain constant within any one group. As architect and art historian L. Prussin showed in her detailed study of the architecture of sub-Saharan nomads, this durability of form is a foil to the ever-changing location of the home. Prussin also pointed out that the perception of space among these nomads is related less to

gender than to life experience; the space perception of nomadic women is as good as or better than that of urban men. Traveling has taught the women to notice subtle differences in the landscape and to position themselves spatially within those geographic and temporal changes.

SOURCES: DOUGHTY (1888); FORDE (1934), 309; PRUSSIN (1995).

Stationary Dwellings

The houses of extended farm families in Japan and Nigeria offer a contrast to the dwellings of the nomadic Basarwa and Bedouin. Although these farm complexes also appear different from one another, they have some similar elements in that they are built to solve similar problems. Yet the nature of the available materials—wood in Japan and mud in Nigeria—affects the final structure, as does the religious and social character of the people. (Chapter 5 looks more directly at the differences in materials.)

JAPANESE FARMHOUSES

In Japanese culture, the term *house* has the meaning—both legal and psychological—of family. Westerners find this significance easier to grasp in connection with the single-family house (the Katsura Villa of Chapter 9) than with the extended- or multifamily farmhouse discussed here. Yet this Japanese farmhouse not only satisfies the basic need of people for shelter, but integrates the people's social, economic, and aesthetic needs. The resulting form, the *minka*, is so elegant that it has attracted the positive attention of such different critics as the late-nineteenth-century American E. S. Morse—a zoologist-turned-anthropologist—and the European modernist architect B. Taut, both of whom lived in Japan and whose opinions are woven into the descriptive analysis that follows.

Physical evidence of ancient Japanese houses, such as postholes, has survived from as long ago as the seventh century C.E. Early houses had wooden frames lashed together with vines, similar to the Japanese and Indonesian dwellings described in Chapters 5 (Interlocking Frameworks) and 10 (Stilt Houses). According to Japanese tradition, lashed houses came before carpenters' tools were invented. But from the early days, people cut wood and prepared it with tools, the development of tools and that of architecture going hand in hand.

The ancient Japanese farmhouse must have been the prototype for both the palace and the castle in two different lines of development. The farmhouse began as a one-story building, a form that reached its fullest development in elegant villas or palaces, such as Katsura (see Chapter 9), a rambling, one-story, country house, while other clans preferred country mansions of several stories, called minka. This second tradition is seen in castles built during the civil wars of the mid-fifteenth to the early seventeenth century—stone variants of the multistory wooden farmhouse known since the fourth or fifth century C.E., with heavy timber framing and thick plaster walls to withstand artillery fire. The castle form continued to influence Japanese architecture until the middle of the twentieth century, particularly for buildings that had to house several families or a great family and its many retainers.

Farmhouses (minka) were built not only as shelters, but to alleviate the cold in winter, to provide storage for farm products, and often to house an extended clan working together to produce silk or some other salable product. A complex could include the dwelling, barns, storehouses, a shrine, and a grove of trees. Builders determined the plan of the complex using the principles of *hogaku*, or "direction-angle" orientation, a system similar to the Chinese geomancy called *feng-shui* and to similar astrologically based locational systems in Tibet and India.

The dramatically steep roof of the Japanese farmhouse was designed to shed water and snow (see Fig. 3.11). Its ridge line could be straight or curved, with the acute angle at the top measuring 40 to 60 degrees. Some roofs,

Figure 3.11. *Yanohara-type farmhouse, Gifu Prefecture, Japan. Behind the auxiliary buildings in the foreground, the main house rises four stories; the upper stories are used for silk production. The thatched roofs are made from local agricultural materials and provide good insulation.*

particularly in the north, were made of tiles, slate, or cedar-bark shingles held in place with stones against the fierce winds of winter. One house might have several different roof coverings, the result of periodic maintenance with whatever material was convenient. Visual continuity was less important than utility.

Originally, a mud or pounded-earth floor at the center of the interior was surrounded by a slightly raised floor or low couch for sitting and/or storage around the sides, similar to the indigenous Tlingit houses of the northwest coast of North America. Gradually, the couch came to fill the interior, developing into a floor of padded tatami, or rice-straw matting, traditional for part or all the house (see Chapter 10, Japanese Floor-level Living). Instead of a large hearth at the center of the rectangular or L-shaped living area, the later houses had a heat pit at the center around which the family gathered.

"The country house is larger and more substantial than the city house . . . some are mansions [whose] massiveness and dignity . . . indicates the position and power of the household," wrote Morse in the late nineteenth century, adding that heavy fixed latticing and dramatic lighting from a window above the rectangular or L-shaped earth-floor entrance room were typical of the minka. One venerable example of this type was the tall, substantial house of a farmer in Kabutoyama, in West Musashi province. The main house stood opposite the gate flanked by storehouses and servants' quarters around the courtyard. At the right, attached to the main house, was the kitchen wing. Both the main house and kitchen wing had thick thatched roofs with an elaborate ridge line, but later additions had tiled roofs. At the left, behind a fence, were a garden and guest house, and behind them was a two-story house for the grandfather of the family.

The auxiliary buildings for one-story farmhouses may include separate quarters for servants, but in the multistory type, such quarters are incorporated into the "family" space of the main building. Although most of the animals lodge outside in their own stables, a prize horse or bull may have a stall at one side of the minka's main hall. The farmyard holds sheds, detached storehouses usually of fireproof materials, a bath hut, and a threshing floor. Some storehouses have stone exteriors and wooden interiors of interlocking planks.

"Some farmhouses . . . are like fortresses, with mighty gates and heavy street walls," wrote B. Taut, who lived in Japan for more than a year in the 1930s. Taut described farmhouses as having a huge central post about 18 inches (half a meter) in diameter, supporting crossbeams 16

inches deep. The post was situated near the fireplace, and a vestige of it may remain in the ornamental post that sets off the tokonoma niche discussed in Chapter 7. Posts and beams were "cleverly interlaced" and secure in earthquakes but, to Taut, not "rationalistic"; rationalism was a European design movement of the mid-nineteenth century that emphasized the development of modern ornaments integrated with structure and the decorative use of materials and texture, rather than added ornaments.

The widely spaced post-and-beam structure of the Japanese farmhouse carried the principal load and made possible the open flooring system, similar to that of the South Seas houses on stilts (see Chapter 10). Partition panels, floors, ceilings, storage units, or ornamental alcoves divided the interior space and ensured flexibility, which helped this type of house remain in use for hundreds of years. Surface finishes revealed the beauty of the wood grain or stucco.

Taut watched a house built from the beginning to completion. He recorded that the workers began by laying out the shape by peg and cord, "as is done everywhere" (see Fig. 2.5). The builders were fine craftsmen; no architect was needed. The owner discussed the house with the master carpenter and then left him and his men to produce their version of the traditional house, with variations according to size, budget, and the owner's preferences.

Multistory farmhouses still standing in Nagano prefecture that have been used for silkworm culture, the industrial base of the extended family, are good examples of the minka. The upper two or three floors had open bamboo latticework floors so that heat from the ground floor could rise to the roof, keeping the silkworms warm enough to grow and spin their cocoons. As indoor-heat sources improved, the house's form and use changed. Before 1750 the cultivators added a summer crop; after 1850, autumn and late autumn crops; finally, in the 1920s, they moved the silk culture out of the house into separate buildings. Thus, the form of the large multistory house was constrained by the farming group's need for large spaces with many possible uses. It also exemplified the social arrangements of the extended family and the aesthetic sensibilities of the Japanese culture (Fig. 3.12).

Living spaces in the farmhouses, as in urban homes, are organized with smaller rooms to the north and larger ones to the south for solar heating. On the ground floor, the hall and the kitchen are either at right angles to one another or share the same long, rectangular space. Family members and servants use the hall for many activities.

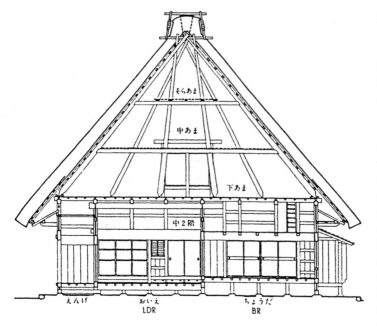

Figure 3.12. *Section of a Yanohara farmhouse, Gifu Prefecture, Japan. Stories 2, 3, and 4 (the attic) were used for raising silkworms; their floors were of latticework to permit the heat to rise. The thickness of the thatched roof is indicated. On the lowest story, the living room-dining room is on the left, and a bedroom is on the right.*

The hall fireplace, developed from the open hearth and smoke-hole of earlier times, and the kitchen stoves are used for both heating and cooking. Heat and smoke affected the design of the roof and facade—the ridge line of the roof is often curved up at both gables to allow for smoke-holes. For many centuries, kitchen stoves were built of stone and lime, with no flue. Smoke was allowed to rise into the thatched roofs, where it killed insects. Since the mid-nineteenth century, however, stoves have included metal flues to control the smoke and reduce the chance of fire. Some households have two stoves—one dedicated to cooking rice, the staple food, and the other for other dishes. In southwestern Japan, the tradition is to build a separate kitchen, so that the fire there will not be polluted by a death occurring in the main house or the house endangered by a kitchen fire. Also, since the climate is milder in the south, cooking fires are not needed for warmth in the main house.

The kitchen is a major hub of activity, opening to the main hall via the wood storage area (see Fig. 3.13). Other storage vats for sake (wine) and pickles take up some of the space on the kitchen floor. Shelves in the kitchen for storing dishes are supplemented by a stair closet, a cabinet placed along a wall or serving as a room divider, with open and closed shelves or drawers of different sizes seemingly piled up into a cabinet, to make a stairway to the story above. Other stairs—very steep—may resemble stepladders with or without railings.

Within the kitchen, a well provides water for both drinking and laundry. Washing tubs stand near the well with a pulley arrangement for raising water; other wells are located in courtyards or gardens. Usually, the latrine and washstand are next to the hall, but in more expensive houses they are located in a separate wing or room off the veranda. The latrine is divided into two areas, a floor toilet in the inner space, and a urinal in the outer space. As in many modern Turkish homes, there is a special set of sandals for use in the latrine. Excrement is stored in a receptacle made of half a barrel or a large earthen vessel set into the ground below the latrine, with access from outside to clean it. These arrangements were "not elaborate but adequate," according to E. S. Morse's late-nineteenth-century American standards. Sewage is not wasted; rather, excrement is sold for use as fertilizer, providing added income to a family. Morse reported, "In poorer tenements, if three persons rent a room together, the sewage pays the rent of one; if five rent a room together, it's free!" Where intensive farming is practiced, people stockpile excrement and garbage for agricultural use. In the Japan of the late 1960s, the countryside still retained the traditional smell, a combination of seaweed, fish, vinegar, and excrement. The residents of modern Japanese cities, however, have standard sewage systems.

Bathing in Japan is partly sanitary, partly aesthetic, and partly helpful in combating the cold of winter in unheated houses. Bathing areas are usually near the latrine but clearly separate from it. The large, deep tubs are heated by a small fire below. Soaping, scrubbing, and rinsing take place outside the tub, which is for communal soaking and relaxing. Japanese culture easily accepts "functional nudity" as part of an activity, such as bathing, and a whole family may soak in the tub together. As a by-product of bathing, the wooden floors of verandas and hallways are polished with a cloth wrung out in bath water, so that body oils in the water give an ivory-like gleam to the floors.

The traditional sleeping arrangements in small houses are also communal. An entire tatami-covered floor can be a "bed," where quilts wadded with cotton or down are spread at night. Tatami mats are "a form of [communal] space, on which anybody may sit or lie without regard to distance' (according to Taut), so that an entire family and their guests may properly sleep in one space at night.

Both Morse and Taut admired the refined aesthetics among the Japanese farmers, unhampered by their relative poverty. "Where these men had settled they had created a garden of the highest culture," wrote Taut, who praised these farmhouses as "the refinement of aesthetic effect" dominated by the ideal of beauty, accomplished by a "display of the genuine material and its weight." The flexibility and the high aesthetic quality helped these houses remain in use for hundreds of years, embodying the survival not just of family lineages but of a culture, yet their simplicity, flexibility, and aesthetic sophistication have made them as attractive to persons from outside the culture as to their original owners. The book by architect T. Itoh and photographer Y. Futagawa more fully describes this unsurpassed domestic architecture.

SOURCES: ITOH AND FUTUGAWA (1980), MORSE (1886), TAUT (1937).

HAUSA EXTENDED-FAMILY COMPOUNDS

Chapter 2 told how the Hausa people of Nigeria make their dwellings of mud. We now examine how people live in these family compounds—the universal Hausa residential units. Similar family patterns, coupled with a similar use of space, are found among the Chinese (see Chapter 11, Hollow Centers: Courtyards). The religious motivations are different, but in both cultures extended families have traditionally found it to their advantage to work and live together, since there was no other "safety net" against disaster. In the following brief account of the economics of the Hausa extended family, we focus on the architectural implications of domestic arrangements.

The traditional Hausa farm household lives in a town or village, within a mud- or stalk-walled area approximately 100 by 100 feet square (30 by 30 meters) (see Fig. 3.14). Both the Muslim religion and Hausa family tradition make marriage mandatory and polygamy common. A domestic unit consists most often of two men (father and son or two brothers) and their wives and children. The extended family contains two or three smaller groups that are based on marriage and occupy separate divisions of the compound. They work and eat as nuclear families or as one group. Within the homestead, each woman has her own round one-room house and shares it with her young children.

Figure 3.13. *Farmhouse kitchen, Kabutoyama, Japan. In the foreground, a woman draws water from a well in the earthen-floor section of the room, while two others work in the raised wooden-floored section behind. The stove is at the left center, and a tall cupboard is at the rear.*

The first act in establishing a homestead is to build the exterior wall or fence (see Fig. 2.1), high enough to block casual views from outside. A homestead has one entrance that cannot be directly opposite a neighbor's entranceway. Thus, the privacy of each household is protected.

The entrance leads into a shallow forecourt. Centered in the back wall of this forecourt is a large, rectangular hut with various uses: a deflecting entranceway for the inner compound, a general work area for men's crafts, a place to entertain neighbors or visitors, and sometimes the sleeping area of the headman. If the compound is big enough, the forecourt may also hold a round hut for adolescent males of the family and another for visitors. Beyond the forecourt wall lies the larger part of the compound.

In some families, a fence divides the large, back area into two sections. On each side of the fence are one household's hearth, granary, a well near the wall that separates the forecourt and rear court, latrines and baths in the farthest corners, and house units. Each woman's

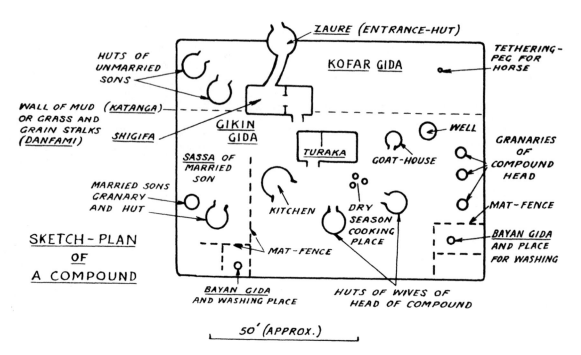

Figure 3.14. *Hausa compound, northern Nigeria, about 1950. A schematic plan of how a rural family organizes the space within the mud wall or fence of branches into a forecourt (kogar gida), with rooms for unmarried sons and space for tethering a horse, and an inner court (gikin gida). The compound is entered through a round building called a zaure. Between the inner and outer courts is the access building (shigifa), a meeting and workplace for the males of the family and sometimes the sleeping place of the head man. Some compounds have an inner building (turaka) for the head man's quarters. The inner court is again subdivided by mat fencing, depending on the number of households living there. Each division has its own living space, granary, latrine (bayan gida), and washing place. Sanitary facilities are separated from the well, located near the fence that divides the outer from the inner court. Both an open-air place for cooking and a sheltered kitchen are available, their use depending on the weather. The basic unit is a round, freestanding room (one per adult) with a thatched roof.*

round house has its own outdoor hearth for cooking; there may be a communal roofed area for wet-season cooking. Within her freestanding but small room, the wife arranges her soft hangings and bed coverings and sets out her cooking and storage utensils. The back area of the compound also encloses granary buildings and perhaps beehives at a distance from the dwelling units and may be large enough to enclose the family's herd as well.

Customary formality between family members increases the interpersonal distance suggested by the architectural arrangement of the separate huts. The married couple maintain a rigid and distant formality between

themselves and toward their first child or first few children. Although most women marry three or four times, a woman may maintain her residence in a former husband's compound—especially if he is dead—to protect her children's claims to a share of that family's wealth. Survival is a real issue in the arrangement and use of the family compound.

These compounds are furnished austerely with a minimum of movable objects, but the residents understand that the tangible arrangements are enriched with symbolic meanings (see Fig. 2.2, detail of house wall with finger patterns and painted decoration; see also the facade of an urban house of Hausa people, Fig. 13.7, and Chapter 15 for a discussion of the symbolic meanings of the houses of the neighboring Batammaliba people). Furnishings include soft, round leather cushions and, for special seating, chairs and stools that carry high status in Africa. Much daily activity takes place on the ground, and built-in seating and sleeping platforms are low. A wife's bed consists of a mud platform at one side of her hut.

Architect N. Macindoe, who lived in Nigeria during the mid-1990s, describes dwellings just north of the city of Kano:

[T]he mud villages no longer had signs of modern materials or services—they were unaffected by development that might have been brought by the presence of the road going by. The villages were made up of walled family compounds with mud huts within and built into the wall [see Fig. 2.1]. Mostly when not attached to the compound wall the huts were circular in plan with conical thatched roofs. Further north the huts were more often rectangular in shape. As we approached Katsina the mud took on a lighter shade and pinkish tinge. Though the huts became rectangular the compounds . . . [they] now had large storage containers round in plan with conical roofs, but the walls were either woven like thatch or of smooth rounded mud like an enormous clay pot. These were set about a foot or more above the ground, I imagine to prevent the entry of rodents. . . . The people here have the appearance of living as they had for many hundreds of years. There is a certain universality about all mud villages dictated by the limits of the material, climate, and time to make them.

In cities, or just outside cities, the noble families from whom the chief is selected live in larger versions of the same compound because it is to their political advantage to maintain a large, cohesive extended family. Hausa living arrangements make a telling contrast with those of the Japanese farmhouses, also built for extended families but without the internal separation into subgroups that the Hausa codify in their architectural forms.

SOURCES: N. MACINDOE, PERSONAL COMMUNICATION (1996), M. G. SMITH (1995).

Underground Houses: Available to Everyone

Dwellings in traditional societies have been made of easily available materials and erected by the community, per-haps under the direction of a master builder or architect. Before modern times, particularly before industrialization, ad hoc local solutions made some kind of interior space generally available to everyone. Even a damp house is better than sleeping outdoors in pouring rain; even a hard-to-heat house is better than sleeping in snow. In the United States today, citizens vehemently argue the issue of affordable housing for all, while Europeans have long assumed that the government or voluntary associations are obligated to provide enough units to house the population. This is a political problem—not an architectural one—although architects may contribute to the solution.

The first response to human need, from which all other architecture has developed, is that of housing. Unlike some other animals that can lock their joints to sleep standing up or clinging to a perch, humans must regularly lie down to sleep, and most of us sleep deeply enough to become oblivious to our surroundings, which means that we need a safe place to sleep. We also find it useful to have a regular place to cook the foods we eat, a place to store food and other things, and a central base for child care. Thus all human societies have developed dwelling units of some sort.

People use different aspects of their environments to create shelter. Where there is a shortage of wood for construction but the ground is easily worked, they have created housing by digging into the ground and hollowing it out into artificial caves. In China, Tunisia (see Chapter 4, Hot and Dry), and other places, such houses have many advantages. Given the population pressure in China, a house that requires few material resources other than the site of the house itself is highly advantageous.

Carved-out dwellings, like cave-temples, date from as early as 7,000 years ago. Two main forms are known. One is the house cut or built into the side of a hill or cliff (see Chapter 9, Agglomerative Cliff Houses). The other is organized around a courtyard sunk into loess soil. In China's western Shansi, northern Shensi, and southeastern Kansu provinces, yellow loess, 10 to 30 meters thick covers an area larger than 144,000 square miles (400,000 square kilometers). Within that area, some 40 million people live in cave houses (see Fig. 3.15).

The nature of the northern loess plains explains the use of these houses. Soil temperatures 6 feet (2 meters) below ground remain stable year round. Air temperatures range from below freezing to extremely hot, but the house excavated below 6 feet remains much cooler than the surface air in summer and much warmer in winter. Inside cave dwellings in Henan, for example, the difference be-

与大地相联系 CONNECTION TO THE EARTH

建筑寓于大自然之中，黄土高原的窑洞就与大地紧密连在一起。

建筑与大地相联系

沿崖式窑洞

地坑式窑洞

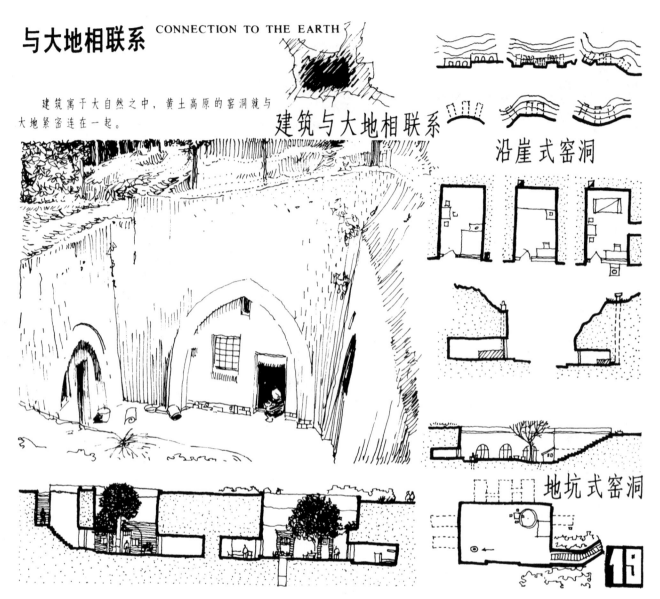

Figure 3.15. *Loess-area houses cut into the ground, northwest China. The large sketch at the left is a view down into the courtyard. Below is a section through two adjacent units: left to right, access stairs, court with tree, two underground rooms, second court with well and tree, another room. At top right, two sets of sketches of plans of hillslope houses like those in Fig. 3.17. Below that, from top to bottom: plans of three units (the left and middle ones having kangs) (see Fig. 3.16); a section showing the relation of rooms to ground surfaces and to the pipelike vents for the kangs; a section of a unit with a bigger court with a tree and a shed near the steps to the ground surface; and a plan of a court with two rooms at the left, three connected rooms at the top, and one room at the right parallel to the access steps.*

tween high and low temperatures was 18 F (10 C), significantly less than the range of 41 F (23 C) for above-ground houses. The cave house offers obvious advantages of thermal comfort and fuel economy.

People also can easily master the techniques of constructing cave dwellings in loess. Using shovels and other farming implements, they cut a house into the soil in a vaulted shape that needs little or no internal support. Vaults may be elliptical, semicircular, parabolic, flat, or pointed; any variant may spring from straight lower walls. It takes workers about forty days to excavate a cave about 20 feet deep by 10 feet wide by 10 feet high (6 by 3 by 3 meters). Such a cave requires at least three months to dry out completely.

Cave houses are economical not just in terms of heating but in their use of materials and their durability. Imported wood is prohibitively expensive in northern China, largely deforested for at least two thousand years. Underground houses cost a quarter of the price of above-ground units and can be used for several generations with proper maintenance. Submerged houses also protect their occupants from the direct path of the wind, which can be punishing, especially in winter.

Of course, there are disadvantages to living underground. Cave dwellings are humid in the summertime. Dampness is a standard problem, which current research is addressing, and seepage may require repair. The lack of light may be depressing. Finally, the size of the house is limited by access to light, ranging from 33 to 66 feet (10 to 20 meters) in front-to-back depth and usually no more than 16 feet (5 meters) high. Greater height and width are possible in places where the soil is highly calcareous, which makes it more coherent and therefore stronger for spanning wider areas.

Ideally, cave houses face south for maximum light and warmth; there is a central doorway to the living room and/or kitchen, and behind these front rooms are the bedrooms needing less light. Small alcoves for storage are often carved into the walls of the main rooms. Subsidiary chambers also have smaller storage rooms opening from their side walls; they are vaulted on a smaller scale.

Stoves in the front corners of the entrance room provide warmth and are used for cooking and heating water. Buried pipes convey heat and smoke from the stoves to the back chambers, where they run under the *kang*, or bed-sitting platform, a standard device known since before 200 B.C.E. in Korea, northeast China (Manchuria), and northern China, whose surface is brick or tile, set about 2 feet (60 centimeters) above the ground (see Fig. 3.16).

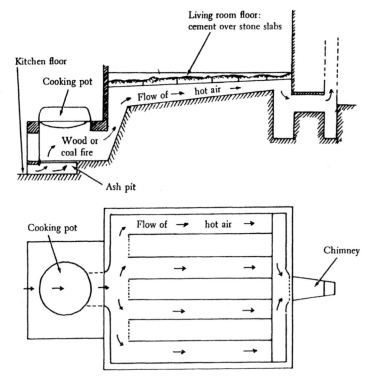

Figure 3.16. *A kang heating system, northern China and Korea. The system is used in loess houses as well as other types of houses. Heat and smoke from cooking fires are captured to warm the brick platform on which people sit during the day and sleep at night.*

During the day, people sit and work on the kang; at night, they cover it with thick quilts to make a bed. Ancient Roman buildings used a similar arrangement, the hypocaust. Any available fuel—wood, plant stalks, dung—works in a kang. A small fire is enough to warm the dwelling, especially since the residents usually pull their feet up from the cold floor when they sit. Each house has a vent to carry smoke and gases out to the upper air.

Both traditional loess houses and modern adaptations are arranged in groups of three or four houses around square or rectangular courtyards that are often larger than 1,000 square feet (100 square meters) and nearly 40 feet (9+ meters) deep. Access stairs lead down into the courtyard from the ground surface. Rain, snow, and dust can fall into the courtyard freely, but some courts are edged at the top with a wall to prevent surface water from draining in. The courtyard contains a well; some have trees or other plantings. The extended family or neighbors who occupy the dwellings use the courtyard as outdoor living space—where chickens, a pig, or small children are secure. The residents can farm the land directly above their houses.

A disadvantage of the cave house is that sun can easily reach only the south facade of the northern dwelling, and in winter the entire courtyard is in complete shade. Thus, no house is cut into the darkest, or southern, wall of the courtyard; the access stair or ramp is located there. It is probably no coincidence that, according to Chinese geomancy—the traditional rules for placing a house in the environment—buildings are never oriented to the north. A south orientation is preferred, and east and west orientations are tolerated.

Entire villages may be built underground as sets of courtyards. Or the cave village may occupy the slope of a hill, with the terrace over one set of roofs forming the porch or street for the houses above (see Fig. 3.17). In front of a row of such houses, adobe brick walls mark the private spaces that open onto the common path. Builders prefer to construct this type of village on a slope that is relatively high but not far from a well for drinking water.

When carving a house into the side of a cliff, Chinese builders start by drawing on the surface of the hill the size and profile of the house they are going to excavate. The facade usually includes a door, a window, and an upper vent. Each local group has its own characteristic geometric patterns of latticework panels for these openings, which can be filled in with rice paper or glass. Sometimes a decorative arch encloses the facade or a tile overhang like a porch roof deflects rain. Usual materials for the facade are adobe or tamped earth, but sometimes baked bricks are used.

Having finished the facade, the owner-builder proceeds to dig out the interior. Like neighboring freestanding houses, the loess-area hillside houses usually have three, five, or seven bays, each corresponding to a room of 16 by 10 feet (5 by 3.5 meters). The extracted soil can be baked to make bricks for the facade or tiles for platforms and stoves. Once the excavation is completed, the walls are coated with a plaster of loess or loess mixed with lime to slow their drying—and consequent flaking. The floor is of compacted earth. In some regions, builders now

Figure 3.17. *Modern hillside houses in loess terrain, northwest China. Soil excavated from the interior is baked as bricks for the facades. The roofs of the lower houses serve as terraces for the upper houses. Doors and windows are screened with latticework lined with translucent paper; every locality has its characteristic latticework pattern.*

reinforce the vaulted roofs of hillside loess houses with concrete, brick, or stone arches to protect against damage from earthquakes.

Whether above or below ground, the houses of wealthier people are distinguished by the number and size of their rooms and courtyards. The bays for two or three rooms may be combined to make one large room, and an affluent family may take over adjacent courtyards, in a pattern similar to the acquisition patterns of aristocratic houses in the old residential quarters of Beijing or Suzhou (see Chapters 11, Hollow Centers, and 14, Blank Walls).

The builder of a loess house may add a latrine as a separate element, especially if the house is enlarged. In earlier times and simpler homes, the activity of excreting had no architectural solution. Today many Chinese villagers use a kind of toilet called a biomass converter, in which human and animal excreta and food wastes are anaerobically digested in a sealed pit. This sensible systemic process produces gas to be burned for cooking and to make electricity; it also yields compost and fertilizer for agriculture. By digging two such pits and using them alternately, sealing one for three or four months after it is filled, the family can use surpluses from some aspects of their lives to supply the deficits in others.

Where space and finances permit, some people—especially those living on slopes—retain the advantages of the cave dwelling while mitigating its drawbacks. They add supplementary surface units of adobe brick or tamped earth near their caves, so that they can use the caves in the winter to escape the worst cold spells and the better-ventilated surface rooms during the heat of summer. They arrange and use space in the same patterns whether above or below ground.

China's loess plains provide not merely the material and sites of houses, but the very houses themselves. As many as 40 million people live in underground houses in this treeless part of China.

SOURCES: C. CHING (1985); R. G. KNAPP (1986); MYRDAL (1962), 45.

FOOD STRUCTURES

As soon as humans had domesticated grains and become full-time agriculturalists, the shape of their settlements was affected by the need to store their harvests. Two of the kinds of structures that people have built to improve their food supply—and thus their chances of survival—are storage units and specialized farming areas. Two storage facilities, one at the archaeological site of Mohenjo-Daro in western India and the other in Japan, illustrate the ways people have responded to this need. In principle, these granaries were not unlike modern farmers' silos. People have also turned to construction to meet the need for more food—for example, by constructing floating gardens in the Valley of Mexico that multiplied food production by as much as thirteen times. Today these floating gardens are used to grow flowers and are a pleasant tourist attraction.

Neolithic clay pots are among the first manmade objects to illustrate that even before shelters were constructed, the preservation of foodstuffs was of primary consideration for survival. While many of these earthenware vessels served as utensils, others were the size of small silos. There were many ancient solutions to the problem of preserving food. A wooden model of an Egyptian storehouse (1800 B.C.E.), in the British Museum shows a two-story granary with shafts for the deposit of grain. A corbelled stone vault defines the storerooms in the citadel of thirteenth-century B.C.E. Tiryns, Greece. In Mali, Africa, and in western Sudan, people built granaries of mud-brick with thatched roofs. In Mexico's Oaxaca valley, earthenware granaries 6 feet (2 meters) high were built on stone bases. These structures tapered outward to keep rodents from scaling them and were topped by conical roofs of interwoven thatch and twigs. Other cultures built multiple storage units. The city of Soltane, Tunisia, has community granaries called *ghorfas*, consisting of hundreds of vaulted masonry cells piled one on top of another, with staircases to the upper levels (see Figs. 3.18 and 3.19). Modern pastoral tribes in Kindo, Ethiopia, construct elevated, grass-roofed granaries, as do other traditional societies, including the Tongo (Africa) villagers who build raised, mud-vessel granaries, as an efficient means to preserve oil, grain, wine, and other foodstuffs (see Fig. 3.20). One of the oldest examples of food-preservation storage is found at Mohenjo-Daro in the Indus valley of Sind, India.

Granaries at Mohenjo-Daro

By about 7000 B.C.E., the hunting-and-gathering way of life had given way to agriculture and herding in western Asia, and agriculture soon spread to the Indus River valley region of Sind, now modern Pakistan. This radical change in survival techniques was accompanied by the de-

Figure 3.18. *The Soltane community ghorfa (granary) still used by villagers. Stacked vaults form the ghorfa walls, accessed by a single entrance. Projecting poles are used to hold rope for raising loads to the various doorways.*

velopment of large, urban centers in Sind, such as Harappa and Mohenjo-Daro, which archaeologists discovered in the early 1920s. Some scholars, such as J. Jacobs, however, have argued that cities came first and caused the development of agriculture.

When our ancestors settled into agrarian community life, each community usually had at least one public structure that was designed to store cultivated grains and other storable agricultural products so that people and animals would have food during expected events, such as seasonal floods, and unexpected ones like droughts and planting failures. Mohenjo-Daro (see Fig. 3.21) was a large town that remained in use during the third and second millennia B.C.E. How did the town survive for so long? Many scholars believe that one of the largest and oldest surviving structures in the municipal complex was a public granary, and the existence of a communal granary also suggests a centralized governing body. Early investigators and current scholars, including archaeologists, D. Chakrabarti and M. Jansen, both of whom have done extensive re-

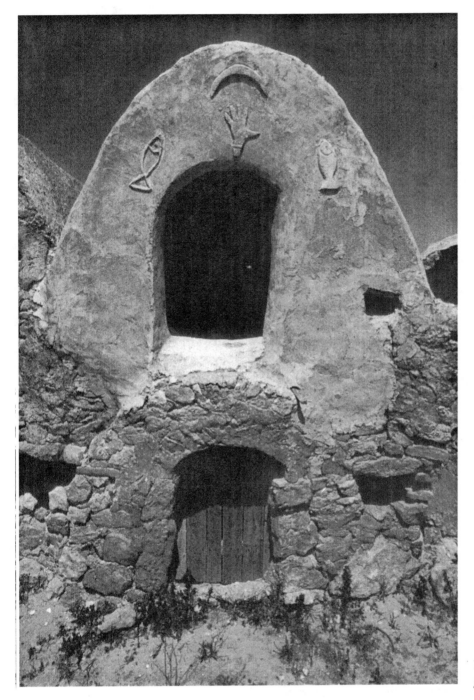

Figure 3.19. *Detail of an old ghorfa, Ksar el Halouf, Tunisia.*

search at the site, support this notion. Recently however, archaeologist J. Kenoyer, challenged this assumption, but did not produce evidence to support the accurate identification of the site; in fact, he stated that "the precise function will likely remain a mystery."

Excavations and research at Mohenjo-Daro reveal one of the most advanced civilizations of the era. The densely populated city, covering about a square mile (1.6 by 1.6 kilometers), had almost 35,000 inhabitants. The dwellings were arranged in variable orthogonal (modified gridiron)

Figure 3.20. *Granary, Tongo, Africa. The mud vessel is raised above the ground on stick supports and is roofed with thatch, as are the houses of the area.*

residential blocks, with sections reserved for public buildings (see Chapter 9, Urban Planning, which contains a fuller discussion of the city plan.)

The structure that is assumed to be the granary (see Fig. 3.22) is one of three buildings, part of the municipal complex. It stands on a 50-foot (15-meter) mound of baked mud-brick, approximately 650 feet wide and 1,400 long (200 × 425 meters); measures 164 feet long and 89 wide (50 × 27 meters); and rests on a foundation of fired mud bricks of uniform size that rises about 5 feet (153 centimeters), from the mound. Archaeologist Jansen suggests that the twenty-seven large, rectangular brick plinths, arranged in three rows dividing the area into sections, may have served as the foundation for the weight of the upper section, probably made of timber, and the stored grain. Mud-brick foundations, which had been built up four times, protected against flooding by raising grain and other materials above the expected water level. Vented shafts allowed air to circulate to the upper granary proper. The original rectangular shape of the building was extended at a later time to include additional plinths. An area at the northwest may have been a loading platform, where grain could be received and processed; holes can still be seen on the ramp for the beams that supported the upper floors. The same elements are found in the granaries of other cultures as well. The size of the granary at Mohenjo-Daro is striking, comparable to that of a large, modern supermarket.

SOURCES: ARDELEANU-JANSEN, FRANKE, AND JANSEN (1983), CHAKRABARTI (1995), JANSEN (1993), KENOYER (1998), R. E. M. WHEELER (1966).

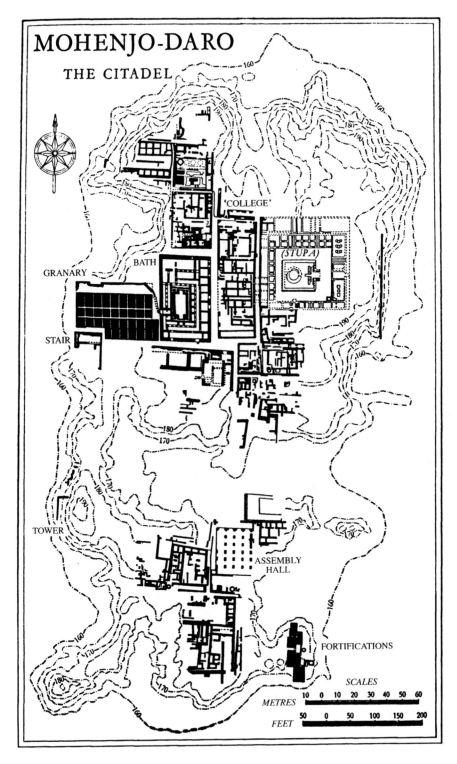

MOHENJO-DARO

THE CITADEL

'COLLEGE'

BATH

GRANARY

STAIR

(STUPA)

TOWER

ASSEMBLY
HALL

FORTIFICATIONS

SCALES
METRES 10 0 10 20 30 40 50 60
FEET 50 0 50 100 150 200

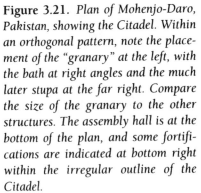

Figure 3.21. *Plan of Mohenjo-Daro, Pakistan, showing the Citadel. Within an orthogonal pattern, note the placement of the "granary" at the left, with the bath at right angles and the much later stupa at the far right. Compare the size of the granary to the other structures. The assembly hall is at the bottom of the plan, and some fortifications are indicated at bottom right within the irregular outline of the Citadel.*

Figure 3.22. *Mohenjo-Daro. Aerial photo of the bath (extreme right) and granary (left). The granary appears older than the bath-complex, since a section of the bath cuts across what may have been a loading platform for grain, at the top of the picture. The square plinths of brick in the granary that originally supported the wooden pillars that held up the second story are clearly visible. The loading platform at the top connects with the inner side of the city rampart.*

Japanese Granaries

In some cultures, food is not only a necessary staple, but a gift from the gods, and granaries were related in style to buildings designed for religious rituals. In Japan, two early Shinto shrines at Ise in the Mie prefecture of central Honshu are similar in design to prehistoric granaries (see Fig. 17.2). In addition to similarity of form, the shrines reflect similarities in construction methods and materials. Fortunately, the custom of rebuilding each shrine every twenty years to preserve the purity of the architectural form allows for the study of the construction of early granaries (see Chapter 17 for a discussion of the Ise shrines).

The Ise shrines were built in a design called *takayuka*, or raised-floor construction (Figs. 3.23 and 5.9). This type of structure was also used to store grain and is known from as early as 250 to 550 C.E. from incisions on pottery shards; bells and mirrors uncovered in Kagawa prefecture also bear reliefs depicting this type of building. The remains of similar ancient storehouses have been found at Toro, in Shizuoka prefecture. A replica of one such storehouse, constructed in recent times, shows the type of ancient granary that is still in use in some parts of Japan (see Fig. 3.23).

Although raised-floor dwellings and shrines coexisted with raised-floor storehouses, each had different functions and building requirements. Elevation on wooden posts was a practical solution for the storehouses. The pillars on which the floor rests were at first, embedded in the ground in early structures, but were later placed on individual stones to protect them from direct contact with the soil; however, in the fourteen principal buildings in the Ise compounds, the pillars still go into the ground in the ancient manner.

Generally, raised-floor buildings were made of wood, for timber abounded in ancient Japan and was the primary construction material. Of the many types of wood available, the durable Japanese cypress was the most favored. It was not painted but retained its natural beauty when local craftsmen smoothed and leveled its surfaces with iron tools.

Beams may have been secured to the vertical supports by ropes. An image of a raised-floor building on a ceremonial bell dating to Bronze Age Japan suggests such a practice, which came directly from the Polynesian ancestors of the Japanese (see Chapter 5 for a discussion of Polynesian houses). Then again, a clay replica of a storehouse from China's Kwantung province, dated to the first or second century C.E., suggests that the elevated storehouse may have come from south China, the Philippines, Malaya, or Indonesia. Wet-rice agriculture was imported to Japan from China, so some method of storing rice reserves could also have been imported from there. The Japanese granaries thus appear to have combined features from several architectural traditions: the post-and-beam fastening from Polynesia and the raised floor from Southeast Asia.

Some of the granaries discovered at Toro featured mortise-and-tenon joinery with corner joints interlocked in an ancient method called *ita-azekura*. There was no provision for windows, partly because none were needed in storehouses and partly because openings would weaken the plank walls, especially if located near the corners, as historian Y. Watanabe observes.

Conjectural restorations at Toro and Sado Island, in the Sea of Japan near the Honshu coast, suggest that these

Figure 3.23. *Raised storehouse (restored), Sado Island Museum, Japan, similar to one at Toro, Shizuoka Prefecture. A circular rodent guard is placed at the top of each support. In front is a removable ladder carved from a single log.*

granaries were small and did not need doorways for loading grain. Instead the grain entered through a triangular space created by an end gable. People climbed to the elevated floor of the granary on a ladder, which was carved in one piece, not constructed with rungs. At the top of the ladder, a small protruding circular or rectangular extension prevented rodents from reaching the interior of the storehouse (see Fig. 3.23). Granaries were limited in size when people had only iron implements, such as sharpened blades and adzes, to shape their supports. As people developed new tools and carpentry skills, they learned to build larger storehouses, for which they found new uses. Eventually, granaries became prototypes for treasuries for the safekeeping of state wealth. In modern times Japan's

Ministry of Finance is called the Okurasho, a term associated with ancient state treasuries.

There are many similarities between the design of the ancient granaries and the Ise shrines: elevated floors, the ita-azekura carpentry method, timber as construction material, and the dedication of the Ise outer shrine to the Goddess of Abundant Food (see Fig. 3.24). The Inner Shrine is dedicated to the Sun Goddess, also important to an agricultural society. Watanabe, an authority on ancient Japanese construction methods, warns that we must be cautious in attributing the development of the Ise shrine buildings directly to granary prototypes. However T. Itoh and Y. Futagawa cite early Japanese beliefs that a divinity dwelled in rice grain. They point out that since the elevated storehouse was both a container and a symbolic residence of the divinity, the prototype of Shinto shrine architecture was the elevated storehouse.

SOURCES: ITOH AND FUTAGAWA (1980), WATANABE (1974).

Floating Gardens of the Valley of Mexico

Granaries house the end product of the food-growing process. The beginning of that process is preparing the land to grow crops. People in the Valley of Mexico performed an even earlier step—they created the farmland itself (see Fig. 3.25). From 1400 B.C.E., farmers learned how to use the swampy edges of lakes as additional land by developing raised-bed gardens called *chinampas*. Chinampas reduced food shortages by increasing and extending productivity, constituting one facet of the urban evolutionary advantage.

In *Mexico and its Religion* (1855), traveler R. A. Wilson described the appearance of the chinampas:

> The chinampas are formed on the fresh-water mud on each side of the canal of Chalco [at Lake Chalco] . . . by laying upon the soft mud a very thick coating of reeds . . . in the form and about the size of one of our largest canal scows . . . the mud is dipped up and poured upon the bed of dry rushes, where it dries, and forms a rich "muck" soil, which constitutes the garden. . . . [I]t gradually sinks down into its muddy foundation; and in a few years it has to be rebuilt by laying upon the top of the garden a new coating of rushes and another covering of mud. Thus they have been going on for centuries, one garden being placed upon the top of another, and a third placed over all [see Fig. 3.26].

This technology of remodeling the land allowed people to use formerly unproductive wet areas during the dry season. The people built small dams to hold water for later use and controlled the closure of drains from fields into lakes or river. The water irrigated the raised fields that they had constructed, extending the acreage under cultivation and the months during the year that farming was feasible. Once year-round farming was possible, farmers could cultivate a greater variety of crops and reap far more abundant harvests without changing their climatic or geographic niche. The genius lay in the orchestration of all the factors.

Raised-bed farming was a response to increased urban population in the Valley of Mexico and elsewhere in Mesoamerica. When people developed chinampas, they substituted intensive for extensive farming, harvesting corn, vegetables, fruit, and flowers. Conserving and reusing former waste products, canals that supported and irrigated the "floating" gardens yielded waterfowl, aquatic animals, and fish. Thus the new system provided a net increase in carbohydrate and protein supplies.

Around 200 to 300 C.E., raised-bed farming also came into use in the Maya areas of the Yucatán, Belize, and

Figure 3.24. *Elevation of Ise Shrine. The marked similarity to granaries, such as the one in Fig. 3.23, is evident in the supporting posts, parallel horizontal siding, deep thatched roof, and pronounced overhang of the roof.*

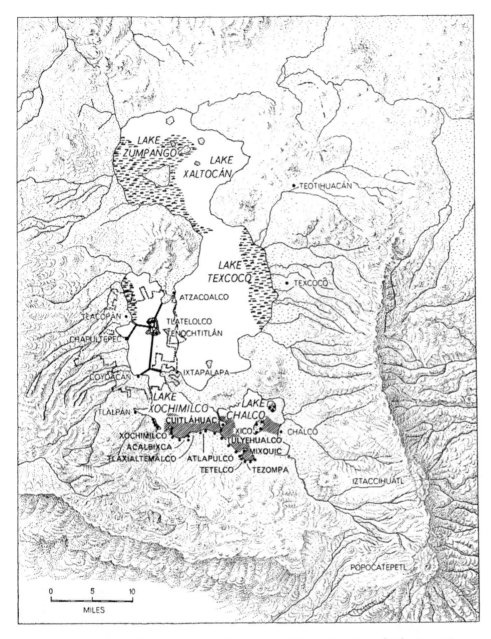

Figure 3.25. *Valley of Mexico, map with its capital Tlatelolco/Tenochtitlán in 1521. In the summers, the five lakes merged into one large lake. Causeways, aqueducts, and dikes are shown by solid lines. Modern Mexico City lies to the west and south of Lake Texcoco. Towns with chinampa (raised fields) are shown in heavy type. The major area of chinampas is hatched; other fields occupied the edges of the capital, and the marshy areas to the west and east (shown by horizontal dashed lines) were potential fields. The springs that fed the chinampas are represented by large black dots.*

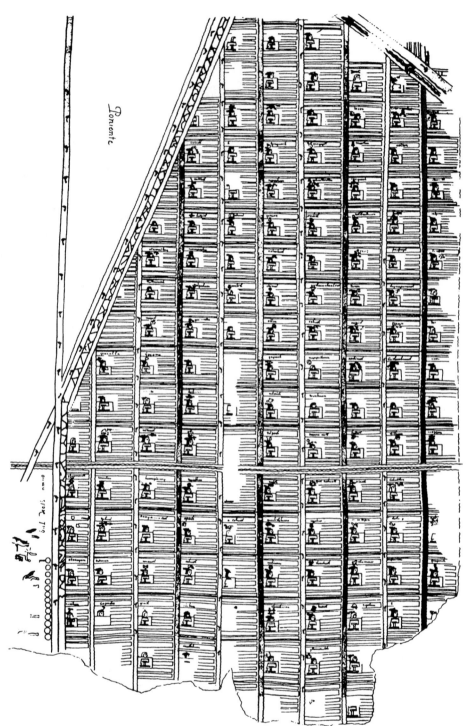

Figure 3.26. *Tenochtitlán, Mexico. Plan of one sector of chinampas, ca. 1560. Streets and causeways are shown by antlike footprints between double lines and canals, by heavier lines. Each group of chinampas is guarded by its seated farmer.*

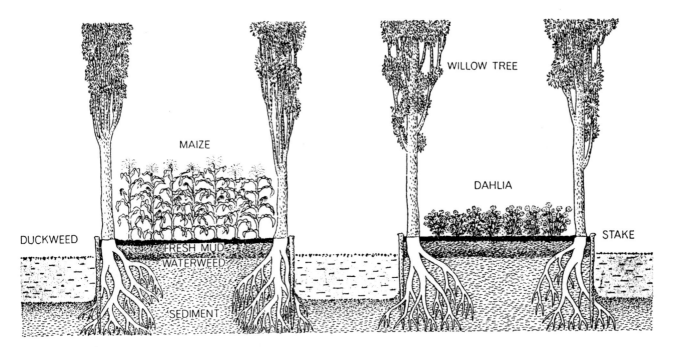

Figure 3.27. *Section of the two chinampas with flanking canals. Trees mark the corners of each plot of constructed land. Canals serve for boat access, irrigation, and fish culture.*

Guatemala. South Americans in Surinam, Venezuela, Colombia, Ecuador, Peru, and Bolivia practiced similar raised-bed agriculture. Anthropologist A. L. Kolata and engineer C. Ortloff showed that raised beds significantly extend the growing season at high altitudes—a fact that may have encouraged the adoption of this technique in the Valley of Mexico, which has an altitude of more than 8,000 feet (2,400 meters). Farmers also practiced raised-bed agriculture in New Guinea, where the practice dates to roughly 350 B.C.E.

The first chinampas in the Valley of Mexico (see Figs. 3.26 and 3.27) developed in the Lake Chalco area because the area had fewer killing frosts, greater rainfall, and more fresh spring water than other parts of the valley. Although immediately north of the mountains, the area had a hot and humid, semitropical climate. The plain where the city of Teotihuacán grew up (see Chapters 7 and 11) was higher and dryer. By encouraging and directing the building of chinampas from an early period, the urban population gained the variety and abundance of foodstuffs from both ecological zones.

Chinampas were built first along lake margins at Claco, Xochimilcco, Tizcocco, and Texcoco, among others. Extension into the marshes was probably ordered and planned by the state, since the system required a complex of grids, feeders, main canals, and dikes at both the regional and local levels. Individual farmers and small communities worked on particular fields, but the major elements of the plan seem to have been determined directly by the ruler.

By 1520, the chinampas reached their greatest extent, covering 25,000 acres (200 square kilometers) in the Xochimillco-Chalco area. By 1520, additional chinampas of Lake Tizcocco and the Lagoon of Xatlocan were also supplying food to the Aztec city of Tenochtitlán. Some chinampas, probably kitchen gardens, were even found in central cities, but larger holdings were developed farther out.

The same technology generated new land for housing by using the waste materials (garbage, trash, building debris) of the valley cities; a dense urban population thus lived on constructed land. Tenochtitlán included nineteen islands built or expanded where lakes were too deep, turbulent, brackish, or saline for crops. Land was laid out in a modular system, in regular grids of long, narrow blocks. New houses and fields continued to be built until the beginning of the seventeenth century. The changing landscape reached its modern form when the entire lake bed was drained in the twentieth century.

TABLE 3.1 Energetics of Food Production in the Basin of Mexico

Type of Agriculture	Soil Type	Family Maize Subsistence Requirements in Kilos	Maximum Work Input	No. of Hectares Cultivatable	Yield in Kilos per Hectare	Total Income in Kilos	Surplus Production	No. of Persons Supported by Surplus
Dry farming	Sandy loam	800	200	2.0	400	800	0	0.0
Dry farming	Clay loam	800	200	1.3	800	1,040	240	1.2
Floodwater farming	Sandy loam	800	200	2.0	800	1,600	800	4.0
Floodwater farming	Clay loam	800	200	1.3	1,000	1,300	500	2.5
Permanent irrigation	Sandy loam	800	200	2.0	1,000	2,000	1,200	6.0
Permanent irrigation	Clay loam	800	200	1.3	1,400	1,820	1,020	5.0
Chinampa		800	200	1.3	3,000	3,900	3,100	15.5

From W.T. Sanders and R.S. Santley, (1983). Reprinted by permission of University of New Mexico Press.

Most of the ancient chinampas have been abandoned or filled in as Mexico City has grown into one of the world's largest urban agglomerations, but a few still exist at Xochimilco, at the southern end of the basin. Restored in the early 1990s as "floating gardens" of flowers, they reopened to visitors in 1994. Physical remnants of the Aztec empire, the chinampas draw residents and visitors to spend an afternoon in the long canoes, boating and singing or buying flowers and fruit from other double canoes that act as shops.

Chinampas farming is one of most intensive and productive agricultural systems ever devised. Farmers could cultivate seven different crops, including two of maize, for a total of thirteen times as much produce as dry-land farming in the same area (see Table 3.1) About 23,000 acres at the south end of Lake Chalco supported at least 100,000 people living on the land and another 100,000 nearby. A family could survive on less than half the food it grew while working only 200 man-days per year, freeing the surplus to support the aristocrats, artisans, soldiers, and bureaucrats of the metropolis. It seems likely that the Texcoco plain, with similar production, supported another 120,000 people. Adding the produce from outlying areas, the farmers of the area could have supported millions at

the capital. The construction of chinampas was a profitable investment of time and energy (see Table 3.2).

SOURCES: DENEVAN (1970); KOLATA AND ORTLOFF (1989); SCARBOROUGH AND ISAAC (1993); A. H. SIEMENS, PERSONAL COMMUNICATION; SIEMENS AND PULESTON (1972); R. A. WILSON (1855), 188–89.

SUGGESTED READINGS

Ardeleanu-Jansen, A., U. Franke, and M. Jansen. 1983. "An Approach Towards the Replacement of Artifacts into the Architectural Context of the Great Bath in Mohenjo-Daro." In *Forschungsprojekt DFG Mohenjo-Daro*, 46–70, edited by M. Jansen and G. Urban. Aachen, Germany: Veröffentlichung des Geodätischen Instituts der Rheinisch-Westfälischen Technischen Hochschule Aachen Nr. 34. (Contents in both English and German.) Plans and other illustrations bring this excavation report to life.

Armillas, P. 1971. "Gardens on Swamps." *Science* 174 (November 1971): 653–61. An investigation of chinampas via aerial photographs, survey reconnaissance, and archival research in sixteenth-century documents. The article reports on a study of settlements, field systems, hydraulic works, roads, and waterways, amounting to landscape archaeology with an emphasis on the impact of humans on the landscape. Compare with Duncann (1990).

Becker-Ritterspach, R. A. O. 1995. *Water Conduits in the Kathmandu Valley*. New Delhi, India: Munshiram Manoharial. At last, a book on the water system of the core of Nepal! Lavishly illustrated.

Chakrabarti, D. K. 1995. *The Archaeology of Ancient Indian Cities*. Delhi: Oxford University Press. A useful summary with a revisionist approach.

Coe, M. D. "The Chinampas of Mexico." *Scientific American*, 211 (July 1964): 90–98. Contains excellent maps and diagrams.

Doughty, C. M. 1936. *Travels in Arabia Deserta*. 2 vols. London, J. Cape (reprint of the 1888 ed.). Doughty caught the real flavor of Bedouin life more than a century ago. The book reads like an adventure story.

Itoh, T., text, and Y. Futagawa, photos. 1980. *The Traditional Japanese House*. New York: Rizzoli. The definitive book on the subject, well written and beautifully illustrated. A list of photos keyed to small replicas of the photos is located at the end of the book, but there is—alas—no key to the drawings.

Kawashima, C. 1986. *Minka, Traditional Houses of Rural Japan*. Tokyo: Kodansha, 1986. Organized by architectural elements, this book is an especially useful reference for this chapter.

Kent, S. 1995. "Ethnoarchaeology and the Concept of Home: A Cross-Cultural Analysis." In *The Home: Words, Interpretations, Meanings, and Environments*, edited by D. J. Benjamin and D. Stea. Aldershot, England: Avebury. What constitutes a home when a group consistently abandons a shelter and moves on? See also Kent's other writings listed in our Bibliography.

Knapp, R.G. 1986. *China's Traditional Rural Architecture: A Cultural Geography of the Common House*. Honolulu: University of Hawaii Press. Knapp is a geographer who has made the Chinese house his specialty. His other writings are listed in our Bibliography.

Lee, R. B. 1979. *The !Kung San*. Cambridge, England: Cambridge University Press. The basic anthropological study.

Lewis-Williams, D., and T. Dowson. 1989. *Images of Power: Understanding Bushman Rock Art*. Johannesburg, South Africa: Southern Book Publisher. Considers paintings and carvings, together with oral history and anthropology, to make a compelling account of the artistic and religious concepts of these people.

Morse, E. S. 1961. *Japanese Homes and Their Surroundings*. New York: Dover (reprint of 1886 ed.). Old but beautifully written and sensitive to the Japanese environment of the late nineteenth century. Morse was a zoologist who stimulated the development of anthropology in Japan. His work is also useful for Chapters 7 (Tokonoma) and 10 (Katsura Palace).

Moughtin, J. C. 1985. *Hausa Architecture*. London: Ethnographica. Well illustrated, with a helpful discussion of construction methods and building types.

Needham, J. A. 1971. *Science and Civilisation in China*. Vol. IV, Part III: *Civil Engineering and Nautics*. Cambridge, England: Cambridge University Press. An extended, interesting study of water management and hydraulic engineering, with both Chinese and Western-language references and excellent illustrations, especially the map of the Huang Ho, Fig. 859.

Netherly, P. 1984. "The Management of Late Andean Irrigation Systems on the North Coast of Peru." *American Antiquity* 49: 227–54. We are indebted to this article especially for information on Peruvian social organization. Netherly is an anthropologist who has worked for years in Peru and Bolivia.

Nicolais, J. 1971. "Nepal: Water as an Element in Urban Architecture." *Architecture & Urbanism* 1: n.p. A photo essay by an architect shows the urbanity of Nepalese solutions.

Ortloff, C. R. 1988. "Canal Builders of Pre-Inka Peru." *Scientific American* (December): 100–07. Easy, fascinating reading.

Ortloff, C. R., R. A. Feldman, and M. E. Mosely. 1985. "Hydraulic Engineering and Historical Aspects of the Pre-Columbian Intravalley Canal Systems of the Moche Valley, Peru." *Journal of Field Archaeology* 12: 77–98. Ortloff is a fluids engineer; his coauthors are archaeologists. Crucial background reading for this unit.

Prussin, L. 1986. *Hautmere: Islamic Design in West Africa*. Berkeley: University of California Press. This lively, well-written, and well-illustrated book will widen one's understanding that the Hausa are a unique, rather than a typical, African people.

Prussin, L. 1995. *African Nomadic Architecture*. Washington, D.C.: Smithsonian Institution Press. A brilliant and well-illustrated study of varieties of architecture designed and built by women of the sub-Saharan nomads. Prussin is an architect and art historian.

Rapoport, A. 1969. *House Form and Culture*. Englewood Cliffs, N.J.: Prentice Hall. The author-architect's beautiful drawings stimulate the readers to compare the arrangements different peoples make for containing their lives. Also useful for Chapter 4.

Silbauer, G. 1981. *Hunter and Habitat in the Central Kalahari Desert*. Cambridge, England: Cambridge University Press. How the Basarwa (!Kung Bushmen) live with their environment.

Slusser, M. S. 1982. *Nepal Mandala: A Cultural Study of the Katmandu Valley*. Princeton, NJ: Princeton University Press. 2 vols. The definitive study of Nepal by a cultural anthropologist. See Vol. 2 for illustrations of the many fountains, baths, and waterspouts. Also useful for Chapters 6, 7, 10, and 12.

Smith, M. G. 1965. "The Hausa of Northern Nigeria." In *Peoples of Africa*, 119–56, edited by J. L. Gibbs. New York: Holt, Rinehart & Winston. A description and analysis of the living patterns of the Hausa people in a major city, Zaria. Smith, an anthropologist, was most interested in family relationships in households.

Tobias, P. V., ed. 1978. *The Bushmen: San Hunters and Herders of Southern Africa*. Cape Town: Ruman & Rousseau. A good introduction.

Watanabe, Y. 1974. *Shinto Art: Ise and Izumo Shrines*, R. Ricketts, trans. New York: Weatherhill/Heibonsha. Written with a deep understanding and love of Japanese architecture.

⊞ 4

Climate and Ecology

"An opportunity comes cleverly disguised as an impossibility." This adage is illustrated by buildings that modify the local climate with local materials. All over the world, builders have met the challenge of extreme climates by constructing ecologically sound, livable dwellings.

Climate and the local geography combine to challenge builders who are concerned with human comfort—or simply survival. Four examples show the range of climatic variations that confronts us as a species. In the northern edges of North America, Eskimo-Inuit builders, faced with snow and cold, used compacted snow to build dwellings in which internal temperatures may be 70 to 90 degrees F (40–50 C) warmer than the outside air. Tibetan architects still face similar problems, although in a more arid climate and at much higher altitudes. Their solution is a dwelling that changes with the seasons.

People living in the hot, dry climate of North Africa and the Middle East require insulation from the intense heat, so builders have created a variety of simple but effective cooling devices in these areas. Builders in New Guinea face still other constraints: a hot, humid climate and many biting insects. Through trial and error—ever the basic human way of learning—they have developed an architectural style that minimizes the discomfort these conditions can cause. Other architectural responses to climate and environment are scattered throughout this book; see Chapters 6 (Spaces for Daily Life), 11 (Hollow Centers), 13 (Symbolic Gardens), 14 (Blank Walls), and 16 (Porticoes).

COLD AND DRY

The Inuit (also known as the Eskimos or Yup'it) of northernmost North America (see the map of North America in the Appendix) live in an area of long, cold, but relatively dry winters and they developed a type of house made of snow. The Tibetans (see the map of Asia in the Appendix) live in a drier but higher area. Their more permanent construction materials—stone, wood, and mud—have let them develop a wider range of building types.

Houses of Snow and Skin:
Inuit Iglus of Northern Canada

The northern rim of North America, northern Siberia, and northern Europe—an area of treeless tundra bordered by sea ice—presented extreme climatic conditions to the Inuit and other hunting or fishing peoples, such as the

Lapps of Finland. The climate of the tundra, above the 53-degree F (10-degree C) isotherm, resembles the climate that prevailed across lower latitudes during the Ice Ages. The mean temperature is below freezing every month of the year. During the short summers, the temperature remains below 53 F, and permafrost (permanently frozen ground) is close to the surface. Eight to 12 inches (20 to 30 centimeters) of precipitation fall throughout the year. To obtain the necessities of life, circumpolar societies dwell each year in several different seasonal settlements, which form a network of complementary locales where they can fish or hunt or visit friends and relatives.

Sometime between C.E. 700 and 1400, the ancestral Thule people of northeastern Canada or western Greenland invented the semisubterranean, well-insulated, lamp-lit underground house with a tunnel entranceway. The variation of this dwelling, called the *iglu* (in Inuit) or igloo—a domed snow house—may have come to the central Arctic region of northern Canada as recently as the nineteenth century. Few human dwellings reflect as clever an adaptation to and use of their ecological niche as does the iglu, a quickly built, safe refuge from the frigid winds and snow of the Arctic, still used by hunting parties.

The iglu widened the range of habitable sites available to the Inuit because it required neither foundations nor soil and because the materials for building it were widely available. An iglu can be located either on sea ice or on land. On sea ice, the builders place the iglu so that its tunnel passage points away from the wind to minimize the chance of snow covering the window or the air vent. On land, they place it in the lee of cliffs for protection from wind, facing the beach.

Builders of an iglu use snow from the site itself. The Inuit distinguish between different kinds of frozen precipitation in ways that are urgent for survival in the Arctic. They have special names for the way snow forms into drifts where its density is suitable for building. The right kind of snow is neither too solid nor too dry nor granular. The best snow for an iglu is from a single storm, wrote ethnologist F. Boas in 1888 in the first ethnological study of any North American people. As the iglu ages in use, its interior develops an icy skin from melting and freezing, improving the tightness of the enclosure.

An iglu's size is determined by how many people use it and for how long (see Fig. 4.1a). An iglu that is 6 feet (1.5 meters) in diameter is big enough for a traveling shelter, but for winter-long habitation, a larger one, of about 15 feet (4.5 meters) in diameter and 10 to 12 feet high, is more comfortable. To reach such heights, the builders pile up a bench of snow to stand on while they finish the upper parts. Small or large, the iglu's profile is a catenary curve, the strongest shape; the dome provides maximum volume with minimum surface area. The shape of the iglu also conserves heat while allowing good air circulation.

Hunters build an iglu quickly if they need temporary shelter while on a hunting trip. In just a couple of hours, two men can build a simple structure about 5 feet high and 7 feet in diameter. Three experienced men can build one 9 feet (2.75 meters) in diameter in less than an hour.

When two people are building an iglu, they begin by tracing a circle of the appropriate size on the ground. One stands inside the circle, the other outside. The inside man is the cutter; he begins by cutting blocks of snow using a serrated knife, taking the blocks from what will be the floor and the passage of the iglu. A good size for the blocks is 4 to 8 inches thick, 3 to 4 feet long, by about 2 feet tall. All the blocks are cut slightly too large, so that the outside man can "custom fit" them to their places in the wall. The cutter passes the blocks to the outside man, who shaves their edges so that the blocks fit snugly and curve slightly inward. As the outside man sets each block in place, he hammers on the top of it. The bangs cause melting and refreezing at the crystalline level, welding the blocks together.

Once the first circle of blocks is complete, the builders slice the tops of the blocks off at an angle to form the base of the spiral that makes the rest of the iglu (see Fig. 4.1c). Then they continue cutting and laying successive circles, each narrower than the last. When the builders reach the space for the "keystone" block, they cut it too large for the hole at the top of the dome, twist it through the hole, bevel it so that it fits flush, and push it into place. The last block or last several blocks may be triangular.

The Inuit then use the same methods to make the iglu's entry, with its tunnel walls and roof. The floor of the passageway yields snow blocks to make its own walls and roof. The passage is lower than the floor of the inner iglu area and usually slopes slightly downward then upward; it may dip as much as 9 inches (23 centimeters) in the center. This dip turns the passage into a trap for cold air, draining cold air from the living quarters. The passage is built parallel to the wind direction or on the windward side of the iglu because drifts forming on the lee side would obstruct the entryway. A wall made of a couple of layers of snow blocks protects the entry and deflects the wind up over it, making a "porch" area. Spherical segments that are tucked into the angles between the passageway and the main dome served as storerooms; they open to both the exterior and the interior (see Fig. 4.1d).

While the men finish the tunnel and any adjacent spaces, such as storerooms, the women and children finish the main iglu. First, they push wedges of snow into large cracks but leave one hole near the top to act as a "nose" for ventilation. Smaller cracks anchor the ties for the skin lining of the iglu before the cracks are filled solid. The exterior is finished by packing loose snow over it. The iglu may have a window, consisting of a slab of translucent ice set into the dome just over the entrance to the tunnel. Freshwater ice is best for this purpose; the Inuit often haul a piece of it from camp to camp. Sometimes a reflecting surface to intensify the light is set up next to the window, in the form of a block of snow inside the dome at a 90-degree angle to the ice window. In the absence of ice for a window, the Inuit may use the translucent linings of seal intestines; they stitch these linings together and mount them vertically (visible in Fig. 4.e). Soapstone lamps within the iglu not only provide additional light, but give off heat and are used for cooking.

Simply because of shelter from the icy winds, the interior of an iglu is much warmer than outside. Lamps and people's bodies add more warmth, which is retained by an inner lining of skins tied to the walls and connected outside to toggles. This lining is usually of sealskin (but could be of caribou hide), and it also serves as the cover for the family's summer tent. In the iglu, it creates a layer of air next to the snow-block walls that increases the insulation of the structure (see Fig. 4.1b). Then the heat from lamps and bodies may raise the interior temperature to as much as 59 degrees F (15 C) even when the external temperature is minus 40 degrees F (-58 C). Yet this heat does not reach the snow-block walls to melt them. At night, the residents hold warmth in by blocking the passageway with a "door" made of another block of snow. This block makes it even more vital that at least one open chink between the snow blocks serve as the "nose" of the iglu; if stale air builds up, the color of the lamp flames changes, so the Inuit know to pierce other small holes for ventilation.

At least half the interior is set aside as a sleeping platform. Boas described this platform as being about 2.5 feet (75 centimeters) higher than the floor, which, in turn, is 9 inches (23 centimeters) higher than the entrance tunnel. Skins cover the sleeping platform, usually piled on a layer of willow, heather, or baleen (the elastic, horny material from the mouths of baleen (whalebone) whales). Flanking the floor passage are two smaller platforms that hold the soapstone lamps (see Fig. 4.1 d and e). Above the platforms hang kettles for cooking, and above the kettles are racks for drying boots and mittens. The simmering of the kettles increases the internal humidity of the iglu, which both improves the comfort level for people inside and contributes to the interior glaze of ice on the walls that helps to exclude the wind. On the floor of the iglu passage are such items as horn dippers, blubber pounders, urine buckets, tools, frozen meat, and garbage.

European and American scholars have recorded as many as nine variations on the single, isolated iglu form. Compound forms ranged from the standard 15 feet (4.5 meters) to 27.5 feet (8.4 meters) in diameter and could be 12.5 feet (3.8 meters) high. These variations appear to correspond with three factors: differences in the size or kinship relations of groups, different geographic regions, and differences in local customs and/or weather. The Eskimos of eastern and western Canada used iglus only as temporary shelters, mostly when hunting, and built only the simple, single-dome-plus-passage version. The central Inuit of northern Canada, between Labrador and the Mackenzie Delta, used iglus as all-winter residences and built the larger and more complicated variants.

By connecting separate iglus, the Inuit could create a complex in which a group of families feasted, sang, and danced during the long hours of winter darkness. The dance room at the center was an important feature of a settlement, for its ceremonial and hierarchical aspects, as well as for the conviviality it allowed. This room was found not only in the snow iglus of northern Canada, but in the sod-house form used by Alaskan Yup'it.

The symbolism of the dwelling is subtly gender related. Its symbolic meaning was evident to the inhabitants from the beginning of construction: If a man wanted many children, he used a serrated knife to cut the first block of the broad side, slicing outward to deflect any bad luck away from the people who were to live within. To ensure good fortune for the children, he cleared all loose snow from the interior space during construction. When cutting the last snow block to fill the "keystone" opening, a man indicated that he wanted a son by cutting that block bigger than the one before it and placing its softest side toward the rear of the iglu. A large keystone opening was thought to ensure easy childbirth for the mother. The floor area was associated with men, their tools, the sea, and sea animals and fish; the sleeping platform was associated with women, their soapstone lamps and gear, the land, and fur-bearing animals, as Nabokov and Easton explained.

Death in an iglu might attract evil spirits to the place. Therefore, the survivors sometimes broke a hole in the wall to remove the body and then either abandoned or destroyed the iglu. Sometimes they sealed the body in the iglu and themselves moved away. In other instances, they went on living in the same iglu without letting the death disturb their tenure. In the latter cases, the symbolism of home was stronger than the association with death.

Iglus allowed the Inuit of Canada to adopt a way of life that involved seasonal changes of habitation. Long ago these Inuit lived year-round in semi-underground permanent houses clustered in the center of their territories, where soil conditions were favorable for such construction. More recently the Inuit lived in groups of iglus in

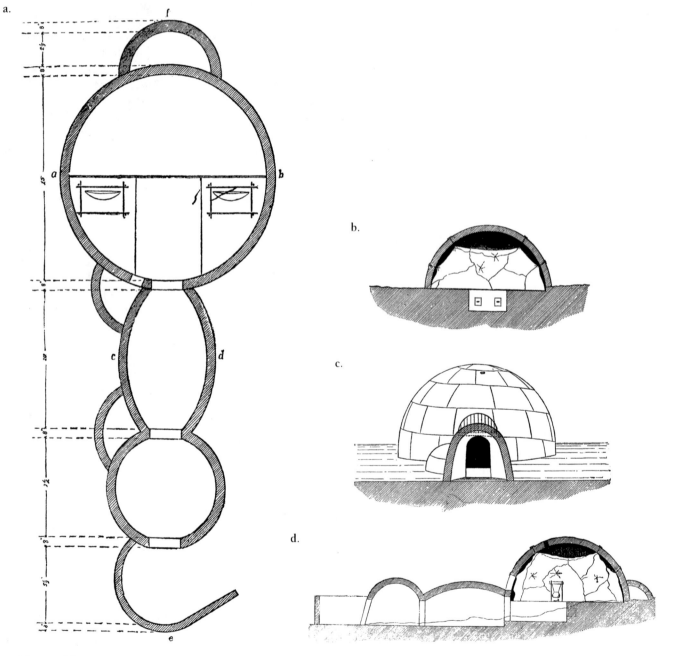

Figure 4.1.

e.

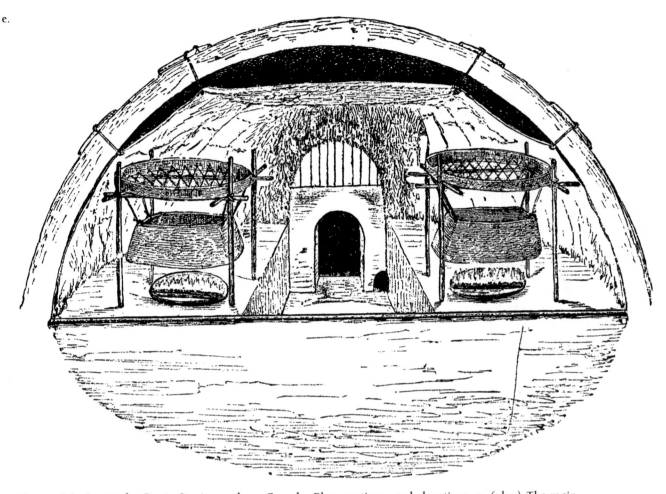

Figure 4.1. *Inuit iglu, Davis Strait, northern Canada: Plan, sections, and elevations.* **a.** *(plan) The main living space is divided into four parts, a platform to hold the stove-lamps on either side of the passage and a higher platform for sleeping and sitting. The entrance passage, in segments with a low roof, leads to a porch protected from wind by a curved wall. Two quarter wedges and one half wedge provide outdoor storage space for frozen meat and furs.* **b.** *(section through the main living space) The interior is fitted with a skin lining fastened to the snow blocks by toggles. The small squares below the sleeping platform are for storage of items that can be kept at or above freezing.* **c.** *(exterior view) The spiral of the snow blocks that compose the iglu is evident, as is the vent or "nose" in a block near the top. At the left is a small storage wedge. In the iglu wall is a window of clear ice or sewn seal intestines—both translucent—indicated by a striped half-circle.* **d.** *(section through the iglu) Left to right: entrance wall, two-part entrance passage, main space with a passage leading to the bed platform and flanked by two quarter-circle platforms with heating lamps, and the outside storage wedge.* **e.** *(enlarged section from the wall opposite the entrance) In the foreground is the sleeping-sitting platform. Stoves, with cauldrons for food and basket-racks to dry shoes and mittens suspended above them, flank the passage to the entrance. The arched window appears above the doorway. Sealskin hangings create an air pocket along the wall, insulating the interior and retaining the heat of lamps and warm bodies. On the floor of the passage is a pile of trash, waiting to go outside.*

winter and tents in summer. They were not confined to the interior of their territories but could live on the coast, convenient for both summer and winter hunting. Changes of house materials gave them more choices about where to live. The reasons for this change of locale are still not well understood, but may have involved climatic variation that called for changes in hunting patterns, coupled with the availability of the iglu, which can be set up on an ice floe, as well as on land, and is ideal for winter seal hunts. In all respects, the iglu was well adapted to the long and cold but dry winters of the Arctic region of Canada.

Most iglus were built to last one long winter, although some were meant for much shorter use—the few days' duration of one hunt. As spring approached, the warmer weather melted enough of the snow blocks so that the iglu's roof caved in. Then the inner hide lining became the roof for a while, while the lower walls and inner platforms of snow remained. Eventually, however, the temperatures of summer mandated moving into a tent on a different site for a few months.

After World War II, the use of iglus declined. Since about 1960, many Inuit have lived in modern houses. Yet they continue to use temporary iglus for hunting and other excursions. Like the Kalahari nomads, the Inuit have abandoned many of their former ways but find themselves ill served by new types of housing that dictate different relations between interior and exterior, as well as the loss of environmental control and fragmentation of personal space.

Summer and Winter Houses in Tibet

The Tibetans have learned to deal with a cold, dry climate, one of the most severe climates on earth. Orientalists Snellgrove and Richardson describe the adaptable Tibetans as "fearlessly accepting existence in its most fearful . . . forms." Their challenge is intensified by the high altitude of their country and has led to building forms and methods suited to local constraints. Some Tibetans use their houses differently in winter and summer; others live in different structures at different times of the year.

Few people in the world reside at higher altitudes than the Tibetans; most live in valleys at 14,000 feet (4,267 meters) above sea level. The most densely populated part of the country lies just north of the Himalayan range and south of the Kunlun, the mountains that border the Tibetan plateau. The rivers that become the Brahmaputra, the Mekong, and the Chang Jiang rise in southeastern Tibet, their valleys providing access to the plateau. Only the

valley of the Yarlang Zangboo river (formerly Tsangpo, also known as the Brahmaputra) is suitable for agriculture, and here the major cities are located. The rest of the plateau is arid pasturage, with an average elevation of 16,000 feet (4,880 meters).

In traditional, pre-Communist Tibetan society, wealthy, aristocratic families—nomads, farmers, and businessmen—owned the land and lived in big houses, up to four stories high; the rest of the people lived in smaller quarters. Many families still have woman chiefs because women usually manage the family home and finances. Some groups practice polyandry, in which a woman has several husbands at once, usually brothers. This domestic arrangement is not reflected in the architecture of the house but is handled by behavioral conventions: "Traditionally the parents' room is either at the rear of the building or on the story above the main part of the house, giving it a level of privacy and importance in the spatial hierarchy. In a polyandrous family, this is the woman's room; when one of the husbands is with her, he leaves his shoes at the entrance to the room, thereby signaling that he is there and the space with her is occupied" (W. Semple, personal communication based on work as an architect in Tibet).

The Tibetan custom is to consult an astrologer before construction, as before any important undertaking. The astrologer's tasks are to position the building on the site, to ask local deities' permission to assemble materials for the house, and to beseech them to aid in its construction. If the astrologer sees unfavorable omens, special rituals can be carried out to counteract them. The patron can then begin to gather the wood and other materials for the structure, which may take four months to bring the long distances from the forested slopes of the Himalayas. The greatest cost is transport of materials, since a village can be five days' travel from the nearest road.

There may be obstacles to a patron's construction plans. Building cannot begin until legal permission has been obtained, a permit system dating from before the seventeenth century. Laws are clear and publicly recognized. For example, a builder cannot block a city water channel or roadway or the sun from a neighboring building (see Fig. 4.2). The drain of the toilet must be carefully located, and the owner must provide sufficient space to clean the toilet. In short, the new structure must not be a nuisance. The owner must provide plans, which are checked on site by someone from the staff of the mayor or council. Should there be a conflict between classes, such as an aristocrat bribing officials for permission to break any of these rules, a poor person can sue to have the original law checked at

Figure 4.2. *Tibetan houses, Lasha. The ground floor is for storage or commerce; here, hand-made rugs are sold. Living takes place above, as the large windows indicate. The tapered window frames are roughly shaped from beams. Notice the carved decoration over the window of the house at the right. Exterior valances are common over doors and windows, their ruffled form resembling the trim along the eaves of Nepalese temples.*

the site. Then the owner is forced to rebuild the structure properly.

The Tibetan farmhouse is the prototype for both urban and rural buildings, whether rich or poor. Buildings are solid in construction (see Fig 4.3a and b). Walls of stone with mud mortar or of bricks made of air-dried clay are laid up with an inward slope to the outer side of the walls. Wooden posts and beams support the roof-terrace. Simple houses are owner built, while large houses are professionally constructed. Only the roofs of some monasteries are gabled; all other roofs are flat, covered with earth for insulation.

Houses may be freestanding or, in the towns, may have party walls. Stairs are usually located on the west and

can be placed either inside or outside. The west side or southwest corner of the house is the preferred location for the toilet room, usually at the top of the exterior stairs leading to the second floor. The toilet is a simple hole in the floor; every night the excrement is sprinkled with ashes, and it later becomes fertilizer.

A typical one- or, more often, two-story house is rectangular in plan with an off-center court oriented to the south. A big room on the north side of the house opens southward onto a balcony; in winter, woven curtains of wool protect the balcony. It and the spaces next to it are the winter living quarters, while the upper roof frequently has a summer living room under a partial roof or arbor. As additional protection from the cold, the family wears

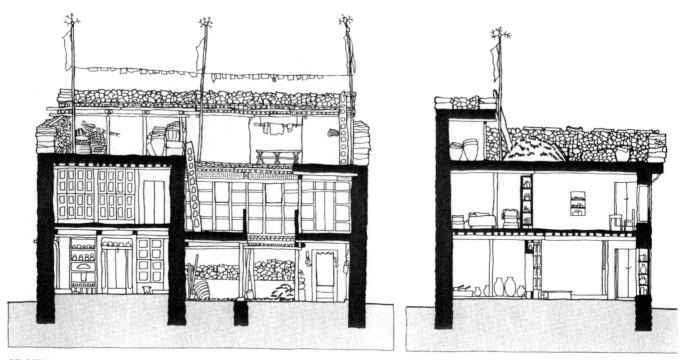

SECTION A   SECTION B

Figure 4.3. *Tibetan-style house, Marpha, Nepal.* **a.** *The heavy walls enclose the open court of the house at the second level and support the roof deck above. Notice the larger windows opening onto the court. On the ground story is the winter cooking room (left), space for the animals (center) and storage (back right), and the summer cooking area (front right).* **b.** *At the lower left is the "pot room" for storage. Above it is the shrine room, also used for grain storage. Opposite is a room for weaving, below it the summer cooking room. Wood is stacked along the edges of the upper terrace, while the central space is used for drying grains and hay. Sheds at the back are for storage or for sleeping in the summer.*

layers of warm clothes and gathers next to the permanent fire of the cooking stove, over which a pot of "two thousand year soup" is always simmering. The Tibetan soup is made of "yak bone, nettles, knuckle-sized lumps of wheat dough, cheese, beans, and radishes," says Narkyid, who grew up in this culture. Anyone in the household is free to serve himself or herself soup at any time, eating it for breakfast and lunch as convenient. The evening meal, on the other hand, is a common meal. The family and any visitors gather near the cook stove to eat and talk together. Furniture in this big room consists of a low table in one corner and perhaps a bench or several benches along the walls. People sleep on a thick carpet on the floor or on the benches, using futon-type quilts for padding and for warmth. At the back of the main room is the family shrine, protecting the sleepers and the grain stored there.

Tibetans generally stay outdoors as much as possible because one's body warms up quickly in the sun, whereas indoor rooms stay cold for a long time. Making the most of the sun for warmth, they use south-facing porches, balconies, and terraces. They position large windows on the south sides of their buildings, small windows on the north. Because of winds, the east and west sides have small windows, too. The ground floor has no windows, since it is used for storage and stabling animals. If possible, the building backs up to a mountain or hill. In fact, whole villages are sited on south-facing slopes for solar warmth and for protection from north winds.

Tibetans who settled in the highlands of what is now Nepal a thousand years ago still preserve their ancestral house forms. In Marpha, a village about a hundred miles northwest of Kathmandu, summer is pleasant but winter is so cold that half the population moves down to lower valleys for three to six months. The village sits in a gorge twice as deep as the Grand Canyon (i.e., 2 miles), in an upland valley between the Himalayas and Tibet. There 720 people live in 162 houses. Vertical in form, the houses are built into the terraced hillside. They are placed at the base of the west wall of the valley but above the arable land, oriented both to minimize exposure to wind and to catch the morning sun (see Fig. 4.3a and b).

The steep terrain seems to have determined both the strong relation of each house to its terrace or terraces and the unusual placement of the kitchen yard, which may be located at either the front or the rear of the house, adjacent to the second floor. In the Tibetan tradition, houses have flat roofs on which people can spread grain to dry. Wood for heating and cooking is stacked along the edge of the roof for later use. The upper floor is an open terrace, with storage rooms at the back that may also be used for sleeping in the summer. In one noticeable response to the climate, people have created both summer and winter cooking rooms. Cooking is done on a low fire box made of clay or on a tin stove (like a Bunsen burner). The winter kitchen on the ground floor has a wooden floor, more easily kept warm than stone or tamped earth. The summer kitchen is on the level above, adjacent to the kitchen yard (see Fig. 4.3a and b).

Tibetan house materials include stone for the foundation and walls and earth for the flat roof, which is frequently resurfaced. Interior surfaces of a mixture of clay and dung are refinished twice a year, except the lower walls and the floor, which are done every two to three days. Besides the roof beams, wood—not locally available—is required for the interior load-bearing columns. When the house studied by architect K. D. Blair was built in 1980, its construction required a team of five carpenters, four masons, and four laborers. The cost was U.S. $4,075 (equivalent then to about U.S. $40,000 in 1996 buying power). This was a house for a prosperous family (additional information on building costs is in Chapter 17). The interior furnishings included a Tibetan tin stove used for heating during the winter.

In the past, all Tibetans were nomads.[9] Today, Tibet's nomads still follow the custom of maintaining both summer and winter housing. During the summer, a nomad family lives in a tent of black goat or yak wool as they follow their flocks. In the winter, they move into their one-room stone house or migrate southward into a warmer valley, where they continue to live in their tent.

Tibet's climate has shaped not only the architecture of private houses but the form of monasteries. Traditionally, as many as a third of Tibetan adults were monks or nuns, creating the need for thousands of large buildings for religious communities (see Fig. 4.4). One of the best known of these monastaries is the Potala palace in Lhasa which for centuries was home to the ruling Dalai Lama (see Fig. 4.5). The true name of the building is the Palace of Avalokitesvara because the Dalai Lama is considered a manifestation of Avalokitesvara, a bodhisatva, or holy person, often identified with Buddha. Two other monuments dedicated to Avalokitesvara are Angkor Wat (see Chapter 11) and Borobudur (see Chapter 5).

Built in 1645 on a high ridge, the Potala palace stretches out in long wings, crowned with turreted buildings at each end. It is thirteen stories in all, each story about 16 feet (5 meters) tall. Wide stone steps lead from level to level.[10] The wings are of whitened stone, with windows that increase in size upward. The dark red central mass of the palace is hung on the outside with an enormous black curtain, the ceremonial equivalent of the curtains that enclose the central balconies of ordinary houses. Many balconies and porches open toward the sun under

[9]When Kuno Narkyiid was a boy at the monastic school in the Potola palace in Tibet (ca. 1960), he was taught that 40,000 years ago, when the Chang Tang (northern plain) was filled with vast lakes, all Tibetans were nomads. There was a civil war between two kingly brothers, and the losing side decided to leave the country. They migrated northeastward, some dropping off to stay in what would become China and Korea, but others continuing across the Bering Straits to North America. (The lakes to which Narkyiid was referring, existed after the last glacial age, from 10,000 years ago, according to naturalist G. B. Schaller, 1993. Thus, they could have existed after earlier ice ages as well.)

[10]It is interesting to note that the approach from the river to the governmental center in Albany, New York, confronts a similar expanse of tall stone wall that was deliberately configured in imitation of the Potola palace (see C. H. Krinskey, 1981).

Figure 4.4. *Tibetan monastery, ca. 1850, based on a domestic housing type. Note the balconies with heavy curtains and the general alignment toward the southern sun.*

overhanging roofs, and small gold canopies and gilded pagodas erupt from the otherwise flat roofs. The palace contains over twelve hundred rooms—offices; residences; a school; a large monastery; temples, including four-story stupas; and a lower area for storage.

HOT AND DRY: SOLAR MANAGEMENT IN THE MIDDLE EAST

Like builders in extremely cold climates, those in intensely hot regions face the challenge of using their available materials effectively. Near deserts, people live in dwellings that range from sophisticated buildings of sun-dried or baked brick and stone to the earth itself. They have adapted a variety of architectural elements to control heat in these dwellings.

Thousands of years ago, people developed systems of natural ventilation for architecture in arid areas of the Middle East, North Africa, and South America. Among the many devices for cooling interiors was the air-scoop, or *badgir* (Islamic wind tower), which projects vertically from the roof bringing moving air into the house through an open space or cavity between two parts of a party wall. The scoop is a vertical shaft that channels exterior air to the interior recesses of the house (see Fig. 4.6). The outlets are usually at floor level where people sit. Historian al Azzawi explains that the wind catcher, the exterior portion of the air-scoop, has an opening facing the strongest prevailing winds. Approximately 3 feet (.92 meter) wide and 3 feet deep, it is usually made of brick or wood with a slanting plane at the opening to direct the wind current down through the shaft. A screen below the opening catches debris. Incoming air is channeled into a cavity

Figure 4.5. *Potola Palace, Lasha, Tibet. The Palace of Avalokitesvara, formerly the residence of the Dalai Lama and the seat of government, is now a museum. The lower parts without windows are for storage. The central part, which is painted red, is the palace, flanked by monasteries, schools, and other functions.*

within the inner wall, which is cooler than the outside walls because it does not come into contact with direct sunlight.

Pictorial evidence shows such devices on roofs in Middle Kingdom Egypt (ca. 1500 B.C.E.). Pottery models of houses from Peru (200 B.C.E.) also have air-scoops, indicating that their use for ventilation was not limited to any one culture or period. The late thirteenth-century Italian explorer Marco Polo observed that in the excessively hot areas, such as Harmoz in southern Iran, that he visited, rooftop ventilators caught and deflected cooling breezes into the house interiors. Today, people in many parts of the world still use the efficient nonmechanical devices.

Unidirectional wind catchers, also called air-scoops, are the most common. But if winds are variable, as in some parts of Iran, multidirectional towers are constructed. These towers capture the wind from several directions, usually four. A sail-like device at the top of the wind catcher rotates on a pivot similar to a weather vane. When viewed from the exterior, such multiple rooftop wind catchers present a jagged skyline (see Fig. 4.7).

Multidirectional wind towers are also used to cool underground cisterns for water storage. In Aghda, for example, wind towers are built over a cistern to cool the water stored below (see Fig. 4.8). Larger buildings may have passive cooling systems that incorporate both wind towers and water by covering the water with a dome. M. Ba-

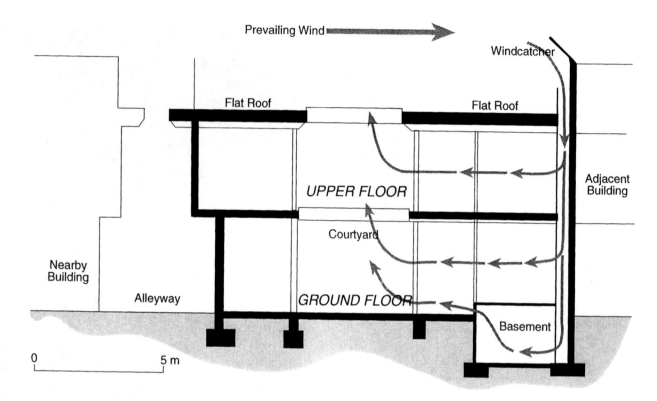

Figure 4.6. *Section of a typical air-scoop cooling system, North Africa and the Middle East. Moving air from the prevailing winds is drawn down through a wind catcher at the right into a channel in the wall; circulates through the rooms of the house, cooling them; and moves out into the courtyard. In the courtyard, the air rises as it is warmed, and more cool air is drawn into the house. The wind catcher can be closed off when it is cold or when there is too much dust in the air. The family room at the right on the ground floor is raised a few feet so that windows below floor level of the family room that open onto the courtyard can provide air circulation for the basement area.*

nadori relates that these cisterns are sunk about 39 feet (12 meters) below ground with a vented dome above. The earth provides insulation from the sun, the domed roof minimizes the surface area exposed to the sun, and vents allow the air to circulate. As the sun heats the roof of the cistern, the air above the water grows warmer, increasing the rate of evaporation, which, in turn, increases the movement of the air. The water vapor is moved by the action of the draft from the towers across the surface of the water. The layers of deeper water are only slightly affected because the heat of the air is dissipated in evaporating the surface water. Another way of storing energy for later use is the Iranian system of making ice during the cold, dry winters for use in the summer. People pour water into a shallow rectangular pond surrounded by adobe walls that shield it from the wind and heat gain. Once the water freezes, they cut the ice and store it in a pit between layers of straw. Both the cistern and ice-making systems can give rise to health problems because the water may be stagnant or impure. However, water from these cooling methods can be used for other purposes, such as irrigation.

People living in hot, dry climates improve their comfort by countering the extremely low humidity. One way they do so is to stimulate condensation within their dwellings. They place porous, earthenware water jugs at the lowest level of the house, sometimes in a basement below ground level and thus least vulnerable to solar radiation. The jugs not only aid in cooling by the evapora-

Figure 4.7. *Wind towers, Aghda, Iran. The high rooftop structures with narrow vertical openings and the shorter, broader ones are wind catchers. The squater ones may span a large living room; some, placed sideways, may feed several rooms. In the foreground is a courtyard of a mosque, with a two-story iwan flanked by classrooms.*

tive process on their surfaces, but provide cool drinking water. The basement also offers a cool respite from the heat of the summer months, and the residents spend much time there. The floor of the room above is raised enough to allow windows on the courtyard side of the basement wall, adding to the comfort level by improving air circulation (see Fig. 4.6).

For thousands of years continuing into the present era, people in the Middle East and other hot, dry regions have designed their traditional dwellings around internal courtyards (see Chapter 11), for both thermal and social reasons. Individual rooms face the courtyard through intervening shaded terraces and galleries, an open plan that increases the potential for air circulation and provides a buffer zone against reflected heat entering the interior of the building. Porches shade the walls of the building, also reducing the interior temperature. At night, heat loss takes place through radiation from the courtyard to the night sky, contributing to a relatively cooler interior during the daytime. In addition, planting the courtyard with vegetation and adding fountains or pools tends to increase the humidity, which, in turn, maintains a lower and more comfortable temperature.

Other structural elements are designed to combat heat. Roofs overhang buildings by 10 feet (3 meters) or more, providing shaded passageways below and aiding in the circulation of cool air to the interiors. In multiple-story dwellings, the floors of succeeding stories project

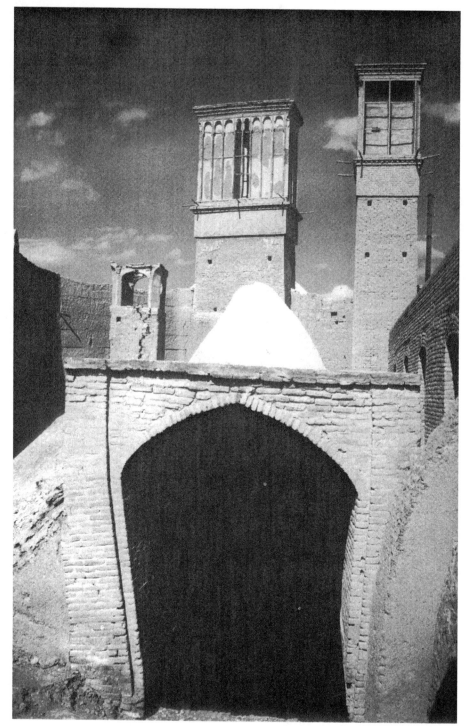

Figure 4.8. *Wind towers over a cistern, Aghda, Iran. Designed to keep the water storage unit cool, the cistern has shallow steps under the arch leading downward where a donkey can be taken to load and carry the water.*

outward, each extending over and providing shade for the story below. Exterior brick walls are thick enough to provide insulation and are painted in light colors to deflect the solar radiation. The choice of materials for walls and roofs is of great importance to the rate of heat transfer. Stone, mud, and brick act efficiently as insulation materials providing resistance to the transmission of heat through the walls and the tiled or flat roofs. Windows facing the public lanes are small, if they exist at all, but those on the interior courtyard are larger to provide ventilation and light for the rooms. Carved wooden screens let the inhabitants control how much light and heat reaches the interior.

People in Middle Eastern countries limit the amount of interior furnishings in traditional dwellings, to allow for freer air circulation. Carpets or low couches provide seating, the practice perhaps inherited from nomadic Arab forebears that places the sitter low where the air is cool. During the hottest months, people roll up the carpets and sit on the cool stone floors.

An alternative to these methods of combating the intensive heat of desert areas is the practice of excavating underground dwellings with natural insulation. Some living quarters—for example, in southern Tunisia and western Libya—are built entirely underground, giving inhabitants maximum protection from solar radiation and severe desert windstorms. G. Petherbridge described these dwellings as a complicated system of underground tunnels quarried from hard sandstone, 23 to 33 feet (7 to 10 meters) below ground level. The dwellings open onto deep courtyards, square or rectangular, with ramps for access to the ground level. Residents can close these approaches with barricades for protection. Living and storage quarters are tunneled into the sandstone around the open courtyard area. Longitudinal tunnels may lead to adjacent courtyards. In principle and in many details, these arrangements are similar to Chinese loess houses (see Chapter 3). Underground survival systems have a long history in North Africa. Roman builders in Tunisia adopted this method two thousand years ago to ameliorate the unfavorable effects of the hot, arid climate.

People in hot, dry areas need to control heat in public structures, such as markets and bazaars. They protect these spaces from the scorching sun by covering them with arched roofs, domes, or cloth. Lantern or cap vents on top of the arches and domes allow the warm air to escape, while cooler air is drawn in from the exterior through the entrances at street level.

SOURCES: AL-AZZAWI (1969), BAHADORI (1978), FATHY (1986), W. JOHNSON (1995), PETHERBRIDGE (1978), RUDOFSKY (1977), YULE (1876).

HOT AND HUMID: BIG ROOF IN THE NEW GUINEA RAIN FOREST

In tropical areas of Asia, Africa, and the Americas, high temperatures and high humidity produce distinct building problems. In some of these places, rainfall can reach 12 feet (3.66 meters) per year. Ventilation is essential for personal comfort. In addition, houses must be elevated to escape the dampness or flooding at ground level. Raised floors contribute to the flow of air around the building and may allow people to shelter their animals and goods in the space beneath the structure (see Chapter 10, Stilt Houses). Open sides let cooling winds circulate within the house. Porches, verandas, and large window and door openings promote air movement, as does the open plan of the interior. Walls and floors are thin to avoid the accumulation of solar radiation. Outdoor shaded areas for many household activities help to minimize the effects of high humidity.

People choose specific building solutions not only for climatic reasons but for cultural reasons. The big-roofed, open-plan, ceremonial house of many peoples in New Guinea is not only a solution to problems of climate, but a reflection of social behavior and ideology.

New Guinea is the second largest island in the world, after Greenland. Its interior erupts into vast mountain ranges as high as 16,500 feet (5,030 meters), a wild and rugged terrain. The many isolated valleys in this terrain have been inhabited for so long that their denizens have developed more than five hundred languages, although large rivers facilitated communication in some regions. Because of its colonial history, the island is now divided into Irian Barat (Jaya), part of Indonesia, and independent Papua New Guinea. Most inhabitants are Melanesians, but there are also Negritos and Papuans. All have had to accommodate their domestic architecture to a hot and humid tropical climate.

Although the languages and cultures of New Guinea differ greatly from those of Southeast Asia, the architectural style of the big-roof building follows Austronesian (from Southeast Asia and Oceania) architectural precedents that are well established throughout the western Pacific. The New Guinea houses are most similar to those on Sumatra, including construction on wooden piles (like telephone poles) and a saddle-roofed profile with ex-

Figure 4.9. *The Great Kan Ravi, men's ceremonial house, Kaimari, New Guinea. Photographed in 1924. Notice the size of the men relative to the house. Such houses could be more than 300 feet long (59–72 feet tall by 33–39 feet wide = 90+ meters long, 18–22 meters tall by 10–12 meters wide). Palm branches screen the interior from view.*

tended ridge lines. This building type, which evolved in New Guinea "on a grand—almost a fantastic—scale," according to anthropologist R. Waterson, is now found in north coastal Papua, along the Sepik River, and on the southeastern coast.

The ideology and climate of the island together dictate house form. This fact is not surprising, as human beings insist on living on several levels of tangibility at once. We have already shown that in a Basarwa camp, two sticks can mark inside and outside, or his and hers, and that a seemingly pragmatic semidome of snow blocks can carry several layers of symbolic meaning for the Inuit. One might expect the big-roofed houses of New Guinea to have similar import.

An umbrella-like, thatched "big roof" gives protection from both sun and rain (see Fig. 4.9). The steep, overhanging eaves of the roof serve as side walls, extending almost to floor level. Many houses have no enclosure walls at all; residents rely on the high stilts for privacy. Under shelter of the big roof, the interior climate is better than that outside. Drafts from open sides carry the air warmed by human bodies or smoke from antimosquito fires up toward the roof (see Fig. 4.10). Unfortunately, these roofs seem also to foster chronic allergic lung diseases from dirt and molds dropping down out of the thatch.

The number of houses that a village needs is based on the activities to be provided for, not on the number of people. For instance, in areas where custom dictates that men must sleep separately from their families, a hamlet containing only one family would consist of two houses. Some hamlets have additional types of houses, such as a collective women's house or temporary or permanent garden houses at the edges of fields. In some villages, all houses are of the same form and size. For example, in Tafalmin in the highlands, the men's houses, family houses, and an ancestor-cult house are all similar in size and structure. Other villages have several different house shapes.

Some villages have one house that is decidedly bigger than the others; anthropologists call it the "men's house." Although the number of house users is relatively small, men's houses are huge in scale and elaborately decorated (see Fig. 4.9). Perhaps they are intended to impress visitors with the size and strength of the village. This emphasis on size and ornamentation parallels a social arrangement that relies on prestige and influence for leadership, rather than the formal hierarchy more commonly found in other societies. Leaders known as "big men" dominate local groups among the different cultures of the island.

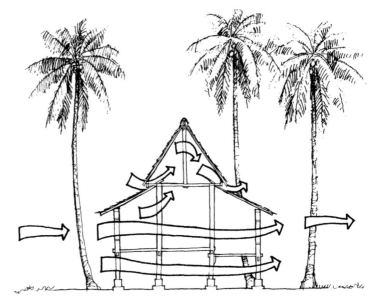

Figure 4.10. *Air movement in a Malay house, adapted to the hot and humid climate. The canopy of coconut trees gives shade; the upper roof is perched over the lower, with a gap to allow breezes to penetrate; and the elevated floor provides a third layer of shade for the ground area. Walls made of shutters and carved panels allow for the continual flow of air within the dwelling area.*

Especially in coastal areas or near rivers, people set up their houses on wooden piles, height adjusted to local circumstances. In general, the higher the house, the more prestigious. Often the houses are on piles over water away from the shore, where mosquitoes cannot easily reach them. Canoes can be stored under the raised living quarters (see Figs. 5.7 and 10.17).

The frameworks of the floor and the roof rafters are attached to stilts. In the Kiwai area of western Papua, ethnographer B. A. L. Cranstone described one men's house as having separate support systems for the roof and for the floor (see Cranstone's Fig. 4). One set of bamboo poles raised the floor, while the roof was borne by an outer row of posts and a second taller row a third of the way into the floor area, leaving the center of the building unobstructed. These bamboo posts were strong enough to support the light ridgepole of the roof and its thatching materials. Bamboo, flexible and available in a wide range of sizes, is ideal for use where great height is desired but only the human energy of the builders is available. (Cranstone's Fig. 5 shows the method of erecting a tall post by tipping it into a prepared hole.)

The most prominent feature of the big house is its roof. Painted decoration fills in the front gable; protecting this painted decoration is an important function of the roof. The upper section of the facade may be nearly upright, may slope outward and upward to meet the gable of the roof, or may slope inward to be better shielded by the roof from the weather (forming a veranda at the front of the house). All three positions give some protection from the rain.

The big roof houses of New Guinea are both architectural solutions to local problems of climate and reinforce the social organization. The houses are not a perfect solution because of the diseases mentioned earlier and gender exclusivity (see Chapter 6, Social Rewards). Yet the people use local materials with ingenuity to produce a satisfactory structure. Indeed, recent studies indicate that this construction tradition is more cost-effective for its intended use than is imported technology.

The houses also suggest Waterson's caution: "Some buildings fall between the western categories of public and private, and others combine functions we would expect to be kept separate." As an example of such a combination, she cites the "house", "temple," and "meeting-place" in the nearby Moluccas Islands, where just one kind of structure is associated with that range of activities. The men's house of New Guinea is a useful example of the distinctive ways of thinking that guide construction outside the Euro-American tradition (see Chapter 6, Social Rewards). These variations remind us that when we apply our own rules to the architecture and urbanism of another people, serious misunderstandings may follow.

SOURCES: CRANSTONE (1972), FORGE (1973), RAPOPORT (1969), RUFF AND RUFF (1990), WATERSON (1990).

SUGGESTED READINGS

Al-Azzawi, S. 1969. "Oriental Houses in Iraq." In *Shelter and Society*, 91–102, edited by P. Oliver. New York: Praeger. A good basic discussion of the vernacular architecture of Iraq.

Bahadori, M. N. 1978. "Passive Cooling Systems in Iranian Architecture." *Scientific American* 238 (February): 134–44. A comprehensive overview; illustrated.

Blair, K. D. 1983. *4 Villages: Architecture in Nepal.* Los Angeles: Craft and Folk Art Museum. Simple and clear, well illustrated, written by an architect. One village of the four is the home of people of Tibetan ancestry, who build Tibetan-style houses. See also as a source for Chapters 6 (Use of Street and Roof) and 10 (Building Types).

Bowden, R. 1990. "The Architecture and Art of Kwoma Ceremonial Houses." In *Sepik Heritage: Tradition and Change in Papua New Guinea*, 480–90, edited by Lutkehaus et al. Durham, NC: Wenner-Gren Foundation, Carolina Academic Press. This whole volume on New Guinea is fascinating.

Cranstone, B. A. L. 1972. "Environment and Choice in Dwelling and Settlement: An Ethnographical Survey." In *Man, Settlement, and Urbanization*, 497–503, edited by P. J. Ucko, R. Tringham, and G. W. Dimbleby. Cambridge, Mass.: Schenkman. A perceptive analysis.

Fathy, H. 1986. *Natural Energy and Vernacular Archiecture: Principles and Examples with Reference to Hot Arid Climates.* Chicago: University of Chicago Press. The author, a noted and prize-winning architect, introduces the reader to the subject of natural energy and how it is used in arid regions.

Fitch, J. M., and D. P. Branch. 1960. "Primitive Architecture and Climate." *Scientific American*, 203 (December): 134–44. This concise article shows how people have met the challenge of living in severe climatic conditions.

Petherbridge, G. 1988. "The House and Society." In *Architecture of the Islamic World: Its History and Social Meaning*, 176–208, edited by G. Michell. New York: William Morrow. An informative discussion of Islamic domestic architecture.

Snellgrove, D., and H. Richardson. 1980. *A Cultural History of Tibet.* Boulder, Colo.: Prajna Press (reprint of 1968 edition). Interestingly written and thorough.

⊞ 5

Materials, Methods, and Architectural Form

We now examine two building methods, carving out and assembling, and two types of materials, permanent and ephemeral. Architecture that has been carved out contrasts vividly with that which is assembled or built up. Carved-out architecture is more like sculpture than construction and has the unique aspect of being seamlessly one with its setting. Most construction, however, is built up of pieces to produce a hollow interior. The process is the same whether the structure is a simple Basarwa shelter (see Chapter 3) or the extensive complex of Nan Madol in the Caroline Islands (see Chapter 8): Assemble the pieces you need, and then put them together by the methods of your artisans.

One building tradition may encompass more than one set of procedures and materials. The Inkas of Peru used permanent materials in one building procedure, ephemeral ones in another. In the building of temples, palaces, and other monumental structures, they were masters of "Cyclopean" stone construction. But the Inkas also used perishable vines and wood for hanging bridges. The strong connection between the materials, methods, and resulting forms is evident in these strikingly opposite solutions.

CARVED-OUT ARCHITECTURE

Carved-out architecture occurs in many parts of the world: temples in India, dwellings in Cappadocia, prisons in Sicily. Our examples are the rock-cut churches of Ethiopia and the "cosmic mountain" at Borobudur on the Indonesian island of Java (see the maps of Africa and Asia in the Appendix).

Ethiopian Rock-Cut Churches

Chapter 1 discussed some early rock-cut temples in India, artificial caves cut into hillsides. In India, the tradition of carved caves led directly to the carving of temples in one piece, as at Elephanta and Ellora (see Fig. 1b). Indian traders who crossed the Indian Ocean may well have brought this concept to Ethiopia, where more than three hundred rock-cut churches are found, each located either in a trench or at the entrance to a quarried cave. Although these churches are Christian, not Hindu, a number of scholars have noted resemblances. Yet it is a giant conceptual step from carving away surplus rock and leaving

Figure 5.1. *A map of rock-cut churches, Lalibela, Ethiopia. The church of Bieta Gheorghias is in the trench at the left, near the river. Light gray represents the River Jordanos and tributaries, and dark gray represents the trenches around the churches.*

a hollow to the more architectural process of carving a freestanding building into a rock outcrop, attached to its setting only at the ground level.

On an isolated hillside near the ancient Ethiopian capital of Lalibela, some 250 miles (400 kilometers) north of the modern capital of Addis Ababa, stands a group of ten rock-cut churches and one chapel (see Fig. 5.1). Monolithic buildings were not uncommon in Ethiopia before these churches were built; for example, there are similar underground tombs on the southwest slope of Mount Abuya Joseph, where the churches are located. These buildings were structurally strong, so they resisted centuries of neglect and the destruction of raids from Egypt, Sudan, and Arabia.

A brief review of history will illuminate the role these rock-cut churches have played in the lives of the Ethiopi-

ans. The peoples of Ethiopia are the result of millennia of invasion, migration, and mixture. Very early, the indigenous population mixed with Egyptian and Sudanese neighbors, but there may have been an even earlier descent from prehistoric people like the protohuman "Lucy" found in East Africa in 1974.[11] The next invaders were Semites from Arabia and a Jewish strain that tradition attributes to the union of King Solomon and the Queen of Sheba. Other influences came from Christian Syrians living at Kerala in India, who were trading partners of the Ethiopians, and from the Nestorian Christians of Syria. The Ethiopians were a cosmopolitan people whose architects could combine many traditions. The ideas of Indian

---

[11]See note 6.

Brahmins, Jains, and Buddhists came to Ethiopia through trade, as did those of Middle Eastern Manicheanism (a religion of dark-evil vs. light-good). Syrian and Egyptian models of early Christianity were preserved in Ethiopia by the country's isolation after the Muslim conquest of North Africa in the eighth century C.E.

The Axum dynasty had dominated Ethiopian trade from the second century C.E. By about 300 C.E., Axum rivaled Rome as a great power, trading as far away as Spain and China. The kingdom disintegrated in the tenth century. Later the Zagwe dynasty came to power. One of its most important kings was Lalibela, who ruled from 1195 to 1220 or 1235 C.E. and adopted visual features from surviving Axumite architecture to reinforce his dynasty's claims to power. His program included the creation of monolithic churches at Lalibela and other sites. The building of the churches contributed to his beatification. The king's assistants in the project were an architect named Sidi-Maskal and—according to pious legend—supernatural workers. These legends also report that God appeared to the king in a dream and revealed the plans of the ten churches. The model of these churches was the Holy City of Jerusalem, which the king was to replicate in the Horn of Africa. The king was also inspired to carve these churches by the tales told by monks who returned from the Holy Land and described the caves, grottoes, and underground tombs incorporated into the Church of the Holy Sepulcher in Jerusalem and the Church of the Nativity in Bethlehem. Like the Holy Sepulcher in Jerusalem, one of the Ethiopian churches had a "Tomb of Adam" and "Tomb of Christ." The king renamed the local intermittent river after the Holy Land's Jordan River, and the hill above became the Mount of Olives.

Ethiopia's rock-cut churches were laid out east to west, as is customary with most Christian churches. Although commonly rectangular, they could also be triangular, cubical, or cross shaped, depending on the site. Using a cave as the site might mean that the builders had to widen the cave entrance or deform the standard geometric plan of the church. Freestanding churches were surrounded by deep and wide trenches forming courtyards on four sides. The core buildings range in size up to 109 by 76 feet (33.5 by 23.5 meters), which means that the trenches range to 140 by 124 feet (43 by 38 meters) in length and width and 32 to 45 feet (10 or 15 meters) deep.

Of the ten churches at Lalibela, Bieta Gheorghias, the church or house of Saint George, is the most famous. Its external simplicity contributes to its beauty. Seen from above (see Fig. 5.2b), the Greek cross shape of the church body is reiterated on its roof, which projects slightly over the plain sides and is embellished with two concentric crosses in relief (see Fig. 5.2b). The same monolithic rock forms the setting, roof, walls, inner pillars, and floor. On the western front of the building, seven steps lead to the main door; the church is raised above ground level on a projecting base of three layers. Along the sides, compound windows are set into pointed arches, with jambs of three layers and projecting capitals. The upper windows are cut in Arabian floral patterns with a small cross in each. Inside the church, where the four arms of the Greek cross meet, are four central pillars.

The largest of the ten churches is Bieta Medhane Alem. It measures some 110 by 77 by 36 feet (33.5 by 23.5 by 11 meters) and is set in a trench that measures 38 by 125 feet (42 by 38 meters). Of the thirty-two rectangular pillars on the exterior that supported the projecting roof, many are now fallen. Like the church of Saint George, it stands on a base. The main door is in the west wall and opens to a vestibule and the nave, which is flanked by two aisles on each side. Four rows of seven pillars, carved from the living rock, support a series of crossings where the archlike ridges between pillars articulate the flat ceiling. A cross-wall joins the side walls to the pillars to form the vestibule, and at the east end a similar wall partially encloses the sanctuary. Along the walls are windows at two levels; these once had stained glass in the shape of a cross below and a star above. On the roof are carved two concentric crosses.

Because the Lalibela churches are set in trenches connected by tunnels, a pilgrimage to them becomes a series of discrete experiences. The pilgrim enters a courtyard by going down a sloping tunnel and then passes from church to church through other tunnels. From within one trench, the pilgrim cannot get a sense of the ensemble or of how the churches relate to one another, which may explain why many early maps of the site do not agree.

Although the builders did not have to bring construction materials from a distance, one should not underestimate the amount of work involved in partially freeing the church from its setting. The stone at Lalibela is red sandstone. Like other sandstones, it is durable but fairly easy to work when freshly exposed to air. Construction difficulties included both excavating and finishing the buildings. According to a personal communication from P. Grossmann, of the German Archaeological Institute in Cairo:

> It is extremely difficult to create a . . . true parallelity of all the walls in carving the interior of an outwardly

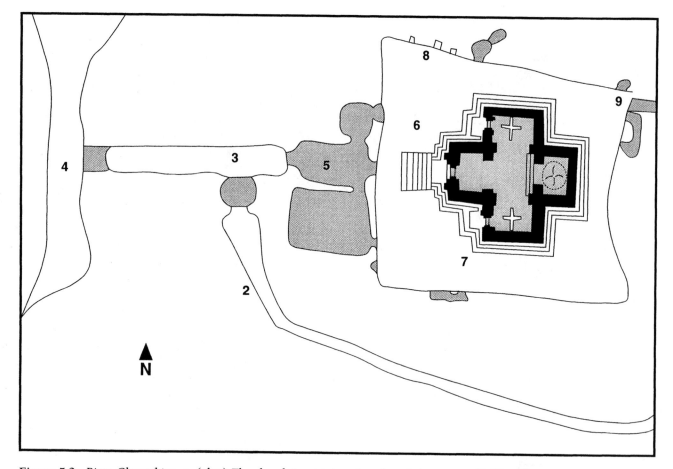

Figure 5.2. *Bieta Gheorghias.* **a.** *(plan) The church is set into a trench or "pit-courtyard" (6). (2) is a tunnel in the rock and (3) is the trench leading to the Jordanos River (4), the Jordanos itself; caves are at (8) and a former exit is at (9). A water tank, probably for baptisms, was once located at (7). Heavy black lines indicate walls of the church.*

defined structure . . . the beginning was to cut some narrow trenches at the level of the windows inside and outside the building [and then] outside and inside were carved [at once]. The doors and windows were needed not only to have some light inside, but to establish the inner design.

The floor of the trench, the staging area for finishing construction, later became the courtyard. Inside the church, the workers carved in place the pillars, capitals, and arches, as well as any interior partitions, taking care to allow sufficient thickness so that the exte-

rior walls would be strong enough to support the roof. The floor, walls, and roof were one continuous piece. Some churches, like Madhane Aläm, also have an exterior colonnade on one or more sides to support a projecting roof. The builders gave other exterior walls perpendicular buttresses or walls with bays. They used a great variety of forms; models included earlier Axum architecture, Roman temples with columns (Medhane-Aläm), and the Greek cross popular in Byzantine times.

The architectural skill exhibited at Lalibela is of the highest order. Historian J. Doresse writes, "In their origi-

Figure 5.2. b. *The concentric crosses on the roof of Bieta Gheorghias are clearly visible, and one has a real sense of the church looming up in its 40-foot (12-meter) deep trench. The stone is a rosy pink sandstone. The church is 72 by 75 feet (22 by 23 meters).*

nality of design and artistic achievement, these remarkable constructions must be ranked among the finest architecture of the Christian world." Only in reinforced concrete could the shapes be equaled.

These churches were the locus not only of Christian rituals, but of dynastic and funerary monuments. Lalibela was long accessible only by mule track—L. Findlay went there in 1944 by mule and wrote about it—or by foot. The churches are still places of pilgrimage, especially at Christmas and Epiphany, when tens of thousands of people gather at Lalibela, with monks chanting, drums beating, and worshippers slowly dancing. The remote past of

Ethiopia remains present today, incarnate in the monolithic churches of Lalibela. It is fortunate for us that these one-piece buildings have withstood eight hundred years of invasions, earthquakes, and neglect. In the late 1960s the United Nations Educational, Scientific, and Cultural Organization (UNESCO) designated them a World Heritage Site.

SOURCES: BIDDER (1959), BUTZER (1982), CAVALLI-SFORZA, MONOZZI, AND PIAZZA (1994), DORESSE (1959), FINDLAY (1944), P. GROSSMANN (PERSONAL COMMUNICATION).

Cosmic Mountain at Borobudur, Java

Borobudur (760–830 C.E.), the largest Buddhist monument in the world, is located on a hill in the tropical Kedu Plain on the island of Java. Borobudur is not a temple in the sense of a place of congregational gathering, since it has no interior chambers. Instead, as archaeologist W. B. Morton explains, it is a three-dimensional model of the Mahayana Buddhists' cosmos.

Borobudur's manmade form—consisting of a shrine atop a hill—is like a stepped pyramid or "mountain" reaching a height of about 85 feet (26 meters) (see Fig. 5.3a). This pile of unmortared andesite and basalt rests on a base about 370 feet (113 meters) square with terraces that diminish in size toward the top. The three uppermost terraces are occupied by individual stupas surrounding a larger stupa at the summit. On each of the four sides, a stairway provides access to the various levels. Together these stairways form an access path that is adorned with hundreds of intricately carved panels and statues depicting Buddha and scenes and events in his life. Pilgrims climb the sacred "mountain" to achieve spiritual enlightenment, inspired by these visual images and by the design of the monument itself (see Fig. 5.3b). The edges of each terrace converge with an imaginary superimposed sphere, recognized but invisible, as we described in the discussion of the stupa form in Chapter 1.

The silhouette of Borobudur, seen from a distance, has been compared to that of the distant mountains. Its relationship to the volcano Mount Meru (or Sumeru), the world mountain and home of the deities, is implied by the hundreds of serene-faced and godlike statues that confront the pilgrim approaching the monument. The numerous figures and ornamental designs enveloping the monument are carved of the same black volcanic stone that forms the manmade mountain. The style of the images is reminiscent of high Indian art during the Gupta period (fourth

to sixth centuries). Java's ancient rulers, the Sailendras, originally came from India, and the classical style of workmanship found at Borobudur has Indian precedents.

Borobudur can also be readily perceived as an immense work of sculpture. As the pilgrims begin their upward journey (ten times around the monument), the sculptural narrative unfolds. As archaeologist J. Miksic relates, this ritual emulates the journey of the bodhisattvas, or Buddhist saints, who passed through ten levels of mortal existence toward their goal of spiritual enlightenment.

The sculptures were designed to be seen in sequence (see Fig. 5.4a). The narrative begins simply, but gradually becomes more complex, paralleling the pilgrim's quest to comprehend life and thus reach a spiritual goal. The balustrade reliefs alone cover 500 panels, varying in size from the upper panels, 40 by 24 inches (100×62 centimeters), to the lower ones, 102 by 26 inches (260×65 centimeters). More than a hundred panels depict the life of the Buddha, The scenes are taken from sacred texts with illustrations of figures, birds, and animals.

A different experience awaits on the upper three levels. The path changes from rectangular to circular, and the low walls and balustrades permit views of the wide expanse of the open land. Visual forms on these terraces are much simpler. The instructional style turns away from reliefs with complex narratives to focus on seventy-two separate stupas, formed of curved, stone-latticework. On the lowest of the three terraces are thirty-two small stupas, twenty-four on the next, and sixteen on the top. These stupas seem to refer to ancient Indian burial practices that were followed when Buddha's ashes and relics from his life were buried in separate stupas. Each of the smaller stupas encloses an image of the Buddha, seated and turning the Wheel of the Law, which refers to his teaching, which continues as a wheel does when set in motion (see Fig. 5.4b). The central stupa does not contain an image of Buddha. Perhaps this is an acknowledgment that ultimate enlightenment cannot be depicted—or perhaps the original image has been lost.

It is easy to recognize some of the symbolic meanings found at Borobudur. Like thousands of other stupas throughout the Buddhist world, the seventy-two smaller stupas and the large one at the center all had pillars, or "masts," extending upward from the top of the dome, signifying the connection between heaven and earth. The presence of the stupas at the summit of the monument represents the attainment of spiritual knowledge through mystical instruction. Yet scholars have not been able to agree on the meaning of all of Borobudur's symbols, and

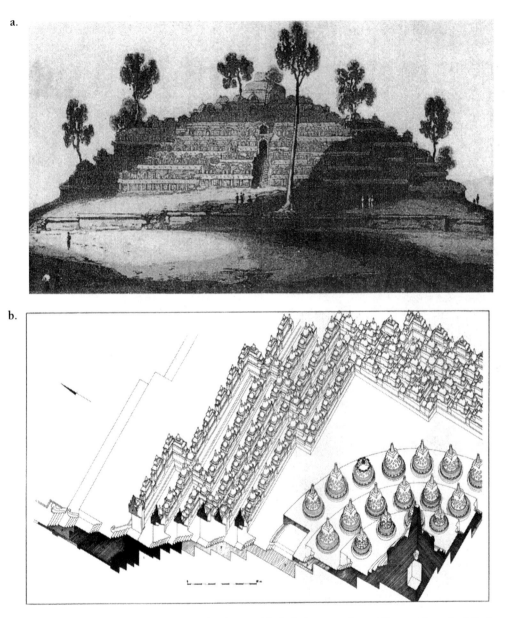

a.

b.

Figure 5.3. *Borobudur, Java.* **a.** *The first published drawing from Thomas Stamford Raffles,* History of Java *(London, 1817). The succession of terraces, axial stairways, relief carvings, and rings of stupas on the roof are plainly visible.* **b.** *Axonometric perspective from the northeast corner. The shadings represent different periods of construction. From the lowest stairs at the left, one mounts terrace after terrace to the roof, where three circles of small stupas surround the large stupa at the center.*

Figure 5.4. Borobudur. **a.** *The relief sculpture along the corridor of ascent depicting a stupa iconographically the equivalent of Buddha—with devotees.*

the Javanese builders left little information to help unravel the complexity of the architecture.

Orientalist A. Snodgrass asserts that Borobudur was built by a Tantric sect who saw the world and their part in it as a creative dance—a world of multiplicity aligned with unity. Its constructional elements reflect the sacred mandala diagram. According to Miksic, an authority on Southeast Asian architecture, the plan of the monument may have been inspired by the Vajradhatu, or "Diamond World" mandala (see Fig. 5.5), which Snodgrass classified as a mandala of Jina Buddhas. By the eighth century, thousands of schematic mandala forms existed, each showing the deities in their sanctuaries. The Vajradhatu, however,

was a popular version taught by Javanese monks who belonged to a sect with wide support in Central Asia. According to Tantric texts, the Diamond World mandala is composed of nine mandalas, the central square being the "Diamond World Great Mandala" itself. The diagram was further divided into smaller sections reserved for various deities. Vairocana, a manifestation of Buddha, presides at the center of a double circle within a square, surrounded by images of Buddhas and bodhisattvas. Hundreds of deities are symbolized on the outer perimeter. The four Buddhas encircling the supreme Buddha of the Diamond World mandala are represented at Borobudur by statues on the balustrades facing the four cardinal directions. The

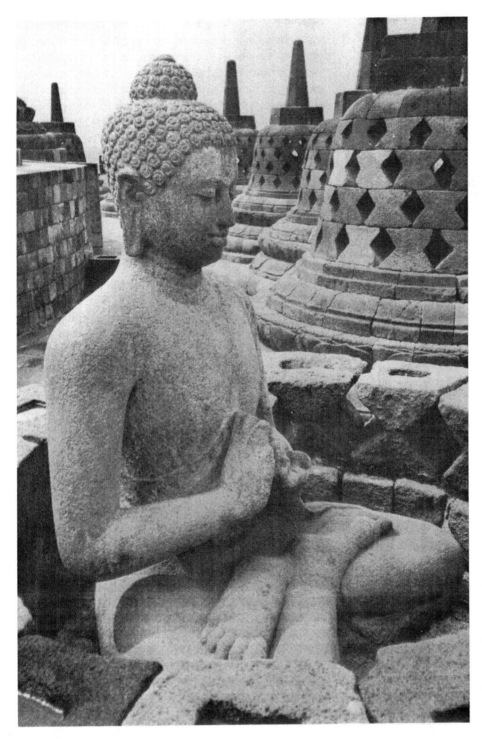

Figure 5.4. b. *A stone image of a seated Buddha which was encased in one of the seventy-two small stupas that suround the crowning larger stupa. Other small, bell-shaped, latticework stupas, many still containing their Buddha figures, are visible behind.*

Figure 5.5. *Tibetan mandala, the Diamond World (Vajradhatu), from the ninth century. This mandala depicts the five Jina Buddhas, who are transcendental beings according to the Advayavajra. The Buddhas are seated in the center cross formed by circles, attended by their bodhisattvas in smaller crosses of circles in the five directions of space (right, left, above, below, and center). On the outside perimeter of the inner square, hundreds more deities are depicted. The Borobudur monument has been analyzed as a Diamond World mandala; see the text for many levels of associated meaning.*

arrangement and appearance of statues along Borobudur's path of ascent seem to match the tenets of Tantric Buddhism, which designates certain types of deities for various levels of spiritual attainment. Numerous other concordances reinforce the idea of a link between Borobudur and a mystical mandala layout.

Who supervised the building of this immense project, which contains more than a million stone blocks? Javanese legend has it that Borobudur was built by a divine architect named Gunadharma, but modern investigations have

shown that it was built in stages, with several remodelings, undoubtedly by skilled and experienced builders. Expert supervision would have been needed to direct thousands of laborers to quarry, transport, and lay the stones, and the richness of decoration attests to the great skill of the artisans who created the hundreds of statues and reliefs covering much of the structure. Scholars suggest that the work was likely carried out under the auspices of the ruling Sailendra dynasty by a number of succeeding architects and religious leaders. Political support would probably have been needed for so vast a project, even though the motivation for it was spiritual, according to Miksic. But even before Buddhists acquired the site and began constructing their cosmic mountain, others, possibly Hindus, had begun building at Borobudur. The purpose of this earlier, unfinished work is unknown, but its three-level stone design may have influenced the plan of the lower three sections of the present monument.

Borobudur continued as a religious site until the tenth century, when the Sailendra court disappeared. Earthquakes, common in the region around this time, may have contributed to the general exodus of the population. Despite the gradual deterioration of the monument, some pilgrims continued to visit Borobudur. Eventually, however, the site was overgrown with tropical vegetation and became a haven for rebels, its original purpose forgotten. Around 1710, a Javanese writer reported the flight of a political dissident into the area. A few others visited Borobudur during the eighteenth century, but the monument provoked little interest, being regarded only as a hill with many statues. In the nineteenth century, European travelers became interested in the ruins, and one investigator, a Dutch engineer named H. C. Cornelius, had a series of drawings made of the site. In the early nineteenth century, Cornelius submitted the drawings, along with a report on the Borobudur sanctuary, to Lieutenant-Governor Thomas Raffles. Europeans, recognizing the significance of the monument and the degree of sophistication that its design and erection would have demanded, carried out excavations at the site from 1814 until the 1870s, although not continuously. Tangles of tropical overgrowth and soil covered most of the site. What finally emerged was an earthen-core hill faced with 6 to 12 feet (2 to 4 meters) of thick stone blocks. Since that time, archaeological and architectural study have gone hand-in-hand with renovation. Morton explains that preservationists painstakingly removed, cleaned, and registered over 800,000 stones in the early 1970s. Some of the work was subsidized by the Rockefeller Foundation. Unfortunately, in 1996—only fifteen years after its renovation was completed—Borobudur was listed as one of the world's ten most endangered monuments, threatened by both its hot and humid setting and by the great number of visitors.

SOURCES: MIKSIC (1990), MORTON (1983), MUNSTERBERG (1970), SLUSSER (1982), SNODGRASS (1985).

ASSEMBLED PIECES

From solid stone buildings, we turn to those made of assembled pieces: two types of wooden houses from two Pacific regions.

Lashed Polynesian Houses

The islands of Polynesia lie in the Pacific Ocean, stretching from Hawaii on the north to New Zealand on the southwest and Easter Island on the southeast—"the largest region in the world ever to be settled by a single ethnic group," according to historian-ethnologist P. Bellwood. The islands were gradually populated from about 1500 B.C.E., with settlements in Samoa at that date and far to the east on Easter Island by 400 C.E. Hawaii appears to have been settled from the Marquesas Islands to the south by about 300 C.E., with later influence from the Society Islands, also in the south.

Caves were the first shelters when the Polynesians colonized Hawaii. Refugees from intertribal wars continued to shelter in caves and lava tubes—the hollows formed as the exterior surface of a lava flow cooled before the interior—on the Big Island of Hawaii until the sixteenth century, after European contact. By that time, however, another housing tradition—that of houses assembled by lashing prefabricated sections together—prevailed across the islands. The durable bamboo, lashed together with fibers, provides a strong, flexible structural material.

Many details of this housing tradition came to the Hawaiians from the ancient Lapita or even earlier ancestors, with strong influence from Tahiti in the Society Islands. This tradition has left traces in the language: The Hawaiian terms for house posts (*pou*), ridgepole (*kauhuhu*), rafters (*o'a*), and thatch rafters (*'aho*) are used elsewhere in Polynesia with only slight differences of dialect. In fact, many Polynesian islands exhibit variations of the lashed house. In Samoa, houses are set on earth mounds, with shrines ("god houses") having more formal rectangular or star-shaped mounds; on Rarotonga (Cook Islands) and in Hawaii, houses are set on stone platforms; in New Zealand,

the houses had partially planked walls, probably because of the cooler climate.

Hawaiian houses varied in size and construction. In precontact times, according to the British explorer Captain James Cook, who died in Hawaii in 1779, houses were for storage or rainy weather; people mostly ate, slept, and lived under the shade of breadfruit trees. This practice was feasible, since the temperature usually varies between 70 and 80 degrees F (21–27 C). In areas of dense settlement, however, people slept indoors, probably to avoid mosquitoes and neighbors.

A careful analysis of Hawaiian house types by anthropologist and native Hawaiian P. H. Buck gives us much more detail than is usually available for Oceanic architecture. Because one can rarely document the traditional construction process from the literature—little of it has been committed to writing—we have paraphrased his account at length. Buck distinguishes four types of Hawaiian houses and tells how builders made each:

1. Without walls. Two posts supported the ridgepole. Straight rafters leaned against it, their lower ends embedded in the ground. A second ridgepole was laid on top of the crossed rafters. Gable posts with oblique ends were equally spaced on each side of a post at the center of each end. There could be a ground plate, and bent rafters were sometimes used to give more interior room (see Fig. 5.6).

2. With stone walls (an intermediate form between the first and the third and fourth types). Piling up stones to clear the ground made wall-like linear heaps of stone over which the roof was placed. An example from Maui measured 29 by 12 feet (9 by 4 meters), with the wall 3 feet (nearly 1 meter) high on all sides. An opening at one end served as a doorway. The ridge was supported by a kind of ridgepole-brace arrangement. The height of the ridgepole was 9.5 feet (3 meters). Main rafters were set along the side walls, with their upper ends lashed to the ridgepole. Smaller rafters were placed between the main rafters. Purlins, some 23 on each side, were made of bamboo. Thatch of pandanus (a tropical pine) leaves was folded about 5 inches (13 centimeters) over the purlins and kept in place by pressure, without pinning. Examples are also known of a hipped roof with stone walls, where the doorway was placed in the middle of the long side.

3. Gable roof with thatched walls (see Fig. 5.7). This type was in general use in 1788, as sketched by Captain

Figure 5.6. *Polynesian house model, at the Place of Refuge, Pu'uohomo Honanna, on the Big Island, Hawaii. The house framework, lashed together, is of Type 2 (see the text) and would have been finished with a thatched roof and walls.*

Cook's artists. The best-known example, with a frame from an old house on Kauai, measures 12.5 by 10 by 8.5 feet tall (4 by 3 by 3 meters) and is in the Bishop Museum in Honolulu. Its roof rises above thatched wood-frame walls. The supporting posts are of hardwood, their lengths corresponding to the overall dimensions of the house, here nearly 5 feet (147 centimeters). This dimension ranged from 3 to 4 feet (90 to 120 centimeters) in small houses and from 12 to 14 feet (4 to 5 meters) in large houses. In a chief's house, the posts were trimmed to round shapes, but in the house in the Bishop Museum, some are round and some are square, averaging 4 to 8 inches (10 to 20 centimeters) across. In poorer houses, the bark was left on the posts. This type of house is a good example of lashed-frame construction methods.

To assemble such a house, two experienced builders lashed the frame together in the traditional manner and thatched it with pili grass. They began by wedging the corner posts in holes in smoothly tamped earth. Ropes strung at two levels between the posts gave the line and height for wall posts, set about 6 feet apart (less than 2 meters). Prefabricated sections of the walls and roof were fastened together by lashing, using braid

of 'uki'uki grass or, less often, coconut fiber. On the Big Island, the lashing was often made of aerial roots; on other Polynesian islands, builders used a finer flat braid of sennit (straw or grass). The lashing patterns produced lozenge and chevron designs; similar patterns were found in Samoa as late as the 1950s. Many connection details seem to have come intact from the bamboo constructions of Southeast Asia and Indonesia. For instance, frame members of Southeast Asian, Indonesian, and Polynesian houses are all notched to receive lashing and cusped to embrace wall plates.

The height of the ridgepole depended on the owner's social rank—*pou hana* (ridgepole) came to mean "important person." In 1828, commoners on Maui had ridgepoles 4 to 6 feet (120 to 180 centimeters) high, while chiefs' houses were 18 to 20 feet (5.5 to 6 meters) tall. The ridgepole of the house in the Bishop Museum is 8 feet 2 inches (2.5 meters) tall. Each ridgepost is lashed only at the top, to the main ridgepole. The ridgepole itself is long and slender, so it can bend upward in the middle for more height. Each rafter and end post is lashed to the ridge posts.

Rafters were made of wood, sometimes detailed with forked ends and a groove on the upper side to re-

Figure 5.7. *Polynesian canoe shed of Type 3 at the Place of Refuge, Pu'uohomo Honanna, on the Big Island, Hawaii.*

ceive the ropes. They were tied to the wall plate and to each other at the ridgepole where they crossed, presenting flat surfaces to each other and being notched on the outer surface for additional lashings. Then a second ridgepole was added above, and the two poles were fastened once on each side of the crossed rafters and twice in the gap between them, making a firm but flexible joining. Just as the sides of the house have rafters, the ends have 2 to 6 gable posts, depending on the size of the house, spaced symmetrically and lashed in place. The resulting framework is shown in Fig. 5.6.

To complete the roof, the builders bound purlins to rafters horizontally at 15-to-18-inch intervals, but did not tie them to the ridge posts. These lashings made elliptical patterns on the interior, combining utility and decoration. Three loops joined purlins to rafters and five joined purlins to wall posts. The final element of

the frame was thatch-purlins, placed 5 to 6 inches (13–15 centimeters) apart, not tied but fixed in place by support rods.

The builders started with the side walls and moved on to the roof, beginning at the back of the house and working from the bottom to top. All the elements of the frame were tied together with a series of clove-hitch knots. Sometimes diagonal struts were used under the roof between the rafters to strengthen the frame; this method is also seen in farmhouses in northern Japan. Although Polynesians used different kinds and sizes of thatch, they all used the same method of roof structure. In central and western Polynesia, sheets of thatch with stiff upper edges were tied to horizontal purlins. Some houses had a double-layered roof, with pandemus on the inside and pili on the outside. Hawaiians preferred pili grass for its green color and fragrance when new. On some roofs in Hawaii and New Zealand, bunches of thatch were tied to the horizontal purlins. The most difficult part of the roof to complete was the line where the top of the thatch met the second ridge-pole because gaps in the seam meant a leaking roof. Polynesians performed a special ritual to ensure that their roofs were properly sealed along this edge.

4. Hipped-roof house. This type of house, in both con-cept and execution, is very like Type 3 except that the end triangles are part of the roof, not the walls, a vari-ation seen in some early drawings: By using wall posts as piles and stretching beams between the wall plates to make a raised floor, the builders created a house suitable for river valley living. The hipped-roof house was common in Hawaii along Oahu's Waimea River in the nineteenth century. After the American period be-gan in 1851, this style became more widely popular, the lower space being used as storage or for a cool re-treat. The lanai, or porch, is also a postcontact feature of Hawaiian houses.

Doorways in traditional Hawaiian houses were small, many just tall enough to crawl through, and often had arched tops, a reference to the crescent moon. Hawaiians, like New Zealanders and Cook Islanders, sometimes used sliding doors.

The elite among the Polynesians lived in a cluster of separate buildings, consisting of sleeping houses, a canoe shed, perhaps a house for menstruating women, a sepa-rate shrine, and often a cookhouse or another special-activity structure. Most people, however, had only one house, used primarily at night. Commoners' cooking was usually done outdoors, where daytime living took place, thanks to the benign climate. Some Polynesians had food taboos that required eating outside or on a special porch so as not to contaminate the house.

Like people all over the world, Polynesians organize their interior spaces according to their mythological sys-tem and their cultural values, the house, according to an-thropologist R. Waterson, being "the intersection of the visible and the invisible worlds." In traditional Hawaiian houses, interior space was divided conceptually (not phys-ically) by gender, age, class, and rank into sacred space, common space where the family gathered to eat, and women-and-children space. Anthropologist S. Kent re-ports that "although physical boundaries such as walls are absent, conceptual ones are rigid and dictate the use of space within the dwellings . . . consistent with the socio-

political organization, gender stratification and division of labor, and economic specialization." Family members all slept together in one big room. Furniture was minimal, consisting of carved wooden seats; headrests; and wooden shelves for household utensils like gourds, baskets, and bowls. Floors were covered with mats or dry grass, and people used thick piles of mats for mattresses, with bark cloth as coverings. For torches or lamps, they used either kukui nuts from the candlenut tree as "candles" or oil lamps carved from basalt.

Although not as dematerialized as the Basarwa shel-ters, Polynesian houses were relatively insubstantial. The houses were readily replaceable, if necessary, after occa-sional tropical cyclones. In Japan, similarly insubstantial but aesthetically satisfactory houses continued to be used uncritically but were far from successful in the harsher cli-mate. In the northern islands of Japan, the lashing of bam-boo and other lightweight materials gave way to mortise-and-tenon methods more suitable to wood construction.

SOURCES: BELLWOOD (1987), BUCK (1964), KENT (1995, 1996), P. V. KIRCH (PERSONAL COMMUNICATION), WATERSON (1990).

Interlocking Frameworks in Japan

Japan stretches for more than 1,900 miles (3,000 kilome-ters) from north to south in the north Pacific Ocean. Over such a range of latitude, climatic conditions can vary, from heavy snowfalls and severe cold to humid, subtropical con-ditions. Few countries have so many environmental varia-tions: torrential rains, seasonal monsoons, and typhoons—destructive forces that ravage the islands. Japan also experiences frequent earthquakes. Traditional Japanese ar-chitects had to counter these conditions with appropriate structural designs using available building materials.

Originally, Japan's rugged mountains were covered with abundant forests. From the earliest times, timber was available for building—cypress, pine, cedar, hemlock, and other species of trees, each with distinctive structural and aesthetic qualities and each responding in its own way to the forces of nature—earthquakes, and climatic differen-tials. Eventually, however, restrictions evolved concern-ing by whom, when, and how the timber was to be used. Under the feudal system, the ruling elite could fell trees as they wished; others had to obtain permission. By the nineteenth century, trees that were desired for construc-tion were marked in the spring for fall felling.

Wood is the material of choice for constructing tra-ditional houses. It is a practical and versatile medium.

Timber can be cut into desired shapes and reassembled from its natural form to become an interlocking framework, the basis of the traditional Japanese house. Builders began by felling timber and cutting it into required lengths for manageability. They followed a standard pattern based on Chinese construction manuals that were brought to Japan by Buddhist monks and merchants around 600 C.E. (see Chapter 2, Chinese Construction Manuals). For example, Japanese builders developed a system of measurement based on the size of the tatami mat (approximately 6 by 3 feet (2 by 1 meter), which corresponded to the unit of length called the *ken* (see Chapter 10, Fig. 10.23).

The tatami system of measurement originated in Kyoto, which was the capital and cultural center of Japan from the eighth to the twelfth century; the city maintained its cultural influence until the nineteenth century. After the seventeenth century, builders in many other cities imitated the Kyoto-style town house, and the tatami module set the standard of room measurement for houses built far beyond Kyoto, although regional variations continued to exist.

Most traditional Japanese houses follow a simple constructional pattern, basically rectangular with a post-and-lintel structural system, that builders could follow with relative ease. As a result, construction projects seldom involved a "professional architect"—a term not used in Japan until the late nineteenth century. Instead, a master carpenter and his assistants built a house according to directions given in carpenters' manuals (Fig. 5.8).

H. Engel, an architect-engineer and authority on Japanese building techniques, described the building of a traditional house from foundation to roof: The house was raised on posts two-and-a-half feet (75 centimeters) above the ground, with no basement (see Fig. 5.9). This elevation kept the wooden floors from coming into contact with the often-damp ground and protected the interior from rodents and other pests. The granaries discussed in Chapter 3 were elevated for similar reasons but with a greater distance between floor level and ground surface. The house posts rested on flat, oblong stones, rather than foundations, protected from the deterioration that would result from contact with the soil. These posts were placed at regular intervals, the distance between them (measured from the center of the column) based on the size of the tatami. The visual effect was of proportional harmony, lightness, and buoyancy. Foundations are now required in modern Japanese residences as a precaution against earthquakes, but earlier they were found only in castles

because those structures were usually made of heavy stone.

The posts or columns, not the enclosure walls, carried the weight in this vertical framework. Most of the exterior wall consisted of sliding panels called *shoji*, removable, light wooden panel frames covered with translucent rice paper. The frames fit into a track, much like the sliding glass doors found in modern Western houses. Such panels are specifically related to houses constructed after about 1600 (see Chapter 9, Katsura, for another discussion of shoji screens).

The interior spaces were divided by *fusuma*, movable wooden lattice-framed paper partitions that can create rooms according to the desired function. Household members could not attain complete privacy in rooms with such thin partitions, but they relied on courtesy, consideration, and psychological distance for comfort. Both the shoji and the fusuma use the same measurement module as the tatami; this standardization of size meant that these building elements could be mass-produced.

Some portions of the walls were solid—although "solid wall" does not have the same meaning in Japanese construction as it does in Western architecture, where it is more often load bearing. For example, above the upper shoji track was a section of fixed, non-load-bearing wall. A floor-to-ceiling solid wall might be placed in the tokonoma (a recess in a wall divided by partitions) or in another desired area. Builders often completed a house with a self-supporting inner bamboo skeleton, similar to the Polynesian houses discussed earlier. The skeleton consisted of vertical bamboo members tied together and coated with clay on both sides. This clay-finishing step was repeated several times, with color added to the last coat for visual effect. The result was interior and exterior wall surfaces that were aesthetically pleasing in both color and texture. To protect the exterior wall from rain and weathering, the builders sometimes covered it with sections of thin timber boards that overlapped and were aligned horizontally. Sometimes protruding roof tiles shielded the walls.

The roof not only served its basic protective function, but held intrinsic symbolic meaning for the Japanese, constituting a link between heaven and earth. The highest point of the house, it was securely attached to the earth by posts and beams. Side and end posts supported the purlins and rafters, and longitudinal beams at the top of the columns made the structural transition from framework to roof; wooden blocks made the structural transition from column or post to beam. In houses with wooden

Figure 5.8. *A traditional Japanese house with carpenters at work. Carpenters were the most important Japanese construction craftsmen. Here, the two at the bottom measure a piece of wood; above them, a worker raises his adze to shape a beam while the man at the left is sighting along a piece of wood to check for warping. Others are their assistants. Note the drawing of what they are building, leaning at the back.*

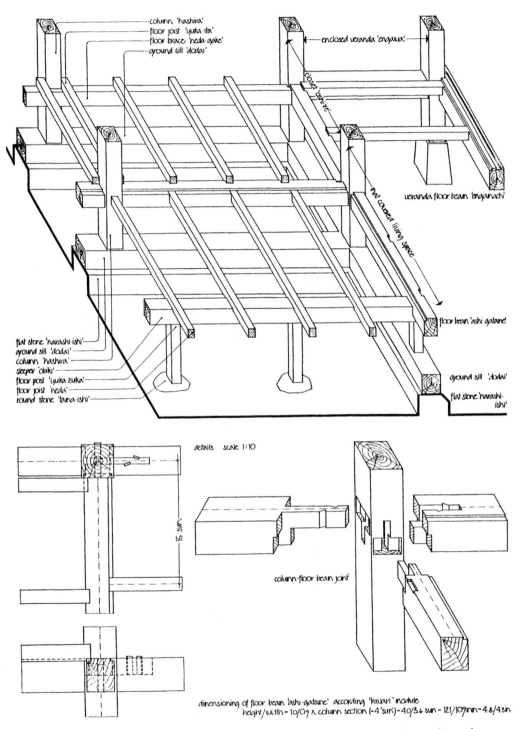

Labels in figure:

column 'hashira'
floor joist 'yuka-ita'
floor brace 'neda-gake'
ground sill 'dodai'

enclosed veranda 'engawa'

closer 'oshi-ire'

veranda floor beam 'engawa-achi'

mat covered living space

floor beam 'ashi-gatame'

flat stone 'narashi-ishi'
ground sill 'dodai'
column 'hashira'
sleeper 'obiki'
floor post 'yuka-zuka'
floor joist 'neda'
round stone 'tama-ishi'

ground sill 'dodai'
flat stone 'narashi-ishi'

details   scale 1:10

15 sun

column-floor beam joint

dimensioning of floor beam 'ashi-gatame' according 'kiwari' module
height/width - 10/09 x column section (~4 'sun') - 40/3.6 sun - 121/109mm - 4.8/4.3in

Figure 5.9. *Details of floor construction for a Japanese house. Note the traditional stone-supported posts of the raised floor. Shown are joists, braces, foundation stones, columns, and an exploded view and plan of a floor-beam joint. (See front cover.)*

or matting ceilings, the occupants could not see imperfections in the underside of the rafters, but not all houses had ceilings.

There were three basic types of roofs: gable, hipped, and a combination called a hipped gable. Separate lean-to roofs covered auxiliary structures, such as latrines or verandas, that were attached to the main house. Verandas especially required separate roofs with lower eaves because the steep slope of the main roof could not accommodate the width of the passage. Engel suggests that the lean-to roof was derived from aristocratic residences of tenth- to twelfth-century Japan—the shinden style. This traditional type featured independent hallways, with separate roofs, linking the various parts of the mansion. In turn, the shinden style had its genesis in Chinese prototypes. However, historian J. Reynolds points out that the builders of some Buddhist sanctuaries used lean-to roofs as early as the seventh century.

The steep pitch of the traditional Japanese roof allowed it to shed rain or snow, and the low-hanging eaves kept excess sunlight out of the interior during summer but did not exclude it altogether during winter. The lower portion of the roof overhang curved upward slightly. Although thatched roofs were common in Japanese farmhouses, the rafters in town houses were often covered with natural bark and tiles. Builders coated the bark with clay and straw to make a plaster in which they set terra-cotta roof tiles. Such a roof was a massive weight for the structural posts to support, especially during torrential rainstorms or earthquakes, and was known to collapse. As Engel notes, "The Japanese house in a typhoon is like a house of cards in a draft."

While wood is relatively flexible during earthquakes, Engel suggests that the traditional house style was inappropriate for the Japanese physical environment, its materials and designs of questionable utility in the face of the many other destructive forces common to the islands of Japan. Wood is an impermanent material, requiring frequent rebuilding. It is susceptible to damage from fire, as well as from insects and rodents, and it offers low lateral resistance to the forces of wind and rain. And the elevated house, based on Southeast Asian or Oceanic prototypes from areas of tropical or subtropical climate unlike Japan's north-temperate climate, produced impermanent structures with less stable foundations than other types of building.

Yet the Japanese relied strongly on traditional methods and were reluctant to deviate from them even when the methods were not the best response to environmental conditions. According to Engel, rather than radically change the design of the traditional house (which people still build in some areas today), the inhabitants adjusted their living habits to meet the challenge of climatic variations. In winter they wore thick, padded clothing; used charcoal braziers for heat; and took hot baths. In summer they donned lighter clothing and removed exterior screens from their dwellings, opening them up for ventiltion

Modern builders have not lost the essence of the traditional form, despite the adoption of many Western practices. The Japanese continue to respect natural building materials, especially wood, and to admire the visual appeal and versatility of the open plan. Although the tatami module no longer serves as the basic measurement for a whole structure, contemporary builders commonly include a "complete Japanese-style room" using the tatami module.

SOURCES: ENGEL (1969), ITOH AND FUTUGAWA (1980), NISHIHARA (1968).

ONE CULTURE, TWO BUILDING TRADITIONS

Dwellings made of permanent materials, such as stone, survive for much longer than those made of bamboo, wood, and thatch; thus we are likely to have a more complete picture of the built environments of societies that use such permanent materials. Many societies, however, use more than one set of materials. The Inkas of Peru built in stone, but they also followed a different building tradition that used ephemeral materials like vines and wood to construct bridges. Both traditions contributed to the stability of the Inka empire, and both required sophisticated methods of handling materials and organizing workers.

Inka Stone Masonry

In the 1200s C.E., the legendary first Inka leader, Manko Capac (see Table 5.1), is believed to have led his followers from Peru's southern highlands to the Cuzco valley in the Andes and expanded his rule over other peoples of the Cuzco area. Eventually, the Inkas gained military and economic control over diverse regions of the mountains and the coast, from the southern reaches of the Maule River in Chile to the northern boundaries of Ecuador. By the time of the Spanish conquest in 1532, they had built a powerful empire covering approximately 650,000 square miles (1,683,500 square kilometers), with a population of about 6 million. It is remarkable that so vast an empire could be united, and massive building programs initiated,

TABLE 5.1 The Inka Dynasty Circa 1200–1572

Lords of Cuzco

Manko Capac	Son of the Sun
Sinchi Roza (son of Manko Capac)	Ruled: ?
Lloque Yupanqui (son of Sinchi Roza)	Ruled: ?
Mayta Capac (son of Lloque Yupanqui)	Child prodigy, Hercules of Inka legend fl. 1290–early 14th century
Capac Yupanqui (son of Mayta Capac)	fl. 1320
Inka Roca (son of Capac Yupanqui)	First to use "Inka" as a noble title
Yahuar Huacac (son of Inka Roca)	Ruled: ?
Virakocha (son of Yahuar Huacac	Began conquests

Emperors of Tahuantinsuyu (Four Quarters of the World)

Pachakuti Inka Yupanqui (son of Virakocha)	First emperor; usurped the throne Ruled 1438–71
Tupa Inka (son of Pachakuti)	Great conqueror Ruled 1471–93
Huayna Capac (son of Tupa Inka)	Ruled 1493–1527
Huaskar (son of Huayna Capac)	Overthrown in civil war; executed by Atahuallpa Ruled 1532–33
Atahuallpa (another son of Huayna Capac)	Captured and executed by Francisco Pizarro Ruled 1532–33

Inkas After the Spanish Conquest

Tupa Huallpa (another son of Huayna Capac)	Ruled 1533
Manco Inka (another son of Huayna Capac)	Ruled 1533–45
Paullu Inka (another son of Huayna Capac)	Puppet ruler Ruled 1537–49
Carlos Inka (son of Paullu Inka)	Ruled 1549–72
Sayri Tupa Inka (first son of Manco Inka)	Ruled 1558–71
Titu Kusi (second son of Manco Inka)	Ruled 1558–71
Tupa Amaru (third son of Manco Inka)	Ruled 1571–72

during the relatively short reigns of three Inka rulers in less than a century, from 1438 to 1527.

In 1438, the Inka leader Pachakuti Inka Yupanqui launched an expansion program that involved the construction of fortresses, public buildings, and palaces in highland Peru and adjacent territories (see Fig. 5.11). This ruler possessed a genius for social organization based on the ethnic blending of peoples, the relocation of subjugated populations, and the sending of forces to colonize conquered territories. The Inkas imposed their institutions and religious concepts on conquered peoples by requiring them to use a common language and to serve in the military. Pachakuti further consolidated the empire by standardizing architectural forms and building an infrastructure of highways, bridges, and agricultural terraces (see Fig. 5.11 and the map of Central and South America in the Appendix). His son Thupa Inka (Tupa Inka) (1471–93) and his grandson Wayna Qhapaq (Huayna Capac) (1493–1527) continued the building program he had begun.

Stone was the building material of choice (see Fig. 5.10). Because the Inka did not have saws, timber construction was limited, although they used some wood for beams, rafters, and roofs or for more elaborate structures. Several kinds of stone, including the fine-grained rocks, rhyolite, andesite, and limestone, were used. The stone was either quarried locally or transported from greater distances in blocks that commonly weighed 75 tons and more.

Monumental Inka architecture was built of massive stone blocks. How did the Inkas quarry the stone, cut and dress it, transport it, and fit the huge blocks with such skill and precision without modern technology? In his study, architect J. P. Protzen shed light on Inka construction methods. Despite a limited range of tools, the Inkas were able to quarry stone. Moreover, because quarry sites often coincided with major rock falls, the blocks did not always have to be cut; workers could select suitable stones from among the fallen boulders and partially work them before sending them to the construction site for finishing. If necessary, such stones could be further broken up by driving a wedge along a fracture to obtain a smaller section. Hammerstones with round smooth surfaces were used to shape the stones on which the laborers worked.

Moving the massive blocks was especially difficult because of the mountainous terrain. Sixteenth-century eyewitness accounts by Spanish chroniclers record that many men pulled the stones with fiber ropes, dragging them up and down steep roadways. Striations on the blocks show how the road's gravel surface ground against the stones.

Figure 5.10. *Fountain near Cuzco, Peru. The water is visible at several levels. In the far background is a wall with trapezoidal niches, characteristic of Inka architecture. Massive stones were cut and laid in straight courses and often fitted without mortar. Such walls were for important buildings and were made by skilled stonemasons. Contrast these walls with the wall of irregular fieldstones in the foreground, where mortar is needed to hold the stones together.*

Protzen describes the transport of these massive boulders to the site called Ollantaytambo once they had been selected and roughed out. Following the path over which blocks of relatively coarse-grained rose rhyolite had traveled, he found ramps that were extensions of roadways leading to slides that were used to slip the stones down ravines into the Urubamba river during the season when water levels were the lowest. This system directed the massive blocks downward with less human effort than if laborers had carried them down. At the bottom of the slope, workers had to transport the blocks across the river before moving them up the opposite incline.

Writing about the construction of the fortress at Saqsaywaman, sixteenth-century observer Pedro de Cieza de Leon (quoted in Protzen) described methods that workers at Ollantaytambo probably also used: "Four thousand [workers] were breaking stones and extracting stones; six thousand were hauling them with big ropes of hide and leaf fibers . . ." How could so many workers manipulate the stones on narrow mountain roads, making the difficult turns? Protzen theorizes that the crews worked

Figure 5.11. *Roads of the Inka empire. Quito, Ecuador, at the north end of the road system, was 2,000 miles (3,200 kilometers) from Santiago, Chile, at the south end. Cuzco, the capital, is at the approximate center. Southeast of Cuzco and northwest of La Paz is Lake Titicaca, the area from which the Inkas originated. About halfway between Cuzco and Quito lies the Chicama river valley, the irrigation of which is discussed in Chapter 3. (Compare with Map III in Appendix.)*

127

mainly at the back of the load, pushing and braking the stone blocks, using levers and some type of lubrication. Efficiently organized overseers controlled the labor force (called *mi'ta* by the Inkas) of tributary workers.

At the construction site, workers cut the rough blocks and dressed them to size before arranging them in a wall or building. They fitted the stones together with great precision, sometimes using a mortar of sand, gravel, and grass, but mortar was used sparingly with precision-cut blocks. Once the blocks were in place, laborers worked their surfaces with hammerstones and then polished them.

The walls of monumental Inka structures were usually thick—24 to 39 inches (60 to 100 centimeters)—and tapered inward from bottom to top to counteract the outward thrust of the roof. According to architectural historian S. Niles, there were three types of construction. The first consisted of large, well-defined, fitted blocks with smooth joints. Walls made of these stones exhibited the most skillful workmanship and were designed for important monuments, such as the royal buildings in the ancient capital of Cuzco. The Inkas generally did not depend on mortar for bonding when working in this technique. The second type, "intermediate" masonry, combined less skillfully fitted blocks, often arranged in two thick layers, with a core of clay and rubble as a matrix. Builders used this type of construction for buildings of lesser importance. The third type consisted of fieldstones held together with clay. Used for smaller buildings, this type of construction required less precise workmanship and a greater amount of the bonding agent. Types 2 and 3 are seen in the fountain shown in Fig. 5.10.

Lifting these weighty stones required ingenuity. Loose blocks found at Ollantaytambo have grooves and bosses (protuberances). Their presence indicates that workers used levers, ropes, and inclined planes to facilitate lifting and to move the cut stones. Other cultures arrived at the same solutions at different times in history: Egyptians used levers to move the stone blocks of the pyramids into place, and Greek masonry bears similar evidence of bosses.

Another way in which the skill of the Inka stonemasons is similar to that of Egypt's master builders is that both cultures could fit stones neatly without a bonding agent, using only a small amount of mortar to provide slipperiness for ease in sliding the huge blocks into their final places and relying upon the minute precision of the stonecutting to provide a snug fit. As in ancient Egypt, the most prestigious Inka buildings had the finest stones, sometimes with smooth, polished facings; joints carved for fitting the stones together; and other features appropriate to the purpose of the structure.

Most Inka architecture, however, was built of mortared masonry (see Fig. 5.10). Fieldstone walls were laid either in courses, using stones of a similar shape and size for each entire layer, or uncoursed, in which a miscellaneous mixture made up the wall. Alternating headers (masonry units laid crosswise) and stretchers (horizontal masonry units laid lengthwise in the direction of the wall) for the corners and wall heads added strength to the wall because these stones tended to be of a greater size and length than the rest of the stones. Because of the regularity of most of the stones in the coursed method, little mortar was needed. Conversely, builders found it necessary to use clay mortar when laying fieldstones of various sizes in uncoursed construction. Mortared, uncoursed walls were less stable than more finely fitted, coursed walls.

One of the most striking features of Inka stone masonry was the forming of trapezoidal niches within the fabric of the wall. Builders had to plan carefully to achieve such uniformly sized and shaped alcoves, with level foundations, in symmetrical arrangements. As Fig. 5.10 shows, the niche blocks are larger than the wall blocks and are evenly finished on the inner side of the niche. The lintel is a large, rectangular stone, and the wall is built up around this frame. The thickness of the wall determines the depth of the niche.

Niles points out that while the niches themselves exhibit the stonemason's desire to maintain a good fit of blocks, the same is not true of the stones that were placed between the niches. Sometimes a thick clay covering was applied to this part of the wall to conceal the inconsistencies between the two wall sections. Murals may have been common in or around the niches. Sixteenth-century documents report wall murals in the palaces of Cuzco (see locations in map, Fig. 8.10). Other than the niches and the texture and individual qualities, such as the color of the construction stones, however, Inka buildings display a notable lack of architectural ornamentation.

Although we know from detailed accounts by Spanish conquerors that the Inka empire had temples, fortresses, administrative centers, dwellings, and other buildings, it is hard to tell what activities took place in a particular room or building of the remaining ruins. The typical structure had a single interior room, usually rectangular, with trapezoidal niches and entrances. Modern scholars' difficulties in determining function are compounded by the accounts of the eyewitness-chroniclers, who may have misinterpreted activities and mislabeled structures according to their own cultural orientation. For example, the building called the "fortress of Saqsaywaman" by a sixteenth-century writer may have been a fortified temple or a "royal house of the sun"—a castle with multiple purposes, as archaeologists G. Gasparini and L. Margolies (1980) claimed (see Figs. 8.8, 8.9, and 16.1, and Chapter 8 for a discussion of this structure).

Because it seemed to later peoples that only superhumans could have built as the Inkas did without using wheels and with only crude stone tools, many myths have developed. Some nineteenth-century visitors proposed that Inka buildings had been assembled by giants or other supernatural forces. Others suggested that the Inkas had secret formulas for melting or softening rocks. In modern times, the credulous have claimed that extraterrestrials built the structures. These unfounded theories show that many observers have been reluctant to credit such fine achievements to New World peoples, as historian L. McIntyre reports. We are indebted, however, to sixteenth-century chroniclers, such as Pedro de Cieza de Leon, whose descriptions preserve a truer picture of Inka culture.

The logical explanation for Inka accomplishments in construction lies in social organization—the division of tasks among a large labor force and overseers, efficiently run by a centralized power. (A similar principle governed the building of the Great Wall of China; see Chapter 8.) The thousands of visitors who travel to see the magnificent stonework at Cuzco, Machu Picchu, Ollantaytambo, and other Inca sites agree that they are among the most impressive monuments the world has to offer. It is a tribute to Inka ingenuity that the same social organization that produced these enduring monuments also produced bridges of perishable materials. Bridges, together with a well-organized road system, served to build and unify the strong Inka society.

SOURCES: GASPARINI AND MARGOLIES (1980), MCINTYRE (1975), NILES (1987), PRESCOTT (1856), PROTZEN (1993).

Inka Roads and Woven Suspension Bridges

Ease of communication affects the success of a political group, so that roads, trails, and bridges were essential to the cohesion of the Inka state, wrote anthropologists D. E. Thompson and J. V. Murra. Owing to the geography of mountain valleys and desert oases, the Peruvians lived in dense "islands" of settlement amid wider areas of little population. If travel along the coast were reckoned at one unit of time, then anthropologists J. R. Topic and T. L.

Topic estimated that travel from mountain to mountain would be 1.3 units and from the coast over the high passes to the mountain valleys, 1.46 units. By making river crossings easier, bridges cut down travel time (see Fig. 5.11).

Traffic on Inka roads consisted of people and llamas. This light traffic made the roads narrower and thus cheaper to build than if they were meant to carry wheeled traffic. Coastal roads were either raised on high embankments retained with clay walls, the edges planted with trees and shrubs for shade and as route markers, or indicated in sandy desert areas by rows of piled stones. Mountain roads were paved with flagstones and often surfaced with a bituminous cement harder than stone. A major challenge of road building was the numerous ravines and rivers to be crossed, which required many bridges and retaining walls. Engineer A. Regal analyzed early Peruvian bridges, dividing them into four groups by materials: (1) stone (whether high in the air or inserted into the bed of a river), (2) wood (logs or planks, often combined with stone abutments), (3) pliable vegetable materials (ropes, cables, and so forth, either floored with wood or not, usually having abutments made of stone or stone and wood), and (4) floating materials (such as balsa, reeds, or cornstalks).

The most primitive bridge consisted of two cables strung at different heights so that a person could hang on to one and walk on the other (compare with Fig. 5.13). Alternatively, a single cable could support a small platform or large basket hanging from a pulley; people or loads could be pulled across. In 1609, Chronicler Garcilaso de la Vega described a hanging bridge—the Cusibamba Bridge at the provincial capital of Accha—that is traditionally considered the first of its kind, built by the fourth Inka Mayta Capac in about 1290. The bridge was 320 feet (98 meters) long and 5 feet (1.5 meters) wide, slung on ropes wound at each end onto wooden posts held in cemented stone anchors. Although replaced periodically during the Inka period, it was neglected under the Spanish, and in 1694 the rope of this bridge fell into the river, possibly because of the lack of maintenance.[12] Vega also reported that the fifth Inka, Capac Yupanqui, built a wider bridge near Cuzco to facilitate conquest. The cables—up to 200 feet (61 meters) long—were "as thick as a man's body," noted Prescott, and threaded through rings or holes in stone buttresses and fastened to huge timbers.

---

[12]See Thornton Wilder's novel, *The Bridge of San Luis Rey* (1929).

a.

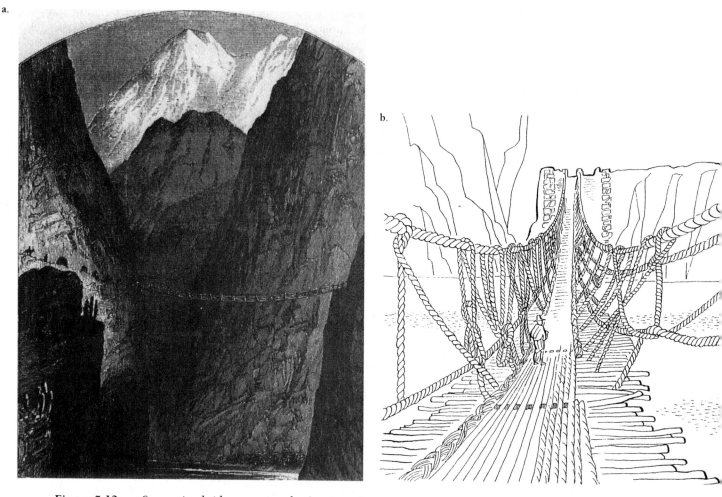

b.

Figure 5.12. a. *Suspension bridge spanning the Apurimac River, near Cuzco, Peru. The experience of crossing the bridge, which is made of vegetable fibers, was fearful because of the wind and the depth of the canyon, according to Squier, who drew the sketch in the 1870s.* **b.** *Detail of the bridge. The floor is of logs, bound together by cables of fiber and suspended by other cables from abutments of massive stones and large logs on each shore.*

Capac Yupanqui built a floating bridge in 1320 on Lake Titicaca (see the map of Central and South America in the Appendix). Garcilaso de la Vega reported that it consisted of boat-shaped clumps of cornstalks, placed in two layers, strengthened by cedar roots, and tied together with hemp ropes. Water ran between the clumps, which people called "the shoes of the bridge." In 1877 North American engineer E. Squier sketched the balsa bridge over Rio Desaguadero and the Totora bridge of reeds over the outlet of Lake Titicaca, both of which belong in the floating category.

Bridges on mountain routes must be propped or suspended over valleys. The most dramatic of these suspension bridges are those made of wood (logs, planks, or sticks) and pliable vegetable materials. One major bridge was described by engineer E. Squier in the nineteenth century (see Fig. 5.12a and b) and studied more recently by anthropologists Thompson and Murra:

Three or four cables form the floor and the principal support of the bridge, over which small sticks, sometimes only sections of cane or bamboo, are laid transversely, and fastened to the cables by vines, cords, or throngs of raw hide. Two smaller cables are sometimes stretched on each side, as a guard or hand-rail. Over these frail and swaying structures pass men and animals, the latter frequently with their loads on their backs. . . . [We crossed] the great bridge over the Apurimac, on the main road from the ancient Guamanga to Cuzco . . . a large and rapid stream . . . crossed at only a single point, between two enormous cliffs. . . . From above, the bridge, looking like a mere thread, is reached by a path which on one side traces a thin, white line on the face of the mountain, and down which the boldest traveler may hesitate to venture. This path on the other side at once disappears from a rocky shelf . . . through a dark tunnel cut in the rock, from which it emerges to trace its line of many a steep and weary zigzag up the face of the mountain. It is usual for the traveler to time his day's journey to reach this bridge in the morning, before the strong wind sets in, for during the greater part of the day, it sweeps up the canyon of the Apurimac with great force and then the bridge sways like a gigantic hammock, and crossing is next to impossible.

Although most suspension bridges crossed rivers with a single span, double forms were also known. The two halves met at a stone pillar in midstream. Another variant was the *hamaca*, or cable bridge, which looks like a suspension bridge but has lower railings—or none at all—and hence requires a wider footpath (as A. Regal illustrated).

The old wooden bridge near Huanuco Viejo in Peru and the connecting section of stone highway have been in continuous use for centuries and are probably originally Inka. Thompson and Murra studied the reconstruction of the bridge, observing both the physical process and the social organization that made it possible. The latter was similar to the social organization reported in Chapter 3 for Peruvian canals, but here our interest focuses on the physical process.

"The bridge over a torrential river was made of very thick timbers," wrote the conqueror Hernando Pizarro's scribe in 1534, noting that the stone abutments were "securely and very well made in the time of the Inka." It had projecting supports made of three tiers of five timber beams, each nearly 6 meters long. Then came very long logs "so big [that] a man could just clasp them in his arms," the biggest nearly 18 meters long. The builders cantilevered these logs over the supports to span the river, laid shorter timbers crosswise on top, and then covered

them with stones and earth topped by sod. This method created a structure that was strong in the center of the roadway but weak at the edges.

Both construction work and maintenance of the bridge were shared. The original work was probably done by two village moieties. Villages on one side of the river supplied and positioned logs 1, 3, and 7, and those across the river supplied and positioned logs 2, 4, and 5. Both groups worked together on log 6. As early as 1534, the anonymous chronicler of Pizarro's trip recorded information about the maintenance of this bridge: "On each side of the bridge there were people who lived right there who had no other trade, nor duty but to repair and maintain the bridge." Other writers, however, did not report such custodians. It is tempting to think that there were two reconstruction systems, one imperial and one local. At least one instance is recorded of local people working with workers from a new Inka settlement to construct a bridge together. Other ancient documents reported that in the past, the villagers of the left bank of the river did not have to be forced to repair the bridge, but in 1596, under the Spanish, they saw no reason to do so because they had lost their lands near the bridge and no longer had any incentive to do the work.

Providing tree trunks was a big part of the labor needed to construct bridges. At places like Huanuco Viejo, both bridges and settlements were well above the tree line. Builders brought wood from about 12 miles (20 kilometers) or even farther away. As an alternative, they could make a bridge of ropes of "straw" from a plant that grew wild locally, but a straw bridge had to be rebuilt every two years. Wood bridges lasted eight years on average, with a minimum life of four years and a maximum of twenty.

The Inka bridge builders knew how to work with the available local materials and where to locate their bridges. They retained the engineering traditions of their predecessors and added their own administrative genius to the construction of these essential links in their communication system. (Compare with the African suspension bridge in Fig. 5.13.)

Ephemeral the bridges certainly were, owing to the combination of materials and climate. Yet they sufficed to link the roads that served the extensive empire, making possible the unity commemorated in the monumental stone constructions of the cities. The Inka post system carried luxuries from different parts of the empire. Trained runners from the villages were stationed less than 5 miles apart along the roads. With runners dashing at top speed for an hour before handing a message or parcel to another

Figure 5.13. *Suspension bridge, Congo-Brazzavilla, Africa. The structure is similar to the Peruvian example, but the details are different. Note that the walking surface is a single strand of fibers bound together for strength; also, the safety of those crossing is ensured by four levels of cables and connecting links, forming a network along the sides.*

runner at the next post, the system routinely covered 150 miles (240 kilometers) a day. The Spanish, in contrast, needed eight to ten days to cover the same distance by horseback or coach. A modern sociologist commented that woven bridges were more efficient and somehow less threatening than the modern road bridges that traverse the same chasms.

The Inkas had the most extensive road system of any premodern, wheelless society in the Americas. It covered nearly 2,000 miles (3,200 kilometers) from north to south.

Expansion of the empire into northern Chile and northwest Argentina alone required more than 600 miles (965 kilometers) of roads. The road network, which consisted partly of new construction and partly of roads built by earlier peoples, such as the Moche and Chimu, combined eleven main or royal roads and many secondary ones (see Fig. 5.11). Remnants of secondary routes are still visible in the Andean back country, while some bridges and sections of royal roads have been in use since pre-Inka times.

Road builders were concerned not only with the problems of running linear routes within basins, but with the steep ascents and descents between basins—especially the climb from the coast to a 12,500-foot (3,800-meter) pass before dropping into a high valley. Just as the irrigation systems (see Chapter 3) were completely laid out before construction began, so would roads be planned and laid out in advance, following ridgelines or rivers. Residents built each local section, thereby having some opportunity to manipulate the route.

Sources: Garcilaso de la Vega (1966); Mundigo (personal communication); Prescott (1856); Regal Matienzo (1972), 124, 129; Squier (1973); D. E. Thompson and J. V. Murra (1966); Topic and Topic (1983); K. Wheeler (1997).

SUGGESTED READINGS

Bidder, I. 1959. Lalibela: *The Monolithic Churches of Ethiopia.* London: Thames & Hudson. Good plans, sections, descriptions.

Buck, P. H. (Te Rangi Hiroa). 1964. *Arts and Crafts of Hawaii.* Vol. 2: *Houses.* Honolulu: Bishop Museum. An architectural study by an anthropologist—typical of the kinds of materials available to scholars at that time. Well done.

Cieza de Leon, Pedro de. 1959. *The Inkas of Pedro de Cieza de Leon,* ed. with introduction by V. von Hagen, trans. H. de Onis. Norman: University of Oklahoma Press. Written in the first century after the conquest of Peru and illustrated by an Inka artist, the book is not only invaluable but lively and informative.

Coaldrake, W. H. 1990. *The Way of the Japanese Carpenter.* New York: Weatherhill. An in-depth study of the aesthetic attitudes and working methods of carpenters in Japan.

Engel, H. 1964. *The Japanese House: A Tradition for Contemporary Architecture.* Rutland, Vt.: Charles E. Tuttle. A detailed study of Japanese domestic architecture with many illustrations. Includes chapters on society, aesthetics, gardens, and philosophy.

Gasparini, G., and L. Margolies. 1980. *Inca Architecture,* trans. P. Lyon. Bloomington: Indiana University Press. This well-written study of Inka architecture contains many excellent photographs.

Hyslop, J. 1984. *The Inca Road System.* Orlando, FL: Academic Press. The key monograph on this subject.

Kirch, P. V. 1985. *Feathered Gods and Fishhooks.* Honolulu: University of Hawaii Press. See especially Chapter 11, Settlements and Societies. Lucid and compelling reading, with many illustrations and a useful bibliography.

Miksic, J. 1990. *Borobudur: Golden Tales of the Buddha.* Boston: Shambhala. The definitive study of this monument.

Morton, W. Brown III. 1983. "Indonesia Rescues Ancient Borobudur." *National Geographic* 163: 127–42. A clergyman-turned-preservationist shows what was worth saving at Borobudur and how the preservation took place.

Niles, S. 1987. "Niched Walls in Inka Design." *Journal of the Society of Architectural Historians* 40: 277–85. Niles discusses the construction of Inka niches, one of the standard components of Inka design.

Nishi, K., and K. Hozumi. 1985. *What is Japanese Architecture?* New York: Kodansha. An excellent, concise overview of Japanese building types.

Protzen, J. 1993. *Inka Architecture and Construction at Ollantaytambo.* New York: Oxford University Press. This well-illustrated monograph is a careful and thorough investigation of Inka building practices. It was written by an archaeologist with many years of experience studying Inka construction techniques.

Schuster, A. M. H. 1984. "Hidden Sanctuaries of Ethiopia." *Archaeology* (January–February): 28–35. Fine illustrations in color.

Squier, E. 1973. *Peru: Incidents of Travel and Exploration in the Land of the Incas.* New York: AMS Press for Peabody Museum (reprint of 1877 ed.). Squier was a civil engineer who had previously studied Native American mounds at St. Louis and elsewhere. Useful also for Chapter 8 (Saqsaywaman and Cuzco).

Thompson, D. E., and J. V. Murra. 1966. "The Inca Bridges in the Huanuco Region." *American Antiquity* 31: 632–39. A careful and interesting study.

Topic, J. R., and T. L. Topic. 1983. "Coast-Highland Relations in North Peru: Some Observation on Routes, Networks, and Scales of Interaction." In *Civilization in the Ancient Americas,* 237–59, edited by R. M. Leventhal and A. L. Kolata. Albuquerque: University of New Mexico Press. Analysis of the social adaptation to the constraints of the terrain, in terms of roads, bridges, and time necessary for communication in these coastal desert and mountain terrains.

PART III

Purposes of Traditional Architecture

Architecture fulfills a great variety of purposes. Among them are daily life, religion, and power. Buildings house the first, shape our experience of the second, and symbolize the third. Traditional architecture makes many physical provisions for the way people live—squeezing into cramped quarters in houseboats, for example, or expanding daily life onto the street and roof. The connection between architecture and daily life goes beyond the physical, however, to reflect and embody social structures. And who receives the social rewards of the use or ownership of architecture? Examples from New Guinea and Nigeria show how two traditional societies answer this question.

Religious architecture can be a space in the home, the street as the site of special events, or a space set apart for religion. Ancient and modern societies in Japan, Mexico, Nepal, India, North Africa, and New Mexico have provided for the religious aspects of life in a variety of architectural forms, some as temporary as a parade, others as permanently a part of the landscape as a volcano.

The monumental stone construction of two "lost cities"[13]—Zimbabwe in East Africa and Nan Madol in the Caroline Islands north of New Guinea, in the Pacific Ocean—suggests architecture's role in the expression and maintenance of power. The Great Wall of China and the Inka fortress of Saqsaywaman in Peru are examples of empire building and enhancement of the imperial image. Another aspect of empire is colonialism, which affects indigenous traditions, as shown in the conquest-related architecture of the Islamic princes in India. Colonialism's effect on urban form is clearly apparent in the rapid sequence of pre-Inka, Inka, and Spanish conquests at Cuzco in Peru.

---

[13]B. Davidson, *The Lost Cities of Africa* (1959).

⊞ 6

Spaces for Daily Life

Daily life—is it meager in its ordinariness or rich in its variety? The latter, as is evident from the few examples in this chapter, selected from many possibilities. There is abundant variety in the way people around the world structure their daily lives through architecture. The houseboat seems a simple-enough arrangement for family life, but even within this arrangement there is variety, as shown by the contrasting styles of houseboat living in the vale of Kashmir and the coastal seas of China. Another custom, common among the Newar people of Bhaktapur in Nepal, is to use roofs and streets as extensions of living space. Both the boat dwellers and the Newars are constrained by the shortage of lots for building, but they have worked out remarkably different solutions to this problem.

Societies sometimes restrict access to parts of the built environment, suggesting that some lives are considered more worthy than others to participate in the use of important architecture. This chapter closes with an examination of the theoretical and political implications of how a society distributes the rewards of architecture. Which groups are excluded from the use of buildings, and why?

LIVING IN TIGHT SPACES

Naval architecture is a legitimate term. Houseboats (see Figs. 6.1–6.4), in which whole families live and work, are ubiquitous in the coastal waters of Japan, South China, and Southeast Asia and are found in the rivers of China and the inland waters of Kashmir as well. In places without enough arable land to support everyone, wrote traveler R. F. Fitch, "[m]illions of people live much like waterfowl, more or less permanently on the water . . . born and reared [sic], marry, bring up families, and finally breathe their last, afloat."

Houseboats of China

Houseboat living has an ancient pedigree. The Tanka boat people of Hong Kong may be among the oldest inhabitants of China; the name Tan (or Tanka, or Tan-Kia) refers to the ancient aborigines of south China. From time to time, other Chinese have joined the boat people, and some boat people have become land dwellers (see Fig. 6.1 for an example of an early houseboat). Countless numbers of

Figure 6.1. *Pottery model of a Chinese houseboat from the later Han dynasty, first century c.e., found in a burial near Kuang-chow. The model is nearly 2 feet (0.60 meters) long. From left to right: the rudder under the overhanging stern, the steersman's cabin, deckhouses roofed with matting, a gallery punctuated with bollards for the polers to walk along, and a projecting bow with an anchor. The mast would have been placed just to the right of the deckhouses.*

Chinese live on river and canal boats, and China's coastal houseboat culture stretches from Shanghai in the north along the coast to the southwest, with its center in Hong Kong. In 1931, Hong Kong had 70,793 boat dwellers—15 percent of the total population. By 1961, the number of boatpeople had risen to 136,802, but they represented only 5 percent of the population of fast-growing Hong Kong. The government began building housing, and people began moving ashore. Since its heyday in the first half of the twentieth century, Hong Kong's houseboat population has dwindled both in absolute numbers and as a proportion of the total population.

In 1967, more than half Hong Kong's boat dwellers were people living on fishing craft (junks or sampans); by the early 1980s, they were less than 1 percent of the total population (see Fig. 6.2 and 6.3). Others lived on ferries, launches, tugs, sailing passenger junks, cargo boats, lighters, water boats, houseboats, hulks and other stationary craft, traditional junks, pleasure craft, ocean or coastal ships, and a few on warships. A larger boat housed a crew of from six to sixty people; smaller vessels housed as many as ten.

The Tanka boat dwellers live mostly in nuclear, patriarchal families. The men are fishers, performing tasks that require male strength and social experience, but women often own and manage small passenger boats. Because their lives depend on their unusual physical environment, the Tanka have more physical mobility than do most workers in China. Like their land-based neighbors, the Tanka set a high value on the model of life based on Confucius's teachings, which emphasize respect for family and for state bureaucracy. This model of social ethics relies on sympathy and respect between ruler and subject, parent and child, elder and younger brother, husband and wife, and friend and friend. Of these relationships, the parent-child relationship is the most important. Etiquette, ritual, and a strong insistence on virtue ensure the smooth functioning of the group.

The Tanka way of life continues today for three main reasons: economic need, discriminatory laws and regulations, and social rejection. Many boaters are too poor to live ashore. A Chinese farm family of five or six can support themselves on two acres of land, but the cost of land is prohibitive for many.[14] A houseboat can accommodate

---

[14]Seventy-five percent of China's population lives on 15 percent of the land, nearest the ocean. This population crunch drives land prices up.

an aged grandparent, his son, the son's wife with a few children, and sometimes additional crew. Usually, the eldest son inherits the father's boat, but in some groups, older sons buy their own boats and the youngest sons inherit the family boats.

"A Chinese fishing junk must be one of the most uncomfortable crafts in the world to live in," mainly because of the crowding. Besides humans, a boat houses chickens, a guard dog, and a cat to catch rats and mice. It has little room for storage. "As the shelters are low, it is difficult for people to walk under them. There are horizontal rails or wooden planks outside the shelters, on either side of the boat, for people to walk on . . . over the boat there are many rods used for drying laundry or nets," according to anthropologist H. Kani. Residents continually clean both their boat and their clothing in the harbor's waters. At least twice a month, they scrape the boat's hull, rub it with tung oil, and polish it. They wear clean black or blue cotton suits every day, donning many layers in winter.

A small stove, efficiently used, provides both heat and a cooking fire. The stove is set into a box 1.5 feet (45 centimeters) square beneath the deck. Fitch called the meal produced on this stove "a culinary feat . . . meats and vegetables cooked separately in succession, and each put aside into a bowl. Then one cooks the rice. Then, place the meats and vegetables over the steaming rice and set in place the deep cover. Steam from the rice warms the rest." Keeping house on a boat requires this kind of ingenuity. Market boats bring supplies to each houseboat, selling rice, vegetables, clothing, medicines, and trinkets.

One of the intrinsic features of life on a boat is the ever-present danger of falling into the water. Boat dwellers have developed safety devices to protect and manage their children. On the upper Chang Jiang river, they secure babies in baskets of bamboo. On the south China coast, they use life belts of bamboo or wood, with a rope tied from the child to the boat. Tanka mothers often tie their babies to their backs, but young children may wear gourds tied to their waists to buoy them up if they fall in the water. Children soon learn their way around the boats and master the skills needed to move safely. Every child helps with the work. At age four, they begin to row; at six, they are adept; and at ten, operating a boat is second nature.

Two vessels commonly used as houseboats are junks (tall seagoing ships with square sails, high sterns, and flat bottoms) and sampans (small, flat-bottom boats, propelled by a single scull or small motor over the stern). Boatbuilders still make these vessels according to traditional patterns. The design responds to local sailing conditions, but the workmanship depends on cost and personal

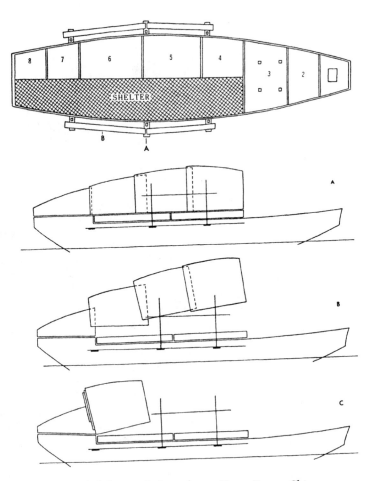

Figure 6.2. *A fisherman's houseboat, Hong Kong, China. Plan (above): At (2) and (3), holds for crabs and fresh fish; at (4), a galley (for cooking); at (5), the family living space; at (6) and (8), the general hold; at (7), the hold for nets. A and B are railings and support on both sides of the boat. Cross-hatching marks the roof (shelter), which actually covers areas 4–8. Sliding roofs (below) A, fully extended forward; B, propped upward for more headroom; C, retracted.*

choice. The best boats are made of heavy teak or china fir. The horizontal beams of the hull retain the natural rounded shape of the tree trunk, to increase strength. The curved keel enables the craft to ride the trough of a large wave easily. Because these boats are duck shaped, not fish shaped, they can plunge into the trough and rise again on an almost vertical wave with far less danger of being submerged than a keeled boat twice the size. Sitting low in the water, they can be sculled (propelled by a long oar) in calm weather. Some still have long sweep-type oars, especially in coastal areas. Sails are made of straw, reed, bam-

Figure 6.3. *Houseboats anchored in Aberdeen Harbour, Hong Kong. Two sets of boats like those in Fig. 6.2 are anchored in concentric circles.*

boo matting, or sailcloth. Although the boats are fast by sailboat standards, since 1961 the boat people have added motors for increased range and safety.

Since the seventeeth century, Chinese boatbuilders have used the balanced rudder, an innovation that came into use in the West only in the nineteenth century. Designed so that the center of water pressure is on the forward face of the rudder, halfway along its length, the balanced rudder made it easier for Chinese sailors to turn and thus steer their craft—a feature that offered great advantages to small boats with small crews in rough seas.

Traditionally, boat people buy only the hull of their houseboat. They then make and rig the mast, the sails, and sometimes the deck shelters that enclose the home. An average boat using about 30 feet (9 meters) of teak and china fir cost $15,000 in 1965 Hong Kong dollars and, if well built, had a useful life of several decades.

Besides the hull, mast, and sails, a finished boat requires decorative emblems. The stern of the boat may bear a painted phoenix, the symbol of immortality, often in red, the color of good fortune. Certain important beams may be painted with flowery garlands and other traditional decorations. After completing a new boat, the boat people celebrate the event with a communal sail making and festive lunch. (Compare with tipi making, Chapter 2.)

Houseboat owners often hire out the boats as living accommodations for other boat people or as a commercial venture. The average small houseboat built for the river passenger trade, for example, has a central cabin, 10 feet by 6 feet (3 by 1.8 meters), in which six or seven passengers may sleep. Sliding partitions separate it from the rear cabin, which measures 3 feet by 6 feet (90 by 180 centimeters) and is suitable for one passenger. When not used for passengers, the cabin space may serve as a home for the owner's family. The boatmen work at the rear, in an 8-square-foot space used for steering, rowing, cooking, and toileting. The crew sleep by turns under the deck in a space 3 feet (90 centimeters) wide (see Fig. 6.2 and 6.3).

Larger fishing junks are shelters for the crew and the catch, sending small boats out to fish but housing family members off-ship in the home port. Medium and small junks are more likely to have shelters on deck for people and underdeck areas for storage. The smaller sampans, perhaps the most common of the coastal houseboats, have no furniture. Rather, the center deck is edged by a ditch-like depression at the bottom edge of the curved roof, where the boat dwellers keep their clothes, tools, and utensils.

At Guangzhou (formerly Canton), boats are still parked more or less permanently in canals, rising up and down with the tides and settling on mud flats at the lowest tides. Recently, perhaps because the men now leave for longer fishing trips, the trend is for old people and mothers with young children to move near shore, where they live in anchored junks, shacks on stilts above tidal flats, or even in conventional houses on land.

Sources: R. F. Fitch (1927), Kani (1967), Needham (1971), Ward (1965).

Houseboats in Kashmir

Far inland is Kashmir, an area on the India–Pakistan border where Hindu and Muslim cultures overlap. There, thousands of people live and earn their livelihood aboard their boats on the lakes of Kashmir. Houseboat living has been a feature of Kashmiri life for centuries; Kashmir existed as a country before the Christian era; a tenth-century Indian text, called the *Rajatarangini*, refers to the Kashmir boatmen, whose name is derived from the Khasi people of India's northern mountains.

Kashmir is located in an ancient lake basin at an altitude of 5,300 feet (1,615 meters) in an intermountain valley of the Himalayas. Snow-capped mountains ring the valley, and Kashmir has been described as an "emerald set in pearls." The scenic valley is a desirable vacation area and has attracted visitors, both domestic and foreign, for centuries. Among the visitors were the Mughal emperors who were enchanted with Kashmir's gardens. In the seventeenth century, Shah Jahan, builder of the Taj Mahal (see Chapter 9) laid out many gardens in Kashmir, the best known being the Shalimar garden at Srinagar on the edge of Dal Lake. The Jhelum River, in northeast Kash-

mir, along with numerous tributaries, lakes, and canals, provided water for these gardens, as well as extensive waterways for the Kashmir boatmen and their families. Gate locks regulate the entrance of water into the canals from the lakes. When the water in a canal reaches the necessary level, the boats glide into the twisting, turning waterways, a never-ending panorama of flowers, shady cypress and chinar trees, shops, and people along the banks (see Fig. 6.4). S. Sanyal, a writer who studied the Kashmir boatmen, reported her findings in 1979.

People called Hanji live and work afloat but are not a homogeneous social group. The boatmen recognize distinctions based on specific occupation, such as fishers, produce vendors, and dredgers. In this hierarchy, the Doonga Ha'enz, who own houseboats and transport tourists or visitors, occupy the top rung. The Bahats Ha'enz live permanently on large barges and transport grain, timber, and other building materials. Other boatmen, such as fishers, may live part time in mud huts along the river banks. Boat-building takes place along the shore; ferrymen bring rafts of logs to the boatyards, where workers saw and shape it according to the type of boat needed.

The various types of boats reflect the economic and social status of the Hanji. The *Doonga* is the most common boat form. Its function is to transport passengers or grain, depending on the season and specific demands. As with most of the boats, the Doonga is constructed of wood. It is flat bottomed, usually about 50 feet (15 meters) long and about 6 feet (2 meters) wide. The framework of the sloping roof is timber, and the walls of the enclosed section are made of matting. Hanjis usually reside in the aft section, which has a kitchen with a dried-clay surface for cooking. The threat of fire is inescapable, but water is always at hand to put out the flames. Sometimes goats and chickens share the living space. The passengers or transported goods occupy the more desirable fore part of the boat, establishing a division based on social status between passengers and boat people.

A second kind of boat, called a *Bahat*, or barge, carries cargo. The living space, a two-room cabin, takes up a major portion of the barge, leaving a little open space for cargoes of timber, bricks, grain, or fuel. Both the Bahats and the Doongas have limited sanitation facilities, relying on the lake for hygienic purposes.

Other kinds of boats are roofless and used mainly for transport. Small boats, called *shikaras*, similar to gondolas, function as pleasure craft for lake and river excursions. A type of raft is used as a floating vegetable garden; it is made of reeds upon which the gardener piles lake-

Figure 6.4. *Houseboats on Dal Lake, Srinagar, Kashmir. The verandas of the houseboats provide scenic views of the snow-capped mountains and lake. Small boats, shown on the right, deliver fresh fruits and vegetables. Primarily used for visitors, the interiors of these houseboats range from simple to elaborate. Some houseboats have modern bedrooms with bathrooms, dining rooms, and Victorian living rooms. The Victorian style reflects their nineteenth-century British origins—a time when foreigners were not permitted to own land.*

weed. He then shapes indentations into the weed, fills them with rich mud from the lake bottom, and plants vegetable seeds. The Kashmiris often tow these rafts from place to place (compare with Chapter 3, Floating Gardens of Mexico). Small boats carry the vegetables they yield, as well as other goods, to sell to other boat people and those along the shore.

Introduced in 1888 by the British, the modern houseboat is among the newest types of boat in Kashmir (see Fig. 6.4). It evolved from the native Doonga to serve the European tourist trade that followed the British occupation of India. According to author A. Denis, an English visitor to Kashmir in the 1930s, politics was the original stimulus for the use of houseboats by foreigners such as the British. Foreigners were not allowed to construct buildings on land, so those who had business reasons for extended visits ordered boats built instead. Many floating houses were built during the period of British rule, and their owners now rent them to visitors for vacations and business trips.

At its best, the houseboat is by far the best equipped of the Kashmir boats in terms of convenience, spaciousness, cleanliness, and modern amenities. Some have a parlor, a dining room, and two or more bedrooms. Windows are glazed, and interior wooden elements exhibit skilled workmanship. Floors consist of planking fitted together without nails. The rooms are connected by doors aligned axially. Of 100 houseboats reported by Sanyal, 24 percent had more than seven windows; boats averaged three windows on each side. The residents use these windows for ventilation, to obtain water, and even for fishing. The boats offer magnificent views of the passing scene. Passengers can read and relax on the roofs; in addition, many boats have verandas. The boat owner and his family live on a small boat towed behind the craft, where cooking takes place. Houseboats fall within a wide range of this ideal, however, and many lack the comfort and cleanliness described here.

Because of their mutual occupation, boatmen tend to be clannish and resistant to outside influence, national or otherwise. Yet Sanyal's comprehensive investigation of modern Kashmiri boatmen offers insights into the daily lives of these amphibious people. Their family pattern relies heavily on the extended family group. Single families (husband and wife only) or primary families (husband, wife, and children) cannot earn enough for normal subsistence, but the extended family (father, sons, grandsons, brothers, and their wives and children) is more economically productive. The average family is thus large. A husband can have an additional wife, especially in case of death, desertion, or divorce, although a wife usually has only one husband. Women do not enjoy a high status, having no voice in their arranged marriages, which usually take place when they are around age fourteen. Limited by various male-biased laws, they have little social mobility. The division of labor separates the genders at an early age. Boys as young as seven help their fathers, while girls remain with their mothers, doing household chores.

With regard to sanitation, education, and economic survival, the boating life is often substandard. Lack of privacy may seem to be one of the greatest problems from a Western viewpoint, but overcrowding is a greater concern to the boat people—as many as fifteen people may be crowded under one roof. Latrines are a luxury that most boat people do not have. Some people have access to community latrines on the river banks, but others just use the river bank. All value cleanliness, however, and bathe in the river or lakes or at the public bathing ghats. Mosques provide bathing facilities in the winter when the natural waters are too cold. Almost all the Hanji boats have a kitchen area, but three-fourths of their drinking and cooking water comes from the rivers and lakes. Some carry water on board from shore, and a few—about 5 percent—have tap water on their boats.

The social and religious lives of the boat dwellers are linked to their economic success as Sanyal explains. Although most of the people of Kashmir are Muslims, the Hindu caste system is reflected in restrictions that custom and religion place even upon the Muslims, such as the sanction against intermarriage among the various subgroups of boat people. Opportunities for social mobility are further limited by the fact that 40 percent of the people are illiterate. The nomadic boating life offers the average family little chance of educating its five or six children, and education is a luxury for people who barely have enough to eat.

The boat people exist at a near-poverty level. Their greatest expense by far is for food, for which they spend, on average about 60 percent of their income. During the tourist season, they have a good source of income, but economic survival is difficult during the rest of the year They rely on loans and other concessions from those in power for their survival. Boatmen's unions try to ensure maximum benefits for their members.

The lives of the boat people are not entirely miserable, however. Compared with Hong Kong, for example, Kashmir's population density is low. Partly because of the high elevation, the climate, even during the summer, is comfortable, with daily temperatures of 80 to 90 degrees F. The fertile valley and floating gardens provide an abundance of fruits and vegetables. Festivals are a joyous part of Kashmiri life, eagerly anticipated by the boat people, as well as other Muslims. The holiday called *Id-ul-fiter* occurs at the end of the Muslim month of Ramadan-ul-Mubarak. Sanyal relates that at this time the boat people wear new clothes when they go to places of worship and enjoy eating delicacies after the month of fasting required during Ramadan.

As with the boat people of China, living afloat is a traditional way of life for the amphibious people of Kashmir. Despite some unfavorable living conditions, boats provide dwellings for people who have few alternatives, and even those who could live ashore sometimes prefer boat life for its travel and variety. The houseboats of China and Kashmir show different ways in which people use boats as homes. They also suggest wider questions: What counts as a house? Indeed, what can be considered architecture?

SOURCES: DENIS (1934), GERVAIS (1954), SANYAL (1979).

USE OF THE STREET AND THE ROOF IN NEPAL

One traditional way of daily life stretches the definition of the house to include spaces adjacent to and on top of the structure itself. In the Himalayan kingdom of Nepal, people extend their domestic lives onto the roof and the street—extensions that may double a family's living space at no extra cost, as well as increase its interaction with neighbors and foster community. Arable land is scarce in Nepal. People have responded to this shortage by building towns of three- or four-story houses with shared (party) walls. These houses line the narrow streets and shelter communal courtyards at the center of the blocks. Roofs, rooftop porches, and the streets have important functions in the daily lives of the Newari residents of the cities of the Kathmandu Valley (see Figs. 6.5, 10.14, and 10.15; Chapter 10 contains a detailed description of the town houses).

In each neighborhood, daily life spills out into the streets. Aside from the time spent sleeping, the people of

Figure 6.5. *Roof-level porches, Bhaktapur, Nepal. People sunning themselves as they do domestic tasks. In the background, a new white concrete building contrasts with the red or gray brick of the older houses.*

Nepal spend some 80 percent of their lives outdoors. Even office work in the Kathmandu Valley is often conducted on a terrace or patio—especially in winter—to take advantage of the sun. Buildings are unheated and chilly at the valley's elevation of more than 4,000 feet. Thus, streets take on many functions, symbolic and practical. In addition to major courts or plazas, each neighborhood has ample public space where the people socialize, especially at the natural or artificial ponds and the taps, where the women wash clothes and bathe themselves and their children (see Chapter 3). Public fountains on the streets, in architectural settings, are especially favored as resting and meeting places, sometimes fitted with a temple or a rest house.

In the old capital of Bhaktapur, people sit just outside their doorways at the edge of the street, spinning or weaving, chopping wood, or making gravel by splitting rock. Here men play cards, talk politics, socialize, or carry on their woodworking while children play. On the level places of streets and plazas, they thresh and dry grains or spread out chili peppers to dry. Ducks, chickens, dogs and cats, and cows scrounge for food in the streets; the streets are home also to goats and sheep that are tethered wherever a little green fodder, such as grass or weeds, is growing around a tree. The narrow streets are well shaded—a relief from early summer heat, but when the monsoon brings its downpours in midsummer, the streets are uninhabitable, and in winter darkness makes them damp and cold.

Daily life extends onto roofs as well as the streets. On cold winter days, people take to their roofs to warm themselves in the sun, compensating for the lack of heating in the houses. They also use their open roofs to dry clothes and food and for some food preparation (see Fig. 6.5). A porch or dormer leads from the kitchen area to the gently slanted roof. Some neighborly interaction takes place as people talk from roof to roof.

A different set of relations to the street is visible in a relatively new village of the plains (Terai), lying at 2,180 feet (664 meters) elevation, about 200 miles (320 kilometers) west of Bhaktapur. Its residents are a tribal people, the Tharu, aborigines of the Indian subcontinent (also found in India and Bengal-Bangladesh). This group once had temporary houses in the malarial swamps, where they practiced slash-and-burn agriculture. Their present home, Budbudi, was founded around 1900 near a bubbling spring that gave its name to the village but is now dry.

In their new settled life, the Tharu kept the housing form and living patterns of their past: Their one-story houses stretch out along the one street. With plenty of arable land, their house lots are less constrained than those of Bhaktapur. The interior of a Tharu house is divided into two rooms, one facing south, the other north, which are, in turn, subdivided. The south room has three doors, two for people and one for animals, and a fence divides the room so that animals can occupy half of it during the night. The other half, large and well lit, is intensively used. There people prepare food, cook, eat, and celebrate family events; they also gather around the corner beehive fireplace in cold weather.

The north room, which occupies about two-fifths of the house, is extremely dark and close, lit only by six or seven small circular openings about 5 inches (13 centimeters) in diameter, a foot (30 centimeters) above the floor in the east and west walls. These openings catch the prevailing wind, ventilating the room and preventing mold. The space is subdivided by huge clay storage pots for grain. At the far end are the shrine room and another kitchen. The eldest man sleeps in the shrine room with his wife; children sleep on the floor between the grain storage jars, close to the central partition of the building. Some cooking also takes place here. Dishes are washed outside to prevent the deterioration of the mud floor of both kitchens. Additional storage is located on overhead platforms and in the area behind the house.

The method of building these houses is strikingly similar to methods that are used from Malaysia to Easter Island (compare with Chapter 5, Lashed Polynesian Houses), suggesting a common origin for the lashed framework. Materials were once easily available in the rain forest and still are not difficult to procure. Builders make a framework with posts, columns, and beams of peeled tree trunks rigidly lashed together. The roof is made of thatch 12 inches (30 centimeters) thick. Curtain walls are composed of small reeds lashed horizontally to the posts and reinforced with a clay covering—a construction method called wattle-and-daub.

Tharu houses are a sophisticated response to climatic extremes. Terai dwellers must contend with hot and dry summers, hot and humid monsoons, chilly winter nights, and an annual rainfall of 5 feet (155 centimeters). The wattle-and-daub walls and the clay storage pots inside absorb heat during the day and radiate it back at night, six to ten hours later. During the worst heat of summer, this radiation produces much heat inside the house, but then most people sleep outdoors in the yard. During the winter, however, the radiated heat is ideal.

Outdoor life is generally carried on in private, fenced areas behind the houses, where people dry grains, socialize, and perform household tasks. Each house also has a kitchen garden. Twenty to thirty houses flank the single street of the village. People use the street only for feeding animals during the monsoon and for children's play; it is not yet the locus of intense activity like streets in Newari towns. A century is not a long time to develop customs about the public use of organized central space, so different from the random space of the previous rain forest habitat. But even the Tharu, who did not have a tradition of dense urban living, are developing patterns of street use now that they live close together.

SOURCES: BLAIR (1983); GUTSCHOW AND KÖLVER (1975): 22; SLUSSER (1974, 1982); M. THAPA (PERSONAL COMMUNICATION); WATERSON (1990).

ACCESS TO ARCHITECTURE—SOCIAL REWARDS AND THE USE OF BUILDINGS

Access to the built environment—the right to use buildings and spaces—is a social privilege. By examining architectural solutions to common problems of everyday life, one sees how a society distributes some of its rewards. History and geography provide many examples, including

Figure 6.6. *Contrasting sizes of a men's ceremonial house and a woman's dwelling in a village of the Kalava people, New Guinea. The large ceremonial building is profusely decorated, while the small domestic building is plain.*

gender-specific architecture from New Guinea and Nigeria, which are far enough away from modern American concerns to give us a feeling of cultural objectivity—perhaps warranted, perhaps not.

Social Rewards and the Use of Ceremonial Buildings in New Guinea

Among the Kwoma, Hiyewe, Yafar, Iatmil, and Abelam peoples who live along the Sepik River and in the highlands of New Guinea, as among the rest of us, "The relative positions of women and men are subject to debate and struggle," writes anthropologist D. Losche, because "opposition over matters of production, exchange, and reproduction is interwoven with their identity of interests"—that is, survival and reproduction. Both opposition and unity are quite evident in the architectural arrangements of different peoples in New Guinea (compare with the Bedouin and the Hausa extended family, Chapter 3, and especially with the big roof houses of these same New Guinea peoples, Chapter 4; see Fig. 4.9).

In the old yam festivals of the Kwomo, a Sepik River group studied by art historian R. Bowden, gender determines access to the ceremonies. It is taboo for women to enter the men's houses of the Sepik River and Ramu valley areas. The big house where men's rituals take place may be only a roof held up by posts, but during the rituals it becomes the connection between men and supernatural bush spirits. Wearing masks or other costumes, men identify with the spirits, who, in turn, personify the yam, the basic food of these people. Costumes, masks, or carved representations of the bush spirits are the most precious possessions of important families who reckon their descent through eldest sons from the first man to acquire them. This ceremonial art, which reflects men's ideology, is carefully hidden from women and children and, in some cases, is even used against women as an instrument of coercion. In contrast to this secret art are paintings on the ceilings of the big house and sculptures representing clan spirits or figures from mythology that decorate the posts. These paintings and sculptures are permanently public and have accessible, identifiable meanings (see Fig. 6.7).

Women are excluded in different ways on three different occasions. During the first celebration, *yena*, women are not allowed near the men's house. During the second, *mija*, women dance in front of the men's house, but a screen of leaves placed across the front allows them to see only the tops of the ritual sculptures inside, not the men performing the ritual (see Fig. 4.9). In the third ceremony, *nowkwi*, the women also dance outside, but a taller screen completely surrounds the building. The men claim that only through their rituals does the essential yam crop mature. Because men are classified as "hot" like spirits and like yams, they, along with the spirits and yams, are easily polluted by women, who are "cold." To avoid pollution, men live apart from their wives. Women, equated with nature, are considered intrinsically polluting and must be kept from the ceremonies and from the buildings and spaces where the ceremonies take place.

The Kwoma and other Sepik river peoples build architecture and assign access to and use of space in ways that reflect their understanding of how the world is organized. Male and female are basic classification categories of the world, not just of humanity. Anthropologist R. Williamson spells out this division in the greatest detail; we include only items with architectural implications:

Men	Women
Men's house taller	Women's house shorter
Men are pure	Women pollute, therefore women don't step over men or their belongings
Men inside	Women outside
Men at center	Women at periphery
Men own ridge land	Women own swamp water
Ridge stays the same	Water changes
Men are permanent residents	Women come and go
Men are "natives"	Women are strangers
Collective	Individual
Public	Private

Because socialization and social formation among Euro-Americans differ widely from the practices of many traditional societies, Westerners often misunderstand women's roles in other societies. Women's status in New Guinea is not only different from Western women's status, it is also different from—and higher than—the place assigned to it in the men's ideology. For instance, because women do the carrying, they have some control over the economy, and they also control eating and sex, so that "control" of the whole society oscillates between men and women. Anthropologist P. K. Townsend suggests that if anthropologists got information about New Guinea societies only from women, they would more readily perceive

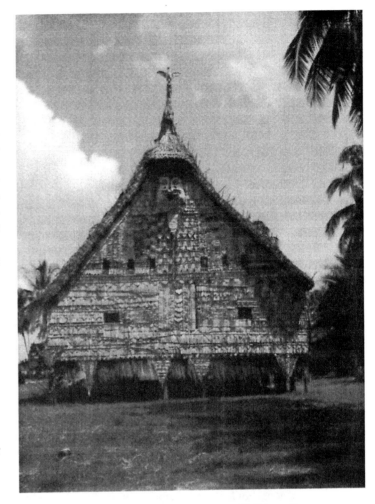

Figure 6.7. *Decorated facade, Korogo, Sepik River, Papua.*

these societies as webs of relationships, not dichotomies or hierarchies of power.

Relations between the genders are more equitable in the Sepik River groups than in the Highland tribes. Until recently, the dominant activities among Highland groups were war and ceremonial exchange, usually by men only. In these groups the dichotomy between men and women is the most extreme. So difficult is the situation of women in some Highland tribes that suicide has accounted for up to 57 percent of their deaths, according to anthropologist M. G. Gebler.

The sweeping cultural changes that anthropologist Margaret Mead began to document in the 1950s have affected the coastal and river peoples more than those in the Highlands. Some groups are now Christians and have abandoned—with their old spirits—the custom of excluding women from intertribal activity and community spaces. An example is the changing access of the Hiyewe women of the Sepik area to trade, politics, and religion and to the new buildings where these activities take place. The new municipal building and church are open to all, and women participate in all group activities, although less frequently than men. The women also have new work relationships with other women, whereas each used to work alone.

The control and use of buildings in New Guinea tribal society reflects tensions between men and women. In particular, the men of the New Guinea highlands confer upon themselves status, power—and preferential access to the most imposing architecture built by the group. Yet in studying the architectural arrangements of these peoples, we must consider that a direct linear chain of causality will probably not do justice to complex interactions, such as those between men and women. These interactions are complicated by physical differences; the demands of economics, and the sanctions of religion, myth, and ideology.

SOURCES: BOWDEN (1984), GELBER (1986), LOSCHE (1990), TOWNSEND (1990), WILLIAMSON (1983, 1990).

Space and Gender in Islamic Society: Kano Palace, Nigeria

The use of space in the Kano Palace of Nigeria's Hausa people illustrates how religion and ideology have given gender-based meanings to architecture. In the traditional Islamic household, there is a generally held belief in the sanctity of domestic privacy. The segregation and seclusion of women is of primary importance. It is a husband's duty to protect his wife, in keeping within Quran'ic (Koranic) teachings. However, the Muslim world encompasses a multitude of diverse cultures with their own histories, as well as different regional and economic characteristics. As a result, there are many types of dwellings in the Muslim world. In general, however, the way people arrange the interiors of their houses reflects the social division between men and women in Islamic culture. Author G. Petherbridge states that the unifying element that determines the arrangement of the "domestic family unit" is the Qur'an, the Islamic holy book, common to all Muslim cultures. It contains specific instructions regarding acceptable social behavior and, consequently, the arrangement of a family's domestic quarters.

A space is set aside within the home for a harem, or women's area. The harem is the architectural solution to the Qur'an's insistence that the husband is responsible for the protection of his wife's honor, so that the wife does not bring disgrace upon his house or to his name. This imperative has resulted in the seclusion of women within the harem, which is also the domestic quarters of the family. In affluent households in some societies, the segregation of the sexes resulted in the construction of individual buildings for this purpose (see Chapter 3, Hausa Extended-family Compounds). For example, people on the island of Djerbanear, off the southeastern coast of Tunisia, built separate houses reserved for the men adjacent to the main dwelling. The tents of the Bedouins also reflect the emphasis on segregation; a central curtain divides the interior into male and female areas when men other than family members are visiting (see Chapter 3). Seclusion is also equated with respect and protection for the Islamic woman, to shield her from unwanted attention.

Under Muslim law permitting the practice of polygamy, the husband must provide each of his wives equally with separate living quarters, according to the importance of his social status. He also has the authority to restrict his wives from leaving their quarters, visiting with other women, or attending social events. These concerns affect the design of the house, which must have space to accommodate all aspects of the women's social lives apart from the social space of men. Some harems are a sequence of apartments, with facilities for cooking, washing, sleeping, a latrine, and other domestic activities for each wife. Segregated rooms are reserved for the men of the household and their male visitors.

Symbolic of the economic status of the household, the reception room is the most lavishly furnished; its decor is an indication of the economic status of the household. This room is used for religious discourse, as well as for social visits, and it is situated near the entrance of the house to ensure that visitors will not come into contact with the women of the family, whose quarters are in the interior. Petherbridge reminds us that the seclusion of women in Islamic society manifests, both architecturally and socially, the principle of enclosure.

An example of gender distinction in the Islamic city-state of Kano in northern Nigeria was recently studied by anthropologist H. Nast in connection with social changes taking place there between 1500 and 1900. During the latter part of this period, from 1807 to 1903, nomadic Fulani Islamic scholars and military leaders waged a "holy war" against the Muslim Hausa aristocracy. Excessive taxation by the Hausa aristocracy gave the intruding Fulani people a chance to win the pagan farmers to their side and to conquer Hausaland, resulting in major changes in the Kano palace compound.

The palace compound at Kano is large—about 1,000 feet wide and 1,600 feet long (300 by 500 meters) (see Fig. 6.8). When built in the 1500s, it formed a rectangular "suburb" connected to the extensive city walls. During the early 1800s, it was divided into three gender-specific sections.

Male slaves and eunuchs lived near the entrance to the palace. Part of the military elite, they were the royal bodyguards and controlled weapons and treasures with the exception of grain. They also occupied an enclave within the female domain where the king's residence was located. Women of the palace were secluded and housed in an area called the "stomach," the inside of the palace, farthest from public contact. A separate male enclosure within the elaborate king's quarters and court chambers was connected by a path around the outer edge of the "stomach" to the male slave quarters near the main gate. A number of compounds for eunuchs surrounded the royal chambers, and Islamic scholars occupied some compounds adjacent to a mosque near the king's quarters, as Nast relates (see Fig. 6.9 a, b, c, d).

The women of the household were classified according to rank: royal wives, concubines, and slaves. Royal wives (up to four) were the most secluded, each with separate living quarters. Next were the concubines, who lived together in a walled compound. Slaves had their quarters together in a third area. They ran errands, did the heavy labor, and guarded the court chambers, and some collected grain taxes.

The concubines were a complex hierarchical group with administrative duties that included advising the king on state affairs. They also occasionally acted as "extensions" of the royal wives, who, as a leisure class and the most precious possessions of their royal husbands, were not permitted outside their domain. One of the concubines held the title of "Master of the Grain Silos," overseeing a group of women slaves who controlled the storage and distribution of grain and collected taxes in the form of grain. These taxes were essential for food consumption at the palace; the grain treasury in the palace fed as many as a thousand people daily, including the royal

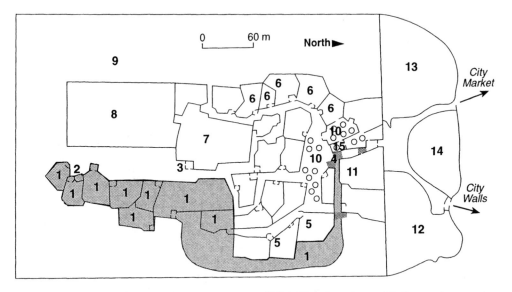

Figure 6.8. *Kano palace, northern Nigeria, ca. 1750. The plan shows (1) the men's area, including the king's residence (largest unit numbered 1), mosque (2), Qur'anic school (3) Islamic court (4), wives' quarters (5), quarters of concubines and slave women (6), kitchen (7), dye pits (8), farm plots of female slaves (9), grain silos (small circles) in the area of (10), arms depot and stable (11), slaves quarters (12), quarters of unmarried sons (13), and quarters of eunuchs (14). The main entrances lead into the palace from the city walls and the city market.*

a.

b.

Figure 6.9. *Sketches of gates and major buildings, Kano Palace, Nigeria. **a.** and **d.** The north and south gates; **b.** the king's quarters, identified by the bulge of the dome; and **c.** the treasury building. All the walls are mud, and the windows are small or nonexistent. The gates and doorways are buttressed for strength. Pictures of the domestic quarters of the palace are rare.*

family, nobility, extended families, slaves, and visitors. Taxes were also necessary for state projects, for defense, and for the increasing extravagance of the royal court. Another female official in the market area was in charge of determining the city's grain prices.

These women were able to hold vital economic and political roles because neither they nor their slave as-sistants were secluded but, rather, were expected to work outside the palace. However, they did maintain communication with some secluded members of the female aristocracy, who played a silent role in commerce. Women's importance was reflected in the large portion of palace that was allocated to them for their quarters.

c.

d.

Figure 6.9. *Continued.*

After the "holy war," however, the city-state became a conservative emirate. The concubines were removed from their positions of power, and demands increased for greater seclusion of women. Eunuchs and scholars were moved from the inside to the outside of the palace, further isolating the women. The emir took over a great part of the women's chambers, adding them to his own quarters, and, as Nast explains, part of the women's domain was walled off and converted into two male domains. An upper story was built in the king's chambers. From its windows, men could look down on the women's quarters for purposes of surveillance, a practice instituted to quell resistance to the new order. In short, the architectural space allocated for the women decreased while that of the men increased. As women's power lessened, the male eunuchs gained authority, and a male slave was appointed

"King of the Grains" replacing the female "Master of the Grain Silos." According to Nast, "Women's political and economic control over grain tax collection and exchange were thus eliminated, severing palace women from the public domain." From then on, women were limited mostly to a reproductive role.

Here it can be seen that giving women less architectural space reinforced the conception of seclusion, even as the transfer of power to male slaves all but eliminated any major efforts by women to resist.

Today, public events take place at Kano, where as many as 50,000 Muslim worshippers may gather in a large open space beside the mosque. During the spectacular religious celebration called Eid or Sallah, thousands of men in varicolored robes fill the streets and surrounding areas, especially on the north side of the palace, where the emir lives. Architect N. Macindoe, who lived in Nigeria, reports that during one festival, the emir circulated around the town, greeted dignitaries at a large square adjacent to the central mosque, and addressed the crowd at the palace gates. Macindoe also visited the old Kano marketplace, with its narrow alleys cutting through many shanties and market stalls. Some of the stalls date from the original market, where the concubine who was "Master of the Grain Silos" went to collect the grain tax.

Traditional architecture fits many purposes. Living space can be confined to a boat or extended into the street. Architecture can make daily life easier—or at least endurable. The question of access to architecture is exemplified here by Oceanic and Islamic societies, in which men and women have different rights to use certain buildings. When we think of how an iglu or a tipi is used and when we come in Chapter 11 to the relatively egalitarian assignment of space in the courtyard houses of China, we see that each society decides how to allocate the advantages of architecture. Architectural solutions respond not only to physical requirements, but to cultural values as well.

SOURCES: NAST (1993), PETHERBRIDGE (1978), PRUSSIN (1986).

SUGGESTED READINGS

Bowden, R. 1984. "Art and Gender Ideology in the Sepik." *Man*, N.S. 19: 445–58. A good introduction to the topic.

Denis, A. J. 1934. *Houseboating in Kashmir*. Los Angeles: Times-Mirror Press. A personal account of houseboat life during visit to Kashmir.

Fitch, R. F. 1927. "Life Afloat in China." *National Geographic* 51: 665–86. Early black-and-white photos and an accompanying article on the geography of China caught the "sleeping giant" just before the upheavals that began in the 1930s.

Gelber, M. G. 1986. *Gender and Society in the New Guinea Highlands: An Anthropological Perspective on An-tagonism Toward Women*. Boulder, Colo.: Westview Press. Eye-opening.

Gervais, P. 1954. *This Is Kashmir*, 80–95. London: Cassell. An informative discussion of canal life.

Kani, H. 1967. *A General Survey of the Boat People in Hong Kong*. Monograph Series No. 5. Hong Kong: Southeast Asia Studies Section, New Asia Research Institute, Chinese University of Hong Kong. With boat plans and village plans.

Nast, H. 1993. "Engendering 'Space': State Formation and the Restructuring of the Kano Palace Following the Islamic Holy War in Northern Nigeria, 1807–1903." *Historical Geography* 2: 62–75. The primary source for the Kano Palace.

Petherbridge, G. 1978. "Vernacular Architecture: The House and Society." In *Architecture of the Islamic World*, 176–208, edited by G. Michell. New York: William Morrow. Discusses gender issues.

Sanyal, S. 1979. *The Boats and Boatmen of Kashmir*. New Delhi: Sagar. Sanyal's interviews with the boatmen of Kashmir make this small volume especially noteworthy.

Strathern, M. 1984. "Domesticity and the Denigration of Women." In *Rethinking Women's Roles: Perspectives of From the Pacific*, 13–31, edited by D. O'Brien and S. W. Tiffany. Berkeley: University of California Press. Causes reflection on our own folkways, as well as those of New Guinea.

Ward, B. E. 1965. "Varieties of the Conscious Model: The Fishermen of South China." In *The Relevance of Models for Social Anthropology*, 113–37, edited by M. Banton. London: Association of Anthropology Monographs. Ward's study group was composed of 600 people on forty boats and nine families living on shore. The author was more interested in how the people thought about their lives than in the boats as architecture, but this is still a valuable study for our purposes.

Williamson, M. H. 1983. "Sex Relations and Gender Relations: Understanding Kwoma Conception." *Mankind* 14: 13–23. Helps to clarify the distinction between sex and gender.

Religious Architecture: A Continuum of Meaning

Depending on the society and its customs, religious space may be located in the home, on the street, or in separate areas especially set aside for this purpose. We have found no society completely lacking in architectural recognition of the spiritual, but the degree of elaboration varies greatly. The seven examples discussed in this chapter form a continuum: The Japanese tokonoma retains the least religious content, while the powerful aura of Mount Taylor escapes the confines of any one religious system.

Our examples of religious spaces in the home are the permanent niche, called a *tokonoma*, in a Japanese house and the temporary altar set up in Mexican households to honor the dead. Both incorporate features that other cultures may not consider strictly religious, but for their users, these features contribute to the spiritual ambience. The street can also be the locus of community religious activity. The main street of Bhaktapur, Nepal, for instance, is not only lined with shrines and temples, but serves as the path of frequent religious processions. Similarly, the streets of India are home to temporary temples, or floats.

Monumental architecture also serves religious purposes. Islamic mosques, sometimes single buildings and sometimes entire complexes, fill a socioreligious role similar to that of the cathedrals of Europe. Even larger are the huge pyramids that flank the great Street of the Dead in the ancient Mexican capital of Teotihuacán. Among the most impressive monuments ever built, these pyramids are deliberate echoes, in form and orientation, of the volcano that rises above the end of the street. A similar volcano, the enormous cone of volcanic Mount Taylor in New Mexico, was once a natural religious focus for the Keresan people who lived to its immediate south, making the landscape itself a form of religious architecture.

SPACE IN THE HOME

In an only partly understood world, it makes eminent sense to have shrines in the home where families can petition and thank the deities and unite in ritual. The Japanese tokonoma and the Mexican Altar of the Dead are two different outgrowths of religious sensibility expressed in domestic architecture.

JAPANESE TOKONOMA

The simplified interior plan of the traditional Japanese house, with its movable screens for defining particular areas as needed, does not emphasize one living space over another—with one exception: Part of one wall contains a niche, called a tokonoma, reserved for the display of art objects (see Fig. 7.1). The tokonoma is not only a special place for the family; it is a space before which an esteemed guest is seated. Originally, this picture recess held a function beyond that of aesthetic enhancement; it added an important spiritual dimension to the house. As an elite architectural form, it was widely used in this sense, but over time, it gradually lost some of its specific religious function.

The origin of the tokonoma is obscure. The concept of building a picture recess into a dwelling has some affinities with Zen Buddhism, which gained importance in Japan from the seventh century C.E. Zen Buddhism called for developing a state of mind in which meditation becomes the key to attaining spiritual enlightenment. It was closely linked to the love of nature and art. Although its exact origin is uncertain, H. Engel, an authority on Japanese domestic architecture, suggests that the origin of the tokonoma may be found in the Buddhist monastery where a Buddhist picture scroll hung above a shelf holding an incense burner and flowers. Here the monks assembled to drink tea and take part in contemplative rituals. At first, people used a low, sepa-

Figure 7.1. *A tokonoma in a traditional Japanese house. The alcove provides a special place for the display of art objects. The tokonoma is often separated by a thin partition and rustic post from an adjacent area used for shelves and cabinets, as is seen on the left. Note the different floor and ceiling levels. Tatami mats cover the main part of the floor, and shoji screens form the walls left and right.*

rate table in front of the wall, instead of a shelf, and the recess was called an *ashi-ita,* but by the late fifteenth century, they were building a shelf into the wall to hold the objects, and the alcove was called the tokonoma. In some contemporary houses that are too small for a formal tokonoma, people still use a low table set before a wall.

Whatever the details of its arrangement, the alcove represented the spiritual core of the household, as it did of the monastery. Perhaps, however, the origin of the tokonoma lies outside the monastery. Architectural historian J. Reynolds points out that one of the oldest surviving proto-tokonomas at Togudo, Ginkakuji, was not related to Zen Buddhism. An 1886 study by anthropologist E. Morse suggested that the tokonoma was derived from a "bed space" on a raised platform of ancient Malay houses, and indeed the word does mean "space for a platform." Contemporary scholars, however, reject the link to Malay houses; Engel notes that the earliest documents and extant buildings show a wide space with a shallow depth—unsuitable for bedding.

Another forerunner of this space was a niche in the main room of a warrior's residence (*shuden*), with a raised platform in front of a wall where the picture alcove was located. The military leaders, or shoguns, of the twelfth through the nineteenth centuries received guests on the floor in front of the alcove. Usually, the highest-ranking person, whether host or guest, sat in front of the tokonoma. Both the nobility and commoners adopted this practice, identifying the spot in front of the niche as the most formal and important in the house. As a place of honor, it parallels a similar special seat in American Indian tipis and Polynesian houses (see Chapters 2 and 5). Japanese warriors' houses and those of the nobility combined elements of the picture recess, an adjacent alcove for shelves, and construction methods used in houses of Buddhist monks. They copied the monks' preferred *shoin* style of residence, in which a wide, elevated sill in a window area served as a study. This area was usually located adjacent to the *toko,* as it is often called, providing light to the alcove.

Although the specifically religious purpose diminished over time, the tokonoma it retained spiritual-aesthetic significance. Paintings, first brought to Japan by Buddhist monks, added visual elegance to that part of the house, and the niche was an ideal place to display them. As Engel notes, members of the nobility used the space to hang important paintings, thus reinforcing the aesthetic effect of the recessed area. By the sixteenth century, the

picture recess had become a standard of the Japanese design vocabulary.

The toko could be located in various areas of the house, usually in the family dining or living room or a formal reception room, less commonly in a special tearoom—a small enclosed independent area for the tea ceremony—found only in the homes of the wealthy. The preparation and drinking of tea was a highly ritualized practice that was based on the teachings of Zen Buddhism, and ceremonial tea drinking became part of Japanese family life. Depending on her status and household structure, the wife of the head of the household was charged with maintaining and caring for the scrolls and paintings displayed in the toko. Usually a single flower or plant cutting, along with a picture scroll, sufficed to create an atmosphere that reflected the family's aesthetic taste and spiritual attitude. These objects could be changed according to season or the family's preferences.

The space alloted for the tokonoma can vary and usually does not occupy the full expanse of the wall. Next to it, separated by a thin, fixed partition and columns, is an alcove for shelves or cabinets called *tokowaki.* Built-in wall shelves evolved from the eleventh-century practice of utilizing separate storage cabinets. In addition to providing storage space, the shelves offer a rare opportunity for ornamental experimentation, since Japanese taste in interior design generally prefers understated simplicity.

The column between the two recesses, *tokobashira,* is the same size and squared shape (sometimes irregular) as a structural post; it may have a supportive role, but generally is purely decorative, with little symbolic connotation. Chosen for its exceptional qualities of wood and grain, the column emphasizes the significance of the tokonoma and reflects the Japanese appreciation of natural forms, as well as the importance and formal significance of the tokonoma. Similar posts, called *daikoku-bashiras* or sacred center pillars, especially prominent in Japanese farmhouses (see Chapter 3), do have a symbolic function in the Shinto religious tradition. These large free-standing columns refer to ancient mythological gods of the fields. The central post at the Ise (Naiku) Shrine (see Chapter 17), for example, represents a complex system of associations; among them is the belief in the divinity of the emperor. Engel, however, does not think that the tokobashira between the two recesses in Japanese houses grew out of these ancient religious traditions, believing rather that its meaning is primarily aesthetic.

The partition dividing the two alcoves is made of natural materials, usually clay or wood, and both floors are of polished wood planks. A small opening near the base admits light from the toko, nearer the outside wall, to the inner space of the tokowaki. The two sections usually co-exist, but builders avoid bilateral symmetry, so that dimensions, elevations, ceiling heights, and other constructional details are not equal. The ceiling of the tokonoma, for example, is usually higher than that of the tokowaki, and its floor is raised above the level of the shelving recess. While a finished beam of the picture recess is situated about a foot from the ceiling, the corresponding beam of the shelving area is somewhat lower.

Because there are no rigid requirements for equality of form in these units, there are unlimited opportunities for variation. Sometimes the tokonoma extends along an entire wall with no adjoining tokowaki. The picture recess—by virtue of its greater importance—usually is larger, designed in proportion to the rest of the room.

According to Engel, the asymmetry of the tokonoma and tokowaki is linked to Zen philosophical ideas that urge the avoidance of symmetry. With external form and order minimized, people can focus their attention on the simplified aspects of the content, rather than on the overt message of the form itself. This does not mean, however, that Japanese principles of construction lacked a sense of order. On the contrary, as we noted in the discussion of Japanese house construction in Chapter 5, builders paid strict attention to modular proportion and standardization of method and materials. The modular system of construction, inherited from the Chinese, evolved into a Japanese linear measurement called the *ken*, generally the distance between the centers of two columns, about 6 feet (2 meters). The ken measurement was not standardized, however; it could vary from region to region. The average toko recess consisted of a section about 1 ken long and half a ken deep. There is a correlation between the standard size of the tatami mat, 6 feet by 3 feet (183 by 91 centimeters) and the basic plan of the toko.

This part of the house was visually enhanced by raising the topmost horizontal crossbeam of the toko above the level of the surrounding room. The shelves themselves were arranged asymetrically, and the patterns of some of the tatamis carried out a similar irregularity. Thus, the toko's variation from the symmetrical module breathed life into what could have been an oppressively rigid scheme.

In Japanese residences with separate teahouses built solely for observance of the tea ceremony, the tokonoma is an important feature. A nonstructural, freestanding tokobashira that is sometimes placed in the middle of the room highlights the importance of the spot where the actual tea ceremony is held. These posts, unlike the sacred central pillars of farmhouses, are mainly decorative. Left unfinished, they manifest the rustic simplicity of *wabi* philosophy, which idealizes refined austerity and spiritual tranquillity.

The tokonoma is an integral part of the design of Japanese houses, a permanent architectural space whose purposes were once spiritual and now are primarily aesthetic—although some spiritual significance still adheres. In their refined and subtle simplicity and use of natural materials, they exemplify the Japanese architectural tradition.

SOURCES: ENGEL (1964), HASHIMOTO (1981), ITOH AND FUTAGAWA (1980), MORSE (1961), NISHIHARA (1968).

Mexican Altar of the Dead

No rite of passage evokes stronger feelings or more varied ways of coping than death. Societies handle death and its burden of negative feelings in many ways. One of them, El Dia de los Muertos, the Mexican Day of the Dead, is among the world's most cheerful festivals, a mixture of All Saints' and All Souls' days that combines a solemn holy day with national independence day and an enormous party. It is the kind of dialogue with death that Anglo-Protestant culture shuns, according to reviewer W. J. Rushing.

Mexico's multilayered attitude toward death goes back to the pre-Columbian past. When the Aztecs ruled much of central Mexico, their religion demanded thousands of human sacrifices annually to appease the gods who ensured the food supply. But the intense awareness of death as a part of life goes back even earlier to the beginning of the Common Era. The Day of the Dead carves out a space—albeit a temporary one—for ritual in the domestic architecture of Mexico. Nowhere is the importance of the home for religious ritual more evident than in the custom of erecting Altars of the Dead (see Fig. 7.2).

Unlike the tokonoma, a permanent architectural feature that has lost most of its religious significance, the altars of the dead are specifically religious but ephemeral, lasting less than a week. For days before and during the festival of the dead in late October and early November, the family is busy setting up an altar, decorating it, symbolically offering food and drink to the deceased, and then going to commune with their dead at the graves. These actions, and the altar that is their focus, display a mix of "reverence for the dead, revelry to welcome them, and mockery to defy death," writes R. R. Beimler. The dead souls are imagined as dancing and having a good time, and their living relatives expect to share in the celebration.

The home altar is called *un ofrenda* (offering). Some are small, some large, but all are elaborate. They are made of wood or bamboo and wire, set on the floor or on a table. Ornamentation of home altars depends on regional traditions, individual wealth, recent deaths in the family, and available wealth for the costs of the altar, write museum curators J. F. Hernandez and S. R. Hernandez. Families decorate their altars with carved and painted wooden figures of saints (*santos*); candles; cut-out tissue-paper banners; "stars" woven of cane; skulls made of bread dough or sugar; flowers; and food and drink, such as chocolate mole sauce, a corn drink, chocolate candy, fruits, and bottles of brandy. They also place photographs or other remembrances of dead family members on the altar and add more offerings each day. They may use burners for copal incense, both on the altar and at the grave site. The result is "an incredibly sensuous art in which laughter and passion commingle with tears and sorrow" notes Rushing.

Especially poignant are the preparations to welcome dead children of the family, from October 31 until noon on November 1. People set off firecrackers to lure dead children back to their homes. Some make special altars for the children, with a new toy for each dead child—a small skeleton, miniature coffin, or decorated sugar skull—and the child's favorite food. Death toys for the living children introduce the children to death in an atmosphere of joyful celebration.

In some places, the celebration includes a reception on October 27 for the "orphan" dead—people who were killed accidentally, have no family to mourn them, or died unrepentant. Their spirits are received outside the house, so that unpardoned souls do not endanger the family inside the house.

When the relatives visit during this festival, they enter the house over paths of fresh marigold leaves—the autumn-blooming marigold was a vivid symbol of death for the Aztecs—scattered from the house door to the altar, for the dead to follow, just as in the cemetery the graves are newly covered with marigold petals and purple cockscomb. Visitors enter the house and inspect and do reverence to the elaborate altar; they may stay with the family and visit the cemetery with them. On the afternoon and evening of

Figure 7.2. *The "Day of the Dead in the Country," a drawing in charcoal, chalk, and pencil, by Mexican artist Diego Rivera. The people are shown gathered at a family grave in the local cemetery. The grave is decorated like the family's home altar, with candles, an incense burner, and offerings.*

November 1, church bells toll for the dead, and all join in a procession to the cemetery for an all-night vigil (Fig. 7.2).

On November 2, priests say a mass for all the dead souls, and families stay in the cemetery all day. The vigil ends with masked mummers appearing to scare away lingering spirits. After returning home, the celebrating mourners exchange the offerings from their altars with

Figure 7.3. *A contemporary domestic Altar of the Dead, Ventura, California. Flowers in a bottle decorated as a skeleton, a photograph of deceased family members, several candles (one in a figurative vase), a woven tablecloth, and offerings decorate a home altar for the Day of the Dead, 1996.*

friends and relatives on November 3. The next day, they remove the altars and decorations, and the festival is over. Thus the rituals pass from generation to generation.

Local communities celebrate the Day of the Dead with vital, distinctive traditions. In the Oaxaca area, people preserve the Zapotec tradition of placing tiny candles on the family altar for the dead children on the morning of November 1. Then they blow out these candles so the dead children will depart. In the afternoon, they place larger candles and offerings for adult spirits on the altar, and in the evening they pray there. The next day, All Souls' Day, everyone goes to the cemetery.

In Tetelco, prayer flags decorate houses and altars in the form of tissue-paper banners with elaborate cut-out designs. These flags developed from a pre-Hispanic tradition of painted paper splashed with rubber. Special breads with appropriate decorations are placed on the home altar, as well as inedible decorations made of a dough of bread and glue, dried and then painted (see Fig. 7.3).

The home altar is a highly personal tribute to the dead in one's own family, but people recently have begun to set up brightly colored altars in public places, such as restaurants, shops, hotels, and town council rooms. In the American Southwest, the Day of the Dead has been celebrated ever since the founding of seventeenth-century Spanish-colonial settlements in New Mexico, and since the 1960s, public and gallery exhibitions of Altars of the Dead here celebrated the area's Mexican cultural roots. These exhibits have come to signify Mexican cultural pride, an important manifestation of Chicano consciousness. But in the larger cities of Mexico, the combination of growing secularity, the rising costs of objects associated with the Altars of the Dead, and the huge increase in tourists attending the festival have made the participants increasingly self-conscious. The growing commercialization of the celebration threatens this domestic feast with the loss of much of its religious meaning. Yet whether in Los Angeles, Mexico City, or a small village, every celebration depends on local and regional traditions related to the mixture that is Mexican religion. The still-strong religious element of the Mexican Altars of the Dead contrasts with the more aesthetic significance of the Japanese tokonoma.

Compare the temporary brush shelters of the Kalahari Desert (see Chapter 3), which we insist are architecture, with these temporary Mexican altars, and compare those, in turn, with the temporary temples of India discussed later in this chapter. Neither ephemerality nor smallness excludes these objects from our definition of architecture as "structures that have been thoroughly thought through before they are built." (See also discussions of the big-roof houses of New Guinea in Chapter 4, the town houses of Nepal in Chapter 10, and the anthropomorphic architecture of the Batammaliba of West Africa in Chapter 15 for examples of domestic shrines.)

SPACE ON THE STREET

Many cultures—particularly in warm climates where people spend much of their time outdoors—furnish their streets and plazas with shrines and temples, so that reli-

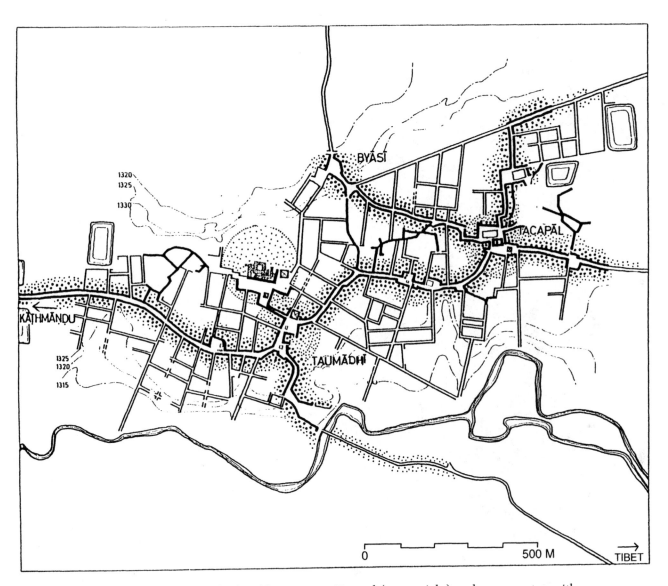

Figure 7.4. *Plan of Bhaktapur, Nepal. The older center at Tacapal (upper right) and newer center, with the Taumadhi plaza discussed in the text, where the processional way down the hill begins. The street eventually comes to the riverbank, where it widens. The 500 meters from the palace to the river are tightly packed with four temples of Shiva in various forms; seven shrines of Ganesh; seven temples or shrines of Vishnu in various forms; three shrines of the mother goddesses; three dance platforms; and three fountains, as well as houses and shops.*

gious ideas and behavior are threaded through daily life (see Chapters 6 and 12 for more on Nepalese religious observance). The main plaza and street of Bhaktapur, Nepal, is a religious space, and many streets in India also become so during festivals.

Bhaktapur's Street Shrines, Nepal

The old city of Bhaktapur, 7 miles (about 11 kilometers) east of Patan and Kathmandu, has kept medieval Hindu

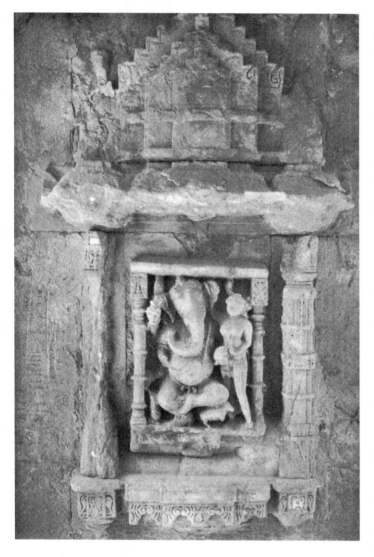

Figure 7.5. *Shrine of Ganesh, Ambapur, India. Townspeople visit the shrine, which is placed in the wall of the stepwell (see Fig. 3.2) on their way to gather water. The god is asked to bless their daily activities, thus ensuring an endless supply of water and other good fortune.*

concepts alive in many rituals. The townspeople see their city as a mirror of the universe (see Fig. 9.4); there is no difference between religious and political history, no distinction between the sacred and the secular. Sanctification is such an integral part of the Nepali concept of space that temples and shrines of all kinds to serve all kinds of gods appear in every street and plaza. It is the custom to honor every shrine, if time permits. People worship at the shrines in passing, on their way to work or school. Primary worship, however, is in the home; people do not go to a sanctuary to worship with a congregation.

Bhaktapur's central Taumadhi plaza and the main street leading downhill from it, are crowded with temples and shrines for all rituals, groups, and castes. The buildings constitute a system dedicated to groups of gods, with much overlapping and borrowing of legends and attributes. As the "realm of the gods," the streets and plazas are open to all castes and all followers of the various Hindu gods, the Buddhas and bodhisattvas, and the aboriginal nature gods. This openness is different from the enclosed shrines and monasteries that welcome their own worshippers more than others. All these holy places work together in the life of the city as a whole and in the particular religions of its inhabitants.

The temples and shrines extend along the sloping road from the central plaza winding down to the river in Fig. 7.4. They include six temples, seven shrines of Ganesh (see Fig. 7.5) and three of the mother goddesses, three dance platforms, and three fountains.

All religious processions follow the main road. The most important procession, which takes place at the Bisket-Jatra festival, is a great parade for the Hindu gods Bhairava and Bhadrakali. Each god rides in his own chariot, made in the form of a temple with wheels. These chariots are so heavy and unwieldy that dozens of people are needed to pull them (see Fig. 7.6 and compare it with Fig. 7.7). The climax of the parade is the ritualized clash of the two chariots, a fertility rite and an acting out of rivalry between the upper and lower sections of the city. By lifting the rivalry from the economic and political to the religious level, the rulers were able to draw on the tolerance that came from the local blend of religions; Nepali religious activity combines Hinduism and Tibetan Buddhism as Japanese religion combines Shintoism and Buddhism.

Taumadhi plaza is not only the focus of the parade, but the architectural focus of the town, the location of its highest building, the Devi temple, and two other temples to major gods of medieval Hinduism: Shiva (as Bhairava) and Vishnu (as Narayana). Like the Ganesh shrines that

Figure 7.6. *Ceremonial chariot, Bhaktapur, Nepal. Constructed of timber, the chariot is waiting to be decorated for a procession.*

Figure 7.7. *Sun-Chariot Wheel, Surya Temple, Konarak, India (thirteenth century). The intricately carved stone wheel and section of the cart from this temple are replicas of those parts in a movable Sun Chariot of the Hindu god Surya. The carved wheel resembles circular mandalas, as well as the cart wheels in Fig. 7.6.*

cluster around the Devi temple, the other shrines of this processional street and of the narrower side streets and courtyards of Bhaktapur are not isolated "facts," but parts of a system that accompanies the people in their daily lives.

Of all the gods of Nepal, the most attended to is the rotund elephant-headed son of Shiva named Ganesh (Ganesha). Children on their way to school stop to pat the god's belly, or climb up to pat his head, or simply bow to say *Namaste!* (I greet you!) Cultural anthropologist M. S. Slusser (the source of all quotations in this chapter unless otherwise noted) wrote:

Ganesha's name resounds on every tongue, and many bear it as their own; he has a temple in every neighborhood and every square; his images are at the roadside, crossroads, and along the pathways, by the rivers, in the forests and on the hills, beside the doors and gateways, in the dharmasallas [rest houses], and in the homes and courtyards; and almost invariably Ganesha shares the shrines of all the other gods. In every public or domestic rite, Ganesha's name is the first invoked . . . his shrine [is] visible or his image circumambulated before commencing the worship of any other deity, even the most exalted. . . . In Nepal, Ganesha's fundamental role is to create—and to remove if it so pleases him—obstacles to success in human endeavors.

His father, Shiva, conceived Ganesh independently, and this so enraged Shiva's wife Parvati that she cursed the child with a monstrous elephant head and pot belly. But Shiva blessed him:

> Success and disappointment shall proceed from thee, and great shall be thy influence amongst gods, and in sacrifices and all affairs. Therefore shalt thou be so worshipped and invoked first on all occasions, or otherwise the projects and prayers of him who omits to do so shall fail.[15]

Like Ganesh, other Hindu gods have noticeable freestanding shrines along the main street with open access. There are also Buddhist stupas of all sizes inside and outside the city, often accompanied by statues of associated Hindu gods. Some Buddhist shrines are freestanding in the open or in courtyards; others are hidden away in monasteries or former monasteries. Individuals often build small shrines for both religions along the street to share with others or in their own houses or yards.

Down by the river at Masan Ghat (the riverbank where the dead are burned), the shrines are mainly to minor gods, gods of death, and other "bad gods" or demons. Between the two groups of gods and shrines stretches the processional way, the one street of the city that is wide enough for vehicles. This road—about 300 meters (less than a thousand feet) long—is also the way of the dead, leading to the river's edge. Regardless of caste, all the dead are brought along the side streets to this main street and then along the main street down to the river, where the dead are burned at three special places called burning ghats, always located on riverbanks or where two rivers join. This lower plaza may be the oldest element in Bhaktapur's urban form. Two temples of Shiva the Destroyer stand at the shore in Chupin Ghat at the end of the route.

The needs of the living, the rituals of the gods, and processions for the dead are conflated on this street in Bhaktapur. The intimate scale and the frequent shrines to

Ganesh anchor this Nepali street firmly in everyday life—and death.

SOURCES: GUTSCHOW AND KÖLVER 1975, 22; SLUSSER (1974, 1982); M. THAPA (PERSONAL COMMUNICATION).

Temporary Temples for Processions in India

In India, many Hindu temples are found along city streets and in plazas. Some temples, however, are replicas, called *rathas*, that are built for mobility and for temporary use; they are floats on which worshippers move an image of a deity through the streets of the town. Although mobile and constructed of wood and bamboo, the ratha follows the architectural pattern of the stone abode of the idol and carries a similar sacred meaning. While the image of the main deity occupies the most prominent place on the ratha platform, other parts of the vehicle, such as the wooden wheels, may be considered temporary dwelling places for minor deities.

The general form of the mobile temple has changed little over the centuries. For example, the thirteenth-century Surya temple at Konarak in Orissa is a stone replica of the kind of processional vehicle still used today. A giant elaborately carved wheel (see Fig. 7.7) suggests a "solar chariot" in which to transport the Sun-god Surya, according to Indian mythology.

Rathas can be massive temples of tremendous weight, according to J. Pieper, an authority on urban festivals, towering as much as 50 to 90 feet (15 to 27 meters) above the platform and weighing over ten tons. Some are ornamented with metal and carved or painted and then adorned with streamers to add to the festive air. Even the tow ropes and wheels have symbolic meaning; all parts of the rathas are considered to be sacred. At midday, when the procession halts for rest, the spectators touch the ropes with respect. The participants carry the smaller, lightweight temples on their shoulders. All the floats are assembled in sheds reserved for this purpose, and when the festival is over, they are dismantled and stored near the temple associated with the deity. Before a ratha is used again, the wheels, chassis, and decorative elements are inspected and refurbished.

Festivals occur at regular intervals fixed by the full moon and pay tribute to a specific deity, season, or regional event. Every temple celebrates at least one festival a year, but some celebrate as many as six or eight. Many festivals are performance oriented, with dancing, singing, and theatrical presentations. Those that include a proces-

---

[15]These two quotations are from T. A. Gopinatha Rao, *Elements of Hindu Iconography*, 2 vols. (New York: Paragon, 1968), 35–47; original work published 1914.

sion offer the populace the opportunity for active participation and are eagerly anticipated.

During the processions, the idol, a symbolic representation of a god or goddess, is made visible to a large number of devotees who otherwise might not be permitted to enter the most sacred areas of the permanent temple, where restrictions apply according to the system of caste. During the festival, however, caste discrimination is relaxed, and all members of the society have nearly equal social status.

The prescribed paths include various routes around the town; the size and shape of shops, houses, and other buildings, as well as their locations, play an important role as the large and often unwieldy chariot (see Fig. 7.6) is guided past them through the narrow streets by sometimes hundreds of devotees. Buildings, spaces, and the procession interact. Historian J. Pieper stresses that architecture and urban patterns become part of the visual spectacle and that the key to understanding the urban and architectural space lies in the processional courses. Skillful manipulation in guiding and coordination in towing the large temple chariots are essential. Twenty people may ride on a ratha to help direct it. The rhythmic beating of a drum attached to the cart sets the pace as the entourage moves along the route.

With the route established, the organizers must arrange the order of the floats and other processional elements. Leading the procession is the temple elephant, a sacred animal of the Hindus. Following the elephant are drummers; people carrying decorated parasols; musicians playing wind instruments; guardians with silver clubs; the flower-bedecked ratha; torch bearers; oil carriers; a canopy; a brass parasol (symbol of royalty); and, finally, the priests or Brahmins, reciting sacred hymns. The practiced circumambulation of the town may derive from customs described in ancient texts, such as the Rig Vedas (ca. 1200 B.C.E.). The route is dictated by the ritual significance of various ceremonial sites, such as ghats (sacred bathing pools). In towns of the Kathmandu Valley in Nepal, the procession follows the ancient lines of defensive walls of each town. According to ancient Indian architectural treatises, such as the Vastu-Sastras, town planning was based on cosmic diagrams, or mandalas, the urban pattern being designed as a replica of the celestial sphere (see Chapter 9). As far as possible, builders sited temples, other sacred buildings, shops, and residences in conformance with religious beliefs. Urban space was specifically designed to accommodate the route of the festival procession.

Often important families sponsor these processions. One member rides on the float to direct the course, and about twenty family members and friends ride to direct the ropes and leverage necessary to maintain mobility. In present-day Kathmandu, the schedule includes traveling to an extramural site for music and dancing; at night the float is guarded. Upon the return there are further celebrations.

India's love of pageantry has its origins in prehistory. Cave paintings of the Mesolithic period show dancing figures. Oral tradition and ancient religious texts teach that there is little distinction between secular and religious life; both are part of the same entity. The celebration of life is an inherent characteristic of the culture, and processions are an exuberant form of celebration.

Festivals and processions have been part of almost all cultures, from the ancient rituals honoring the goddess Athena on the Greek acropolis to the annual Rose Parade in Pasadena, California, a modern Western version of a symbolic procession carrying out specific themes, complete with music, flowers, and enthusiastic people. In India and Southeast Asia, an atmosphere of joyous celebration prevails as processions of temporary temples through the streets bring images of deities to the people. The result, as Pieper observes, is an experience in which the Asian religious beliefs are most enthusiastically expressed.

SOURCES: PIEPER (1983), SLUSSER (1982), M. THAPA (PERSONAL COMMUNICATION).

SPACES SET APART

Some spaces are set apart from everyday life and dedicated to religious use. We examine three such entities, one distinguished by its distinctive architectural form, one by the enormous scale and monumental structures that distinguish it from the surrounding built-up area, and one by its aniconic but immense natural form.

Size was certainly a factor in setting each of these entities apart as "sacred." The Great Mosque in Qairawan, Tunisia, was the largest and tallest building of the city when it was built. The Street of the Dead in Teohuatican, an ancient complex north–northeast of Mexico City, points toward a now-missing former cone of the volcano Cerdo Gordo and thus preserves the memory of this fearsome geographic feature. New Mexico's Mount Taylor is a volcano that gave spatial organization to the religious life of early inhabitants in the region. "Set apart" space, then, can be either natural or manmade, as the religious and physical realities require and make possible.

Special Buildings: North African Mosques

One of the most significant Islamic architectural forms is the mosque, the Muslim house of worship. Its basic shape is derived from early Christian churches, with their important entry courtyards, and from Middle Eastern courtyard houses (see Chapter 11), possibly because the Prophet Mohammed, Arab founder of the Islamic faith, addressed his first followers in the courtyard of his house. The mosque is one of the most enduring forms in Islamic architecture. Its general plan and function have changed little from the seventh century C.E. until the present, although there are regional variations. Because the mosque is such an important part of Islamic architecture, we briefly review the historical background of early mosque construction before we examine the Great Mosque at Qairawan, one of the earliest in North Africa.

In 622 C.E., Mohammed (ca. 570–632 C.E.) migrated from Mecca to Medina. This journey, called the Hijra of Mohammed, marks the official commencement of Islam. Thereafter, through military conquests and religious zeal, Islam spread rapidly throughout the Near East and into Asia, Africa, and the Iberian Peninsula. Not only Islamic religious beliefs, but Arab political convictions and social values were transmitted to these new areas. Islam—submission to the will of Allah, or God—is more than a religion, it is a way of life for the Muslims. Its unifying elements are the holy book called the Qur'an (Koran) and the Arabic language in which it was written. In the Qur'an, which contains messages revealed to Mohammed from Allah, proper religious conduct is codified. The *hadiths*, a collection of edicts by the Prophet, his immediate followers, and others, outline a system of social behavior. All the various regions of Islam observe the hadiths, but each interprets them differently, which accounts for the diversity in unity that characterizes Islamic culture.

The holiest Muslim city is Mecca in Arabia, Mohammed's birthplace. At the center of the city is the Ka'ba, a cubical shrine enclosing a sacred black stone (thought to be a meteorite) located in the courtyard of the Great Mosque. Mecca is the hub of a symbolic wheel extending outward through the whole Muslim world (see the map Spread of Islam in the Appendix). In addition to this horizontal connection with the world, there is a vertical, spiritual axis, which Islamist J. Dickie calls "the axis mundi of Islamic cosmology," defining the Ka'ba as the geo-graphic and spiritual center of the world. In every mosque, the focus of the interior is the *mihrab*, a niche indented in the *qibla* (wall) facing Mecca that gives the direction for prayer. The mihrab, then, emphasizes the importance of the qibla, oriented toward Mecca.

The most important architectural form of Islamic culture was the central place for prayer and social interaction, which evolved into the focal point of the Islamic city—the mosque. The transfer of design elements from one region to another, together with the insistence on having every mosque directed toward Mecca, helped maintain the unity of Islam. For an example of an early mosque, we turn to the Great Mosque of Qairawan in North Africa, a major monument of early North African Islamic architecture, with its central aisle (sometimes called a transept plan) plan, sanctuary, hypostyle hall, aisles perpendicular to the qibla, and courtyard surrounded by colonnades according to historians, N. Alsayyad and G. Boostani.

The fundamental religious concepts governing Islamic society determined the importance of the mosque. Prayer is established at four levels: the individual, the congregation, the total popultion of a town, and the entire Muslim world. Muslims must pray five times daily. Dickie explains that while this daily prayer can take place anywhere, mosques are designed for specific functions. The small mosque or, *masjid,* is for individuals or small prayer groups; the large mosque, *jami masjid,* is the Friday mosque for the weekly congregational service. Although it is not a mosque, an open space, called a *musalla,* serves as the site for community prayer on special occasions, including the two chief Muslim festivals. Rituals are simple. In keeping with the religious belief in egalitarianism, there is no formal hierarchy. Usually the only religious dignitaries involved in the organization of spiritual practices are the *khatib,* or teacher, and the *imam,* or prayer leader.

In North Africa, the Romans had established cities in the Maghreb, the region that includes Tunisia, Morocco, and Algeria (see Fig. 7.8), but many were destroyed in the wars of the fourth, fifth, and sixth centuries. After the Arabs conquered Tunisia and eastern Algeria and gave Africa the new name Ifriqiya, they established settlements and began constructing buildings. Their use of the enclosed, arcaded courtyard reflects Greco-Roman temple courtyards and early Christian church courtyards, both derived from earlier house forms. These models were widely adopted in North Africa and elsewhere in the Islamic world, where both the indigenous peoples, the pre-Arab descendants of North African people called the

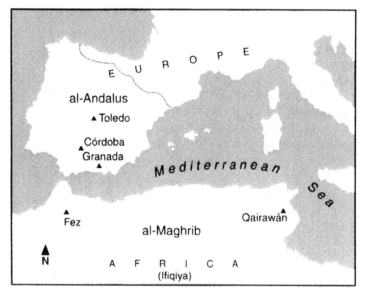

Figure 7.8. *A map of key monuments in the Islamic portions of North Africa (al-Maghrib) and Spain (al-Andalus) in the tenth century.*

Berbers and the conquering Islamic culture were nomads with limited architectural traditions.

The earliest Muslim city in Tunisia was Qairawan, dating to c. 663 C.E. Historians D. Hill and L. Golvin explain that the early history of the city is not well known, but Sidi Akba built a mosque there in 676. The mosque was a modest affair, rebuilt several times on an earlier Romano-Byzantine site as the growth of the city brought the need to accommodate larger congregations. The existing Great Mosque was a further rebuilding by Ziyadat Allah in 836, during the Aghlabid period, and represents an important early step in the development of North African Islamic architecture. It has been called the gem of the emerging Maghrebi style, that is, the architecture of Morocco, Algeria, and Tunisia. After several major additions and remodelings, its plan became an irregular quadrangle, with a courtyard enclosed by porticoes (colonnaded porches) (see Fig. 7.9). It was the prototype for many courtyard mosques with a prayer hall, common in parts of North Africa. The building contains seventeen aisles, including a wider central aisle, aligned with the mihrab, which indicates the direction of Mecca; readings from the Qur'an or other liturgical messages are given from the nearby pulpit, called a *mimbar*.

There are three basic types of mosques: the courtyard type, the transept or central aisle type, and the type with

a large, domed interior space. The Great Mosque of Qairawan belongs to the transept type, with features of the simple courtyard plan: a large hall with its roof supported by many columns (a hypostyle), a courtyard surrounded by colonnades on three sides, and with a plain entrance wall (see Fig. 7.9a and b). According to architect al Asayyad, in the Qairawan mosque the qibla portico is divided in the center. The transept on the axis facing Mecca has a wider span than the other aisles, with clerestory lighting. Domes over the mihrab and the center of the transept emphasize the direction of Mecca. Similar plans are found in the Friday mosque (al-Hkim) at Cairo and during the Umayyad dynasty in Syria (ca. 700s), as well as in many later North African mosques.

The Qairawan mosque has two small domes above the central aisle; the one over the mihrab, built in 862, is curved in a melon shape, a form based on Roman examples. Early mosques typically used small domes raised on squinches or pendentives, depending on the region. These methods adapt a round dome to a square base by building transitional supports at the corners (see Fig. 16.3a, b). In general, the domes also punctuate the exterior form to indicate the position of the mihrab and the qibla, admitting light through a ring of windows at their base into the otherwise dark interior. Symbolically, domes represent the vault of heaven, a cosmological reference known also in the Romano-Byzantine cultures that preceded Islam in this area.

Another adaptation in Qairawan was the square-based minaret (tower), situated at the center of the entrance wall, opposite the sanctuary. The minaret continues the earlier practice whereby someone called the faithful to prayer by shouting from a rooftop, but its form may have derived from Roman watchtower prototypes. Other Roman architectural elements remain: Some of those of the tower at Qairawan, such as a reused lintel, have Roman carvings.

Mosques and, later, palaces were the major buildings of the emerging Maghrebi style. Both usually had rectangular courtyards surrounded on three sides by arcades, with the entrance on the fourth side. Ceilings were flat, roofs pitched. Unlike the carved-out structures in Ethiopia and Indonesia or the wooden frameworks of Japan and Polynesia, the structural system combined uniform pieces of stone or brick into load-bearing masonry. With these materials, the North African Arab builders continued earlier Roman and Byzantine ways of enclosing space.

The walls were stone or brick, but the roofs were wooden—except for high domes. Specific aesthetic refinements, spatial possibilities, and functional opportunities

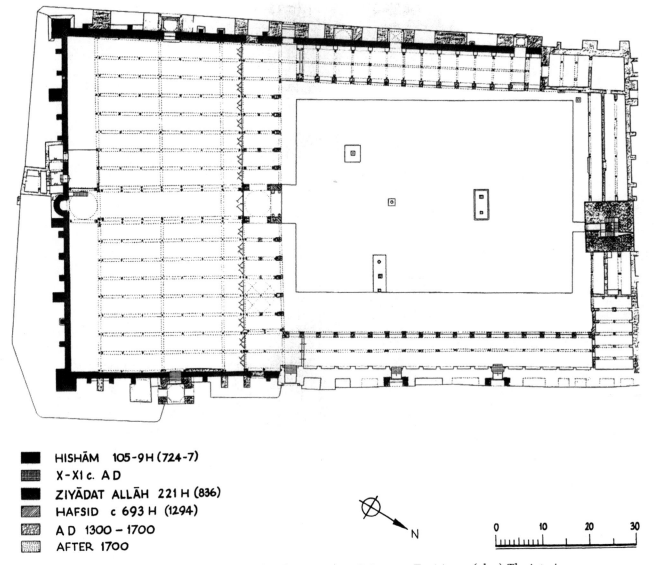

HISHĀM   105-9H (724-7)
X-XI c. A D
ZIYĀDAT ALLĀH   221 H (836)
HAFSID   c 693 H (1294)
A D 1300 - 1700
AFTER 1700

N

0   10   20   30

Figure 7.9 *Plan and view of the Great Mosque (ninth century) at Qairawan, Tunisia.* **a.** *(plan) The interior of the flat-roofed congregational space of the prayer hall is about 236 feet (73 meters) wide. It has a nine-transept plan with seventeen aisles (a wider one in the center) running perpendicular to the qibla wall. The roof is articulated with two domes, the larger at the main entrance and the smaller over the mihrab in the wall.*

grew out of this construction method. In parts of Central and West Africa, where stone or wood are not the traditional building materials, builders relied instead on mud-brick (see Chapter 16, Old Traditions, New Materials).

Ornamentation of the early North African monuments was limited; the painted ceilings of the Qairawan mosque and the marble on the mihrab are exceptions. Sometimes builders of mosques covered surfaces with plaster and incised designs. After the twelfth century, glazed tile work became popular, letting craftsmen work creatively with a colored medium. Artistic motifs were geometric, vegetal, or epigraphic forms, in keeping with the Islamic prohi-

Figure 7.9. b. *Aerial view of the Great Mosque. The wall encloses a spacious courtyard with arcaded porticoes, allowing a generous preparation area for prayer and for accommodating enormous crowds for important holy days. There is a basin for ablutions in the center of the courtyard. Over the entrance to the courtyard rises the minaret, a vertical element in an otherwise horizontal design. Its cupola is on axis with the two domes of the mosque.*

bition against figural decorations. The high point of Maghrebi architecture was attained under the indigenous Berbers. Low, flat ceilings and pitched-roof buildings with T-shaped sanctuaries continued to dominate.

From the ninth through the twelfth centuries, mosques and minarets were the major monuments at Qairawan, although the city also had some excellent palaces and tombs. Political upheaval began in the eleventh century, and the ruling Zirids abandoned the city to nomadic Bedouin tribes. The Great Mosque began to deteriorate for lack of mainte-

nance. In the late thirteenth century, a new dynasty, the Hafsids, accomplished some major rebuilding.

In the Iberian Peninsula, known then as al-Andalus, the Qairawan mosque plan became popular after the tenth century, and hypostyle types were built there. Until the thirteenth and fourteenth centuries, al-Andalus exerted a major influence on Maghrebi architecture through the mosques built at Cordoba, Granada, and Seville. The Great Mosque at Cordoba, enlarged in the eighth, ninth, and tenth centuries, was the most influential building of western Islam in plan, elevation, and decoration. The al-Qarawiyyin mosque at Fez (859–1143); the Great Mosque of Algiers (1096); and palaces, such as that of Ali ibn Yusuf in Marrakesh (1131–32), also greatly influenced architectural development in North Africa. However, domes were modest architectural features in North Africa until the twelfth century Almoravid period; after that time, they became the focal point of Islamic architecture and had elaborate interiors. The treatment of the vaults with multiple ribs in the dome over the mihrab, elaborate stone and stucco decorative motifs, and the invention of stucco stalactites called *muqarnas* (see Fig. 10.5)—especially notable in the twelfth century Kutabiyya Mosque in southern Morocco—produced attractive effects. The ultimate in dome construction was reached in Turkey and Egypt in the magnificent domed mosques, such as the Shezade and Suleymaniye in Istanbul of the sixteenth-century Ottomans (see Figs. 16.14 and 16.15).

SOURCES: ALSAYYAD (1988), ATASOY (1990), DICKIE (1978), FRISHMAN (1994), HOAG (1975), MICHELL (1978), DE MONTEQUIN (1982).

Ceremonial District: Teotihuacán, Mexico

Teotihuacán[16] was the first true city in Mesoamerica. In its monumentality, sophisticated planning, and overall size, it stands among the greatest preindustrial centers of the world. The city was larger than its contemporary, imperial Rome. Civic architecture included streets, plazas, religious buildings, palaces, apartments, factories, water-supply facilities, and storage for food and other materials. The size and orientation of streets and buildings indicate sophisticated planning—streets were laid out in a grid pattern requiring both planning before construction of buildings and a determination to maintain the pattern over time. This geometric pattern contrasts with the "campus plan" of the Maya cities discussed in Chapters 10 and 14, although both are thought to have an astronomical base. Design elements used at Teotihuacán were simple—esplanades, platforms with altars or small buildings, pyramids with small temples on top, courts, staircases, quadrangles—but the combination of the elements was masterful.

[16]The name of the site, given by the later Aztecs, means "place where gods or lords are made." Aztec rulers made respectful pilgrimages here nearly every month. The names of buildings are from the Aztec language, Nahuatl, or the Spanish or were applied by modern archaeoelogists; the ancient names are unknown.

Pyramids were the focus of regional, municipal, and neighborhood life. Large pyramids up to 150 feet high, of varied profiles, lined the main street, and courtyards contained smaller ones up to 12 feet high. Each of the three central pyramids had its own courtyards and auxiliary buildings, and they made a most impressive grouping along the axial main street (see Chapter 11, Teotihuacán, Mexico, Street of the Dead, Figs. 11.11 and 11.12). Grouping together a large pyramid, small temples on platforms, and auxiliary buildings within the architectural precision of enclosure walls produced a unity lacking in Egypt, making the pyramids of Teotihuacán more readily experienced by a modern visitor as a forceful religious environment. Indeed, the pyramids along the Street of the Dead demand awe, according to A. Mundigo, a sociologist who lived in Mexico City for a number of years. This effect was intended by their builders, for whom the pyramids had at least two meanings: They were places where the worship of gods took place and the gods themselves were encountered, and they resembled volcanoes, the most awesome natural features of the landscape.

All the pyramids of Teotihuacán have a core of earth and lava stone, with a masonry skin of stone panels that, in some cases, forms a surface with strong shadow patterns. Archaeologists have found that Middle American cultures usually rebuilt temples by adding an outer layer to the pyramid and replicating the shape of the crowning temple or temples. As a result, the pyramids grew larger over time. Use of lava stone increased the pyramids likeness to volcanoes.

At the center of Teotihuacán are three large pyramid complexes. The Pyramid of the Moon is the termination of the axis, while the Pyramids of the Sun and the Feathered Serpent lie along the east side of the main street.

The Pyramid of the Moon is 150 feet high with a 490-foot-wide base (45.24 meters high by a 149.4-square-meter base). Its architectural form consists of interlocking, truncated pyramids and stairs, echoing the volcanic mountain of Cerro Gordo behind it in the distance. Platforms surround the pyramid, and an altar stands in front. A statue of Chalchiuhtlicue, the Great Goddess, was found nearby, which suggests that the pyramid may have been dedicated to her. This goddess ruled earthly waters and was both the patroness of warfare, who required sacrifice; the mother of the gods; and the fertile mountain itself. Anthropologist J. C. Berlo reproduced an ancient depiction of the goddess as a fertile mountain (see her Fig. 5).

The Pyramid of the Sun (see Fig. 7.10) is more than twice as large as the Pyramid of the Moon and probably

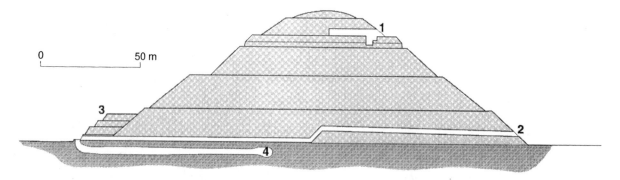

Figure 7.10. *Section of the Pyramid of the Sun, Teotihuacán, Mexico. Beneath the pyramid (darker gray) the ancient cave enters from the left. In the base of the pyramid are the two tunnels excavated by archaeologists—1920 at right (2) and 1933 at left (below 3)—the latter marking the combination tomb and approach stairs added some time after the original construction. A third tunnel (1), dug in 1962, is located near the summit.*

took thirty years to build, compared with twelve for the latter. Possibly begun as early as 250 B.C.E. and finished by 200 C.E., the Pyramid of the Sun consists of 2.5 million tons (2.3 million metric tons) of sun-dried bricks (adobes) made from clayey-lime sediments, the great pile faced with stone and then covered with concrete, surfaced with lime plaster, and decorated with sculpture. Its size is overwhelming. As tall as a modern twenty-story building and some 700 feet (213.4 meters) square at the base, the pyramid almost equals the Egyptian pyramid of Cheops in area, but is only half as high. Visitors are often impelled to climb to its top, an experience analogous to the ancient rituals—especially since one is likely to meet devotees of the modern pyramid cult. In antiquity, the Pyramid of the Sun was probably taller, with one or two temples on top. It faces a little north of west, with its stairs oriented to the point on the horizon where the sun and the Pleiades both set on the day when the sun's course reaches its northernmost point. This pyramid was probably the focus of an ancient creation myth.

Only recently have modern archaeologists realized that the Pyramid of the Sun was built over caves (see Fig. 11.11). One of these caves, a cloverleaf-shaped sacred cave, was sealed around 450 C.E. when additional structures and a stair were added to the west side of the pyramid. Archaeologists rediscovered the entrance in the late 1980s, a pit some 23 feet (7 meters) deep under the central stairway that leads to the top of the pyramid. From the pit, a steep and partly rock-cut stair leads down to a cave-tunnel in the bedrock that led in prehistoric times to an

important shrine in the ritual cave (see R. Millon's Fig. 4). Later, people carved or enlarged the tunnel and the four rooms of the cave, probably to extract volcanic scoria fragments (tezontle) to use as construction materials, according to L. Barba P. They also plastered the walls with mud and installed some basalt ceiling slabs. Halfway along, the tunnel widens to form two more rooms; the tunnel itself is divided by partitions into about twenty sections. This linear cave lies so close to the central axis of the pyramid that the location was surely not accidental. The cave here became the outlet for a spring, or at least a resurgence; ancient stone drainpipes and manhole covers found inside the tunnel handled the water flow. Modern aerial photographs show a line of vegetation extending from the front of the pyramid, indicating persistent underground water seepage.

In Mesoamerican mythology, as in some other cultures, a cave symbolized the womb of the earth. People went to caves to visit the gods, who gave water and germinated seed and fruits, especially if the cave had a spring. Such a cave was considered a place of emergence into this world (see Keresan religious concepts discussed later). In their books and oral tradition, the later Aztecs preserved the idea of a sacred cave at the foot of the pyramid stair, an entrance to the underworld and to the Earth Lord's home. Manuscripts depicted one cave as a cloverleaf, which, according to anthropologist D. Heyden, could symbolize both the House or Realm of Maize and the four quarters of the world. Oracles were associated with caves; a map from 1580 locates an oracle in Teotihuacán between

Figure 7.11. *Teotihuacán, looking north. The axial street is aligned with the Pyramid of the Moon at the north and is flanked by other pyramids and their courts on the right and apartments with viewing platforms on the left. Towering over them is the cone of the volcano behind Cerro Gordo, on which the form of the pyramids was modeled.*

the Pyramids of the Sun and the Moon. It was thus the existence of caves that determined the placement of the Pyramid of the Sun, affecting the geometry of the civic core.

The group of buildings to the south of the Pyramid of the Sun is now called the Citadel. It consists of a pyramid, many altars, and three palaces. An enclosed court measured 643 by 775 feet (196 by 236 meters). The entire complex is oriented to the northwest horizon like the Pyramid of the Sun (see Fig. 7.11). The pyramid of Quetzalcoatl, the Feathered Serpent, was the central and most important building of the complex. Teotihuacán residents believed that their security depended upon propitiating this warrior deity, usually by blood offerings, even human sacrifice. Archaeologists found evidence that more than two hundred people had been entombed within the pyramid during construction as dedicatory sacrifices—young soldiers (probably captives), priests, and women, buried singly or in groups of 8, 18, and 20, the numbers of the Venus calendar (a Venus-cycle year is eighteen months of twenty days; eight years make a full cycle, equal to five solar years; for these people, the planet Venus was a male

war god). Investigators also found an important burial pit under the center of the pyramid and a second one under the stairway in front of the pyramid that seem to have been for the ruler who built the pyramid and for his successor, respectively. (Compare with Tikal's pyramids as royal funerary buildings, Chapter 14; see Fig. 14.9).

The Pyramid of the Feathered Serpent is the most successful integration of architecture and sculpture at Teotihuacán. Its walls, 66 meters long, considerably shorter than the Pyramid of the Sun, were elaborately arranged in terracelike layers, decorated with hundreds of carved heads of gods, which seem to erupt from discs described as mirrors edged with feathers, and further set off by the shadow patterns of the architecture. Originally, the pyramid was covered with lime plaster and painted, as were most wall surfaces in Teotihuacán. The background was dark blood-red with blue-green circles for the bulging eyes of the god. This complex also included twin palaces to the north and south for rulers and a third palace that may have been for priests.

The pyramids drew the eyes and attention of the Teotihuacán people and the pilgrimages of their neighbors, enhancing the status of the site as a true city. Religion absorbed major resources of the state and the devotion of the people. In addition to public monuments, every apartment complex of the city had at least one temple, as well as altars that were miniature versions of the monumental pyramids.

SOURCES: BARBA (1995); FUSON (1969); HEYDEN (1975A), FIG. 12; MILLON (1992), FIGS. 4 AND 10; SANDERS, PARSONS, AND STANLEY (1979); SUGIYAMA (1992), FIG. 6; TAUBE (1992B).

Without Buildings: Mount Taylor, New Mexico

From a monumental architectural complex, we turn to a place of religious focus but not of enclosed space. Not all places of intense religious experience are buildings constructed by humans. For thousands of years, a large volcanic mountain in New Mexico has inspired the awe of people living near it. In pre-Columbian times, it was a fo-

cus of religious belief for the Keresan people who lived in the area.

Perhaps as early as 4,500 years ago, ancestors of the Keresan people came to what is now northern New Mexico and settled along the river now called the Rio Grande and to the west of it. The river cuts through a region of canyons, mesas, mountains, and one peak different from the others— a wide cone of black lava and basalt, covered with the dark green of firs and spruce. Smaller cones are scattered on its lower slopes; on the eastern flank, basalt cores stand like sentinels, some as much as 2,000 feet (600 meters) high. The volcano, Kow-i-stchum-ma Kote, known as Mount Taylor, is nearly 12,000 feet (3660 meters) in elevation and almost five miles (8 kilometers) wide, towering more than 5,000 feet (1524 meters) over the plains and more than 3,000 feet (914 meters) over the nearby mesas (see Fig. 7.12).

The prominence of mountains played a significant role in Keresan creation legends, which relate that people and all other living creatures came up to this world from the underground through an opening called *sipapu*. E-yet-e-co, the mother of life, lived and created at the deepest depth of this pit, so the people revered volcanic craters especially. A. Ortiz described the creation of the mountains this way:

> "Now we are going to make the mountains," Tsitcti-nako[17] [the original earth mother] said, and showed them how to throw a certain stone from the basket toward the north while speaking certain words. There a large mountain arose. They did the same in the other directions, and mountains appeared all around them.

Over centuries or millennia, people spread out to occupy the valleys, canyons, and mesa tops along the Rio Grande, Rio San José, and Rio Puerco east and west— always within sight of the great volcano. Their languages grew more separate, but seven of the groups maintained enough contact to retain a common language: the Keresan, now settled in the pueblos of Acoma; Laguna,[18] Sia

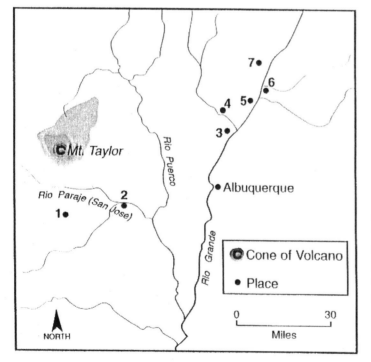

Figure 7.12. *Map of Mount Taylor, New Mexico, with the pueblos of Keresan people. Acoma (1), the oldest of this group, and the one in most dramatic relationship to the mountain, lies directly south of it. The other Keresan pueblos are Laguna (2) (a post-Conquest settlement). Santa Ana (3), Sia (4), San Felipe (5), Santo Domingo (6), and Cochiti (7).*

---

[17]We have not been able to reconcile spellings as transliterated by different authors, although Ortiz, a Native American from this region, is most likely to be correct.

[18]Laguna itself was created by the Spanish governors as a synoikism (union of several villages into a city, frequently under duress) of several defeated puebloes after the seventeenth-century Pueblo Revolt, which implies that before Spanish domination, there were more than seven Keresan pueblos.

(also known as Zia); Santa Ana; Cochiti; Santo Domingo; and San Felipe. The people of Acoma Pueblo remember that their ancestors once lived to the north, near Cubero, but that about three hundred years before the Spanish came to New Mexico, they had to leave this open site near the river because of danger from Apache and Navajo wanderers. According to their oral history, they lived on Katsimo, now known as Enchanted Mesa, and some of them moved to Acoma about 1200 C.E. Their name for the new settlement is reported as Acoma, Acu, Acuo, Acuco, or Ako—"place that always was"—indicating the longevity of the site, according to historian W. A. Minge, although according to anthropologist P. Nabokov, the name means "place of preparedness." Other sources suggest that Acoma means "people of the white rock." From these discrepancies, we see that the Keresan culture does not reveal all its truths.

Like other Pueblo peoples, the residents of Acoma defined their home as the center, or navel, of the sacred geography of the world. The edges were the mountains of the horizon to the north, east, south, and west, and to those four points the Keresans added "above" and "below" and sometimes "at the center," a way of reckoning used by agricultural peoples since Neolithic times. The Acoma people think of the universe as having three or four levels—the sky, the earth, and the underworld, which has up to four subdivisions—and have elaborated the idea of the center. Figure 7.13 is a schematic version of Pueblo orientation, showing the settlement at the center surrounded by a limited terrain with firm edges, both geographic and conceptual. At the center live "The People."

Mountains have a continuing physical and symbolic presence in the lives of those who follow the agricultural cycle. Figure 7.14 is a horizontal calendar of the neighboring Hopi people, similar to the way both residents of Acoma and the Inkas of Peru organized their world. According to C. D. Forde,

[t]his calendar . . . is provided by the daily shift in the position of sunrise on the horizon. The smallest irregularities on the southern sky-line are well known, and the more significant within the sun's path, probably some twenty or more, are named with reference either to their form, to ceremonial events, or to agricultural operations which fall due when the sun rises immediately behind them.

The religious and political head of Acoma still watches for the appearance of the rising sun over a particular mountain, hill, or mesa, using it to synchronize rituals and farm activities with the solstice or equinox calendar. This ancient tradition, which mixes the practical, the beautiful, and the divine, is found also at other mesas.

Acoma is also surrounded by springs and many hidden sanctuaries connected by well-worn trails that link Acoma and its neighbors, the Laguna and Zuni pueblos. Like the mountains, the shrines are associated with specific colors, plants, birds, animals, seasons, and spirits. North is connected to winter and yellow, west to spring and blue, south to summer and red, and east to autumn and white.

Figure 7.15 is a schematic depiction of Pueblo world levels and the connections between them. Architect D. G. Saile writes:

But house [sic] in the sense used here was not solely a place of residence. It was a place of potential communication with the spirit world. Each of these houses are [sic] situated such that they could form a break or channel through which a connection could be formed between the three levels of the Pueblo world.

Although it is misleading to represent this idea in a fixed visual form, figure [our 7.15] may clarify some of the general spatial relationships. It should be remembered that for any one Pueblo group, this arrangement was much more intricate, that much depended upon the particular geographical location, and that aspects of the power of the spirits varied through the Pueblo year. The village itself is a very important place of contact with the spirit worlds. It is, in effect, the centre of the networks of communication. . . . At the center was great potential power in a controlled form. With proper prescribed ritual and prayer the power would benefit and ensure the survival of all the villagers. At greater distances from the village and at greater depths or heights the power was potentially more dangerous and uncontrollable. . . . A mountaintop seems to be important because it can concentrate power at a point and because [the mountain] cuts or transcends levels.

The El Malpais area of intense lava flows west of Acoma is especially important as a locus of sacred shrines. Rain clouds follow a path from St. Johns, Arizona, to the west, to Acoma Mesa, moving "like approach lights at an airport," wrote anthropologist and historian Minge. The rain path runs across Zuni Salt Lake by way of El Malpais, through shrines and natural rock formations in the Berry-

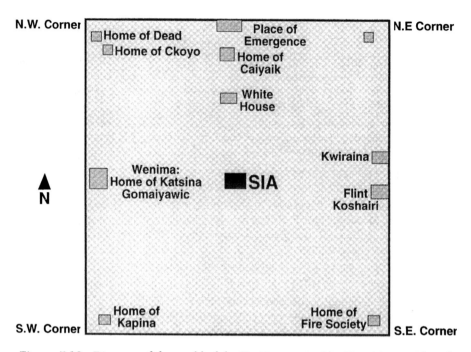

Figure 7.13. *Diagram of the world of the Sia Keresan pueblo, New Mexico. The village is at the center of the world, and all the corners and the midpoints of the sides are attributed to persons or groups. Most important of these places is the Place of Emergence. At Acoma, Mount Taylor is located exactly at this northern point.*

The earth, according to Sia belief, is square and flat; and, since it has thickness, it may be assumed to be a cube. It is divided into four horizontal layers: the lowest one is yellow; the one above, blue-green; the third, red; and the top layer, white. [Note that different colors are allocated to these levels by the various Keresan groups.] Everything in the world above is arranged according to directions. . . . These points constitute a ritual circuit. . . . In the middle-north is the Place of Emergence. . . . Also in the north, but between the middle and the northern edge of the world, is Kacikatcutiya (White House), the place in all Keresan origin myths where the people lived after their emergence and where they obtained most of their institutions and other cultural items. . . . In the northwest corner is Gyitibo-kai, the home of the dead. . . . In the middle-west is Wenima, the home of the Katsina, the anthropomorphic rainmakers . . . in the southeast is a tunnel, or cave, called Mawakana Rainbow House. It is here that all the spirits created by Tsityostinako gather at Hanyiko to receive the prayers of the Sia people.

—*abridged from L. White (1962)*

hill ranch area, and on to Acoma through a region symbolically important for the Keresans. A major religious duty for the Acoma people is to visit the shrines associated with the rain path, carrying out rituals to ensure rain.

Unlike the Navajo religion, which has been described in detail in the literature, the Keresan religion is recorded in contradictory fragments. Traditional secrecy is reflected in the lack of agreement among accounts of the names of the mountains on the boundary of Acoma territory. In

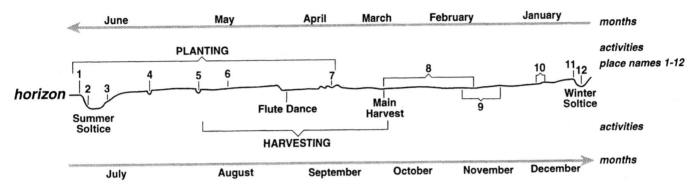

Figure 7.14. *Geographic calendar of the Hopi pueblo of Sihmopovi, west of Acoma, New Mexico. The calendar coordinates agricultural activities with the position of the sun and moon, in relation to mountains and other geographic markers, to designate the passing of cyclical time. The horizon of hills and mountains is the heavier line at the center. The cycle begins at the upper right, moves to the left with months and activities correlated, and then moves to the right along the bottom of the drawing from the summer solstice until the end of the year. Note that the native peoples of Mexico and Peru project similar calendars onto their own landscapes; exactly such a geographic calendar is known at Cuzco, Peru, from Inka times, according to Aveni (1982).*

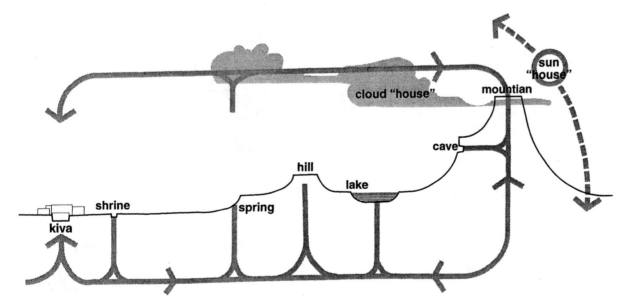

Figure 7.15. *New Mexico. Pueblo world levels and the connections between them. Each place of potential communication with the spirit world is thought of as a "house." In the diagram, there are "houses" in the kiva, at shrines, springs, hilltops, lakes, caves, and mountain tops. The clouds and the sun have their own "houses."*

many cultures, true names are unmentionable, to preserve their potency. Mountains, especially volcanoes, are sacred because they are often associated with a lake or pond—always miraculous in this arid desert—and because they have an earth navel on top that gathers blessings, directing them to the settlement. A second kind of sacred eminence is a flat-topped hill, particularly if it is dark and foreboding, with a cave or tunnels. The orientation of the Acoma people in their landscape is first to the mountains, and because Mount Taylor is the closest, it is the most immediate object of awe.

Geological as well as anthropological insights give us another explanation for the awe Mount Taylor inspires (see Fig. 7.16). Some of the basalt flows on the south slopes are very recent, possibly even post-Colombian, and look as if they may still be hot, according to geologist J. Shomaker. A volcano that has erupted, sending out lava during the past five hundred years from vents so close to Acoma, requires the precaution of daily observation by the pueblo leader. It is practical to direct the little side streets of the mesa community to the north so that people can easily see the volcano as well as the sun. The desire to

Figure 7.16. *View to Mount Taylor from the church at Acoma Pueblo, ca. 1900. In the foreground are the other buildings of the church complex, and in the middle ground, the row houses, with their access ladders to upper stories. A few roofs of the last row of houses to the north are barely visible. Mount Taylor stretches out along the horizon.*

avoid flowing lava and bombardment by airborne debris from the volcano was a strong incentive for siting the settlement far south of the mountain's slopes and high on the mesa, rather than down in the river valley. (See Chapter 14, on Acoma houses, for a discussion of the arrangement of the Keresan village itself.)

The boundary mountains of the Acoma world and Zuni Salt Lake are still places of pilgrimage among the Keresans. Along the way, devotees perform rites, such as footraces to the top of a mesa. One wonders whether the courses of these races lead to places made unhealthy by the radioactivity from the uranium ores that are plentiful in the area. If so, experience may have taught the devotees to acknowledge the force of the place but protect themselves by staying there as short a time as possible—in other words, by running.

Mount Taylor's spell is not limited to the Acoma people, its closest neighbors. It is the focus of pilgrimages from the Zuni to the west and the Hopi farther west.[19] It also exerts a strong attraction on outsiders, who are mesmerized by its beauty of form and by the daily play of light across its slopes.

Human responses to the numinous and the sacred form a continuum: the Japanese tokonoma, more aesthetic than soulful; the overtly folk-religious arrangements of the Mexican Altar of the Dead; and the shrines and chariots of religion in Nepal and India, where religion permeates all life. Islam's religious responses are more codified and more architectural. A walk among the pyramids of Mexico's great Street of the Dead compels awe. So do certain landscapes: The numinous space around Mount Taylor, the least tangible of the religious foci we have examined, is enclosed only in the mental ordering imposed by the Keresan people. These examples suggest the great variety both of human responses to spiritual impulses and of architectural provisions for the spiritual life (compare with Taoist ideas of being and nonbeing as related to architecture, Chapter 15.)

---

[19]In 1999, the Hopi lost their peace emissary, Thomas Banyacya, the last of four such emissaries chosen in 1948 by the Hopi elders when they learned that uranium for the atomic bombs dropped on Japan had been mined in northeastern Arizona. Banyacya warned in many public venues that the world faced global cataclysms if people failed to live in harmony with nature. "What have you as individuals, as nations, and as the world body been doing to take care of the Earth?" he asked in his address to the United Nations General Assembly.

Sources: Aveni (1982), Forde (1934), Guidoni (1975), Gunn (1917), Harvey (1972), Minge (1991), Nabokov (1986), Ortiz (1972, 1984), Saile (1977), Sedgwick (1926),Shomaker (1967), Tainter and Gillio (1980), Trauger (1967), Tyler (1964), White (1942).

SUGGESTED READINGS

Berlo, J. C., ed. 1992. *Art, Ideology, and the City of Teotihuacan.* Washington, D.C.: Dumbarton Oaks Research Library and Collection. An important volume of recent investigations; see the Bibliography for its various chapters.

Carmichael, E., and C. Sayr. 1991. *The Skeleton at the Feast: The Day of the Dead in Mexico.* London: British Museum Press. The best study to date, and well illustrated.

Colcutt, M. et al. 1988. *Cultural Atlas of Japan.* New York: Facts on File Publications. A good source for an overview of Japanese culture. Divided into topic sections with specific sites highlighted; many color plates.

Dickie, J. 1978. "Allah and Eternity: Mosques, Madrasa and Tombs." In *Architecture of the Islamic World: Its History and Social Meaning,* 15–47, edited by G. Michell. New York: William Morrow. A valuable reference.

Engel, H. 1969. *The Japanese House, A Tradition for Contemporary Architecture.* Rutland, Vt.: Charles E. Tuttle. See the section on the tokonoma.

Frishman, M., and H.-U. Kahn, eds. 1994. *The Mosque: History, Architectural Development and Regional Diversity.* New York: Thames & Hudson. A highly stimulating and well-written study of mosques, with contributions from eminent scholars in the field.

Gutschow, N. and B. Kölver. 1975. *Ordered Space Concepts and Functions in a Town of Nepal.* Wiesbaden, Germany: Kommissionsverlag Franz Steiner GMBH. The urban design of Bhaktapur, analyzed with great intelligence and close attention to the social meaning of the spaces. See also Gutschow (1982) for many excellent plans and photos of this city.

Harvey, B. 1972. "An Overview of Pueblo Religion." In *New Perspectives on the Puebloes,* edited by A. Ortiz. Albuquerque: University of New Mexico Press. A good short account, but note that not all has been revealed.

Hashimoto, F. 1981. *Architecture in the Shoin Style: Japanese Feudal Residences.* Tokyo: Kodansha. An informative discussion of a particular style of early Japanese architecture.

Heyden, D. 1975a. "An Interpretation of the Cave underneath the Pyramid of the Sun in Teotihuacán, Mexico. *American Antiquity* 40: 131–47. An innovative study, especially when combined intellectually with Barba's (1995) geological work.

Hill, D., and L. Golvin. 1976. *Islamic Architecture in North Africa: AD 800–1500.* Hamden, Conn.: Anchor Books. The history and architecture of Tunisia, Algeria, and Morocco.

Marcus, J. 1983. "On the Nature of the Mesoamerican City. In *Prehistoric Settlement Patterns: Essays in Honor of G. R. Willey,* 195–242, edited by E. Z. Vogt and R. M. Leventhal. Albuquerque: University of New Mexico Press. Clear, interesting, significant—a model of urban design history, from an anthropologist.

Michell, G. 1988. *The Hindu Temple.* New York: Harper & Row. A highly informative treatment of forms and meanings.

Millon, R. 1964. "The Teotihuacán Mapping Project." *American Antiquity* 29: 345–52. A brief report on a mammoth mapping project that changed American archaeology permanently.

Monsias, C. 1987. "Look Death, Don't Be Inhuman": Notes on a Traditional and Industrial Myth" (Introduction). In M. T. Pomar, *El Dia' de los Muertos: The Life of the Dead in Mexican Folk Art,* 9–16. Fort Worth, Tex.: Fort Worth Art Museum. Catches the macabre humor of the celebration.

Ortiz, A. 1972. "Ritual Drama and the Pueblo World View." In *New Perspectives on the Puebloes,* 135–61, edited by A. Ortiz. Albuquerque: University of New Mexico Press. An insider's view of pueblo ritual.

Pieper, J. 1983. "Festivals as a Matter of Course in the Public Life of Traditional India." In *Reports on Field Work Carried Out at Mohenjo-Daro, Pakistan, 1982–83. Vol. 1: Interim Reports,* 119–29, edited by M. Jansen and G. Urban. Aachen, Germany: Forschungsprojekt "Mohenjo-Daro." Processions and other active manifestations of piety.

Pieper, J. 1975. "Three Cities of Nepal." In *Shelter, Sign and Symbol,* 52–69, edited by P. Oliver. London: Barrie & Jenkins. By an eminent authority on the subject and well written.

Tainter, J. A., and D. A. Gillio. 1980. *Cultural Resources Overview: Mt. Taylor Area, New Mexico.* Santa Fe, N.M.: Bureau of Land Management. A combination of anthropological and geological insights into the region and its residents.

White, L. 1942. 1964 reprint. "Cosmology and Pueblo Life." In *The Pueblo of Sia, New Mexico.* Bulletin 184. Washington, D.C. US Government Printing Office: Bureau of American Ethnology, An early study, still valuable.

⊞ 8

Expression of Power

Ever since the first city walls were built, two of the primary tasks of monumental architecture have been to express power and to maintain it. Architecture has fulfilled these purposes in several ways: through the sheer size and finish of such monuments compared with structures for daily life, through walls and fortresses that literally solidified imperial power, and through the effect of the conquerors' architecture upon the conquered.

The monumental structures of Nan Madol in the Caroline Islands in the western Pacific and at Zimbabwe in East Africa are so impressive that early foreign visitors were often unable to believe that the indigenous people had built them (see Chapter 15, Writing Architectural History). In both cases, the size and sophistication of these stone structures set them markedly apart from the ephemeral domestic buildings that surrounded them.

The Great Wall of China, one of humankind's most imposing and enormous constructions, reflects the military aspects of empire. So does Saqsaywaman near Cuzco in Peru. The military force, religious sanctions, and royal presence that emanated from this hilltop fortress helped the Inkas

maintain their uneasy hold on other peoples and dominate trade routes and urban settlements. By examining the ways in which the Inkas and later the Spanish changed Cuzco, we see how each group, in turn, imposed its culture and architecture upon the conquered. Similarly, the Muslim conquerors of northern India introduced their own architecture when they built forts at Agra and Delhi. Conquest and colonization are not unique to the Europeans, who have been the most recent conquering culture. (See also Chapter 3, Irrigation Systems, in Peru, and Chapter 13, Islamic Gardens, for architectural manifestations of power.)

MONUMENTALITY

Individuals or groups can use architecture as remembrance devices. The first duty of a monument is to remind people of a person or an event. Many effective monuments appear in this book: the columns topped with portrait statues in Durbar Square, Patan (Chapter 12), Asian stupas that remind viewers of Buddha or Buddhist saints (Chapters 1 and 5), Mexican altars of the dead (Chapter 7), the Taj Mahal (Chapter 9), and the memorial mosques built by architect Sinan for the Ottoman emperors (Chapter 16).

Another kind of monumental architecture, however, is intended to impress viewers with its own size, permanence, and excellence. Such structures are often erected as political statements, to secure or prolong the dominance of one group over others, or to make a statement about what the rulers value. In this category belong the cosmic "mountains" at Borobudur and Angkor Wat (Chapters 5 and 11), the pyramids at Teotihuacán and Chichen-Itzá (Chapters 7, 10, and 11), and the plans of Chang'an and Heijo (Chapter 9). This category also includes the monumental stone architecture of Nan Madol and Great Zimbabwe.

Stone Architecture in the Caroline Islands

Monumental architecture is an effective manifestation of power, as rulers everywhere have discovered. Powerful stone architecture is not limited to large empires or to cultures with long written histories. A culture with no written history, virtually unknown to the outside world, built the complex of monumental structures called Nan Madol on the southeast side of Pohnpei (Ponape) in the Caroline Islands of the Pacific region called Micronesia.

"No site in Oceania surpasses the dramatic beauty of Nan Madol"—an abandoned stone settlement set in a mangrove jungle—wrote architect W. N. Morgan. Nan Madol is the collective name for ninety-two islands, mostly manmade, covering 200 acres (80.92 hectares), or about one-third of a square mile (0.86 square kilometer). The name means "place of intervals" (between houses or buildings) or, loosely, "place of crowded buildings," suggesting that Pohnpei's usual settlement pattern was the isolated family homestead.

Pohnpei, Micronesia's third largest island (see the map of Oceania in the Appendix), is a picture-perfect Pacific paradise with forested central volcanic mountains and coastal lagoons fringed by coral reefs. Its interior provides wood and other organic building materials. Fertile soil and ample water made life easy enough to allow the leaders to divert labor into the construction of monumental architecture. And because the island is volcanic, it also has basalt, which the Pohnpeians learned to use for their monumental architecture.

From the dating of ceramics, we know that Pohnpei, specifically Nan Madol, was populated in the early centuries C.E.; the oldest archaeological deposit found here

dates from 232 C.E., while the oldest date from coring is 227.

About a thousand years ago, the island's settlers were building stone platforms, house foundations, walls, pavings, and tombs, as well as earth terraces and mounds, along the coasts, in the valleys, and on the hillsides and mountaintops of the interior. During the eleventh century, the island seems to have been unified, and around 1150, Pohnpeians began to build elaborate architecture of basalt megaliths for their chiefs, who were entitled to architectural supplies and labor as forms of tribute. All the men of the island were organized to quarry, move, and erect the stones. The peak period for both the society and the architecture was 1400 to 1800, although the most impressive buildings apparently date from before 1600.

Human nature, with its predilections for competition and display, produces psychic and physical energies that may usefully be absorbed in some kind of community project. In India, for example, the building of stupas drew on those energies to make mammoth structures. Such projects could also create or strengthen a state, as K. Mendelssohn suggested for the ancient Egyptians. As information about the Micronesians of Pohnpei accumulates, we may see whether the state-building pattern applied there.

The political system was altered when a new dynasty was founded in the early seventeenth century by a foreign adventurer named Iso-Kalakal (Isokekel), who called himself the son of the chief god of Pohnpei. After the reigns of his six successors at Nan Madol, the kings moved their residence to the shore, although priests and their families continued to live at Nan Madol. After European contact, the island's population dropped rapidly from 20,000 or even 35,000 to between 6,000 and 10,000. In 1854, smallpox killed another 2,000 to 5,000 people. By the 1870s, the population was reduced to only 300, and the ancient system was effectively gone. As the people reported in 1910, "Because of smallpox we have forgotten much."

Nan Madol's original spatial configuration (see Fig. 8.1b) is hard to perceive because under humid tropical conditions, jungle and mangrove swamps choke the site, in spite of frequent efforts to clear it. The ruins stretch for 4,600 feet (1,400 meters) along the southeast side of the central island and 2,450 feet (381 meters) into the lagoon. Organized on an axis that runs northeast–southwest, the islets of the monumental group have been amplified or built up with coral fill to form platform bases, standing now up to 7 feet (more than 2 meters) above high tide. Most islets are quadrilaterals; only six or seven are irregular in shape. On each one, walls that range from 6 to 30 feet (1.8 to 9.1 meters) high rise above the base to define the human space. From the walkway outside, stairways penetrate to the inner space. On the platforms inside the walls, the people built large permanent structures of stones up to 20 feet (6 meters) long and weighing up to 50 tons (45 metric tons). The architectural repertory consisted of walls, fortresses, tombs, temples, platforms for ceremonies, meeting houses, houses and palaces, tunnels, canals, breakwaters, and seawalls. The stone structures were supplemented by buildings of wood, bamboo, and other perishable materials.

As the chief monumental area of Pohnpei, Nan Madol has three groups of ruins: Madol Pah, which includes the kings' residence on Pahnkadira Islet and the administrative center, southwest of the central waterway; Madol Powe, the northeast sector, residence of the priests and site of important tombs; and, finally, the complex of retaining walls, sea barricades, and canal levees that constitutes the outer seawall. Nan Madol's physical separation from the main island symbolized and reinforced the elite status of the residents and the import of ritual activities there.

The kings' residence is the most complex and impressive compound (see Fig. 8.1a). Under Iso-Kalakal, a master of controlling communications for personal power, Pahnkadira became a holy shrine that the high priests and the subking entered once a year to offer tribute. The shrine was equipped with spear racks, offering altars, and special stones on which a ritual narcotic drink was prepared. As late as the mid-nineteenth century, Pohnpeians annually performed a ceremony that involved dancing in canoes facing the islet.

Within the mammoth wall that bordered the entire islet was the residence of the king and his family. The king's chief attendants lived within the lower enclosure walls. In the center of the large enclosure stood a three-tier platform with three firepits, the site of the Temple of Nan Zapue, the Thunder God. Two separate buildings flanked an open area containing a pool for rituals or possibly for swimming. In the west corner was the house of the king; his family lived opposite him, in the southeast corner; each house had its own guardian wall.

Other houses were like the king's house but smaller. Coastal houses of Pohnpei were generally built on rectangular stone platforms that rose above high tide. Such platforms were usually about 60 feet (nearly 6 meters) square for commoners, up to 800 feet (74 meters) square for nobles, and up to 1,470 feet (136 meters) square for

kings. The houses usually faced to the northeast to catch the prevailing winds. Ranging in size from 10 by 6 feet to 20 by 40 feet (3 by about 2 meters to 6 by 12 meters), they resembled Polynesian houses (see Chapter 5). The walls had open spaces for windows, closed with wickerwork shutters. The floor, also of bamboo wickerwork, was "soft as a carpet," according to descriptions from early nineteenth-century travelers. A firepit in the center of the house floor was used not for cooking, but for warming the old and the ill, whose bodies are more sensitive to slight changes in temperature. People slept on mats with blankets woven of tapa cloth from the bark of mulberry trees. Cooking and many other activities took place outside the house.

Monumental Nan Madol was built of two permanent materials, basalt and coral. The Pohnpeians quarried and hewed basalt on the main island at several quarries. Carbon-14 studies show that basalt was in use by 1260 C.E. at the latest. During construction, the builders used levers, inclined planes of coconut palm trunks, and strong ropes of hibiscus fiber to move the basalt blocks from the quarries to bamboo rafts, which ferried them to the individual island. On the island, they were placed to form the outline of a podium or platform (see Fig. 8.2). Several basalt rocks still lying on the floor of the lagoon show that the Pohnpeians did not always manage these rafts successfully.

Coral, mostly in the form of loose rubble from the reefs of the lagoon, was used to fill and pave the islet cores. Lightweight, easy to pass from hand to hand, and (slowly) self-replacing, it was a reliable material. As flooring, it was porous, a great advantage for a seaside site that also received heavy rainfall.

Builders filled in the frame with coral until it reached the planned height, usually about 6 feet above high tide. Peripheral walls and the interior structures of basalt rose from the podium. Builders pried these stones off the rafts, moving them up a series of ramps made of palm logs as many workers heaved on ropes. So difficult were the stones to move overland that a series of islands that could be reached from every side by water were the obvious choice as the site for this complex.

Construction shows two variants of edge and fill. One type was platforms or walls made of basalt logs interlaced at right angles, like log cabins, then filled with coral rubble and earth (see Fig. 8.2). The other was double walls linked by crosspieces—the outer face appearing as giant headers and stretchers, the inner space similarly filled with coral and earth.

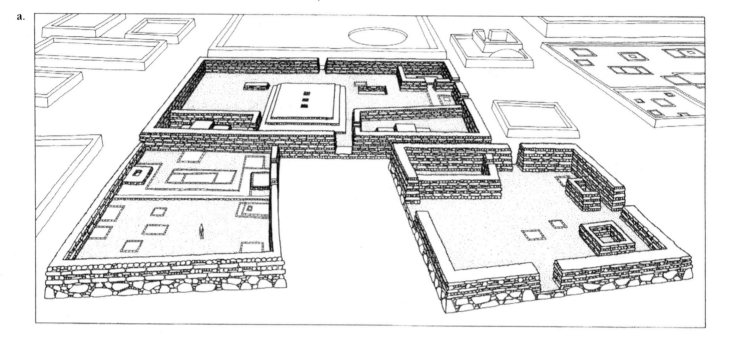

a.

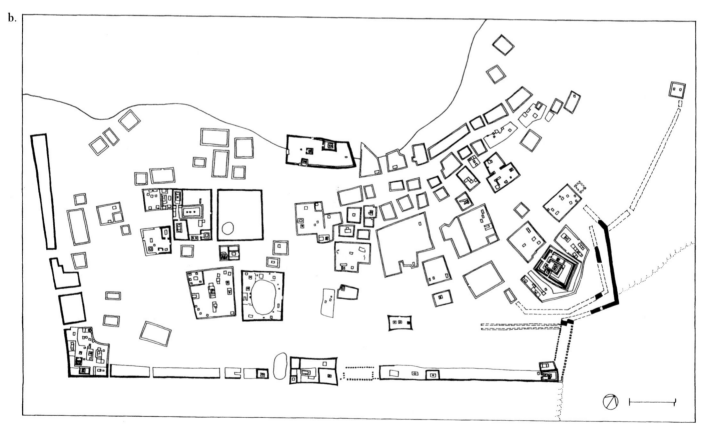

b.

Micronesian Nan Madol is visually different from the extant monumental architecture of Melanesia and Polynesia. Its richness suggests that it may be profitable to sample the architectural history of the other 25,000 islands of Oceania. The first archaeological investigation of Pohnpei using scholarly methods took place as recently as 1963, under the auspices of the Smithsonian Institution. W.N. Morgan's 1989 study is not only the first of Pohnpei by an architect, but also a pioneer study of Oceanic architecture by someone with the relevant architectural background.

SOURCES: ASHBY (1987), ATHENS (1983), COIFFIER (1990), LEHNER (1996), MORGAN (1989), L. POLK (PERSONAL COMMUNICATION).

Great Zimbabwe in East Africa

Zimbabwe (formerly Rhodesia), located in southeastern Africa between the Kalahari Desert and Mozambique, about 250 miles from the Indian Ocean, has fascinated historians and archaeologists since the rediscovery of ancient stone ruins there in the early nineteenth century. Zimbabwe was settled during the Iron Age (ca. 1000 B.C.E.), and a flourishing culture existed there centuries before Arab or European explorers had learned of the riches of the area, especially its gold mines. Once gold from these mines began to be traded through markets in Kilwa, Tanzania, in the late sixteenth century, treasure seekers were lured from afar. Within a few centuries, Zimbabwe was an important trade center with links to the Indian and coastal trade routes that connected East Asia,

India, Arabia, and East Africa (see the map of Africa in the Appendix). According to archaeologist D. Beach, from the beginning of stone construction at Great Zimbabwe until about 1550, when the area was abandoned, its Bantu-speaking population steadily increased to a high of around 18,000, with a ruling class of about 500.

Great Zimbabwe's importance in the history of architecture lies in its stone monuments, covering about 60 acres, which attest to the sophisticated architectural development of a unique society and are unsurpassed by those of any other sub-Saharan African culture. The ruins, including towers and walls, lying about 17 miles (27 kilometers) southeast of Fort Victoria, offer evidence of a society whose monumental architecture was designed to express power.

A Portuguese historian wrote in 1552 about the ruins of a stone fortress located in the mining country in Zimbabwe. The local inhabitants called the fortress Symbaoe—"house of stone"—but knew little about them. In 1867 an American hunter rediscovered the mysterious stone ruins. Others came to investigate, including K. Mauch, a German explorer (1871), who believed that the hill fortress represented the biblical Solomon's temple on Mount Moriah and that an elliptical building in the valley below was modeled after the Queen of Sheba's Jerusalem palace, which, according to the Bible, she occupied in the tenth century B.C.E.. English journalist R. Hall supported Mauch's theory about the origins of the Zimbabwe ruins, a theory that was probably based on thirteenth-century (or earlier) Arabian or Ethiopian legends and the prevailing climate of nineteenth-century romanticism. In 1890, the English statesman and financier

Figure 8.1. *Nan Madol, on Pohnpei in the Caroline Islands, Micronesia.* **a.** *View of Pahnkadira, the royal residence compound, oblique view. These structures are from 1300–1600 C.E.. The rectangular main enclosure (top) of the islet measured 105,500 square feet (9,709 square meters). In the west corner of the large rectangle at the top center of the view is the secondary enclosure of the house of the king; its 8-foot-thick (2.44 meter) walls surround a courtyard 63 by 107 feet (19.2 by 32.6 meters), in which stands a house platform, 32 by 42 feet (9.75 by 12.8 meters). The king's family lived opposite him, in the southeast corner, within an enclosure 94 by 135 feet (28.65 by 41.15 meters) in which there is a dwelling platform, 64 by 67 feet (19.51 by 20.42 meters). At the center is the platform for the sanctuary of the chief god, and in the open area between the sanctuary and the family's house there is a pool for rituals or possibly for swimming. A western extension (bottom left) of another 33,500 square feet (3,112 square meters) housed the king's chief attendants inside lower enclosure walls.* **b.** *Plan of the ceremonial center and residence of priests and kings, erected on islands artificially enlarged and heightened to lift buildings above high tides and storms. The royal residence is at the left center.*

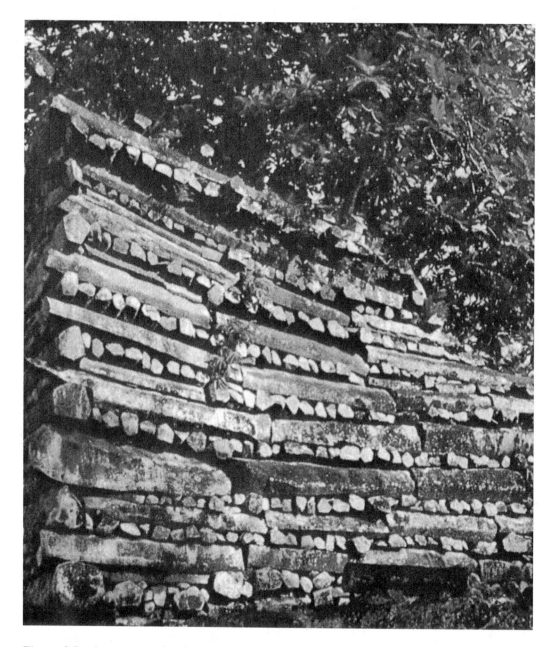

Figure 8.2. *Construction detail, Nan Madol. The platforms were designed to raise buildings above storm tides. The "logs" are basalt prisms up to 19 feet (5.8 meters) long. The basic construction method for foundations and walls consists of cages of basalt logs up to five tons (4.5 metric tons) in weight, filled with lighter coral, with buildings on top.*

Cecil Rhodes became fascinated with the ruins and sponsored an investigation.

A more scientific approach began with 1905 excavations by Egyptologist David Randall-MacIver, who deemed the ruins African in origin and dated them to between 1000 and 1500 C.E. After excavating at Zimbabwe, English archaeologist Gertrude Caton-Thompson agreed in 1929 that the ruins were ethnically African origin but dated them to the ninth century C.E. Caton-Thompson concluded that the plans and details of the site were "typically African Bantu," indicating "a mature civilization of a high kind, originality, and amazing industry." Yet these findings were not generally accepted, possibly because they conflicted with prevalent racial and cultural biases. More recently, archaeologists, historians, and the general public have acknowledged that the site's creators were Bantu-speaking Africans.

Great Zimbabwe has two sets of buildings. One group is situated on an eminence called the Acropolis because of its 350-foot (107-meter) height (see Figs. 8.3 and 8.5). Below the Acropolis is the second group, known as the Great Enclosure, an elliptical area about 300 feet long by 200 feet wide (90 by 60 meters). It is surrounded by a granite wall four feet (1.3 meters) thick and about 830 feet (253 me-ters) in circumference. Pierced by three entrances, the wall varies in height to a maximum of 35 feet (11 meters). Its sections were built between existing granite boulders, making it almost impenetrable. Some 15,000 tons (13,600 metric tons) of stone were used in the construction of the wall. In the earliest phase, 1000–1300 C.E., the courses were laid irregularly with untrimmed stones and without foundations. The sections built between 1300 and 1400 are of cut stones laid in courses without mortar and are straighter and are secured in trenches. Workers broke the granite stone into sheets by heating it with fire and then used iron and stone tools to shape the sheets (see Fig. 8.3). The top layer formed a decorative chevron pattern that reflects similar examples from the east African coast.

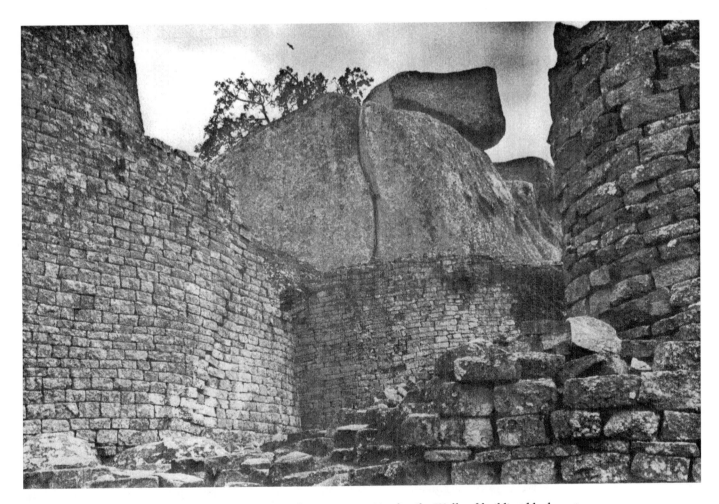

Figure 8.3. *Acropolis, Great Zimbabwe, southern Africa, construction details. Walls of building blocks cut from thin granite sheets are fitted closely together around a huge boulder, making the interior space almost impenetrable.*

One of the major structures in the Great Enclosure is now called the Great Temple. Investigators believe that it served as a dwelling for the ruler, his wives, and courtiers, as well as the center of ceremonial and political activities. Within the outer perimeter, other walls created labyrinthine corridors. Archaeologists have found huts, granaries, and shrines within the enclosure, as well as many rooms whose purposes are not known.

One of the most intriguing shapes is a solid conical tower whose use has not been identified (see Fig. 8.4). Once rumored to have been a hollow reservoir for royal treasures, it proved to be solid. Adventurers tried to gain access to its interior—to no avail. Another suggestion is that the tower is a phallic symbol; still another is that it was Muslim in origin, perhaps inspired by the minaret. It is possible that Zimbabwean traders could have seen examples of Muslim minarets and imitated them without

adopting the Muslim faith. This cone is 17 feet (5.18 meters) across at the base and 34 feet (10.36 meters) tall. It has been described by R. Summers, as "the finest technical and architectural achievement in these, or any other, Rhodesian ruins."

The other major group of ruins at Zimbabwe, the so-called Acropolis (Figs. 8.5 and 8.6), presents an image of strong defensive works. Beach believes that it was primarily intended to convey absolute power—an appropriate image, as Zimbabwe's rulers exerted political control over much of the surrounding area. Although stones of the Acropolis were initially laid to fill in the spaces between natural outcrops, eventually individual walls were laid separately to form a continuous manmade wall similar to the wall of the Great Enclosure. (See also the fortification wall at Saqsaywaman, Peru, discussed later.)

Carbon-14 dating has documented a sequential, soci-

Figure 8.4. *Great Zimbabwe. The completely solid conical stone tower is one of the most perplexing elements in the Great Enclosure, a large area below the Acropolis. Standing 30 feet (9 meters) high and located near an outside wall, its purpose is unknown. Is it a signal tower, granary, phallic symbol, or celestial observatory?*

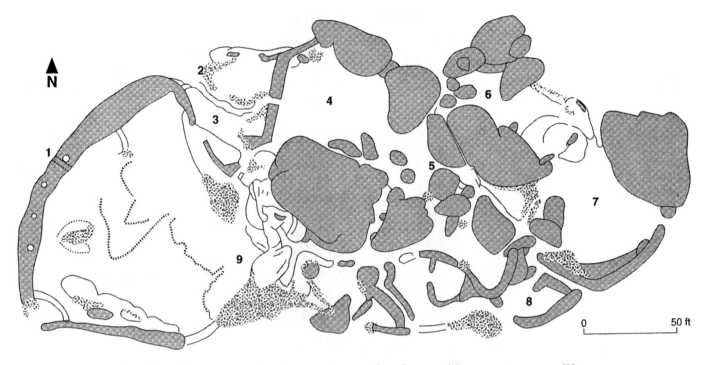

Figure 8.5. *Plan of Great Zimbabwe. Acropolis, showing the central enclosures: (1) western entrance, (2) entrance from the northwest ascent, (3) platform enclosure, (4) cliff-rock enclosure, (5) central passage, (6) balcony enclosure, (7) eastern enclosure, (8) recess enclosure, and (9) covered passageway. This 350-foot (107-meter) high "hill fortress" overlooks the elliptical Great Enclosure and the valley below. Although the location seems to be ideal for defense, many believe it was constructed as a royal compound for Shona leaders and their families.*

etal evolution between the first occupation, in the first millennium, and the fourteenth to fifteenth centuries, when many stone walls and stone houses were constructed. According to Beach, the final version of the Acropolis probably dates to a period between the eleventh and fifteenth centuries, the high point of Zimbabwean culture.

The Acropolis plan is divided into four sections: eastern, western, and southern enclosures and covered passageway. We do not know the purposes of some of these enclosures, but their elevated location suggests that they may have been used for defense. The most sacred area was in the Eastern Enclosure, where archaeologists have discovered stylized replicas of long-necked birds carved in soapstone. This area may also have contained a ceremonial site where priestly offerings were prepared.

By the end of the thirteenth century, several other settlements with elevated fortified areas had appeared in the region, as had smaller villages. The clustered ruins of many buildings and small stone enclosures are scattered across the Zimbabwe valley floor for 99 acres (40 hectares). The dwellings in these villages originated as structures of mud and straw; later builders translated them into stone. The number of dwellings indicates a large, settled community.

Some of the buildings were probably the dwellings of the Shona, the ruling class from the thirteenth to the fifteenth centuries as the Bantu-speaking population steadily increased. The Shona controlled the economy, especially the lucrative gold trade, and expressed their political and economic control in architecture. Merchants in the service of the Shona exported metal jewelry and textiles. In turn, foreign imports—"prestige goods," such as glass, shells, and porcelain—came to Great Zimbabwe, where they became symbols of Shona importance and authority relates archaeologist A. Shernatt. After 1500, however,

Figure 8.6. *Great Zimbabawe, view from within the Acropolis.*

there was a general decline in both the population and the quality of building. Builders used stone of lesser quality and laid it less skillfully. By about 1550, the site had been abandoned, and for years, persistent myths about hoards of ancient treasure led gold seekers to ransack the ruins. By the beginning of the nineteenth century, treasure hunters looking for the legendary King Solomon's mines had registered 114,000 gold claims, which included claims for the gold thought to exist there, but no one uncovered the hoped-for legendary treasures. In 1895, two Johannesburg investors formed the Ancient Ruins Company, Limited, to investigate the monuments at Great Zimbabwe, and the British South Africa Company granted them the right to exploit the ruins. In 1902, however, the legislative council of Southern Rhodesia passed an ordinance to protect the ruins, and scientific study began.

Africans continued to build stone walls as late as the 1700s in other parts of southern Africa, but none of these constructions matched the significance of Great Zimbabwe. Like the stone structures of Nan Madol, Great Zimbabwe—culturally and geographically miles from Oceania—is an expression of localized sociopolitical power.

SOURCES: BEACH (1993), CATON-THOMPSON (1931); DAVIDSON (1959), 250–52; FAGE (1978); MCINTOSH (1998); SHERRATT (1980); SUMMERS (1963).

EMPIRE BUILDING

Expressions of imperial power take many forms. One form is the war of aggression against neighboring countries that exhibits and enhances military might. The Chinese, in the interests of preserving and building their empire, took another path. They chose to enclose their country within a monumental wall. And on the other side of the world, in Peru, a fortress helped first the Inkas and then the Spanish to exert their power over an extended South American empire.

The Great Wall of China

Chinese rulers of the Han, Sui, and Ming dynasties built walls in the mountainous regions of northern China as expressions of political policy. A wall can be defined as a structure built for defense and security or to enclose an area; simply put, it keeps something in or keeps something out. The walls protecting China were intended to do the latter.

Immense mountain ranges have isolated China from her neighbors in the north for centuries, serving as natural barriers against the incursion of invaders. As early as the fifth century B.C.E. and for several centuries thereafter, the Chinese found it necessary to supplement these natural boundaries by building small wall sections as additional defenses on the north and west sides of the mountain ranges. Although these early wall sections served to separate warring Chinese kingdoms, the primary purpose was to keep nomadic herdsmen from invading the cultivated fields of the central plain, where the sedentary Chinese practiced agriculture. Constructed to link watchtowers and battlements, at strategic points, historian J. Needham explains that some sections of wall had eight to twelve towers per mile. The walls both deterred attacks and provided a vantage point from which sentinels could warn if an attack appeared imminent. They were the embryonic beginning of one of the world's greatest architectural accomplishments (see Fig. 8.7).

At first, the threat of invasion was sporadic and isolated. Over several centuries, however, the nomadic invaders grew stronger and more unified. Counterattacks on the marauders' camps by Chinese farmers were not practical, and appeasement was of questionable success. The Chinese saw no alternative to the construction of walls as a protective measure.

In the second century B.C.E., military strategists suggested the establishment of strongly fortified walled towns, to be administered by the army, along the borders. The towns would include farmers who could provision the army and aid in defense against the Xiongnu tribes, made up of a group of nomadic herdsmen. By the third

century B.C.E., the first Ch'in emperor, Qin Shi Huangdi,[20] had unified China. His army of approximately 300,000 warriors defeated the northern invaders and was pressed into service to construct connections between earlier walls to form the original Great Wall. Later rulers undertook reconstructions of the walls in the Ordos region of northern China and the northeast corner of the Huang Ho River in the sixth and seventh centuries C.E.. For several centuries as Dai W. observes, after that time, the Chinese kept up the walls but did little additional building. As historian J. Needham observes, there were "periods of importance and periods of decay" as political policy fluctuated. Nonetheless, conflict between the nomads and the farmers requried the Chinese to maintain a continuing system of defense throughout many centuries.

During a period of internal conflicts (ca. 500–221 B.C.E.), the country itself split into warring kingdoms. Widespread construction of walls and fortifications, some connected to the Great Wall and visible on maps of that wall, resulted from this localized civil strife.

By the early Tang dynasty (618–907 C.E.), the government was more stable and interest in wall building decreased. The emperor Taizong (also called Li Shih-min; 626–649 C.E.) believed that the Great Wall was of little strategic value and eliminated the patrols guarding it. Military strategists now questioned the need to maintain the wall, suggesting that offensive, rather than defensive, measures provided the best protection for China, as Wenbao points out. Interest in wall building lagged; instead, China expanded her borders into other areas, such as Manchuria and Korea.

Leaders of later dynasties were constantly being threatened by the ever-increasing strength of invading armies, especially the Mongolians, who had conquered some northern Chinese border kingdoms. The wall sections, however, had become fragmented and ineffective, so China resorted to bribery and other methods of appeasement. These methods failed in the long run, and in the thirteenth century the Mongolian leader Genghis Khan conquered the area around present-day Beijing. Although

---

[20]The first legendary Emperor Huang Ti (Yellow Emperor) ruled in 2697 B.C.E.; the Ch'in dynasty Emperor Shih Huang-ti ruled in 221–206 B.C.E.; Shih was his surname, and he probably adopted the given name Huang-ti or -di as a claim to be like the first legendary emperor. *Encyclopedia Britannica*, 15th ed., Vol. 3, 220–22.

Figure 8.7. *Great Wall of China near Beijing. A nineteenth-century engraving shows members of a German expedition studying portions of the wall. The average height of the Ming wall is 25 feet (8 meters) and the width is from 15 to 30 feet (5 to 9 meters) at the base, sloping upward to approximately 12 feet (4 meter) at the top. In many sectors, the wall is topped with battlements and interspersed with towers. This section of the wall continues to the tops of the mountains in the background.*

the Chinese strongly defended the wall at key points, most sections were minor impediments to Genghis's campaigns of conquest throughout China and beyond. His grandson Kublai Khan, who became emperor of all China in 1279, developed a strong military force, which resulted in Mongolian rule over China; in general, his reign was one of economic and cultural advances.

The Mongols ruled China for almost ninety years until the Chinese finally drove them out. The Ming dynasty (1388–1644 C.E.) arose and took a new interest in the wall: Mongols outside China still posed a military threat, and the emperor's military advisers suggested that the Great Wall should be rebuilt. The Ming program of repairs and extensions to the wall, the most ambitious architectural project that the world has known, eventually evolved into a defense system that stretched across northern China for almost 4,000 miles (6,000 kilometers). Although construction of the Great Wall continued under several different dynasties, the Ming sections are the most well preserved.

In his discussion of the Great Wall, historian Luo Z. traces the 170 years of collective effort by both patrons and laborers to strengthen the wall—a time span similar to that required for the building of St. Peter's basilica and piazza in Rome during the Renaissance and Baroque periods. The latter project took over 200 years and involved numerous popes, architects, and workmen. Both projects reflect the determination of a concentrated imperial effort.

Work on the rebuilding started on the defensive line near Jiayuguan Pass on the western perimeter. From there, the wall twists, as Luo Z. has observed, like a dragon, eastward through the mountainous regions of the Hexi Corridor, skirts parts of the Gobi Desert, and then advances toward the town of Wuwei, where it branches to the south following the contour of the terrain. The wall winds through greatly contrasting terrain—vast deserts in the northwest; forests and farmlands in the northeast; valleys, hills, rivers, and lakes to the south; and immense mountain ranges. Thousands of fortresses, gates, watchtowers, and settlements were built along the wall (see Fig. 8.7). Their placement suggests that in those days the perceived danger was from Manchuria.

The wall ends at the Manchurian border (now Liaoning province). But during the Song dynasty (960–1280 C.E.), as Luo Z. points out, a fence of trees extended it 300 miles (483 kilometers) farther east. The 400-mile (644-kilometer) portion of the Great Wall near Beijing is the best preserved.

The preservation of any man-made structure depends on many factors. Among the most important are the materials used and the methods employed in construction. The builders of the Great Wall used readily available local materials that differed from place to place. The Ming wall, of fired brick and tile, is south of the Qin dynasty's tamped-earth wall. Other sections were of stone or timber.

The average height of the Ming wall is 25 feet (7.6 meters), and the width is 15 to 30 feet (4.5 to 9 meters) at the base, tapering up to about 12 feet (3.6 meters) at the top. Where the wall rose steeply, the builders broke wall sections into steps. Thousands of military and civilian laborers wound their way up narrow mountain roads carrying rocks and bricks in baskets that hung from horizontal rods on their shoulders; sure-footed animals brought more materials. The civilians were either peasants press-ganged into service or convicts. The organization, direction, and provisioning of so many laborers was a major accomplishment, comparable in scope to building the Egyptian pyramids.

From its beginning and continuing through the Ming dynasty, the Great Wall was primarily a military undertaking. Generals were charged with overseeing the work, relying on the collective effort that is characteristic of the Chinese. References to the cooperation appear on stone inscriptions giving names, dates, and other information about the completion of a particular wall section. The chain of command was well organized, and there was efficient communication between military and civilian authorities, attesting to the collaborative effort that produced positive results.

Beacon towers were designed so that no obstacles would obstruct the view of the signal from a distance, much like the third-century C.E. eastern Roman frontier, where a series of forts defended the empire against invaders from the northeast and Persians from the east. Roman fortresses were set approximately 50 miles (81 kilometers) apart and manned by soldier-farmers whose families lived with them; the Chinese also followed this practice. Roman fortresses evolved into settlements, as did those established by the Chinse along the Great Wall.

The Great Wall's planners benefited from the experience of previous builders, studying written texts and military manuals, as well as the terrain. Some of the guidelines and manuals provided drawings from which builders could select stylistic details, so that fortresses and watchtowers varied in style and decoration, adding an aesthetic element to the purpose for which they were constructed. The wall was intended to offer an imposing visual display of military power to those on its far side—with decorative details chosen to display the strength of Chinese culture and to overawe the nomads.

The cultures on the two sides of the wall were not always at war. They traded, the nomads bartering horses for grain and silk, and sometimes commerce even had governmental sanction. Migration between the two groups was not uncommon during peaceful periods. According to historian Dai W., during the time of the Han dynasty (third century C.E.), members of the Xiongnu tribes turned to agriculture and moved into Han Chinese territory, while some of the Han people crossed over to live in the nomadic regions. Intermarriages, often unions between royal families, also took place. The wall that was built to keep the enemy out in times of war may have served as a meeting place for social integration between the two cultural groups in times of peace.

Was the Great Wall an effective defensive barrier? Yes—at specific times and in specific places. Historian J. Needham argues that it was quite effective in keeping out troops of nomadic horsemen. Storming the wall or building ramps over it took time during which the Chinese could muster reinforcements. However, against strong, unified invading forces, such as those of Genghis Khan, the wall slowed but did not prevent the enemy advance.

Modern technology has made the original purpose of the wall obsolete, of course. Yet two-fifths of Mongolians today are nomads who roam with their caravans, as they did centuries ago, following their ancient practices of trade and animal husbandry. China still keeps a watchful eye on the Mongols when they cross over the Chinese border into Tibet and limits the amount of merchandise they can trade.

Neglect, lack of funds for maintenance, and other problems have taken their toll on the Great Wall. Only portions of it are now open to the public as tourist attractions. It is astonishing not only that so large an undertaking could have been conceived as necessary and possible but that it was completed, given China's immense size and the multiple challenges the builders faced. Considerations of topography, planning, organization of labor, materials, methods of financing, and a host of other concerns attest to the determination of the Chinese to erect such a monumental barrier for the protection of their empire.

SOURCES: DAI (1981), LUO (1981), NEEDHAM (1971), WALDRON (1990).

Saqsaywaman Fortress, Peru

On a spur of the plateau above the city of Cuzco, Peru, stands the fortress and shrine called Saqsaywaman (Saccsayhuaman, Saccsauma). In plan (see Fig. 8.10), ancient Cuzco resembles a giant mountain lion, with Saqsaywaman as its head. One of many fortresses in the Inka empire, Saqsaywaman is attributed to the ruler Pachakuti (Pacchakuti, Pachacutec), who also built Inka Cuzco. Yet the fortress has been dated to as early as 1400, and Pachakuti came later, in the mid-fifteenth century. Perhaps Pachakuti transformed an existing complex; his project supposedly consumed the labor of twenty thousand men for thirty years.

Although only 3,280 feet (1000 meters) from Cuzco's central plaza, the fortress is about 768 feet higher (234 meters) and is thus conspicuous from every part of the city. The physical proximity of fortress to city was dramatically evident during the 1534 battle for control of the city, when the attacking Inkas showered missiles from the fortress onto the Spanish troops occupying the city below.

We suggest that the massive structure of Saqsaywaman was intended to manifest and maintain power, symbolizing and enhancing the Inka conquest of the valley, the city of Cuzco, the whole central portion of Peru, and the coastal areas. This control was religious, royal, and military, so it is no wonder that all three realms are apparent in the structure.

Saqsaywaman is surrounded on three sides by mountains rising to 13,000 to 16,000 feet (4,000 to 5,000 meters) high, shaped by glaciers, temperature changes, and rain. Toward the south edge is the fort with its extensive walls (see Fig. 8.8). To the north rises the mountain of Rodadero with the rock called the "Inka throne," natural slides (probably surface evidence of faults), and terraces. The available building site consisted of two hills and a plateau at 11,700 feet (3,566 meters), culminating in a precipice—the name Saqsaywaman refers to falcons or hawks, and certainly the brink of a tall precipice would be an ideal launching place for birds of prey. The archaeological area occupies about 124 acres (0.5 square kilometer), centered on the fortress near the edge of the cliff. The pageant known as the Inka Feast of the Sun took place on the rectangular area between the two hills, on the opposite side of the fortress from the cliff.

Like the builders of Zimbabwe (discussed earlier), the Inkas put their greatest effort into walls (see Figs. 8.9 and 16.1), rather than complete, roofed buildings. On the plateau of Saqsaywaman, natural outcrops determined the

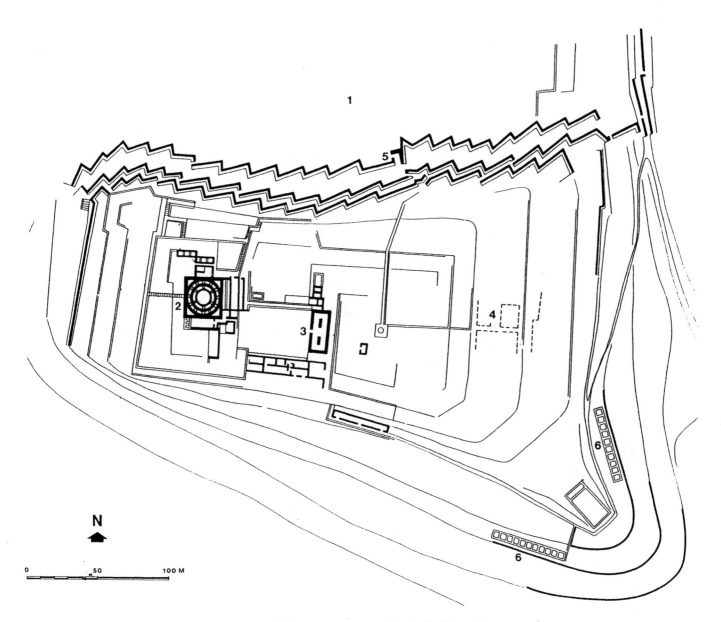

Figure 8.8. *Plan of Saqsaywaman fortress complex, Cuzco, Peru. This plans shows the terrace for ceremonies (1), towers (2, 3, 4), the principal entrance (5), and storerooms (6). Three lines of massive walls, totaling 1,800 feet long and up to 59 feet tall (548.64 by 17.98 meters), with terraces and parapets (see Fig. 8.9), make up the structure. An entrance passage led into each enclosure. Salients (zigzag walls) ranged in size from 27 by 14 feet (8 by 4 meters) to 15 by 12 feet (almost 5 by 4 meters) by 10 to 12 feet (3 to 4 meters) tall.*

Figure 8.9. *Wall of Saqsaywaman fortress, showing exquisitely hewn stones. One stone, abandoned before use, was over 1,000 tons (900 metric tons) and might have taken 20,000 men to move, while the largest stone built into the fort is 361 tons (328 metric tons). Compare the size of the stones to the figures in the photograph.*

form of the fortress. The builders artistically combined natural features with man-made walls. They hewed massive blocks of limestone from quarries to the north and east, as well as from the site of the fortress itself; the largest stone in the walls weighs 361 tons (328 metric tons). The stones were fitted together into three lines of massive walls with terraces and parapets (see Fig. 8.8). Additional walls stood on the higher land north of the fortress and on the brow of the cliff to the south toward Cuzco.

These walls were bonded at the inner corners, and some—again like those at Zimbabwe—incorporated outcrops of living rock. Two of the projecting masses of rock were hollowed out for rooms, one square and one round.

(Geologist V. C. Kalafatovich reports the outcrops and the rooms built in hollowed-out rock, but archaeologist J.-P. Protzen does not see the spaces as man-made—what we see depends on what we know.) Of the three towers in the fortress, one has been traditionally assigned to the Inka, the other two to the garrison. The outer walls of the fortress had roomlike niches built into them, and in some places drains pierced the walls. Cisterns were carved into the surface of the rock within the fortress.

Additional ramparts stood on the height behind the central group and on the brow of the hill, toward Cuzco. An entrance passage led into each enclosure; modern excavation and living tradition suggest that the complex consisted of a religious sector, a military sector, a reservoir and canals for water distribution, dwellings, walls and their gates, and storehouses. In the ancient language, the entrance gates were called, "of sand," "of the engineers," and "of the god Viracocha-puncu." Between them stretched the zigzag salients of the strong ramparts.

Saqsaywaman's builders knew how to combine natural and man-made forms artistically. In Chapter 5 we described the stone masonry of the Inkas. A brief examination of the geological basis for this building tradition will illuminate the constraints and opportunities the Inkas encountered. We know of two well-graded roads used for transporting cut limestone from cliffs that edge the plateau some three-quarters of a mile (1,200 meters) away. The limestone here splits off in irregular blocks, unlike the granite at the Inka refuge Machu Pichu, which breaks into regular forms. The quarriers at Saqsaywaman used the natural fractures in the rock. Their working method seems to have been to excavate the earth and debris below a block that had already begun to split off, forcing the block to drop. Then they partly hewed the block before dragging it to the building site. Limestone slabs still lying at the quarry vary in size up to 30 by 8 by 6 feet. (approximately 9 by 2.5 by 2 meters). To fit the stones into place, workers hammered them precisely to break off the edges, then ground the edges for a proper fit.

Rarely do we have detailed information about the geological characteristics of building stones. Saqsaywaman is an exception. Its ramparts are of the local bluish marine limestone, soluble in rain, with poorly preserved fossils, of three varieties—a compact black-and-gray stone; a sandy black-and-yellowish gray stone; and a conglomerate/breccia with cemented veins of calcite and calcarinite. A green diorite with veins of an igneous mineral was also used. Volcanic stones, such as gray and dark gray andesite, brought from a quarry about 18.6 miles (30 kilometers) to the southeast were also used for buildings within the fortress.

Karst caverns and shafts, the products of weathering and erosion of the limestone terrain millions of years ago, are notable features of the plateau. There are two well-known caves on the north face of Rodadero Mountain, one of which, according to local legends, was connected by means of a long tunnel to the site of the Inka Temple of the Sun, now the church of Santo Domingo. But geologist Kalafatovich reports five obstacles to such a connection, the most telling being the fact that the tunnel would often be filled with groundwater. It is unlikely that the Inkas had to rely on secret passages between the fortress and city palace to maintain their power.

Spanish conquerors called the fortress of Saqsaywaman the "ninth wonder of the world." Yet they began to demolish it immediately after the conquest, probably to keep it from being used by the newly subdued Inkas. Today only the largest stones survive in situ, the smaller ones having been reused elsewhere in Cuzco.

Saqsaywaman manifested the power and sophistication of the Inkas to design an enormous structure; to find and organize materials and manpower for construction; to control the quality of design and finish; to carry out the construction while also building many large palaces, temples, and festival halls in Cuzco; to divert waters that could have been troublesome at the site to the city where they were needed; and, especially, to preempt a potentially threatening site for a dynastic monument that combined fortress and shrine. Its later history reminds us of the power of the Europeans, who invaded with guns and horses, displaced the Inkas, and succeeded to their power. Yet although it is largely a ruin, Saqsaywaman has, to some extent, survived the brief Inka empire and the longer-lasting empire of the Spanish.

SOURCES: BRUNDAGE (1967), GASPARINI AND MARGOLIES (1980), KALAFATOVICH (1970), PRESCOTT (1856), SQUIER (1973).

COLONIALISM AND NATIVE TRADITIONS

In the mid-twentieth century, as World War II ended, many cultures successfully revolted against colonialism. All over the world, people who had long been ruled by foreigners rose up and demanded sovereignty. Given the polemics of the time, it was easy to believe that Europeans were the most nefarious colonizers, with the Americans not far behind.

It is instructive, therefore, to examine the colonizing behavior of other cultures. In Peru, the Inkas took over the middle Andean territory in the fifteenth century, but within a century were displaced by the Spanish. In India, the Mughals, a mixed group of Middle Eastern peoples, were one of a series of invaders of which the Europeans have been only the most recent.

Inka and Spanish Changes at Cuzco

Cuzco is the original pre-Inka name of the Peruvian settlement, but the impressive capital that was discovered by the Spanish in 1532 was constructed after the Inkas conquered the valley in the early fifteenth century. The Inkas rebuilt Cuzco in their image, and the Spanish who conquered them, in turn, changed it to suit their own needs, especially during the sixteenth and seventeenth centuries.

An enormous central plaza was the focus of Inka social life (see Fig. 8.10). After 1450, the ninth ruler, Pachakuti Inka Yupanqui, laid out this plaza, punctuated by a tower and a stepped platform used as an altar, shrine, and throne. The area was originally swampy, but his

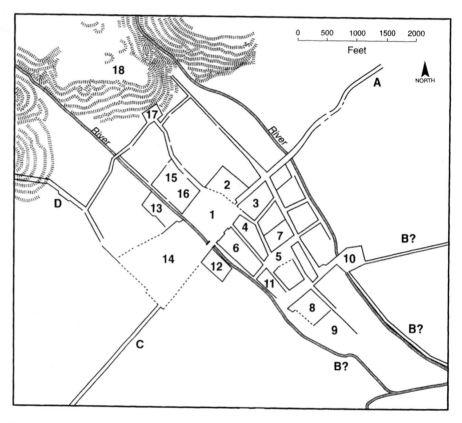

Figure 8.10. *Map of Inka Cuzco, with arrangements before 1532. The map shows (1) the Great Plaza, 400 by 300 feet in size (120 by 90 meters), called Haucaypata, with Suntuiwasi Tower and other shrines; (2) the palace of Cuysmanco/Kiswarchanca (Quishuarkancha) with Temple of Viracocha; (3) the palace of Hatunkancha/ Yupanqui; (4) the palace of Aqllawasi/Aclla Huasi, compound for Chosen Women; (5) small Intipampa plaza; (6) the palace of Amarukancha (Dragon Yard)/Wayna Qhapaq lineage palace); (7) the palace of Pucamarka or Calis Pucyo Huasi; (8) Coricancha (Qorikancha) or Golden Enclosure, oldest part of city; (9) Puma's Tail/ Pumapchupan, a park; (10) Rimac Pampa plaza; (11) the possible site of the Pound, where sacrificial animals and children were kept until needed; (12) the palace of Mana Huanunca Hauasi; (13) the palaces of Patallacta and Illapakancha; (14) Cusipata plaza; (15 and 16) the palaces of Coracora, Cassana/Pachacatic (or Condorcancha) and Yachawasi; (17) the palace of Colcampata; (18) Saqsaywaman fortress, palace, and shrine; A, B, C, D are the four major roads leading to the four quarters of the empire; the location of B is disputed. Two rivers bracket the oldest part of the city, the one through the center is the Sapi.*

builders tamed the spring (now visible in a fountain be-hind the Holy Family chapel of the cathedral). However, water control had begun even earlier under the sixth ruler, Inka Roca, who planned and began an irrigation system for the area. His engineers built a fifteen-foot-wide (5 me-ter) stone channel about 68 miles long (over 100 kilome-ters) to carry the Huatanay river through the city. In the urban core, the channel ran 20 feet (6 meters) below the surface, with footbridges of large stones cantilevered over it.

Large palace enclosures and festival halls of the rul-ing and noble Inkas dominated the urban core. The ap-parent chronological order of these palaces helps us to un-derstand the development of the city, although caution is necessary, since the fifteenth-century rulers built palaces then for their predecessors' lineages. The "Golden Enclo-sure," set in an open area called Field of Pure Gold, was in the oldest area of city ([8] on Fig. 8.10). It encapsu-lated the house and a small shrine of the first Inka, Manko Capac, and his four sister-wives. A holding area for lla-mas and children—both awaiting sacrifice—also stood in the Golden Enclosure [11].

To the west of the Golden Enclosure, around an enor-mous plaza, stood palaces for the lineages of the second, third, and fourth Inkas, who, like the first Inka, died long before the Inka conquest of Cuzco. The palace of the fifth Inka, Capac Yupanqui, stood to the northwest [15], up-stream along the Huatanay River; the sixth ruler, Inka Roca, later used it as a school for boys. Inka Roca began the palace called Coracora (Weedfield), the northern part [16] of which Pachakuti later finished. At the northeast end of the plaza stood the palaces of the seventh and eighth Inkas [3]. Next on the northeast side [2] stood the tem-ple of Quishuarkancha (Kiswar-chanca), a universal cre-ator god; then an audience and council house separated the palace of the eighth ruler, Viracocha, from the street and plaza. Pachakuti completed the northwest facade of the plaza, building his own palace in the angle next to Coracora and uniting the two structures with a council house facade (the southern part of [16]). This was the largest hall in Cuzco, able to shelter three thousand peo-ple. Another hall was big enough for sixty Spanish horse-men with lances to maneuver in, and several other halls measured 200 by 50 or 60 paces. Each hall was the cor-porate headquarters of a lineage.

The simple limestone facades of these royal palaces contrasted with their rich interiors, as described by Gar-cilaso de la Vega, the son of a Spanish conquistador and an Inka princess. Garcilaso migrated to Spain, where he

had a distinguished career. In the late sixteenth century, he wrote:

> The royal mansions of the Inkas were second to none in the grandeur, opulence, and majesty of everything that pertained to the service of these princes. . . . The sides of the apartments were thickly studded with gold and silver ornaments. . . . Niches, prepared in the walls, were filled with images of animals and plants curiously wrought of the same costly material. . . . The king slept between two sheets made of vicuna wool, which is so fine and in so much demand, that the Spanish brought some to King Philip II for his bedchamber. . . . All the tableware in the house . . . was of solid gold. . . . Each one of these mansions has its bathing suite, with large gold and silver basins into which the water flowed through pipes made of the same metals.

Other palaces belonged to non-Inka nobles who were forced to reside as honored hostages in the southern part of Cuzco. Their servants lived in nearby villages, along roads that led to the parts of the empire from which they came. Greater Cuzco thus became a microcosm of the en-tire empire. Wrote, Pedro Sancho de la Hoz, a contempo-rary and biographer of the conqueror Francisco Pizarro, "It is full of the palaces of magnates, for in it reside no poor folk."[21]

Cuzco was central to Inka mythology. "The Inkas held the whole city as itself a sacred thing. It was one of their paramount idols," according to Garcilaso. From the cen-ter of Cuzco radiated many imaginary lines called *ceques*. The word means ray or sight line, but came to have sec-ondary meanings like the cluster of meanings associated with the English word *place*, which can refer to both spa-tial and social organization.[22]

The concept of ceque informed the Inkas' social and metaphysical structures. As a physical place, a ceque was the region where a ruler's corporate descendants and the groups that supported them lived. A group descending from one ancestor, male or female, formed a marriage class

---

[21]Sancho de la Hoz (1534) was one of the first of a group of writers, including an anonymous writer of 1535, the 1543 re-port of Juan Ruiz de Acr, and Pedro Pizarro's work of 1571; the latter two works describe the rebuilt colonial city (see Rowe and Menzel, 1967).

[22]Descriptions of the ceque system are from ethnohistorian R. T. Zuidema unless otherwise noted.

and could marry only according to the rules of that class. This whole system was devised to regulate marriage, which, in turn, regulated access to property and power. For instance, an Inka ruler typically, came to power at the time of his marriage and served until the marriage of his successor.

Ceques were also thought of as lines along which holy sites were distributed, some four hundred shrines being known near Cuzco. Noble families were responsible for ensuring the holiness of the shrines because there was no separate priestly class. Originally, ceques formed the boundaries between irrigation zones, each linked to a source of irrigation and a direction. The four major roads linking city and hinterland were the dividing lines between the four political sectors and met at the southern edge of the central plaza of the city. Each road had a shrine where Cuzco first came into view and another where it entered the central plaza. The plaza and the nearby Coricancha (Temple of the Sun) were the geographic and political focuses of the ceque system. Ceque "permitted . . . mapping of the values of the culture, in a flexible manner" onto the physical setting of that culture, according to R. T. Ziudema. By associating physical space and mythological meaning in the ceque system, the Inkas converted the environment of their city into a natural agricultural clock and a kind of map, where every person knew his place (compare with the Pueblo Indian calendar, Fig. 7.14).

In 1532, forty years after Columbus discovered the New World, adventurers under Pizarro invaded Peru. Inka society was exhausted from civil war and accustomed to autocratic rule. With the advantage of horses and guns, Pizarro and his men were able to trick the Inka Atahualpa, steal his wealth, murder him, and take over Cuzco. In an attempt to dislodge the Spanish, attacking Inkas burned the city in 1535, but the Spanish were victors and carried off to Spain the silver, gold, and other valuables of the Inka empire. From Cuzco alone, the loot amounted to 580,000 gold pesos and 215,000 marks of silver, not counting the "royal fifth" of gold items too unusual to be melted down into ingots, as the chronicler Sancho de la Hoz reported in 1534.

Prescott, citing Garcilaso and others, wrote that Cuzco "astonished the Spaniards by the beauty of its edifices, the length and regularity of its streets, and the good order and appearance of comfort, even luxury, visible in the numerous population." Estimating the value of their conquest, the Spanish noted that there were 100,000 buildings in the valley, as Sancho de la Hoz recounted:

When the Spaniards [sic] first entered it, there was a great quantity of people . . . more than 40,000 property owners in the city alone, for [including] the suburbs and neighboring districts around Cuzco to [a distance of] 10 or 12 leagues, I believe that there would have been 200,000 Indians, because this was the most densely populated [part] of all these kingdoms. . . . Cuzco, because it is the capital city and residence of the Inka nobles, is large enough and handsome enough to compare with any Spanish city.

In the conquest of 1532, the thatch-roofed buildings of the city suffered from fire and destruction. In 1538, the first bishop of Cuzco commented that most of the city was tumbled down and burned. Extensive rebuilding was necessary. Cuzco's huge central open space was now divided by the Spanish into three sections. The northern section became the Plaza Mayor (A), separated from the next plaza to the south (B and C) by houses, which included that of Garcilaso de la Vega [9]. Finally, the last section of the original open space became a large plaza in front of the university and the church of San Francisco [8] (see Fig. 8.11). R. Rivera Serna records the distribution of house lots to the Spanish. It was easiest to assign new house lots in the destroyed areas of the city or in the south section of the central plaza called Cusipata, not previously built upon.

Most of our knowledge of early colonial Cuzco comes from sixteenth- and seventeenth-century documents and from the surviving walls of the city that the Spanish rebuilt using Inka builders, methods, and materials (see Figs. 8.11 and 8.12).The new houses, like the old ones, were of rough stones with clay mortar, stuccoed and possibly painted; occasionally, a sixteenth-century coat of arms over the entrance or balconies for the windows survives. Temple platforms and council houses were reused as the sites of Christian churches and governmental buildings (see Fig. 8.12). The first cathedral was established on the site of the Temple of Viracocha [1], and Viracocha's palace became the site of the adjacent Chapel of the Holy Family. The Temple of the Sun was replaced by the church and convent of Santo Domingo [6].

Some Inka structures were pressed into service with little change, such as the council house of Inka Huayna Capac, 800 feet long (243.84 meters), reused as the church and convent of the Jesuits ("La Compania"); the same was true of a barracks and a prison [4]. At the foot of the hill of Saqsaywaman, the Spanish built the church and plaza of San Cristobal [12] in front of the earlier granaries and

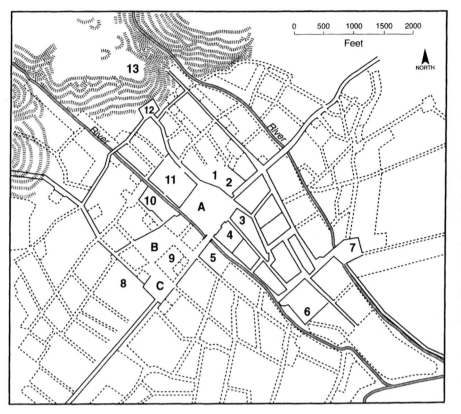

Figure 8.11. *Map of Cuzco as changed by the Spanish in the sixteenth and seventeenth centuries. The map shows A the plaza Mayor or Plaza des Armas; B and C remnants of Cusipata Plaza; (1) the first cathedral, on the site of Temple of Viracocha; (2) Triunfo, governmental offices in Inka Viracocha's audience hall (galpon); (3) Santa Catalina church and convent, in Aqllawasi palace compound for Chosen Women; (4) La Compania, the Jesuits church, also a school, and at the east end, a prison, used for a while as a barracks; (5) La Merced, the later cathedral, on site of the galpone of Mana Huanca Huasi; (6) Santo Domingo church and convent—on the probable site of the Temple of the Sun; (7) Rimac Pampa/Plaza; (8) San Francisco University and Church; (9) the house of chronicler Garcilaso de la Vega; (10) Prefectura (governmental offices), on the site of the galpone Peta Llacta; (11) schools; (12) San Christobal church on the site of the palace of Colcampata; and (13) fortress of Saqsaywaman.*

from the materials of a former royal-lineage palace at Colcompata. Other structures were partially destroyed and rebuilt. The streets of the colonial town continued to be lined with the old masonry walls 35 to 40 feet (9.1 to 12.2 meters) high shielding buildings of one to three stories. Indeed, at eye-level Cuzco still seems an Inka city (A. I. Mundigo, personal communication; see Fig. 16.1). Because of the futility of removing all these walls, the street pattern continued to be quadrilateral but not regular, paved as before with pebbles or stone and centered with stone-lined water channels.

Colonial Cuzco continued as the capital of Peru until the late 16th century and later the capital of its own province, but the decline of political power—indicated by the decay of the road system (see Chapter 5)—eventually isolated the city. Power shifted to the coastal city of Lima, which Pizarro had planned as the new capital housing the viceregal court. In 1877, Engineer E. Squier commented

that for close to three hundred years before his time, it was easier to travel from Lima to New York City than from Lima to Cuzco. The people of Cuzco, still mostly Native Americans, retained during colonial times much of the social system that made survival—if not power—possible in difficult ecological niches (see Chapter 3, Irrigation Systems in Peru).

Because Cuzco was a natural center for control of the string of Andean "islands" of settlement, blessed with a good water supply and a southwest exposure, it became, during fewer than two hundred years, the capital, in turn, of pre-Inka, Inka, and Spanish power in Peru. In each phase, buildings and spaces carried the message of who was in control, as is seen most poignantly in the construction and destruction of Saqsaywaman.

SOURCES: BRUNDAGE (1967), GARCILASO DE LA VEGA (1966), PRESCOTT (1856), RIVERA SERNA (1966), SANCHO DE LA HOZ (1534), SQUIER (1973), ZIUDEMA (1964).

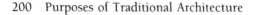

Figure 8.12. *View of Spanish Colonial Cuzco, Peru, from the northeast. In the early seventeenth century, Haucaypata Plaza (at the upper center) was reserved for Spaniards with horses, while the lower square, Cusipata, was for Inkas, their llamas, and market booths. Between the squares is a row of Spanish buildings erected over the river Sapi. At the upper left, Saqsaywaman (here called Senca Urco) is indicated schematically, and just below it San Cristobal, a church built in the ruins of the palace of Colcampata. Near the bottom center, Coricancha is the old Intipampa Plaza, with the tower of the later Dominican church. The tower to the right represents the Church of San Francisco; kneeling figures to the right of the tower indicate the nearby Inka prisons, called Sankayhuaci (the building above the prisoners) and Pinas Huasi.*

Mughals in India: Red Forts at Agra and Delhi

> That wealth and power could make an earthly
> paradise even in the scorching plains . . .
> *Inscription carved in an Audience Hall,*
> *Red Fort, Old Delhi*
> *—quoted in Watson (1975), 118*

Colonialism is the control—political or economic—of one culture by a group of transplanted people from another. The Mughals—Turks, Persians, and Mongols in origin—are a classic example of colonialism. They conquered the greater part of India, settling in enclaves as privileged rulers. Nowhere can there be found more opulent displays of imperial wealth and power than in the buildings that were constructed during Mughal rule (1526–1858). These Islamic rulers needed permanent fortresses to maintain their political power, but the defensive structures they built far exceeded their utilitarian purpose. Mughal society expressed its values in the luxurious fortress-palaces that three rulers—Jalal ud Din Akbar (reigned 1556–1605), his son Nur ud Din Jahangir (1605–1627), and Akbar's grandson Shihab ud Din Shah Jahan (1627–58)—built in the conquered regions of India.

Akbar established the institutional basis of the Mughal empire, with administration in the hands of the military and political elite. This body was made up of Afghans, Persians, and Turks who formed a well-organized ruling class; Indian-Muslims made up a small majority. Mughals were not intolerant, but they did impose hardship on the settled population through taxation to support the building programs and extravagances of the court.

Akbar also set Mughal cultural policy, which provided for a "synthesis between Hindu and Muslim." The ruler acquired his taste for art, literature, and poetry from his Persian mother and expressed it in his patronage of the arts, especially in the decoration of the palace in the Agra fort. From his Turkish father, a military man, he learned how to "command, assimilate and integrate aspects of diverse cultures," traits that he used to advantage in the administration of his government, according to historian I. Lapidus. This attitude is expressed in architectural styles that sought to combine features of each society.

The Mughal conquest began when the first Mughal emperor, Zahir ud Din Babur (reigned 1526–30), gained control of Agra and Delhi. Akbar, Babur's grandson, enlarged and consolidated the empire, which eventually included all northern India and parts of the Deccan, Kashmir, and Sind (Fig. 8.13). He took possession of the Indian Rajput fortresses at Chitor (1567) and Ranthambhor

(1569), invading and annexing prosperous provinces. In 1565 he began building the Red Fort, so-called because of its red sandstone, in the capital city of Agra (see Fig. 8.14). This impressive stronghold was one of his greatest architectural achievements. The fort, located on the banks of the Jumna River in north central India about 124 miles (200 kilometers) south of Delhi, replaced the earlier brick citadel of the Sultan Iskandar Lodi. There may even have been ancient Hindu structures on the site, since many Indian monuments were destroyed during the Mughal reign. Little remains today of Akbar's buildings but the outer walls, gateways, moat, and the Jihangiri Mahal palace.

The Red Fort was both a military fortress and a luxurious palace. Its external appearance was a powerful symbol of military authority. The fort is enclosed with massive double sandstone walls extending 1.5 miles (2.4 kilometers) in circumference. Seventy feet (21 meters) high and 10 feet thick, they are built of solid stones linked with iron rings, pierced with slits for defensive artillery, and protected by crenellated battlements and turrets. A drawbridge over a 40-foot (12-meter) moat leads to the Delhi gate, which is flanked by two octogonal towers inlaid with white marble designs. A staircase leads to the top of the inner gate, from which the marble domes of the Taj Mahal (see Chapter 9) can be seen in the distance. The guarded gates reinforced the message of authority.

The lavishly decorated buildings inside the fort (see Fig. 8.15) expressed another type of power, in direct contrast to the stark military appearance of the exterior. Here, the Mughal princes and their retinues enjoyed a life of luxury that excluded all but a chosen few of the indigenous Hindus—who were, however, provided with a Hindu temple near the fort. Within the palace complex were the emperor's residence, administrative headquarters, military garrison, arsenal, and royal treasury. No strong distinction was made between military and civil service, so the bureaucratic body acquired a militant character.

Of the several palaces built by Akbar within the Red Fort, only the two-story Jahangiri Mahal survives. The Muslims respected the artistry and skill of Hindu craftsmen and employed them in the construction of the palace, which was built in the Hindu tradition. Many Hindu architectural characteristics are evident, such as intricate carvings on the facade and elegantly carved white marble reliefs and brackets that contrast strikingly with the red sandstone pavement of two adjacent courtyards. The main courtyard is surrounded on three sides by a series of symmetrically aligned rooms, such as those found in Hindu palaces. Mughal artistic taste is reflected in rectangular piers with a thin overlay of Islamic floral patterns and geo-

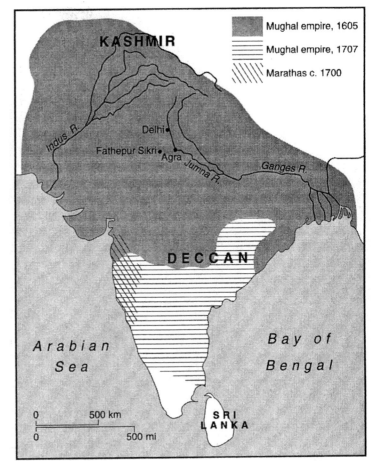

Figure 8.13. *Map of the Indian subcontinent showing the extent of Mughal control in the seventeenth and eighteenth centuries. In 1605, the region was ruled by Mughal emperors, (dark gray). The Marathas of western India were finally conquered about 1700. Horizontal lines indicate their increased territory by 1707. Note that Sri Lanka and the tip of the subcontinent retained their independence.*

metric designs. One side opens onto a courtyard that has three *iwans* (large vaulted niches or portals) facing the court interior, each with marble veneers covering arches and niches, typical of Islamic architecture. On the roof are two pavilions ornamented with similar carvings and inlays of marble. The roof also holds cisterns (tanks) that supplied the palace with water; numbered copper pipe-holes indicated which section of the palace received the water. The integration of indigenous styles with that of the Muslims exhibits the royal policy of conciliation.

Akbar built two other impressive forts, replete with sumptuous furnishings and gardens—one at Allahabad

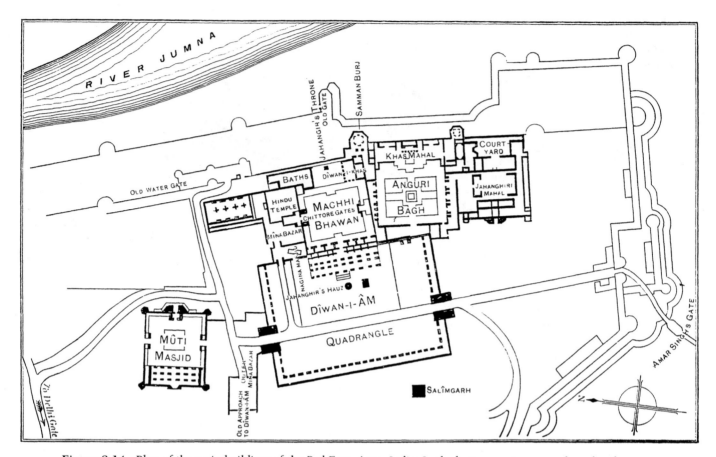

Figure 8.14. *Plan of the main buildings of the Red Fort, Agra, India. In the bottom center, a quadrangle adjoins the Diwan-i-Am, or Hall or Public Audience, begun by Shah Jahan. To the left is the Muti Masjid, or Pearl Mosque, with octogonal pavilions at the four corners. Directly behind the Diwan-i-Am is the Machhi Bhawan, a courtyard with flower gardens, water channels, and shrubbery. To the right of this courtyard is the Anguri Bagh, a typical Mughal garden with a fountain and terraced walkways. This building stands in front of the Khas Mahal, or emperor's private apartments. To the left of the Khas Mahal is an octogonal building believed to be where the imprisoned Shah Jahan died. To the right is the Jahanghiri Mahal, an earlier palace possibly planned by Akbar.*

and the other at Lahore. Many of the gardens mirror the Islamic *char-bagh* layout of Qur'anic gardens (a four-part garden divided by water channels), which, in turn, derived from earlier biblical sources related to the four-part arrangement of the garden of Eden. Akbar's favorite palace was Allahabad, the largest fortress. Little of it remains today, however, because it was demolished in the nineteenth century under British rule. As in the Red Fort, the interior spaces functioned as both living quarters and governmental offices. Akbar's crowning achievement in architecture, however, was the building of a new royal city,

Fatehpur Sikri, his capital from 1570 to 1585. Fatehpur Sikri (1569–1680) is located on a hilltop twenty-five miles southwest of Agra. Following earlier Mughal examples, Fatehpur Sikri, with its splendid palaces, halls, and Great Mosque that exemplified the highest achievements in Mughal architecture, was much like a great palace and mosque. Historian A. Bannister Fletcher relates that skilled laborers formed marble and sikri stone into buildings and pavilions of great delicacy, with carved grilles and windows and wide platforms supported by thin columns and domed roofs. The inhabitants later aban-

Figure 8.15. *Red Fort at Agra. A palace facade within the Red Fort with a decorative surface treatment in tiles that is characteristic of Muslim architecture, with its pointed arches and large iwan marking the entrance. Also note the roof pavilions.*

doned the town because its hilltop location was a poor site for the maintenance of an inadequate water supply provided only by an artificial lake. Yet the elaborate stonework of the buildings that remain is a testament to the technical skills of the builders, shown in the detailed sandstone carving of the palace, the marble screen of a tomb, and the treatment of the porch columns of the Jami Masjid (see Fig. 2.7).

The reigns of Jahangir and Shah Jahan were periods of architectural activity and economic prosperity. Both rulers continued the tradition of royal patronage in the construc-

tion of magnificent buildings that reflected their extravagant taste. When Shah Jahan became emperor, he destroyed most of Akbar's buildings within the Red Fort and built the Di-wan-i-Am (Public Audience Hall). The hall featured a white marble alcove from which he held court and administered decisive judgments seated on a raised throne. In 1648 he added the Pearl Mosque to the complex. Situated in a court-yard paved with white marble, the Pearl Mosque is one of the most beautiful buildings in the fortress.

In 1638 Shah Jahan moved his capital, which he called Shahjahanabad, to (Old) Delhi, where he built a new

Figure 8.16. *A bird's-eye view of the Red Fort and palace, Delhi, India (1639–48). At the front of the sandstone structure is an octagonal tower with an onion dome. The Lahore and Delhi, the two high, main gates, are located at the centers of the side walls. Within the complex, the throne hall (Diwan-i-Am), for public audiences is centered on the axis. In the third courtyard from the front, polo players are seen. Courtyards, gardens, bazaars, pavilions, and other buildings, including a treasury and an arsenal, fill the interior space. Not only a royal residence, the fort served as a center for the administration of governmental affairs.*

palace-fortress (Figs. 8.14 and 8.16). Built of sandstone, it, too, was called the Red Fort and, like the earlier fort, it had high walls and fortified gates. Again, the luxurious interior contrasted sharply with the forbidding exterior. The plan of the fort was orthogonal, with bazaars and gardens leading to the center court of a music pavilion. Legend has it that music was played continuously on the chance that Jahan might appear. The Public Audience

Hall, a single-story pavilion, was at the back of the complex. From the gardens, the Jumna River could be viewed, and marble terraces overlooked sites where elephant fights and other forms of entertainment took place. Cooling waters flowed through channels of interconnecting pavilions, and exquisite marble carvings ornamented cornices and other architectural elements. Every sort of luxury proclaimed the emperor's power and prestige.

One of the more costly examples of imperial indulgence was the Peacock Throne. Studded with sapphires, rubies, emeralds, and other precious stones, it was flanked by two solid gold representations of peacocks. Twelve emerald pillars supported a canopy of beaten gold, studded with pearls. The throne's lavish ornamentation was yet another expression of the extravagant use of state finances for personal pleasure and prestige.

Shah Jahan, who ruled for thirty years, was ruthlessly ambitious, both politically and artistically. Mughal architectural capabilities reached their full extent during his reign; the Taj Mahal was his greatest accomplishment (see Chapter 9). The Mughal empire survived Jahan's extravagance, although it began to decline after the reign of his son, Aurangzeb (1658–1707). Ironically, Shah Jahan died a prisoner of this traitorous son in the Red Fort at Agra in 1666.

"Monuments validate and define the social hierarchy, justifying the social system that built them in a way that words and deeds cannot. They provide a symbolic means to reinforce and preserve social institutions far beyond the life spans of individual leaders," wrote archaeologist J. S. Athens, referring to the important monumental architecture built by the Micronesians of Nan Madol. Similarly, durable and costly stone architecture demonstrated the power of the rulers in Zimbabwe, China, Cuzco, and India. Buildings of mud or bamboo, no matter how practical, do not carry monumental stone architecture's conviction of power and the willingness to exercise it.

SOURCES: BANNISTER FLETCHER (1987), HAMBLY AND SWAN (1968), KING AND LEWCOCK (1978), LAPIDUS (1988), LATIF (1981).

SUGGESTED READINGS

Asher, C. 1992. "Architecture of Mughal India." *The New Cambridge History of India*, Vol. 1. Cambridge, England: Cambridge University Press. High-quality writing and a lucid and thoughtful treatment of the subject.

Athens, J. S. 1983. "The Megalithic Ruins of Nan Madol." *Natural History* 92 (Decmber): 51–60. A good short account; illustrated.

Aveni, A. F. "Horizontal Astronomy in Inkaic Cuzco." In *Proceedings of the Symposium Space and Time in the Cosmovision of Mesoamerica*, 175–79, edited by R. Tichy. Munich: Wilhelm Finkl Verlag. Discusses the use of the landscape as a calendar, similar to its use at Acoma.

Brandt, J. H. 1962. "Nan Matol: Ancient Venice of Micronesia." *Archaeology* 15: 99–107. Contains some information not in the Athens article.

Caton-Thompson, G. 1983. *Mixed Memories*. Gateshead, Paradigm Press. Written by an early excavator, whose analysis of Zimbabwe was rejected for a long time for political reasons.

Davidson, B. 1959. *The Lost Cities of Africa*. Boston: Little, Brown. An early account that takes the history of African building seriously. Well written, with a few illustrations.

Garcilaso de la Vega, G. S. ("The Inka). 1966. *The Royal Commentaries of the Inka*, trans. by X. Livermore. Austin: University of Texas Press. The earliest account of Peru in a Western language by an indigenous person.

Gernet, J. 1981. Forward. *The Great Wall*. New York: McGraw-Hill. The book includes chapters by Dai, pp. 42–51, 158–67, 168–83; and Luo, pp. 140–57. Written by both Western and Chinese scholars, handsomely illustrated with many color photographs and graphics, this book traces the history of the Great Wall, providing a fresh approach to the study of Chinese architecture.

Hambly, G., and W. Swaan. 1968. *Cities of Mughal India: Delhi, Agra, and Fatehpur Sikri*. New York: G. P. Putnam's Sons. Wonderful illustrations in an older but still useful introductory book.

Lapidus, I. 1988. *A History of Islamic Societies*. New York: Cambridge University Press. Basic reading.

Morgan, W. N. 1989. *Prehistoric Architecture in Micronesia*. Austin: University of Texas Press. A pioneering study of Pacific architecture by a person trained in architecture and architectural history. Valuable.

Needham, J. 1971. *Science and Civilisation in China*. Vol. 4, Part 1: Physics and Physical Technology. Cambridge, England: Cambridge University Press. This section discusses the Great Wall.

Pal, P., J. Leoshko, J. Dye, III, and S. Markel. 1989. *Romance of the Taj Mahal*. London: Thames & Hudson and Los Angeles County Museum of Art. A handsome catalog with many color photographs and informative text.

Prescott, W. H. 1856. *History of the Conquest of Peru*. New York: Modern Library. Originally published in 1856. A tour de force of scholarship, beautifully written.

Sherratt, A. 1980. "Zimbabwe. In *The Cambridge Encyclopedia of Archaeology*. New York: Crown. Illuminating and authoritative.

Summers, R. 1963. "City of Black Gold." In *Vanished Civilizations of the Ancient World*, edited by Edward Bacon. New York: McGraw-Hill. A well-illustrated account of Zimbabwe. Conveys the excitement people felt when it was first realized that much had been missing from the conventional histories of Africa.

Waldron, A. 1990. *The Great Wall of China from History to Myth.* New York: Cambridge University Press. In this scholarly work, the author questions previously held assumptions about the building of the Great Wall and presents new insights into its construction and history.

Whitty, A. 1957. "The Origins of the Stone Architecture of Zimbabwe." In *Third Pan-African Congress on Prehistory,* 366–77, edited by J. Clark. A serious early study.

Zuidema, R. T. 1964. *The Ceque System of Cuzco.* Leiden, the Netherlands: E. J. Brill. An account of the several layers of meaning of the ceque system. Not easy reading, but well worth the trouble.

PART IV

Planning and Design

Planners and designers have many concerns, among them land use, building types and uses, and the organization of structures. Possible land-use patterns are myriad, ranging from the ancient city of Mohenjo-Daro in Pakistan, where the same society endured for a thousand years, to the more recent cities of Cuzco in Peru and Toledo in Spain, both of which have seen drastic changes of culture. Other communities illustrate the contrast between cities laid out symbolically and those that seem to have grown by agglomeration. Landscaping, too, offers contrasts: the formal iconography of the Taj Mahal garden and architecture against the precisely informal gardens of the Katsura Villa in Japan.

Building types and uses are as varied as the Mesoamerican ball court, unique to one culture and region, and the house, at once the most universal and most varied type of building. The way people use the space inside buildings also differs. The Mayas, for example, used benches for seating, whereas floor-level living was standard among the Japanese, who knelt on tatami mats, and among the Islamic peoples, who sit on cool, stone floors in summer and warm rugs in winter.

Structures are organizations of mass and void. Some buildings have a void in the center, while others have solid cores. In a third type of organization, buildings can be stretched out along an axis. The great American city planner Edmund Bacon contrasted two types of axis: one, in which buildings are arranged like beads on a string, and another, in which buildings are arranged like beads flanking the string. We examine the former in the Forbidden City of China's capital and the latter in Teohuaticán's Street of the Dead in Mexico.

These examples relate to the question: What do people need? Through architecture, people display their beliefs, relate to nature or overpower it, and place usefulness somewhere on a continuum between merely utilitarian and far above such issues. Do the cities described in these chapters show evidence of professional builders who planned for sustainable architecture, allowing for human variation and sometimes producing the intimate or the sublime? Or was architectural planning merely a tool of the rulers to keep people quiet?

⊞ 9

Land Use

Both urban planning and landscape settings reflect decisions about land use. The persistence of the grid pattern at Mohenjo-Daro in Pakistan illustrates the theoretical basis of some arrangements. In contrast, changing forms of settlement in Toledo, Spain, were affected during many centuries by the different peoples who lived in and altered these communities.

Our Asian examples reveal self-conscious urban forms. Mandala diagrams (see Chapter 2) provide a basis for the organization of Indian cities as well as temples. The Chinese worked out axial plans several millennia ago and used such a plan for their capital city of Chang'an (now Xian); the Japanese borrowed the plan for their new capital, Heijo. These geometric, political plans contrast with the apparently unplanned but subtle adjustments of the Anasazi cliff dwellings at Mesa Verde, Colorado.

Architecture can include landscape. Combined with the formal iconography of the royal tomb, called the Taj Mahal, gardens contribute to the monumentality of the extremely beautiful building. Equally beautiful—but embodying different criteria of expression and a vastly different aesthetic sense—are the gardens and architecture of the princely villa at Katsura in Japan, much admired by the Euro-American modernists for the many layers of meaning incorporated in its simplicity and lack of ornament.

URBAN PLANNING

In considering how any culture uses land, we first ask, To what extent does this society plan its settlements consciously? In colonial America, the settlers of many northeastern towns recreated the winding roads and central common space of the late-medieval English towns from which they came; elsewhere in the world, the impulse to replicate the known, however informally, repeatedly resulted in the re-creation of the urban type called "organic." Two hundred years later, in the very different terrain west of the Mississippi River basin, town builders turned instead to the checkerboard grid pattern focused on a main street—so simple, so easy to lay out. The desire to make a new town simple, clear, and practical in form—as well as approximately equal in economic advantages to all the initial settlers—resulted in the grid type in many areas of the world.

We have some documentary evidence of conscious urban planning in the Americas before and just after European contact. The Spanish conquerors of Mexico City wrote of official Aztec architects whose job was to ensure conformity to accepted standards in the former Aztec capital. Spain had its own solution to town planning in the Americas: In 1573 the Spanish promulgated the Laws of the Indies, which—among other things—guided the physical development of new colonial towns. Spain revised these laws about once a century thereafter. Colonial administrators recorded the actual plans of their new cities and the hoped-for growth of those settlements in a series of maps filed with the Archives of the Indies, at Seville, Spain.

Formal or Organic: Mohenjo-Daro and Toledo

Our knowledge of Mohenjo-Daro comes from archaeological excavations. Although excavation records tell us what has been discovered, they are the observations of later people, not the original builders, so they cannot tell us infallibly how Mohenjo-Daro's inhabitants created or used their buildings. Unlike Mohenjo-Daro, Cuzco and Toledo have been inhabited from their earliest days to the present—but not continuously by the same people. Conquerors and migrants changed these cities. There has been little archaeological excavation at Cuzco, but we can learn much from the unintended survival of old walls, the information garnered from repairs after earthquakes, and sixteenth-century descriptions and drawings. For Toledo, we have even less archaeological information; people have been reluctant to disturb the fabric of a modern Spanish city.

In each of these cities, the unit of agglomeration has been the city block, which can form either a grid or a freer organic form. We use the term *grid* to mean not only the checkerboard, in which blocks are square and regular in size, but other right-angle and quadrilateral patterns. Blocks may be long, narrow rectangles or irregular quadrilaterals; streets can meet at T-intersections, at four right angles, or at oblique and acute angles. Organic growth, on the other hand, is a type of development similar to the natural growth of living things, in which curved shapes predominate. As applied to architecture, it refers to buildings or cities in which form meets the needs of function in a way that is unified, clear, and well integrated but not geometric. Toledo is organic because of its winding streets and blank walls (see Fig. 9.1), perfectly suited to the urbane life of the Moors who configured the city this way (see also Chapter 14, Blank Walls). Similarly, the scattered

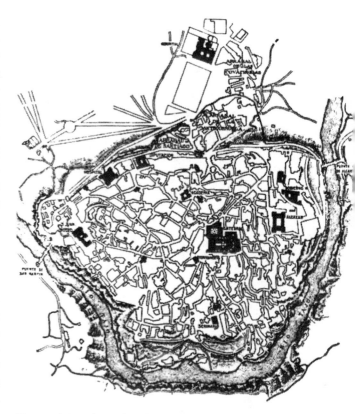

Figure 9.1. *Plan of Toledo, Spain, showing its irregular street pattern from the Moorish period in the Middle Ages. Although the organic plan of the city was not considered suitable for Spanish colonies in the New World, the city's municipal ordinances were the basis of the Laws of the Indies. The tradition of combining medieval and Islamic ideas with Italian Renaissance and Spanish Baroque concepts of urban form strongly influenced the culturally inclusive cities of the Spanish empire.*

mud houses of the Batammaliba (see Chapter 15, Anthropomorphic Architecture) and the bipolar villages of New Guinea (Chapter 4, Big Roof) show irregular development rather than formal plans. Yet organic does not necessarily mean planless.

The simplicity of any two-dimensional plan is contradicted both by the richness of the three-dimensional city and by local variations. Think, for instance, of the grid of eighteenth-century town houses in Philadelphia, set at the edge of the sidewalk and occupying the entire street frontage of each parcel of land. How different from another place—perhaps a twentieth-century suburb of the same city—where houses are set in green lawns, back from the street. Or the different effect in the central blocks of the same city that are now occupied by huge skyscrapers, their dense occupancy overburdening the narrow streets of the first plan. Perhaps all three versions of the grid show conscious planning, but the criteria were different in each case. And, as usual, each plan yielded unintended consequences.

We can describe urban land use both in terms of density, with its benign or harmful effects on economic vitality and physical health, and in relation to many other issues—privacy, for instance. In Mohenjo-Daro, Toledo, and Cuzco, families achieved privacy through the use of blank outer walls.

The recovered ruins at Mohenjo-Daro reveal not only the ancient city, but the modern political truth that it is easier to excavate a dead city than one still in use. Mohenjo-Daro is about 250 miles (400 kilometers) north of Karachi, Pakistan, along the Indus River (see the map of Asia in the Appendix). The site was accidentally discovered early in the twentieth century by investigators who were examining a Buddhist stupa of the second century B.C.E. that stood on its highest point. Finding that the stupa was made of reused ancient bricks, the investigators[23] expanded their search and found a large town with plazas, quadrangular blocks, monumental buildings, and a sewer system—the complete city of a previously unknown civilization, now called the Harappans (see Chapter 3, Granaries at Mohenjo-Daro, and Figs. 3.18 and 3.19). The city flourished from around 2800 or 2500 to 1800 or 1700 B.C.E., overlapping the eras of the Egyptian pyramids and the Mesopotamian city of Ur (roughly 2600 and 2100 B.C.E., respectively).

The contrast between ancient Mohenjo-Daro and the nearby modern town Karkana is extreme, partly because there was such a long time between the two occupations. The walls of Mohenjo-Daro's large houses averaged 5 feet (152 centimeters) in thickness. Most ancient houses also had their own wells and bathrooms with latrines, served by a municipal sewer system (see Fig. 9.2). The modern town has thin-walled houses—some are merely posts connected with wires strung with grass, symbolizing, rather than providing, domestic enclosure. From the standpoint

of thermal comfort and privacy, the earlier people had the advantage. Mohenjo-Daro was not laid out as a perfect grid, but its overall form and individual structures reveal a search for order. So do the engineering projects, such as drainage, that made the settlement possible. The city appears to have been divided into a "citadel" and a lower, residential area with straight streets running north–south and east–west, with sewers set into them to collect household wastes. Between the streets, the houses fill the blocks, which measure 1200 by 600 feet (365 by 183 meters). Although the houses were built at different times, the builders maintained this orthogonal arrangement as periodic floods raised the town level. The citadel on the hill was a complex of municipal buildings, the great bath, pillared hall, the so-called granary, and official or priestly living quarters (see the discussion of the granary in Chapter 3). Excavator M. Jansen estimates that twenty thousand workers could have built these buildings in two years.

The overlay of one culture on another may affect land use, but this did not happen at Mohenjo-Daro—the same culture occupied the city for 1,000 to 1,500 years and rebuilt it by using the melted heaps of their flood-ravaged houses as higher bases on which to build the next set of houses after major floods. Elsewhere, however, changes in culture affected the visible form of cities.

***

The Spanish city of Toledo (see Fig. 9.1) was settled as the fortress-town of Tolentum by the Romans around 190 B.C.E. and still existed in 550 C.E., when it became the capital of a Visigothic kingdom. Both the Romans and the Visigoths appreciated the strategic advantages of the site: a granite hill surrounded on three sides by the gorge of the Tagus (Tajo) River.

In 712 C.E., however, the city came under Islamic rule when a north African people, called the Moors, conquered the site and gave it a walled nucleus called a *medina*, which enclosed the main mosque, international bazaar, and local commercial center. The irregular terrain was conducive to an irregular plan—organically winding pedestrian streets still distinguish Toledo. Through the ninth and tenth centuries the Muslim town prospered, gradually absorbing the surrounding villages.

The Spanish Christians reconquered Toledo in 1085–86, but the town kept its Moorish culture until Spain and Portugal expelled the Moors and Jews at the end of the fifteenth century. At that time, the mosque and other

---

[23]The most famous of the Mohenjo-Daro excavators was M. Wheeler, who worked there from the 1920s. Important contributions were made in the 1960s by the American anthropologist G. Dale. Since 1979, UNESCO has worked to preserve the site, and the Technical University (M. Jansen and others) in Aachen, Germany, has been excavating there since 1983.

Figure 9.2. *Mohenjo-Daro, Pakistan. View of a street at the site, from the second millennium* B.C.E. *or earlier. Note the covered drain, which received waste waters from domestic bathrooms. The walls of houses, usually made of an outer surface of baked brick and a thickness (up to 5 feet, nearly 2 meters) of sun-dried brick, presented blank walls to the passing pedestrians, beginning a venerable Asian tradition.*

Muslim buildings were rededicated to Christian service. The plaza, a horse market since 1176, was later enlarged and still later destroyed by fire. By 1605, it had been rebuilt, but it was never evenly and uniformly arranged because of the difficult terrain.

The last major change was Charles V's sixteenth-century rebuilding (in a Renaissance mode derived from Italian models) of the Alcázar castle, off to the east of the town. The Spanish adopted Toledo's medieval and hence Morisco administrative and municipal ordinances—but not its organic pedestrian pattern—in Seville and from there transposed it to the Americas as the governmental pattern for new cities there. These ordinances ultimately helped shape the compound culture being generated by the mixed populations of Latin America.

One such Spanish colonial city is Cuzco, which has several historical layers and where change continues to-

day. Little is known of the pre-Inka settlement, but we can develop a fairly accurate idea of the Inka capital of the fifteenth and early sixteenth centuries. Many Inka walls of large, beautifully worked stones are still in situ (see Chapter 8). During the Spanish colonial period, builders reused many of the old religious and governmental sites, as well as their walls (see Fig. 16.1), or at least their stones, for the new activities of the developing colonial culture. They also inserted new houses, churches, and governmental buildings into the old urban fabric.

As these three examples show, each culture organizes both family space and community space to suit its social needs, in balance with the physical conditions of the chosen site. People may choose a site for its defensive potential, as in the use of Toledo's hilltop as a fortress for nearly 2,200 years (compare with Chapter 8, Saqsaywaman). The equally careful siting of Cuzco on the mountain slopes facing south–southeast was greatly to the thermal advantage of the residents. The pragmatic decisions of the Harappans of Mohenjo-Daro to rebuild according to original patterns meant that the city survived on the same site for a millennium. In their persistent struggle against the river that supplied water to their fields even as its very abundance threatened death and destruction, they turned disaster into new beginnings.

SOURCES: EDMUND BACON (1974), CROUCH, GARR, AND MUNDIGO (1982), DALES (1966), GUTKIND (1967), JANSEN, ARDELEANU, AND FRANKE (1983), R. E. M. WHEELER (1966).

Symbolic Creation or Gradual Agglomeration?

Religious and political authorities have often determined to build with symbolic meaning. We look at two examples, an Indian city laid out according to a mandala and a Chinese city whose builders used a spacious grid to reinforce their claim to dominion. In contrast to both is the settlement of Mesa Verde in Colorado, which lacks the appearance of a formal structure but was nevertheless subtly adjusted to the constraints of its site in a large cave high above a valley floor.

RELIGIOUS PLAN: A MANDALA CITY IN INDIA

A mandala is a small diagram, yet it can determine the placement of features in a large city and illuminate both the principles of organization of the universe and the processes of building and living in a city. In Chapter 2 we noted that the mandala could be a mnemonic device for passing on architectural knowledge, precisely because it is a powerful symbol that is not limited by the space-time constraints on individual human lives; we must live in one era and a particular area, but the knowledge embedded in a mandala is both portable and enduring. The mandala also provides a pattern that both represents the cosmic city and sanctifies the human city, so that the human city manifests the cosmic.[24]

Borobudur, built as a residence of the gods, may have been based on the Vajradjatu or "Diamond World" mandala as its plan (see Fig. 5.5). The dimensions of Angkor Wat (see Chapter 5) exhibit space-time—namely, an extended period called a *yuga* (age of time) in Hinduism,

mapped onto the path between the entrance pavilion and the core sanctuary. A number of Indian monuments use mandalas to coordinate the zodiac, human time, orientation, and hierarchical order. Thus, the divine reality, which is formless, takes form through visible creation. The South Indian tradition points out specifically that the center of the mandala symbolizes Brahma, surrounded by lesser gods; then the world of humans; and, finally, the region of demons. By the sixth century C.E., Indians had realized complete forms for these concepts—forms that were equally useful for symbolizing mythology or organizing architecture. Earthly things, both terrestrial and demon worlds, testify to the power of Brahman through the physicality of mere cities and temples when organized as mandalas. The many variants of the mandala provide not only spiritual guidance, but pragmatic plans for cities and temples, making theological symbolism concrete and utilitarian.

Archaeologists have not recovered the most ancient cities of India, largely because these cities were built of perishable materials like clay and wood. Not until the Mughal era of the seventeenth century did builders commonly use stone for secular structures. Yet Varahamihira, a noted astronomer and scholar of the sixth century C.E., described the use of the mandala—and hence a plan—for laying out cities in his treatise on astronomy, *Bhrat Samhita*. For cities, he recommended a mandala of 9 by 9 (81) squares, the most powerful mandala, while for temples, he recommended the 8 by 8 (64) mandala. Other mandalas were used in south India, the most important having 7 by 7 or 16 by 16 panels.

The mandala-based temple cities of south India, such as the city of Shrirangam (see Fig. 9.3), were centered on a temple (sometimes two) set in concentric rings of streets surrounded by walls. This rectilinear mandala is different from the flowerlike one of Bhaktapur, Nepal (see Fig. 9.4). A short, gilded tower marks the temple, which is surrounded by shrines and prayer halls. In the second ring stand priests' houses and stalls for selling flowers, incense, and fruit for the worshippers' sacrifices. Farther out are the residences and businesses of the people, in a pattern that replicates cosmology (compare with Chapter 2, Mandala Diagrams). The tallest and most splendid architectural elements are the gate towers, which, in their height and decoration, magnificently display the human element of the plan, while the modesty of the central sanctuary alludes to the impossibility of physical form revealing full divine truth.

Shrirangam has five concentric ring walls; in the outer three walls are sets of gates, two along the north–south

---

[24]Note that not all mandalas are Hindu. Mandalas are used frequently in China and Africa as well.

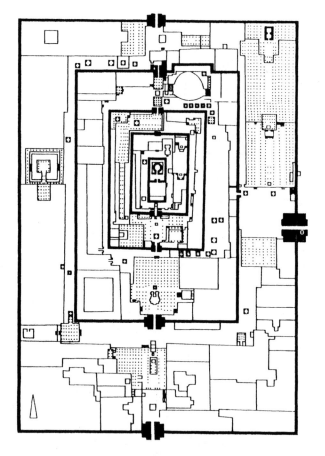

Figure 9.3. *Plan of Shrirangam, India. The city is shown as an image of the universe, arranged in concentric rings around Brahman, represented here by his modest shrine at the center. Like the mandala on which it is based, the city organizes the most sacred elements (shrines and priests houses) closest to Brahman, with progressively less venerable elements farther and farther away. The tallest elements are the gate towers at the north, east, and south. Here, there are two major streets and eight large roads 20, 16, and 13 feet (6, 5, and 4 meters) wide.*

axis and one on the east side (see Fig. 9.3). The north–south axis extends to connect with the bathing ghats along the two moatlike rivers that edge the city. The population lives within the area of the three outer walls, and the city's central core contains the temple, pillar halls, stores, and stables.

Building a new settlement according to the traditions embodied in the mandala involved the following steps:

- Choosing an astrologically auspicious day on which to begin.

- Choosing a mandala with a number of squares corresponding to the number of residential quarters planned.

- Finding a site. Indians prefer a site that slopes to the north or northeast, the opposite of the south-facing sites preferred in China. Perhaps a north slope is cooler and has the protection of the hill against the monsoon storms, which come generally from the south. Builders avoid siting a city in a hollow, however, lest it become a lake during the monsoon rains.

- Laying out the rectangular or square plan, the task of the priest-architect. The outer edge of the mandala becomes the city rampart. An area next to the wall is kept clear for a processional way and for troop maneuvers.

- Leveling the site. At this time, the people make offerings.

- Plowing a furrow along the east–west axis; the priest performs this task, followed by the lower castes, who plow the entire site and sow grain. When the grain is ripe, they bring their cattle there to graze, sanctifying the ground with the holy aura of cattle.

- Drawing the plan on the ground, another task for the priest-architect. The north–south and east–west axes, which are royal ways, are laid out by the use of shadows cast from a gnomon, a method used also by the Egyptians, Chinese, and others (see Chapter 2). The width of these major and lesser streets depends on whether the place is to be a city, town, or market with streets 40, 33, or 26 feet (12, 10, or 8 meters) wide, respectively. Usually there are two major streets—eight large roads 20, 16, and 13 feet wide (6, 5, or 4 m.) used only by carriages and elephants and many narrow streets, simple carriage ways with footpaths on each side for pedestrians. A town should have at least four gates at the cardinal points.

- Carefully purifying temple areas.

- Marking out residential blocks with informal alleys and footpaths.

The height and orientation of houses depend on the caste of the residents. Indians prefer a courtyard house for privacy and coolness. Such houses are similar to the ancient houses at Mohenjo-Daro. From four basic house plans, builders have developed 14,000 variations. Indians

Figure 9.4. *Mandala diagram of Bhaktapur, Nepal. The design is based on triangles at the center and the form of a lotus for the overall plan. Neither of these motifs bears any resemblance to the actual city plan (see Fig. 7.4).*

215

regard this multitude of variations on a simple form as a perfect example of how human life and the cosmos reflect each other. "Truth, in order to be operational and penetrate into men's hearts, must be refracted in a thousand modes," as Tucci comments.

SOURCES: CHANDRA (1980), G. HOUSTON (1976), MORON (1978), TUCCI (1988–89).

IMPERIAL PLAN: CHANG'AN COPIED AT HEIJO

The grid plan, one of the oldest forms of urban design, has an orderly, efficient street pattern that serves all inhabitants equitably. The third-millennium Harappan settlements in the Indus Valley had a semblance of regular street patterns. So did Greek cities, such as Priene and Miletus, from the third and second centuries B.C.E. The logical grid arrangement of public and private spaces served as a model for colonial cities that were established during imperial Rome's territorial expansion, and, as a result, modern European cities, such as Lyon, France, echo the nuclear grid design of Roman military encampments, which they once were.

In China, a long tradition placed the highest importance on the capital city as a symbol of imperial power. A rectangular, walled enclosure with spaces clearly articulated within a spacious grid reflected a controlling, organized system of rule. Builders carefully orchestrated the siting and planning of imperial palaces and governmental structures to preserve this image.

The capital of the Tang dynasty (618–906 C.E.), Chang'an, reflected this architectural tradition and served as a model for the design of Japan's first permanent imperial capital, Heijo (710–787 C.E.). Chang'an, today known as Xian, was located on the Wei River in Shaanxi province. Earlier settlements in the vicinity date from around 4000 B.C.E. Some of them served as capitals—among them the third-century B.C.E. Qin (Chin) Dynasty capital at Zianyang and the following Western Han dynastic town of the first century in approximately the same location. The Sui dynasty (581–618 C.E.) built Chang'an.

A text called the *Rituals of Zhou* (Zhou Li), around the first century C.E., describes the ideal of the Chinese city: it would be enclosed by an exterior wall with three gates in each side of the wall and major avenues running east–west and north–south. There would also be an inner wall. N. Steinhardt, an authority on Chinese urban history, thinks that this inner wall enclosed the palace city, although it is not specifically referred to in the Records of

Trades portion of the *Rituals of Zhou*. The arrangement of buildings, such as temples, markets, and audience halls complied with an overall scheme. However, Steinhardt has shown that not all Chinese imperial cities shared a common lineage stemming from the guidelines in the *Rituals of Zhou*.

Chang'an's builders did not strictly adhere to these guidelines. The ideal palace quarter was located near the city center (see Chapter 11, Beijing), but at Chang'an the palaces were in the north-central part of the city next to the outer wall. Steinhardt attributes this deviation from the ideal to the difficulties of building on an earlier city site and to limitations imposed by the Zao River, a tributary of the Wei river. Another possibility is that the palaces were built near the outer wall to defend the rulers against a possible uprising of the townspeople and to give them an easy escape route into the countryside—a common strategy in the ancient Middle East and in Medieval Europe, as historian L. Mumford demonstrated.

The Tang dynasty continued to build Chang'an according to the basic grid design (see Fig. 9.5). The city is impressively large, 6 miles (9.6 kilometers) wide in some places. In the seventh century, its outer wall was 23 miles (37 kilometers) long, and by the eighth century, its population numbered about 1 million. The map of modern Xian shows the enclosed geometric street pattern, defended by a surrounding wall. Even in modern China, Xian's wide, tree-lined streets and its rectilinear plan are distinctive.

The plan and arrangement of Chang'an's buildings became a visual expression of imperial power, serving as a model for other Chinese cities, such as Luoyang, also built by the Sui and Tang dynasties. Not only was the rectangular grid plan a logical solution to spatial organization, but it demonstrated how intellectual concepts could successfully be translated into concrete form.

In the late 600s, Japan's rulers were planning to build a permanent capital city. For years, they had shifted their capital from one palace site to another, according to the desires of successive rulers, with courtiers in random settlements around the palaces. Upon a ruler's death, his successor abandoned the old settlement and established imperial quarters elsewhere to avoid the negative connotations of the former ruler's death—and to escape the threat of political rivalries that might develop in the old city. In 645 and 667, attempts were made to establish permanent capitals at Naniwa and Otsu.

But political activity and centralization of power were increasing in Japan, and by the end of the seventh cen-

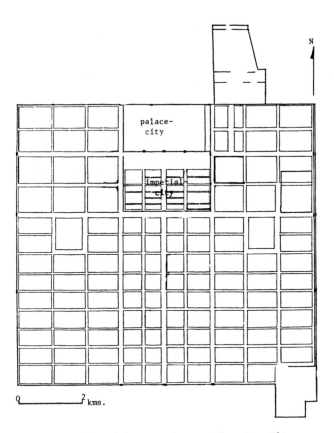

palace-
city

imperial
city

N

0 _____ 2 kms.

Figure 9.5. *Plan of the Tang dynasty Chang'an, China, seventh to tenth centuries* C.E. *Within this walled city, the emperor's residence, or palace city, is at the north and governmental offices are in the imperial city sector immediately to the south. The remainder of the city was segregated by local walls into over a hundred wards. The city covered about 30 square miles (78 square kilometers).*

the Asuka valley. The capital was laid out on a regular grid plan resembling Chang'an but was at a much smaller scale; it lasted little more than fifteen years, in part because its geographic location proved unsatisfactory, possibly for commerce. In 710, the ruling Empress Gemmei moved the imperial court from Fujiwara to a new site at Heijo, near the present-day city of Nara (see Fig. 9.6), a location favorable for commerce at a time of increased international trade.

The Chinese influence was strong from the beginning. Heijo's builders chose the site using rituals based on Chinese geomancy, a form of divination through the interpretation of various natural phenomena. Chang'an was the city's model, but although the city was designed on a larger scale than Fujiwara, it was much smaller than Chang'an. Major arteries extending 2.5 miles (4 kilometers) east–west were crossed by broad avenues stretching approximately 3 miles (4.7 kilometers) north–south, creating a grid that divided the city into eight north–south zones and nine east–west zones. Each zone was divided into eight quarters, which were, in turn, divided into sixteen blocks 394 feet (120 meters) wide. These blocks were divided again into smaller units.

The plan was organized efficiently and was nearly symmetrical except for two sections: the Outer Capital, which extended to the northeast, and the North End, a northwest portion. Authors K. Nishi and K. Hozumi explain that these two irregularities, both of which seem to have been adjustments to the terrain, affected the regularity of the overall design, as shown in Fig. 9.6. The southern, or Rampart (Rajomon), Gate was the main entrance to the city, opening onto the great Suzaku Avenue, which divided Heijo. This thoroughfare ended at the northern Suzakumon Gate, facing the Imperial Palace compound. Within the compound were assembly halls, governmental buildings, and related structures for the eight ministries of government, all symmetrically aligned on the main axis. Additional governmental halls, offices, and service buildings were located within the Inner Palace compound and the imperial residence in the northernmost part of the city. To the south were the residences and commercial areas. Dwellings for both commoners and nobles were located according to importance, with the highest-ranking personages situated closest to the Imperial Palace compound. Powerful figures could command several blocks for their living quarters.

Along with the network of roads that linked the capital to the provinces, the use of the Chinese grid plan for the capital city helped to modernize Japan. Heijo remained

tury, rulers recognized the need for a more stable seat of government. At the time, China exerted much influence on Japanese culture and institutions: Buddhist priests from China and Korea strongly influenced Japanese religious beliefs and practice; commercial trade with China expanded the Japanese economy; Chinese artisans and scholars provided cultural stimulation; and contacts with the Asian continent greatly advanced the Japanese art of building. China's system of political administration—a strong centralized government with palaces and administrators in close proximity—was also influential. As Japan emerged as a power and sought to develop its own governmental institutions, it turned to the Chinese for a model.

In 694, Japanese rulers established the first imperial city (that was intended to be permanent) at Fujiwara in

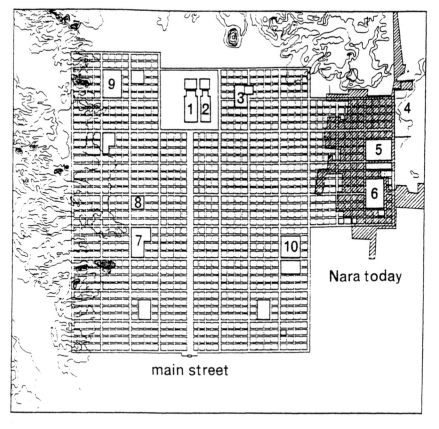

Figure 9.6. *Plan of Heijo-Kyo (Nara), Japan, as seen in the early eighth century* C.E. *Heijo-Kyo, although much smaller, replicates the plan of Chang'an, a grid divided into sectors. Modifications were introduced because of differences in terrain—in the addition of a section to the northwest (North End) and to the eastern Outer Capital. A further irregularity is also evident in the plan of the Imperial Palace compound, where a major building terminates the axis of the main street. These modifications result in less symmetry but a closer relationship of the plan to the site: Imperial quarter (1 and 2), Hokke-ji Temple (3), Todai-ji Temple (4), Kofuku-ji Temple (5), Ganko-ji Temple (6), Yakushi-ji Temple (7), Toshodai-ji Temple (8), Saida-ji Temple (9), and Daian-ji Temple (10).*

the capital until 784, when the population is thought to have numbered as many as 200,000. After 784 the new Emperor Kammu moved the capital to Nagaoka for a short time, finally establishing his imperial city on a site north of Heijo that he named Heian-kyo (today, Kyoto). Heian remained Japan's cultural capital even after the political capital moved to Tokyo in 1868. Heian also followed Heijo's grid plan using even more regular rectangular shapes (see Fig. 9.7).

Similarities in the plans of Chang'an, Heijo, and Heian far outnumber the differences—with two exceptions. Chang'an was a walled city; Heijo, Heian, and other Japanese grid-plan cities were not. Geography is the main reason for this difference. China, a continental country with great expanses of flat land, needed protective walls (see Chapter 8, Great Wall of China). The mountainous islands of Japan, in contrast, are protected by the sea and have numerous defensible sites. In Japan, the use of Chang'ans grid plan was more important to imperial identity than were great walls.

SOURCES: MUMFORD (1961), NISHI AND HOZUMI (1986), STEINHARDT (1986).

AGGLOMERATIVE: CLIFF HOUSES AT MESA VERDE

The Four Corners region of the United States is the junction of the states of Colorado, New Mexico, Utah, and Arizona. It contains thousands of archaeological sites, six hundred of which are cliff dwellings. One of the best known of these cliff dwellings is located in Mesa Verde National Park in southwestern Colorado (see the map of North America in the Appendix). It was a population center of the pre-Columbian Anasazi, native American Indians, and its approach to settlement organization is different from the orthogonal layout of Chang'an and Heijo. Mesa Verde's high-density, agglomerative planning, no less than its unique setting in lofty cave-niches, has fascinated people ever since the site's rediscovery in the nineteenth century.

The Anasazi people—or "ancient ones," as the later Navajo called them—settled in the region as early as 700 C.E.. At first, they found shelter in carved-out spaces of the sandstone cliffs, sometimes 2,000 feet (610 meters) above the valley floor. Then, for several centuries, they clustered in small settlements on the tops of mesas, living in pit houses, shallow dwellings dug into the ground. Around 950 C.E., there was a shift back into the cliffs, possibly for reasons of defense.

The Anasazi built multistory pueblo structures fronted with plazas in open caves in the cliffs. Archaeologists have studied their water-management and agricultural systems, marveled at their engineering expertise in masonry construction, and concluded that the Anasazi culture was highly sophisticated despite the fact that it left no written records and used only simple tools. Elements of Anasazi architecture and material culture reveal religious practices and social customs that the present-day Pueblo people of the American Southwest apparently inherited.

The Anasazi's social structure, religious orientation, and relation to nature influenced their structures. That there is no physical evidence of a ruling class that imposed military force, economic control, or royal leadership has led some scholars to think that the Anasazi practiced social equality. Ritual and social mores governed their actions. After extensive studies comparing the egalitarian society of the modern Pueblo people to that of the Anasazi, archaeologist W. Ferguson and anthropologist A. Rohn concluded that the customs have not changed drastically. The key to the successful social system of the modern Pueblo community is the equality and security of its members, who select the individuals who control rituals, customs, and decisions. To be ostracized from the rest of the group is severe punishment. The ancient Greeks had a similar philosophical outlook—Socrates chose death rather than face the prospect of banishment from Athens, his communal group.

The ancient Anasazi distinguished household members, kinship groups, the community in general, and the moieties called the Summer and Winter People, who were seasonally responsible for rituals and other activities. As in the related Acoma communities (see Chapter 14), the nuclear family—father, mother, children, and sometimes other close members—constituted the household group, which lived, ate, and worked together. The second, or kinship, category included several matrilineally related households. In the community, or pueblo group, all members shared a special relationship because of their common goal of survival. Not all modern pueblos, however, follow the matrilineal pattern or have Summer and Winter moieties.

The kiva was (see Fig. 9.8) the Anasazi's most important structure. Kinship groups gathered in the kivas for many activities, religious rituals among the most im-

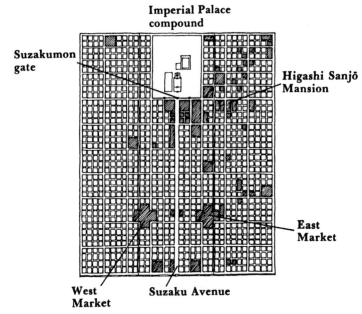

Figure 9.7. *Plan of Heian, Japan's Capital during the eighth to twelfth centuries, C.E., now called Kyoto. The original plan replicates that of Heijo-Kyo and refers to more distant sources in the plan of Chang'an. Like Heijo-Kyo, Heian is much smaller than Chang'an. Changes in later centuries resulted in less symmetry than is shown here.*

portant; other activities included weaving; toolmaking; and storytelling, which preserved the history of the people for the younger members of the community. Sometimes, however, groups were restricted to men only, as is true today among the Pueblo peoples where only the men participate in kiva activities. At Acoma, men's ceremonial and political life balances women's domestic life and ownership of the houses and fields.

The kiva—a semisubterranean, usually circular, roofed chamber with masonry walls (see Fig. 9.8)—developed from the earlier pit house, common in the seventh to ninth centuries C.E., although the function shifted from dwelling to ceremonial center. Kivas that were designed for the kinship or clan groups were approximately 7 feet high and 20 feet or less in diameter (2.13 by 7.10 meters). Great kivas, for use by the wider community, were larger. Entrance was by ladder through a flat or corbel-vaulted log roof supported by columns and by a series of masonry pilasters placed around the circumference. There was a bench or storage area at the junction of the wall and floor and a draft deflector on the floor, perpen-

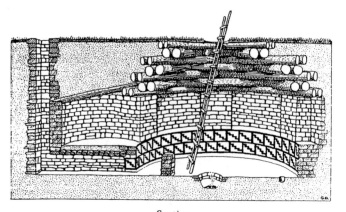

Section

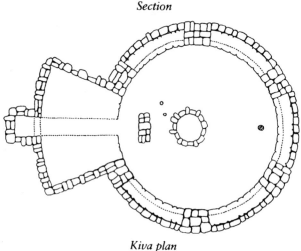

Kiva plan

Figure 9.8. *Kiva plan and interior elevation twelfth century* C.E. *The Anasazi-type kiva illustrated here has a "keyhole" plan, usually about 20 feet (8 meters) in diameter and about 7 feet (2 meters) in height. Kivas were subterranean rooms entered by a ladder through the roof of corbelled logs, where communal ceremonies, both sacred and social were held. A bench or storage platform surrounded the interior wall. Behind the fire pit in the center of the drawing is the sipapu, or hole symbolizing the place where the Anasazi believed that their ancestors emerged from the underworld. The extension at the left of the drawing is a ventilator shaft with a draft deflector in front.*

dicular to the ventilator shaft that channeled air into the interior. Pictographs and petroglyphs sometimes ornamented the walls. In the absence of a written history, these ornamentations have provided some cultural information about the daily lives of the dwellers. Anthropologist P. Nabokov and architect R. Easton explain that the Anasazi

believed that spirits migrated upward from within the earth through a *sipapu* (hole in the earth), so each kiva has such a hole in the floor to show a symbolic link with the spiritual and ancestral underworld.

Spruce Tree House at Mesa Verde is one of the best-preserved examples of a cliff village. Experts have estimated that as many as two hunded people lived at the site, which has 114 rooms and eight kivas. Nestled under a great sandstone cliff overhang, a cavern 425 feet long and 80 feet deep (122 by 24 meters) provided a sheltered space on which the Anasazi could build, although they had to level some parts of the cavern floor to accommodate their structures. There, two- and three-story rooms or storage chambers with shared walls were constructed about 1,000 feet (300 meters) above the valley floor. The rooms are square, rectangular, or D-shaped to fit into the curved cave walls. Many have fireplaces, smoke-holes, and window spaces. Some of the upper stories had balconies with ladders for access. In front of the structures was an open plaza, where people could cook or work outdoors; smaller plazas were tucked in among the units. Kivas were located among the dwellings. Some of their roofs served as floors for courtyards or upper-level rooms.

Building materials were adobe, timber, and sandstone. At the northern part of Spruce Tree House, the rooms extended to the top of the cavern. Ferguson and Rohn relate that one enterprising mason built a stone column to support a log that provided a horizontal base for the wall of the uppermost room, a practice followed by other builders of the Spring House at Mesa Verde. Builders plastered some walls and decorated them with geometric designs or pictures of animals and people. The network of rooms, some interconnected, illustrates how the Anasazi used limited space efficiently with a plan fitted to the site.

The Cliff Palace (see Fig. 9.9) was even larger than Spruce Tree House; the twenty-three kivas here, one of the largest dwellings at Mesa Verde, follow a similar architectural pattern. This ancient site (1100–1300 C.E.) is one of several in the Cliff-Fewkes Canyon Settlement in Mesa Verde, named after an early (1908) investigator of the Anasazi ruins. Archaeologists estimate that about 2,500 Anasazi lived in the Mesa Verde area during the peak of their culture. The Cliff-Fewkes Canyon region was inhabited by about 800 people in 33 apartment-type lodgings with 60 kivas.

The Cliff Palace, with three hundred residents, was the largest settlement of the group. More than two hundred rectangular rooms, twenty-three kivas, towers, and

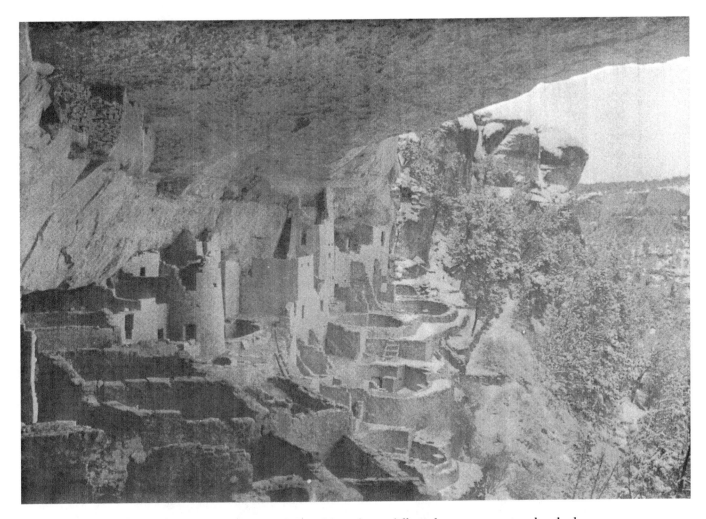

Figure 9.9. *Mesa Verde Cliff Palace, Colorado. Sheltered by a huge cliff overhang are over two hundred rooms and twenty-three adjacent kivas. By leveling the cave floors, the inhabitants were able to build shelters, some three stories in height. At center are two circular kivas.*

storage chambers were built on a sheltered ledge high above the valley. The towers have asymmetrically placed windows and may have had religious significance. Or perhaps they were lookout posts; at this height, the breathtaking view extends for more than 100 miles (170 kilometers). The location suggests that the Anasazi appreciated both the landscape's beauty and the advantages of a natural defensive vantage point.

At Chaco Canyon, New Mexico, multiple-story complexes were constructed with thick walls on the lowest level to provide additional support. Mud-plastered, pine-beam floors were built with offsets and balconies gracing the upper levels (see Fig. 9.10). Nestled under a cliff overhang, the White House Ruin of Canyon de Chelly, Arizona (see Fig. 9.11), on the valley floors, has been dated, from tree rings used in construction beams, to between 1060 and 1275 C.E., when the site was abandoned, according to Ferguson and Rohn.

No one knows why people chose to live so precariously above the canyon floor. It may have been for reasons of defense or climate or because natural shelter already existed. The architectural remains, however, give ample proof of sophisticated adaptation to a distinctive environmental setting. Yet by the end of the thirteenth

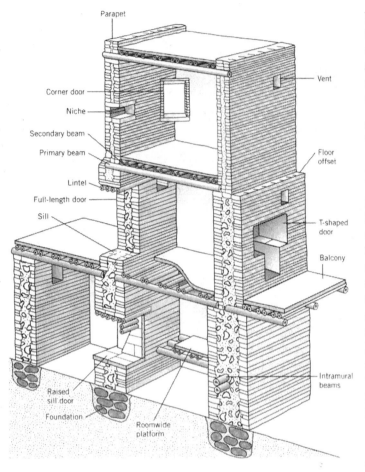

Figure 9.10. *Cross-section of Anasazi architecture (ca. 1150 C.E.), Chaco Canyon, New Mexico. Built five rooms deep and four to five stories high, a complex could have as many as three hundred rooms. At the lowest level, wide walls of stones with mud mortar bear the weight of the upper stories; walls narrow as the structure rises and were reinforced with embedded wooden beams. The floors, balconies, interior platform, and roofs are made of layers of pine beams plastered with mud. The doors are either T-shaped or made with raised sills.*

century, at the peak of their culture, the Anasazi began to abandon their cliff dwellings. They migrated to areas of the Rio Grande valley with other indigenous people, eventually constituting the Hopi, Zuni, and other pueblo cultures. Little concrete evidence supports any of the theories about their decline, which occurred before the arrival of the Spanish conquerors in the sixteenth century. Was it droughts? There were some serious ones. Was it attacks by hostile enemies? Or was it socioreligious dissension that changed their way of life? Many historians and archaeologists think that it was a combination of all three: a widespread drought lasting several decades or even a century weakened the society, triggering enemy attacks and dissension.

SOURCES: CANBY (1982), FERGUSON AND ROHN (1988), NABOKOV AND EASTON (1989), STURTEVANT (1978).

LANDSCAPED SETTINGS

Landscape, like urban architecture, is subject to both political and design control. The history of landscape architecture is just beginning to be written, and we do not attempt to deal here with large concerns, such as the relation of the scale of landscape to the zeitgeist or ethos of a time and place, the use of foreign materials in landscape design, and the maintenance or destruction of historical styles of landscaping. We look at two examples of aristocratic landscape, each responding to the aesthetic and political circumstances of its patron and designer: formal iconography and patterning at the Taj Mahal in India and the elegant informality of the grounds of the Katsura Villa in Japan. (See also the discussion of Sri Lankan landscapes in the Introduction.)

Form and Meaning: Taj Mahal, Agra, India

> The Taj Mahal complex stands as the logical culmination of the earlier Mughal architectural tradition, combining bold engineering and massive scale with formal elegance and a totally coordinated design of flawless visual symmetry.
>
> *Begley and Desai (1989), xli*

A mausoleum and memorial for Mumtaz Mahal (1593–1631), beloved wife of emperor Shah Jahan (1592–1666) the Taj Mahal (see Fig. 9.12) has long been considered one of the most impressive and beautiful works of Mughal architecture. It was modeled after the first important Mughal monument constructed in Old Delhi in 1564: the tomb of Shah Jahan's great-grandfather, Emperor Humayun (1530–56). The size of Humayun's tomb and the design that coordinates it with the surrounding garden set the direction for much Mughal architecture, promoting, as historian D. Carroll suggests, "Persian ideals as an enduring influence in Indian architecture." Those ideals are well represented in the Taj Mahal, where the al-

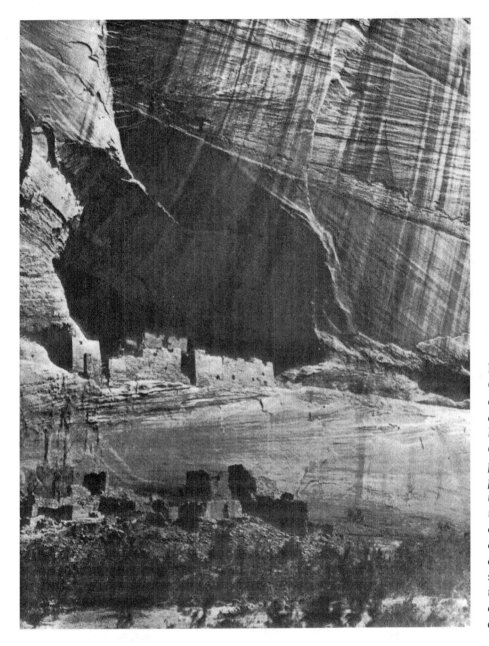

Figure 9.11. *The White House, Canyon de Chelly, Arizona. One of many cliff houses in Arizona and New Mexico, this was the home of Basket Marker, then Cliff Dweller, then Pueblo peoples, who lived here for a longer period than at any other ruins in the Southwest. The village, dating from approximately the eleventh century* C.E., *is set on the canyon floor and in a great cave at the base of sandstone cliffs, stained red by manganese and iron oxide. The upper houses could be reached from the roofs of the lower ones.*

legorical significance of the layout arises from a thematically unified visual plan.

The complex, adjacent to the Jumna River, was laid out on a grid plan with the garden constituting an important part of the overall scheme (see Fig. 9.13). The garden follows the typical Persian design, although the tomb stands at one end of the complex, rather than at the center, as in most earlier Mughal tombs. Within the grid lay-

out, all buildings and spaces are systematically proportioned to achieve an overall harmonious effect.

Ustad Ahmad Lahori, the chief architect for the Taj Mahal, was an engineer and scholar who worked on many architectural projects for the emperor, including the vast palace of the Red Fort in Delhi (see Chapter 8). Here, he followed the paradisiacal themes of earlier garden tombs. With his assistants and a highly respected calligrapher of

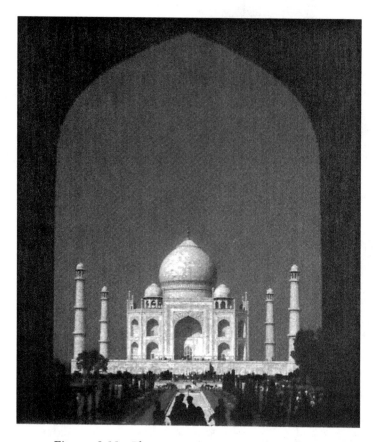

Figure 9.12. *The Taj Mahal, Agra, India. This tomb of Begam Arjumand Bano (Mumtaj Mahal) (d. 1631), wife of Emperor (Shah) Jahan, was begun in 1632. The monument and extensive formal garden complex cover 42 acres (17 hectares). The water axes lead the eye to the Taj Mahal, which rises 280 feet (85 meters) and is crowned by a pointed dome, 63 feet (19 meters) high with a gold pinnacle. At each of the four corners of the platform is a minaret crowned by a stupa. Buildings and landscape combine to form an allegory of the Gardens of Paradise, according to the Qur'an, making the Taj Mahal a masterpiece of Mughal architecture.*

Qur'anic inscriptions named Amanat Khan (see Fig. 9.14), he orchestrated the building program under the overall direction of Shah Jahan, whose great interest in architectural projects and desire to outdo his grandfather Akbar in this regard are well documented.

By turns benevolent and ruthless, Shah Jahan always saw himself as an exalted ruler, manifesting his power in monumental architecture. Historian W. Begley suggests that his self-importance may have been inspired by pop-

ular Sufi tenets that expounded the medieval Doctrine of the Perfect Man; Akbar had been called the "Perfect Man of that age" and believed that he was almost divine. Shah Jahan's excessive vanity made him especially vulnerable to this type of celestial association.

Official seventeenth-century court histories describe the Taj Mahal, emperor Shah Jahan, and his wife, Mumtaz Mahal in florid and grandiose prose, extolling the magnificence of the undertaking inspired by the great love that Shah Jahan had for his wife. Writers of the following centuries echoed the romantic theme of unequaled marital bliss as the guiding principle behind the construction of the tomb. Begley, however, believes that the Taj Mahal was as much a monumental symbol to enhance Jahan's power and prestige as it was a memorial tomb for his dead wife. Shah Jahan had always been obsessed with asserting his prominent role in history; under the title King of the World, he ruled Islamic regions covering an area almost half the size of Europe.

Begley suggests that the garden is an important key to understanding the allegorical importance of the Taj Mahal's overall plan and its program of Qur'anic inscriptions. It was common to describe Persian gardens in metaphorical terms, linking them to the "Gardens of Paradise" of Qur'anic passages (see Chapter 13). He quotes one inscription on the entrance gateway to the tomb of the emperor Akbar (1543–1605) in Sikandra, near Agra, which claims: "These are the gardens of Eden, enter them to live forever!" Nearly all the many carved inscriptions on the Taj Mahal are verses from the Qur'an, many of them related to the gardens of paradise (see Fig. 9.14).

The complex of the Taj Mahal covers 42 acres (17 hectares) and is enclosed by a lofty wall. At the center of the southern wall, an entrance gateway leads to a courtyard that opens onto the Great Gateway, a massive portal leading into the garden. The Persian garden scheme, called a *char-bagh*—a garden divided into four parts by water courses or pathways symbolizing the Four Rivers of Paradise and a marble basin at the intersection of the channels—refers to the heavenly "tank of Abundance," believed to be envisioned by Muhammad as he ascended to paradise. Flanking the tomb at the northern extremity are ponds, a mosque, and a hall that preserves the symmetry of the plan by its similarity to the mosque. The design also incorporates shops, verandas, and porticos. With its central canal and courts inspired by the char-bagh arrangement, the garden provides a visual axis that culminates in the monumental mausoleum and adjacent buildings. The plan's rigid symmetry is softened by cypress trees that

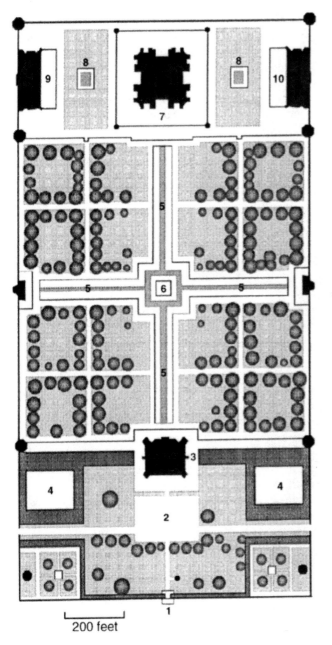

Figure 9.13. *Plan of the Taj Mahal and adjoining garden. The garden is formally arranged with long intersecting pools on the axis and cross-axis and square beds of trees and other vegetation, evoking the Garden of Paradise described in the Qur'an. The marble mausoleum is supported on a masonry terrace, approximately 983 feet (300 meters) long, 367 feet (112 meters) wide, and 50 feet (15 meters) high. The entrance to the tomb (1), opens onto a quadrangular court (2), dominated by the great gatehouse (3), flanked by symmetrical courtyards at (4). Tree-lined canals (5), and a central fountain (6) articulate the longitudinal and horizontal axes elaborated with flowers and shrubbery. At the far end is the tomb (7), with flanking pools (8), a mosque (9), and a matching hall (10). Grey areas are gardens and trees.*

200 feet

stone; skillfully carved marble screens and inlay work, *muqaranas* (three-dimensional ceiling-niches of stucco and tile), and calligraphic inscriptions from the Qur'an adorn much of the surface area (see Chapter 13, Symbolism and Ornamentation).

The "Illumined Tomb," as Mughal sources call the mausoleum, is the focal point of both the allegorical and architectural programs. Begley interpreted it in symbolic terms as the Throne of God from which Judgment will be made on the Day of Resurrection. The dome is seen as a crown, similar to those in contemporary Mughal paintings showing ceremonial crowns. Begley supports this interpretation with references to medieval Islamic cosmology, in which the Throne is described as "an infinitely vast structure situated upon a raised plinth . . . [and] directly beneath the terrace of the Throne, God created the celestial Gardens of Paradise . . . [which] are filled with beautiful palaces and sensual delights." Although Mughal court poets made metaphorical references to the Divine Throne as an example of "architectural perfection," figural depictions of the Throne of God are rare in Islamic art, partly because of orthodox Islamic restrictions against the figurative portrayal of God or any of his attributes.

Shah Jahan was particularly attracted to the image of a ruler on a throne. The lavish Peacock Throne (in the Red Fort in Agra) that commemorated his coronation was raised on a platform and bejeweled, as was the Taj Mahal. Begley claims that the plan of the Taj complex, with its apocalyptic Qur'anic inscriptions, represents allegorically the concept of the Day of Resurrection, when the dead assemble for Judgment at the Divine Throne. A copy of Ibn al Arabi's 1238 manuscript *Futuhat al-Makkiyya*, which

shade the approach to the mausoleum and by the fragrance of orange blossoms, jasmine, and roses. As the visitor proceeds through the garden toward the mausoleum, the ever-changing colors reflected in the long pool and on the marble dome of the Taj Mahal add visual splendor to the scene.

In opulence, the Taj Mahal is difficult to surpass. Jewels and semiprecious stones are embedded in floral designs on the facade; white marble contrasts with black

At each corner of the 313-square-foot (29-square-meter) platform bearing the tomb is a tall, slender minaret. On each side of the square tomb, a richly ornamented, 63-foot-high *iwan* (see Chapter 10) enhances the feeling of grandeur. The corners of the building are cut off so as to form an eight-sided shape. Over the tomb, an inner dome is surmounted by an outer dome with a gold pinnacle that soars to 280 feet (85 meters) above the cenotaph of Mumtaz, the focal point of the tomb.

Within the tomb, an octagonal carved marble screen encloses the cenotaph itself. Qur'anic inscriptions offer further evidence for the suggested allegorical interpretation; the verses seem to be recited by angels supporting the Throne of God that the dead will see on the Day of Resurrection. The cenotaph may have symbolic meaning beyond that of an elaborate architectural monument honoring Mumtaz. Traditionally, the messages of the Qur'an and the hadiths are meant to be interpreted on two levels—the literal and the symbolic. Connections between iconography and features of Islamic architecture are common in Mughal literature, poetry, and architectural practice.

The notion has persisted that Shah Jahan planned for his own memorial a monument of even greater beauty and symbolic content than the Taj Mahal. As early as 1654, twelve years before the emperor's death, Jean-Baptiste Tavernier, a French merchant, wrote that the Shah had planned a similar monument to be constructed on the opposite bank of the Jumna. His claims were likely based on hearsay; no evidence supports them.

Shah Jahan's extreme pride in himself and his accomplishments suggest that the logical place for his burial was beside Mumtaz Mahal within the allegorical and architectural setting that attested to his greatness. Indeed, he was buried there in 1666. The cenotaph of the "Perfect Man" was placed beside that of his beloved wife, and the epitaph carved on his grave describes him as the "Guardian of Paradise"—a description that some believe he may have written himself. Nothing could more surely point to the Taj Mahal and its gardens as a symbolic representation of the divine world.

SOURCES: BEGLEY (1979), BEGLEY AND DESAI (1989), CARROLL (1978), HAMBLY AND SWAAN (1968), LATIF (1981), PAL (1989).

Continuity with Setting: Katsura Palace (Villa), Japan

The formal plans of Islamic buildings and their garden settings focus on the control of nature, subordinating the

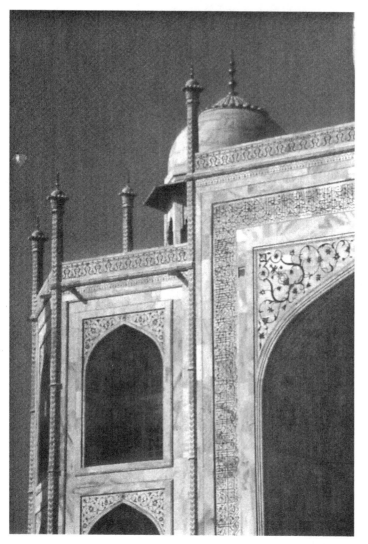

Figure 9.14. *Detail of the south portal (iwan) of the Taj Mahal inscribed with verses from the Qur'an devoted to revelations by the Prophet. Surya 36 Ya Sin (verses 1-21) is considered to be the "heart" of the Qur'an. Verse 21 reads: "Obey those who ask no reward of you (for themselves) and who have themselves received guidance" (translated by Yusef ali, 1977). The calligraphic inscriptions were carved into white marble after a design by the renowned calligrapher Amanat Khan.*

was owned by Shah Jahan's father, Jahangir, contained a "Diagram of the Plain Assembly on the Day of Judgment." The diagram depicts the Throne, Tank of Abundance, and other eschatological references that have been interpreted through analysis of spatial relationships in the drawings, as echoed in the architectural plan of the Taj Mahal.

landscape to geometric designs. In contrast, the Japanese house-garden relationship is one of intimacy, blending the two entities into a harmonious coexistence of human beings and their natural surroundings. A rich example of this harmonious integration of architecture and garden design is the Katsura palace (goten) or villa and its expansive garden setting near Kyoto.

The imperial family built Katsura in the mid-seventeenth century. The palace was originally planned as a modest structure in wooded surroundings on land owned by Prince Toshihito (b. 1579–d. 1629). Following the fashion of the Japanese aristocracy, Katsura was intended as a country retreat, a place away from the city in which to relax, enjoy the natural surroundings, and pursue aesthetic interests. The two architectural styles then prevailing were the elaborate and ordered shoin (literally, library) design, preferred by the ruling military government, called the Tokugawa shogunate military government, and the Sukiya style, which reflected the simple and freer rustic taste associated with ordinary people (see Chapters 3 and 5). Aristocrats like Prince Toshihito had limited political power at this time and may have felt affinities with the common people as well as the with shogunate. The Katsura villa incorporates aspects of each style.

During the fifty years after Toshihito's death, the villa was enlarged in several stages but without a governing design. Variety in its architectural mode and expressions of taste reflect a number of political, religious, literary, and Chinese cultural influences, resulting in a combination of various styles and construction methods. Yet as the villa grew, its patrons and architects achieved a balance between the old and the new, creating an outstanding example of the kind of house and garden design that members of the Japanese aristocracy enjoyed during the Edo period (1615–1857).

The main divisions of the palace are the Old Shoin (library area), the Middle Shoin, the New Goten (palace), and the Music Suite. Each section is arranged to offer the finest view of the pond and garden, the major focus of the compound. The builders accomplished this goal, in part, by varying the floor and roof levels of each new addition (see Fig. 9.15), as historian A. Isozaki notes.

The Old Shoin, which dates from 1624, was the entrance block and has two guest rooms and two smaller rooms, perhaps storage areas. Facing the pond, it was angled so that the autumn moon reflected on the water's surface. Toshihito's son Toshitada built the Middle Shoin in 1641. Connected at right angles in a stepped arrangement to the Old Shoin, it has broad vistas of the garden. The rooms of the Middle Shoin are smaller than those in the

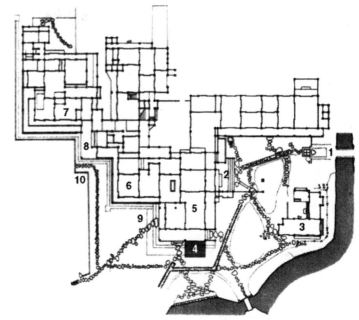

Figure 9.15. *Plan of Katsura, the imperial villa (palace), Kyoto, Japan. The villa was built by Prince Toshihito (1579–1629) and Prince Toshitada (1619–1662). The plan shows the main gateway (1), entrance (2), Gepparo tea pavilion (3), veranda (4), Old Shoin (5), Middle Shoin with music suite behind (6), New Goten (7), veranda (8), moss (9), lawn (10). The "flying geese" pattern of the stepped-back design of the villa offers many views of the garden from different angles. Verandas provide a subtle transition between house and garden, both physically and visually.*

Old Shoin, but there is one alcove for the display of works of art or flowers (see Chapter 7, Tokonoma). The Music Suite and the New Goten were added later. The former is a transitional section with a storage area for musical instruments and a small tearoom; in the latter are several small rooms and service areas. The New Goten was remodeled in 1663 in anticipation of a visit from the retired Emperor Gomizuno-o; teahouses and small pavilions were added to the garden area.

The exterior profile of the three major sections presents a configuration known as the "flying-geese" design (see Fig. 9.15) that resembles the triangular pattern of geese flying in formation. Not only did this plan permit more views, it allowed ample ventilation and sunlight to reach the interior. The same design was used earlier in the construction of Kyoto's Nijo Castle (1626), which reflected the military government's taste and sense of order. At Katsura, the flying-geese pattern evolved after plans for the New Goten were formulated and apparently was not the result of a preconceived design, archiect R. Isozaki explains.

Recent literature supports the theory that the villa, rather than being based on one guiding principle, combines many styles, construction methods, and ideas. Yet it has a unity that has influenced modern design. As early as 1933, the German architect B. Taut saw in Katsura design concepts that were relevant to the movements taking place in Europe in the 1930s; for example, the emphasis on post-and-lintel construction with simple vertical and horizontal lines brings to mind the paintings of Piet Mondrian, then painting in the Netherlands. Taut linked Katsura not only to European modernism but to the development of modern Japanese architecture; since his time, K. Tange, the noted Japanese architect, has written extensively about the palace, linking it to the European modernist movement of the 1930s.

The interiors at Katsura exhibit an open plan broken up by screens and room dividers (fusuma), movable partitions of paper or cloth. Room divisions follow a unified spatial pattern based on the tatami module, with little emphasis on symmetrical room size. Pale yellow painted walls contrast with the dark blue tatami bindings on the floor, stressing the vertical and horizontal lines, as architect A. Isozaki suggests. Some of the interior screens are painted with landscape scenes, leading the eye from the interior to the natural landscape beyond the window (see Fig. 13.1). Other windows act as frames for selected views of the landscape. Both devices serve to connect interiors with exteriors. As another connection, one open veranda has a "moon-viewing" platform. Construction materials—wood, stone, bamboo, and cypress—used for the walls further emphasize the continuity between the house and garden, where similar natural materials are found (see Fig. 10.22).

The garden abounds in many shades of green, from dark evergreens to bamboo; however, with the exception of plum and cherry trees, there are few colorful plants and flowers, which may diminish the serenity of the scene. Nature was transformed in this man-made landscape into an aesthetic ideal to be enjoyed in the "stroll garden," where one travels a predetermined route. Such gardens evolved in the Edo period, and Katsura is the oldest surviving example. At each turn of the winding path, a new scene unfolds to delight the eye. The path, made of hundreds of stepping stones to protect the surrounding moss, circles the pond, whose small islets are linked by bridges, and leads past miniature mountains, streams, dry stone gardens, cultivated areas, pavilions, and teahouses.

Occasionally, part of the scenery is "borrowed" from beyond the compound, such as a view of distant mountains or valleys. In this way, the builders made the natural panorama an extension of the garden. Although there were no strict rules for garden layouts, designers at Katsura and elsewhere employed shakkei, the use of "borrowed" scenery, and followed some standard techniques in planning views. These techniques, as landscape architect W. Adams tells us, come from landscape painting, in which a foreground leads through the midground into the background. By applying these principles to garden design, planners linked the expanded view of nature to the intimacy of the Imperial garden. Sometimes, to present a picturesque scene without too much sky in the "picture," they trimmed trees in such a way that an overhanging limb screened out some of the sky. They applied the same method to enclosures, such as fences, planting trees or shrubs to screen and balance long stretches of fencing.

When Katsura was built, Japanese builders and planners had employed shakkei for several hundred years, which they had adopted from the Chinese; a Chinese garden treatise, called Yuan Ye, written during the Ming dynasty (1368–1644), refers to the method (W. Adams, 1991). Numerous manuals and treatises on garden arrangements, including those of Chinese origin, attest to a profound interest in the cultivation of nature. The use of ponds, dry gardens, bridges, and other elements to reflect deep—but foreign—religious and philosophical ideas is one of the most significant of the many Chinese and Korean contributions to Japanese conceptual landscaping; from these sources the Japanese developed their own style.

The Katsura compound contains five teahouses. Koburi Enshu (1579–1647), a tea tutor and adviser on the building of Nijo castle, is said to have influenced some of the designs of the villa, including the teahouses. The Zen-inspired teahouse, popular from the 1500s, is one of the most interesting traditional structures in Japanese gardens (see Chapter 7, Tokonoma). Teahouses were little more than simple, rustic huts—small, with low doorways that forced one to crawl through the entrance as an act of humility. Inside, the small space gave those attending the ceremony a feeling of enclosure and intimacy (see Figs. 9.16 and 9.17). The room was bare except for a tokonoma, the hearth over which the teakettle was heated for the tea, a few utensils, and tatami matting. Its simplicity was intended to produce a tranquil atmosphere in which the cultured elite could drink tea, admire the beauty of the tea utensils, and discuss such subjects as literature and poetry. The tea ceremony developed into a highly ritualized

Figure 9.16. *Entrance to the ceremonial teahouse at Manshu-in, Kyoto, Japan. The asymetrical design is intentional as are the placement and small size of the door, which force guests to crawl into the teahouse— an act of humility. Each boulder is precisely placed for maximum aesthetic and spiritual effect. The boulders' irregular surfaces force mindfulness of the relation of body to foot to stone.*

affair, beginning with the approach through the garden, where basins were provided for ritual cleansing. Stone lanterns lit the way to evening ceremonies (see Fig. 9.18).

The growth of Zen Buddhism had a profound effect on Japanese cultural tastes. Zen descriptions of a celestial paradise garden (different in concept from the Islamic paradise gardens discussed in Chapter 13) inspired man-made counterparts, places for meditation in an idealized natural setting. The meditative and introspective aspects of Zen Buddhism also influenced the principles of the tea ceremony.

The Katsura garden design also reflects literary sources. For example, M. Shikibu's classical Heian novel *The Tale of Genji* contains many passages describing landscapes, some of which inspired the plans at Katsura. The educated Japanese court read and absorbed other master-

Figure 9.17. *Teahouse built by Japanese carpenters, now in the Art Museum, University of Michigan. Clarity and a sense of order derive from the geometric pattern carried throughout the elevated teahouse. The tokonoma with scroll and flower arrangement sets a contemplataive mood for the tea ceremony. Tatami floor mats provided for guests also articulate the room's dimensions, since the mats are usually 6 feet by 3 feet (2 meters by 1 meter) in size.*

pieces of the time, such as the Buddhist priest's Kenko's *Essays on Idleness*. Adams relates that Kenko taught reverence for all phases of natural growth, including the imperfect and the impermanent.

Despite these later influences, however, the ancient Shinto religion was the original source of the Japanese love of nature. The Japanese term for garden is *niwa*, meaning a sacred space. Belief in the sacredness of the landscape began as the ancient fear of natural phenomena but evolved into the perception that all living things are interconnected, spiritually and metaphysically. Zen Buddhism later stimulated the deep reverence for nature that became an essential part of the Japanese character. The continuity between the Katsura villa and its garden set-

Figure 9.18. *A bird's-eye view of a Japanese teahouse. A fence divides the area into inner and outer sections. To the left is a shelter for waiting. Stepping stones on the right lead to a place for washing one's hands and then to the teahouse door. The building fits into the landscape through the subtle integration of water, greenery, and architecture.*

ting mirrors the spiritual link between the Japanese people and their natural environment.

SOURCES: W. ADAMS (1991), BRING (1981), ISOSAKI (1987), MASUDA (1970), NISHI AND HOZUMI (1986), OKAWA (1975).

SUGGESTED READINGS

Adams, W. H. 1991. *Nature Perfected: Gardens Through History*. New York: Abbeville Press. Sections on eastern and western garden history. Many beautiful color plates.

Bacon, Edmund 1974. *Design of Cities*. Harmondsworth, England: Penguin Books. A classic. Note particularly the many fine analytical drawings of urban features.

Begley, W. E. 1979. "The Myth of the Taj Mahal and a New Theory of Its Symbolic Meaning." *Art Bulletin* (March): 8–37. The author supports his theories with convincing documentation.

Begley, W. E., and Z. A. Desai, compilers and trans. 1989. *Taj Mahal: The Illumined Tomb, An Anthology of Seventeenth Century Mughal and European Documentary Sources*. Seattle: University of Washington Press. The wide scope of the documentary sources in this anthology—court histories, documents, inscriptions, calligraphy, and related topics—makes it indispensable for the study of Imperial Mughal architecture. Many illustrations.

Bring, M., and J. Wayemberg. 1981. *Japanese Gardens: Design and Meaning*. New York: McGraw-Hill. A well-written examination of the development of Japanese gardens.

Canby, T. Y. 1982. "The Anasazi: Riddles in the Ruins." *National Geographic* (November): 562–92. Excellent photographs.

Chandra, L. 1991. "Life, Space and Structures." In *Concepts of Space Ancient and Modern*, 211–18, edited by K. Vatsyayan. New Delhi: Abhinav Publications. A thoughtful presentation of the meaning of architecture for Indians.

Ferguson, W. M., and A. H. Rohn. 1988. *Anasazi Ruins of the Southwest in Color*. Albuquerque: University of New Mexico Press. The exceptional photographs and accompanying text make a valuable contribution to the study of Anasazi architecture.

Gutkind, E.A. 1967. *Urban Development in Southern Europe: Spain and Portugal*. Vol. 3 of *International History of City Development*. New York: Free Press. See the entries on Toledo and Salamanca.

Houston, G. 1976. "Mandalas: Ritual and Functional."

Tibet Journal 2 (April–June): 47–58. A good short account of how mandala diagrams embody and lead to truth.

Isozaki, A. 1987. *Katsura Villa*, trans. J. Lamb. New York: Rizzoli. A comprehensive study of the Katsura Palace.

Jansen, M., "The Concept of Space in Harappan City Planning—Mohenjo-Daro." In *Concepts of Space Ancient and Modern*, 75–82, edited by K. Vatsyayan. New Delhi: Abhinav Publications. A succinct and interesting account of the urban arrangements at Mohenjo-Daro.

Masuda, T. 1970. *Living Architecture: Japanese.* New York: Grosset & Dunlop. A useful source for various aspects of Japanese architecture and urbanization. Contains plans and elevations, as well as photographs.

Nabokov, P., and R. Easton. 1989. *Native American Architecture,* New York: Oxford University Press. See pp. 356–65 for information on Mesa Verde.

Nishi, S., and K. Hozumi. 1986. *What is Japanese Architecture?* trans. M. Horton. New York: Kodansha International. An excellent source, a must for basic information on Japanese architecture. Good structural organization, many drawings.

Okawa, N. 1975. *Edo Architecture: Katsura and Nikko.* New York: Weatherhill/Heibonsha. Stimulating introductory essays.

Steinhardt, N.S. 1986. "Why Were Chang'an and Beijing So Different?" *Journal of the Society of Architectural Historians* 45 (December): 339–57. A thought-provoking, authoritative, and detailed essay on the development of Chinese urban plans. Essential also for Chapter 11 (Beijing).

Steinhardt, N. S. 1990. *The Chinese Imperial City.* Honolulu: University of Hawaii Press. Thorough. The only monograph in English on the topic. Many plans and maps.

10

Building Types and Uses

Examples from around the world can only hint at the immense range of building types and uses. We begin with a building type unique to a geographic region, the Mesoamerican ballcourt and then examine a building type unique to a religion and culture, the Islamic school or university, adapted from the plan of the early mosque courtyard. We look next at forms more widely used: combinations of pyramids, altars, and platforms in such different cultures as the Mesoamericans and the Oceanic peoples of the Tuamotu Archipelago. Finally, we turn to housing. People meet the universal need for housing with a multiplicity of forms; our examples come from urban Nepal and (mostly) rural Southeast Asia. To parallel the variety in building forms, we suggest the similar variety in uses with two different arrangements for floor-level living, one Japanese and the other Islamic.

UNIQUE TYPES

Some building types are linked to specific places, cultures, or times. In use or meaning, they may have analogues in other places or among other peoples, but in form, they are distinctive, arising from the way particular people met a particular architectural need.

Ballcourts of Central America

The earliest examples of constructed ritual ballcourts can be traced to the Olmecs; a recently excavated site at Teopantecuanitlán, 100 miles (161 kilometers) south of Cuernavaca in Mexico, has two ballcourts from approximately 1200 B.C.E., and at Paso de la Amada, Chiapas, Mexico, a ballcourt was discovered that dates to 1400 B.C.E. The Maya, who came later, also played team sports, particularly one ballgame, known as Pok-a-Tok. The rules, scoring, and general conduct of this game have been lost in time, but sculptural reliefs and hieroglyphics on the walls, benches, and markers of the ballcourts suggest that the game was similar to the modern game of soccer. Most of the large Classic Maya cities—Tikal, Uxmal, Palenque, Copán, and Chichen Itzá—had one or more ballcourts that were close to the main ceremonial precincts where large crowds could view the contests. The Maya had a rigid social system, but evidence suggests that all levels of society attended the ball-games (see Fig. 10.1).

There were many types of ballcourts. Some were closed, and others were open ended. The most common were shaped like a capital I, with sloping or vertical parallel walls enclosing a stone-paved playing court. The playing areas varied in size, but some were about the size of a modern American football field (100 yards long and 40 yards wide). The largest court excavated at Chichen Itzá is 548 feet (167 meters) long and 230 feet (70 meters) wide with vertical walls.

Carved stone rings were inserted at an angle high on the walls, almost out of the players' range; they were ball hoops or markers for scoring. The rings varied in form.

Figure 10.1. *Maya ballcourt, Copán, Honduras. The court is situated below the Acropolis from which this photo was taken. The playing field is bracketed by two sloping areas leading up to two platforms with buildings. On the left, at the upper center of the ramp, is a stone hoop for the ball. At the right end is a set of stairs, possibly for viewers, and beyond that lies the Main Plaza.*

Some of those at Chichen Itzá were stone circles; macau (bird) heads were represented in stone at Copán. The difficulty of sending a ball through one of these rings would have been compounded by such elements as the ring's height, size, and angle to the wall. According to archaeologists L. Schele and M. E. Miller, some of the solid latex rubber balls weighed as much as 8 pounds (3.6 kilograms) and measured 18 inches (46 centimeters) in diameter; others were similar in size to a modern basketball (see Fig. 10.2).

Round stone markers along the center of the playing field may have been used for scoring. These markers varied in size. Some were about 3 feet (1 meter) in diameter. At Copán, three markers—each carved with images of two ball players—stood along the ballcourt's alley, suggesting that the game was played by two contestants. Experts do not know exactly how many players constituted a team, however.

Early Spanish chroniclers in the Valley of Mexico wrote that the players could use neither hands nor feet to propel the solid rubber ball through the hoop but used their shoulders, forearms, and hips to bounce the ball back and forth among the players. Evidence at Chichen Itzá, however, suggests that the players kicked the ball. M. G. Robertson, an authority on Maya ballgames, writes that a player wore an open sandal on one foot and a sandal with a closed toe on the other. Wall paintings and illustrations in codices at Tepantitla suggest that players may also have used bats.

Uniforms and equipment were an important part of the ballgame. The player wore a heavy, horseshoe-shaped pad, called a yoke (made of leather or basketry stuffed with cotton), around the waist for protection from contact with the hard ball and padding on his knees and forearms. Experts have discovered and studied innumerable sculptural, bas-relief, and figurine images of the game, but they have not reached a consensus on the use of several puzzling pieces of equipment, *hachas* or *palmas,* that were associated with it. Relief panels of Late Classic ballcourts at Tajin (Classic Veracruz civilization) show players wearing these items. Hachas are thin stone blades; a stone stela (ca. 300 C.E.) shows them being strapped to a player's hands. Archaeologists have found some Classic Veracruz hachas carved in the shape of a human head in profile wearing a headdress, which may have been used as markers or placed inside the yoke for protection from the impact of the heavy balls. Some scholars believe that the U-shaped carved stone yokes that have been found imitated the heavy belts that players wore.

Figure 10.2. *Clay model (200 B.C.E.–300 C.E.) of a Mexican (Nayarit people) ceremonial ballgame, showing spectators watching two teams of players. The model is 5.5 by 13 by 8 inches (14.0 by 33.0 by 20.3 centimeters).*

The Mesoamerican ballgames were sometimes played as demonstrations of skill, but they usually represented much more than a contest among competing athletes— they reenacted Maya mythological beliefs. The game became an elaborate ritual, motivated by pervasive Maya and other Mesoamerican religious beliefs, symbolic confrontations between humans and divinities, and visual metaphors for the struggle between Life and Death. Miller cites passages in the Popol Vuh, a Quiché Maya text, that refer to Life and Death as contestants in a ballgame. Walls, stelae, and monuments at many ballcourts that are decorated with reliefs depicting scenes of the game, the players, and religious rituals emphasize the link between the game and Mesoamerican religious life.

Abundant evidence shows that the ballgames also provided victims for sacrificial rituals. The priesthood exerted a powerful influence over Maya culture, for example, from the Late Preclassic period (ca. 100 C.E.) until the Spanish conquest in the sixteenth century. The Maya worshiped many deities with complex roles; the priest's function was to interpret the will of the gods, to which human sacrifice was believed to be the appropriate response. Sacrifice, especially of captives taken in warfare, became an integral part of religious rituals throughout Mesoamerica. Sometimes captives were pitted against each other in ballgames, with the unlucky losers offered as sacrifice. The carved panels on one of eleven ballcourts at Tajin graphically reveal the gruesome consequences of defeat. There on the south court of the wall, two members of the winning team are depicted excising a victim's heart. Ballplayers are decapitated in bas-reliefs at Chichen Itzá, and similar scenes are depicted at other sites where stelae show victims' heads being used as balls on the playing field or human figures bound within a ball-shaped form. Thus winning was usually a matter of life and death, and highly skilled players were greatly regarded.

Some ballgames, however, produced less violent outcomes. Ritualized games were the highlight of various festivals. Much wagering accompanied these events, but the losers forfeited only their clothing and jewels. Since there was no form of currency, the winners confiscated the losers' clothing, causing the hasty exodus of the spectators after the winning team was announced.

Many cities had more than one ballcourt; Chichen Itzá, for example, had thirteen. Three of its smaller ballcourts had vertical walls and were arranged near a market that has been dated to the Postclassic period (900–1100 C.E.). Archaeologists have not firmly established the date of the main ballcourt, but they link it to the same period on the basis of sculptural reliefs on platforms between the Castillo (pyramid of Kukulcán) and the ballcourt. (See the discussion of Chichen Itzá later in this chapter).

The location of the ballcourts within the core of the city attests to their architectural importance, as well as to the great appeal that the games and their grisly outcomes had for the populace. The largest pyramid was next to the ballcourt, presumably because it was the site of rituals associated with the games. Games held a similarly important place in ancient Rome, where gladiatorial contests originated from funerary games that culminated in human sacrifice. According to M. E. Miller, the large number of courts at Tajin suggests that the city may have been the site of major games, like the Olympic games of the classical Greek world.

Succeeding rulers may have supported existing ballcourts to preserve religious rituals or commissioned new ones as the population increased. The Maya continued to build ballcourts over a long period in the major lowland Maya cities—from 250 B.C.E. to between 600 and 900 C.E. (in Chichen Itzá to as late as 1100 C.E.). Maya culture, however, gradually declined after 800. The decline led to the abandonment of entire cities, some left unfinished and, as Miller points out, even the ballplayers' equipment was left on the courts at Palenque and Copán.

SOURCES: FERGUSON AND ROHN (1990), M. E. MILLER (1990), SCARBOROUGH AND WILCOX (1991), SCHELE AND MILLER (1986).

Islamic Educational Buildings

Originally, mosques were not meant to be important visual symbols. Their function was primarily to provide a place for public worship, usually in a walled, rectangular precinct enclosed by covered porticos around an open courtyard. Yet mosques also had a secondary educational function, intended to strengthen the ties between Islamic religious and secular thought. Because literacy in Arabic was important for Islamic cohesion, the complexes that Muslims built to house the activities of their faith in all parts of the Islamic world included schools.

After the expansion of Islam in the seventh and eighth centuries, Muslims established a system of higher education. In addition to their own appetite for learning, their intellectual resources included Classical and Hellenistic manuscripts on mathematics and the sciences that Muslim scholars translated into Arabic and circulated widely. In the mosques, they taught theology, jurisprudence, logic, physics, astronomy, algebra, geometry, medicine, and the art of building. By the tenth century, the educational system had matured, and students received degrees from these mosque-universities.

As the Muslim world continued to expand, the complexities of Islamic intellectual pursuits required greater specialization. Teachers of jurisprudence began to instruct students privately in this subject, first in their own homes. Later, communities established private academies of jurisprudence. The buildings they constructed solely for specialized teaching in Quran'ic, philosophical, and administrative law are known as *madrasas*. The word is derived from the Arabic darasa, meaning "to read" or "to learn." Madrasas were separate from, but adjacent to, the mosques.

The origin of the madrasa form has been traced to tenth-century domestic courtyards in the province of Khurasan, in Iran (Persia until 1935), where believers maintained their allegiance to the orthodox Islamic faith despite contemporary political questioning and the appearance of new doctrines. The Seljuk rulers of Khurasan, who made education the key to a return to basic Islamic ideology, modeled their mosques on the Khurasanian cruciform house plan: a central courtyard with four arched openings forming an axis-cross-axis design (see Fig. 10.3). As the Seljuk Empire grew, it carried the classic madrasa type of mosque to other parts of the Islamic world. According to architectural historian F.-A. de Montêquin, the

traditional mosque-university was the main center of higher education, but its failure to incorporate quickly new specialized courses in jurisprudence contributed to the development of the madrasa. By the end of the eleventh century, Baghdad had its first large madrasa, which was an official part of the state university system—Qur'anic law was no longer taught at the mosque-university. Rulers soon recognized that the madrasa had political value in addition to its role in religious instruction; it was the place where future governmental officials were educated to prepare them for battle against heretics and other enemies. Frequently, a wealthy governmental official, a royal benefactor, or even the ruler himself paid for the construction of a madrasa as a gift to the state.

Although the madrasa could include a small mosque, it was a building specifically built for teaching and learning. The classic madrasa is a two-story building with classrooms, service rooms, and a chapel on the first floor and student dormitories above. The cruciform plan is defined by a square courtyard and four large halls, with arched openings called *iwans*, which terminate the two axes of the complex. Just as in a mosque, the most impressive iwan was opposite the *qibla* wall facing the holy city of Mecca; this iwan serves as a chapel. Again, as in a mosque, the wall facing Mecca also has a prayer niche, or *mihrab*.

In a madrasa, a master assigned to each iwan was responsible for instruction in "religious sciences" and jurisprudence, explains Islamist J. Dickie. Each master taught one of the four orthodox legal institutions of the Sunni Islamic tradition: the Hanafi, Shafi'i, Maliki, and Hanbali. In 1234 the first four-rite madrasa (the Mustansiriya) was built in Baghdad with professsors, teaching associates, a library, kitchens, and other facilities. After several years of instruction, the students became Islamic society's legal and administrative officials. Eventually, the curriculum expanded to include a broader field of instruction, and the madrasas became Islamic colleges. At first, the administration of activities in the madrasa was often the responsibility of the imam, who conducted the prayer ritual. As the educational institution grew, however, a dean and faculty members took over responsibility for its internal affairs. Schools were autonomous; they had their own regulatory system and were maintained with support from private donors, explain al Faruqi and al Faruqi.

Although the cross-shaped plan was well suited to the four aspects of Sunni instruction, it was not designed specifically for this purpose. The plan had existed well before the development of the madrasa. The four-iwan plan

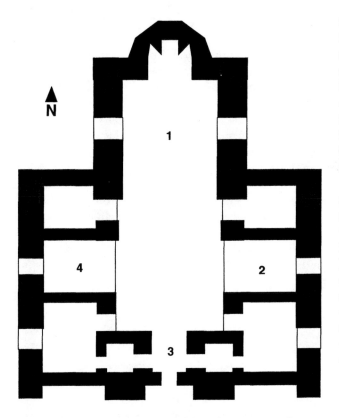

Figure 10.3. *Plan of a typical Islamic four-iwan madrasa— a cruciform plan with a central courtyard. Iwans are situated in the transverse and longitudinal axes of the cross plan. A madrasa is the college of jurisprudence of the traditional Islamic university. Traditionally, the madrasa, like a mosque, is oriented toward Mecca and has a mihrab (prayer niche) to indicate the direction of prayer. Iwan (1) is the largest and functions as a chapel. Iwan (3) is a vestibule, while iwans (2) and (4) serve as classrooms.*

was popular and came to be used for palaces, infirmaries, hospitals, and caravansaries, as well as mosque courtyards. Nevertheless, the arrangement and use of these oversized vaulted halls was not limited to the four-iwan plan. The halls could vary in number and purpose; for instance, the madrasa complex of Dayfa Khatun at Aleppo, Syria, has only one iwan. In early madrasas, the number of iwans was chosen in response to political and local conditions, according to Islamist J. Dickie.

The iwan developed over time into a vehicle for dramatic visual impact. Some iwans were so huge that they required buttressing from the rear, as in the Great Mosque of Isfahan, a classic eleventh-century example of a collegiate mosque (see Figs. 10.4 and 10.5). The large openings blurred the distinction between inner and outer space, reducing the sense of confinement. The courtyard facades might have smaller iwans, contrasting in size but still maintaining an overall unified architectural scheme as they moderated between the huge axial iwans and the small cells of the students. Some tombs also had these large portals; one well-known example is the massive entrance to the celebrated Taj Mahal (see Chapter 9).

Maya ballcourts and Islamic educational buildings seem to have little, if anything, in common. Each, however, was intended to serve a unique function, and both were designed on a monumental scale of similar materials. Although their uses were dramatically different, the ballcourt and the mosque expressed politico-religious beliefs. In both cases, the long-term use of these specific building types shows that their plans admirably fit the purposes for which they were created.

SOURCES: AL FARUQI AND AL FARUQI (1986), ALSAYYAD (1988), DICKIE (1978), MONTÉQUIN (1978).

PYRAMIDS, PLATFORMS, AND ALTARS

People in every part of the world devised ways of raising sacred buildings above the mundane world and making ceremonies more visible to the assembled faithful. Some of these structures were platforms elongated to hold linear buildings. Others were terraces. Still others were pyra-

Figure 10.4. *The Great Mosque, Isfahan, Iran. The iwan features a stalactite-type vault (muqarnas). Three-dimensional shapes in various combinations of corbeling or stucco work produce a honeycomb effect. This unique feature is an original Muslim design.*

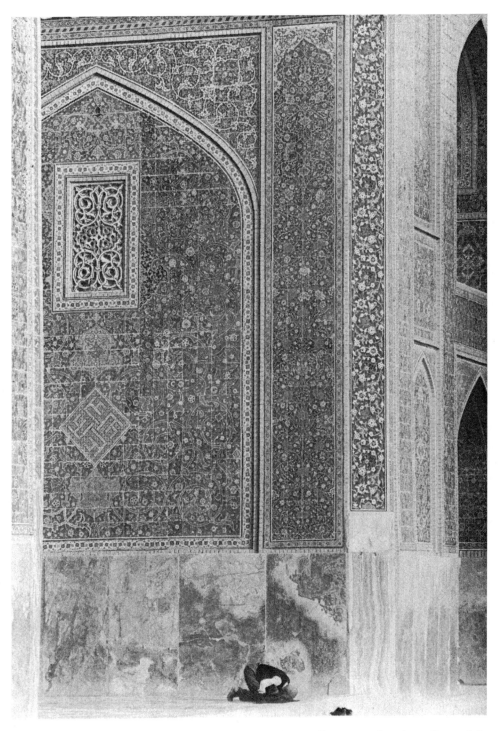

Figure 10.5. *The Great Mosque, Isfahan. Detail of iwan illustrating the tile surfaces of the design. Characteristic of Islamic architecture, all surfaces are decorated with calligraphy and floral motifs.*

mids or cones, with or without temples on top. The pyramids of Mesoamerica and the platforms and altars of the Pacific islands suggest the wide variety of these forms.

Pyramids in Mesoamerica: La Venta, Monte Albán, and Chichen-Itzá

The earliest known pyramidal structure in Mesoamerica is found at the archaeological site of La Venta on the east coast of Mexico. The Olmecs ("people of the rubber country") lived here from around 2250 until 500 B.C.E.[25]

By 1200 B.C.E., the Olmecs had mastered techniques of monumental building and were trading throughout Central America. They were the first Mesoamericans to build ceremonial centers with large architectural groupings oriented to the direction of the magnetic pole, decorated with statues and reliefs in hard stone, for their religious and civic rituals.[26] The earliest platforms for shrines, groups of horizontal slabs (probably altars), and vertical stelae were Olmec creations, as was much of the symbolism used in Mesoamerica until the Spanish Conquest—some of it still surviving. This symbolism included the human/feline form of the jaguar god and death in the form of a skeleton interacting with a human. Olmecs also created the first glyphs for writing, developed fully by their successors, the Zapotecs and Mayas.

Following this rapid development, La Venta flourished from approximately 900 to 500 B.C.E., the capital of a loose-flung society. During those centuries, the island site in the riverine environment and the society that inhabited it were changing with equal rapidity. Amid a 50-kilometer stretch of villages and towns, the Olmecs built their ceremonial area on a formation called a salt dome, a stone plug of gypsum or anhydrite, about 1 mile (1.6 kilometers) long. Today, it is an island in a swampy rain forest.

The most prominent building at La Venta is conventionally called a pyramid (see Fig. 10.6a and b), but it is actually a fluted cone with ten deep grooves between ribs. Recent excavations indicate that there were a stair or ramp on the south side and numerous large and small platforms, such as the one under the cone. Because of its appearance—and because the basalt used in its construction was floated on rafts from the Los Tuxtlas volcanic region 80 miles (130 kilometers) away—some experts have speculated that the Olmecs originally came from that area. The structure is a modest prototype for the later Sun and Moon Pyramids of at Teotihuacán (see Chapter 7), which were 50 to 100 percent larger.

North of the "pyramid" was a large court enclosed by prismatic basalt columns also rafted from the Los Tuxtlas area, weighing up to 1 ton (0.9 metric tons) each. Invisible below the court's clay surface were tons of semiprecious stones, and some pavings arranged as gigantic jaguar masks. Above the buried paving were other treasures under precise layers of sand and clay in several colors.

Olmec architecture may have inspired later Classic buildings at other sites in the central plateau of Mexico and in the Maya lands of Mesoamerica. After the third century C.E., Olmec customs, symbolism, and architectural ideals from La Venta and nearby San Lorenzo were adopted by the Classic-era cultures that succeeded them. Despite the similarities, Monte Albán in Oaxaca, Mexico, was built not by the Olmecs but by an independent trading partner of La Venta. Similarities include the practice of using layers of clay in contrasting colors beneath the surface of the monumental plaza. Ideas, as well as goods, passed between the two sites.

Monte Albán was occupied for 1,500 years after 500 B.C.E., mainly by the Zapotecs. It is situated in the dry southern highlands of Mexico on a ridge rising 1,000 to 1,300 feet (300 to 400 meters) above a valley between two rivers. Settlers, drawn to the area by abundant deposits of magnetite, a kind of iron ore, set up workshops to produce objects from the refined ore—small mirrors, earposts, and other trade items. Later they expanded production to make large, concave mirrors of other iron ores, apparently used in religious rites. Their technical innovations also benefitted agriculture; the Zapotecs were responsible for several major breakthroughs in canal technology, such as the earliest Mexican reservoir-fed canal and the earliest floodgate known in the country, both facilitating irrigation.

Zapotec architecture, like Olmec, included platforms. Yet the Zapotecs had easier access to their building materials—limestone and sandstone—a fact that made an immediate difference in the appearance and massing of their platforms. At Monte Albán, they leveled the ridge to form an enormous paved plaza and placed the major pyramids on platforms near the edges, some with walls more than

---

[25]These are 1992 versions of the dates; carbon 14 dating in 1957 gave uncalibrated dates from 1160 to 580 for La Venta.

[26]Maya architectural groups were similarly oriented to the magnetic pole, and as the pole shifted location, so the orientation changed, as R. H. Fuson demonstrated in 1969.

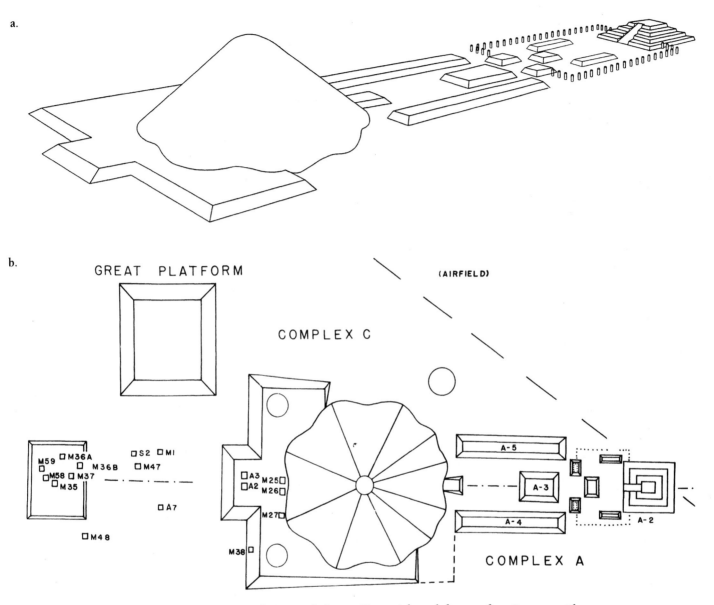

Figure 10.6. *La Venta, Mexico, reconstructed view and plan.* **a.** *From right to left are a four-tier pyramid, which probably supported a houselike shrine; a large court, 131 by 164 feet (40 by 50 meters), edged by platforms that served as either the earliest formal ballcourt or the site of palaces or administrative buildings. On the left, a fluted (scalloped) cone is now thought to face another group of buildings out of the drawing, farther left. The cone, 360 by 460 feet, was made of 130,000 cubic yds. of beaten earth and clay and set on a broad low platform (110 meters tall, 140 meters in diameter, and 99,000 cubic meters).* **b.** *The plan shows a group of buildings at the left that are now thought to be the focus of the composition. The fluting of the cone is indicated by the array of radii.*

20 feet (7 meters) high (see Fig. 10.7). Like their Olmec models, these pyramids and platforms were oriented to the magnetic pole. Stairs were common on the pyramidal sanctuaries and on the platforms with or without temples or palaces. Outer walls and stairways were made of stone, inner walls of rubble. Because foundations were placed on the ground or just below the topsoil level, earthquake damage was common. Lest repairs weaken a structure, the custom was to enlarge the platform or pyramid, masking the damage. A large platform of stone formed the basis for each temple or administration building made of ephemeral wood and clay (see Fig. 10.8). Some of the pyramids seem to have served as tombs, for under Pyramid 7 was found the exquisite gold jewelry that is now the great drawing-card in Oaxaca's regional museum. Along the west side, one pyramid platform was enriched with figural reliefs (see Fig. 10.9).

The combination of temple, patio, and altar on a platform was a Late Urban Period (up to 750 C.E.) building type at Monte Albán. Typically, a two-room temple stood at one end of a platform, with an enclosed patio in front of it, in which stood an altar. Beyond the patio was an open space for those attending a ceremony, located at the far end of the platform and reached by a broad stairway from the plaza. This configuration was later adopted at Chichen Itzá, where it is now called a Gallery Patio Structure.

In its heyday, Monte Albán was home to some thirty thousand people. After 750 C.E., the population moved down to the valleys, and the ridge site became a fortress. The canal and reservoir system that made early settlement possible are no longer visible on the mountain.

***

The building tradition of the Olmecs and Zapotecs reached a climax in the magnificent Maya pyramids of Chichen Itzá in the Yucatán peninsula of Mexico. Gradual development of the Yucatán began with the first human occupancy about ten thousand years ago. By 2500 B.C.E., people were establishing farming communities, making pottery, and building houses of a type that is still used in the region: posts supporting a thatched roof, set on a plastered earthen platform. This form served as the prototype for religious and secular buildings over two millennia.

The form of settlement in the Yucatan changed dramatically between 750 and 450 B.C.E. A village center with

Building over
Tomb 104

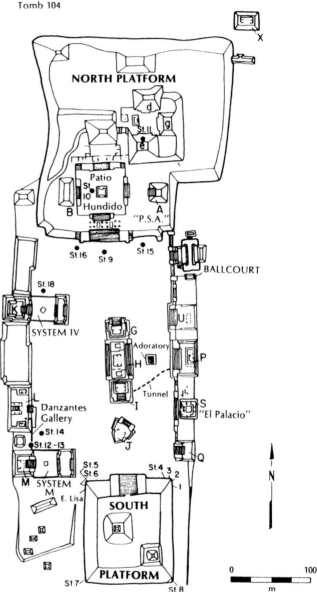

Figure 10.7. *Plan of the main plaza, Monte Albán, Mexico. The architecture is pulled to the edges of the artificially leveled and extended hill top. Outcroppings were used as bases for the north and south platforms, on which pyramids and patios were built. At least one ballcourt was placed at right center, one of the structures lining the right side of the main plaza. The pointed building at J was an observatory. For Danzantes Gallery on left; see Fig. 10.9.*

Figure 10.8. *View of Patio Hundido, Monte Albán, looking south. This patio backs up to the North Platform group of the Acropolis and overlooks the large open spaces, platforms, and stepped pyramids in the center and south along the ridge. No trees shaded the plaza—the dazzling brilliance of the sun made strong shadows to set off the forms of the architecture.*

wooden buildings on a platform surrounding a courtyard was replaced by a broad open platform with a small pyramid at the west end. Set in the center of a town, the plaza and its platform alone required 130,790 cubic yards (100,000 cubic meters) of limestone. Local rulers and priests performed rituals in the plaza; nearby they built the wooden prototypes of later stone palaces. From 200 B.C.E. onward, these rulers, controlling a larger population and wielding more power, began to build pyramids more than 100 feet (30 meters) tall. The placement of these structures was perhaps more important than their size as an indicator of advancing civilization: Already by 100

B.C.E., some pyramids were oriented to the paths of astronomical events. By the fourth century C.E., a group of structures at Tikal, in present-day Guatamala, had sight lines based on the observation of equinoxes and solstices.

Chichen Itzá was built and occupied by an increasingly cosmopolitan nobility—some Maya, some Mexican—whose public art inccrporated diverse political expressions to reinforce and consolidate their authority. Founded about 850 C.E., the city ruled most of the northern lowlands until about 1200. The center of the archaeological site covers 3 square miles (5 square kilometers) and contains a dense collection of architectural ruins (see

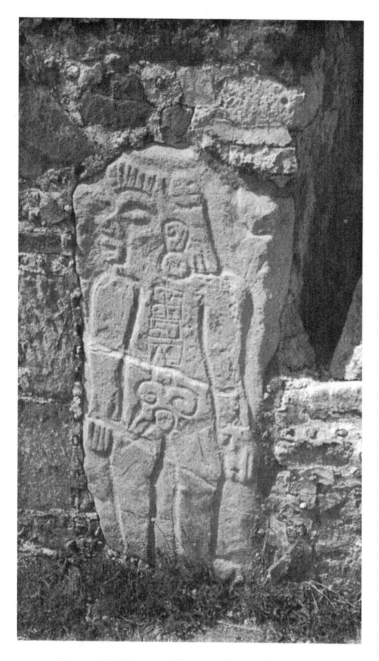

Figure 10.9. *Monte Albán relief, one of the approximately three hundred reliefs called "Dansants," a series of upright stelae along the west side of the central space, the Danzantes Gallery shown in Fig. 10.7. Today they are thought to represent the contorted bodies of slain captives; however, themes of self-sacrifice, veneration of ancestors, and human suffering from unpredictable forces in the cosmos is also inherent in these images.*

Fig. 10.10). Although the site has been excavated for more than twenty years, much about it remains unknown—population size, settlement patterns, building functions, and chronological scheme. Any account must be considered tentative. (Compare with Chapter 14, Tikal.)

Chichen Itzá's planners and builders developed a number of architectural styles. One, named for the early Chenes people, had a decorated lower facade and masked doorway; it is visible in the facade of the extension of the so-called Nunnery. Next to it, the building now called the "Church" or "Iglesia," is in the Puuc style, named for another Maya group. Dating from before 300 C.E., this style features smooth, veneered lower walls topped by decorative friezes of stone mosaics; the plain wall and the frieze are separated by a horizontal molding that is repeated at the summit. Puuc decorations, more geometric than the Chenes style, are also colorful, with red backgrounds and green motifs against whitewash or stucco. Builders in this style employed a few columns to support the lintels of the doorways.

In addition to early Yucatán styles, the rulers of Chichen Itzá used Mexican architectural plans and ideas like those from Tula, 62 miles (100 kilometers) to the west—stone altars with animal friezes, pillars with reliefs of warriors on the four faces, life-size caryatids, sloping embankments combined with vertical walls of temples, freestanding serpent columns, feathered serpent balustrades, and carved wooden lintels and beams. At Chichhen Itzá, however, these devices were built in new materials with new methods. The earlier Yucatan architecture had emphasized mass in the piles of heavy materials that made up the pyramids, but at Chichen Itzá, a new architecture of space used columns and piers, combined with vaulting, to produce immense roofed structures, parallel corridors, open along the facade, measuring as much as 300 by 50 feet (91.57 by 15.25 meters) in a single building. Up to ten times as big as earlier Mayan rooms had been, some were as large as 8,000 square feet (743 square meters). In some colonnades, thrones have been found, indicating that these buildings may have served as council halls. (Compare them with the audience halls of Inka Cuzco, Chapter 8.)

The earliest surviving structure at Chichen Itzá is the High Priest's Grave, a pyramid variously dated to 842 or 999 C.E. It was built over a seven-lobed cave, similar to the cave under the Pyramid of the Sun at Teotihuacán, suggesting that it was the "origin" building in the cosmic landscape here. Entry was by an artificial shaft, filled by the bones of seven graves and many sacred objects of rock crystal, jade, and pottery. Perhaps the graves are tied to a legend involving an alternate name for the city: Uucyabnal, meaning "seven great rulers."

Because of the regular Mayan renovation of pyramids and temples by enclosing an earlier sanctuary in a new outer layer of masonry, excavators have discovered, at several places in the Yucatán, Classical Maya pyramids encased within later versions. The Temple of the Chac-Mool[27] at Chichen Itzá, for instance, was found enclosed in the Pyramid of the Warriors, while a red throne in the form of a jaguar was found in the sanctuary of the earlier temple buried under the Castillo (see Fig. 10.11).

Central to the latest version of the city (950–1200 C.E.) were the rebuilt Temple of the Warriors, Court of the Thousand Columns, and the Castillo pyramid. The Temple of the Warriors was 180 feet long and 100 feet high, surrounded by an 8,000-square-foot columnar hall (55 by 30.5 meters, 743 square meters). Four flights of 92 stairs ascended the pyramid, one on each side, with an extra step at the entrance to the temple, for a total of 365 steps. The temple on top was approached through paired serpent columns and square piers with relief carvings. This monument resembles those at Tula but is larger and better built. Anthropologist R. J. Sharer thinks that Tula may have been an outpost of Mexicanized Maya—a reversal of a long-popular theory that invaders from Tula built Chichen Itzá. With regard to our understanding of the Toltec and the Maya, C. B. Kristan-Graham writes that with "more data on the internal evolution of each, there is less reliance on 'foreign influence' to explain the culture"—and the architecture.

Considerably larger than the Temple of the Warriors is the so-called Castillo (see Fig. 10.11). Four stairways led to the well-preserved, corbel-vaulted building at the top. The Castillo is similar to the late Twin Pyramid Groups at Tikal (see Chapter 14). It was dedicated to Kukulcan, the Maya equivalent of Quetzalcoatl. Like such central Mexican pyramids as Quetzcoatl in the Citadel at Teotihuacán, it has monster mask reliefs on the exterior and carvings of war captains on the door jambs.

---

[27]A chac-mool was a statue made in human form, its knees drawn up and leaning back on its elbows with its head turned over one shoulder; its hands were spread out on either side of a "plate" laid flat on its abdomen, between the chac-mool's shoulders and knees, to receive the heart cut from a living victim.

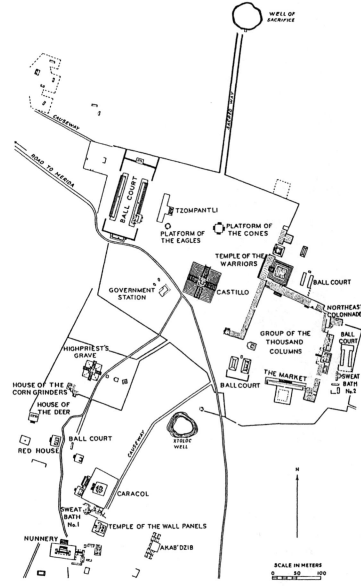

Figure 10.10. *Plan of the central core, Chichen Itzá, Yucatán, Mexico. The Xtoloc Well (center) was one of many karst shafts that served as water sources, but the Well of Sacrifice (top of the plan) seems to have been used only for religious ceremonies. Modern roads and historic raised causeways for pedestrian traffic are shown by double lines. (See R. H. Fuson, 1969, Fig. 4, for the astronomical orientation of these buildings, with particular reference to the solstice sunrises and sunsets.) Pyramids, ballcourts, and other structures are loosely grouped in a "campus plan."*

Figure 10.11. *View of El Castillo, Chichen Itzá. This the largest and tallest of the pyramids here, the base measuring nearly 200 feet (60 meters) on a side and the height measuring approximately half that. Stairs on all four sides lead to the temple on top, now missing its original tall crest.*

The architecture of Mesoamerica became larger and more intricate over time. The builders had a flexible vocabulary of spatial expression to make statements of grandeur that ranged in scale from individual buildings to entire civic complexes. Elevations gradually came to emphasize the interplay of masses, the subordination of units to the whole, and unification. Stairways were important, whether tall and narrow or short and wide. Because of powerful light and large scale, deep shadows formed against the gray limestone of Chichen Itzá, and the builders included the effects of these shadows in their plans for the structures. From its fairly modest beginnings in the clay cone at La Venta and the stone platforms shaped like truncated pyramids at Monte Albán, Mesoamerican traditional architecture moved toward its grand finale at Chichen Itzá. Throughout this sequence, the builders continued to develop variations on the theme of the terrace, pedestal, and platform that separated the sacred precinct

from the mundane world while they simultaneously provided a visible link between the supernatural world above and the natural world below.

SOURCES: KRISTAN-GRAHAM (1989), 95; SHARER (1994); WINTER (1989), 45.

Oceania: The Tuamotu Archipelago

Some architectural elements used by the Maya recur in the religious architecture of the Polynesian people of the Tuamotu Archipelago in the southeastern Pacific Ocean. Religious spaces, called *marae*, are of the simplest form—stone platforms and altars sometimes surrounded by walls (see Fig. 10.12). Yet the variation among them testifies to the human delight in differentiation and individuation.

Large numbers of marae are scattered over each atoll. Among traditional Polynesians, every lineage built its marae on its own land, convenient for feasts and other rituals. Judging by the bones found in the refuse pits, the primary ritual carried out at the marae was feasting on turtles. As ethnologist K. P. Emory noted in 1934,

> [t]he elders went with great pomp to the marae, taking their lances and grouping themselves in a semicircle [around the altar], each one with his back against his special long stone, at the foot of which was his smooth and shining stool made in one piece from the trunk of the tou tree.

After the elders offered the sacrificial turtles, they closed off the marae with coconut ropes. Women and commoners were allowed at the open end of the court. Other ceremonies took place to the right and left of the altar, where offerings were made especially to the warriors and chiefs. An 1874 observer reported:

> [The] chief priest begins the ceremony by sitting with his back against the [altar]. His principal assistant was on the right and two others on the left. Out on the court, opposite the chief priest, knelt the "kneeler." All these priests were of chiefly blood. Left and right of the "kneeler" sat two parallel rows of warriors on stools. The assistant gave the ceremonial cap and staff to the headpriest who took a bunch of leaves and struck the ground to awaken and call the god. Then he turned toward the ahu and invoked all the gods with deafening yells. Later he sat out in the court and was presented with the head of the turtle."
>
> —Emory (1934/1971), paraphrasing
> A. R. Montiton (1874)

If a hurricane, a war, or simply the desire for better land led people to occupy new lands, they established new lineages with new sanctuaries. They abandoned their earlier marae, which often fell into ruin. Each marae had a name; Emory listed 274 different names for 344 marae; in only two cases were duplicate names used on the same island. Repetition of a name indicated strong links between places and groups. The list included five names each used for more than five marae, each on a different island. Even when the name is repeated, however, the architectural form of the marae is different.

A Spanish visitor to Tuamotu in 1606 was the first to describe these sanctuaries to the Western world. He wrote:

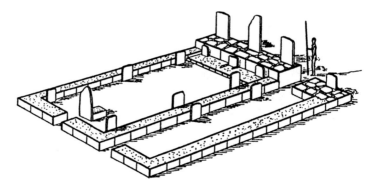

Figure 10.12. *Drawing of a marae at Manhina-i-te-ata on Takaroa in the Tuamotu archipelago. The entrance is from the left, facing the altarlike platform at the far end, with its upright slabs. Stones form an enclosing wall. At least one ceremonial stone chair was placed on the longitudinal axis, just inside the entry, facing the center of the platform.*

> In groves of coconut and Pisonia trees were raised slabs of a marae. The ground was kept very clean. From a tree hung plaited coconut leaves which fell over the upright of the stone altar.
>
> —quoted by Emory (1934/1971)

In 1765 a visitor to a marae on Takaroa saw near it "many neat boxes full of human bones," which the people kept as relics of their forebears. In the western islands of Tuamotu, house-shaped boxes of such relics, called *fare heiao* (*fare* was the local word for "small house," and *heiao* is related to the Hawaiian term for this kind of sanctuary, *heiao* or *heiau*) were stored separately in a niche or in a special house for use in religious or patriotic ceremonies. On occasion, people took out these boxes, dusted and decorated them, and raised them on forked posts in the marae. They also stored feathers of rare birds, considered treasures, in other boxes at the marae.

Emory was the chief investigator of these religious spaces in the Tuamotuan Archipelago, finding a total of ninety-nine on the atolls of Takaroa, Takapoto, Fagatau, Fakahina, Makatea, Reao, and Hao (see Figs. 10.12 and 10.13). He also drew maps of the locations and plans of the forms of marae on all the inhabited islands north and east of the archipelago. In Hawaii and the Marquesas Islands he found the greatest complexity of marae form. In the Society Islands, Tuamotu, the Australs, Tongareva, and Easter Island, the marae forms are simpler and easier to identify.

Some of the marae Emory found in the Tuamotuan Archipelago were grouped on the sea side of an island

Figure 10.13. *Heiau (marae) on Huanine, French Polynesia. The platform has four levels, constructed of irregular stones without mortar.*

(Reao); others were on the lagoon side (Fagatau). Most were in or near villages, often built in the shade of trees and sited to receive the cooling trade winds.

Central and western Tuamotuan marae exhibit some common features: an unpaved rectangular court, often enclosed in a low coral wall; a tiny stone or coral platform with an upright slab in its center within the court, and a platform, called an *ahu* (roughly translated as "altar") and more upright slabs at the far end of the courtyard from the entrance. The ahu measures 10 to 80 feet in length, 2 to 10 feet in width, and 1 to 5 feet in height (3 to 24 meters by 0.6 to 3 meters by 0.3 to 0.8 meters). Behind the ahu are three or more upright slabs, ranging in height from 2 feet to 9 feet (60 to 275 centimeters), erected in groups of uneven numbers, set 8 to 18 inches (20 to 45 centimeters) apart.

One long wall of the court may end in a small circular enclosure used as a refuse pit. Some marae, such as the one on Reao, have another special feature: a small vault or niche in the ahu or in the step in front of it for stor-

ing of scared objects. Some marae contain special altars for particular gods—on Fagatau Island, an oblong pile of branch coral on one side of the court is an ahu to the god Ruahatu, lord of the ocean. Such altars are also known at Hao and Vairaatea.

On Reao, Emory studied twenty-one marae, ranging from 25 to 100 feet (8 to 31 meters) in length and 4 to 10 feet (122 to 305 centimeters) in width. The small platform in front of the ahu normally measured 5 by 3 feet (150 by 90 centimeters) and stood at least 20 feet (6 meters) from it. Courts, defined with stone or coral edges, were 100 to 300 feet long (30 to 90 meters). Marae vary in the placement, number, and size of upright stelae along the rear edge of the ahu. Emory suggests that many of these differences arose from variations in the local availability of materials.

On the western islands, the court was not enclosed, but the ahu was faced with one course of squared slabs placed on edge, from 2 to 6 feet (61 to 193 centimeters) long. The slabs overlapped at the corners. The interior was filled with coral rubble, with a top dressing of fine coral pebbles or sometimes flagstones, similar to the construction methods used at Nan Madol (see Chapter 8).

Some marae have small platforms to the right or left of the ahu. In the western marae, these tiny platforms bear uprights next to or opposite the ahu to serve as backrests for the gods or their representatives. The upright of greatest veneration is reserved for the chief or chieftess. According to a Spanish visitor named Varela, who described the stones in 1772:

> [They] do duty as leaning stocks when those who meet together for their religious ceremonies sit down at these spots; but only in Epure, priests and their *arii* and his brother do sit down there, and although some of these stones remain vacant they pertain to the deceased fathers and ancestors of these personages and nobody may seat himself against them.
>
> —*quoted in Emory (1969)*

Tuamotu's location holds clues to the evolution of the marae form. Far south of Hawaii, sandwiched between Tahiti and the Marquesas Islands (see the map of Oceania in the Appendix), this archipelago has some marae that resemble those of Hawaii and others that resemble those of Tahiti. Emory (1969) wrote:

> [E]ast Tuamotu marae, in differing from the western and Tahitian, exhibit a number of the differences which distinguish the archaic marae ruins [ca. 1000 C.E.] of Necker Island, at the northwestern extremity of Hawaii, from the inland marae of Tahiti. . . . It is easy to believe that the marae of the eastern Tuamotus are survivals of the same culture which left the prehistoric marae on Necker Island, and therefore that the[y] . . . represent a form employed by the earliest settlers both in Hawaii and in southeastern Polynesia. The discovery . . . of prehistoric marae . . . is conclusive evidence that the marae form is an ancient one.

The oldest form of marae has uprights without an ahu, with or without paving. At least one "seat" (backrest) was provided, considered essential for the meeting of gods, ancestors, and men. Some of these seats were sculpted with abstract human elements. In the eighteenth century, Captain James Cook described similar backrests with painted human faces on Kauai, in the Hawaiian Islands.

On some islands, coastal and inland marae have different forms. None of the western marae of the Tuamotus

differ much from the more ancient, inland marae of Tahiti and Moorea except for the use of local basalt instead of limestone (compare with the marae at Huanine in French Polynesia, Fig. 10.13). Yet many variations are known within this type. The largest Tuamotan marae, found on Tubuai, are rectangular courts, 65 by 160-feet (20 by 49 meters), enclosed on three sides by a fence of stone slabs as high as 10 feet (3 meters); these marae have no ahu, but the court is paved. At the other extreme, people on Rapa built miniature marae, probably because the village was crowded onto a hilltop. Ahu on Easter Island, like those of the Marquesas, contain earlier types of platforms. Some marae are roughly built with found—not shaped—stones, while others are carefully built with platforms faced with neatly fitted slabs of even height and megalithic uprights trimmed to convenient size. And the New Zealand Polynesians completely abandoned the building of marae during their several generations of nomadism after they migrated to the islands.

The sanctuaries were often built in or near groves of Pisonia trees, whose shade was particularly appreciated in the hotter climates of near-sea-level atolls. At certain times of festival, the celebrants closed the marae court with a garland of coconut leaves skillfully woven together.

Both these Polynesian sanctuaries (see Fig. 10.13) and the pyramids of Mesoamerica were built for ceremonies honoring the gods. Not accidentally, they also reinforced the power of the elite who were both priests and kings (see Chapter 8). Ceremonies that took place in these sacred enclosures made up in their elaboration for the simplicity of architectural form.[28]

SOURCES: EMORY (1934/1971, 1969).

HOUSING VARITIES

People have invented many kinds of houses. We examine a common type of housing found, among many other places, in Nepal: the urban town house that shares party walls with neighbors on two sides. Another widely used

---

[28]For comparative materials on early modern attempts to deal with non-European architecture, see J. Rykwert, *On Adam's House in Paradise: The Idea of the Primitive in Architectural History* (MIT Press, 1981), a brilliant romp, or B. Stafford, *Voyage into Substance: Art, Science and Nature in the Illustrated Travel Account 1760–1840* (MIT Press, 1984), a prize-winning and illuminating study.

form is the house on stilts, usually freestanding, especially common in the tropical and subtropical area in Southeast Asia and across the western and central Pacific.

Town Houses in Nepal

Nepal's three historical capitals, Kathmandu, Patan, and Bhaktapur, have complex and intricate social systems. Kathmandu, the capital today, is the most cosmopolitan, while Patan (see Chapter 12) is mainly Buddhist and Bhaktapur is the old Hindu center. In the best Nepalese tradition, however, members of each group live among the others in the three cities and in small country villages.

The different peoples of the valley share a few basic housing patterns—a unity of form all the more remarkable because Nepal is home to forty main ethnic groups, each with its own language and culture. The town houses of the Newari people of Bhaktapur show how the Newari have traditionally organized their domestic spaces.

Bhaktapur is divided into many neighborhoods, to some degree by status and by caste (the occupational group into which one is born). On one hand, the organization of communities by caste defines and limits individual opportunities; on the other, it creates an environment of mutual support within each neighborhood. Shopkeepers, teachers, officials, courtiers, and other high-status people live along the main road and around the three major plazas. Farmers live in the middle zone. People of the lower castes and untouchables, such as street sweepers, live along the river near the bottom of the town, in one-story freestanding structures, not town houses. This difference seems to indicate that these residents were originally ethnically distinct from the Newaris of the upper town (see the plan of Bhaktapur in Fig. 7.4).

The town is densely urbanized. Daily life centers on the neighborhoods, in which 150 to 300 brick houses, three or four stories tall, share party walls. Congestion is in the same range as in Cairo or Tokyo, although there are far fewer inhabitants. The chief reasons for crowding seem to be to preserve land for agriculture (only 17 percent of the land in this mountainous country is arable), to maximize urban sociability, and to reduce the demand for fuel in the winter. Although Nepal's latitude is that of central Florida, its altitudes range from plains of 650 to peaks of 26,000 feet (198 to 7,925 meters). The lowland areas have a tropical, humid climate, but the entire country is cooled by winds from the Himalayas. In Bhaktapur, Patan, and Kathmandu, at an altitude of 4,600 feet (1,400 meters), winters are chilly. Tall, narrow townhouses (see

Figs. 10.14 and 10.15) are a practical response to both the climate and the shortage of fuel.

A Newari family of parents, sons, sons' wives, and children lives in each town house. Another reason for families to live together is that there is no social network or governmental program to assist families in times of emergency or long-term need. The family is a patriarchy under the control of the eldest man. Each gender has a defined role. Women's work is child care, cooking, collecting water and firewood, animal care, nursing the sick, planting, and harvesting. In the past, women stayed mostly within their neighborhoods, but more recently they have been participating in the wider life of the community. Most men work at the whole range of agricultural tasks; in the 1980s, 70 percent of city dwellers were still farmers who were occupied with crops and animals—as well as trade, crafts, or construction in the off-season. Because construction trades in Nepal are not caste specific, they offer job opportunities to many people.

Most housing in Bhaktapur was built two hundred to three hundred years ago, when the city was the capital of an independent kingdom. Materials were the same as those used in the palaces of the Kathmandu Valley—dark red baked brick or gray sun-dried brick with brown wooden grillwork for windows and door frames, topped by a tile roof (see Fig. 10.14), make an attractive streetscape. Fired brick is still used for the visible parts of the house, sun-dried brick for the rest. House builders use mud mortar, which is cheap but not durable; it cracks easily, allowing walls to bulge alarmingly and the cold winter winds to blow into the house. Foundations are usually of limestone, forming a platform at least 9 inches (23 centimeters) high for protection against flooding by the torrential rains of the monsoon. Because there is no vapor barrier between the platform and the walls, the houses are damp and cold in winter. A wooden or brick partition on the second floor and columns on the third and fourth floors divide the space but are separate from the load-bearing brick walls. Floors are coated with clay over wood. These houses are inexpensive to build but require more maintenance than would a house made entirely of baked bricks with cement mortar.

The completion of a town house is followed by a ritual consecration, during which the priest may recite a prayer, such as the following:

O my son! . . . build a house as follows: assemble carpenters and brick makers and other incarnations of Visvakarma as necessary. Then, choosing an auspicious

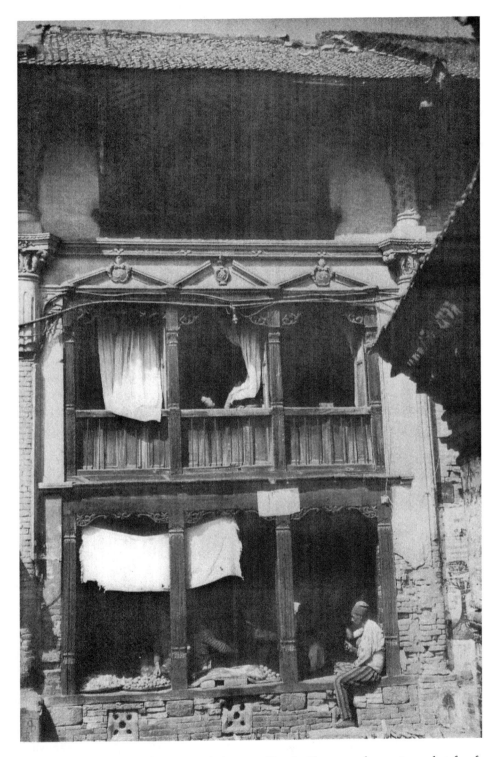

Figure 10.14. *A small house in Bhaktapur, Nepal. The town house is made of soft red brick with window frames of wood painted dark brown. The ground floor is used for commerce.*

Figure 10.15. *A typical Newar house, Kathmandu Valley, Nepal. Load-bearing walls of brick support the four-story structure, with the central wall replaced by columns or piers on the two upper stories. The lattice windows permit cross ventilation and may be sealed with wide shutters that hook out of the way against the ceiling. The kitchen and eating area are in the attic, and there is often a roof terrace (see Fig. 6.5). This house is unusual in having street doors on a long side instead of at the end.*

time, prepare and bake bricks. Have the auspiciously ordained foundation laying ceremony . . . putting in [models of] a fish, a turtle, an elephant, a horse, and a golden lotus. Then build a magnificent house with the proper auspicious marks and proportions. If a man does this, I call him great . . . O my client! You have built a house to live in; your house is finished . . . may your construction always remain firm. May all the gods protect it for as long as the gods live on Mt. Meru. . . .
—from the Sthirobhava-vākya,
quoted in Slusser (1982)

Family housing is remarkably similar wherever the Newari live. All town houses occupy the same width on a street, but the depth depends on the particular family. Space is used in an identical manner within each house. The ground floor is for animals and storage of things that can withstand dampness or for a shop or two spilling over into the street. On the second floor, a longitudinal partition wall of mud brick separates sleeping spaces from stor-

age areas, and the third floor consists of one large room with several columns arranged above the partition wall of the second floor. The third floor is used for feasting with family and neighbors and often for extra sleeping. During the daytime, sleeping mats are rolled up and stored at the edges of the room. Clothing, such as easily rolled saris, is kept in wall niches. Also, with more light than the lower floors, the third floor is the place for weaving and other craft activities. The fourth, or top, floor (if there is one) is again a large room with columns down the middle, but its use is restricted to family members who sleep, cook, and eat there. They use the roof terrace for preparing and drying some foods, such as grain, and perhaps for keeping chickens in a chicken coop. Because warm air rises, the top story may collect some heat from the floors below. In addition, the living-room kitchen is the most private space of the house, where visitors go only upon specific invitation, and is therefore as far as possible from the street door. This space may also be used at night for sleeping (see Fig. 6.5).

The urban town house is not without its shortcomings, but, for the most part, it has proved satisfactory in the Newari cities of Nepal. It accommodates people's desire for community and is frugal with building materials and fuel. The house and the life of the people are mutually well adapted.

SOURCES: BLAIR (1983), GUTSCHOW AND KÖLVER (1991), P. OLIVER (1987), SLUSSER (1982).

Stilt Houses in Indonesia

Houses on stilts are ubiquitous on the islands of Indonesia. (See also the accounts of elevated buildings in Chapter 3, Granaries, and Chapter 5, Japanese Houses.) Anthropologist R. Waterson's illuminating book on the vernacular architecture of Southeast Asia shows that dwellings raised on posts are a logical regional response to climatic conditions and frequent seismic activity. She introduces us to a "complex of related cultures" having many differences but sharing the practice of living in elevated structures (see Figs. 10.16, 10.17, and 10.18). Stilts keep houses from contact with the damp earth in tropical regions, offer protection from rodents and other pests, allow ventilation, and defend residents against intruders. Chickens, goats, and other animals are also sheltered under the elevated house (compare with Fig. 10.19)

The stilt house is elevated on vertical posts that can either be set directly into the ground or rest on flat stones that serve as foundations. The posts support the floor and enclosing walls, above which rests the roof—although not all Indonesian dwellings have walls.

The diameter of the posts varies. R. Waterson reports that in 1862, Sir Spencer St. John, an authority on Borneo colonial history, in observing a Kenowit (Sarawat, north Borneo) village, explained the advantage of thick posts: If the village was attacked, the enemy hauled a war boat to the village, where about fifty of the attackers used it as a shield. Gaining access to the area underneath a house, they proceeded to cut the posts. If the posts were sufficiently thick, the defenders had time in which to retaliate. Posts of modest size had their advantage, too: A group of people could pick up an entire house and move it to another location. Anthropologist, C. Snouck Hurgronje (1906) relates that in Aceh, Sumatra, builders commonly made pegs smaller than the posts' holes and then wedged them in place, allowing them to dismantle and reassemble the house quickly.

There are many variations, but the general house plan uses a post-and-lintel system to support the load of both floor and roof. Builders attach architectural elements to one another using the mortise-and-tenon technique, not nails (see Fig. 10.18a and b). Natural materials, such as fibers, bamboo, and rattan, lash the constructional elements together. Builders in some areas, mainly North and South Nias, use diagonal posts as well as vertical ones. Their V-shaped floor supports resist seismic activity and offer greater support to the structure, especially when the weight of the heavy roof is a factor. Walls of leaf and split bamboo panels, which are not load bearing, function as screens to enclose the interior living space. As noted, they are optional; builders often omit them, increasing air circulation through the house (see Figs. 4.10 and 10.21).

Large, sloping roofs with extended eaves, characteristic of many Southeast Asian dwellings, are a dominant feature of the Indonesian stilt houses. They give the impression—not always justified—of ample interior space. An oversized roof is also a symbol of the wealth of the household. Roofs may have other symbolic decorative elements that have little to do with construction. For example, many saddle-roofed, pile-built houses in Sumatra, north Thailand, and northeast India have gable finials shaped like crossed water-buffalo horns (see Fig. 10.19). These finials are meant as symbols of protection for the household—the water-buffalo uses its horns for defense, as well as offense, and is important in terms of wealth and sacrifice. Roof finials can also have decorations shaped like birds or water serpents, as in south Sulawesi.

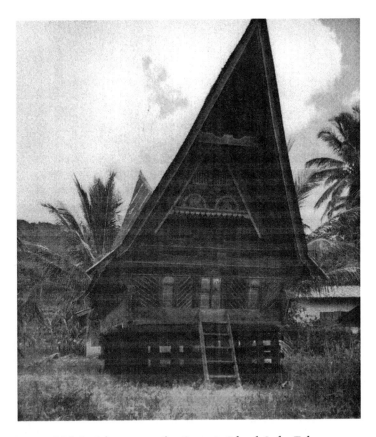

Figure 10.16. *A house on stilts, Samosir Island, Lake Toba, Sumatra. Under the steep roof's tall gable (although not quite as high as those in Figs. 4.3 and 6.6), decorated with symbolic paintings, a veranda stretches across the front. A wide ladder allows access. The stilts elevate the building several feet. Chickens and pigs may be sheltered under the house.*

Like the Batammaliba of Togo and Benin (see Chapter 15), some Indonesian societies metaphorically relate parts of houses to human anatomy. They think of a house as having a head, legs, body, and other elements like those of a living organism. When a house is built, it is "given life." When fire or some other calamity destroys a house or it is thought to be inhabited by evil spirits, the house loses its vitality or "living force." A healthy house is thought to be "cool," while an unhealthy one is "hot"— an understandable analogy with temperature, given the tropical equatorial climate.

Elevated houses need not be on land. For more than four millennia, people have lived in pile-supported habitations over water. Such dwellings are still being built in

Figure 10.17. *Kenowit, Sarawak, north Borneo. A village of tall houses on stilts. Much of the same ecological rationale for building is found here as in the Amazon region (see Fig. 10.20), but the tall piles here were also for defense against attacks.*

some regions of the Southwest Pacific; architect J. Fitchen relates that Papuan river dwellers live on a river branch not far from the Waropan coast and build houses of grass and palm slats with bamboo floors, supported on pilings. The houses are in midstream, and residents reach the shore by swimming or by boat. Some houses over water are designed to accommodate large communal groups and require combined effort in their construction. In Humbolt Bay in New Guinea, entire villages are set on pilings aligned in a street pattern. Building determinants include the depth of the water, the necessary depth of a stable foundation for the posts in the lake—or river—bottom strata, and the desired height of the floor above the water level (compare with Fig. 10.17, 10.20). Builders must consider these points when estimating the length and width of the pole supports and the labor they will require. These problems are compounded in coastal areas with tides; these fluctuations have a fairly constant pattern, but over time, they may change the depth of the local waters.

European visitors to Southeast Asia from the fifteenth century onward noted the skill and ingenuity exhibited in the construction of pile-supported platform houses. But they did not so readily understand the interrelationship between local social patterns and built forms. In Indonesian societies, Waterson explains, the house is the most important principle in the organization of kinship systems. Complex "House societies" encompass patrilineal, matrilineal, and bilateral systems and are made up of kinship groups who either live in the dwellings or have some affiliation with them. Names and titles are inherited through generations, a practice not unlike that of the Western world. The principle of kinship and the idea of the "living house" is carried over into state systems in which the ruler's house is equated with the "navel" or center of his domain. Waterson quotes ethnologist Shih Lei (1964), who wrote, "The family as institution is recognized by three aspects: the house, the name attached to it, and the people living in it."

We do not yet know for sure when or where the raised-pile dwelling originated—physical evidence is incomplete; tropical climates are hard on timber buildings. Yet early studies and later ones indicate that the pile-built,

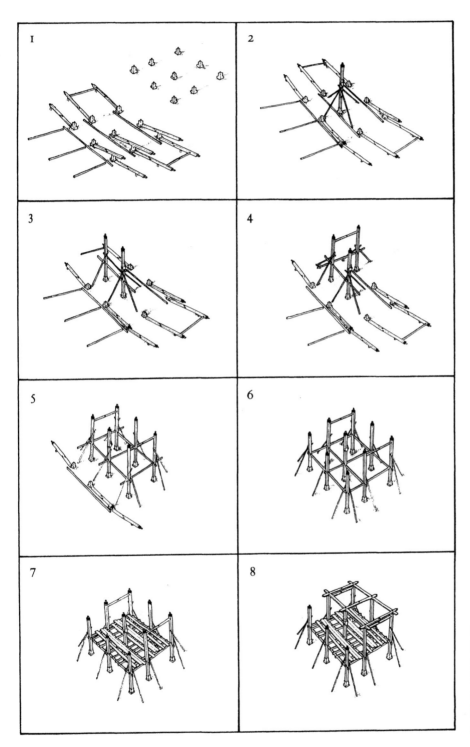

Figure 10.18. *Malaysia. Steps in building a traditional house on stilts. The pieces are first cut to size, laid out on the ground, assembled in order, as depicted from top left to lower right (1–8 and 9–16). The last elements are the lower walls.*

255

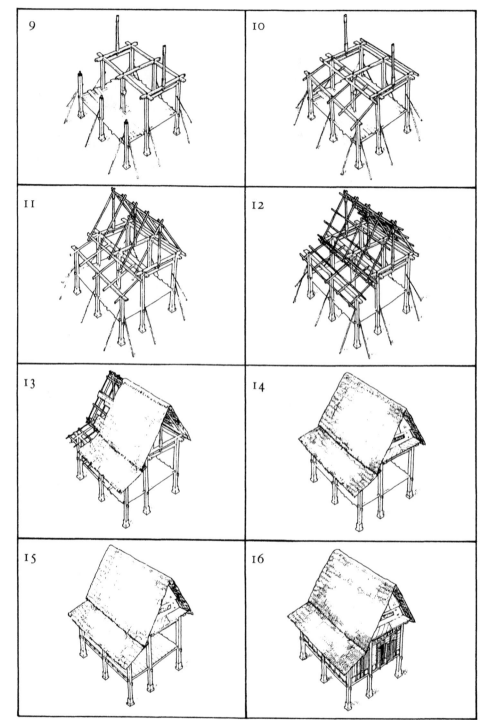

Figure 10.18. *Continued.*

Figure 10.19. *Examples of Indonesian buildings with gable horns and saddle roofs. Nos. I–VII are from eastern Indonesia; VIII, from east Java; IX–XII, from Sumatra; XIII, from Vietnam; XIV, from northeast India; and XV, from Micronesia.*

Figure 10.20. *Farmhouses on stilts, Amazon region, Brazil. The larger one is for an extended family, as is common here. Built on the highest part of the floodplain, the houses are sited to take advantage of river transportation. The piles lift them above high water, which in the rainy season is about 4.5 feet (1.5 meters) higher than shown here, within a few inches of the floors. The walls of the houses are wood, and the roofs are asbestos paneling.*

saddle-roofed house of Southeast Asia was the source of Indonesian forms. Information also comes from linguistic studies that have allowed scholars to track human migrations. In addition, Waterson explains that archaeological evidence found at Nong Chae Sao in 1966 indicates that Neolithic elevated houses were known in Thailand. The example discovered at the site was about 31 feet (9.5 meters) long, with a raised floor and ladder access. It was not unlike the homes of modern Thai hill dwellers.

The people of tropical-subtropical South China may have developed the pile-supported dwelling during the

Neolithic era; it then spread along patterns of migrations that began thousands of years ago in those regions of the world. The many variations of house form and decoration produced by complicated migration and interaction patterns are reflected in developments in ancient Japan, where people moved from pit dwellings to gable-roofed pile buildings by the late Neolithic and early Metal Age. The Yayoi people came to Japan from South China by way of Taiwan around 300 B.C.E., bringing the cultivation of rice and the use of granaries built on piles, as well as other features of Austronesian culture (the language spoken by most Southeast Asian peoples) that is common to Malaysia and Oceania. The dominant Yayoi architecture can still be seen in the Ise Shrine (see Chapter 17). The link between Japan and the peoples of the Pacific Islands first became clear when investigators noticed the emphasis on a post-supported framework in Japanese traditional architecture; only more recently have most Western scholars learned from Japanese linguists that the Japanese language has a strong substratum of Austronesian, although scientist E. Morse noted this connection in the 1880s.

South China's effect on Japan was indirect, but the contributions of Vietnamese people show how complicated migrations and interactions could be. The Dong Son of North Vietnam, who appeared during the Bronze Age (after 3500 B.P.) and flourished from about 500 B.C.E. to 100 C.E., were noted for their bronze mirrors and traded with both Indonesia and South China. Many of these mirrors were decorated with images of people in a three-level pile house with sloped gables, like those still seen in Sumatra. The figures wear costumes of China's Han dynasty of the first centuries B.C.E./C.E.

From early times, then, the house on stilts was common in humid areas. Today, more than half the world's people live in the triangle that connects India, Southeast Asia, and China, the supposed center of human life since the end of the Ice Age. Given this density of population and the popularity of the elevated dwelling, the lashed-together house on stilts may be the most common building type in the world.

SOURCES: DOMENIG (1980), FITCHEN (1990), P. GIBBS (1987), JUNSAI (1991), WATERSON (1990).

USING SPACE

The use of space is culturally determined—a surprising idea to many who believe that everyone in the world puts things away as they do; unites studying with sleeping, as in an American college dormitory; and separates grandparents from young children, as is customary in residences for American senior citizens. But the use of space is a construct, not a "given," as we show in two different versions of floor-level living: that of the Japanese and the Muslims.

Japanese Floor-Level Living

Many societies rely on minimal interior furnishings. Nomads keep possessions simple so as not to impede mobility. Individuals or families who share dwellings with others may have limited space and, in some traditional societies, custom works against the accumulation of large amounts of furniture. In traditional Japanese homes, for example, the floor itself is the main piece of furniture.

The traditional Japanese house is built to accommodate people who are seated or kneeling on the floor. This position establishes the eye-level plane both for the architectural focus and for household activities. Windows are placed for viewing at this angle; in fact, the Japanese so value the viewing experience that it has determined the form of the house. The view of the garden when the movable exterior screens (shoji) that make up much of the outer walls are pushed aside or removed is an important aesthetic experience (see Fig. 10.21). The open plan of residential interiors is arranged for maximum viewing of the garden from the interior, so that an occupant can contemplate the garden from a seated position at a level slightly higher than the ground—a view with a pleasant psychological and aesthetic effects. The garden scene is another room to be enjoyed from a seated position within the house.

Japanese builders make a distinction between interior and exterior space by raising the floor of the dwelling about 2.5 feet above ground level (see Fig. 10.22). Sometimes the veranda is built lower than the interior floor, as a transitional space. The separation places an appropriate value on each space.

The interior floor space is organized around the 6-by-3-foot (2-by-1-meter) mat known as a tatami (see Chapters 5 and 7). The tatami is a pad made by stuffing the interior of a woven mat with rice straw and stitching the long border with a strip of dark binding. Users place mats on the floor to produce decorative geometric patterns that unite the floor with the vertical and horizontal structural arrangement of the rest of the house interior.

Originally, the tatami was portable and could be folded because the grass filler was more pliable than the straw used today (see Fig. 10.23). The word tatamu, "to fold," evolved into tatami. Eventually, in some parts of Japan, the mat's standardized shape and size determined certain architectural features of the house, such as the distance between columns. (Although the size of rooms was based on the size and proportion of the tatami, architect-engineer, H. Engel points out that the tatami was not a distinct module for overall construction, as is often thought.) By the Muromachi period, from the late fourteenth to the late sixteenth centuries, movable mats were replaced by floors completely covered with tatamis.

Figure 10.21. *View from the interior of a traditional Japanese house. The translucent shoji screen is pushed aside, providing an intimate view of the garden. The uncluttered interior is conducive to serenity. The horizontal and vertical geometry of the tatami mats and screens contribute to the clarity of design and act as a foil to the garden outside. The women arrange flowers for the tokanoma.*

From the use of the padded floor arose a custom to prevent damage to the fragile, textured surfaces of the mats: People remove their wooden clogs or other foot coverings and put on heavy slipper socks of light cotton before they enter the house—a practice in use today.

The interior space is unified by the relationship of the mats to the movable interior wall sections and the exterior screens; the heights of both are determined by the length of the mats. Wall units fit into a groove with a molding that continues around the room. The floor-level

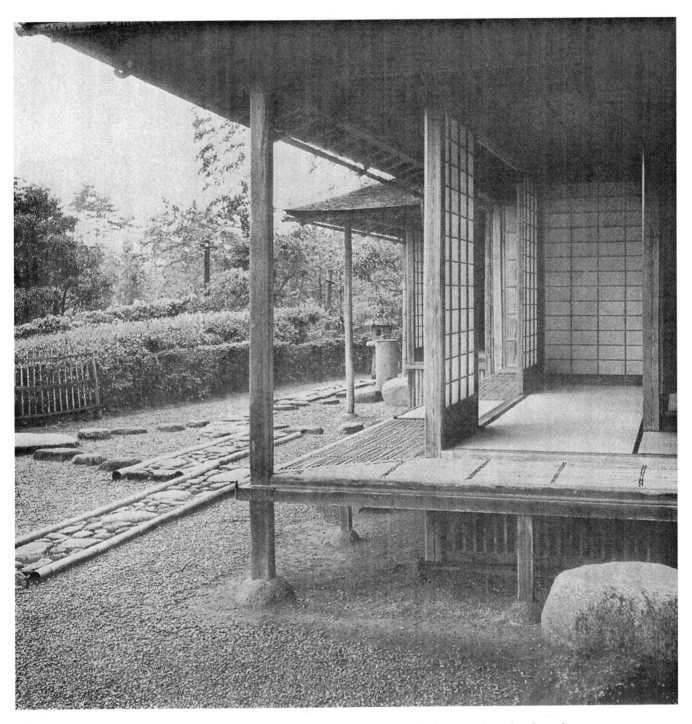

Figure 10.22. *Arisawa villa, Matsue, Japan. The spatial connection between the house and garden depends upon shoji screens to open the house to the garden or close it off. The elevated floor of the room (covered with tatami mats) is continuous with the bamboo flooring of the narrow veranda. A deep overhang shelters the veranda and the interior. The garden "borrows" its distant view from neighbors.*

Figure 10.23. *Detail of a Japanese house from the Kasuga-gongen Rugen-ki Scroll (1309). In the foreground, a man carries a tatami mat—at that time, the tatami was still carried from place to place. The house is raised above the ground level . The veranda surrounding the houses provides a transitional space between the garden and house.*

view thus offers an uninterrupted and unifying series of commensurable elements that tie the floor to the walls to the ornamentation provided by the molding.

People cook and serve meals—and sleep, read, and socialize—at floor level. Bedding consists of mattresses or quilts placed on the floor at night and folded and stored in closets (the size of one tatami) when not in use. No chairs are needed; people kneel on the floor. This arrangement has affected the relationship of building space to human scale; a standing person is out of place in this low-scale environment.

For heating, the floor incorporates a *kotatsu*, a small, low table draped with a quilt. Underneath the table, often in a recess in the floor, is a small box holding pieces of burning charcoal. People sit around the table reading or conversing, with their legs under the quilt, which traps the warmth from the charcoal fire. The floor-level kotatsu is practical in that it uses only a small amount of fuel.

The important ritual of the tea ceremony (see Chapters 5 and 9) also takes place at floor level, in the recep-

tion room where the tokonoma is located or in a separate teahouse (see Fig. 9.17). The dimensions are determined by the number of mats used, usually four and one-half. These mats are placed around a central hearth that rests on a half-mat called the "hearth-mat." The placement and size of the mats give spatial orientation to those seated on the floor.

Traditional Japanese dress is suited to floor-level life. The kimono, a loose-fitting robe worn by both men and women, is a practical garment—allowing greater flexibility than more restrictive clothing. One style and size fits almost any shape. Long-sleeved and floor-length kimonos also keep the arms and legs warm. In present-day Japan, some people who wear Western-style clothing for business change into traditional kimonos when they relax at home and don more than one kimono to keep warm during the winter, especially if most of their seating is on the floor.

Sources: Engel (1964), Morse 1886 (1961).

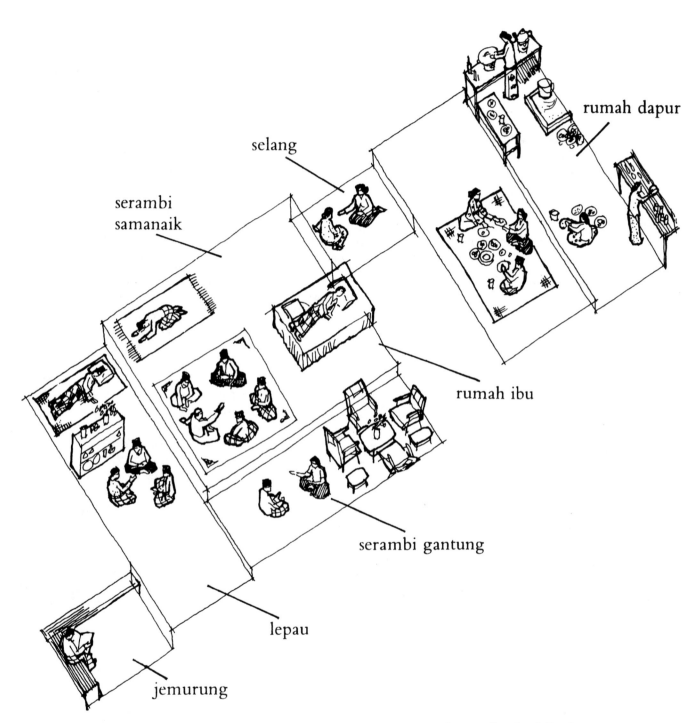

Figure 10.24. *Interior of a Malaysian house illustrating various activities carried out at floor level. People sleep, talk, pray, entertain, cook, and eat using little furniture. Note that the floors are at different levels, depending on the importance and privacy of the activity.*

Islamic Floor-Level Living

Floor-level domestic arrangements may be the result of a migratory or nomadic way of life in which personal possessions are necessarily few. Some indigenous African and South American tribes have complex social and religious structures that place little value on household furnishings in the Western sense and that focus on architectural elements with symbolic meanings. For example, some Malaysians and Indonesians—who spend much of their time carrying out daily activities at floor level (see Fig. 10.24)—perceive profound symbolic connections between their houses and human activities.

Many Islamic peoples were originally nomadic, and the interiors of their dwellings still reflect, to some extent, their former way of life, in which household goods were few because it was difficult and costly to transport them. People use the floor for sitting and eating, softening the surface with carpets, cushions, rugs, and mats that can be easily folded and stored in cupboards when not in use. Islamic rooms, like the Japanese, have interchangeable uses and a minimum of furniture. What is lacking in furniture is made up in the quality of the decoration exhibited in the carpets, cushions, and wall coverings.

Because of the extremely hot climate in most Islamic regions, people sleep on the flat roofs of their houses. They use rugs or mattresses, eliminating the need for beds or divans, although in some areas—notably Arabia, Egypt, and Turkey—people do use divans or beds. Also, courtyards serve as places for outdoor cooking, socializing, and other domestic activities, further reducing the need for cumbersome furniture. In some palaces and other monumental buildings—the fourteenth-century Alhambra at Granada, for example—inscriptions around fountains are placed at eye level for those seated on the floor. Architectural historian J. Hoag observes that fountain basins "are flush with the marble floors," reminding us that major architectural works were designed by and for people who sat on the floor. The gardens, too, were planned to be enjoyed by people sitting in the porticoes.

The effective use of architectural space is determined by a number of factors. As architect A. Antoniades states, "Space becomes meaningful for architecture only when it creates 'certain feelings', the ones which are demanded by the function [users' needs] and enhanced by the architectural solution."

SOURCES: ANTONIADES (1992), HOAG (1987), JUNSAI IN VATSYAYAN (1991).

SUGGESTED READINGS

Danien, E. C., and R. J. Sharer, eds. 1992. *New Theories on the Ancient Maya.* Philadelphia: University Museum, University of Pennsylvania. Contains many well-illustrated and interesting essays, including: Ashmore (pp. 173–84), a clear exposition of the kind of organization found in Maya cities, and Rust (pp. 123–39), which places La Venta in its geographic and social setting. See our Selected Bibliography.

Dickie, J. 1978. "Allah and Eternity: Mosques, Madrasas and Tombs." In *Architecture of the Islamic World: Its History and Social Meaning*, 15–47, edied by G. Michell. An especially useful section on madrasas.

Emory, K. P. 1971. *Tuamotuan Stone Structures.* New York: Kraus Reprint Co. (reprint of 1934 edition). The original study of these sanctuaries.

Emory, K. P. 1969. "A Re-examination of East Polynesian Marae: Many Marae Later." In *Studies in Oceanic Culture History*, Vol. 1, 73–92, edited by R. C. Green and M. Kelly. Warner-Gren Symposium on Oceanic Culture History. Honolulu: Department of Anthropology, Bishop Museum. Emory had been thinking about marae for thirty-five years by the time this was written. He quotes many other early travelers and scholars.

Engel, H. 1964. *The Japanese House: A Tradition for Contemporary Architecture.* Rutland, Vt.: Charles E. Tuttle. An excellent discussion of floor-level living.

Fitchen, J. 1990. *Building Construction Before Mechanization.* Cambridge, Mass.: MIT Press. The author's exploration of traditional construction methods is useful for understanding how structures—including those of Southeast Asia—were built before modern methods were introduced.

Gibbs, P., Y. A. Rahman, and A. Kassim. 1987. *Building a Malay House.* Singapore: Oxford University Press. An enlightening approach to the practical study of Malaysian architecture.

Junsai, S. 1991. "Cave Man Space versus Boat Man Space." In *Concepts of Space Ancient and Modern*, 185–88, edited by K. Vatsyayan. New Delhi: Abhinav Publications. A thought-provoking and scholarly work on early migrations.

Kolb, M. J. 1992. "Diachronic Design Changes in Heiau Temple Architecture on the Island of Maui, Hawaii. *Asian Perspectives* 31: 9–38. Historical in approach.

Pendergast, D.M. 1988. "Engineering Problems in Ancient Maya Architecture: Past, Present and Future." In *Engineering Geology of Ancient Works, Monuments and His-*

torical Sites, Vol. 3, 653–60, edited by P. Marinos and G. Koukis. Boston: A. A. Balkema. The author, a structural engineer, concludes that between the climate and the weakness of corbel vaulting, it's a wonder any pyramids are still standing.

Schele, L., and D. Freidel. 1990. A Forest of Kings: The Untold Story of the Ancient Maya. New York: William Morrow. A well-documented discussion of Maya history. Fascinating, amply illustrated, well written, and closely argued.

Schele, L., and M. E. Miller. 1986. Blood of Kings, 241–54. New York: George Braziller. A discussion of the Maya ballgame. Illustrated.

Sharer, R. J. 1994. The Ancient Maya. 5th ed. Stanford, CA: Stanford University Press. Do not settle for an earlier edition. This one sums up and includes the relevant research up through 1993, explaining how many earlier ideas have been proved false or incomplete.

Waterson, R. 1990. The Living House: An Anthropology of Architecture in Southeast Asia. New York: Oxford University Press. An extensive and scholarly study of the culture and architecture of Southeast Asia. Also pertinent to the Introduction and to Chapter 6, Ceremonial Buildings in New Guinea.

⊞ 11

Organization of Structures

Architecture can be organized around a center point or a line. Each of these categories, in turn, can be divided. Buildings organized around a point can be a void or have a solid core at the center. In linear organization, the axis or line can be either a space or a row of buildings.

Courtyard houses that are organized around a void offer a contrast to Cambodia's Angkor Wat, which is organized around a central mass. This pairing is also a vernacular-monumental contrast. The houses represent architectural solutions to the problems of everyday life; Angkor Wat is a ceremonial sanctuary, reminiscent in some ways of another structure with a solid central mass: the "cosmic mountain" of Borobudur in Java (see Chapter 5)—a narrative building that is not only a monument to certain religious and royal points of view, but one of the largest structures ever built.

In *The Design of Cities*, planner Edmund Bacon pointed out that an axial arrangement can have either a solid or a void as its focus. He used the term *beads on a string* to describe the row of palaces at the heart of the Forbidden City in Beijing; these buildings stand squarely on the imaginary line of the central axis. Perceptually and experientially different is linear organization, in which the central axis is a void, as exemplified in the Street of the Dead in Teotihuacán, Mexico (see Chapter 7). The edges of the slightly irregular void are punctuated by the huge blocks of three great pyramids, two on the east side and one at the north end of the street. Less imposing structures stand on the west. The void of the street is emphasized in three or even four dimensions—if the fourth is taken to be time—by the missing cone of the volcano toward which it points.

HOLLOW CENTERS: COURTYARDS

Some buildings are organized around hollow spaces, more conventionally called courtyards: enclosed, roofless outdoor rooms. Such spaces existed in ancient Mesopotamian houses as long ago as the third millennium B.C.E., in the Indus valley at Mohenjo-Daro no later than the second millennium, and among the Greco-Roman peoples of 800 B.C.E. to 600 C.E.. Their Byzantine and Islamic successors in the Mediterranean basin and western Asia continued to build houses and other buildings around courtyards, as do their descendants today. Various cultures have found that walling off private living or working space from the surrounding urban fabric or from the relative emptiness of the rural countryside offers certain advantages.

North Africa and the Middle East

The open courtyard (see Fig. 11.1) has wide application in Islamic architecture. Mosques—for example, the hy- postyle type, such as the Great Mosque at Qairawan (see Chapter 7)—madrasas (see Chapter 10), and palaces (see Chapter 8, Red Fort) inevitably have courtyards. Among the recently excavated ruins at Qasr al-Hasyr in Syria is one of the earliest known caravanserai, or lodgings for travelers; numerous rooms open onto its interior paved courtyards. In hot regions, many courtyards have arcades, or columned covered walkways, attached to the interior

Figure 11.1. *Courtyard houses, Afghanistan. Although uniformity of style is notable, the courtyards of various houses differ in shape. The private interior, often with a tree, provides flexible space that moderates the severe hot and dry climate. Roofs provide additional living space.*

walls to offer shade. The air that enters the interior through open doorways and latticed windows is cooled by these arcades or by fountains and pools in the courtyards; this type of outdoor-indoor living is highly energy-efficient (see Chapter 4, Hot and Dry). Other elaborate courtyards, constructed for public display, are modeled after descriptions of the "Gardens of Paradise" in the Qur'an (see Chapter 9, Taj Mahal, and Chapter 13). According to architectural historians N. Alsayyad and G. Boostani, the courtyard "plays the role of establishing the Muslim's place in space." Among the mostly Islamic peoples of North Africa and the Middle East, with few exceptions, the millennia-old, traditional courtyard-house is still the commonest type of urban dwelling, reflecting the high value that Islamic societies place on seclusion and privacy.

The courtyard can range from an elaborate Mughal garden courtyard to a small outdoor space attached to a humble dwelling. Courtyards of the wealthy may be enriched by luxurious gardens, tiled pavements, fountains, and pools, just as the interiors of the homes are embellished with elegant carpets and floor coverings.

The ideal plan of a house and courtyard is a hollow square or rectangle, with a single row of rooms surrounding the open space. In practice, however, constraints of terrain, street patterns, and adjacent buildings often require builders to make adjustments. In areas with multistory houses, a courtyard may be situated on an upper level with skylights illuminating the interior below, or surrounded by upper-level galleries and balconies on which people can sleep or eat. Paving of tile or stone offers an aesthetic advantage; the integrity of the original design is preserved when the surface is covered with pavement, more difficult than lawn for subsequent owners to change, as scholars have observed.

In less common building types, the courtyards surround the house or stretch along one side of it. This form is more commonly found in rural areas, where land is more available, fewer building restrictions apply, and there is less need for privacy than in cities. Islamic courtyard dwellings are not practicable where outdoor activities are restricted because of a cold climate or for other reasons. The courtyard form offers so much in terms of social interaction, practicality, and symbolism that it continues to thrive in areas where the climate permits.

SOURCES: ALSAYYAD AND BOOSTANI (1988), W. JOHNSON (1995), P. OLIVER (1987), PETHERBRIDGE (1978).

China

The Chinese house customarily faced onto a courtyard, whether it was the one- or two-story urban home of a wealthy family in Beijing or Suzhou or the multistory, round, communal dwelling of Hakka farmers in the southeast. Even freestanding houses often have an attached enclosure that functions like a courtyard; to create usable but private space, the enclosure is outlined by spur walls from the ends of the building, low walls, or merely a stalk fence. Some villages that have been rebuilt since the 1970s have a pattern of rear courtyards entered from narrow alleys; here, the space includes a pigpen, woodpile, latrine, and bathing area. Other southern courtyards include chicken coops and biogas converters[29] for methane production.

The earliest surviving houses in China are those of merchants and gentry from the Ming (1368–1644) or Qing (1644–1912) periods. It is reasonable to assume that the features of these houses were also found in the modest peasant houses of the day. Like the Han dynasty models and many southern houses to this date, the surviving examples had only small courtyards for ventilation. Many were two-story structures.

Yet the courtyard type of house was known in China long before the Ming dynasty (see Fig. 11.2). It appears in models from the Han Dynasty (202 B.C.E. to 220 C.E.) that show L- or U-shaped dwellings around small courtyards for ventilation. U-shaped courtyard dwellings are also known from paintings of the Sui Dynasty and are still common in South China. Traditional housing in Fujian, in southeast China, consists of a row of one-story buildings extending to the same depth between windowless exterior walls and separated internally by courtyards, like the rungs of a ladder laid flat on the ground. The main hall of such a house has a broad veranda that is reached by large doors and latticed windows, so it is well ventilated even during heavy rains. Wide eaves protect all rooms from the tropical sun. One-story bedrooms, kitchens, and storage spaces are parallel or perpendicular to the main hall; the bedrooms are usually in a separate hall to the rear. Such houses frequently grow—in depth for the gentry and in width for farm households—to ac-

---

[29]Biogas converters combine organic wastes and excrement in a sealed unit. After about three months of fermentation, methane gas is available for fuel, and the solid material left over makes excellent fertilizer.

commodate an extended family. Houses of this type were built also in Taiwan from the eighteenth century on. A fully developed example may have five courts, each with a big hall on the north side and smaller rooms or suites around the other three sides. The roofs of the halls make a receding row from the entrance, their height increasing away from the main entrance, while the courtyards decrease in size.

The degree of architectural articulation given the main entrance depended on the family's wealth. The outer doorway, shielded by a small roof, led into a vestibule space. A barrier wall prevented the eyes of visitors and the ill-will of evil spirits from affecting the family directly. Beyond this, circulation patterns could be complicated, depending on the size of the house. The tapestry of light and shade as one walked from the front of the house to the back or from the interior to the exterior enriched daily life in such a house, particularly important for the women who were mostly confined to the home.

Writer N. Waln conveyed the importance of the courtyard house in Old China in *The House of Exile*. In the 1920s and 1930s, Waln lived in Hebei Province with a Chinese family who had been partners in trade with her own family in Philadelphia for more than a century. The house was begun seven centuries before, and over the years, the residents' tastes and efforts had made the courtyards both serviceable and beautiful. They added gardens, ponds, a new pavilion here for a poet, a new doorway there through the wall to the neighboring family when the neighbor's daughter married a son of the family. The enclosure wall was 6 feet thick and about 22 high (1.8 by 6.7 meters), with only two openings: a door of solid planks large enough for a horse and carriage (the "To and From the World" gate) and a small window (the "Gate of Compassion") cut in the north wall, through which the residents handed charity to the needy.

The six-generation family of eighty-three lived in the 1920s in a series of one-room units arranged around courtyards that were connected by internal gateways shaped like flowers, fans, vases, or full moons. The house could accommodate such a large number of people because the rooms and the courtyards—outdoors yet private and protected—had multiple uses and lent themselves to many activities. At the center of the network of courtyards and intervening pavilions, the double-roofed, story-and-a-half Hall of Ancestors sheltered the ancestor tablets of twenty-nine generations.

After the Communist Revolution of 1949, the authorities turned such houses over to many unrelated fam-

Figure 11.2. *A traditional courtyard house, Beijing, China. The street entrance is not aligned with the inner doorways. Large halls are parallel to the entrance wall, separated by courtyards. Smaller rooms open onto gardens in the courtyards.*

ilies, usually at higher density and with fewer resources available for maintenance. Today, as land prices escalate, tall apartment buildings are replacing the old courtyard houses, especially in Beijing.

Still, the courtyard house endured for well over two thousand years in China. Neither exceptional materials nor exquisite furnishings made it so satisfactory. On the first stone of the house that Waln describes, these words were carved:

Glazed brick, white mortar, and blue roof-tiles do not make a house beautiful; carved rosewood, gold cloth, and clear green jade do not furnish a house with grace; a man of cultivated mind makes a house of mud and wattle beautiful; a woman, even with a pock-marked face, if refined of heart, fills a house with grace.

Indeed, courtyard houses typically use simple local construction materials and methods, whether mud brick with bearing walls or post-and-beam with brick curtain walls. Tile roofs are stable and fire resistant. The organization of the courtyard house, whether Chinese, Middle Eastern, or North African, makes it adaptable for variations of use and changing social patterns, ensuring its longevity.

SOURCES: A. BOYD (1962), KNAPP (1990), RASMUSSEN (1969), WALN (1933).

The American Southwest

New Mexico has courtyard houses from both the preconquest and Spanish Colonial periods. Spanish Colonial culture was a hybrid born from the blend of two parent cultures: the culture of Renaissance Spain by way of seventeenth-century Mexico, which was itself a development from Moorish and earlier Roman models, and the culture of the Pueblo peoples. Like the professional architecture of Europe and America, traditional architecture—wherever it is found—unites disparate influences into a new creation. In New Mexico, those influences are more than 800 years old on the Native American side and at least 2,500 years old on the European side. Since both ancestral forms used courtyards, it is not surprising that these forms appear in the eighteenth-century synthesis. Whether that synthesis is itself old enough to be considered traditional depends upon your frame of reference.

Fig. 11.3 is a plan of Santa Fe made in 1848, soon after the conquest of the area by the United States in the war with Mexico. The sizes and relationships of buildings and spaces are those of the end of the Mexican period. The plaza was the central gathering place of the community, where the market took place. People strolled there in the evening and followed the porticoed street to the little plaza in front of the church (lower right). The surrounding porticoes made the main plaza a kind of public courtyard. Native Americans presented petitions at the Governor's Palace[30] at the top of the plaza and sold their crafts under the palace portico. This portico lined what had been the southern side of the presidio, the fortress-like rectangle that had housed the seventeenth-century settlers, soldiers and civilians alike. The Governor's Palace could be shut off or opened up to the public space out-

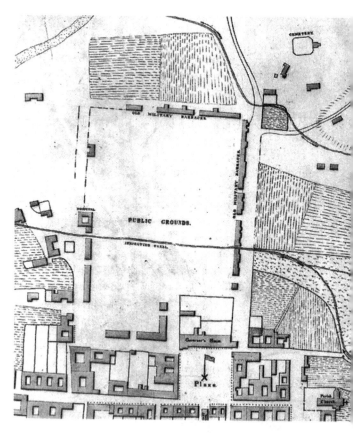

Figure 11.3. *Courtyards of three sizes, Santa Fe, New Mexico. Dating from Spanish Colonial times (of the eighteenth to early nineteenth centuries), the smallest courtyards are in private houses. The central plaza, a medium-sized public courtyard, is surrounded with porticoes, represented here by rows of dots. The largest open space is the Public Grounds, or Commons, at the north, where the original Presidio of the settlement was located within walls composed of a file of rooms. The Commons lay immediately south of the earlier village of Native Americans, where the trapezoidal fields are shown at the top of the map.*

side—a characteristic shared with the courtyard farmhouses discussed later. Small businesses, the homes of important people, and even a chapel were united visually behind the porticoes lining the east, south, and west sides of the plaza. Most of the buildings around the plaza had courtyards at the center of their plans. These outdoor spaces, enclosed within the homes, were on a domestic scale.

The community's largest enclosed outdoor space was the "Public Grounds" or "commons," formerly the court-

[30]See the discussion of this name in Crouch, Garr, and Mundigo (1982), 85.

yard of the Presidio. Only the scattered and crumbling structures labeled "old military barracks" remain. Even after the orientation of the part of the presidio that was reserved for the governor was switched to open southward onto the plaza, the rest of the area remained military. Soldiers were garrisoned in it, soldiers and militia drilled in the open area labeled Public Grounds, and a hospital with its own inner courtyard stood at the center of the west side. An irrigation canal divided the commons into two parts, and the main bed of the Santa Fe river (at the bottom of this part of the map) divided the Spanish Colonial town from the original Mexican Indian annex farther south.

The core of the town shown in this plan seems to refer mostly to Spanish Colonial examples from northern Mexico, yet it was built to attract the local Indians to the Spanish way of life. Many observers do not realize that the Pueblo dwellers had already developed a way of life compatible in many details with that of the Europeans. The Santa Clara Pueblo dating from before 1600 (see Fig. 11.4) shows that the Indians, too, had a tradition of organizing settlements around plazas. The Mesa Verde settlement of the Anasazi, ancestors of the Pueblo peoples (see Chapter 9), also provided smaller and larger open spaces for communal life.

Why were courtyards attractive to residents in this desert climate? A courtyard or plaza with a portico around the inner walls let residents control their exposure to the blazing sun. During winter, they could rest or work in the full sun, while during summer, they could do so in full shade. The roof of the portico also shielded the courtyard walls from the heat, while the enclosure provided privacy for the residents and safety for young children. Many activities, from cooking to manufacture to nursing a baby to celebrating a wedding, took place in the family's courtyard.

In Santa Fe houses, the rooms encircled the courtyard (see Fig. 11.3). Being nonspecific in form, they could be used for various purposes. An extended family could live peaceably under one roof because a married son and his wife or several teenagers could withdraw into their own space. The family could store food or even shelter animals in other rooms.

The courtyard of a country house might be larger, just as the spaces for animals, storing farm products, and housing relatives for long or short periods were more numerous. This form is a distant descendent of the late Roman farmhouse, from regions as far apart as Britain and North Africa. Residents preferred the safety of living in a mod-

LEGEND

⬜ 1 STORY
▨ 2 STORY
K KIVA
A ABANDONED ROOM
† CHURCH

0' 50'   250'

Figure 11.4. *Plan of the Santa Clara Pueblo, New Mexico. The pueblo dates from before 1600; the Colonial-period church is shown at the left, outside the core of settlement. The organization of the dwelling units in rows around courtyards was clearly earlier than the Spanish period.*

est fortress, able to turn in on itself, with strong doors that could be barricaded and space to stable domestic animals. Such a house form enabled people to persevere in settling regions not yet pacified. Functionally, if not in physical form, such a farmhouse resembles the traditional Japanese farmhouse (see Chapter 3), which also had defensive as well as domestic features.

The Spanish and Indian courtyard houses shared additional features, among them building materials and methods. The builders used adobe bricks or sometimes flat stones for the walls and made roofs of clay piled on logs. Outer surfaces were covered with adobe (mud) plaster, frequently renewed. (Compare with Keresan houses at Acoma, Chapter 14.)

Even more important were the similar organization of solid and void, with the rooms of the house relating to an enclosed outdoor room of many uses. The Chinese and Islamic houses may have influenced each other's development, and the Islamic house, the Spanish house, but this "family tree" of influence does not account for the Pueblo Indians' use of a similar pattern. Rather, architecture seems to have followed what biologists call convergent evolution, in which apparently similar structures are found in organisms from different lines of descent.

Human beings like to have a special place to gather, a place that embodies and symbolizes their common life. The courtyard in all its guises is one of the most satisfying of these gathering places. Even the Americans who conquered New Mexico—Easterners and Middle Westerners whose architectural vocabulary did not include courtyards—saw how Santa Fe's central plaza could be used for propaganda. By inserting the United States flag into the plaza and recording this symbol on their maps, they established new dominance over the local people. In Santa Fe, as elsewhere, the enclosed central space has survived partly because of its practicality and partly for symbolic reasons.

SOURCES: CROUCH, GARR, AND MUNDIGO (1982), STUBBS (1950).

SOLID CENTER AT ANGKOR WAT, CAMBODIA

Some structures have solid centers. They may have smaller attendant buildings, as does the great stupa at Sanchi, or subsidiary parts attached to the solid core, as at Borobudur, Java (see Chapter 5). Like the enormous sanctuary of Angkor Wat in Cambodia, these are ceremonial buildings, not dwellings that need ventilation and privacy. The name is used for the funerary temple we discuss here, but also for the entire capital district of the Khmer state.

Angkor Wat (*wat* means temple) consists of a central mass with auxiliary galleries, gateways, and smaller buildings attached to it, built between ca. 1110 and 1150 C.E. It is the world's largest religious structure, so vast and intricate a building that it cannot easily be photographed as a whole from the ground (see Fig. 11.5 a and b). Visitors today find the Angkor Wat complex awesome, both for its size and for the high quality of its architecture and sculpture.

Around 800 to 1000 C.E., the Khmer people came to dominate much of Southeast Asia from their homeland in present-day Cambodia (see the map of Asia in the Appendix). They created one of the great civilizations in history, comparable to the Classical Maya of 300–900 C.E., who lived half a world away in the similar tropical terrain and climate of the Yucatan Peninsula (see Chapters 3 and

10). Just after 1000 C.E., Khmer monumental art and architecture flowered rapidly and spectacularly in the region north of the Tonle Sap, or Great Lake.

Early Classical Khmer buildings had developed from local wooden forms in the ninth and tenth centuries. These early temples—isolated sanctuaries for deified dynastic ancestors—were of brick with carved brick exterior reliefs, an idea imported from India (see Fig. 11.6). Regional variations came together in the high classical style: from the south, tall towers with angular or pyramidal roofs; from the north, walled galleries joining towers. Later ideas included multiple sanctuaries on one terrace, the cruciform tower plan (see Chapter 1, Ananda Temple), and the cella (the central sanctuary of a temple) atop a stepped pyramid.

Khmer cosmology incorporated the royal cult, centered on the king as a kind of divine incarnation. The religion of the Khmer period, like modern Nepalese religion, seems to have been a blend of Hindu and Buddhist beliefs. Like Indian and Chinese Buddhist temples (see Chapter 1), Khmer temple complexes were raised on a series of five terraces, ringed with towers to resemble a chain of mountains with foothills. This variant of the stupa is called the stepped terrace, or cosmic mountain. The religious pilgrim sees the terraces as physical images of the cosmological series of worlds.

Angkor Wat was built as the dynastic temple and cenotaph of King Suryavarman II, who dedicated it to the Hindu god Vishnu. It was conceived as a microcosm of the divine world, center of the capital, the empire, and the universe. Like its neighbors—the Bayon (Angkor Thom), Preah Khan and Neak Pean, Ta Prohm, Pre Rup, and others (see Fig. 11.7)—Angkor Wat was decorated with some of the finest sculptural reliefs known anywhere. Angkor Wat alone has half a mile of relief sculptures arranged in long narrative strips, once gilded and painted, with additional rich carvings over and beside every doorway and corner.

Angkor Wat's scale is immense. Sandstone walls, signifying the rock wall around the universe, enclosed 7,900 acres (3,200 hectares) of flat land and a water-filled moat 625 feet (190.5 meters) wide, signifying the great ocean (see Fig. 11.5b). The rosy or gray sandstone was transported to the site by elephants.

Approaching the central triple outer gateway of Angkor Wat, one sees a long causeway over the moat, leading to the main buildings, culminating in a triple pavilion with a triple gate. After entering the gate one goes through another long passage between two large libraries and two ceremonial water tanks to a cruciform platform outside the main entry. There one enters an intermediary structure shaped like a cross within a square. Both the square and the cross are composed of long shrine galleries with corbelled roofs, supported by square pillars with richly carved square capitals. Over the centuries, many of these galleries have served as sanctuarries for statues of Buddhas and gods, of many sizes and poses, brought here for safekeeping. Worshippers place flowers or burning incense in front of favorite statues, some of which have knees or shoulders polished to a luster by centuries of caresses from the faithful. Flanking the intermediary structure are twin smaller buildings, probably libraries. On the farther side of the intermediary space is the first terrace, its corners marked by four towers.

Steep flights of stairs lead to the next terrace, which again has corner towers, shrine galleries, entrance pavil-

Figure 11.5. *Angkor Wat, Cambodia.* **a.** *The towers and walls of this enormous religious and funerary monument are reflected in the waters of the moat that surrounds it. The central tower is 215 feet (66 meters) tall, but the moat is even larger—625 feet wide (190.5 meters). Like the great reservoirs (barays) of the area, this moat was designed to retain water for irrigation. But an equally important function was to make the building more visible. The reflective surface gathers our scattered impressions of its length and richness of detail into one image.*

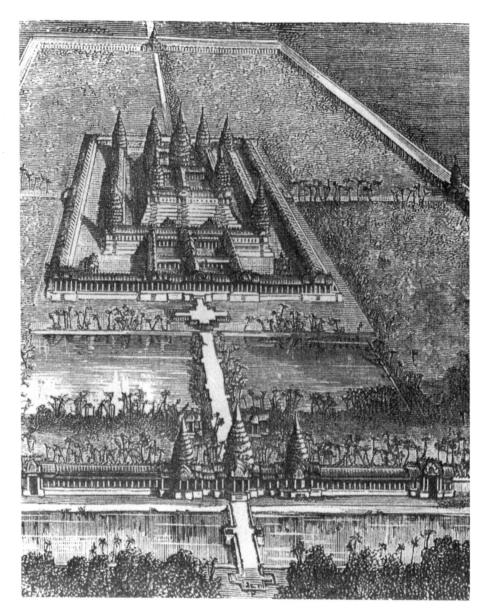

Figure 11.5. b. *A nineteenth-century engraving of Angkor Wat. The outer gate with three towers, flanked by galleries, is at the bottom of the picture. Just inside are two buildings, probably libraries. The causeway leads over the moat to a cross-shaped platform in the inner moat surrounding the monument. Within the walled inner enclosure is a four-part entrance suite, flanked by two large libraries. The entrance suite leads to an inner wall from which steep stairs, again flanked by libraries, lead up to the central core, which is again divided into four parts. There are towers at the four corners of the inner wall and again at the higher corners of the central core. The climax of the whole design is the largest tower at the center.*

ions, and triple aisles in a cross shape leading to the high central tower. Galleries are repeated at each upper level. Roofs are carved into convex curves with recurved eaves. One climbs the highest flight of stairs to the portals of the central tower, at the fifth level. The central chamber is entirely filled, not by the statue one would expect, but by a resonant void; there is no evidence of a cult figure having been installed within it. From the top terrace, one looks out over the monument itself, the surrounding canals and fields, and the nearby structures in their jungle setting.

Here and there, in the silent sanctuary and along the moat, walk Buddhist monks in their saffron and burgundy robes. The silence is intensified by the heat and humidity.

Not far from Angkor Wat are the temples, reservoirs, moats, roads, terraces, and causeways of other Khmer building complexes. Some are still entangled with jungle; some show the marks of recent and ancient wars, although J. Listopad, curator at the Los Angeles County Art Museum, reports that in a two-week visit in 1990, he saw only one damaged temple. Some temples radiate graceful

Figure 11.6. *The miniature temple of Banteay Srei, not far from Angkor Wat. Dedicated in 967 C.E., this memorial temple was enriched with the earliest surviving Khmer relief sculptures, depicting episodes of royal mythology—the finest Khmer sculpture in the full-round. The building depicts Mount Meru as the source of creation and the divine origin of water. This temple is part of a pink sandstone group consisting of sanctuaries, libraries, and monastic quarters. The patron was a Brahmin descended from the royal family, his architect influenced by the architecture of the Pallava Dynasty of southeast India. The temple is well preserved, partly because it was long hidden in the jungle, located more than 15 miles (25 km) from the main concentration of buildings at Angkor Wat. As the photograph shows, the architect was equally adept at the development of full and empty space and in the fantastic inventiveness of the decorated gables of the roof.*

beauty in their proportions and sculptured decoration. All combine to induce a feeling of respect for the Khmer creators.

"To understand Angkor," says B. P. Groslier, the long-time excavator of the site, "you have to understand that the important thing was not the temples but the waterworks. Angkor was a hydraulic city. The Khmer Temple . . . is only a chapel built on a reservoir of water, [which] is the source of life." This admonition from a man who devoted his life to extricating the temples from the jungle, restoring them, and publishing accounts of

them for the Western world alerts us to consider carefully the interaction of natural environment and cultural history. Indeed, one's first impression of this area is that it is the greenest place on earth—at least during the three-month rainy season. Abundant vegetation testifies to the hydrological features that are central to any understanding of Angkor. Large and elaborate reservoirs, canals, moats, sluices, and irrigated fields still survive from the ancient centralized system for controlling and storing water. So important to Khmer culture was water that the king was not crowned but anointed with the wa-

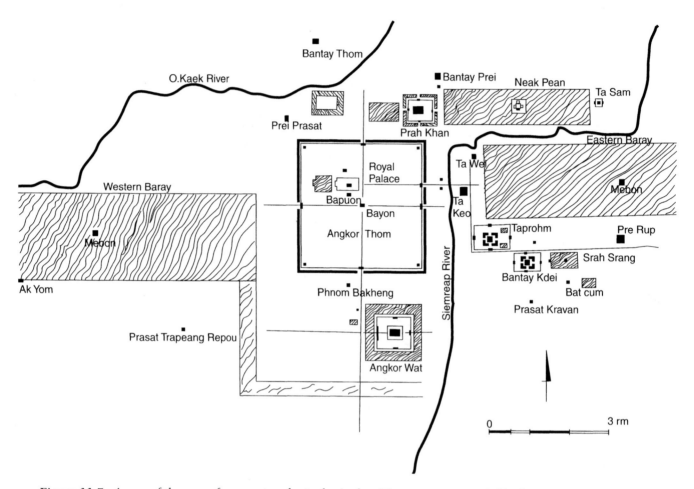

Figure 11.7. *A map of the many funerary temples in the Angkor Wat area, accompanied by huge reservoirs and moats. The temple of Angkor Wat is at the center bottom. The moat around Angkor Wat extends seven-eighths of a mile (2.6 km) along each side.*

ters from the rivers of all the countries that paid tribute to him.

Angkor Wat lies upstream from the Tonle Sap (Great Lake) on the Siem Reap River on a relatively flat, low, inland plain, heavily forested and watered by both the annual monsoon rains and snowmelt from the Himalayas in the Mekong River. The main crop is rice, supplemented by staggering amounts of fish from the Great Lake, since the concentration of fish is the highest in the world, ten times that of comparable areas in the North Atlantic. Fishing supports thirty thousand workers—just as it did when the reliefs were carved on the walls of Angkor Wat.

Yet we cannot assume that an abundance of food automatically generated a city at Angkor Wat. Some inves-

tigators think that, like Tikal in Central America (see Chapter 14), the area may have had only enough specialized labor to build and maintain a ceremonial center, not to sustain the long-distance trade that is usually postulated for a true city. It is more likely, however, that Angkor Wat was the urban center of a population of approximately 1 million. Endowed with natural resources, it also grew rich from taxes, tithes (a tenth of income, paid to the gods), and commerce from a much larger area. Khmer sovereignty reached into the hinterlands of Laos, Thailand, and Vietnam, where resources, such as metal ores, were extracted to make splendid buildings, ornaments, and the tools of everyday life at Angkor Wat, an urban center.

The first Khmer city, Hariharalaya, was built in the Angkor Wat area between 877 and 889, not long after King Jayavarman II unified the Khmer state in 802. The early Khmer kings built new capitals as their royal residences and abandoned older ones, a practice they shared with the rulers of China and Japan (see Chapter 9, Imperial Plan). Each ruler first built a set of canals and waterworks and then erected his temple. Each new city probably overlapped the older ones, as did the series of cities at Xian and Beijing in China.

The years 1000 to 1200 were the dynasty's richest period. By the thirteenth century, elaborate public spectacles still involved parades of soldiers, musicians, waiting women, carriages, ministers and princes on elephants, royal wives and concubines, and finally

> the king, standing on an elephant, his precious sword in hand. The elephant's tusks are sheathed in gold.
>
> *Chou Ta-kuan, a Chinese visitor,*
> *—quoted in C. Pym (1963)*

But by the sixteenth century, Angkor Wat had been abandoned. One explanation is a "brittle" or rigid social order, unable to adapt to change; another is a population decimated by malaria. The Khmers also underwent religious change from Hinduism to Buddhism and many attacks from Thailand, the last in 1431–32. The abandoned temple became a Buddhist monastery; perhaps at that time it was dedicated to the Buddha Avalokitesvara (like Borobudur in Java and the Potola Palace at Lhasa, Tibet). Then for many centuries, the ruins of Angkor Wat were lost in the jungle, although in the early seventeenth century, Spanish missionaries heard rumors of them. It was not until the 1760s that H. Mount, a French botanist, rediscovered the site, which was almost perfectly camouflaged by jungle.

The work of Groslier and other French experts to rescue the ruins from the jungle was cut short by war in Southeast Asia during the 1960s and 1970s. Ironically, American bombings in 1973 disturbed the jungle and revealed previously unknown temples. Two years later, French archeologists were forced to leave when Khmer Rouge and Vietcong forces took over the area and destroyed the archaeological records. In recent years, new experts, who add the disciplines of cultural anthropology and soil science to those of art history, philology, and politics, have resumed the study of Angkor Wat.

Transcending changes in political rule and religious content, the solid core of Angkor Wat speaks to us as an architectural form. Penetrated by galleries and richly ornamented with fine sculpture, it seems to incorporate much of the complexity of human beings—those who constructed it, those who fought over it, and those who visit it.

SOURCES: BRANDON (1978), M. D. COE 1961, 84; GROSLIER AND ARTHAUD (1957), PYM (1963), LISTOPAD (1996 PERSONAL COMMUNICATION).

AXIAL ARRANGEMENTS

An architectural axis can have religious meaning or embody an understanding of the geographic setting. Or, as with the Main Street of a small American town, it can be an economic fact. Here we discuss two axes with important symbolic meanings: the royal axis of the capital of China and the axis of religious pilgrimage at Teotihuacán.

Beijing, China: Forbidden City

Unlike the urban designs based on the grid or organic schemes discussed in Chapter 9, some city patterns, such as the monumental core of Beijing, the capital of China, are strictly axial. The ancient Chinese method places buildings of greatest importance farthest to the north.

Stretching north–south for five miles (7.5 kilomters), the axis of Beijing determines the placement of the imperial buildings. The architectural components are laid out formally like beads on a string (see Fig. 11.8), rather than being bilaterally symmetrical. The structures are independent of one another but aligned. Like the ancient capital at Chang-an, Beijing was built on a site where major cities have existed since the first millennium B.C.E.. Since the tenth century C.E., through several name changes, they have served as China's capital. The nucleus of the present city can be dated to the time of Kublai Khan (1264 C.E.). By the sixteenth century, the walled city occupied 24 square miles (62 square kilometers) and had an estimated population of 1 million. At the center, an inner and an outer city were grouped together along the axis.

The Outer, or Chinese, City is an east–west rectangle contained by a low wall. Testifying to the antiquity of this quarter, the two most important temples of the entire country, dating from prehistoric times, flank the axial way in this sector—on the west, the Temple of Agriculture, and on the east, the Temple and Altar of Heaven.

The Manchu (Mongolian) emperors (1644–1912) created a "twin" city in a square area north of the Outer

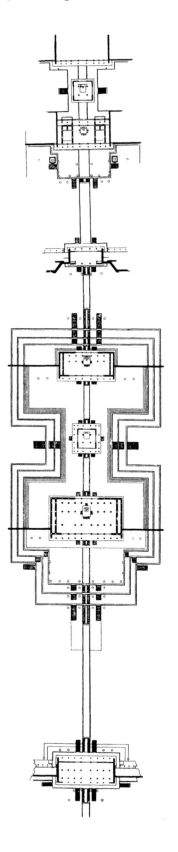

City, separating it from the Chinese section by a 50-foot-high (15 meters) wall, guarded by numerous towers and pierced by several gates, of which the southern gate on the main axis is the most important. The wall was different from the walls of other cities in that it was made of three layers of brick on each side of a core of rammed earth. The large, expensive bricks—24 by 12 centimeters, weighing 24 kilograms each—were made of "settled clay," so heavy that a mason could lay only a limited number in a day. The interstices were filled with mortar that was also smoothed over the walls as a finish.

Within the Inner City is the walled Imperial City, where courtiers lived; within it, the Forbidden City, containing approximately eight hundred palaces, halls, pavilions, and shrines, with a total of about nine thousand rooms. It was home to a series of twenty-four emperors, their wives, concubines, children, and servants during the Ming and Ching (Chhing) dynasties between 1369 and 1911 (see Fig. 11.9).

The street that runs between the two major temples of the Outer City continues northward as the organizing principle of the Inner City. In an elegant play on expectations of axiality, this street becomes a processional way—that is, a void—or is flanked by palaces, a series of solids. The most important punctuation of the axis is a group of three halls in the center of the Forbidden City, two rectangular halls flanking a smaller, nearly square one (see Fig. 11.9). All three straddle the axis, and are visible only from within the courts of the Forbidden City. A little farther north, another set of three halls, the official quarters of the empress, repeats the pattern, but because these halls are set amid gardens, the design is less evident. Spaces between the buildings of the Forbidden City interact with the structures to provide a visual progression northward to Coal Hill, which is crowned by a tower. Stairways and terraces lead through various spatial levels.

Figure 11.8. *Forbidden City, Beijing. Plan of the north–south axis with the three imperial audience chambers: the Hall of Heavenly Purity, the Hall of Middle or Complete Harmony, and the Hall of Preserving Harmony. The halls are elevated on terraces, protected by marble balustrades, and bracketed by gateways that emphasize the north–south axis. Each of the major buildings and gates is centered on the axis, quite the opposite of the relationship between buildings and axis at Teotihuacán. At the top of the plans, are smaller axial halls from the palace of the empress.*

Figure 11.9. *Forbidden City, Beijing. View of the north–south axis, from the Hall of Preserving Harmony to the Hall of Supreme Harmony. The marble pavement in the immediate foreground, carved in high relief, is preserved because no one was allowed to walk on it. Bearers carrying the sedan chair or litter of the emperor walked on the smooth marble on either side. This single piece of stone weighing 200 tons was transported by sliding it along ice.*

Thus the physical plan emphasizes the importance of the rulers, whose chambers alone are allowed to interrupt the axis.

Unlike the builders of cities, such as Istanbul, where mosques with tall minarets are the focal points, the architects of the Imperial City did not use height to emphasize the importance of the palaces. Their architectural vocabulary combined seclusion and opulence with an insistent axial pattern. All Chinese architecture is based on a modular system, whatever the variation of form and function. The number of bays (large vertical divisions of walls) determines the dimensions and proportions of the buildings. Color denotes hierarchical position within the overall plan—the palaces are lavish in their use of white marble for terraces and railings and of imperial orange for roof tiles.

West of the Imperial City, an irregular string of lakes surrounded by parks contrasts with the monumental axiality of the architecture and provides welcome greenery as a foil to the dense urban fabric (see Fig. 11.10). Water from the lakes feeds a winding canal that carries water to the Imperial City, filling a moat with a stone base and marble rim, along its south edge.

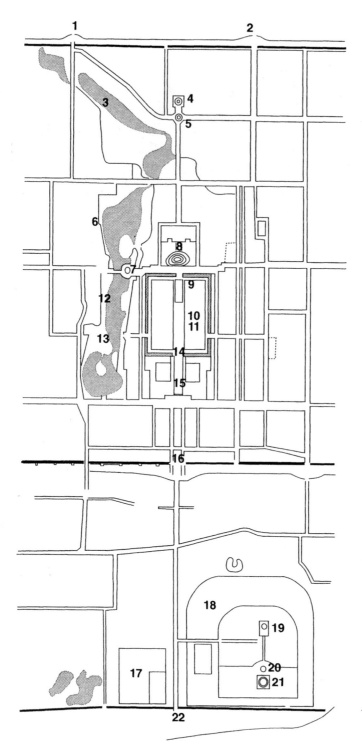

Figure 11.10. *Plan of the core of the city of Beijing, China. The axial movement progresses from the entrance to the Imperial City in the south to Coal Hill in the north, complemented by the irregular string of lakes set in gardens, to the west. Beijing occupied an area of 24 square miles (62 square kilometers). From the top to the bottom of the plan: North Gates (1 and 2); lakes and park (3, 6, 12, 13); Drum and Bell Towers (4 and 5); Coal Hill with tower (8); inner palace apartments, now a museum (9); three imperial halls (10 and 11; see Fig. 11. 10), Gate of Supreme Harmony (14); Gate to the Forbidden City (15); Gate of the Inner or Manchu City (16); Altar and Temple of Agriculture (17); Altar and Temple of Heaven (18–21) (17 and 19–21 are from the pre-Manchu Chinese capital); and South Gate (22). Note the moat that runs around the Forbidden City.*

As many as twenty thousand visitors a day now traverse the brick walkways of the Forbidden City to enjoy the visual drama of progression through the axial layout of the city. Their experience of axiality is both satisfied and thwarted by the arrangement of the major buildings straddling the axis.

SOURCES: EDMUND BACON (1974), KRUPP (1989), NEEDHAM (1971).

Teotihuacán, Mexico: Street of the Dead

Teotihuacán, the ancient capital of Mexico, is centered on a long, straight, 300-foot-wide street, today called the Street of the Dead. The pyramids and palaces that lined the Street of the Dead made an appropriate setting for civic and religious events on this windy plain northeast of present-day Mexico City. As the House of the Gods, the Pyramid of the Moon was the goal of pilgrimages and processions. Priests clad in feathers, masks, and mirrors led soldiers, kings and nobles, drummers and other musicians, and finally public crowds to the precinct, where celebrations of festivals were held. Bright sun and clear air at more than 8,000 feet of altitude made the vivid colors of celebrations still more intense as a hundred thousand people poured into the street from the Citadel courtyard, joined by nearly two hundred thousand from the Great Compound (city market and administrative center) across the street and tens of thousands more from the Pyramid of the Sun courtyard. Others stood along the way or lined the platforms and flat roofs of apartments along the street. The gods being honored were fearsome, demanding warfare and human sacrifice to ensure plentiful crops and governmental stability. It was essential that the people participate enthusiastically in parades and other rituals.

The scale of the Street of the Dead was uniquely magnificent in the New World (see Fig. 11.11). No other American city could rival it in the size, volume, and plan of its imposing buildings. "Monumentality on this scale magnifies both the religion and the polity," wrote anthropologist J. Marcus. In Chapter 7 we described the pyramids that flank this street; here, we concentrate on the street itself. Why were the city's major buildings—more than a hundred temples, shrines, and altars on platforms—located there?

The core of Teotihuacán was a dense mix of civil, religious, and residential buildings, divided into quarters by the Street of the Dead and two major streets running east and west from the center. The regular grid of the core governed more than 1 square mile (3 square kilometers), while in an adjacent zone that covered nearly 2 square miles (5 square kilometers), streets at 187-foot (57-meter) intervals enclosed apartment buildings. Around this center was a residential zone of 1 to 3 square miles, concentrated but less regular. Farther out was a less dense zone of residences, workshops, and some ceremonial structures covering about 5 square miles (12 square kilometers).

An early origin for the construction of the Street of the Dead and other major parallel streets is suggested because the same alignment—15.5 degrees east of astronomical north—is also standard for fields in central Mexico and northern Vera Cruz. Both the Street of the Dead and the cross-streets reached out from the core toward the mountains. South of the city, the Street of the Dead aligned with a concavity marking a pass across the ridge that bounds the valley; the northern vista is closed by the truncated volcano to the west of Gordo Hill (Cerro Gordo) (see Fig. 11.12). The street extends nearly 2 miles from the city center in each direction. From south to north, the street gradually rises 82 feet in 1 mile (25 meters in 2.5 kilometers). Because of the monumental buildings, the east and west streets (6 and 7 on Fig. 11.11) no longer intersect the Street of the Dead and now point toward low mountains at their outer extremities. Called now East and West Avenues, these streets date from the later first millennium B.C.E. Once East Avenue terminated in the Street of the Dead, but in the third century C.E. the rulers developed or enlarged the Citadel sanctuary over the crossing, so that no there is no direct connection to the central axis from the east. The final form of the cross avenues dates from no later than 200 to 450 C.E.

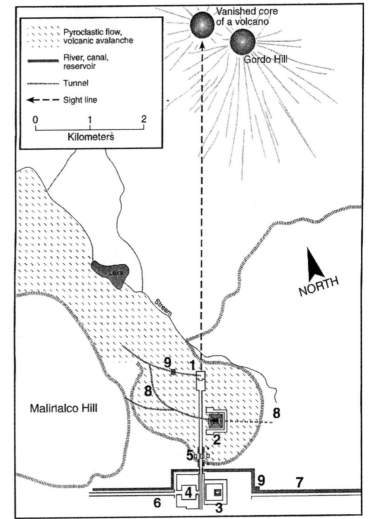

Figure 11.11. *Map of Teotihuacán, Mexico, about 2000 B.P. The city's setting in a basin surrounded by volcanoes determined the design. Man-made tunnels led toward the Pyramid of the Moon (1), and to a resurgence beneath the Pyramid of the Sun (2). The Street of the Dead aligns with a long-vanished cone of volcano, to the north (top of the map). The distance from the Pyramid of the Moon at the north to the Great Compound and Citadel at the center is 1.5 miles (2.5 kilometers); the street, some 300 feet wide (91 meters), continues for about 2 more miles to the southern edge of the city. Other features are the Citadel and Temple of Quetzalcoatl (3); the Great Compound (4); the Street of the Dead complex (5); West Avenue (6); a canalized river, running just north of East Avenue (7); tunnels (8); and reservoirs (9).*

Figure 11.12. *Axial view of Teotihuacán, from the Street of the Dead near the center of the city, northward to Cerro Gordo. The Pyramid of the Moon mimics the shape of the volcano. Other platforms pertaining to the buildings that flank the street are also visible.*

The Street of the Dead was made special by its width and by the accompanying architecture. Although a version of the Street of the Dead had existed earlier, during the second century C.E. it was enlarged and flanked with several large pyramid complexes. At its northern end is the Pyramid of the Moon, whose form echoes the volcano behind it in the distance (see Fig. 11.12 and Fig. 7.11). Architectural historian S. Tobriner suggested that the Street of the Dead aligns not with the visible cone (Gordo Hill) but with a huge, long-vanished original cone somewhat west of the surviving cone. (Compare with the orientation of Acoma to Mount Taylor, Chapter 7, fig. 7.16.)

The Mexican volcano, like Mount Taylor in New Mexico, last erupted in the 1490s, just before the Spanish arrived. Given the mountain's central importance as the feared source of volcanic disaster and the blessed source of water, it is no wonder that the main street of the community pointed toward it.

The three central pyramids memorialize ancient geographic features of the site. The Pyramid of the Moon in front of the volcano is shorter than the Pyramid of the Sun, but rises to the same height because of the increase in ground level. The Pyramid of the Sun, on the east side of the street (see Fig. 11.11) was built over a spring; this fact may explain why there are pyramids on only the east side of the street. Both the Pyramid of the Sun and the Citadel are aligned with the cross-axis, which is oriented 17 degrees south of east, following the path of the sun on two crucial dates that coincide with the rising and setting of the Pleiades.[31] The need for a clear vista from the Pyramid of the Sun and the Citadel to the setting sun seems to have precluded any massive building on the west side of the street. Construction of the Pyramid of the Sun and perhaps the Pyramid of the Moon probably began just before the common era.

Looking south from the Pyramid of the Moon (see Fig. 11.1), one sees on the left the larger and simpler Pyramid of the Sun, then the later complex now called the Citadel, containing the much smaller but more richly decorated Pyramid of Quetzalcoatl; to the right, palace apartments stand nearest the Pyramid of the Moon, followed by the Great Compound with its huge open court. Where the major axes crossed at the physical center of the city, the religious, administrative, and economic centers of Teotihuacán faced each other across the Street of the Dead. The Citadel complex (3 on Fig. 11.11) seems to have been a political center in a religious setting, with strong geographic and symbolic meanings; the people probably did not differentiate between those aspects of communal life.

Across the street from the Citadel, the Great Compound (4 on Fig. 11.11) served, Millon thinks, as the central market. In its present form, it dates from 200–450 C.E., although there may have been an earlier market on the same spot. In form, the Great Compound is different from the other monumental compounds along this street. Two large raised platforms, or wings, flank the plaza, each with several buildings facing inward toward the court. Millon postulates that they were connected with the administra-

_____

[31]See Millon (1992) for the astronomical basis of this plan.

tion of the city's economy. The entrance to the compound was at street level from the east, with an equally wide opening leading to the west. If Teotihuacán was a pilgrimage site, as many suppose, a large gathering space like this would have been useful.

The linear space flanked by buildings of this Mexican axis is the obverse of that at Beijing, where the major buildings constitute the axis and the space flows around them irregularly. At Teotihuacán, although the monuments are imposing, the emphasis is on the long void between them. The creators of both axes went beyond the manipulation of single buildings, revealing an urbane understanding of architectural interaction and extension. Compare the straightforward axiality of these arrangements with the winding processional path of Bhaktapur (see Chapter Fig. 7.4), equally rich in monumental buildings.

The hollow-center complexes of courtyards and the solid-center complex of Angkor Wat, though rich and complicated, are more self-contained. In that sense only are they simpler than the grand axial streets. Also interesting is the contrast between the convexity of these monuments, which rise above the ground on which they stand, and the "concave" Ethiopian churches that disappear into their settings (see Chapter 5). The latter add a further degree of elaboration—the pilgrimage experience is shaped by not a single church, but by a set of ten, among which the pilgrim travels by climbing stairs and passing through tunnels. In all these examples, the organization of space contributes directly and significantly to the experience of architecture, to the kaleidoscope of built forms. (See also Chapter 15, Being and Nonbeing in Chinese Architecture, for yet another way of thinking about spatial relations.)

SOURCES: BERLO (1992); BRAY (1972); J. MARCUS (1983); MILLON (1992), 381; TOBRINER (1972).

SUGGESTED READINGS

Bacon, Edmund 1974. *Design of Cities.* Harmondsworth, England: Penguin Books. A sensitive analysis of the architectural form of Beijing.

Barba, P. L., L. Manzanilla, R. Chavez, L. Flores, and A. J. Arzate. 1990. "Caves and Tunnels at Teotihuacán, Mexico: A Geological Phenomenon of Archaeological Interest." *Centennial Special Volume* 4: 431–38: Geological Society of America. Exciting reading.

Bronson, B. 1978. "Angkor, Anuradhapura, Prambanan, Tikal: Maya Subsistence in an Asian Perspective."
In *Pre-Hispanic Maya Agriculture,* 255–300, edited by P. D. Harrison and B. L. Turner. Albuquerque: University of New Mexico Press. Stimulating.

Chang, S.-D. 1970. "Some Observations on the Morphology of Chinese Walled Cities." *Annals of the Association of American Geographers* 60 (March): 63–91. A geographer examines the standard patterns of Chinese traditional cities, with special reference to their enclosure by ramparts and to their accommodation of different ethnic groups, especially the native Chinese and the conquering Manchus. Also relevant to Chapter 10, Imperial Plan.

Coe, M. D. 1961. "Social Typology and the Tropical Forest Civilizations." *Comparative Studies in Society and History* 4: 66–85. An interesting comparison of the geographic settings of Tikal (Mexico) and Angkor Wat (Cambodia).

Groslier, B. P., and J. Arthaud. 1957. *Angkor, Art and Civilization,* Trans. E. E. Shaw. London: Thames & Hudson. Groslier was the foremost excavator of Angkor Wat.

Johnson, W. 1995. "Keeping Cool." *Aramco World* 46 (May–June): 10–17. A brief, illustrated article summarizes methods—including courtyards—for keeping cool in hot, dry climates.

Knapp, R. G. 1990. *The Chinese House.* New York: Oxford University Press. Knapp is a geographer who does justice to his subject. The book discusses and illustrates rural and urban houses and their courtyards.

Marcus, J. 1983. "On the Nature of the Meso-American City." In *Prehistoric Settlement Patterns: Essays in Honor of G. R. Willey,* 195–242, edited by E. Z. Vogt and R. M. Leventhal. Albuquerque: University of New Mexico Press. The best brief analysis of Mesoamerican urban patterns.

Millon, R. 1992. "Teotihuacán Studies: From 1950 to 1990 and Beyond." In *Art, Ideology, and the City of Teotihuacán: A Symposium at Dumbarton Oaks, October 8–9, 1988,* 339–419. Washington, D.C.: Dunbarton Oaks Research Library and Collection. An interesting review that reflects Millon's many years on the site and a great deal of thought.

Needham, J. 1971. *Science and Civilization in China: Part 3, Vol. 4: Physics and Physical Technology.* Cambridge, England: Cambridge University Press. Needham discusses the axial plan of Beijing under "Civil Engineering." Especially good for its bibliography.

Pym, C. 1963. "Collapse of the Khmers." In *Vanished Civilizations of the Ancient World,* 105–38, edited by Edward Bacon. New York: McGraw-Hill. Good pictures, plans, and maps, and a diagram of the development of the Khmer temple plan from Bakong in 881 to Bayon ca. 1200.

Stubbs, S. A. 1950. *Bird's-Eye View of the Pueblos*. Norman: University of Oklahoma Press. An analysis of aerial photos of southwestern pueblos. Convincing evidence of courtyards in pre-Hispanic times.

Tobriner, S. 1972. "The Fertile Mountain: An Investigation of Cerro Gordo's Importance to the Town Plan and Iconography of Teotihuacán." *Teotihuacán* 11:103–13. Mesa Redondo, Mexico: Sociedad Mexicana de Anthropologia. This seminal early essay is now complemented by that of Barba et al. (1990).

Waln, N. 1933. *The House of Exile*. Boston; Little, Brown. This fascinating book describes traditional Chinese family life and the changes that occurred during the 1920s and 1930s.

⊞ PART V

Cultural Values

Built structures overtly express cultural values. Outsiders can never completely and intuitively understand the symbolic languages of architectures all over the world as "native speakers" do, but we can raise and examine some of the cultural issues at stake. These issues include the fusion of monumental and vernacular elements into a functioning whole; symbolism and ornamentation, including the question of who controls and carries out the decorative program; the relationships between architecture and social structure; theories of architecture; and the ways in which class, gender, and ethnicity have affected the writing of architectural history and theory. Our survey concludes with two different responses to architectural decision making and two different ways of considering the economics of building.

The architecture of other cultures reveals something of the builders' cultural values—for example, the kings of Sri Lanka built their large, artificial lakes not for the welfare of the people but for glory, although this fact may tell us more about the nature of one-person rule than it does about a particular society. But in looking at other cultures' architecture, we may also gain insight into our own values. In the United States, at the beginning of the twenty-first century, it may seem obvious that economics is always the basic problem, but in other times and places, people have based important architectural decisions on kinship systems, personal prestige, dynastic necessity, opportunities for intercultural action, missionary religion, resource constraints (even when no money changed hands), and generous feelings toward loved ones. Buildings that house daily activities or are the goals of special occasions may reveal—or hide—these values. And in the process of changing the built environment, values themselves evolve. Architectural differences ultimately reveal the underlying consistency of human behaviors.

◫ 12

Vernacular and Monumental Combinations

Architecture is often classified as monumental or vernacular. Monumental architecture is massive, imposing, great in either quantity or quality, of heroic scale, of enduring significance, and made to cause remembrance. Vernacular architecture is "everyday" architecture, made with the commonest techniques, decorative features, and materials of a period, region, or group. Monumental buildings include palaces, many religious buildings, and some governmental buildings and are usually expensive, large, durable, and weighted with symbolism; columns, obelisks, and other structures whose only function is memorializing are also monumental architecture. Vernacular buildings include houses, markets, schools, depots, and other structures of everyday life, often with their own symbolism.

Monumental and vernacular architecture can serve similar ends. For example, the monumental architecture of Sri Lanka (formerly Ceylon) includes massive domed Buddhist stupas, called *dagobas*, dating from as early as the third century B.C.E., some larger than the great Egyptian pyramids. Containing a small inner chamber for a relic or memento of the Buddha, the dagoba was symbolically and religiously the equivalent of the Buddha, significant for the people. The faithful, however, also built simpler, smaller neighborhood and domestic shrines for local religious observances—examples of vernacular architecture.

The uses of monumental and vernacular architecture are exemplified in the water-supply system of the Sinhalese culture of Sri Lanka and the lively central plaza of Patan, Nepal. As we show, the vernacular and the monumental form a continuum, not a dichotomy.

WATER SYSTEM: SRI LANKA

Anthropologists and historians know that the range of solutions for any social problem extends from extremely simple to highly sophisticated, without a firm boundary between the vernacular and the monumental. This is exactly the case with Sinhalese water provisions. Just as people built shrines that were huge, expensive, and monumental and shrines that were small, domestic, and vernacular, they used both monumental and vernacular elements in their water-supply system. Local dams, temporary weirs, tanks and reservoirs, and vast lakes—with the canals and channelized rivers to connect them—were all parts of a system that grew to encompass nearly all the arable land of the island. Some were built by villagers for their own use, some by engineer-monks for regional use, and some by professional builders for the kings's cities and agricultural estates. Hence, these water elements could be vernacular or monumental.

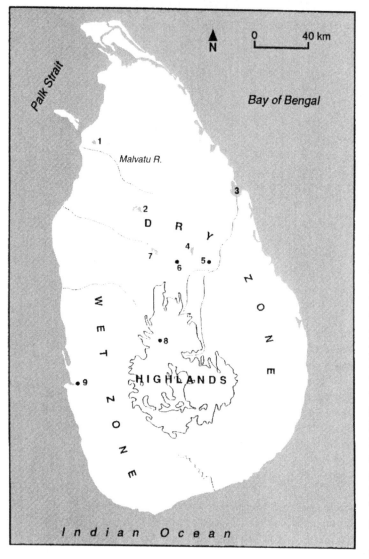

Figure 12.1. *Map of irrigation works, Sri Lanka. The map shows (1) Yodavava, (2) Anuradhapura, (3) Trincomalee (Gokunna) port and city, (4) Minneriya Tank, (5) Polonnaruva, (6) Sigiriya, (7) Kalavava, (8) Kandy (the nineteenth century capital), and (9) Colombo (the modern capital). Elements of the water system at 2, 4, 5, and 6 are discussed in text as is Sigiriya (6), which is also illustrated in Figs. 12.3 and 12.4.*

The first Sinhalese settlements appeared along the Malvatu River in the third century B.C.E. (see Fig. 12.1). There people supplemented the early pattern of slash-and-burn agriculture, adapted to a low population density and alternating wet and dry seasons, with a new pattern of permanent villages based on technology imported from India, where people had already been using tanks, dams, and canals for water control for about three thousand years. Eventually, earthen cisterns and village water tanks became so ubiquitous in Sri Lanka that they seemed not to have a history or a style; by the late nineteenth century, the southwestern part of the island had one small tank for every square mile of surveyed land, with 440 tanks in the Mau Ara river basin alone. These were modest structures for local use: "The first essential requirement of the agriculturist is not irrigation on a grand scale but simply a little modest conservation of local water resources," that is, drainage and diversion of flood waters, wrote hydraulic historian E. R. Leach. Village people built the tanks and collectively owned the water and fish they contained.

The builders of water-system elements, such as tanks and canals, had one goal in mind: a more dependable and abundant supply of water in a land of periodic drought and uneven natural distribution of water. These structures remained usable over long periods when administered and maintained at the village or district levels. No major bureaucracy managed the irrigation system; rather, local people took responsibility for daily cleaning and necessary repairs in a social arrangement similar to that of traditional Peru (described in Chapter 3), especially the nonmonetary basis of the work (see Leach's bibliography). For more than fourteen hundred years, Sinhalese people built and maintained water-system elements in local efforts directed by professional engineers, many of them Buddhist monks. Modern engineers find that premodern water systems in many countries show a high level of hydraulic understanding and engineering skill. The water system of Sri Lanka, which flourished at about the same time as Angkor Wat (see Chapter 11) and Pagan (Chapter 1), may be the most complete one to survive from earlier times.

The first Sinhalese engineer whose name is recorded in inscriptions was Uparaja Mahanaga (250–210 B.C.E.), a brother of the king. Mahanaga expanded the idea of the village water tank into the earliest Sinhalese monumental reservoirs. These royal water works supplemented the local systems on a large scale that made them engineering, rather than plumbing, projects, according to Leach. Although kings often received credit for entire tank-and-canal systems, in many cases they only initiated or completed these projects.

Either local communities or kings using forced labor could build water-system elements of all sizes and degrees of elaboration (see Fig. 12.2), from the family cistern and village tank to enormous shallow tanks held by thick earthen dams and braced with stone and brick. Early inscriptions mention weirs, canals, and reservoirs, as R. Gunawardana noted. A king in the third century B.C.E. built the enormous Tissawewa tank at Anuradhapura. By the first century B.C.E., the tanks and canals exhibited sophisticated engineering, as we can see from their remains, although no engineering texts have come down to us. Reservoirs could be as large as 6,400 acres (2,590 hectares) in area, with embankments up to 7 miles (18 kilometers) long and 40 feet (12.19 meters) high. Canal systems up to 200 miles (300 kilometers) long connected the reservoirs, linking tanks to each other and to perennial rivers, with spillways to handle excess water. By the second century C.E. or even earlier, the engineers knew how to release water from the tanks without causing a surge that would destroy the earthen banks. They used simple, effective devices, called valve pits, that contained sluices at staggered levels in the embankment with connecting channels and valve mechanisms. These devices controlled the release of water under tolerable pressure.

In the first century C.E., King Vasabha built twelve tanks and twelve canals. The greatest of these was the Alahara Canal, which carried water 30 miles (48.3 kilometers) from a river to land in the dry zone. Improved irrigation allowed people to grow as many as three rice crops a year on hundreds of square miles of land (1 square mile = 259 hectares), producing an agricultural surplus that financed cities and monasteries. Because of additions to the water supply, cities had piped water, including enough for ornamental pools. It is likely, however, that only about 10 percent of the Sinhalese population lived in cities, so this urban improvement benefited only a few.

The great tank-building phase of the late third century C.E. produced some sixteen tanks near the capital.

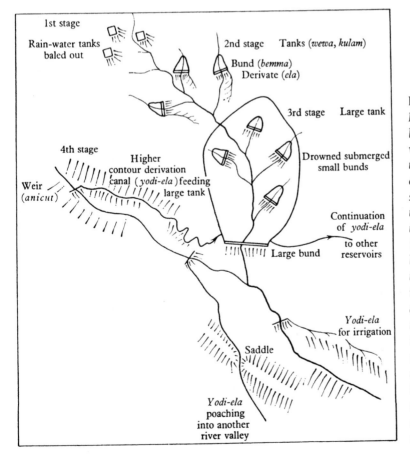

Figure 12.2. *Evolution of a reservoir in Sri Lanka. The first stage (upper left) was the collection of rainwater into tanks from which it was baled out for personal use or for agriculture. In the second stage (upper center), larger collectors were built by damming across a stream and building a contour channel along the hillside, from which short canals fed the water to fields along the slope. In the third stage (center right), an enormous bund created a large reservoir submerging the early small tanks. At about the same time, a fourth stage involved increasingly sophisticated temporary dams (weirs) across streams, coupled with contour canals to divert water toward the giant tanks of the third stage. Small local canals continued to water hillside fields. At bottom right, one sees the development of this system into long canals that can obtain and deliver water to more than one valley. The Sri Lankan canals are comparable to the Chimu system of Peru, discussed in Chapter 3.*

The largest was the Minneriya Tank. Fed by perennial rivers and monsoon rains, this system included existing and repaired village tanks, huge tanks, and medium-sized feeder tanks that received water from the rivers and fed smaller tanks through canals. Also from the third century are the twin Kuttam Pokuna ponds, a double settlement tank: heavier particles in the water sank into the first pit; the discharge flowed over the rim into the second pit. In the fifth century, a king dammed the Mahaveli River anew, building many tanks, the most notable being the Kalavava, south of Anuradhapura. Kalavava was created by a dressed-granite dam 3 miles (5 kilometers) long and nearly 50 feet (15 meters) tall and fed by a 50-mile-long (80 kilometers) canal.

Throughout these centuries, kings were glorified by having their names associated with huge water projects, rather like honorary chairmen. Sinhalese rulers cherished the reputation of being irrigation engineers, not conquerors or city builders. The most notable waterwork in this tradition of royal patronage was the palatial pleasure garden called Sigiriya, built by King Kasyapa I (473–91 C.E.). It was located near the Kala Oya headwaters, on terraces surrounding a tall rock promontory (see Figs. 12.3a and b and 12.4a and b). The complex included a palace on top of the rock mesa, a boulder garden that exploited the natural forms of smaller rocks, eastern and western precincts with large moats, and a large tank south of the palace rock. The surviving tank is only a small part of the original pool, which was enclosed by a 5-mile-long (8 kilometers) dam.

Sigiriya's western precinct had the largest water gardens in Asia, including swimming pools, ponds, and reflecting pools fed by pipes from the moats (see Fig. 12.3a). The pools helped the king and his courtiers endure the hot and humid climate. A narrower stretch of garden, flanked by fountains and incorporating large moated islands (possibly for royal pavilions), led to the stairway up past huge boulders (see Fig. 12.3 b). Another huge cistern at the southwest corner of the great rock fed these higher pools and fountains. A natural gallery in the rock, decorated with vivid paintings of beautiful women (few of these paintings survive), led to the royal retreat (Fig. 12.4a). More cisterns, pools, and a reservoir on top supplied the palace with water (see Fig. 12.4). The mesa top also exposed the king and his chosen few to the breezes that mitigated the heat and humidity.

Sinhalese civilization flourished from 200 B.C.E. to 993 C.E. and survived until the thirteenth century. Originally, the kings granted water rights to individuals or to monasteries. From the beginning of the common era, tank owners bought and sold water, buying a volume of water as it entered their tank, selling some to local customers, and sending the rest to owners of the next tank along the system. Tank owners, often members of the warrior caste, were liberal patrons of Buddhism, so that monasteries came to control up to a quarter of the island's land and water resources, according to Gunawardana.

Water management was not centralized under autocratic control until the tenth century or so. Before that time, local control meant that the water system could survive invasions and even the disarray of prolonged instability in the national government. Then came a period when the royal design and building of huge dams and canals were extended into royal and elite ownership. During a brief but brilliant cultural renaissance, from the eleventh to the thirteenth centuries, Sinhalese rulers proclaimed a new capital, supplied with water by the Parakrama Samudra (tank). This "sea" incorporated two earlier tanks and was connected by canals to the huge Alahara canal system dating from the first century. The Parakrama Samudra's enclosing dam was of the finest stonework—an appropriate final effort for this hydraulic society.

Concentration of power and ownership in the hands of kings and their favorites eventually supplanted the broad base of local control and led to the downfall of the system and of the society. A series of invasions by Turks/Mughals defeated the Sinhalese in the thirteenth century. These disasters coincided with an upsurge of malaria, which further restricted life in the plain. The water-supply system fell into disrepair. Its monumental elements survived, though many did not remain operational. Its vernacular elements first suffered from the collapse of the national economy and then were reestablished in a "one tank, one village" ecological pattern that has persisted until modern times.

In the landscape of nineteenth-century Sri Lanka, the king and nobles struggled over whose interests, whose "story," would be embedded in the landscape. The rulers manipulated the very appearance of the landscape, masking the ideological nature of its form and content, so that their values seemed objective and natural—indeed, taken for granted. J. Duncann calls this activity "reductive normalizing," the attempt to make what is patently cultural appear free of manipulation. Cultural amnesia allowed the landscape to become a powerful tool in the struggle for dynastic supremacy.

After World War II, the cycle turned again to rebuilding. Buddhism had helped the people of Sri Lanka

a.

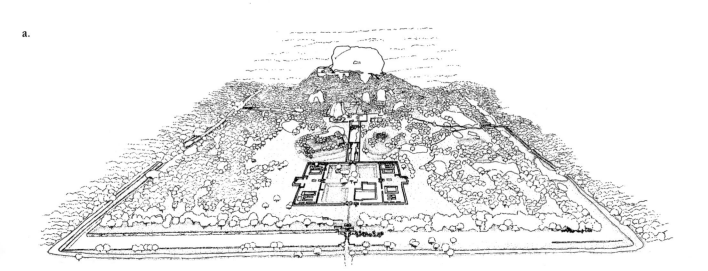

b.

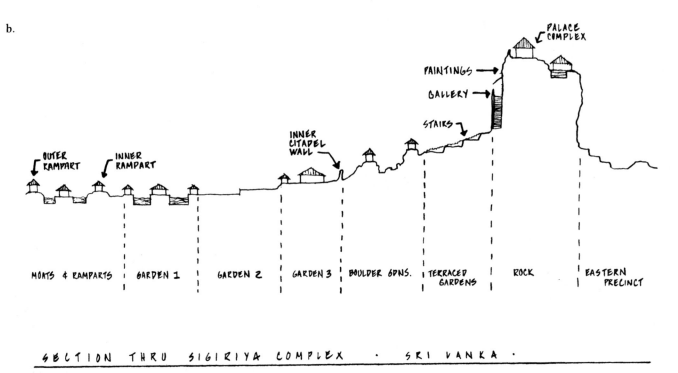

PALACE
COMPLEX

PAINTINGS

GALLERY

STAIRS

INNER
CITADEL
WALL

OUTER
RAMPART

INNER
RAMPART

MOATS & RAMPARTS · GARDEN 1 · GARDEN 2 · GARDEN 3 · BOULDER GDNS. · TERRACED GARDENS · ROCK · EASTERN PRECINCT

SECTION THRU SIGIRIYA COMPLEX · SRI LANKA ·

Figure 12.3. *The Sigiriya water gardens (restored), Sri Lanka. **a.** View along the central axis. At the lowest level are buildings and pools and a wide walkway leading toward the rock outcropping on which the palace was built. **b.** A section showing the elevation of walls, gardens, pools, small buildings leading up to two flights of stairs decorated by the famous paintings and, finally, the upper palace, with its own cisterns at the summit of the 650-foot-high (± 200 meters) rock.*

Figure 12.4. *Sigiriya.* **a.** *Schoolchildren climb the stairs to the palace at the top of the rock, a total of 1,200 steps. They entered between the lion paws at the bottom.*

survive defeat and economic collapse by minimizing their wants and needs. It now encouraged the building of water-system elements as good deeds that would benefit the builders in both the present existence and the next life. Now that malaria is under control, builders of huge irrigation projects in Sri Lanka aim to turn the central plains into wet rice areas again, thereby restoring ancient economic riches. Modern politicians have been reexamin-

ing ancient ways of administering water use. As the cycle turns to rebuilding, people again consider the building of water-system elements a good deed that will benefit their next life.

SOURCES: DUNCANN (1980), GUNAWARDANA (1971), 21; LEACH (1959.

DURBAR SQUARE, PATAN, NEPAL

> As an ensemble the Durbar Square in Patan probably remains the most picturesque collection of buildings that has ever been set up in so small a space.
> —*P. Landon (1928)*

In Durbar Square in the heart of Patan, Nepal, monumental buildings are grouped with vernacular, elite buildings with those of commoners, and planned effects with spontaneous ones. *Durbar* means place of royal assembly—a royal plaza, one might say—and all three of the capital cities of the Kathmandu Valley have such squares. Market activities and animals have been banished from Bhaktapur's Durbar Square since the renovation around 1980, but Patan's ensemble of buildings and activities does not have to be cleaned up to look its best. Indeed, the plaza is at its best when it holds the full range of human activities, including recently added tourist activities that extend the meaning of *vernacular.*

The urban design of Patan's Durbar Square developed over many centuries. Since it is unusual to find in the study of traditional architecture such a detailed written record as this, we linger on the historical changes in this plaza. The works of M. S. Slusser and of E. Sekler have given us a rare opportunity to follow its changing patterns. However, although the plan in Figure 12.5 illuminates the subtleties of the composition, it cannot reveal the three-dimensional relations of the buildings to one another (see Fig. 12.6a and b) or the greater complexity of their development in time. Nor does a plan reveal the interaction of the various materials used: fire bricks (*inta* in the Nepali language), wood for roofs and trim, and sandstone, quartzite, or limestone, with the latter two used for foundations.

Patan's plaza developed where the road between east and west Nepal crossed the north–south Tibet–India route. Before 300 C.E., a market plaza stood at that crossing, complete with the necessary shrines. The people of those days were mostly Buddhists, but with underlying beliefs in local gods from long before the birth of Gautama. Over many centuries, the Buddhist element gradu-

Figure 12.4. b. *Aerial photo of the promontory. The platforms on which the palace was built and the large tanks for water are plainly visible.*

ally receded and Hinduism reasserted itself, but the ordinary religion of Nepal has remained a fascinating mixture of the two overlying the original nature-religion. Of the three capitals of the Kathmandu Valley, Patan has been the most persistently Buddhist, yet its role as a crossroads town has brought many other religious ideas to mingle with the simplicity of Buddhism. For instance, the shrine of Shiva (according to Slusser) or Vishnu (according to M. Thapa, personal communication) at the bottom of the plan (A) is an old shrine to a Hindu god. Texts from the seventeenth century tell of a large sacred stone that was lodged in the site across the street (at number 6); from prehistoric times, as Slusser noted, natural stones of un-

usual form or size were thought to be places where the terrible Shiva could be encountered, and for a long time people have worshipped him at this corner of the square. A boulder and a market are not what Euro-Americans usually regard as religious monuments, yet together they are just that in this context. (Buildings in the plan of Fig. 12.5 are numbered in chronological order.)

Early Historic Period
(Licchavi Dynasty 300–879)

Next to the crossroads, the ruin of an early marketplace lies under the scant remains of a monastery of the first

Figure 12.5. *Plan of Durbar Square, Patan, Nepal. The numbers identify the buildings by chronological order; all dates are* C.E. *The names are both the current names and the ancient Sanskrit names.*

Oldest elements: A *Lokshmi Narayann—the oldest shrine to Shiva (Vishnu?)*; B *Mani Ganesh (Ganesha) shrine*; C *Candika shrine (chaitya)*; (1) *Manidhara fountain (570).*

Sixteenth-century elements: (2) *Cara Narayana temple (1566)*; (3) *Narashima/Narsingha temple (1589).*

Seventeenth-century elements: (4) *Krishna Temple with Garuda Pillar/Garudadhvaja (1637); (5) Biswanath/Visvesvara temple (1627); (6) Sundari-chowk/palace (1647); (7) Bhandarkhal garden with Lohan Hiti (pond) (1647); (8) Narayana small temple (1652); (9) Degutale tower and temple (1661); (10) Mul-chowk Taleju tower and temple (1666); (11) Mul-chowk/Yantaju palace (1666); (12) Nasal-chowk/palace; (13) Taleju temple and tower (1671); (14) Bhai Dega/Bhaidevala/Visvanatha temple (1678); (15) Agama Chen (or Chem), palace chapel (1679, destroyed 1934); (16) Shiva/Bhimasena temple (1680); (17) Yoganarendon Pillar (1693).*

Eighteenth-century elements: (18) *Mani Mandapa/ council "hall" (1701), now one of a pair of resting places; (19) Hari Sanker/Sankara-Narayana temple (1706); (20) Simhadhvaja/Lion Pillar (1707); (21) Cyasing-devala/Krishna temple (1723); (22) Mani Kashar Narayan Chowk/Caukot/Lumjhya Palace (1734); (23) Ghanta/Taleju bell (1737); (24) Small shrine.*

Miscellaneous elements: E *is a monumental gateway; W1 and W2 are additional fountains; The space to the left of 8, 3, and 19 is a garden, with a small shrine to Vishnu; b1, b2, and b3 are stages for performances (dance platforms); D is a modern apartment building.*

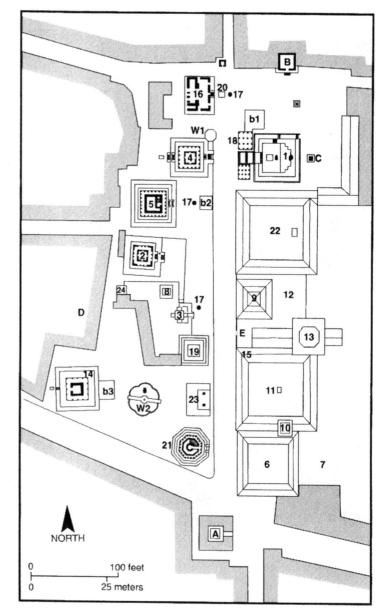

294

historic dynasty. In 570 C.E., to serve the assembled traders and others, Bharavi, the grandson of King Manadeva I, gave a deep fountain (1 on Fig. 12.5) (see Chapter 3 for a description) to Patan. Rebuilt later as the Manidhara Fountain, it is still an important focus of life in the plaza. The negative stepped-pyramid of its hollow form makes a superb foil to the positive stepped forms of the later temples across the street. From the steps leading down into the fountain, D. P. Crouch, author, first began to assimilate the complexity and subtlety of the plaza's design.

Also dating from this early period may be the Ganesha (Ganesh) shrine at B (compare with Fig. 7.5) and the Candika Chaitya (shrine) at C. Kings of this dynasty worshipped both Shiva and Ganesh, and Candika was their tutelary goddess, also honored under the names Taleju and Durga. The shrines of Shiva and Ganesha bracket Patan Square to the north and south. Candika's shrine is on the south side of the upper cross street, in the small plaza behind the Manidhara Fountain, aligned with its axial entrance stairs. These early shrines suggest the edges of the shape that became the plaza.

Figure 12.6. *Durbar Square, Patan, Nepal.* **a.** *Nineteenth-century engraving. Palaces form a firm edge to the north-bound street, while temples make an undulating arc along the left edge. The complex spatial and stylistic arrangements of this triangular plaza are evident in the juxtaposition of Indian and Nepalese temple forms and the guardian lions and pillars with honorific portraits of kings.*

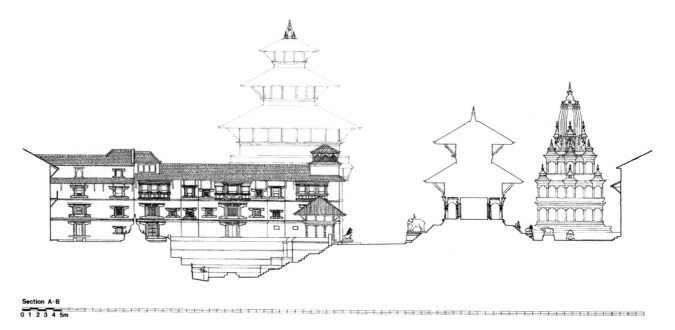

Section A-B
0 1 2 3 4 5m

Figure 12.6. b. *A section of the plaza looking south, running through the Manidhara fountain of the sixth century (on the left), across the palace street, and then through a seventeenth century temple. Profiles of the palace, the shadowy tower-temple behind it, and the pagoda-type Cara Narayan, with the Indian-type Krishna (4 in Fig. 12.5) to its right and behind it, reveal the many cultural influences at work in the architecture of this crossroads city.*

Transitional Period (879–1200) and Malla Period (1200–1482)

By the close of the Licchavi period, nobles had built houses along the east side of the square. The turbulence of dynastic change produced a fortified palace (22 on Fig. 12.5) at the north end of this complex; another palace (11), was also begun in this period. In the 12th century or earlier, a second monastery appeared at (6), according to Slusser. In the Malla period, the row of houses began to grow into palaces. Inscriptions from the fourteenth through sixteenth centuries refer to particular palaces, but their remains have not been identified because no one is eager to disturb the existing buildings.

Independent Patan

In the late fifteenth century, the Malla dynasty broke into three independent kingdoms with capitals at Patan, nearby Kathmandu, and more distant Bhaktapur. In the late sixteenth century, a royal chamberlain built two temples in the Patan plaza—the first permanent buildings in the center space. In 1566 he erected at (2 in Fig. 12.5) a Newar-style temple with tiered hipped roofs (similar to a pagoda),

dedicated to Vishnu. In 1589 he built a second temple at (3), using the tower-shaft form called sikhara, developed in India about the sixth century C.E. and known in Nepal since the ninth century (see Chapter 1 for a discussion of this form at Khajuraho). In these first plaza temples, the outward-protruding roofs of one and the upward-tapering tower of the other set up a three-way tension with the stepped cavity of the deep fountain across the street.

The Malla symbolized their temporary takeover of Patan in 1597 by building or rebuilding a Taleju temple, probably the one at (9 in Fig. 12.5), thought to date from the sixteenth century or earlier. Taleju was the heavenly patron of the Mallas, as she had been of the Licchavis. The tower is still the tall, graceful focus of the ensemble.

The Seventeenth-Century Builder-Kings

The seventeenth century was the great period of Patan construction. The major builders of Durbar Square were three outstanding kings: Siddhinarasimha, his son Srinvasa, and his grandson Yoganarendra. In 1619 King Siddhinarasimha began to replace the old palace at (12 in Fig. 12.5), a program that his son was to continue until 1684, when new palaces lined the entire east side of the street. Siddhinarasimha also built temples: a brick Krishna temple at (4) in 1627, followed by a stone temple to Visvesvara at (5) in 1637. In front of the Krishna temple, he placed a pillar topped with a portrait statue of himself as the guardian bird-spirit called Garuda, the inevitable companion of Vishnu. Siddhinarasimha's palace building may have been spurred on by the burning, around 1642, of the Taleju temple (9). In 1646–47, the king built a completely new palace (6), known as Stone-court after the ancient boulder earlier. This palace replaced the medieval monastery, which had replaced a monastery from the first centuries of our era.

Also in the 1640s, outside the plaza proper and east of the palaces, Siddhinarasimha laid out the Bhandarkhal garden (7 in Fig. 12.5), now the Patan Archaeological Garden, with many sculptures. Originally, the garden, with a large fountain and tank and pavilions carved with reliefs, was dedicated to Taleju. The genre scenes of the carved reliefs may be thought of as an eruption of the vernacular into the monumental, as Slusser stated.

The Narayana temple (8 in Fig. 12.5), built in 1652, has been attributed to Siddhinarasimha's son Srinvasa, in honor of his brother, but since Srinvasa would have been only eleven years old at the time, the temple was more likely a project of the royal parents, who also built the tomb at (24). The temple is a small cubical structure set at an angle in front of a small garden—another reason for attributing it to Siddhinarasimha, the only garden builder of the group.

Between 1661 and 1684, the entire row of palaces on the east side of the plaza was renovated (see Fig. 12.6a). The renovation included rebuilding, around 1661, the public temple (9 on Fig. 12.5) atop a three-story palace wing. It also included the 1666 restoration of the central palace, with its shrine and the royal "chapel" whose roofs (at 10) erupt from the south wing of the courtyard (11). In 1671 King Srinvasa added a new Taleju temple for the royal family in the south corner of the old northern palace (13). Later that decade, he collected many religious relics into a clan sanctuary that stood at (15) until an earthquake destroyed it in 1934. Srinvasa completed the enlargement and modernization of the palaces by restoring and enlarging the defense tower and its palace (22) around 1680. Having thus provided a serene and stately backdrop for Durbar Square, Srinvasa finished by erecting a new temple for the god of good fortune (16). In front of the temple is a sunken fire-pit mandala.

In 1678 Srinvasa's chief minister built a temple dedicated to Visvanatha at (14 in Fig. 12.5). The Nepalese had a strong tradition of conveniently located substitutes for inconvenient pilgrimage sites, and this new temple was a substitute for pilgrimages to the Visvanatha Temple in Benares, India, then recently destroyed. Elevated on a high plinth and rebuilt with a dome after the 1934 earthquake, it holds down the western corner of the plaza and, together with the king's temple (16), brackets the diagonal side of the plaza. The placement of these two temples mimics that of the other pair of temples half hidden in the palace (at 10 and 13), built during the same reign.

The last of the seventeenth-century builder-kings, Yoganarendra, set up his portrait pillar at (17 in Fig. 12.5) in 1693. The same year, the south wing of the northern palace (22) fell down and was not rebuilt for forty years. But in 1701 Yoganarendra replaced the earlier council hall (18) in front of the deep fountain with one of a pair of open but roofed platforms now mostly used as a resting place (see Fig. 12.6 b). There, one can buy a few vegetables or a single cigarette or sit for a while after bathing at the fountain below. Yoganarendra also replaced the paving of the dance platform immediately to the north (b1); another dance platform is located between the street and the Garuda pillar of the Krishna temple (b2, near 5), and still another is on the east side of site 14 (b3). Kings of Nepal have been fond of appearing in the public dance-dramas that enact the stories of their mythology.

The Eighteenth Century

Members of Yoganarendra's family added to the square during the eighteenth century. In 1706 his sister built a temple to Hari-Hara (19 in Fig. 12.5), completing the arc of buildings that curves westward from the street. In 1723 Yoganarendra's daughter built another sikhara dedicated to Krishna (21) at the southern point of the plaza opposite the Sundari-chok palace. The octagonal shape of this sikhara repeats the forms of the roofs of the Taleju temple (13) and of the water sources at W1 and W2.

The finishing touches of the square date from the first half of the eighteenth century. The last honorific column, the Simhadhvaja or lion pillar (20 in Fig. 12.5), appeared in 1707, closing the northern vista of the palace street and setting up a fine visual dialogue with the Vishnu/Shiva monument at the other end of the row of palaces (A). In 1716 King Radhinarasimhamalla donated a great doorway (at E) leading to the royal Taleju temple, set back from the street within the row of palaces, in line with (13). In 1734 King Visnumalla rebuilt the fallen wing of the palace at (22), and three years later, he and his queen offered the bronze bell in honor of Taleju that remains at (23).

All these buildings form a splendid background for rare royal marriages or stately meetings. Contrastingly frequent vernacular scenes are the market and craft activities that still make this plaza the center of Patan life—the vivid colors of food and clothing; the wandering cows, small boys, dogs, and chickens; motorcycle repair in this corner, paintings being sold on that doorstep, carpets disguising the new apartment building to the west (at D in Fig. 12.5). The water of the fountains and the enclosed small garden behind shrines 19, 3, and 8 offer refreshment. Figures 3.3 (in Kathmandu) and 6.5 (in Bhaktapur) give some hint of the three-dimensional quality of this architectural interaction, accompanied by the lively cadences of ordinary life. In its capacity to provide a superb setting, where the eye and the spirit never weary of the combinations of forms, Patan Durbar Square achieves its real excellence.

That the square could develop over centuries into a masterpiece of urban design speaks well for the underlying unity of concept in this culture. Succeeding generations of royal builders and ordinary people shared a similar vision of what the urban center should be. The lack of ego did not produce the superb effects visible here; kings were quite eager to memorialize themselves in pillar-statues, temples for their favorite deities, and palaces. But a strong building tradition incorporated various styles, sizes, materials, and meanings, harmonizing them aesthetically and practically. There is no finer example of urban design—a well-executed blend of the vernacular and the monumental.

SOURCES: NICOLAIS (1971), PRADHAN (1991), SEKLER (1980), SLUSSER (1982) PL. 6, 127–28, 532–33.

SUGGESTED READINGS

Clarke, A. C. 1978. *The Fountains of Paradise*. New York: Harcourt, Brace. Science fiction set in the water gardens and palace at Sigiriya, with great sensitivity to the ancient place.

Gunawardana, R. A. L. H. 1971. "Hydraulic Society in Medieval Ceylon." *Past and Present* 53: 3–27. Supplements Leach (1959), with an excellent bibliography.

Landon, P. 1928. *Nepal*. 2 vols. London: Constable. The pre-Slusser classic.

Leach, E. R. 1959. "Hydraulic Society in Ceylon." *Past and Present* 15: 2–26. A refutation of Wittfogel's (1972) hydraulic society thesis, with an excellent bibliography.

Silva, K. M. de. 1981. *A History of Sri Lanka*. Delhi: Oxford University Press. Draws together a lot of information.

Slusser, M. S. 1982. *Nepal Mandala*. Princeton, N.J.: Princeton University Press. Although written by a cultural anthropologist, this is the primary source for the architecture of Nepal. We have rearranged her material and placed our interpretations on it, based on several visits to the city and critical reviews by M. Thapa and J. Thapa. Slusser is relevant also to Chapter 10 (Town Houses, Nepal).

13

Symbolism and Ornamentation

Many designers of architecture and landscape architecture deliberately set out to embody symbolism in their constructions. Indeed, they often leave documents explaining their intentions, as at the Taj Mahal (see also Chapter 17 on costs). Symbolism can be either personal or general, belonging to an entire culture. Chinese and Islamic gardens offer scope for speculation about how personal or general their symbolism may be. Some architects use those conventional symbols called the alphabet or other characters of a culture's written language for ornamentation. Not all ornamentation is produced by professional architects, however. Some is the work of artisans who earn their living decorating for others, and some is the work of the owners and users of buildings, like the Ndebele women who decorate their homes and their persons with similar colorful motifs.

SYMBOLIC GARDENS

Gardens express relationships between human beings and their natural surroundings. The earliest known gardens were practical, situated near simple dwellings to provide food. From these beginnings, elaborate pleasure gardens evolved for a variety of reasons: to express religious or philosophical concepts, to evoke subjective responses to the beauty of nature or to express power. The designs of Chinese and Muslim gardens reveal the religious, philosophical, and aesthetic principles that guided their designers.

Chinese Gardens

"All facets of Chinese culture are evident in the Chinese garden," observes landscape architect E. Morris, who describes the garden as a symbolic record of the history of the country's art, architecture, poetry, and philosophy. One of the earliest references to pleasure gardens was Ch'u Tz'u (*The Songs of the South*), from the third century B.C.E. In this collection of poems, the author describes the beauty and joy found amid natural surroundings. Other works of Chinese literature similarly express the affinity between nature and humans, endowing nature with profound symbolic meaning, as in the great pleasure the poet, Tang Yin expresses in viewing a garden scene:

Jade-fresh bamboos,
Rare-shaped stones,
Blue ancient pines,
Old gnarled branches—
Sighting all these,
Through a window,
On a fine-day,
What a joy!

Tang Yin 1470–1525
(Quoted by Johnston, 1991)

In the natural beauty of their surroundings, the Chinese found a model for garden designs. Planned to reflect untouched nature, gardens were a microcosm of the natural landscape within their walls, in contrast to the geometric Islamic layouts discussed in Chapter 9 and later in this chapter. Chinese gardens also reflect the inspiration of Confucianism, Taoism, and Buddhism—all philosophies that upheld reverence for and unity with nature. A garden tradition evolved that combined spiritual qualities with the aesthetic sensibilities of the artist and the poet.

Confucius (551–479 B.C.E.), whose philosophical teachings were dominant factors in establishing a sociopolitical system for much of China's history, believed that the cosmos and humans are united. He taught that when harmony exists between the social and natural domains, a sense of well-being results. The teachings of Confucius linked the garden with the tradition of the literati, or well-educated persons, whose gardens, known as scholar gardens, often had adjacent study rooms or libraries. The scholar-patron designed the garden layout and engaged carpenters, horticulturists, and others who were skilled in the arts to carry out his scheme. Designed as an intimate retreat, enclosed and isolated by high walls, the garden was a peaceful, even rustic, place for relaxation, intellectual discourse, or solitude and contemplation.

Whereas Confucianism is concerned with social systems existing harmoniously with nature, the Taoists (exemplified by Lao-tzu, sixth century B.C.E.) believe in the total unity of the universe. Humans respond to the passive and active forces preserved in contrasts in nature (yin and yang), not opposing principles of natural elements, balanced but always in a continuous state of change. Thus, garden space should be irregular, with meandering paths and curved sections imitating an uncontrolled landscape. Just as in the natural landscape, what is ahead is unknown; in a Chinese garden, one is surprised at every turn by the arrangement of the setting. Taoists place less emphasis on intellectual pursuits, believing that "intuitive knowledge" is the best approach.

The third important influence was Buddhism, imported from India about the first century C.E. Buddha's teachings stressed the union between the natural and spiritual worlds; his reverence for sacred mountains, as well as the image of a paradise garden for immortal souls in a Pure Land, fit well into the Chinese philosophical framework.

The Chinese created many types of gardens, from small private retreats, covering an acre or less, to expansive imperial hunting parks. The Han dynasty (third century B.C.E.) marked the beginning of unified China, and its royal pleasure parks became symbols of imperial power, some covering as much as 300 square miles (460 square kilometers). Ancient poems tell of aristocratic hunting parties in luxurious preserves with rare animals and birds, trees, and plants. In the first century C.E., within a vast park in Chang'an (see Chapter 9) were more than thirty palaces and other buildings set amid lakes and gardens, stocked with many imported birds and animals. Private gardens of great pretension grew out of this early hunting-park tradition.

It has been said that Chinese gardens are planned with a "painter's eye" (see Fig. 13.1). Beginning in the fourth century, landscape painting became a major art form in conjunction with the development of garden art. Just as painting was monochromatic, the gardens were composed mainly of green plants, rather than varicolored flowers and shrubs. Geomancy guided the choice of site, ensuring favorable cosmic signs, water and wind direction, suitable terrain, and other factors that might affect the success of the undertaking. The division of space was not symmetrical. Walls could curve or have openings through which a partial view of a garden scene would surprise the stroller. Plantings were chosen for symbolic content as well as beauty. A lotus flower, for example, could evoke thoughts of Buddhism because Buddhists view the world as a giant lotus blossom, the petals representing the four corners of the cosmos. A group of rocks might suggest the mountains where deities lived. Water was an important feature. Buddhists regarded lakes as celestial sanctuaries, so most gardens had a pond or stream, often bridged, to replicate heaven. There were no lawns because gardeners and patrons agreed that lawns tended to define space and decrease a garden's perceived size. Pavement or some other non-plant ground cover was used instead. A garden might in-

Figure 13.1. *The Zhouzheng Yuan (Humble Administrator's Garden), Suzhou, China. The largest garden in Suzhou, is seen from the lower floor of a two-story hall. Typical of the scholar gardens of the city, this one combines green plantings, water, winding paths, and a stone pavilion. The interaction between architecture and landscape is enhanced by the play of light and the effect of changing seasons on buildings and their natural surroundings.*

clude, however, small structures, such as pavilions or covered terraces, integrated with the house.

Suzhou, located in the Yangtse delta about 50 miles (85 kilometers) west of Shanghai, is known as China's city of gardens. Suzhou has long been admired for its beauty because of the many scenic gardens and temples that are carefully arranged along its canals and waterways. It has often been referred to as the Venice of China. One immediate impression of the Suzhou gardens is their denseness. In a limited space, not defined by rigid symmetry, may be found many textures of greenery, small mounds of rocks evoking distant mountains, bridges, and abstract sculpture.

The Suzhou garden is an attempt to unite the Buddhist vision of paradise with the Taoist belief in the union of nature and the cosmos. First established in the Sui dynasty (581–618 C.E.), Suzhou's gardens were the product of a highly literate community that included many artists and scholars. One scholar, Chi Cheng, wrote a garden manual called the *Yuan Ye* during the reign of the Ming emperors (1368–1644). In the eighteenth century, another scholar, Shen Fu, claimed that in planning the Chinese garden and its architectural components, "the aim is to see the small in the large, to see the large in the small, to see the real in the illusory and to see the illusory in the real," quoted by C. Jencks.

The Zhuozheng Yuan (Humble Administrator's Garden) is one of the most beautiful gardens in Suzhou (Fig. 13.1). Its history is well documented, dating from the early Tang (Thang) dynasty (618–906). Historian S. Johnston relates that in 1533, a book was written extolling the beauty of the Zhuozheng Yuan; during the years between 1872 and 1911, members of the Manchu dynasty used Zhuozheng Yuan as a meeting place. The wall-enclosed garden has an irregularly shaped rectangular lake divided into sections, with individual islands each with its own pavilion and private part of the pond. Some of the pavilions are shaped like boats to correspond thematically with the setting. Bridges link the islands with the main part of the garden. As the visitors wind their way along zig-zag paths through dense foliage, the concealed view suddenly opens to reveal miniature temples or rocky shores suggesting cliffs. Characteristic of many Chinese gardens, the walkways change levels so that the eye level is also constantly changing. Patterns of natural elements, like ribbed bamboo, are echoed in the gently curving eaves of the adjacent buildings, which are situated close to the water's edge. Reflections in the pond of the buildings and greenery subtly tie together the built and natural environment. Many of the pavilions have thought-provoking names, such as the Leaning-on-the-Rainbow Pavilion, Embroidered-Silk Pavilion, and the Distant-Fragrance Hall.

The Shi-zi-lin Yuan (or Lion Grove) garden in Suzhou is another garden greatly admired for its natural beauty. Like many other gardens in the city, the Lion Grove garden was designed to represent symbolically one part of the universe. Its name derives from the arrangement of two large rocks at the entrance to the garden that look like lions. The beauty of the Lion Grove garden was captured in a fourteenth-century scroll painting by a master of idyllic scenes. In this painting, the eye is led into the garden through a gate flanked by bamboo, past a group of trees where the focus is on several halls and pavilions; beyond, one sees a rockery above which is a small pavilion surrounded by trees. The restrained simplicity of the architecture contrasts with the visual delight of the natural elements. Pond, rockery, distant trees, and plantings are the traditional components of the scholar's garden. Various families have owned the Lion Grove garden. The most recent was the Pei family, of which the internationally known architect I. M. Pei is a

member. The Pei family donated the garden to the Chinese people.

Of the twenty or so gardens that survive in Suzhou, one of the oldest is the Wang Shih Yuan (Garden of the Master of the Fishing Nets), dating from 1140. It is one of the city's smaller gardens, covering just an acre. M. Keswick, who lived and worked in China for many years, describes a visit to the Wang Shih Yuan complex. A summary of her experience tells us that from a busy street one turns into a passageway and through a gate. The first of three courtyards is at a right angle to this entrance; the interior of the double-story house is not visible from the exterior, giving the occupants privacy. Courtyards wind out of sight around corners. Some are cul-de-sacs. Space is broken into a maze of shapes articulated with rocks, shrubs, bamboo, flowers in pots, roofed areas, buildings, high and low walls—visual delight greets the visitor at each turn. The ground is cobbled with stones of gray and dusty pink or other paved surfaces.

The transition from garden to house is subtle. Two steps lead up to a library, which has a stone floor that relates to the paving outside. One of the culminating experiences is the slightly elevated view of the garden through the library door, over to a pond with an inviting pavilion. Keswick notes that after a tour, the visitor cannot recall a specific garden plan because there are so many parts left to explore. The integration of all components tends to blur the perception of pattern.

The Chinese thought about their gardens from many viewpoints: philosophical, aesthetic, and spiritual. S. Johnston, author of the standard work on the subject, aptly characterizes the Chinese garden as "the very poetry of architecture." Chinese garden design had a great impact on the evolution of Japanese gardens (see Chapter 9, Katsura Palace). Although the garden concept had a long history in Chinese culture, its importance has not diminished over time. New gardens are continually being created following ancient philosophies that perceive human beings living in harmony with nature.

SOURCES: ADAMS (1991), BROOKES (1987), GRABAR (1978B), JELLICOE AND JELLICOE (1986), JOHNSTON (1991), KESWICK (1978), LEHRMAN (1980), MORRIS (1983), WANG (1998).

Islamic Gardens

The Islamic garden was based on early Greco-Roman and Persian prototypes. The Greco-Roman hortus, which is described in such ancient treatises as the *De materia medica* of Dioscorides (ca. 40–90 C.E.) refers to the Latin word hortus—the cultivation of bushes, ornamental trees, flowers, fruits, and vegetables. The Persian prototype was the formal garden with pools within a walled enclosure, like the one Cyrus the Great built in the sixth century B.C.E. at Pasargadae. After Arab nomads, with little experience in the art of garden maintenance, conquered Persia in 642 C.E., they adopted Persian garden design and repeated it wherever Islamic culture flourished.

As the Islamic faith spread throughout the Mideast, North Africa, India, and Spain, so did the Islamic garden. The Qur'an frequently mentions gardens as symbols of a heavenly paradise, a reward for the faithful where cool shade, fruit, vegetation, and fountains were pleasurable images for inhabitants of intensely hot and arid regions. The paradise garden or *char-bagh* (also *chahr-bagh*) is dominated by a pool divided into four water channels, symbolizing the rivers of paradise providing water, wine, milk, and honey. Indeed, the word *paradise* is anglicized from the pre-Persian *pairidaeza* (enclosure or burial place); later the Greek paradeisos expanded the meaning to refer to a place of bliss, as well as to an ideal garden. The synonymous words for garden, *firdaws* and *rawda*, also mean "paradise" and "burial place." Islamic artists and poets extolled the beauty of the garden and its inherent reference to paradise. Poems about gardens, executed in stone inlay or ceramic calligraphy, adorn many public secular buildings. Art forms, including paintings, miniatures, carpets, pottery, and fabrics, depict stylized garden scenes.

Muslim concepts of garden design were partly based on Qur'anic scriptures, but the physical models were the royal pleasure gardens of the Middle East, which had existed since the second millennium B.C.E.. These extravagant gardens were designed to be enjoyed by the elite, often as expressions of power. The royal garden, usually geometrically ordered, illustrated the extent of the ruler's control over nature in the manipulation of the environment and especially in the management of large-scale water systems for irrigation for the gardens, fountains, and pools. Sometimes the palace garden served as a place for receiving guests. A porch (*tatar*) or colonnade provided a shaded area between house and garden, sometimes with an *iwan*. Historian J. Brookes explains that the tatar has a metaphysical meaning, as well as a functional one, being the "locus of the soul moving between garden and building, where garden is spirit and building body." Features of royal gardens were translated into more modest gardens for the average Muslim. The garden sanctuary represented a vision of

paradise to be enjoyed in the coolness of enclosed courtyards (see Chapter 11).

Traditional Muslim beliefs relate the intellect to the Divine Order of the universe; human beings and nature are related mathematically through shape and proportion. As a result, measurement, symmetry, and other mathematical processes govern the design of Islamic gardens, as J. Lehrman noted. Although the guiding principle in Islamic gardens is one of order, seen in axiality, uniform parterres, and straight watercourses, there is room for natural growth (see Fig. 13.2). Spatial components are linked through watercourses that flow through changes in levels of terrain, through colonnaded terraces, and through the visual continuity of surfaces decorated with trees, flowers, and organic forms.

Space and scale were crucial. Gardens were designed to complement buildings in color, structure, and scale and could be conceived of as a transitional space offering a harmonious and restful passage between the interior of the Muslim house and the external world—symbolically, a transition between earthly paradise and eternal paradise. The beauty of nature in the Islamic garden is intensified by the contrast with the harsh realities of the desert environment that surrounds it.

Every detail was carefully considered, and all components—height, color, odor, vegetation—orchestrated. Paths were usually elevated, giving one the impression of walking on a carpet of the surrounding flowers. Scattered rose petals also enhanced the beauty of the path. Instead of lawns, designers used pavements of stone, brick, or tile, often arranged in striking geometric patterns. The pavements were practical, too—lawns would had required too much water.

Water—whether moving or at rest in pools—was a key element in Muslim garden design. The Qur'an offered spiritual inspiration for the use of fountains and pools; its scriptures describe gardens as having "flowing rivers and gushing fountains." The chahr-bagh, or formal paradise garden, described earlier, characterized by waterworks, often had a pavilion, fountain, or tomb at the center. The tomb of Akbar, Mughal emperor of India (1556–1605) lies in the center of such a garden at Sikandra, and Shah Jahan's paradise palace, the Mughal Khas Mahal, lies within a courtyard of the Red Fort at Agra in north-central India (see Fig. 8.14) above a narrow incline over which water once cascaded. At the Shalimar gardens at Lahore, landscape architects G. and S. Jellicoe state that 144 fountains were built to delight Shah Jahan as he viewed them while strolling on terraces above.

Figure 13.2. *A miniatuare showing the Mughal ruler, Babur (c.1526 C.E.) inspecting the building of his garden, Bagh-i-Vafa in Kabul (Afghanistan) then the capital of the Mughal Empire (1504–26). The garden is being laid out in geometric form.*

The Alhambra, a Moorish citadel in Spain, is an excellent example of the Islamic gardening tradition. It was built in the thirteenth century by Mohammed I al Ghalib, founder of the Nasrid dynasty, on a hilltop overlooking Granada, a city already known for its gardens. Its buildings and arcaded courtyards with fountains and pools are evocative of the Qur'anic Gardens of Paradise—and through symbolism and ornamentation epitomize Islamic spiritual beliefs and artistic developments. In the Courtyard of the Lions, for instance, the focus is on the fountain at the center, a basin supported by twelve carved lions spouting water. O. Grabar, an authority on Muslim architecture and author of *The Alhambra*, suggests that the lions represent soldiers of a victorious holy war who are rewarded by their prince, and the inscription surrounding the basin supports this interpretation. Floral motifs and geometric patterns on walls, arches, domes, or almost anywhere a surface could be embellished reflect the natural elements of the garden, tying it to similar ornamental themes in the buildings.

Yet, what we see today is not what the original planners intended in terms of parterres and vegetation. F. de Montêquin, an authority on Islamic architecture, notes that the Courtyard of the Lions, for example, had become almost bare of plants by the eighteenth century. However, in the nineteenth century, the citadel was designated a national monument, and governmental appropriations for its upkeep were officially established. A concentrated effort has been under way since then to restore the palaces and gardens further, but they are still far from what they were during the reign of the Nasrid sultans who built the Alhambra.

As the Islamic world expanded to the east, rulers, such as Akbar (1542–1605) and his grandson Shah Jahan (1592–1666), continued the garden tradition by building extravagant parks for pleasure and to express their power (Fig. 13.2). The sixteenth and seventeenth centuries were the Golden Age of the Mughal garden, and those they created in the Kashmir valley of India, especially around Lake Dal, are famous. At Lake Dal, the ample supply of water made possible dramatic displays of cascading streams and water channels integrated with flowers, trees, and other plantings for the delight of the emperors and their guests.

The Mughals also built pavilions and gardens along travel routes—resting places where the business of the court could be carried out. These temporary quarters, where power could be lavished and conveniently displayed, were a "traveling show" for local residents. In addition, they served as places for the emperor to review

military units while seated in his pavilion within these impressive garden settings. According to W. Adams, an authority on garden design, the magnificent and costly manipulation of nature might easily suggest that the ruler possessed divine powers.

Chinese and Islamic gardens were more than just "settings for architecture," as they have been called. They greatly contribute to our understanding of the cultural orientations of those who planned them. Currently, the study of landscape architecture is receiving more scholarly attention as an important factor in the interdisciplinary approach to architectural research.

CALLIGRAPHY AS STRUCTURAL ORNAMENTATION: ISLAMIC ARCHITECTURE

The development of landscape architecture elevated utility to a high aesthetic plane. Similarly, Islamic artists turned the useful scripts that could record dynastic annals and tax collections into major elements of unified aesthetic designs by adorning mosques and other buildings with calligraphic inscriptions. The flexibility of letter formations contributed to the application on various surfaces. Calligraphy, or the drawing of script as a fine art, derives from the Greek words *graphein* (to write) and *kallas* (beautiful). Muslims considered calligraphy to be not only one of the highest art forms, but one of the most important and beautiful ways of transmitting information. Through its medium, admonitions from the Qur'an and other revered writings became patterns of refined decoration, and it had a strong influence on all facets of Islamic culture. Ornamental words transferred knowledge and religious values from one generation to another.

As structural ornamentation, calligraphy can be found everywhere in the world of Islam—on the exteriors and interiors of buildings, on walls, doors, windows, and niches of mosques, madrasas, and palaces (see Figs. 13.3 and 9.14). Ceramic tile, stone, painted plaster, and wood are all surfaces for inscriptions in which words intertwine with arabesques, floral motifs, and geometric patterns. Often these designs completely cover a surface, so that a building's structural and ornamental elements appear to be one entity. Because words or decorative patterns may flow from one architectural element to another, calligraphy has helped unify parts of buildings, linking internal and external facades.

In Arabic, calligraphy is called the "geometry of line," alluding to the careful precision and proportional execu-

Figure 13.3. *A stucco panel from the mihrab of Oljaytu, the Friday Mosque, Isfahan, Persia (1310). Qur'anic phrases and the names of the leaders (imans) of the politico-religious group called Shia are here interlaced in the vegetal forms of the ornately carved stucco mihrab—a combination that suggests a sectarian message. Here the words are both content and ornament.*

tion of the strokes. According to historian A. Özdural, the science of geometry, in fact, influenced calligraphers, who often conferred with mathematicians to strengthen their understanding of the geometric principles that they applied to their programs of ornamentation. An artisan had to be competent in geometry to design these intricate patterns, since the proportions of letters and curved strokes were dependent on mathematical proportions. Illustrated books on the subject were written specifically to aid the ar-

chitect-artisans. The eleventh-century poet-mathematician, Omar Khayyam wrote a treatise on the subject of interlocking figures. Often geometers worked directly with artisans to solve problems in the architectural application of geometric principles.

The practice of calligraphy, executed by Buddhist priests and scribes, originated in China during the second millennium B.C.E. The spread of Buddhism and commerce eventually brought the concept of script as an art form to the Middle East, where two main types of Islamic calligraphy evolved. Some scholars believe that an angular form of writing developed in Iraq during the eighth century C.E. It was called *Kufi*, possibly after the city of Kufah, where important calligraphers practiced their art (Fig. 13.4). The letter forms of Kufi are stylized, blocky, and elongated (see Fig. 13.5a). Letter proportions became regularized over time, but by the eleventh century, a more elegant and refined style, with letters curving gracefully into one another, had appeared in Baghdad (see Fig. 13.5b). This form, called *Nashki*, became more popular and was widely used. There were many regional variations of both styles. Historian W. M. Thackston notes that "over time [the Kufi style] . . . became more and more ornamental . . . and simultaneously less and less readable—with the incorporation of foliation, floriation and knotting into the letters." The lack of legibility did not matter; people knew most of the Qur'anic passages by heart.

Some of the religious messages on buildings were borrowed from Persian mystic sources, while the Qur'an and other writings of Mohammed and his followers were used especially on mosques. Calligraphic ornament also encompassed themes of love, beauty, gardens, politics, and architecture. The use of poetic inscriptions as ornamentation in Islamic architecture stems from an enduring love for the "lyrical language of poetry." Historians I. Al Faruqi and L. Al Faruqi note that as early as the sixth century C.E., Arab nomads recited accounts of their lives and their surroundings in verse and even instructed foreigners in the Arabic language through poetry. By the eighth century, poets were using verse to focus on love and political themes: holy wars, urban concerns, and praise for the ruling elite. Verse was among the most esteemed forms of expression; poets received honors from princely patrons, often becoming wealthy and influential in their own right. Poetry had the highest priority among aesthetic tastes. People wrote and recited thousands of verses, and the enjoyment of poetry belonged to all levels of society.

Skilled calligraphers were highly valued by patrons and architects. Rulers sought their services, especially because printing was not available in the Islamic world until the eighteenth century. Calligraphic inscriptions had widespread application. Calligraphers were responsible for the patterns that sculptors and stonemasons transferred to the exteriors and interiors of buildings and to many other surfaces The role of calligrapher was not limited by gender or class—many women and even children produced calligraphic works that earned them widespread reputa-

Figure 13.4. *Portrait of Mir Abd Allah, a calligrapher (1602). This type of perspective and the illllustrations of plants were conventions of Indian art at that time.*

tions. Slave girls with calligraphic skills could hold positions as scribes.

From its earliest use as inscriptions extolling Allah's uniqueness, inscribed on the interior of the seventh-century Dome of the Rock in Jerusalem, calligraphy as a means of conveying information has endured throughout the Islamic world. The Dome of the Rock is an important identifying form for Muslims because it was the site where Mohammed embarked on his night journey to heaven. But Jerusalem is not a holy city only for Muslims; it is also revered by Jews and Christians as a city of profound biblical importance (see Fig. 16.4).

The Alhambra is another excellent example of Muslim architecture with calligraphic decoration. The intricate calligraphy in most of the interior rooms of these buildings exemplifies the purpose of poetry as part of the didactic decorative program. The floral and arabesque patterns that cover niches, walls, and doorways incorporate

Figure 13.5. *Pages from the Qur'an.* **a.** *A page from a ninth-century Qur'an in Kufic script, with characteristic short strokes and straight-lined execution.* **b.** *A page from a sixteenth-century Qur'an, in the elegant Bihahi form of calligraphy in which the script flows in an ornamental pattern.*

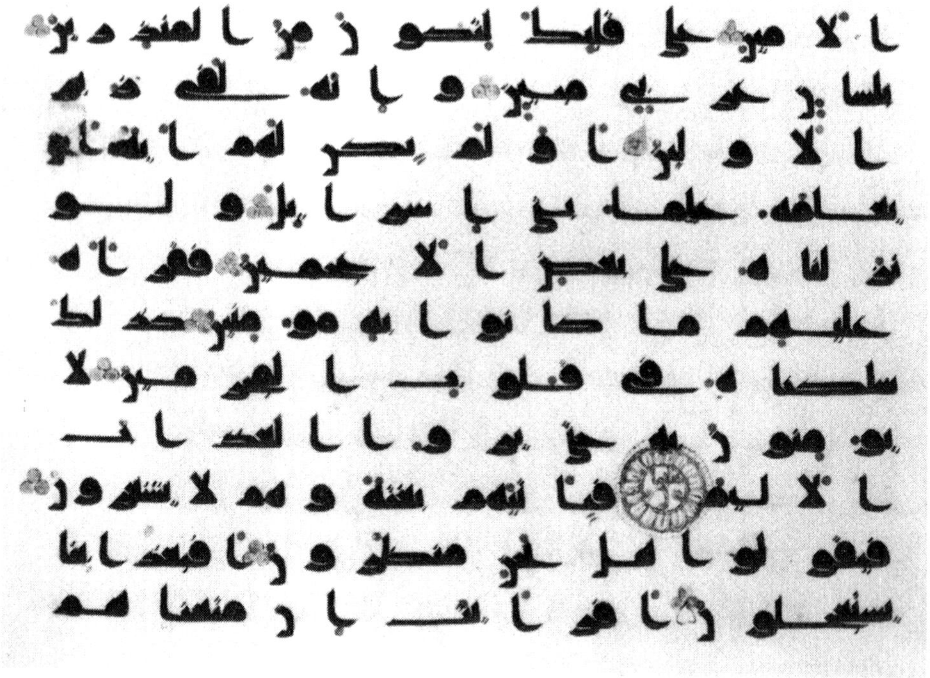

dozens of poetic verses, some of which are at eye level for those seated on the floor in Islamic fashion.

Words are repeated, paralleling the repetition of architectural forms that is inherent in Islamic building design. The beauty of the buildings and adulation for the rulers are expressed in metaphors. The great poet Ibn Zamrak (1333–ca. 1393) composed many of the poems found throughout the palaces, inscribing, as historian S. Meisler notes, in one of the chambers "I am the garden, I awake adorned in beauty. . . . The patient man who looks here realizes his spiritual desires."

Verses above some of the windows in the Hall of the Ambassadors of this palace create the effect that architectural elements themselves are speaking: "My master Yusuf has decked me . . . in garments of pride and flawless artistry." An inscription in another chamber reads, "She is the high-domed hall and we are her daughters" quoted by S. Meisler. Still other verses compare architectural elements to celestial bodies. For example, in the Hall of the Two Sisters and its adjacent court, verses adorning the walls suggest that the stars would rather be there than in the sky.

Not all the Alhambra's inscriptions are poetry. Many are quotations from the Qur'an or provide information on construction, prayers, and other didactic messages. Together with the poetic inscriptions, these inscriptions eloquently evoke the cultural environment of fourteenth-century Muslim Spain. Grabar suggests that the messages were intended to ensure that the Alhambra's meaning would be preserved during the declining years of Muslim rule. In 1492, the last Islamic sultan surrendered the citadel to Christian forces. Some of the buildings have been preserved, but only about one-fifteenth of the original structures inside it remain. The ravages of war, pilfering, and earthquakes have taken their toll. Still, thousands of visitors have come to Granada to admire the beauty of the remaining palaces and their decorative programs.

Elsewhere, Muslim builders considered certain inscriptions appropriate for particular locations. Islamicist Thackston describes an entrance gate to the mosque complex built by emperor Akbar in 1575 in his new north Indian city of Fatehpur Sikri as being ornamented with carved Qur'anic phrases, that solemnize gateways, as Thackston observes, such as "And the gates thereof shall be ready set open." Often the mihrab, or niche in a mosque wall facing Mecca, has inscribed directions for performing the prayer ritual, as in the twelfth-century Congregational Mosque in Bistram, Iran.

O. Jones, a nineteenth-century writer, said in the *Grammar of Ornament,* that one of the first principles of architecture was to "decorate construction, never to construct decoration . . . every ornament arises naturally from the surface decorated."[32] In the Islamic world, architectural surfaces decorated with beautiful calligraphic inscriptions that are woven into arabesque and vegetal designs not only have a didactic purpose, but illustrate how well the integration of ornament and architecture serves to reinforce cultural identification.

Other Forms of Structural Ornamentation

Calligraphy was not the only way in which Islamic architecture was enriched with decorative motifs. Because of its prominence, the iwan became the locus of elaborate ornamentation that enhanced its architectural importance in the collegiate mosque, madrasa, and other types of buildings (see Chapter 10). Marble, ceramic tiles, brick, stone, and even gems adorn the vaults and sides of many iwans. Although decoration applied to architecture may seem mere embellishment from a Western viewpoint, such is not the case with Islamic ornamentation. A designer who applies Muslim calligraphy, vegetal reliefs, or geometric patterns to architecture desires, above all, to create visual patterns that will convey symbolic meanings to the viewer. Muslims believe there is no division between the spiritual and the secular; Islamic theology affects all aspects of life. The continuous patterns produced by intertwining vegetal, geometric, or calligraphic motifs are intended to "lead the viewer to an intuition of divine transcendence," as one writer observes (see Figs. 13.3 and 9.14). A similar principle applies to other elements of ornamentation.

The methods and materials used to decorate architectural forms, such as iwans, are subject to denaturalization, a technique in which the appearance of a form is changed but not the materials of construction. Al Faruqi and Al Faruqi call this process "transfiguration," explaining that although surface decoration alters a structure's

---

[32]In his discussion of the Alhambra in *The Grammar of Ornament,* Owen Jones (1842–45) asserts "The Moors ever regarded what we hold to be the first principle in architecture—to decorate construction, never to construct decoration: in Moorish architecture not only does the decoration arise naturally from the construction, but the constructive idea is carried out in every detail of the ornamentation of the surface."

exterior appearance, basic structural materials, such as wood or stone, retain their inherent qualities of support. Decoration simply reduces the importance of structural elements by drawing attention away from natural materials to the abstract denaturalized ornamentation of buildings. The viewer is led to reflect on a divine, rather than a secular, world. The presence of calligraphy and other decorative elements reflecting cultural beliefs enhances this experience.

In the entrance to the Great Mosque at Isfahan, a *muqarnas*, or stalactite-motif, decoration of the vault consists of a masonry core from which an ornamental brick shell is suspended (see Fig. 10.4a and b). The muqarnas, a grouping of three-dimensional units resembling a honeycomb, attracts attention to its decorative materials, often of stucco. The three dimensionality of the murqarnas serves to de-emphasize the difference between decoration and load-bearing elements. Other examples of abstraction use intricate carving to make stone facades look like lace, contradicting the basic strength of the material. Regardless of material, technique, or regional variation, the surfaces of Islamic buildings have ornamental layers of design that uniquely identify their architecture.

SOURCES: W. ADAMS (1991), AL FARUQI AND AL FARUQI (1986), GRABAR (1978A, 1978B), A. GUAR (1994), HOAG (1987), JELLICOE AND JELLICOE (1986), LEHRMAN (1980), MEISLER (1991), OZDURAL (1995), THACKSTON (1994).

PAINTED WALLS: THE NDEBELE OF SOUTH AFRICA

The Ndebele people of South Africa's Transvaal highlands have developed a tradition of architectural decoration in which women ornament their houses, mural style, with brilliant colors. These painted walls do not merely serve aesthetic purposes. They express both personal accomplishment and community resistance to the domination of the Boers, the Dutch colonists who controlled the land for more than a hundred years after 1872. The painters, trained informally by other women, rather than in art schools, use abstraction as their medium of resistance and self-expression. During apartheid, the government strove to control opinion, imposing secrecy as a way of life. Artists sometimes responded with "innocent" actions, such as combining the black, green, and yellow of the African National Congress—the political arm of black resistance to apartheid—in clothing and on house walls, leaving governmental officials wondering how to arrest a house. Resistance was secret but transparent.

Among the Ndebele people, it is the responsibility of the women to repair, maintain, and decorate the houses, according to M. Courtney-Clarke, one of the first to photograph and write about the Ndebele. When the women adorn their houses and use similar motifs to adorn their persons, they say this is "good work." The Ndebele language has no general words for art or beauty, but it has many terms to describe specific aesthetic aspects. "Good" work maintains not only the house, but the woman's standards of quality. The woman decides how to invest her time and energy, how to enhance the home or decorate the body. Each woman who completes a beadwork or painting project has distinguished herself from the others in her area—but at the same time has identified with them—and she has fulfilled certain magico-religious activities her culture expects of her.

The people of the KwaNdebele region numbered nearly half a million at the end of the twentieth century. Ethnically, the Ndebele belong to the Nguni people, as do the Zulu, Xhosa, and Swazi; their language is close to Zulu. When the Boers conquered these peoples in 1872, the Ndebele became indentured servants on what had been their land. After 1955 the apartheid government of South Africa moved the Ndebele and Zulu into "homelands," but the reversal of the homelands policy in the 1990s freed them from those constraints.

Despite these disruptions, the Ndebele have retained their customs and language. The gender distinction that kept most women at home and out of the labor market probably contributed to this retention; ironically, segregation under apartheid may have done so as well. Although many Ndebele have converted to Christianity, local customs still include major ceremonies and rituals, such as first-fruits ceremonies, both traditional and Christian marriage rituals, dowry feasts, and traditional ideas like witchcraft and totemism.

Even more important artistically are the women's puberty-seclusion rites and the men's initiation rites every four years; these rites apply to everyone. Small groups of men aged eighteen to twenty-two gather for the initiation rites, which culminate—like the girls' rites—in circumcision. This male initiation ceremony, or *wela*, is the most important incentive for a woman decorator, who is impelled to commemorate it by painting the family house: "Before the young men leave for the initiation rites, the women carefully re-plaster the outside walls of their homes, and reconstruct the entranceways. They then paint . . . their impressions of everyday life, interspersed with geometric designs, on the wall surfaces," as Courtney-Clarke wrote.

For girls, the ceremonial focus is more domestic and personal, as Courtney-Clarke noted: "When girls reach puberty . . . they perfect the arts of beadwork and painting . . . under the supervision of their mothers. . . . Painting is not taught in [public or missionary] schools, so it is only through this mother-daughter tradition that the art survives." The women explain, "I learned it from my mother" and "It is the law of the Ndebele." Non-Ndebele commentators, such as G. van Wyk, suggest that Bantu mural art and the practices of the neighboring Sotho-Tswana influenced the Ndebele, who consciously promoted mural art to express pride in cultural identity and resistance to colonialism.

Both archaic and contemporary house forms and painting styles are known. The older tradition produced round houses of mud with thatched roofs, similar to the mud houses of the Hausa (see Chapter 2) Beginning in the early twentieth century, houses became rectangular and cement-block walls and corrugated iron roofs replaced mud and thatch, according to G. Elliott. Although the Ndebele cook in the back courtyard in good weather, in bad weather they cook indoors, in a hollowed-out part of the floor, with the inevitable production of smoke. Because houses have no chimneys, the smoke that used to fumigate thatched roofs is now just a nuisance in houses with corrugated metal roofs.

The women gather the materials and provide much of the labor, but the men do the heavy construction work. Before building such a traditional house, they perform a ceremony to bless the site. As construction begins, the men set the wooden poles of the frame into the earth. Then the women weave twigs and sticks between the poles to make walls. The men climb up to tie on the roof beams and then thatch the roof as the women pass up bunches of grass. The women plaster the walls with ubulongwe, a mixture of clay and cow dung that makes a smooth surface and repels insects. While the walls dry for several months, the people erect low walls surrounding the house, with solid benches along them. Inside the house, the women cover the earth floors with the same clay mixture in a fan pattern. After the floors dry the house is ready for painting.

The women usually work on mural decorations after the summer rains and the harvest. A family occasion, such as a wedding, is a good excuse to repaint the house. The painter's choice of patterns and colors, the execution of her design, and the finished effect "denote her unique and intimate relationship with the home, and her . . . response to being exploited socially and politically," according to Courtney-Clarke. Individuality is shown in her style of decoration, her building methods, and especially her colors. Still, women often copy new or refined ideas from one another, but with individual stylizing of the motifs. They decorate the back and sides of the house with plain color but may include black borders or an incised surface. A woman's passion for pattern appears on the front of her house, where she is likely to use colors that echo those of the beaded skirts and other clothing she makes. Painting is done freehand, without preliminary drawing or measuring. The artist's main tool is her inventive spirit.

Until the 1950s, women also painted the interiors of houses (see Fig. 13.6a); such work is rare now. Most painted interiors are simple and muted. The interior of one of the old round mud houses consisted of a round core room surrounded by a wide, round passageway. Both were painted, but the parents' core room was more elaborately developed ornamentally. Today the single interior room of a rectangular house may be used as a bedroom, kitchen, and storage area. People divide this room with a curtain and rearrange mats and furniture as needed for daily use. Small platforms across the roof beams provide storage; people also store objects by hanging them from the beams. The house always has an ikumba, the mother's private refuge, which even her husband must ask permission to enter, and few outsiders are allowed to do so. When a woman dies or abandons her family, her ikumba is left to disintegrate; it is not reused.

A household has a main round or rectangular house and several attached or freestanding outbuildings. These outbuildings include separate dwellings for sons and for daughters and a separate cooking hut or place. The cluster of buildings is set in a low wall with a gateway that may be flanked by a pair of uprights, sometimes bridged by a decorated lintel. A separate enclosure for animals is outside. The front yard is the reception area. Inside the boundary, low walls divide the space into courtyards. The backyard is for cooking and for keeping chickens.

For both old and new house forms, however, women have been responsible for painting the exterior and interior. They still use the traditional earth colors, made from clay and other earths. These paints are inexpensive but water soluble and must be renewed every year. Brown and yellow (ochre) clays are common, as are white and sometimes dark gray. Cow dung yields brown. A combination of soot and earth from the local riverbank produces black. For the best red, a clay called Rust de Winter, women walked as much as 100 miles (160 kilometers) to get enough for half a lifetime. Rolled into compact balls while

a.

b.

Figure 13.6. *A Ndebele house.* **a.** *The interior, painted by the woman who lives there. In traditional houses, this kind of round living room was at the center, where the parents slept. Young children slept in the hall between this room and its rectangular enclosure. The paint used to decorate this room was in colors made from natural clays.* **b.** *A Ndebele woman painting the exterior wall around her house wears a beaded garment in the same colors—her own handiwork. A son's initiation is frequently the occasion for a complete re-painting of the house, inside and out. The work is done free-hand and includes both geometric designs and motifs from modern life.*

wet, the clay dries to a solid pigment and lasts indefinitely. Bluing, available for laundering, was added as a new color early in the twentieth century. The women apply these colors with their hands and fingers or with brushes made of chicken feathers or chewed twigs.

Nowadays Ndebele women also use commercial colors when they are available. Such paints are more expensive but last several years; acrylic paint is the most common. The painters can mix acrylic with slaked lime or earth to obtain pastels. They use commercial brushes with these paints. Although the traditional colors were brown, ochre, red, and black, red, green, yellow, purple, and blue have been popular since the 1960s.

Designs are bold, linear, and abstract, with a composition logic unique to the Ndebele (see Fig. 13.6b). As Courtney-Clarke notes, apparently abstract elements—diagonal, horizontal, and vertical lines—may be read as representational motifs, reiterating the structural features that support walls and roof and integrating them with other geometric designs.

Patterns are concentrated on the front of the house, the centerpiece of the composition. The tradition continues of scratching geometric designs with the fingers while the clay is still soft, creating a three-dimensional surface. Such designs may be executed in subtle earth colors accented by black and white. Those who use the modern paints often produce more complex designs and geometric patterns. Both the traditional abstract and modern motifs appear in certain highly stylized forms, such as images of flowers and trees that are conventionalized and simplified. Today painters also incorporate Western images, such as razor blades, airplanes (called *ufly*), light-bulbs, and the architecture of the white towns with their two-story houses, swimming pools, and the like. Critic Van Wyk sees the airplane motif as "Western speed sabotaged and frozen in the painter's gaze," and "the travel of machines and energy . . . as a metaphor of the spirit that animates them. . . . The painter physically materializes what she's thinking." Although Courtney-Clarke claims, "Many of these newer images are known to the women only by hearsay," Van Wyk perceives cultural sophistication: "In Ndebele murals, the Western viewer is even more strongly conscious that the women painters are both articulating their own culture and closely observing the world of the West."

For more than a century, the Ndebele lived in individual homesteads on their employers' farms. Modern Ndebele houses built in governmental "camps" from government-provided materials, such as corrugated metal and cement blocks, are formally and thermally different from the traditional houses. Yet the continuity of decorative motifs and colors has ensured the continuity of cultural and individual identity. Even more pervasive than the house murals is the Ndebele woman's passion for making beadwork clothing, which has a stunning unity with the decorations on her house. Beadwork occupies most of the free time of Ndebele women and girls, since beaded clothing has a high value in their culture.

The mural art of the Ndebele has several messages for non-Ndebele. It derives strength not only from tradition, but from nonverbal statements about local political and cultural situations. This mural art alerts us to "separate [adjective] worlds of knowledge, belief, and experience [which] exist and must be thought together." African, Asian, American, Oceanic, and European philosophical systems offer different explanations of the universe. In modern-Western science, ideas about the rational and material must increasingly incorporate indecidability, unpredictability, and the measurement of purely conjectural distances. Unaccustomed ways of thinking—and innovative media, such as painted walls and beaded clothes—may give us new insights, even new solutions. In an ambiguous world, we need all the insights we can gather.

Ndebele painters subtly comment on the constraints of life. The linear designs incised into their houses not only limn zones of decoration, but connect the female body with its labors, the house with the field, the natural with the supernatural—a universe of epistemology and politics through inscribed lines. When a woman uses her fingers to make parallel grooves into earth surfaces of the outer walls, the walls become a linguistic and visual echo of the fields, a landscape painting. Compare this patterns with the painted reliefs decorations of Hausa dwellings (see Fig. 13.7).

As we have shown, architectural symbolism and ornamentation can take different forms in different cultures. Sometimes the symbolism is overt, as when a door jamb "speaks" about its function. Sometimes it is subtle, as in a Chinese garden. And sometimes, as among the Ndebele, it is vested with double meaning. Consider the Ndebele approach to architectural ornamentation in contrast to the attitudes of the Batammaliba described in Chapter 15 and the Islamic examples discussed earlier in this chapter. Each pattern of ornamentation carries cultural meaning that enriches the aesthetic form.

Sources: Courtney-Clarke (1986), Elliott (1989), Van Wyk (1993).

Figure 13.7. *A decorated Hausa dwelling, Kano, Nigeria, about 1960. The house walls and the geometric decoration are of mud. Note the paucity of openings in the wall to preserve privacy in the urban setting and to interfere as little as possible with the strenngth of the walls.*

SUGGESTED READINGS

Al Faruqi, I., and L. Al Faruqi. 1986. *The Cultural Atlas of Islam.* New York: Macmillan. Comprehensive; an excellent source of information on Islamic decoration.

Begley, W. E. 1985. *Monumental Islamic Calligraphy from India.* Villa Park, Ill.: Islamic Foundation. A major contribution to studies of Islamic calligraphy.

Brookes, J. 1987. *Gardens of Paradise: The History and Design of the Great Islamic Gardens.* London: Weidenfeld & Nicolson. A detailed history of the development of Islamic gardens.

Courtney-Clarke, M. 1986. *Ndebele: The Art of an African Tribe.* New York: Rizzoli. A book of stunning photographs and insightful comments.

Gaur, A. 1994. *A History of Calligraphy.* New York: Cross River Press.

Johnston, S. 1991. *Scholar Gardens of China.* New York: Cambridge University Press. Small but indispensable for an analysis of the scholar garden.

Lehrman, J. 1980. *Earthly Paradise: Garden and Courtyard in Islam.* Berkeley: University of California Press. A thorough survey and good reference work.

Ozdural, A. 1995. "Omar Khayam, Mathematicians, and Conversazioni with Artisans." *Journal of the Society of Architectural Historians* 54 (March): 54–71.

Thackston, W. M. 1994. "The Role of Calligraphy." In *The Mosque: History, Architectural Development and Regional Diversity*, 43–54, edited by M. Frishman and H.U. Khan. London: Thames & Hudson. The essay on calligraphy is one of the many fine contributions in this excellent book on Islamic architecture.

Van Wyk, G. 1993. "Secret Resistance in the Murals of Sotho-Tswana Women." In *Secrecy: African Art that Conceals and Reveals*, edited by M. H. Nooter. New York: Museum for African Art. This essay includes several pages on the similar mural art of the Ndebele women.

14

Architecture and Social Relations

C lothes, food, behavior, and personal belongings can be seen as expressions of social status and structure. It is not surprising that the built environment also carries that meaning. Architecture is intrinsically a social art. A building is erected by a group of people. It stands among their other buildings and houses—a subsection of the group for work, recreation, ceremony, or residence. We interact with our buildings individually and collectively. As Winston Churchill said, "We make our houses and then our houses make us." Two versions of that interaction occupy us here: the manifestation and protection of privacy in Chinese and Islamic cities, contrasted with the overt expression of status in Keresan pueblos, Native American tipis, and royal Mayan structures.

BLANK WALLS FOR PRIVACY: ISLAMIC AND CHINESE NEIGHBORHOODS

In some societies that place a high value on privacy, houses turn blank walls to the street. Traditional Sicilian culture, for example, is based on apartment living in multifamily dwellings, two or three stories high, in small towns. Building exteriors look older than their age because people spend little to decorate or maintain them. Houses sit at the edge of the street or may be pulled back just the width of a narrow sidewalk. Inside, however, are marble floors, elegant furniture, and frequently a private terrace. These accoutrements display the family's taste and economic status—but only to those entitled to be received within. This pattern persists even in areas where there is plenty of room for single-family houses. The tradition may derive from Sicily's centuries under Arab rule, which introduced the Muslim preoccupation with privacy[33] to an Italian predilection for apartment living that is at least two thousand years old.

Traditional Mediterranean (see Fig. 14.1) and Chinese (see Fig. 14.2) cultures cultivate reticence to the point of anonymity in the facade turned toward the public. Nothing on the exterior of a house indicates the character or composition of the family inside.

---

[33]See E. Guidoni, *Vicolo e Cortile: Tradizione Islamica E Urbanistica Populare in Sicilia* (Venice: E. Giada, 1982).

Figure 14.1. *Blank exterior walls in an Islamic Village, North Africa. The exterior walls of houses are severely plain, analogous to the plain black wrappers of the women at the right; both envelopes ensure privacy to those within. The covered streets protect pedestrians from the heat and glare of the sun.*

Among one group, the Muslims of North Africa, privacy of the family and seclusion of the women within the family courts have been mandatory (see Chapter 11)—an environment of inwardness, as de Montêquin writes. Both the individual house in the Muslim world and the residential quarter in which it is embedded maintain a balance between isolation and self-sufficiency. The govern-

ment considers a neighborhood or ward to be an administrative unit of the larger city, with its own headman, council, and possibly a defense force. People living in a ward tend to be united in the religion, ethnicity, and occupation; they often form an extended family or clan. Each ward is enclosed by a wall with a single gate, kept locked at night, just as the gate of the whole city was tradition-

Figure 14.2. *A blank exterior wall, Suzhou, China, with a small entrance to Ou Yuan (twin garden). The austere appearance of the wall preserves privacy and gives little evidence of the beautiful gardens within the enclosure.*

ally locked at night. This pattern has eased recently. Now houses are likely to be linked physically with those in nearby administrative units. Climate has shaped neighborhoods, too—the streets are narrow and winding so that the houses shade pedestrians from the scorching sun. Streets are local access routes, rather than thoroughfares.

The blank walls of Islamic and Chinese neighborhoods display similar cultural values despite geographic and religious differences. In even as open a Chinese city as Suzhou, the spacious gardens (see Chapter 13) are enclosed within private walls. Passersby see only blank white walls and an occasional door. Only along the canals, where no pedestrian can intrude, do the garden walls include occasional openwork screens, allowing glimpses of the greenery within. In the old district of Beijing, near the palaces of the Forbidden City, an intensely monotonous series of gray brick walls and gray terracotta roof tiles safely conceals both personal and family individuality. Most houses are one story, but where they rise to two stories, the outer wall also rises to preserve interior privacy from the eyes of neighbors (see Chapter 11, Courtyards).

The Chinese motivation for privacy is more social than religious, derived from Confucian prescripts for the orderly conduct of life. People protect the family life inside their houses not only from view, but also from evil spirits, who are believed to move only in straight lines. Screens inside entryways force people to enter at an angle and keep the spirits out. This arrangement may also help defend the house from marauders and thieves—someone who passes while the door to the street is open will see only the wall inside that blocks the view of the first courtyard. In the home of a wealthy family, this screen wall could be 22 feet (7 meters) tall and even wider, covered on the outer side with richly decorated tiles; in a more modest house, it would be smaller and plainer.

Another aspect of privacy in these societies, another advantage of blank exterior walls, is that wealth and status are not publicly displayed. Among Muslims, the Qur'an stresses the equality of all believers, and proper modesty means not exhibiting differences. In many societies, exhibiting one's assets to the envy of the poor or the malice of the tax collector could be unwise. Families who endure for centuries have learned to risk as little as possible to the whims of others.

Although some elaborately developed societies with many ranks of status manifest social differences in their architecture, an equal number of such societies enforce architectural modesty in the interests of social unity. Religious and philosophical constraints, as well as the practical desire to exclude enemies, noise, and dirt, account for the blank exterior walls that ensure privacy in Chinese and Islamic cities.

Source: de Montequin (1983).

Overt Expressions of Status

In contrast to the hidden quality of domestic life in Chinese and Islamic cities, other cultures state their social relations in visible architectural forms. These forms include the modest mesa-top houses of the Keresan people of Acoma, the vividly painted tipis of the people of the Great Plains, and the costly tombs and homes of the rulers of Tikal.

Acoma Pueblo: United States

The Acoma pueblo in New Mexico is a settlement of flat-roofed Native American dwellings. Its outward appearance reflects the interior organization of the village, an organization that fosters both equality and survival. Pueblo peoples commonly live in extended families with the grandmother, her married daughters, and the daughters' families in attached or adjacent units. When they build a new house or refurbish an old one, it is usually for a daughter who is getting married. The family, which functions as an economic unit, has common use of adjoining rooms and terraces, convenient for cooperative labor on many tasks. The maternal lineage controls the land and its resources, while the men's ceremonial and political life balances women's domestic life and ownership of houses and fields. Only the men participate in religious and political kiva activities. (See Chapter 7 for the religious life of the pueblo people; gender isolation is discussed in Chapters 4, 6, and 15.)

Fixed settlements, but not necessarily villages, appeared in the deserts of the American Southwest about four thousand years ago. Development would have been impossible without the available physical resources—a fine balance between grown and gathered foods, water sources, and special agricultural techniques for desert soil—and social resources, such as kinship groups. Establishing settlements in this area was a great achievement after centuries of trial and error and much thought. The survivors created the pueblo dwellings, whose strong architectural image reflects the sturdiness of their culture, different from that of their Navajo neighbors, latecomers to the area who relied on dispersion and movement for survival.

Acoma and Oraibi pueblos are the oldest continuously occupied communities in the United States, having been settled for more than a thousand years. Acoma, the westernmost Keresan pueblo (see Fig. 7.13), sits on a mesa south of the main road running west from Albuquerque to the Arizona border—but this is to give its coordinates in modern terms. There was an ancient trail in this area, along the river valley, later followed by the railroad and now the highway. On the eve of the Spanish conquest, Antonio de Espijo reported in his 1582 *Expedition*, as cited by Nabokov, that the population of Acoma pueblo was about six thousand. The residents lived by farming irrigated fields six miles (10 kilometers) away, along the Rio Parque. A secondary trail led from those fields to the mesa. Rising 367 feet (112 meters) above the plain, at an altitude of 7,000 feet (2,134 meters), Acoma was easily defended as long as the Keresans had food, water from their cisterns, and warriors (see Fig. 14.3).

By 1934, few families lived on the mesa year-round. The mesa had become a ceremonial center, occupied, in turn, by each matriarchal lineage. In earlier times, Acoma had two centers of population on the mesa top (see Fig. 14.3): the one that still survives and another south of the church around the Rock Cistern.

Acoma is the only complete pueblo that has been recorded in modern architectural drawings. A team from the Historic American Building Survey (HABS) made a de-

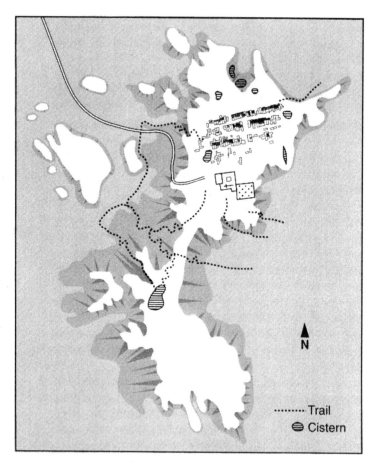

.... Trail

⊖ Cistern

Figure 14.3. *Plan of the Acoma pueblo, New Mexico. From south to north, South Mesa (inhabited before the Spanish conquest); a large cistern (horizontal stripes); trails (dashed lines); the seventeenth to nineteenth-century cemetery (dotted rectangle) and the church (marked with a cross); irregular governmental buildings from the Spanish Colonial period; three rows of houses (white indicating the ground story and black, the top story); more cisterns; and, at the left, the road to farms near the river.*

tailed study of the pueblo in the 1930s, and Nabokov published an edited version of their drawings, with comments, in 1981.

Of the pueblos west of the Rio Grande, Acoma and Oraibi consist of rows of town houses and parallel streets not centralized on a plaza or court. In this respect they are like the five Keresan villages along the Rio Grande—Zia (Sia), Santa Ana, Cochiti, Santo Domingo, and San Felipe. They have unbroken outer walls, an inward focus,

concentric boundaries, an orientation to the compass with buildings facing south, a centralized location of kivas, and standard organizational patterns within the housing units.

Three parallel main streets survive on the northern part of the Acoma mesa, running east–west along the uneven rock surface. House fronts and streets are uneven. The north row of buildings is the longest. Short alleys divide it into three sections and focus the view toward Mount Taylor to the north (see Fig. 7.16). The northern side of the buildings is plain adobe, with a few roof beams protruding at floor and roof levels.

The buildings step up in three levels to the north (see Fig. 14.4). The long north row brackets the inner rows of the site from wind and from inspection by enemies or strangers looking up from outside, but rarely shades the terraces where people work. As the units step down to the south, the terraces form a sort of "front yard," intermediate between inside and outside, under the control of the householders and useful for household work and seating for processions and other communal activities.

The house units face south, turning their high backs to the cold north winds, an important consideration at Acoma's altitude and in a climate where temperatures range from minus 20 to plus 100 degrees F (-29 to 38 C). R. L. Knowles studied this solar orientation and reports that the units are warmed by the winter sun on south-facing walls during the day; at night these walls radiate warmth into the sleeping rooms. It is probable that one group of Acoma ancestors lived at Mesa Verde—conspicuous for its solar orientation—and brought with them to Acoma knowledge of the older solar technology. The addition of a corner fireplace makes the sleeping areas comfortable all night.

All three rows of houses are unified by their use of materials and their form. They are flat-roofed, rectangular units. The 12–15-foot-high (4–5 meters) ground story was for storing food and could hold enough for several years. Traditionally, there were no windows. The only doors were trapdoors, entered from the terraces above by removable ladders. People added doors and windows in the Spanish period that began in the seventeenth century. The first windows were slabs of translucent selinite (crystallized gypsum). Today, windows on the north sides are much smaller than those on the south, a solution that is thermally correct.

Acoma exhibits a strong sense of order, with house walls parallel or perpendicular to the main axis of the settlement. Each house unit is separated from its neighbors

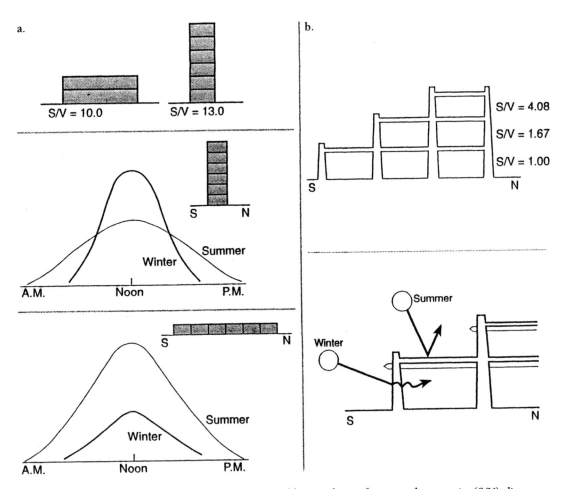

a. S/V = 10.0   S/V = 13.0

S   N   Summer   Winter   A.M.   Noon   P.M.

S   N   Summer   Winter   A.M.   Noon   P.M.

b. S/V = 4.08   S/V = 1.67   S/V = 1.00   S   N

Summer   Winter   S   N

Figure 14.4. *A thermal analysis of the Acoma pueblo.* **a.** *The surface-to-volume ratio (S/V) diagram. (top) S/V related to shape and position. (center) The difference in heat takeup in summer is greater than in winter. (bottom) The pattern of heat gain during summer and winter is similar, but the amount of heat gain in summer is much higher.* **b.** *The shape of the pueblo moderates between the two extreme shapes. More surface is exposed to the south than to the north, increasing heat gain in winter. The ground floor, where temperature is less variable, is used for food storage; the thick walls contribute to thermal as well as structural stability. The second floor, used for sleeping, has the advantages of being safer and more private and of having more openings for fresh air; its higher S/V means more variable temperatures. The highest S/V (and the most variable temperatures) is at the top story, which serves as space for cooking and eating, so that cooking fires add heat during inclement weather. Ventilation is good in summer. Low winter sun hits the masonry walls that store and transmit the heat efficiently, while high summer sun strikes horizontal roof terraces with lower heat transmission and storage capability. Heat stored in the walls during the days helps to warm the building in the cold desert nights, by radiation.*

321

by partition walls, sometimes in the form of steps leading upward. The adobe walls of the apartment blocks abut, rather than being bonded—a structurally weak solution, but one that facilitates the reuse of materials. The sense of order is reinforced by the interiors. Ceilings are about 7 feet (2 meters) high, with spans to 15 feet (4.5 meters). As Nabokov noted, in 1871 G. Gwyther described the house interiors as very clean, unornamented, and sparsely furnished with adobe benches for sitting and sleeping.

Only the church of San Esteban Rey is wider than the standard 15 feet; its 30-foot (10-meter) beams are said to have come from Mount Taylor. The church is also unique in that it is oriented east–west and has its living areas to the north, proving architecturally that it was an imposed, rather than an indigenous, structure. Possibly also dating from the Spanish period are the two freestanding buildings south of the southernmost block of surviving houses. They are much older than the houses, because the houses have been renewed periodically. One of these structures is the Komanina, or council house, which was a requirement of Spanish rule.

Protruding ladders reveal the presence of semisubterranean rooms buried in the house blocks (compare with Chapter 9, Mesa Verde). These are kivas for the men's religious and social meetings. Unlike the homes, which may now have ground-level doors as well as the traditional ladders, the kivas retain the ancient pattern of entrance from above, usually by a double-width ladder (see Figs. 7.15 and 14.5).

The work of building and rebuilding at Acoma is communal, as is the process of collecting house materials. An Acoma resident describes the building process that occurs after the dimensions of the row houses are paced out:

> When they came to the top of Acoma . . . (a row) was built on the north side running east, and in the middle running east, and on the south side running east. Everybody helped with each building. . . . The building materials were carried up from down below, things like fine sand being carried on the back to be used for plaster. This is how adobe bricks were made. Bark, sticks, and ashes were mixed together. Then they mixed the adobe with this and the bricks were made. When the bricks were dried, they built around (laying the foundation), and they kept on (going up) . . . they used to haul pine and oak from Pine Mountain for beams, and they used them for the crossbeams. . . . And the beams used to be beautifully carved. And then . . . willow and scraped cedar were used on top (of the main beams for crossbeams) . . . And for the middle part (that is, the second floor) they used mica for that which was going to be made on the sides (that is, windows). . . . And today it can still be seen in some places. And formerly, I believe, all the people up at the village helped, and it was built as a single unit. And each building, I believe, was distributed (divided up among families), and they were (each) entitled to be in it.

> *Garcia, recorded by W. Miller (1965)*

Today, the living architectural tradition of Acoma includes glass windows, doors with their frames, stovepipes, commercial paints, nails, and locks. Many people now have ovens on the first terrace or have adopted the Spanish corner fireplace with flues made of old pottery stacked up and mortared with mud. Yet construction tradition retains some early features. As noted in 1892 and quoted in Nabokov, "plastering . . . is done by women, who . . . lay the mud on with their hands." They regulate the consistency by spraying the work with water from their mouths. The floors and dados (the lower part of an interior wall, treated with a special finish) are of clay, but the interior upper walls are whitewashed with gypsum. This tradition was still active in 1934, when the HABS team noted that replastering took place in July and August and was completed before the September feast of their patron, San Esteban (St. Stephen).

At any given time, some Acoma buildings are being newly finished or refinished, some are disintegrating, some are being razed so that their materials can be recycled—but most are quietly enduring. The architectural environment has been remarkably stable during the past four hundred years in spite of changes of detail, furnishings, and equipment, and in spite of incentives to disperse.

That stability is likely due to the correlation between the Keresan worldview (still imperfectly known by outsiders) and their daily activities. (See Chapter 7 on Mount Taylor and the Keresan religion.) Families have houses with units of approximately equal size. Building these houses on a mesa several hundred feet above the plain required community cooperation. Over the centuries, people seem to have sacrificed exterior differentiation for internal security. The limited area of the mesa top and the difficulties of carrying building materials to its summit on human backs constrained even the most ambitious family to abide by the local traditions of reusing materials and being satisfied with minimum space. Because the window- and doorless ground story was traditionally a storage

Figure 14.5. *Acoma Pueblo, view from the top of the church tower over the town to the northeast. At the left edge, the lower flank of the volcano, Mount Taylor, is just visible. At the right, in the distance, is Enchanted Mesa, where Acoma tradition says the people once lived. On the rocky surface of the mesa top, in the center of the photo, one can see the remains of the governmental buildings from the Spanish Colonial period.*

space, there was little reason to elaborate the lowest facade, and even if the recessed facade of the second- or third-story terrace differed markedly from its neighbors, little or none of it would be visible from the path. Some individuality is evident in the arrangement of the terrace spaces, more in the interiors. This gradation from street-level anonymity to third-story individuality corresponds to the street-to-inner-most-courtyard gradation in Islamic and Chinese house

arrangements. Egalitarian ownership of land and houses fosters social stability, as evidenced in the pronounced similarity of house sizes and shapes. The Keresan of Acoma have attained unusual equality in housing.

SOURCES: BUNTING (1976), CORDELL AND PLOG (1979), EGGAN (1950), HAURY (1956), KNOWLES (1974), W. R. MILLER (1965), NABOKOV (1981, 1986), ORTIZ (1972), REED (1956), SAILE (1977), STIRLING (1942), L. WHITE (1929–30).

Great Plains Tipis: United States

Native Americans of the Great Plains lived in skin-and-pole space frames called tipis (see Chapter 2). Painted decorations distinguished some tipis from the rest. The two tribes most noted for their painted decorations were the Blackfoot and the Kiowa, although many Siouan tribes also produced fine work (see Fig. 14.6). Perhaps only one Blackfoot tipi in ten or one Kiowa tipi in twenty was decorated, making the status and role of that family visible.

On Blackfoot tents, designs on the bottom and upper panels combined traditional patterns with innovative forms. Designs for the central part represented visionary experiences and supernatural guardians suggested by an individual dreamer-owner or battle scenes from his life.

Each painted tipi had a song repertoire, a sacred "medicine bundle," and a recorded lineage of successive owners, passed down for generations. "Kiowa warriors were remembered long after they had died for the magical power of the tipi designs which they had received in visions. For instance, the design belonging to Chief White Man's Hugging Bear healed the sick, while the painted tipi of Black Cap's Porcupine was believed to keep children healthy," Hungry Wolf reported. He also described a yellow medicine tipi with large drawings of deer on its sides and a lining painted with traditional geometric designs in several colors (see Fig. 14.7). As the skins wore out, the design was transferred to a new set.

Both the inside and outside of the tipi could be decorated with geometric motifs, sacred symbols seen in a vi-

Figure 14.6. *Sioux tipis in 1819, Great Plains, United States. The tipis show characteristic Native American designs, with borders of geometric patterns and a large emblem probably related to the owner's personal history.*

sion induced by fasting, or historical scenes of warfare. Paintings could carry heavy symbolic meaning, either narrative or didactic. Types of designs included all-over repeated images, such as horses or circles (representing stars), or single images, such as a huge bear placed upright along the rear axis and reaching out its four limbs to embrace the whole tent. A painted scene might depict a hunt, a battle between two bands of Indians, or a skirmish with an American army unit. Geometric patterns might form bands along the lower and upper edges of the tent, with stylized images of animals or people filling the space between.

Physically and symbolically, the tipi mediated between geographic and tribal reality, personal and ancestral myth, and personal and group history. Whether painted or not, tipis were sometimes placed with their four main poles oriented symbolically to the four cardinal directions. In other cases, only the doorway was oriented, usually to the east.

In contrast to the Ndebele of South Africa, among whom the women decorate the houses (see Chapter 13), the Native Americans placed tipi ornamentation in the hands of male experts, assisted by the entire family. They spread the tipi cover on grass with the exterior side up. Specialists "outlined figures and border designs in charcoal, using red willow rods for straight-edges," and the family did the painting. Traditionally they bound mineral or vegetable colors to the skins with glue made from buffalo hooves; later they preferred the white man's pigments. Brushes were sticks with chewed ends, buffalo hair, or bones.

According to E. Guidoni, the portable dwelling projected an image of the family. A well-painted tipi exhibited the success of the individuals of the family and their accomplishments in working together. Among the Plains Indians, a womanly woman physically created and erected her family's tipi; a manly man commemorated his dreams and most important hunts or battles in the paintings on his home for his lineage and tribe to treasure. This division of labor and ownership was congenial to the Plains groups. As M. Williamson has observed, "There are certain expectations, norms, and behaviors that are linked to being a man or a woman in a given society. . . . Sex is biologically determined; gender, though linked to sex, is culturally determined"—and so are the activities appropriate to each gender.

SOURCES: FORDE (1934), 61; GUIDONI (1975), 62; HUNGRY WOLF (1972), 25–30; NABOKOV AND EASTON (1989), 161–63; RAPOPORT (1969), 119–29; TALAY (1994); M. WILLIAMSON (1983).

TIPI OF NIKUCIBCAN'S THUNDER VISION   FIRE CHIEF'S CORNSTALK TIPI

SACRED PIPE-STEM TIPI OF WAQAGA

Figure 14.7. *Three tipi designs, Great Plains, United States. Left to right, a dark storm cloud over a rainbow, a pair of cornstalks, and a pair of long-stemmed pipes decorated with feathers.*

Royal Buildings: Tikal, Guatemala

Chapter 8 looked at how the conspicuous display of architecture can legitimate power. Rulers in some pre-Columbian American societies maintained their royal status and strengthened their power by building monumental works of architecture. Archaeological investigations and the deciphering of hieroglyphic writing at Tikal in northeastern Guatemala have revealed the close correlation between the prestige of the ruler, the buildings he erected, the demands of ritual, and the dominance of a patrilineal lineage.

Only a few square miles of Tikal have been extensively explored, but archaeologists believe that the city was immense, covering perhaps 50 square miles (125 square kilometers), and during its height in the Classic period (250–900 C.E.) had 75,000 to 100,000 inhabitants—it was the largest Maya center. We use the term *city* with caution, for Tikal did not have the street patterns that Western scholars assume are basic to a "city" (see Fig. 14.8). Numerous monumental buildings, randomly placed, made up the central area. At its height around 750 C.E., Tikal's public buildings and structures were numerous—pyramids, palaces, temples, courtyards, reservoirs, causeways (raised roads), plazas, shrines, altars, and ballcourts. According to noted Mayanist, M. G. Robertson, more than two thousand structures are now visible. The University of Pennsylvania and the Guatemalan government have excavated the site and reconstructed many of the structures.

Communities probably did not develop until 5000 to 2000 B.C.E., although some researchers suggest that there were settlements as early as 10,000 B.C.E. (Chapter 10, Mesoamerica). During the Preclassic era, from 1500 to 250 B.C.E., these communities became more complex with chiefdoms and socioreligious institutions. Tikal's history reaches back to at least 500 B.C.E. By the 700s C.E., Tikal was the major lowland Maya ceremonial and community center.

Archaeologists have traced Tikal's dynastic history from the 200s to the 700s C.E. through epigraphs, including emblem glyphs, which are symbols inscribed on upright monumental stones called stelae. Together with archaeological studies of royal monuments, tombs, and other structures, these inscriptions give us a picture of powerful ruling families, believed to be semidivine and having both political and supernatural control. As early as 300 C.E., the Maya had made great strides in mathematics, astronomy, hieroglyphic writing, and the development of a calendar. Their engineering skills are evident in the clay-lined reservoirs, irrigation systems, and causeways they built in and near Tikal. A privileged few, members of the ruling elite and the priesthoods, directed the use of this body of knowledge.

The Maya believed that cosmological deities presided over all aspects of life. These supernatural forces had dualistic traits, both animal and human. Their attitudes could range from benefic to vengeful. The system was too complex to be mastered by any but appointed shamans who used mystical powers to interpret signs and appease the deities. In time, a form of patrilineal dynastic leadership developed, in which religious and political power were united in the person of the king, who dictated the building of major works of public architecture—huge projects that reinforced their claims to power by their very scale and magnificence. The king also directed the economic life of the community by dominating trade, food production, and the use of natural resources.

Scholars have recently studied the expenditure of energy and labor necessary for the construction of Maya buildings at Copán, for example (see Chapter 17). At Tikal, the impressive amounts of energy expended for construction projects of competing rulers seem to have been more important than the acquisition of new territory, but the rulers also maintained prestige by constant warfare. Carved stelae at Tikal and other Maya sites depicting captives and scenes of bloodletting were effective propaganda devices intended to perpetuate power.

Water was another route to and symbol of power. The collection and storage of water was vital for the survival of densely populated Tikal, which had no nearby permanent water sources. V. Scarborough and G. Gallopin, authorities on water-management systems in the Maya lowlands, point to the four-month dry season as the impetus for the building of reservoirs and cisterns to collect and store rainfall during the wet season. Channels carried runoffs of rainwater from catchment areas into a central precinct reservoir and smaller residential ones. Other basins were located outside the densely populated areas. Officials controlled the release of rainwater from elevated reservoirs for agriculture. In karst regions (areas of limestone where erosion has enlarged fissures and underground streams), they set stairways and ladders into natural shafts to reach the water table, obtaining freshflowing water for drinking. The streets/causeways that connected sections of Tikal also served as dams for water control. The rulers maintained their authority by controlling the water sources.

Scholars agree that the most important architectural features and functions at Tikal centered on such structures as pyramid temples, necropoli, palaces, and twin pyramid groups. Next in importance were elevated platforms used as public plazas. Third came market areas. Communication and defensive installations included the causeways and encircling walls. For protection from tropical humidity and dense jungle overgrowth, most buildings were elevated on platforms with rubble and earthen foundations, faced with masonry or plaster. Steps and paving, as well as carved ornamentation, were of stone.

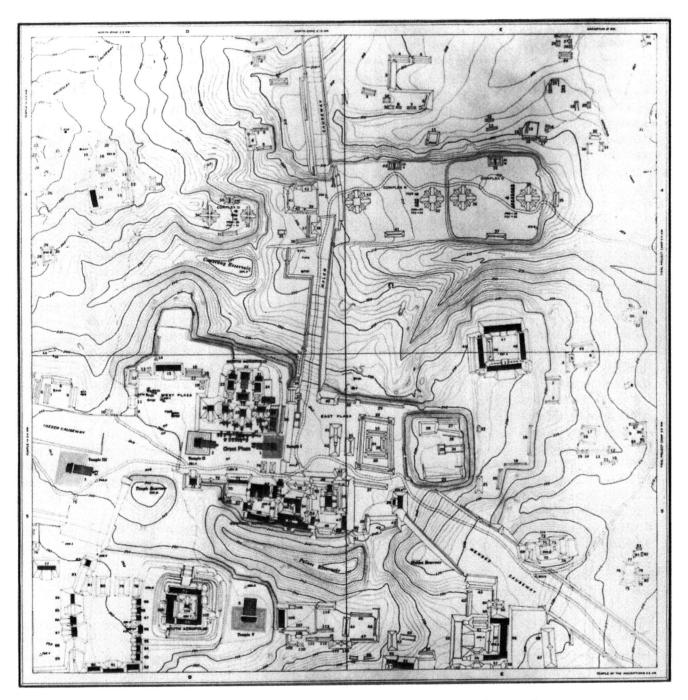

Figure 14.8. *Tikal, Guatemala. Plan showing the Great Plaza, the North Acropolis (top), the Central Acropolis, and the South Acropolis (bottom); the palace and temple reservoirs (center) and other structures—including several pairs of pyramid-temples—in the ceremonial center. Set on level areas amid the hills and valleys of the site, the building complexes are grouped in a "campus plan" without major streets.*

Interior spaces were small. Some interior and exterior surfaces were painted.

Some public works have acquired modern names derived from general characteristics not yet substantiated. For example, some rectangular multichamber structures with windows are called "palaces" when they may have had another function altogether. The so-called nunnery in Uxmal in western Yucatán was almost certainly no such thing; the term was acquired after the Spanish conquest and has no Maya connotation. We should keep this fact in mind in referring to Maya architectural complexes as "ceremonial centers."

Of the many structures at Tikal related to elite status, none are more impressive than the pyramid-temples located on the Great Plaza, dating from 250 C.E. and later. The intentional contrast of architectural mass and space appears in two main sections, the Great Plaza and the North Acropolis. The Great Plaza is a partially enclosed, paved, rectangular platform that covers 2.5 acres (1 hectare). It is flanked by two major stepped pyramids that are symmetrically placed on the plaza's east and west sides (Temples I and II). Multilayered temples and "palaces" occupy the north and central areas (see Figs. 14.8 and 14.9).

Temples served as focal points because kings were buried beneath them, just as commoners were buried under their houses. Temple I, the temple on the east side of the Great Plaza (see Fig. 14.9), consists of nine levels ascending to a height of 145 feet (44 meters). According to Mayanist M. E. Miller, the number nine refers to the nine levels of the underworld in Maya mythology. A steep stairway used by the priests led up the west side to the top, where a chamber was reached through a single doorway. The chamber was crowned by a roof comb, a hollow element that added height to the structure. Temple I is also known as the Temple of the Giant Jaguar. The jaguar was a symbol of power and the image carved on the door evoked the power of the deceased chieftan, Ah Cacau, whose reign was marked by the construction of monuments as settings for public ceremonies that reflected the Mexican-Maya ideology. Influence from central Mexico was strong at Tikal, as at other Maya cities, and economic and cultural ties between Teotihuacán (see Chapter 7) and Tikal had existed for several centuries.

The burial chamber under the base of the pyramid is corbel vaulted. (Because the Maya used the corbelled arch, which can support less weight than the true arch, building heights were limited and stability was compromised.) Under this vault of masonry and rubble, Au Cacau was interred around 731, along with mortuary offerings of pottery, pearls, jade, and other ornaments reflecting his wealth and status. The skeletal remains indicate that he was placed on a stone bench and adorned with a large jade necklace, ornaments, and shells. Opposite Temple I on the Great Plaza is Temple II, a three-terrace pyramid 125 feet (38 meters) high. No tomb has been discovered beneath it, but it may have been the funerary monument of Ah Cacau's wife. Tombs of rulers' wives—even of ruling queens—are known from other Maya sites. Temple II is also known as the Temple of the Masks because of the monstrous masks carved on its facade. Stylized sculpture was an artistic vehicle for depicting Maya figures of humans and gods. A carving of a masked man spearing a captive illustrates the Maya religious practice of human sacrifice. (See Chapter 10 for a discussion of ritual sacrifice in connection with Maya ballcourts.)

Other funerary monuments occupy sections of the North Acropolis, all raised on an elevated platform that measures 330 feet (101 meters) by 260 feet (79 meters) and is reached by a wide expanse of stairs. The symmetrically arranged group on this platform was built over a thousand years ago. Once there were at least a hundred buildings at this site. Some temples are buried beneath the present surface.

The Central Acropolis, covering about 4 acres (1.5 hectares) afforded a view of the great plaza. It is covered with over a dozen multilevel, rectangular buildings with many interior rooms grouped around a series of courtyards. Investigators have described these interconnected, elevated buildings as residences, administrative offices, or royal quarters.

During the late phase of Tikal history, the growing number of the elite and their demands for material expression of power put a heavy burden on the people. More temples meant that more labor was required, but food resources became strained and settlement patterns changed as the population increased. Rituals that glorified the leaders became less meaningful to the people who did the work. These factors contributed to the decline of Maya civilization—eventually, the propaganda of elite architecture and art lost its effectiveness in the society.

Among the Maya, the ruling elite (through patrilineal succession) directed the monumental building programs and controlled economic resources. Among the Native Americans of the Great Plains, distinction and status were achieved not through the size of the dwelling but by its ornamentation. There was less social distance between a Blackfeet chief and a young girl of his tribe than between a Tikal leader and a village farmer, but there was a dif-

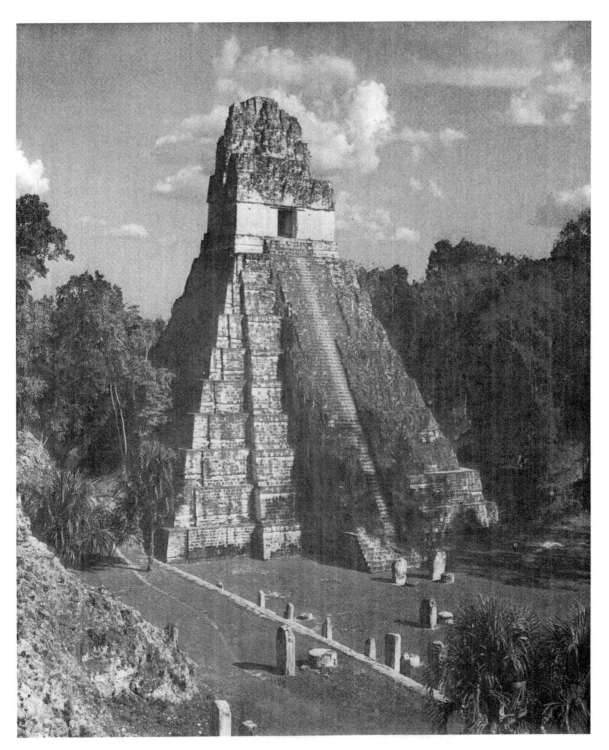

Figure 14.9. *Temple I, Tikal, Guatemala. The temple rises in nine levels to the summit and the funerary temple, topped by a roof comb. The temple was built as a memorial to ruler Ah Cacau whose body was interred at the base.*

ference in status. In both cases, this difference was marked by details of the dwelling unit, constructed and decorated to engender respect. The pueblo people of Acoma had a more egalitarian system of ownership and lived in dwellings that were only mildly differentiated. These examples do not begin to exhaust the range of variation in the relations between architecture and social structure. Yet we think they vary sufficiently to suggest the diversity that is the human hallmark.

SOURCES: MILLER (1990), PENDERGAST (1988), SCARBOROUGH AND GALLOPIN (1991), SHARER (1994), SCHELE AND FREIDEL (1990).

SUGGESTED READINGS

Ferguson, W., and A. Rohn. 1990. *Mesoamerica's Ancient Cities.* Niwot, Colo.: University Press of Colorado. Beautifully photographed, with an informative text.

Hungry Wolf. 1972. *A Tipi Life.* Fort MacCloud, Alberta: Good Medicine Press. Written by a Plains Indian, this little book has an air of authenticity.

Knapp, R. 1990. *The Chinese House.* Hong Kong: Oxford University Press. One of a series of books on this general topic by this geographer. Copiously illustrated.

Knowles, R. L. 1974. *Energy and Form.* Cambridge, Mass.: MIT Press. Knowles's group studied the thermal arrangements at Acoma in great detail. The book is a useful combination of mathematics and architectural drawings.

Knowles, R. L. 1981. *Sun Rhythm Form.* Cambridge, Mass.: MIT Press. A seminal study with historical examples of the relation between the forms of buildings and their solutions for environmental problems.

Minge, W. A. 1991. *Acoma: Pueblo in the Sky.* Acoma, N. Mex.: Pueblo of Acoma. Rev. and expanded ed. (original work published 1976). Thoughtful. Good data on the Keresan religion as it relates to the land.

Montêquin, F.-A. de. 1979. "The Personality and Morphology of the Islamic City." *Action* Vol. 10 (no. 21): 6 ff. This article relates the physical form to the social content of the city.

Ortiz, A., ed. 1972. *New Perspectives on the Puebloes.* Albuquerque: University of New Mexico Press. Ortiz is a Tewa and an anthropologist with an insider's knowledge of pueblo societies.

Petherbridge, G. T. 1978. "Vernacular Architecture: The House and Society." In *Architecture and the Islamic World: Its History and Social Meaning,* 176–208, edited by G. Michell. New York: William Morrow. A good discussion of Islamic living arrangements.

Saile, D. G. 1977. "Making a House in the Pueblo Indian World." *Architectural Association Quarterly.* 9 (2–3): 72–78. A study by an architect with a sensitive appreciation for the nuances of Pueblo architecture.

White, L. 1973. *The Acoma Indians: 47th Annual Report of the Bureau of American Ethnology.* Glorieta, N.M.: Rio Grande Press. Reprint of 1929–30 ed. An excellent report, not surpassed by later work.

15

Theories of Architecture

The Chinese and the Batammaliba people of West Africa have widely divergent concepts of architecture. The Chinese have analyzed architecture from the loftiest spiritual and intellectual levels with the aim of making the intangible perceptible, of creating an architecture suitable for humans who are both physical and spiritual. Batammaliba architectural thought is much more physical, yet it is transcendent in its symbolic content. Male architects and female decorators create mud-and-thatch houses in a collaboration that is analogous to creating a child. The house embodies their understanding of what it means to be human: Parts of it are equated with parts of the human body, and it has a life cycle like a person's, as well as being a dwelling for gods. As different as they are, both points of view contrast with the common North American nonchalance toward architecture. They also show how theories about architecture underlie the built environment.

Our review of the ways in which architectural history is written is in keeping with the reappraisal of history that has occurred since the mid-1900s. We wondered whether the historian's class, gender, or ethnicity alters the methodology or content of presentations of architectural thought. The answer is yes—and the news is good. A wider "gene pool" of historians and a bigger toolkit of methods are producing more vivid histories and a better understanding of the past. Architectural history now includes different kinds of buildings, methods, and architectural theories in wider geographic areas. Here we use the feminist view, one of several new and more inclusive views of intellectual history, to reflect on how architectural history is written.

THEORETICAL DIFFERENCES

Architectural ideas are cultural constructs, not facts, yet we use them so unconsciously that they are nearly invisible to us. Among Westerners, one such idea is the assumption that space is Cartesian, that any point's location is determined by its position relative to the x, y, and z axes of Descartes's mathematical space. Another is that objects, such as the towns along Interstate 90, and processes, such as the construction of a college dormitory, are connected in a linear series. We may recognize that we need to accumulate more data, but we do not usually consider

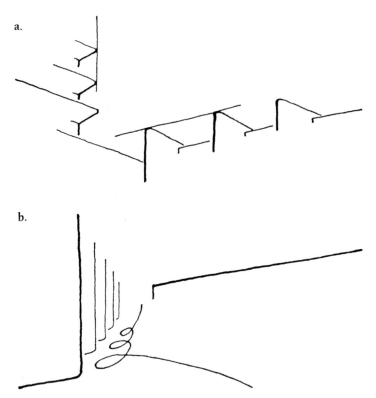

a.

b.

Figure 15.1. *Diagrams of architectural paradoxes.* **a.** *A series of horizontal lines (at the left) add up to a vertical. A series of vertical forms (at the right) form a horizontal.* **b.** *An architectural pause is indicated by the largest loop in the foreground, where the flow of space slows and spreads out, to awaken awareness of the transition, like a retardation in music.*

that there may be valid and valuable questions and postulates that we have never encountered.

Each culture has characteristic ways of thinking but is not completely conscious of them. L. Prussin noted in 1986 that in architecture we lack a "technical language common to both 'us' and 'them'"—whoever those others are. We lack this knowledge partly because words and concepts do not translate directly from language to language. "Each house understands the language of the people who live there," according to Yafoata Tano of the Batammaliba people of Togo and Benin (quoted by S. Blier).

We want to do more than respectfully describe and appreciate architectures that are not based on the Euro-American tradition; we are also trying to notice other sets of ideas about architecture. Looking at what is built and

how people use it, we begin to learn how to think about architecture in more than one way. We see, for example, that Plains Indians and Kalahari Bushmen have similar ideas about claiming space temporarily. We are impressed that Chimu engineers of Peru built irrigation systems using a mathematical system quite different from ours. And now we contrast two ways of theorizing about architecture because different slices through a problem can reveal different aspects of it.

SOURCES: BLIER (1987), D. LEE (1966), PRUSSIN (1986).

Being and Nonbeing in Chinese Architecture

We are fortunate to have A. I. T. Chang's 1956 book, *The Tao of Architecture*, a short but endlessly stimulating volume; the quotes in this section are from this book unless otherwise noted. What is the "Tao" of which Chang writes? The Chinese philosophical principle of Tao—literally, "the way"—can be understood as the first cause of everything in the universe or as the rational basis of human activity or as a simple life not interfering with the course of natural events—in short, a universal ideal. Chang goes further in his application of Taoism to architecture, investigating architectural theory in terms of the epigrammatic philosophy of Lao-tzu, founder of Taoism, who lived in sixth-century B.C.E. China and taught that nature is an "organic whole in which the intangible part is the most vital." Lao-tzu expresses his ideas in paradoxes, as when he states

The way to be is not to be.

Chang helps us grasp this paradox manifested in architecture. The basic architectural task is "embodying intangible content in architectonic form" (see Fig. 15.1). Architecture can be enriched by the play between complicated and simple, between solid and void—as a Chinese philosopher observed, the spaces between the spokes of a wheel are as important as the spokes themselves. The Euro-American tradition offers an example in the sculpture of Henry Moore, in which solids and voids have equal value. Always capable of being filled, drawing on the intangible as a permanent reservoir, the void is real and infinitely viable. The solid is restricted and deadly because it is too definite and seems to nullify all reality but itself.

The architect creates rhythm through changes between uniform shapes and empty spaces and delight through the use of different natural materials. The power of negation can give richness without unnecessary complication; for example, one way to create architectural nonbeing is to provide flowing space between two adjacent environments that have contrasting openness (se Fig. 15.1b). A perpendicular to the direction of flow creates a result between being and nonbeing, like a retardation in music. Such a design, like nature itself, uses minimal means for maximal ends.

Chinese Taoist architectural thought[34] recognizes an important difference between tangible construction and intangible structure. Visible, tangible construction deals with matters of minimum materials and maximum load; like gravity, structure is never fully manifest and is therefore called intangible. Lao-tzu's active negativism, the philosophy of intangibility, gives some useful answers to what Chang considers the two central problems of architecture—the human quality of the physical environment and the harmony and unity of different buildings.

What we think we see is affected by our previous experience and by the light that modifies what we are looking at. In Fig. 15.1a, Chang shows how repeated horizontal elements in architecture create a vertical, and vice versa. To open a confined space, Chang uses a series of lateral planes (Fig. 15.1b), such as a vertical venetian blind or a row of buttresses. Groups of buildings can be integrated by providing an extra void between unifying elements. An excellent example is the generous series of voids between the buildings along the central axis of the Forbidden City in Beijing (see Fig. 11.8). An architect who wishes to make the intangible present may avoid vivid color that dazzles us, choose clarity achieved through grayness, or soften harsh light by the choice of materials. The best architectural composition includes change by time and natural processes, as when architectural detail becomes more visible as it ages and dirt collects to make permanent "shadows" that emphasize the details of the form. The architectural form and the natural deposit of dirt together reveal the passage of time (see Fig. 11.9).

The pace of life should decide the degree of elaboration in any setting: "From a humanitarian point of view, complexity in a subway tunnel and simplicity in a prison are both undesirable." Monotony fatigues the eye, so that a monotonous object, not energetically perceived, becomes nonexistent.

To make possible the existence of intangible content in architectonic form, it is first necessary to know what not to do. Lao-tzu tells us:

> The way to learn is to assimilate.
> The way to know is to forget.

When we forget constructively and affirmatively, we are not inhibited by knowledge; rather, we are released by creative forgetfulness. Creation consciously avoids repetition and subconsciously searches for truth, actively accepting differences as natural, "by an innate respect for each element and its unbounded possibilities for vital development and combination. Crowded massiveness indicates decline . . . but there is liveliness when each building has surrounding space and uniqueness. Then each building radiates in space, and its meaning grows in time."

As the history of Chinese architecture becomes more widely known, many examples of buildings informed by the intangible spirit of the Tao will be analyzed. Eventually we may be able to differentiate Confucian-inspired buildings from Taoist ones through their manifestations of different intellectual positions.

SOURCES: A. I. T. CHANG (1956), LAO-TZU (1972).

Anthropomorphic Architecture in West Africa

The Batammaliba people of Togo and Benin, in West Africa, call themselves "those who are the real architects of earth" (all quotations in this section are from S. P. Blier). Their culture and society reach their clearest expression through architecture, which includes cosmogony, religion, psychology, society, politics, and theater, as well as built form. The Batammaliba take traditions of design, construction, and maintenance seriously. Architects are important people among them. They not only design houses, but work with owners and their families to erect them. Each house is individual in form but must meet standard design requirements and be accepted by the master architects of the village; each is signed by its designer-builder. The large role architects play in Batammaliba society is borne out by numbers: A village of 450 people living in 91 houses has 25 architects.

Village houses are symmetrical (see Fig 15.2). Each stands within a small, irregularly circular courtyard. The

---

[34]The Tao of Architecture deals with Taoist thought, but Chang pointed out (in a personal communication) that the dominant thinking in traditional Chinese architecture has been Confucianist, which he considers a much more static and less adaptable body of thought.

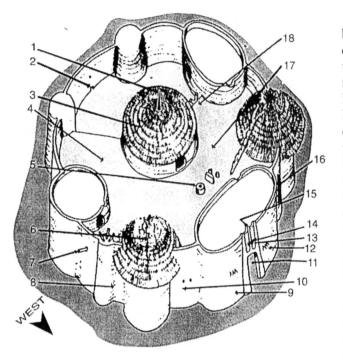

Figure 15.2. *A Batammaliba house, Togo, West Africa. The parts of the house are equated symbolically with parts of the human body: (1) backbone—axis from the pinnacle to the ground; (2) anus—the drain from the terrace; (3) womb/vagina—the house where the mother sleeps; (4) large intestine—the terrace area where meals are served; (5) fontanel/solar plexus—the hole from the terrace to the cattle room below; (6) stomach—granary; (7) penis—the drain spout; (8) bile—the wall surface; (9) legs—the wall flanking the door; (10) joints—the undulating surface of wall; (11) mouth (lips, tongue, and teeth)—the doorway; (12) knees—the chevron decoration on wall; (13) navel/arteries—reinforcing around the doorway; (14) eyes—decoration above the doorway; (15) testicles—the crowning element above the doorway; (16) nose—the pinnacle on the wall; (17) chest—another area of the terrace; and (18) head/jaw—another part of terrace, with a hornlike ornament. A typical house is 18–54 feet wide and 13–16 feet high (6–18 meters wide and deep and 4–5 meters high), with two stories.*

facade has a central door topped by horns and flanked by granaries. The women and children sleep at the terrace level; the men sleep in the lower part of the house with the animals to provide security for the family against the threat of raids by enemies.

Ceremonies during construction ensure the well-being of the house and its inhabitants. These rituals demonstrate the role of the house as cosmology, paradise, temple, social diagram, psychological complement, fortress, and theater, reinforcing the parallels between the house and the human being. Building the terrace of the house, the most difficult and important task, takes several days. The terrace is completed when the family elder pierces the terrace floor to make a ceremonial opening from the terrace to the cattle room below. The flat stone that covers this hole is used daily to serve the main meal to the family, and eventually it becomes the elder's grave stone. This piercing ritual is called "killing" the house and ends with payment to the architect. It is the only ritual that takes place at noon, bringing the sun at the peak of its power into the core of the house and thus defining the house as a cosmological model.

Anthropologist S. Blier, who has studied the Batammaliba closely, writes, "In African architectural traditions as in those of the West, human analogies in architecture are based partially on the use of the body as a paradigm or metaphor for comparable structural, mechanical, decorative, and symbolic forms." Among the Batammaliba, the house is an integral part of the family, defining and maintaining each member's well-being. Psychological problems, as well as important life passages, often require architectural changes—a new tower, renovation of the facade, maintenance of the roof terrace. Architecture serves as a model of physical and psychological balance and completeness, which cannot be achieved without the house.

The house becomes human as it is built. The male architect and female plasterer-decorator create the house as if it were a child, and each step of construction parallels a stage of human development. The earthen core is flesh, the water that moistens the earth is blood, the pebbles are bones, and the clay-plaster surface is skin. And just as a human has a soul, so does a house. Daily rituals reinforce the anthropomorphic identification: birth; the house being fed; the house being dressed in the same patterns as the women's skin; and, finally, the funeral of the elder, when the house ritually becomes the elder. The house is the final resting place for the souls of the elders, deep within the cattle room of the ground floor. At funerals the Batammaliba perform the Dance of the Drums, using the dead person's house as the crucial staging area and stage set, dressing it with funeral cloths. The climactic performance takes place on the upper terrace of the house.

The Batammaliba remember that they once lived in one-story houses, that the simple house form became complex, and that their open huts became fortified; the current house embodies recent historical changes. It also has spiritual meaning. The Batammaliba build their houses not only for their earthly families, but also as temples for the gods. In particular, the house is the temple of the creator god Kuiye, who is both male and female, corporeal and spiritual: "Through architecture, the invisible power dimension of each deity is made visible."

This multiplicity of purposes gives each architectural element multiple meanings. For example, the *lisenpo*, an earthen mound in front of the house door, is at once a copy of the great altar of Kuiye, a memento of his earthly altar at Linaba, a shrine for him and the Earth god Butan, the place of the soul of the house and its members, a memorial to the family lineage (especially the dead), and a symbol of the house's power and autonomy.

Blier sums up her findings: "Architecture is concerned with not only different aspects of human life but also with the variant categories of human thought and expression . . . [it] encourages those who move within it to reaffirm the essential features of human identity and activity."

Chinese Taoists and African Batammaliba demonstrate different aspects of human thought about architecture. Though very different from each other and from conventional modernism, they substantially agree that

The power of the visible is the invisible.
—*Marianne Moore*

SOURCE: BLIER (1987).

WRITING ARCHITECTURAL HISTORY

"Time is not a continuum" for African peoples, writes E. Evans-Pritchard; it is a structural arrangement that coordinates relations, not events. This observation appears in a discussion of African groups in which orally transmitted, valid historical knowledge (as an outsider might see it) extends over several generations, for perhaps one hundred years. Beyond knowledge lies tradition, which has a depth of ten to twelve generations. Beyond lies myth. In contrast, many Americans know two kinds of history. One is the official history taught in school, which covers about twenty five hundred years of the Greco-Roman-European-American continuum, and which they may soon forget. The other is the personal history of their own families, which, barring genealogical research, reaches three or, at the most, four generations into the past.

Until this century, there have been few links between official written histories and personal histories on any continent. Official histories have focused on the governmental and military activities of dominant men and have largely ignored the lives of conquered peoples, women, minorities, and the lower classes.

But what is history? At bottom, it is "all human activity in the past." An all-encompassing definition, however, is too unwieldy to be useful, so it is more helpful to define history as "the stories we tell ourselves about our past." Who tells these stories? We all do, but we have designated specific persons as our official historians, which leads to a third definition of history: "what historians tell us about the past."

Many official historians are lodged in history departments in colleges and universities, where their special interests are pruned by institutional demands.[35] As part of the tradition of the profession of history, each generation of scholars is supposed to question its predecessors. We now examine some of the challenged and challenging ideas about history as they relate to traditional architecture.

We live in an era of "rising contemporary skepticism about Eurocentric perspectives," according to the philosopher S. Harding. This book is evidence of that skepticism. Its authors agree with Harding, who writes:

[N]ot all reason is white, masculinist, modern, heterosexual, Western reason. . . . The extent of human rationality is neither restricted to nor, most likely, paradigmatically exhibited by the modern West. Listening carefully to different voices and attending thoughtfully to others' values and interests can enlarge our vision and begin to correct for inevitable ethnocentricities. . . .

---

[35]As Thomas Kuhn reminds us in *The Histories of Science*, in describing the problems of would-be historians of science in mid-twentieth-century America, "Departments of history had not traditionally provided a home for historians of other disciplines: art, music, or literature, for example. Why should they do so for science?" Therefore, some historians of science went to philosophy departments, where they dealt with the philosophy of science. In history departments, they studied the social and institutional aspects of science, as art historians did the social aspects of art, because these aspects were considered more "historical" and because their audience (students, colleagues, and readers of scholarly journals) were not interested in science or music or the development of painting or civil engineering per se.

We have [as yet] no conception of objectivity that enables us to distinguish the . . . "best descriptions and explanations" from those that fit most closely (intentionally or not) with the assumptions that elites in the West do not want critically examined.

Indeed, we must evaluate critically which social situations generate the most objective descriptions, whether the subject matter is botany or architectural history.

Class, Gender, and Ethnicity

Why do we discuss houses in so many parts of the world? The invisible life of people in their houses is the basic unit of human existence and culture. By making this life and its domestic container explicitly visible, rather than ignoring it, we challenge the dominant, official culture that emphasizes seats of male power, such as palaces or mosques. Women's situations at home and in public can be a resource for fuller and less partial descriptions of architectural history. "Men's theories exclude everyday life and are therefore incomplete and distorted abstract concepts," Harding warns. Looking at any subject matter from a woman's point of view widens the field by adding other experiences, attitudes, and insights to the dominant white-male information and attitudes. Men, according to Harding, have tended to devalue contextual modes of thought, among them the emotional components of reason. Emotion is naturally refractory to analysis or lends itself uneasily to analysis because of its complexity. Above all, emotions of collective origin defy critical and rational examination, as L. Hanakainson-Nelson, Durkheim, and Mauss pointed out. But anyone who strives to see from a second point of view sees things that were invisible before. As J. C. Berlo wrote:

> During the past twenty-five years, feminist scholarship has transformed and revitalized many disciplines, including art history, literary studies, and anthropology. Although feminist scholarship is protean and too wide in its scope to be easily characterized, two main thrusts have been evident: the inclusion of new data on women, often by women scholars, and the re-analysis of long-existing data according to new paradigms in order to yield fresh interpretations.

Harding suggests a further widening of the scope of inquiry to include the intellectual contributions of minorities—racial, sexual, or economic. Those who are newly admitted to the discourse can raise what Harding calls "usefully uncomfortable questions" about canons of knowledge.

In this book, we have studied more houses than fortresses. The house is no more real than the fortress, but it has the advantage for us of pertaining to the lives of women and children, as well as men. By paying more attention to houses than to fortresses, we question the gender assumption that men and their preoccupations are the human norm. In addition, the house is of all cultural artifacts the most resistant to change, yet the easiest for a stranger to relate to. When we study the house, we may look long and hard at other cultures without the density of strangeness that may interfere with our understanding of the mosque, the khan, or the cave-temple.

When Vitruvius wrote architectural history two thousand years ago, he could be excused for assuming that the Mediterranean area was the whole world. Now we know that we share the planet with peoples as different from one another and from Euro-Americans as the Chinese and the Batammaliba. By reporting on the architectural concepts of Chinese Taoists and the "real architects" of the Batammaliba people, we echo, in the field of architectural history, the anticolonial movements of the last half of the twentieth century.

We are only gradually escaping old ideas about cultures and their architectures. Those old ideas are represented here by anthropologist J. G. Frazer and are part of a tradition going back to Heraclitis of Ephesus in the 6th century B.C.E. This tradition saw all human history as cycles of slow change leading to positive improvement ("progress"). But when the passion for scientific classification and description blossomed in the nineteenth century, Frazer's historical methods—based on literary documents and theories—were found wanting: Because history as it was then understood dealt only with particular actions and events, nineteenth-century critics of the historical method believed that no generalizations equivalent to scientific laws could be made.

For a time, the anthropologists and sociologists tried to make general historical inquiries, studying primitive peoples (nonliterate and therefore "historyless") in search of clues to the early history of European culture, and incidentally avoiding chronology. Soon, however, these investigators became convinced that "historical processes could not be depicted in the absence of historical evidence," yet they were unwilling to submit to the "tyranny of chronology" and not methodologically ready to use archaeological and scientific data. Eventually, dissatisfied with their results, anthropologists and sociologists relinquished scientific history as an aim.

One critic of the nonchronological approach was F. W. Mailtand, who showed that sociologists and anthropologists were explaining away any difficulties they found, disagreeing on criteria, and not being specific. G. C. Lewis, another critic, advocated the concept of a plurality of histories, exposed the fallacy of "progress" as social change, and ridiculed scholars who looked for origins but despised dates and dating criteria. G. L. Gomme insisted that "the connection between contemporary savagery and ancient peoples was not easily established" if one insisted on historical verification, and he pointed out the "need for dated historical materials related to a specific geographical area." After surveying the works of these writers, K. E. Bock concluded:

> Comte, Spencer, Mill, and others, worked in an intellectual climate, that they had inherited but had not examined carefully. They already knew what science was. They already knew what the general course of history had been. The "nature" of society and culture was spelled out for them as an elementary lesson handed down by elders . . . [as] the only way to handle such data.

It is difficult to learn anything new when one insists that one already knows everything! But perhaps one reason why some have disliked or rejected history is that all too often it has consisted of a set of obsolete answers, rather than new and cutting-edge questions.

P. Robertshaw's *A History of African Archaeology* gives us a vivid example of preconceptions in history, one in which European notions of Africans as extremely limited "savages" interfered drastically with the perception and collection of accurate historical data (see Chapter 8, Great Zimbabwe). Humans have lived in sub-Saharan Africa for more than a million years. The gold trade there dates back thousands of years, and impressive stone buildings survive from a thousand years ago. Yet the newly arrived Europeans literally could not see the connections between the built and the builders. They managed to ignore Caton-Thompson's 1929 excavations because they could not accept evidence that an African people had a richly developed culture. Such attitudes were useful in justifying economic exploitation.

As recently as 1963, H. Trevor-Roper, Regius professor of modern history at Oxford University, clinging to the definition of history as only or mainly what academic historians do, stated, "Perhaps, in the future, there will be some African history to teach. But at present there is none: there is only the history of the Europeans in Africa. The rest is darkness . . . and darkness is not a subject of history," as cited by Fage. Six years later, the United Nations Educational, Scientific, and Cultural Organization began publishing a multivolume African history, which became "a well-established activity [whose] continued development will be ensured by inter-African exchanges . . . and by the struggles for freedom in all the African colonies [which] gave the African peoples the opportunity of renewing contact with their own history and organizing its study," according to historian J. D. Fage. He went on to define history as the stories we tell about our past. Anthropology and archaeology can reach this history even when there is no written record.

The inclusion of women's perspectives and the widening of history to include indigenous data and viewpoints are as important as learning to interpret and use scientific information.[36] New viewpoints enliven and enrich history for all of us. And if we fail to incorporate these new understandings? The case study, presented next, a delicious example of a paradigm shift, illustrates the effects of bias in reporting historical data.

SOURCES: BERLO (1992); BOCK (1956); CATON-THOMPSON (1931); EVANS-PRITCHARD (1973); FAGE (1981); FRAZER (1907–15); HANAKAINSON-NELSON, CITED IN DURKHEIM AND MAUSS (1973), 32–37; HARDING (1991); ROBERTSHAW (1990).

Case Study: Maya Historiography

> Neither the Mexicans nor Peruvians [were] entitled to rank with those nations which merit the name civilized . . . they [Aztec and Maya cities] . . . [were] more fit

---

[36] Another example: the authors of two articles on the historical records of earthquakes in the eastern Mediterranean studied unpublished Ottoman court documents that record claims for earthquake damage and the amounts spent by the central government on local repairs—a kind of evidence that has rarely been considered. See N. N. Ambraseys and C. F. Finkel, The Seismicity of the Eastern Mediterranean Region during the Turn of the Eighteenth Century," *Istanbuler Mitteilungen* 42 (1991): 323–43; and N. N. Ambraseys, "The Value of Historical Records of Earthquakes," *Nature* 232 (August 6, 1971): 375–78.

to be the habitation of men just emerging from barbarity than the residence of a polished people.

W. Robertson,
History of America (1777)

After the fall of the Maya civilization in the early 1500s, the Spanish conquerors made a concentrated attempt to eliminate all vestiges of the Maya culture by subjugating the Indians and converting them to Christianity. The imposition of Spanish rule and Christianity prompted the destruction of Maya cities, shrines, temples, and altars. Under the influence of the Inquisition, the Franciscan friar Diego de Landa ordered ancient Maya hieroglyphic books destroyed, and with them much information about the Maya culture.

Some of the Spanish conquistadors wrote accounts of the splendors of the Maya cities; European readers greeted these accounts with skepticism, thinking them exaggerated or misinterpreted impressions by overzealous chroniclers. Eurocentrism, with its claim of racial superiority, would not permit Europeans to think that "savages" were capable of such majestic works, as the foregoing quote from Robertson illustrates. Europeans were interested, however, in descriptions of great riches in gold and silver and in opportunities for economic exploitation in the New World. Expeditions into Maya territory multiplied.

Sixteenth- and seventeenth-century references to Maya culture appeared mainly in the official reports of the conquistadors; churchmen, such as Landa (*Relación de las Cosas de Yucatán*); or historians, such as Diego Lopez de Cogolludo (*Historia de Yucatán*), all of whom had traveled in Maya regions. Later eyewitness accounts verified the existence of a high culture with developed cities and infrastructures that clearly required great engineering skill and high organization. But it was one thing to admit the existence of an advanced society outside the Eastern Hemisphere and another to believe that such a civilization could have originated outside the European tradition. When interest in pre-Columbian cultures heightened in the nineteenth century—by which time, of course, the cities lay in ruins and the native cultures had long been subjected to foreign domination—European historians, obsessed with the past and influenced by Romanticism, came to startling conclusions concerning the origins of the Maya people.

A German engraver and explorer named J. F. Waldeck made a series of drawings while traveling in Mexico in 1838 and used them to illustrate his book *Voyage Pittoresque et Archeologique dans la Province d'Yucatan*. The drawings depicted Maya monuments as Egyptian pyramids (see Fig. 15.3.). In a nine-volume work on pre-Columbian archaeology (1831–48), E. King stated that the Maya were descended from the Lost Tribes of Israel, citing cultural similarities. About the same time, a plethora of papers, books, and articles advanced theories that linked American Indian ancestry and culture variously to the Chinese, Hindus, Norsemen, Greeks, Romans, Irish—just about any source other than an indigenous one. At a time when Europeans were avidly collecting and studying the antiquities of many lands, people freely drew analogies between the Maya and other cultures. Augustus Le Plongeon, a nineteenth-century amateur archaeologist who saw an Egyptian connection, published several books on New World architecture and suggested that the Maya had built colonies in Mesopotamia and India thousands of years before. More often, though, observers thought that people from the Old World had colonized the New. As recently as 1988, D. Grable contended in *The Egyptians and the Inca Gold Traders* that Egyptian travelers arrived in South America several thousand years ago and passed on ideas about pyramids to the Americans

The supposed "pyramid connection" was the basis for many notions about cultural ties between the eastern and western hemispheres. So basic and substantial a geometric form is the pyramid, however, that we need not assume a "common origin." In fact, except for shape, the Egyptian pyramids and those of the American cultures have little in common. Archaeologists have pointed out that the Maya pyramid is more like the Mesopotamian ziggurat: Both are earthen substructures for summit temples. But we now know that the Maya examples differed from both the solid stone pyramids of Egypt and the solid mud-brick ziggurats of Mesopotamia, since they were of earth faced with stone.

One of the more imaginative theories about the origin of Maya culture surfaced often in the context of racial origins and concerned the legend of the lost continent of Atlantis. The ancient Greek philosopher Plato had fantasized an idyllic island of great beauty to illustrate a story of human fallibility, but his Atlantis became for some a real continent and the subject of historical investigation. In 1814, A. Brasseur de Bourbourg, wrote *Quatre Lettres sur le Mexique* suggesting that Atlantis was the founding civilization for Mexico and Central America. The ne plus ultra of fanciful theories, however, may have been that of H. P. Blavatsky, who claimed that the egg-laying giants of the lost continent of Lemuria had evolved into various strains of mankind, the ancestors of the American Indi-

Figure 15.3. *Yucatán Peninsula, Mexico. A fanciful drawing of a Maya pyramid in which Chinese and Mesopotamian motifs join the Mesoamerican ones portrayed by to the artist. When this drawing was made (ca. 1829–34), Maya pyramids were covered with tropical vegetation and had not yet been studied by scholars.*

ans. Such publications spread erroneous information about the origin of the Maya and other pre-Columbian cultures, feeding the Europeans' generally accepted attitude of racial superiority.

We now know, with archaeological certainty, that pre-Columbian cultures were indigenous in origin. A few early scientifically oriented explorers, such as John L. Stephens, understood this origin in the nineteenth century. Stephens's eyewitness accounts, published in his pioneering works *Incidents of Travel in Central America, Chiapas and Yucatan* (1841) and *Incidents of Travel in Yucatan* (ca. 1843) invited later systematic investigations that dis-

pelled the widely circulated myths about the origins of pre-Columbian peoples.

Since the 1950s and especially since the 1990s, scholars have published an enormous amount of information about Maya culture. We know that the Maya had a rich written history and a calendar whose precision equals our own. It is likely that still more good popular histories will appear as researchers continue to study the available data and work proceeds at the untold number of major sites waiting to be excavated.

Why did the Europeans, who studied Western history in such detail, form such unsubstantiated theories about these people? A historical bias in writing about an exotic civilization reflects many religious, territorial, and social attitudes. Historian R. Wauchope observes that myths and speculation that are not based on scientific fact can infiltrate the literature at any time, bringing about a popular bias among readers. The case of Maya historiography shows how attitudes and misconceptions can distort perception and with it, historical fact.

SOURCES: GALLENKAMP (1976), SHARER (1994), STEPHENS (1949), WAUCHOPE (1962).

SUGGESTED READINGS

Begley, W. E. 1985. *Monumental Islamic Calligraphy from India*. Villa Park, Ill.: Islamic Foundation. A major contribution to studies of Islamic calligraphy.

Blier, S. P. 1987. *The Anatomy of Architecture: Ontology and Metaphor in Batammaliba Architectural Expression*. New York: Cambridge University Press. A careful and thorough study of ascribed architectural meaning, which could have been strengthened (for our purposes) by additional analysis of how daily life is accommodated by the provided spaces.

Bock, K. E. 1956. *The Acceptance of Histories: Toward a Perspective for Social Science*. Berkeley: University of California Press. Traces the change from a monolithic idea of history to a pluralistic one.

Chang, A. I. T. 1956. *The Tao of Architecture*. Princeton, N.J.: Princeton University Press. Deserves careful and repeated rereading. A good guide to one of the oldest literate architectural traditions.

Danien, E. C., and Sharer, R. J., eds. 1992. *New Theories on the Ancient Maya*. University Museum Symposium Series Vol. 3. Philadelphia: University Museum, University of Pennsylvania. An excellent discussion of new understandings based on new data, such as translations of ancient glyph writing.

Fage, J. D. 1981. "The Development of African Historiography." In *General History of Africa: I. Methodology and African Prehistory*, 25–42, edited by J. Ki-Zerbo. Essential for a fresh and clear understanding of the continent's history.

Gallenkamp, C. 1985. *Maya: The Riddle and Rediscovery of a Lost Civilization*. 3rd rev. ed. New York: Viking Press. Original work published 1959. Still useful as an overview of what we understood when.

Harding, S. 1991. *Whose Science? Whose Knowledge?* Ithaca, N.Y.: Cornell University Press. Excellent for those who are willing to have their minds stretched by careful arguments.

Richards, P. 1978. "Spatial Organization and Social Change in West Africa—Notes for Historians and Archaeologists." In *The Spatial Organization of Culture*, edited by J. Hodder. London: Duckworth. The whole book is worth reading.

Robertshaw, P., ed. 1990. *A History of African Archaeology*. London: J. Currey. A cautionary tale, to warn those who "already know."

R. J. Sharer. 1994. *The Ancient Maya*. 5th ed. Stanford, CA: Stanford University Press. Completely rewritten with new data; replaces S. Morley's (1938) book of the same title and publisher.

16

Architectural Decision Making

New architecture grows from the idea bank of former architectural ideas that builders possess, an idea bank that is the basis for architectural decision making. One kind of decision making involves the reuse and concomitant evolution of symbols and concepts. The other is original creation.

Two examples of reuse come from Rome and one from India. The first is the vault or dome. The Romans and the Byzantines after them made many innovations in covering space with vaults. The rounded shape took on imperial connotations and then came to symbolize Christian religious power. Later, Islamic architects adapted it for both purposes but with variations in shape. The mosques of West Africa allude to the domed form but are roofed in mud, not stone, requiring entirely different structural arrangements. This combination of old and new ideas shows how architecture renews itself.

The urban portico is another Roman form, set free from its early use on exteriors of temples and interiors of courtyards to stretch out along a city's major streets. Medieval Europeans continued to build such porticoes; later the Renaissance Spanish carried this architectural practice to the cities of the New World, where, despite local variations in form, it continued to signify important public space for the new hybrid culture, part Native American and part Spanish.

Even more drastic changes of form followed the migration of the stupa from India to Southeast Asia and then northeast to China and Japan. What had begun as a semisphere acquired a mastlike pinnacle. Later the sphere shrank and the pinnacle grew. As the pinnacle acquired elaborations and was subdivided into stages that became separate stories, the vertical form dominated and the hemisphere became a flat base. Over about fifteen hundred years, the pagoda became a separate building type, but its use and meaning refer back to its stupa origin (see Chapter 1, the Stupa).

Originality appears in architecture whenever builders develop new architectural solutions to the needs of human life. In both modern and traditional cultures, some practitioners of the building arts are notable for their originality. The sixteenth-century Turkish master-architect Sinan, widely recognized for the excellence of his work, was a prolific builder of mosques, palaces, aqueducts, and fortifications for the Ottoman rulers of Turkey, especially in and near their capital at Istanbul. He represents the many creative builders of pre-Industrial Revolution architecture.

ADAPTATION

Builders may adapt entire buildings, parts of buildings, or ideas about buildings to serve new uses for new peoples.

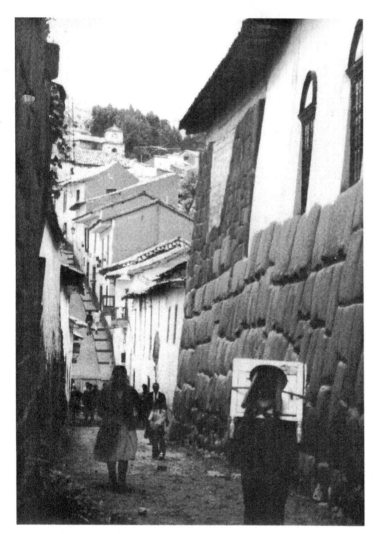

Figure 16.1. *Cuzco, Peru. At eye level, Cuzco is still Inka. Here, a Spanish Colonial building sits atop ancient Inka walls. The large, interlocked stones of the lower wall—probably the wall of a palace of an aristocratic lineage—contrast strongly with the stucco finish of the lighter wall above.*

Some buildings in this volume exemplify adaptive reuse, and we review them briefly here. Then we examine the dome, seeing how different combinations of construction materials and methods produced different solutions; the portico, a European architectural motif adapted for use in the hybrid cultures of Latin America; and the stupa, noteworthy for the metamorphosis of a religious concept and memorial intention into different architectural forms.

Symbols and Concepts—A Review

As architectural ideas turn up in new contexts, they become new through the process of adaptation. Builders of various cultures or periods see the idea differently, use it to solve different problems, shift it a little, change the emphasis, and can rightly claim originality in the result.

Some of the buildings we have discussed reveal how builders have reused an original concept or given a building a new set of uses unconnected to its original purpose:

Artificial caves. Perhaps the most unexpected result of human fascination with caves has been the manufacture of artificial caves in the cliff faces of India, such as those at Lomas Rishi and Karli.

Granary as treasury. Japanese Shinto shrines, such as the one at Ise, have preserved the ancient granary form and added to it a second similar function as treasure house, the storage place for valuable items given to the shrine and treasures of the imperial family. Private families also have treasure houses.

Incorporated walls. Inca walls and platforms in Cuzco became parts of Spanish Colonial buildings. It is easier to reuse than to move large, heavy stones—and if they are exquisitely finished and handsome, like Inca stonework, there is all the more reason to reuse them. The Spanish conquerors were pragmatists; their reuse of the walls and platforms they found in Cuzco and elsewhere in Peru was based on convenience. For ideological reasons, however, they made a point of replacing Inca temples with Christian churches (see Figures 8.11, 8.12 and 16.1).

Multicultural transfer. Like the Austronesian contributions to the Japanese language, the Polynesian house type reused in Japan offers an important clue to the place of Japan in the millennia-long colonization of the Pacific Ocean islands. The house type was an ecologically reasonable solution for the southernmost islands of Japan, but markedly less satisfactory in the northern parts of the archipelago. Not all reuses are reasonable and beneficial.

Pragmatic solutions transformed into tourist attractions. Houseboats, originally homes for those who were too poor to live on land, were copied in elegant versions for the tourist trade, especially since the mid-nineteenth century in Kashmir, but also on the rivers of China, although less so on the South China coast. The royal burial ground and religious center of Nan Madol in the Caroline Islands and the stone ruins of Zimbabwe in East Africa have more recently been turned over to the tourist trade.

Conversion to a museum. In a process not unlike "touristization," the Chinese government has turned the Potala Palace in Lhasa, Tibet, once the home and governmental center of the Dalai Lama, into the country's central museum. Before war began in the 1970s, the Cambodian funerary temple of Angkor Wat functioned as a de facto museum for many Buddhas and other religious statues found in the countryside. Part of the Chinese city of Suzhou, containing the elaborate gardens of upper-middle-class houses, is now a sort of national park, heavily patronized by both local people and visitors.

One form with multiple evolutions. Shelves attached to walls still appear in Hawaiian traditional houses. We do not know how ancient this form is, but there seem to be other descendants—such as the tokonoma—from the original Oceanic house with shelves and niches. Malay houses, for example, have bed niches known to be descended from an original Polynesian house type. The pagoda is another variable form, like the Chinese-Indian version in Nepal (see Fig. 16.2).

Taboo area. Mount Taylor, which we discussed as a sacred place needing no human constructions, retains its sacred function while accommodating modern uranium mines—both tabu. Some think this is not an improvement.

Grid-planned city. Chang'an (modern Xian) was an early capital of China. Builders in Beijing, China, and Heijo, Japan, deliberately copied its form, which meant "imperial capital." In both cases, though, the new users modified the original plan. The grid plan of Teotihuacán, a Native American center in Mexico, developed independently.

Symbolism. The Taj Mahal, that supremely Islamic tomb, not only reuses a dome based on earlier Islamic copies of Roman domes, but punctuates the four corners of the base with towers topped by "stupa" forms that refer to the ancient use of the stupa as an Indian funerary monument. Many builders have reused and adapted the dome as a symbol of power.

Translated forms. Builders have found ways to reuse a form even though they must use new materials. In the absence of masonry or concrete, West Africans have used mud-brick and vegetable materials for the arched roofs of mosques and palaces.

Changing economics. Once the lowest floor of the Newari town house in Nepal was convenient for stabling animals and storing heavy items like agricultural tools or bulky products. Today, with more emphasis on trade and commerce, many ground floors are shops (see Fig. 10.4).

Renovation of dormant forms. The Sri Lankan government has recently refurbished ancient and medieval Sri Lankan water tanks or reservoirs, which had been allowed to decay or even go out of use. The storage of water for nonpotable uses—bathing, irrigation, and the like—increases the productivity of the land.

Reuse of decorative concepts. The women painters of the Ndebele in South Africa have transferred the decorations of their houses to shops. The government has provided small shops in the hope of stimulating markets, and the women "take possession" by painting the shops in characteristic vivid patterns, reusing an idea and skills instead of a building or building type.

Sites. Even a site can be reused ceremonially. The Ise shrine in Japan is really two sites side by side. Every twenty years or so, builders erect a completely new manifestation of the shrine on site A and tear down the one on site B (see the discussion later in this chapter and Fig. 17.1).

The architecture of the future will have more old ideas, from more parts of the world, in its idea bank. If architecture can incorporate the Taoist concept of intangibility, the anthropomorphism of the Batammaliba, and other non-Euro-American ideas that are waiting to be noticed, then we may begin to create a more interesting and satisfying built environment.

Domes of Stone in Islamic Architecture

The dome—a roof that is usually hemispherical but can be pointed or bulbous—is one of the most important

Figure 16.2. *Street scene, Bhaktapur, Nepal. The shrine at the center and another to the right behind it are much smaller than the temple at the rear, and all three are causally juxtaposed to the fabric shop in the left foreground shrine. The mixture of mundane and sacred is typical of every street and open space in each of the three cities of the Kathmandu Valley.*

structural elements in the history of building practice. The Mesopotamians and Egyptians may have placed domed roofs of thatch or sun-dried brick on their circular huts in the second millennium B.C.E. The Greeks used barrel vaults, but about the third century B.C.E., the Romans rotated the arch to form a dome after learning arch building from the Etruscans; they then exploited this architectural feature to its fullest potential. Persians of the Sassanian period (ca. 226–640 C.E.) also built with hemispherical or ovoid domes, a construction method introduced by the ancient Parthians.

Symbolically, domes represent the vault of heaven, a cosmological reference appreciated by both Romano-Byzantine and Islamic cultures. A distinctive feature of these domed structures is the large interior space unencumbered by columns, piers, or supporting walls. Muslims found these interiors well suited to Eastern Islam's spatial requirements for prayer and liturgy, and domed congregational mosques and universities became the hallmark of Eastern Muslim architecture (see Chapter 10).

The Roman dome easily fits over a circular base. When a dome was to sit atop a square or rectangular base, however, the transition from dome to base presented a problem. This difficulty was solved by the invention of the squinch in Persia and of the pendentive in Syria. Both were perfected by the sixth century C.E., when Byzantine architects used squinches and/or pendentives to support domes. A squinch consists of lintels, arches, or corbels that bridge the angles of a square, providing a foundation across the four corners and using wall segments to support the dome. Pendentives are curved triangles of masonry built up at the corners of the base to form a circular arch that supports the dome (see Fig. 16.3).

The Roman Pantheon (ca. 125 C.E.), a concrete cylinder topped by a hemisphere, represents one stage in the development of the dome. Gravity causes domes to exert immense downward and outward pressures, and the Romans counteracted the pressures of the great weight of this and other domes by building thick supporting walls. This simple but structurally sophisticated form was the

conceptual ancestor of the massive dome of the rectangular Byzantine church of Hagia Sophia (532–37 C.E.). Byzantine architects modified the Pantheon model by using pendentives and other methods to support their domes and to accommodate the quadrilateral base upon which the Byzantine church domes rested. Their sixth-century domes, in turn, inspired the monumental domed buildings of the later Ottoman Empire in the fourteenth through sixteenth centuries, discussed later in this chapter. The Romans solved the problem of providing interior lighting without weakening the spherical dome when they used a single opening (oculus) in the Pantheon dome. From the sixth century on, Byzantine builders constructed domes with a ring of windows at their base to illuminate the otherwise dark interiors. The Dome of the Rock, however; is wooden (see Fig. 16.4).

Although it is not a mosque, the Dome of the Rock in Jerusalem discussed previously, is the oldest surviving Islamic monumental domed structure (692 C.E.). It is an octagonal building with two ambulatories surrounding a sacred rock (see Fig. 16.4). The structure has great religious significance for Muslims, Christians, and Jews and served as a model for later Islamic domed buildings.

The successful use of pendentives also inaugurated a succession of buildings with domed roofs, especially in countries and areas that fell under Muslim rule: North Africa, Spain, India, Egypt, Persia, and Turkey. Builders developed domes of various shapes—pointed, bulbous, and ribbed. The Taj Mahal (see Chapter 9) is one of the most celebrated pointed domes (Fig. 9.12).

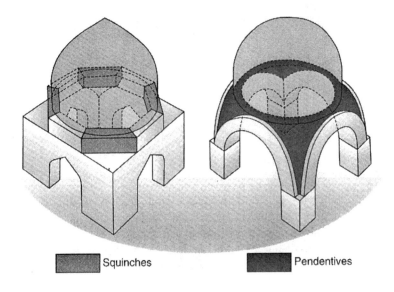

Squinches   Pendentives

Figure 16.3. *Architectural supports for domes. Squinches* (left) *bridge the angles of a square base to form an octagonal support for a small dome or drum. Pendentives* (right) *are built up spherical triangles arising from the four corners of base supports and are primarily used in Byzantine and Islamic construction to carry the weight of monumental domes to the ground.*

Figure 16.4. *Dome of the Rock, Jerusalem (begun 688). The double-shell timber dome rests on arches forming a stone arcade. The arcaded aisles surrounding the dome form an octagonal plan. The exterior was originally ornamented with mosaic and gold, replaced with tiles in the sixteenth century.*

The continued practice of building massively domed structures to enclose large, unemcumbered interior spaces has resulted in such architectural monuments as Santa Maria del Fiore, in Florence (1420); St. Paul's Cathedral, London (1675); and the U.S. Capitol, Washington, D.C. (1855).

SOURCES: GRABAR (1976), KOSTOF (1985).

OLD TRADITIONS, NEW MATERIALS: NORTH AND WEST AFRICA

As we noted in the discussion of early North African mosques (see Chapter 7), Muslims found it necessary to borrow and adapt building techniques and concepts because their nomadic heritage provided no architectural models in stone. New and unprecedented architectural and decorative forms emerged from this amalgamation. Archaeogist A. Segal cites many Roman settlements and buildings in Muslim lands such as Alexandria, Antioch, Damascus, Gerasa, Philadelphiaa, and Philippoppollis, which provided Islamic builders with models of structures, such as domed bath complexes. Islamic builders combined Roman ideas with Eastern Muslim ones. Later, Islamic architects drew on early Christian and Byzantine structures as well to expand the possibilities of domed structures beyond those known to any earlier cultures.

When Islam reached West Africa at the end of the medieval era, the Hausa people of Nigeria already had a lively tradition of mud architecture for houses, ramparts, and sanctuaries. Their builders tackled the problem of producing a mosque that would satisfy the ritual requirements in circumstances quite unlike those in the Near East and North Africa. The biggest difference was that the Nigerian construction tradition used mud, not stone, in roofing the mosques.

Communities in more central Saharan regions, such as Chad, had made some efforts to import builders from the northeast and to develop a local method of building with burned brick. But what developed in Nigeria was a monumental architecture closer to the indigenous past, such as was also found on the southern, desert fringes of Tunisia (see Figs. 16.5 and 16.6). In the Friday Mosque at Zaira, the builders reinforced the walls and the span connecting the walls and roof with wood beams laid in two directions. Some pieces radiate from the roof into the wall, while others are embedded in the length of the wall. A white-painted interior both lightens the space visually and symbolizes holiness. Decorative plasterwork on piers, walls, and ceilings bounces the light around the surfaces. The interior remains dim, however—the nature and weight of the materials required builders to keep windows and doors to a minimum—and this dimness speaks to the mysteries of the religious experience.

SOURCES: DE MONTÉQUIN (1983B), MOUGHTIN (1964), PRUSSIN (1986, 1994), SEGAL (1981).

USE AND REUSE OF ARCHITECTURAL FORMS

A simple concept like a row of posts with beams across the top can have many uses, many details of decoration, and associated meanings, as well as many names. In this section, we look at the portico, often thought of as a Mediterranean or European concept, but appearing early in Asian and American cultures, as we reflect on the transmission of culture. Considering the stupa, whose transformation into the pagoda seems to defy the usual processes of architectural evolution, we take into consideration the transmission of religion. In both cases, the ripples of change returned to their origins and wrought further changes.

Porticoes of the Old and New Worlds—Traditional?

Like the courtyards of the American Southwest (see Chapter 11), the porticoes discussed here represent a hybrid architectural tradition, now five hundred years old, that fused European and Native American ideas. Beginning in Tenochtitlán/Mexico City in the 1520s, the incoming Spanish worked out how to use, reuse, rebuild, and replace the Aztec architecture of their new conquest. They left the existing open space at the heart of the city, but added to it the porticoes of European tradition.

A portico is a horizontal, linear structure with a back wall, a roof, and a row of columns supporting the front edge of the roof. Straight beams usually link the columns at the top, but the version called the arcade has arches. The portico's solid back wall may consist of the front walls of buildings behind the portico, or it may be simply a screen wall that either separates the roofed portico from an inner space open to the sky or acts as retaining wall to a hillside. The Greek stoa, a linear building faced by a colonnade and often incorporating small shops on the ground floor and offices above, was the ancestor of the portico.

Porticoes are a common feature of urban design in Mediterranean lands. They surround public plazas and line important streets. Since antiquity, they have been linked to public space. The Greco-Romans used street porticoes in Syria and slightly later in Rome, in the first centuries B.C.E. and C.E. During the Middle Ages, the portico continued to have the same uses and meanings, although often with pointed arches. An associated medieval form was the monastic cloister, a courtyard formed by the portico; this colonnaded courtyard remained in use into the nineteenth century (see Chapter 11, Hollow Centers). Europeans were not the only ones to use these forms. The portico became an integral part of the architectural vocabulary of the Muslim world.

In a climate with brilliant sunshine and torrential rain, the portico offers important protection from the weather. Yet this is not its only advantage. The portico also gives

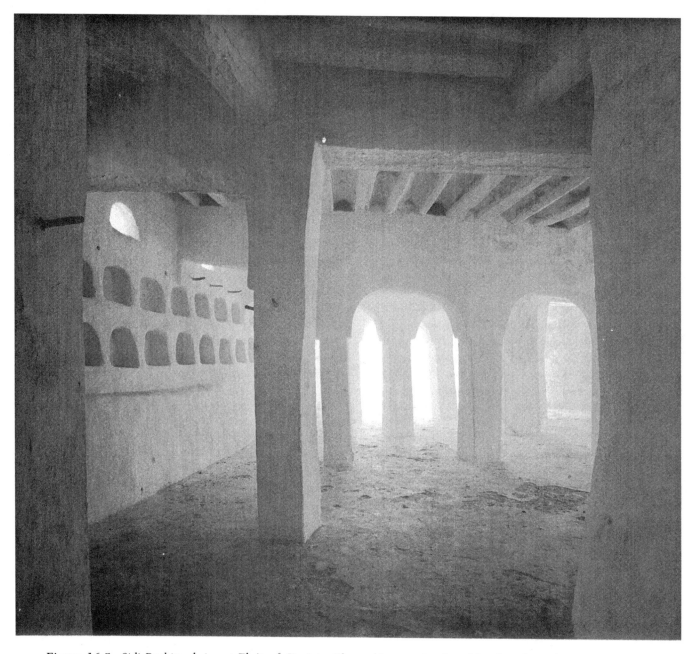

Figure 16.5. *Sidi Brahim shrine at El Ateuf, Tunisia. The architecture is of mud brick and wood, painted white inside and out. The niches add decorative shadows to the interior walls.*

unity to the street, plaza, or courtyard that it serves, for it produces rhythm by the use of columns along the sides of a plaza. Through the alternation of sunlit columns with shadowy spaces, simple elements produce a rich architectural experience. Large and small businesses, civic of-

fices, houses, shrines, eating places, and other buildings can be grouped behind the portico.

The Romans carried the architectural concept of the portico to Spain. The importation into Spain of Italian Renaissance ideas in the sixteenth century renewed the im-

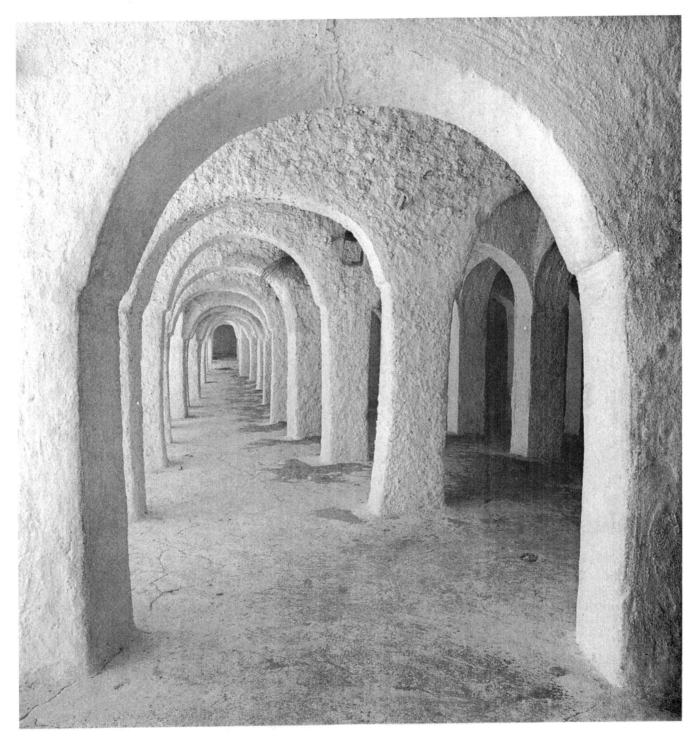

Figure 16.6. *Beni Isguen mosque, in Tunisia. The visual effect of the forest of columns results from structural necessity: mud brick is a weak support and must be multiplied as well as reinforced with wood. This mosque is built partially into a hillside.*

Figure 16.7. *Aerial view of the plaza, Salamanca, Spain. An eighteenth-century construction, this plaza reflects the development of regular plazas in the New World during the previous two hundred years. The colonnaded courtyard has six gateways leading to the city. It inserts a Renaissance rationality into a dense medieval urban fabric.*

portance of the portico. Both small villages and major cities of Spain have at least vestiges of public porticoes. An excellent example is the Plaza Mayor of Salamanca in Spain (see Fig. 16.7). For seventy years, beginning in 1729, the city fathers renovated the buildings surrounding the plaza, creating the perfect achievement—unrivaled in elegance, unity, and refined simplicity, perfect in the proportions of height to plaza area and in articulation of the buildings. The porticoes give the edges of the spacious

plaza the appearance of one continuous building, "an unending arcade of great architectural beauty," according to novelist J. A. Michener. Cafés that spill over into the plaza, bookstores for the university students, lawyers' offices, fine shops, and many other urban facilities share the porticoed buildings around the plaza, and all look out to the middle of the plaza. Passersby and those seated at tables become "scenery" for each other, and much informal education and business takes place through casual encounters in this enclosed space. Two large gateways interrupt the north and south arcades, while the east and west sides have one gateway each.

In traditional societies outside Europe, the portico was often an imported design feature. Such is certainly the case in Mexico City, where the Spanish transformed the main plaza during the sixteenth and early seventeenth centuries. When Hernán Cortés and his men arrived in 1521,

they found the plaza so large that it could have held five hundred houses. Pyramidal temple-platforms crowned with fire altars, long narrow houses for several thousand priests and attendants, schools for boys and girls, granaries, and storehouses were set in a paved, walled area next to Montezuma's palace (see Fig. 16.8). There was also a large mansion for visiting dignitaries, where the Aztecs lodged Cortés and his captains.

The plaza suffered the same destruction as the rest of the city during the battles for possession of the site in the 1520s. When the Spanish finally controlled the city, they made a series of changes to the main plaza. Plans and drawings from this period mirror these changes for us (see Fig. 16.9).

The earliest drawing, made by a fifteenth-century Aztec, shows the plaza surrounded by a wall with gateways that encloses six temple-platforms (see Fig. 16.7). By 1562–66, when the second drawing was made, the temples and their platforms were no more, the stones having been used to build the cathedral. Cortes's palace had taken the place of Montezuma's central palace (see Fig. 16.8). The open space itself is the only part of the Aztec plaza that remains. Porticoes and the cathedral claimed the central plaza for the new population, with new demands and expectations of urban form. This population and its architectural forms were hybrid, as architectural historian N. Neuerberg demonstrated for the later California missions.

The porticoes of the plazas embodied in their enduring physical form the cultural systems of Greco-Romans, medieval Christians, Muslims, and Renaissance Europeans. Later, porticoes signified the new culture that the Spaniards and the Native American peoples produced together. Domes and porticoes are only two of the many architectural forms that the Europeans copied and adapted in new settings (see Chapter 8 on Cuzco's transformation).

SOURCES: BOETHIUS (1960); CROUCH, GARR, AND MUNDIGO (1984), FIGS. 12–14; GUTKIND (1967); J. A. MICHENER (1968); NEUERBERG (1977); PRESCOTT (1856), 337–39.

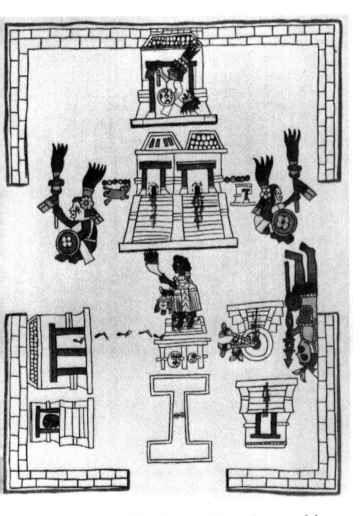

Figure 16.8. *A fifteenth-century Aztec drawing of the central plaza of Tenochtitlán (Mexico City). The walled plaza includes six temples or shrines, an I-shaped ball court, a skull rack, and a dance platform. Blood from human sacrifices stains the steps of three pyramids, and bloody footsteps lead from one shrine to the skull rack and dance platform. Four people are shown participating in a ritual, and what is probably a giant statue guards the entranceway at the right.*

Stupas Become Pagodas

As it moved through time and across geographic space, the rounded hemisphere of the stupa became the elongated tower of the pagoda, yet it kept the same meaning for its Buddhist builders. Architecture was essential to the Buddhist presence in many different societies. Those who made decisions about Buddhist construction clung to the idea of the axis that connects the earth, human life, and the heavens, but they expressed their ad-

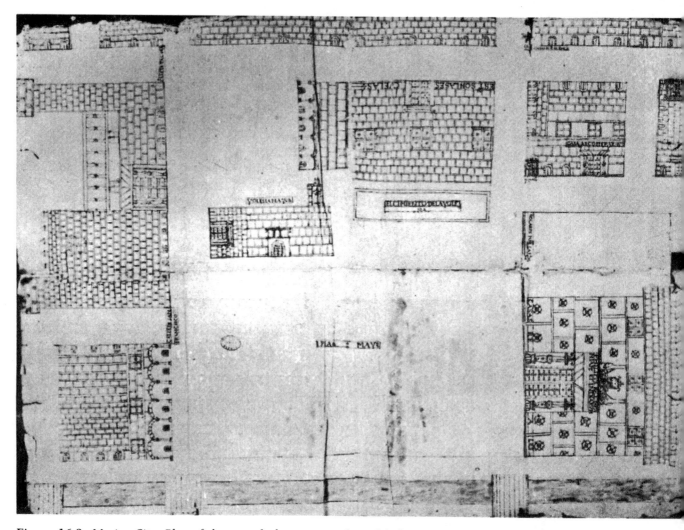

Figure 16.9. *Mexico City. Plan of the central plaza as transformed before 1562–66 and renamed Plaza Mayor; this is typical of plans sent to the Council of the Indies in Seville to report on management of the Spanish empire. Porticoes edge one end of this plaza and the lesser plaza of the cathedral to the left. This arrangement became the prototype for many Spanish Colonial plazas.*

herence to this concept in a kaleidoscope of changing forms. For this reason, although the central beliefs of expanding Buddhism were unchanged through time and across cultures, the appearance of buildings varied according to local traditions and the aspect of Buddhism being emphasized.

In Chapter 1 we examined the earliest Indian stupas, derived from earlier burial mounds. The oldest extant example at Sanchi consisted of a square platform with a large, solid, hemispherical superstructure supporting a relatively small, treelike pillar or mast. In early times, the stupa sym-

bolized nirvana of the Buddha, or a saint, symbolized by a relic and by the form of the structure and it commemorated the life and teaching of Buddha.

Over time, stupas shed their funeral connotations and related rather to mystical concepts. The central post of the original stupa or the extended upright form of the later pagoda carried the consistent meaning "world axis." This architectural entity was the confluence of visible and invisible concepts, and believers experienced the architecture with eyes and spirits attuned to both. Whereas Westerners have postulated an evolution from the hemisphere to the tower (see Fig. 16.10a), Asians have expected that sometimes the rounded form of world-within-world and sometimes the axis that is the path to enlightenment would be tangibly present. They were prepared to read both meanings from whichever architectural element they saw (see Fig. 16.10b).

Of all the variations on the stupa, the pagodas of China, Korea, and Japan differ most strikingly from the original form. These towers developed from small single- or multi-story watchtowers of the Han Dynasty (206 B.C.E.–220 C.E.) into three main variants. One is a tall tower with a smooth stone skin. Another is the multistory, multieave timber tower. The third is also multistoried and multieaved but is made of masonry. The second and third types appeared in the sixth century; people stopped building the timber towers in the nineteenth century but continue to build the masonry ones.

a.

b.

Figure 16.10. *Evolution of Buddhist stupas.* **a.** *Variation from original domed/egg form to world-axis/mountains forms. Left to right: Indian stupa like Sanchi, third to first century* B.C.E.; *Indian stupa, second century* C.E. *and later; Chinese masonry pagoda, fifth to seventh century* C.E. *and later; and Japanese pagoda, seventh century and later, based on Chinese (and possibly Korean) prototypes.* **b.** *Analytical semicircles enclosing a domed stupa (left) and a tower-stupa (right). To the believer, the egg and the mountain forms exist in both buildings, but different parts are visible. The dome is the world egg in which the invisible mountain-axis is contained; the tower is the mountain contained in an invisible egg. In both, the progression is from the physical layers of ordinary worlds below to less tangible layers of metaphysical worlds above.*

The timber towers resemble the Nepalese temples of Patan Durbar Square (see Chapter 12). An early Chinese example was a nine-story pagoda at the capital Loyang, known from written descriptions of its wooden frame. Built in 516 C.E., it was 1,000 feet tall (about 300 meters), including its mast, which represented the cosmic tree that grows from the sum-

mit of Mount Meru. (Compare with Fig. 16.11, the pagoda at Ying Xian and Fig. 16.12, a pagoda model).

From the time the Chinese built the earliest wooden pagodas, they were translating and transforming Indian and Tibetan Buddhist ideas into a Chinese building idiom. At first, the pagoda stood alone, the main building of a

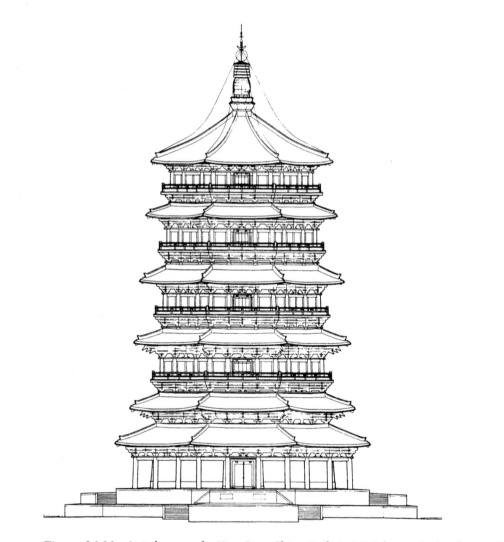

Figure 16.11. *A timber pagoda, Ying Sian, China. Built in 1056 during the brief Mongolian dynasty of Liao, this timber pagoda, part of a Buddhist monastery, is about 100 feet (over 67 meters) high, the tallest wooden structure in China—an early masterpiece. The pagoda has wide eaves that indicate six stories, although there are ten interior stories. The building achieves harmony and structural unity by maintaining the octagonal shape at each level and by strong roof lines that emphasize the horizontality of the stories, which thereby balance the upward thrust of the height.*

temple precinct. Later architects adapted it to a layout that resembled the plans of an imperial palace, displacing the pagoda from the center of the temple grounds and replacing it with an icon hall similar to the imperial audience hall. This hall was often flanked by not one but two pagoda towers; twin pagodas diluted the significance of the singular form as the unique world axis. At some Chinese sites, the pagoda was demoted to the status of a mere gate-tower. In the long run, these alterations may be considered victories of the Chinese secular state over a foreign religion.

The wooden pagoda was the only Chinese building type that was exclusively religious, although it was a product of secular builders, elements, and techniques. Ancient sources as quoted by J. Needham repeat a story about the master builder Yu Hao, who built the Khai-Pao Pagoda in Kaifung in 989 C.E. About ten years later, Yu Hao gave useful advice to another artisan-architect:

> When Chien Wei-Yen was governor of the two Chekiang provinces, he authorized the building of a wooden pagoda at the Brahma-Heaven Temple in Hangchow, with a design of six stories. While it was under construction General Chien went to the top and was worried because it swayed a little. But the Master-Builder explained that as the tiles had not yet been put on, the upper part was still rather light, hence the effect. So then they put on all the tiles, but the sway continued as before. Being at a loss what to do, he privately sent his wife to see the wife of Yu Hao with a present of golden hairpins, and (to) inquire about the cause of the motion. (Yu) Hao laughed and said: "That's easy, just fit in struts to settle the work, fixed with (iron) nails, and it will not move any more." The Master-Builder followed his advice and the tower stood quite firm. This is because the nailed struts filled in and bound together (all the members) up and down so that the six planes [above and below, front and back, left and right] were mutually linked like the cage of the thorax. Although people might walk on the struts, the six planes grasped and supported each other, so naturally there could be no more motion. Everybody acknowledged the expertise shown.

Figure 16.12. *Chinese jade pagoda (ca. 1795). This model is said to have been made for the Manchu emperor of China, Ch'ien-lung (reigned 1735–96), to celebrate the birth of his heir. Carved entirely of jade, in pale green and delicate gray, it is about 8 feet tall. In type, it strongly resembles the timber pagoda (Fig. 16.11).*

J. Needham, historian of Chinese science and technology, comments, "Surely we have to deal here with slanting struts inserted in an otherwise purely rectangular reticulum—[that is,] diagonal wind bracing." This is a good example of innovation in traditional building.

The timber pagoda type from early in the Common

Era, now rare in China, traveled to Japan with Chinese and Korean Buddhist missionaries and became the prototype for the late-seventh-century wooden Horyu-ji tower (see Chapter 1, Fig. 1.10) and many others. A central pagoda, such as Horyu-ji, served in place of both stupa and icon hall, its ground-floor area occupied not by the mast of the world axis but by statues of Buddha carrying the same meaning. The mast, which originally penetrated the entire building from its base in the relic chamber deep below the ground, still functioned as the central beam to which the upper levels of the pagoda were tied when it

was later cut off above the ground story. Just so, in stupas, the mast could penetrate deep into the ground, be embedded in the mass of the stupa, or merely penetrate the upper skin of the hemisphere.

China's first architectural historian, S. Liang noted non-Chinese pagoda forms, the "bottle shaped" (Sinhalese or Mongol) pagodas (see Fig. 16.13) and the "Vajra-based" pagodas like the Ananda Temple in Myanmar (see Fig. 1.11 a, b and c). These types testify to the historical influence of non-Chinese Buddhism as far north as Beijing, an influence that still persists.

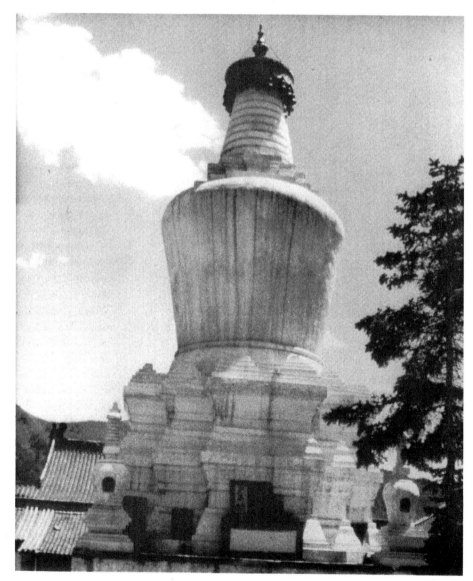

Figure 16.13. *Miao-Ying Ssu (stupa), Beijing, China. Built in 1271, this vertically elongated bell-shaped stupa shows a Mongol influence. It stands in the gardens near the palaces of the Forbidden City.*

Adaptation can mean something tangible, such as building a strong masonry core to lift the central tower-stupa high on the roof of the Ananda Temple. Or it can be as intangible as attributing the meaning "civic space" to a public portico. Reuse can motivate a group of builders, as when the newly sedentary Muslims of the late seventh and eighth centuries C.E. learned to erect domes by studying Roman and Byzantine buildings and working with people who were trained in old methods. Through adaptation, builders may produce something new that looks old or something old that looks new. What matters is how the people of the new society will use the architecture—and how well it will satisfy them.

SOURCES: LEDDEROSE (1980), 238–42; S. LIANG (1984); NEEDHAM (1971), 141; SECKEL (1964), 249; SNODGRASS (1985).

ORIGINALITY: THE TURKISH ARCHITECT SINAN

Many of the traditional architectural forms we have discussed were planned and built by craftsmen whose names are unknown to us, who learned building skills through apprenticeships in guilds or received knowledge handed down within extended family groups. In contrast to their anonymity, we now turn to one of the greatest and best-known architects of the Turkish world, one whose originality and accomplishments have earned him the high esteem of architectural scholars throughout the world.

Koca Sinan, better known as Sinan the Great, served from 1538 to his death in 1588 as chief architect to three Ottoman rulers: first, to the powerful Suleyman I, called the Magnificent, one of the most powerful Ottoman rulers of the sixteenth century, and then to Suleyman's son Selim II and his grandson, Murat III.

In 1512 the twenty-year-old Sinan was recruited to serve in the elite Turkish military corps called the Janissaries. Under the system known as *devsirme* (a form of tax on Christians), the brightest and most physically fit non-Muslim youths were taken from their families to become Muslims and trained, not only to learn military skills but to serve in civil service positions. At that time, Sinan lived in the village of Aginas near Kaseri not far from Thessaloniki (N. Greece) in the Ottoman empire. The Janissaries offered more opportunities than the life of poverty and menial labor that was the usual lot of youths in the outlying districts of the empire.

After eight or nine years with the Janissaries, during which time he learned carpentry skills, Sinan saw military action in Belgrade (1521) and Rhodes (1522) and received military commissions serving as captain of the Royal Guard and commander of the Infantry Cadet Corps. His participation in important campaigns attracted the attention of Sultan Suleyman I, and in 1538, the sultan appointed him Architect of the Abode of Felicity—that is, court architect. Architecture might seem an abrupt change from soldiering, but Sinan had some engineering experience during his military service. Architectural historian G. Goodwin points out that Sinan assisted in the building of bridges for the transport of artillery and constructed military defenses, proving himself adept in areas that required engineering skills. The respect that he had gained as a military leader, together with his experience in practical building projects, such as converting Christian churchs into mosques, made him a likely candidate when the post of court architect became available.

Sinan held that post for more than fifty years, living and building into his nineties. Architectural historians have estimated that he built or supervised the construction of more than one hundred mosques and numerous palaces, schools, hospitals, public baths, bridges, and aqueducts. His official capacity also included overseeing public works and supplying architects and workers for the many projects under his control that he had little time to direct personally.

What formal education in the building arts did he have for such an array of projects? Very little, but during his war campaigns, he visited most of southeastern Europe and the Middle East, and had the opportunity to see or study the architecture of major cities, such as Baghdad, Tabriz, Cairo, and Belgrade. He lived and worked in Istanbul for the greater part of his life and visited other important Turkish cities, such as Edirne, an early Ottoman capital. His first major work was the Shezade (also Sehzade) mosque in 1543. As was generally true of architectural training everywhere until the late nineteenth century, the practice of architecture was pragmatic; plans were simple and buildings were based on earlier examples. Sinan learned by observing and doing. Experience and his native talent eventually produced numerous architectural masterpieces.

Before Sinan, Turkish architecture was simple in plan, with a strong reliance on traditional construction skills and standardization of measurements and materials. Interest in innovation was scant. Scholars agree that Sinan's originality lay in going beyond the expectations of his craft and his patron to unite the Asiatic and European traditions of architecture into buildings of unprecedented harmony.

In designing those many mosques, Sinan neither repeated his major works (the Shezade, Istanbul; the Suleymaniye, Istanbul; and the Selimiye, Edirne) nor clung to early solutions. As Islamist scholars have observed his mosques reveal two main approaches to design: those influenced by architectural ideas from the West and those from the East or southeast—Roman, Greek, Persian, Syrian, Byzantine, and Austro-Hungarian. Among the Western-influenced mosques were the nearly square plans with a single dome on four supports and those with a dome supported by two opposite half-domes and four piers (Suleymaniye, based most likely on the Byzantine Hagia Sophia, and the Bayazit II, both in Istanbul); those with four half-domes on four supports (Shezade, Istanbul, based on Fatihpasha in Diyarbakir); and those with eight supports (the Selimiye, based on the Byzantine church of Saints Sergius and Bacchus in Istanbul). A key architectural idea from the eastern and southern parts of the Ottoman Empire, where Islam had ruled for nine hundred years, was the long qibla wall (see Chapter 7) set in a rectangular plan. Combined with this wall were multiple domes (Piyalepasha in Istanbul, based on Ulucami in Bursa and Eskicami in Edirne), one or three half-domes on four supports (Üsküdar-Mihrimah-Sultan in Bursa), and single domes with six supports (Sokollu-Kadirga in Istanbul, probably from Üchsherefeli in Edirne).

Christian domed churches throughout the Islamic world had become mosques after the Islamic conquest. Older buildings and ruins from Roman times also offered examples of arch and vault construction. Thus, the dome, a derivative of the arch, became a common element in Ottoman architecture. The most important example of a church-turned-mosque in Istanbul was the Hagia Sophia, or Church of Holy Wisdom, built by Anthemius of Tralles and Isidorus of Miletus in the sixth century C.E. The building centered on a large space, capped by a monumental dome. Scholars differ on the extent of its influence on Sinan's work, but it would be naive to ignore its stimulus to his architectural thought and practice. For his own Suleymaniye (1550–57), he probably noted but redesigned the Byzantine support system and generally produced a better-engineered but arguably less intriguing edifice than the great predecessor. Sinan reportedly considered the Suleymaniye masterly but not his greatest work. A family friend's memoirs quote Sinan's own evaluation: "In the Shezade he [Sinan] proved his journeyman level; in the Suleymaniye his mastership; and he showed all his skills and capacity in the Selimiye." We examine these three complexes as definitive examples of the architect's major works.

Shezade (also Sehzade) Cami (1543–48), Istanbul

Sinan's first major commission was to build a mosque in honor of Shezade Mehmet, Suleyman's son and heir, who had died at the age of twenty-two. The structure, the Shezade Cami (a Friday, or congregational, mosque; see Fig. 16.14), consists of two nearly equal sections. Arcades with domed bays surround the square central courtyard. A fountain for ablutions stands in the center. Adjoining this area is the square prayer sanctuary of the mosque. Four massive pillars, assisted by four half-domes, support the central dome.

The Shezade differs considerably from, for example, the Hagia Sophia. The treatment of the Byzantine church focused on spatial complexity produced by domes, half-domes, arcades, and galleries—illusory vistas and symbolic, otherworldly effects. The Shezade—like mosques in general—used simply planned interiors to create a large congregational area in which the faithful could gather. One fundamental requirement of Islamic liturgy is the orientation of the mosque (see Chapter 7), with the mihrab (niche in a wall indicating the direction of prayer) in the qibla wall (the wall facing the holy city of Mecca) as the focal point. Here, the imam, or prayer leader, delivers liturgical messages to the congregation. The mosque has no need for the basilican plan required for Christian processions. Sinan designed the Shezade's interior space for maximum visibility of the minbar (pulpit) and mihrab, achieved through clarity of the spatial composition, according to J. Hoag.

The Shezade Cami is modeled after some earlier mosques, especially the Fatih Pasha at Diyarbakir, which Sinan had probably seen, which featured four small corner domes with four half-domes buttressing the main one. In the Shezade, Sinan demonstrated the sense of symmetry and concern for the harmonious relationship of parts that his later works further developed.

Suleymaniye (1550–57), Istanbul

High on a hilltop above the Golden Horn, the Suleymaniye mosque complex (Kulliye) stands as a prominent visual symbol of the achievements of Suleyman the Magnificent. (see Fig. 16.15). The Kulliye included separate buildings for theological colleges and social service centers, such as

Figure 16.14. *Shezade Cami (1543–48) Istanbul, Turkey. This magnificent mosque was Ottoman architect Sinan's first major commission. Slender minarets frame the view of the multiple domes of the mosque.*

a hospital, schools, baths, soup kitchens for the poor, and guest quarters for travelers. The mosque, at the center of the complex, represented the spiritual focal point for the charitable institutions that clustered around it, so that the provision of charity was tied to Sinan's best-known architectural work. The difficult site, sloping downward, required massive stone foundations for the buildings.

Like Hagia Sophia, Suleymaniye has two semi-domes along the main axis of the central dome, but it also has five cupolas, situated on the sides. Architectural historian J. Hoag explains that the top of the dome is approximately 174 feet (53 meters) from the ground with a diameter of 87 feet (27 meters). The central dome has 32 lights in the drum; an additional 249 windows at the base provide illumination for the broad expanse of open space under the dome. The dome's seeming lightness is deceptive. Four piers support its immense weight, and it is braced with two half-domes and two large arches that transfer the

Figure 16.15. *Suleymaniye Mosque (1550–57), Istanbul, Turkey. The mosque on its hilltop soars above the schools, hospitals, shops, cemeteries, and living quarters for governmental and religious officials that cluster around it. The structural arrangement of the mosque centers on the dome, over 85 feet (26 meters) in diameter, 170 feet (52 meters) high. The minarets are located at the four courtyard corners; two are approximately 180 feet (55 meters) high, with two balconies each, and the remaining two are almosts 250 feet (74 meters) high, with three balconies each.*

forces from the two other sides to the piers. The interior area covers a square of nearly 1,873 feet (174 meters) subdivided into sixteen units, four of which make up the central square. The outer columns are much thicker than the wall between them, so they appear as buttresses against the tremendous outward thrust.

Islamist A. Hatipoglu states that of the four minarets located at the four courtyard corners, two are approximately 180 feet (55 meters) high, with two balconies each. The other two are almost 250 feet (74 meters) high with three

balconies each. The four minarets refer to Suleyman's reign as the fourth Ottoman ruler since the conquest of Istanbul (previously Constantinople), and the ten balconies indicate that he was tenth in succession to the Ottoman throne. Sinan's orchestration of supporting members, buttresses, piers, arches and vaults, and other elements, along with his supervision of rich tiling, carving, calligraphy, and stone inlay, produced an interior space of great clarity and beauty and an exterior of great elegance and aesthetic interest.

The Suleymaniye is a prominent visual memorial to

the great ruler's achievements. It is also a metaphysical allegory. In it, Sinan symbolically achieved the union of heaven, the upper dome, with earth, the lower cube. Yet he did not regard the Suleymaniye as the culmination of his work, calling it his "mastership" but not his greatest achievement. That would come with the construction of the Selimiye mosque.

Selimiye Cami (1569–75), Edirne

After Suleyman's death, his son Selim II commissioned Sinan to build the Selimiye Cami. In doing so, the eighty-year-old architect solved one of the most vexing problems facing Turkish architects: the problem of creating large, domed, open spaces without the obstruction of massive supporting columns or piers. Sinan finally solved the problem in the Selimiye Cami by placing the supporting columns of the central dome so close to the walls that they appear to be part of the wall system. Many large windows contribute to the resulting feeling of airy lightness. At the same time, the play of light on the gold and marble surfaces "dematerialized" the massiveness of the supporting columns, seeming to dissolve the load-bearing elements and to unify the interior space (see Fig. 16.16).

From the exterior, the mosque rises in pyramidal fashion to the octagonal dome. At almost 103 feet (31 meters) in diameter and 138 feet (43 meters) high, this is the largest of the Ottoman domes. Four corner minarets, approximately 230 feet (70 meters) high, complete the impression of architectural unity among all the components

Figure 16.16. *Selimiye Cami (1569–75), Edirne, Turkey. Interior view of Sinan's masterpiece. The massive dome is supported by faceted piers and half-domes. The well-lit interior space flows from one geometrical form to another, an impressive unification of architectural elements.*

of the mosque. Many other architectural refinements, such as the integration of structural components and decoration—red stone and white marble articulate interior arches, the dramatic placement of the mihrab in an impressively large apse, and the skillful organization of all apects of the interior space—validate Sinan's reference to the Selimiye Cami as his masterpiece, for which he used all his skills and expertise.

Sinan's career has been compared with that of Michelangelo in longevity and excellence. Like Michelangelo, he was fortunate to have the support of wealthy and discerning patrons. When he died in 1588, Sinan left students and followers, but none ever achieved what he had accomplished during the classical phase of Ottoman architecture.

SOURCES: GOODWIN (1971), GRUBE (1967), HATIPOGLU (1993–94), HOAG (1987), KURAN (1987), ÖZIŞ (PERSONAL COMMUNICATION).

SUGGESTED READINGS

Dallapiccola, A. L., and S. Zingel-Avé Lallemant, eds. 1980. *The Stupa: Its Religious, Historical and Architectural Significance*. Wiesbaden, Germany: F. Steiner Verlag. The entire book is worth reading, but see especially J. Irwin. "The Axial Symbolism of the Early Stupa: An Exegesis," 12–38; H. G. Franz, "Stupa and Stupa-Temple in the Gandharan Regions and in Central Asia, 39–58; L. Ledderose. "Chinese Prototypes of the Pagoda, 238–48; and D. Seckel. "Stupa Elements Surviving in East Asian Pagodas," 249–59; Other essays discuss the development of Indian and Southeast Asian stupas. Each has a useful bibliography.

Foster, G. M. 1960. *Culture and Conquest: The American Spanish Heritage*. New York: Quadrangle Books. The process and results of colonization in the Spanish New World.

Goodwin, G. 1971. *A History of Ottoman Architecture*. Baltimore: Johns Hopkins University Press. Treats the subject with authority; excellent photographs.

Grabar, O. 1976. "The Umayyad Dome of the Rock in Jerusalem." *Islamic Art and Architecture*, Vol. 13, 33–62. New York: Garland. A detailed analysis by a noted Islamic scholar.

Kuran, A. 1987. *Sinan: The Grand Old Master of Ottoman Architecture*. Washington, D.C.: Institute of Turkish Studies. One of the best and most detailed studies of the architect Sinan; many excellent illustrations.

Lavin, I. 1980. *Bernini and the Unity of the Visual Arts*. New York: Pierpont Morgan Library and Oxford University Press. See the entire book for art history methodology in action; the chapter on the chapel dedicated to Saint Teresa of Avila (in Rome) is an exemplary treatment of architecture as the perfect setting for sculpture.

17

The Economics of Building

Are buildings meant to last? Contrast the ephemeral shelters of the Basarwa with the durable Ise Shrine in Japan, which has a different kind of durability from that of the pyramids at Teotihuacán. The latter endure because of their great massiveness; Ise has endured by being replicated approximately every twenty years for nearly two millennia.

These examples lead us to the underlying question of the costs of building. The economics of building is a suitable topic with which to complete our study because it signifies the bottom line of any architectural culture. There are several ways of evaluating building costs. One is the descriptive approach, exemplified by the court chroniclers who kept the records of income and expenditures for the Taj Mahal. These accounts offer a rare case of detailed information on the economics of premodern construction. Another method is the numerical-analytical approach of R. Bon, who studies the proportion of the gross national product that can or must be devoted to construction; this share changes as the society matures economically. The most promising approach that we have found is that of E. Abrams, who has studied Maya con-struction in terms of what he calls architectural energetics—the analysis of construction in terms of how many person-days it took to build a structure, given the procedures and tools available to the builders. This method permits cross-cultural comparisons that we think will prove highly useful.

DURABILITY: REBUILDING AT THE ISE SHRINE, JAPAN

A building's durability depends largely on its materials. The Mexican pyramids, as we noted, have endured for thousands of years because of their massiveness—and their stone facing. Architecture that is made of impermanent materials, such as wood, however, has limited durability. The Japanese have developed a unique method of faithfully preserving some of their ancient shrines by periodically reconstructing them, thus maintaining the integrity of ancient wood building forms and methods. Our example is the ancient Shinto shrine compounds in Ise Prefecture in Honshu.

There are two major shrine compounds at Ise Jingu that are located about 4 miles apart. The Outer Shrine,

Geku, is dedicated to a local god called the Great Deity of Abundant Food. The prestigious Inner, or imperial, Shrine, called the Naiku, is dedicated to the goddess Amaterasu Omikami, from whom the imperial family is believed to be descended. Y. Watanabe, an authority on Japanese architecture, relates that eighth-century court documents refer to the worship of Amaterasu Omikami beginning in the first century B.C.E. when a shrine was built for the goddess near modern-day Nara. After a time, the shrine was moved to Ise, where it has remained. Scholars have estimated that the Naiku Shrine may be dated to the fourth century. The ritual of periodic reconstruction every twenty years is intended to keep the spirit of Amaterasu alive for the Japanese people. Less is known about the origin of the Geku, except that accounts about the deity of grain were written during the Heian period (794–1185), suggesting that it was not established until the latter part of the fifth century. In addition to these two major shrines, other adjoining sanctuaries at Ise Jingu have a connection with the Naiku and the Geku, but because of the great cost, the Naiku and Geku are the only shrines in Japan that are rebuilt on a regular basis.

Watanabe explains the procedure for rebuilding: Each of these Ise compounds covers approximately 3.5 acres,

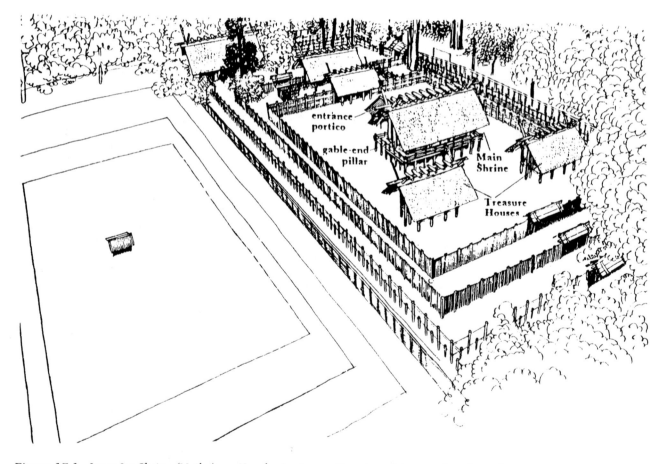

Figure 17.1. *Inner Ise Shrine (Naiku), on Honshu Is., Japan. Drawing of the complex. According to ancient ritual, the shrine was rebuilt every twenty years on an adjacent site to preserve structural continuity. A small roofed structure (left) marks the location of the earlier shrine, which was dismantled after construction of the new shrine (right) was completed. In the past, Shinto shrines were rebuilt periodically, but the Ise Shrine is the only one that is still rebuilt regularly. Besides the main building, the complex includes treasuries and storehouses.*

surrounded by a series of four fences, and each has treasuries, storehouses, gates, and a shoden (main sanctuary). The shrines are reconstructed by first dividing each into eastern and western sections (see Fig. 17.1). The shrines are located on one of these sections. Construction takes place on the empty half of the site. After the new shrine is completed, the earlier shrine is dismantled, and the empty plot is covered with white gravel. A "heart" pillar buried under the floor of the old shrine and a small protective shed over the pillar are the only signs of the former site until the next rebuilding when the process again takes place. Observers first thought that the heart pillar was a structural element, but they now recognize that it is an important religious symbol dating to a period in antiquity before such shrines were erected. The honoring of deities in the physical form of a pillar eventually developed into the building of shrines as dwellings for the gods in their visits to earth. The Ise shrines are closely connected in design to the form of the ancient storage granary (see Chapter 3). As the most prominent Japanese shrines, Ise has influenced the design of shrines since the seventh century.

According to Watanabe, the systematic reconstruction and rededication of the Ise shrines dates from 690 C.E., when the Naiku was first rebuilt. The Geku was rebuilt two years later. A document dated 804 called the *Record of Rituals for the Imperial Shrine of Ise* stipulates: "A new shrine shall be constructed once every twenty years." The Japanese have followed this dictate ever since, interrupted only once for about 130 years, starting in the late fifteenth century when war and other factors interrupted the sequence. The rebuilding program for Inner and Outer shrines were reinstated in 1585.

The passage of time brought changes to both buildings and sites. For example, an ancient construction technique that used a type of lap joint to connect notched horizontal wall planks at the corners (see Chapter 3) gave way to mortise-and-tenon joinery. As the shrines grew in importance, other modifications were made, such as the heightening of the compound fences to distance the sacred precinct from the secular world. The addition of metal fittings and other decorative elements to the buildings in later centuries further supports the notion that the shrine had attained major importance, making greater elaboration desirable.

But the shoden, or main building (see Fig. 17.2), in both precincts has changed little in style since the eighth century. Rectangular with gabled ends, it is supported on piers that raise the building several feet above ground

Figure 17.2. *Inner Ise Shrine (Naiku model). A wide step-ramp leads to the veranda and entrance on the long side of the shrine. Massive posts support the structure; the largest, at each end, prop up the ridgepole. The ornamental rafters of the gables draw attention upward, like the pinnacles of a French Gothic church.*

level. These piers do not rest on a foundation but, following ancient practice, are embedded in the earth. A veranda surrounds the structure. The entrance is on the side, rather than at one end, and is reached by a staircase. The shoden still features the *chigi*, the ancient element of rafters that cross at the gable ends over the ridge (see Fig. 17.3; compare with Indonesian forms in Fig. 10.19). Scholars think that these forked finials projecting up past the ridge of the roof originated before the use of nails as extensions of bargeboards (boards hanging from the roof and covering the gables). Another traditional motif is formed by horizontal logs placed along the roof ridge for security. With rare exceptions, these elements give Shinto shrines a different appearance from Buddhist temples.

A third distinguishing feature is a freestanding supportive post at the gable ends of the Ise shrine. Thicker than others in the building, this post supports the ridgepole. A surviving bronze ceremonial bell from the first or second century C.E. (referred to in Chapter 3, Japanese

Figure 17.3. *Shinmei-gu Shrine, near Matsumoto, Japan. This rural shrine is built in the same architectural style (shimmei) as the Inner (Naiku) Ise Shrine in its raised floor, roof, and use of massive timber supports. Strong, simple elements evoke Japan's ancient past, continuing Shinto aesthetics and practices in the religious life of the modern people.*

Granaries) bears an incised image of such a pillar on a building; Watanabe sees this image as evidence of the ancient origin of Japanese shrines.

Because of the frequent rebuilding, Ise is spared major weathering damage. Carpenters who are charged with the task of replicating each architectural element preserve the continuity of form by copying intact visual structural members when they begin work on the replacement. Yet since the fourth or fifth century, a gradual transfer of architectural elements from function to ornamentation has taken place, comparable to the Roman use of Greek columns as decorations for vaulted structures.

The sixty-first rebuilding at Ise took place in 1993 at a cost of $3 million. Eight million visitors flocked to the site for the rededication, but only the emperor, priests, and special dignitaries were permitted to enter in the compound. The emperor presented a gift of rice from his personal harvest to honor the spirit of Amarterasu Omikami in a ritual that establishes a symbolic link between the imperial household and ancient granaries. Ancestor worship also forms a part of the periodic rededication ceremonies. Thus, the recurrent rebuilding of the shrines preserves architectural form and style and contributes to religious continuity.

Sources: Munsterberg (1973), Nishi and Hozumi (1986), Watanabe (1974).

Construction Costs

How do traditional societies pay for architecture? What is the relation of architecture to the local system of economic power? It is difficult to get exact answers to these questions. The general lack of architectural data for many of the areas and topics we have discussed in this book poses special difficulties in aspects of construction for which anecdotal accounts, aesthetic criticism, and a limited number of case studies are insufficient. Our consultant in building economics, Ranko Bon, professor of economics at the University of Reading, England, summed up the situation in a 1995 interview: "We can understand more than we can explain."

The mechanics of payment for architecture are more easily grasped than the social costs. The costs of land, materials, and labor may be met by taxes, confiscation, tithes, barter, or corvee labor. Status competition, secular or familial appeals to their generosity and altruism, or necessity may induce the rich to donate generously. Sometimes the authorities are clever enough to impose a tax increase when a society's economy is growing rapidly.

How much can a preindustrial society really afford to spend on architecture? Alas, data sets are drastically incomplete. The total costs of architecture include the cost of land, materials, workers' training, daily wages, workers' sustenance and housing, decoration, and necessary rituals. Economists encourage us also to incorporate the cost of income foregone when resources are devoted to architecture instead of to the production of widgets or the enjoyment of leisure time. Socioeconomic costs may include exhaustion after strenuous building, as cultural historian and anthropologist J. A. Tainter postulates for the Romans and Maya.

We have approached the matter of building economics from four points of view: First, we consulted with Bon, a noted expert on the economics of the modern construction industry in advanced and less advanced countries, and learned about trends and relative proportions of wealth spent on building today. Second, we reviewed what is known about building economics in premodern societies, such as ancient Greece. Several dependable modern studies of the cost of Greek temples exist, and it may be possible to extrapolate these costs to other premodern building programs. Third, we examined reports of the costs of the Taj Mahal, taken from court records. Although the reliability of late-nineteenth-century publications of these documents is questionable, we have used them in the same way that one would use Irving Stone's biography of Michelangelo—they may not be true in precise detail, but they are likely to be plausible. Fourth, we consulted E. Abrams's book on the energetics of Mayan construction. Abrams's study suggests promising avenues for exploration: How much time and energy are involved in producing a particular building? Through approximations and analogies, our fourfold approach points to areas where further work could be useful.

Sources: Bon (1986, 1988, 1991, 1992, 1993), Tainter (1988).

Economics of Construction

Poor countries, like poor people, are more numerous and need more buildings than do rich countries, but they can afford fewer. People and countries at the economic midrange spend a lot on construction, but once they break through into their mature economy, they need to spend less because they have already supplied themselves with many of the buildings they require. Even so, there is no country, however rich, that is not continually erecting public and private structures—buildings and civil engineering projects, such as bridges and airports, residential and nonresidential complexes, and monuments. The ubiquitous built environment becomes man's natural environment.

MODERN RESEARCH ON COSTS

According to Bon, construction is essentially an assembly activity, including engineering as well as everything needed to produce buildings, from finance to robotics to agriculture (all quotes are from Bon unless otherwise identified). The building industry has direct and indirect aspects, visible and invisible services and technologies, and branches out into supply industries. In every country, construction mobilizes a large share of the natural resources and has an even greater impact on the national economy through interaction with other industries. The "complex interdependence between the construction sector and its main suppliers and clients . . . requires both structural analysis at given points in time and intertemporal analysis of structural shifts." Such analysis has almost never been carried out for the traditional societies in which we are interested.

Yet the question of how individual income is divided among available goods has at least been tackled by G. Pyatt and A. Roe under the label "social accounting matrices." Some additional fragments of information are presented in a 1961 study by the United Nations Economic Commission for Asia and the Far East. The investigators compared the construction cost per square meter (1 square meter equals 3.3 square feet) with workers' daily wages to get ratios ranging from 150.9 for a brick house in Indonesia to 11.7 for a concrete block house in Taiwan (chart, their p. 7). They also ascertained the ratio between the total cost of a dwelling and the average annual wage of a male worker in Europe and the United States; this ratio ranged from 2 in Portugal to 16.7 in Turkey (their chart, p. 22).

We found Bon's analyses to be the most insightful. Bon classifies countries in Africa, South America, and Oceania as lesser developed (LDC); in Asia, as newly industrialized (NIC); and in Europe and North America, as advanced industrialized (AIC). He explains, "The construction sector plays different roles at different stages of economic development. In early stages . . . its main function is to create the capital stock; in later stages . . . its function shifts toward maintenance and repair of the capital stock [see Fig. 17.4]. These two functions have quite

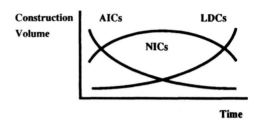

Figure 17.4. *Diagram of construction relationships. This diagram reads as follows: In AICs (advanced industrialized countries), the volume of construction decreases over time; in NICs (newly industrialized countries), it first rises and then falls; and in LDCs (less developed countries), it rises.*

The individual lines of this diagram may also represent several other relationships affecting construction volume. For instance, the inverted semicircle diagrams the share of construction in the gross national product (GNP)—being low for LDCs (left), high for NCIs (center), and low again in mature AICs (right). Both the share of construction in the GNP and the volume of construction over time (regardless of the initial degree of development) also follow this curve.

The partial curve that declines from left to right also indicates the share of new construction in total construction, while the share of maintenance and repair rises over time, represented by the line that rises from left to right.

different technological requirements." As a society matures, the share of new construction goes down, while maintenance and repair (M/R) increase.

M/R, which is labor intensive, has less of an effect on the whole economy than does new construction but has a strong effect on trade, which dominates services and thus construction output. Much of the present construction value in AICs lies in financial services and construction management, not in materials. Noneconomists may wonder whether the same kinds and amounts of funding are available for construction and for maintenance (probably not) and whether the same kinds of economic analysis are done for both. Surely life-cycle costs and infrastructure costs accrue to someone.

Bon's diagram reproduced here (Fig. 17.4) is a pictogram with no numerical significance. It shows the relation over time of elements of the construction industry. Note particularly the inverted-U curve Bon uses to represent several concepts that all develop in the same general way: the share of residential construction in the gross national product (GNP); the volume of residential construction and, therefore, volume of all construction, since residential construction accounts for more than 50 percent of the total, the share of total construction in GNP, and per capita GNP. The general shape of the inverted U holds true, Bon asserts, whether one is comparing LDCs, NICs, or AICs or considering changes in one country over time. The gross domestic product (GDP) in construction first rises to 13–14 percent, then levels off at 7 percent per year. (Other scholars have reservations about the shape of the construction-volume curve over time.)

The curve tilting upward to the right represents the share of M/R, which steadily increases. Like the manufacturing industry with which it is so closely allied, construction's share in the GNP first increases and then declines (see Fig. 17.4) as a society matures, but services (such as M/R) only increase. M/R "includes all forms of construction activity other than new construction—that is, maintenance and repair proper, reconstruction, refurbishment, etc.," according to Bon. In the United States, construction's contribution to GNP is 6–8 percent, of which value added, mainly by labor, is about 3–4 percent. In Japan, the corresponding contribution is 21 percent, up 100 percent since 1980. Value added accounts for about half the value of output.

S. Ganeson investigated the construction industry in Sri Lanka and learned that it went through three stages that could be expressed by the same curves. It is significant for our purposes that Ganeson found traditional Sri Lankan methods and materials to be better for the growth of the construction industry and for the economy of the island-state than imported modern materials and methods. This conclusion was somewhat unexpected (at least in the West) because people often assume that modern materials and methods are, by definition, more efficient and therefore less expensive.

As a student of the present hundred-year span in construction, Bon prefers current data and looks for projections, rather than past data. To compensate for deficiencies in present data, he can use analyses of structural relations, while we, as historians happy to have even past data, must turn to documented historical examples. In this book, we have attempted to study the percentage of GNP spent on the built environment. The reader may remember that in Chapter 6 we discussed the economic reasons for living on houseboats and compared boat dwellers' incomes and hence the amount they can spend on housing, with those of land dwellers. In the same chapter, we discussed the close relationship between access to economic-political power in Nigeria and North Africa and access to

architecture, specifically housing; in that case, gender divided the haves and have-nots. Later in Chapter 6, we noted that religious buildings absorbed a large share of the resources of the early Mexican city-state of Teotihuacán, but also made the city a pilgrimage site for the entire region, thereby benefiting all residents. In Chapter 14 we took a different approach to the economics of building, describing the ways in which the residents of Acoma, constrained by the limits of their mesa-top village, recycle materials and cooperate in construction. Their practices contrast vividly with those of the Maya. In Maya states, the elite controlled all economic resources in excess of those needed for survival and used these resources to build large edifices, perhaps contributing to the collapse of their society (see Fig. 17.5, which depicts the carving of a stelae to commemorate one of the elite).

We have not discussed the even more difficult problem of short-term costs versus long-term benefits. Some comparative figures are available from B. Taut, who reported in 1937 that Japanese laborers' houses cost 500 yen, less than the 600–700 yen they earned in wages each year. At that time, a European laborer had to pay three times his annual wage for "serviceable lodging," and the same cost ratio applied to middle-class European housing. Japanese farmers were poor but adequately housed: Japan had 5.6 million farmhouses that housed 80 percent of the population, although the farmers earned only 18 percent of the gross national income, averaging about 290 yen per year. Some farmers were rich enough to afford mansions: T. Itoh and Y. Futagawa show that in 1979, it cost $3,000 per square meter (about $330 per square foot) to rebuild the three-hundred-year-old Yoshijima mansion, excluding modern utilities. An interesting aspect of this range of costs is that the few expensive mansions did not allocate to themselves all the available construction money; poorer farmers were also decently housed. Compare these figures with those for the elite of Tikal, the building of whose houses consumed 10,000 times as much human energy as those of the peasants.

SOURCES: BON (1986, 1988, 1991, 1993, 1994), GANESAN (1982), ITOH AND FUTAGAWA (1980), PYATT AND ROE (1977), TAUT (1937).

ANALOGIES FROM ANCIENT CONSTRUCTION

Greco-Roman examples give us some clues about the costs of premodern construction. Plutarch, a Roman writer of about 100 C.E., wrote that the Greek city Athens undertook public works projects, especially from 447 to 432

Figure 17.5. *Carving and setting up a Maya stela. Upper left: quarrying the stone, center: transporting the block, lower left: raising the stone and setting it in place, and lower right: carving the reliefs.*

B.C.E., to alleviate the lot of those who were no longer employed after the Persian Wars. Pliny, the Younger, another Roman of the same period, wrote that the remodeling of the Acropolis of Athens generated six thousand jobs per day, at 1 drachma per man, for fifteen years; wages depended on status and skill. Four-fifths of the cost was spent on labor because most materials were free. The Parthenon alone cost 500 talents. And its great gold-and-ivory statue of Athena cost 850 talents; most of the gold treasury of the Athenian state went to form the statues' draperies. Extraordinary funds were always available for Greek and Roman building, such as the 400 talents the Athenians retained from the tribute of 800 or 900 talents their allies had paid them to fight the Persian War. More common sources of money for temples were special taxes; gifts of kings; state resources, such as the Laurion silver mines that belonged to Athens; pious contributions of individuals; and sacred revenues from both pilgrims and temple lands. Additional sources of income for the Parthenon were the treasury of the goddess, money of fraternal associations, fees from the baths, and the sale of surplus materials. Costs were subject to market fluctuations in prices and in the value of money, but pious contributions often kept them down.

The most urgent problem of these building programs was not financing but finding skilled workers. At Selinus in Sicily and Paestum in southern Italy, the huge scale of the work demanded a great number of unskilled laborers. In contrast, only about two hundred qualified workers built the Temple of Asklepeion at Epidauros (Greece) in a mere four years and eight months. The Temple of Asklepeion is the only temple whose costs we know with certainty. It cost 24 of the 240 to 290 talents spent on the entire complex of buildings; compare this figure with the total cost for the Periklean buildings on the Acropolis at Athens: 2,000 to 2,500 talents. The Syracuse ramparts in Sicily, ca. 401–400 B.C.E., were perhaps the largest building project of the fifth century, with sixty thousand workers.

Years of effort, integrating evidence from literary sources and inscriptions with the results of excavations, have produced this wealth of data on ancient Greek construction. Philologist M. A. Burford asserts that there are fewer that six literary references to the total cost of a temple and even fewer to the economics of temple construction. Most of our information comes from the buildings themselves, not from documents. Unfortunately for a historical survey of building costs, not enough similar work has been done with other building traditions.

What makes modern construction different from ancient and premodern construction? Bon and others claim that the difference lies in the relationship of technological advances to costs, especially visible in developed countries. Advanced building technology is a consistent feature of advanced societies:

> Technical progress consists not only of inventions and innovations that require heavy capital investments but also a stream of relatively cheap changes and improvements whose cumulative effect is a drastic reduction of input of resources accompanied by increases in output. The major capital stock of an industrially advanced nation is not its physical equipment; it is the body of knowledge amassed from tested findings of empirical science and the capacity and training of its population to use this knowledge effectively. One can easily envisage a situation in which technological progress permits output to increase at a high rate without any additions to the stock of capital goods [machines and tools used in the production of other goods].
>
> —S. Kuznets (1968)

The traditional building knowledge of nonindustrial peoples includes the ability to utilize readily available natural materials, adapted to the local climate. We argue that these skills are economic resources for their countries, although they have not always been recognized as such.

SOURCES: BURFORD (1965); FRANCOTTE (1979), 54–115.

Describing Costs: Taj Mahal Construction

It is difficult to come up with a true picture of building costs in premodern societies. On the one hand, official recorders tended to exaggerate details of construction expenditures to impress. For example, legend says that the stones of the Suleymaniye complex (see Chapter 16) were mixed with jewels. On the other hand, exaggeration was sometimes unnecessary. Rulers, such as Shah Jahan, spent lavishly, even though the Qur'an condemned extravagance because—for one reason—it increased the tax burden on the poor; the Qur'an also forbade the construction of buildings for questionable purposes as a wasteful use of funds. As with the Egyptians, whose hieroglyphic records tell us much about their culture but not how they built their pyramids, we lack extensive or reliable data on building costs for the architectural works produced by many peoples. Yet we do have some information about the cost of the Taj Mahal.

Documentation of expenditures for the construction of the Taj Mahal at Agra, India, (see Chapter 9) is not always dependable and may not be based on primary sources. Scholars argue that the available copies of court records were made by different scribes at different times and do not always reflect the same conclusions about building procedures. When original court records are lost and only copies remain, inconsistencies result. Much data are merely representative, often meager. We must use caution in evaluating data unsupported by original documentary evidence.

To investigate some of the construction costs paid from the royal treasury, architectural historians W. E. Begley and Z. A. Desai summarized accounts of expenditures that appear in Mughal histories or are inscribed on buildings (ca. 1650 C.E.) and came to general conclusions. Uninfluenced by reports of "sky-touching edifices, heart-pleasing gardens, [or] Paradise-resembling tombs," they relied on data taken from an analysis of governmental expenditures, especially the records of a contemporary scribe. In citing Lahori, the designer of the Taj Mahal, they found that the largest amount paid from the royal treasury was for military campaigns, although the exact amount is unknown. The next largest amount was for bequests and gifts, 10 crores of rupees (95 million rupees). Last was money spent on architectural projects, 2.5 crores (25 million rupees). Of this amount, 50 lakhs (5 million) rupees were spent to build the Taj Mahal. Begley and Desai suggest that Lahori revealed a wry sense of humor when he wrote that the treasures the emperor Akbar had accumulated during his fifty-one-year reign were spent by his son Jahangir in only twenty-two years.

These expenditures could be balanced against general estimates of the amount and quality of gems, gold, and silver in the royal treasury, vaguely described by historian E. Havell, as "not being . . . found in the possession of all the other rulers of the world." For instance, one diamond, of about 280 carats thought to be the famous Koh-i-nur, was valued by a judge of diamonds at "about half the daily expense of the whole world."

Despite religious sanctions against spending excessively, those in power considered it vital to impress the populace, regardless of the burden placed on the economy. Important monuments, such as the Taj Mahal, were expected to be expensive. The often-repeated statement that the upkeep of the Taj Mahal consumed the revenues of thirty villages may one day be supported by fact as interest in the building costs of traditional architecture increases.

Historian A. Chatterjee studied the wage structure of artisans and laborers who were employed in the construction of the Junagarh Fort at Bikaner, India, at about the same period (1670–1761). He found that payments for labor and materials were recorded daily and monthly and that laborers were divided into two groups, "superior" and "ordinary." The superior workers earned up to three times as much as the ordinary workers. Women received only half as much pay as men for the same kinds of work, the excuse being that a woman usually belonged to a family group with a male wage earner. Specialists who were brought to the site from other cities earned more than twice as much as the local workers. In times of famine, as in 1757–61, wages were sometimes supplemented with grain. Chatterjee attributes the low wages of the local workers, 4 annas per day (16 annas equaled 1 rupee), to the low subsistence level.

Great gaps remain in our knowledge of how traditional cultures spent money on architecture. Yet the records of many such cultures will reward greater scholarly attention to the financial aspects of architectural history.

SOURCES: BEGLEY AND DESAI (1989), CHATTERJEE (1985), HAVELL (1904).

New Analysis of Costs: Energetics in the Yucatán

Since the 1960s, architectural studies have broadened to include anthropological data that give historians a social perspective on earlier cultures. This perspective, in turn, has prompted inquiries into the costs of architecture and the economics of building in these cultures. Success in determining building costs for modern architectural projects has stimulated general interest in the question of costs among both students of modern architecture and those—such as specialists on the Maya—in other disciplines. Anthropoloigst E. Abrams developed a method, which he calls "architectural energetics," that has great potential for computing the costs of traditional construction.

Abrams quantifies the costs of constructing buildings into units of comparison, that is, energy "in the form of labor-time expenditure." In his exemplary study of the Maya, he has determined two sets of facts that are useful to us. The first is that workers who were experienced with both ancient stone tools and modern steel tools gained about 30 percent in output by using the latter, a fact that allowed him to estimate the time necessary for construction tasks in premodern times. Abrams also carefully estimated the number of person-days required to build various types of houses at Copán in Honduras, the largest Maya site. One could use his method to estimate the effort required to build Copán's monumental pyramids and temples.

Abrams studied two types of dwellings. The first is the basic wattle-and-daub or pole-and-thatch house, built on a low platform of earth, stone, or debris. Four to eight posts serve as a frame for walls of mud and aggregate. A gabled roof of thatch or grass shelters a porch, and a thinly applied coat of lime wash covers the exterior. The design and materials produce the simplest and most economical type of dwelling. A simple house of this type, built with traditional tools and without beasts of burden, requires 20 person-days in energy costs: 2 for procurement (earth), 4 for transport, 1 for manufacture (cobbles), and 13 for construction (walls, superstructure).

The second type of house is larger and more elaborate. The substructure is higher and longer, and a dressed masonry platform supports the walls. Wall materials consist of more stone and less earth. The interior is often completed with benches, the exterior is decorated with sculpture, and there are terraces. Not only style but utility is improved. The thermal properties of stone permit the better regulation of interior temperatures, the greater height of the platforms makes damage from flooding less likely,

Cumulative Costs of Residences

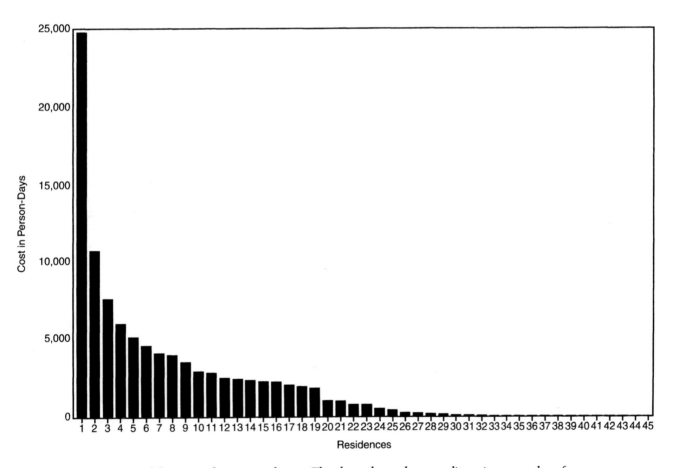

Figure 17.6. *Diagram of the costs of Maya residences. The chart shows the expenditure in person-days for the most elaborate structures contrasted with the simplest residences. For example, five houses cost 5,000 person-days each, only one house cost nearly 25,000 person-days, and 36 houses took only a few days to build.*

and the building materials are less flammable than those used in the first type of house. In this category, one of the largest palaces at late classic Copán cost 24,705 person days: 2,731 for procurement (earth, cobbles, tuff), 10,343 for transport, 10,971 for manufacture (masonry, plaster, sculpture), and 660 for construction (walls, fill, cobble and plaster surfaces)—nearly 1,500 times more person-days than a modest house (see Fig. 17.6). The figures for both types of buildings pertain only to three primary components—the platform, superstructure, and roof—not to decoration or furnishings (see Fig. 17.5). Abrams acknowledges the possible reuse of structural elements or the demolition of earlier works, for which data are not available, and suggests that further studies may provide alternate methods for determining the costs of reuse.

Architectural energetics can help archaeologists and historians determine not only how a structure was built, but its costs to society; this method will be especially helpful in studying cultures that have not kept written records. When building records do exist, those like the ones for the Taj Mahal can give us additional insight into society's economic power structure. We wish that we had these kinds of analyses for all the architecture we have discussed in this book. Future developments in the study of building economics, especially developments that will allow cross-cultural comparisons, will enhance our growing knowlege of the architectures of the traditional world.

SOURCE: ABRAMS (1994).

SUGGESTED READINGS

Abrams, E. M. 1994. *How the Maya Built Their World: Energetics and Ancient Architecture.* Austin: University of Texas Press. A new way of thinking about traditional architecture, yielding a widely applicable method.

Begley, W. E., and Z. A. Desai, compilers and trans. 1989. *Taj Mahal: The Illumined Tomb, an Anthology of Seventeenth-Century Mughal and European Documentary Sources.* Seattle: University of Washington Press. An excellent presentation of information from historical documents.

Bon, R. 1988. "Direct and Indirect Resource Utilization by the Construction Sector." *Habitat International* 12: 49–74.

Bon, R. 1992. "The Future of International Construction: Secular Patterns of Growth and Decline." *Habitat International* 16:119–28.

Bon, R. 1994a. "Whither Global Construction? Part 1." *Building Research and Information* 22:109–14.

Bon, R. 1994b. "Whither Global Construction? Part 2." *Building Research and Information* 22:118–28.

Burford, M. A. 1965. "The Economics of Greek Temple Building." *Proceedings of the Cambridge Philological Society* 191:21–34. See his notes for further bibliography.

Stanier, R. S. 1953. "The Cost of the Parthenon." *Journal of Hellenic Studies* 73: 68–76. At least some of the information on the construction of the Parthenon should be transferable cross-culturally. However, Classical Athens provides both more textual documentation and more accrued excavation data than is common in the traditional societies studied here.

Tange, K. 1965. *Ise: Prototype of Japanese Architecture.* Cambridge, Mass.: MIT Press. A summary of the development of Japanese architecture as typified in one building.

Watanabe, Y. 1974. *Shinto Art: Ise and Izumo Shrines,* Vol. 3, trans. R. Ricketts. New York: Weatherhill/Heibonsha. The lack of an index and bibliography detract from an otherwise good introduction to Shinto shrines.

⊞ Conclusion

This book has been about people outside the Euro-American tradition—how they live in architecture and why they built what they did. Whatever their cultural orientation, people have similar basic needs, although these needs are tempered by a wide range of climatic conditions, available building materials, religions, and social mores. The human race is but one entity, and everyone is part of it, so it is of paramount importance that we try to understand some of the concerns we all share, from obtaining food and shelter to decorating our built environment. Yet each culture responds to these concerns in its own way. Architecture, which expresses the "enduring values of collective human life," as philosopher J. Dewey postulates, is a window into a myriad of past and present societies.

Research on diverse aspects of architectural history has escalated in the past few decades.[36] Since the late 1980s, there has been a tremendous outpouring of data on the Maya culture; for instance, anthropologist E. Abrams devised a new investigative method for estimating traditional building costs that offers great potential for similar research in other societies. Since the late 1970s, archaeological studies in China have added greatly to our knowledge about that country. Tools, such as infrared photography and aerial remote sensing devices, may produce more accurate surveys of the Great Wall, as A. Waldron suggested, and in 1994 the radar on the space shuttle Endeavor found two previously unknown parallel segments of the Great Wall of China, covered by desert sand and invisible from the ground.[37] Thus, modern methods yield information not found on the eighteenth-century charts from which the route of the Great Wall had previously been largely determined. As still newer techniques develop, they will give us still more accurate knowledge about architectural phenomena.

Thanks to this rapid advance of technology, anyone with access to a computer can now use the resources of libraries, museums, and other institutions around the world—resources that might have been difficult or impossible to access in the past. The sheer amount of information on architectural and cultural topics is growing almost beyond computation, and it is available to a wider audience than ever before. Museum-oriented programs, such as the Getty Information Institute, can put the public in touch with a wealth of information that was unimaginable to earlier generations of scholars. Youth-oriented museum programs stimulate young people to develop an interest in the art and architecture of other cultures. The way we receive information has also changed dramatically. We still have books, plans, and drawings, but now we also have CD-ROMs, the Internet, computer-aided design, digital video discs, and more. These and other audiovisual materials enrich the study of architectural history by letting more of us see buildings in three-dimensional form.

Some research now focuses on areas outside the Euro-American sphere, although there are persistent gaps in historical reporting. A great deal has been written about the

---

[36]Reported in *USA Today* (April 19, 1996).

[37]Another example: the authors of two articles on the historical records of earthquakes in the eastern Mediterranean studied unpublished Ottoman court documents that record claims for earthquake damage and the amounts spent by the central government on local repairs—a kind of evidence that has rarely been considered. See N. N. Anbraseys and C. F. Finkel, "The Seismicity of the Eastern Mediterranean Region during the Turn of the Eighteenth Century," *Istanbuler Mitteilungen* 42 (1991): 323–43; and N. N. Ambraseys, "The Value of Historical Records of Earthquakes," *Nature* 232 (August 6, 1971): 375–78.

Indian subcontinent, for example, but European perspectives often shaped the authors' perceptions. Nevertheless, the focus of architectural literature is broadening; a more diversified agenda is now enhancing the former emphasis on formal characteristics. Thus, this book contains interdisciplinary ideas as well as the details of specific structures. We cannot understand the sophisticated water-management systems developed in Sri Lanka (250–210 B.C.E.), for example, without data from anthropologists, hydraulic engineers, and sociologists, as well as architectural historians (see Chapter 12). As the scope of our understanding broadens, it is no longer sufficient to study architectural works within the narrower confines of earlier research patterns. Our argument throughout this book has been that architecture expresses cultural values, including technology, and that those values are as worthy of study—and as essential to a full understanding of architecture—as is its form.

But the formal description of architectural works remains an extremely important element in historical narrative. Human beings, after all, see the world and everything in it as form and space: the postive forms of buildings or landscapes and the negative space that surrounds or is integrated with these masses. The Ottoman mosques of the sixteenth century illustrate spatial unity; their massive domes, silhouetted against the sky, present a vision of solidity that contrasts with the vast open spaces inside them. Space and form "together . . . form an inseparable reality, a unity of opposites, just as the elements of form and space together form the reality of architecture," according to architect F. D. Ching.

From a human standpoint, visual scale can evoke a wide range of responses: awe in response to images of power (the Great Wall of China), devout spiritual reverence (the temples of Borobudur or Angkor Wat), or deep-felt aesthetic appreciation (Japanese gardens or the Taj Mahal). Allied to scale is proportion, the physical relationship between the parts of a building. The formal aspects of many constructed works include plans, either oral or written, with proportions that are suitable for the function, whether symbolic or practical.

The organization of architectural components "promotes design economy, as similar functions share similar services," as architect A. C. Antoniades argues. Composition requires the control of multiple interactive constraints. The repetition of elements, as in arcades or porticos (see Chapter 16), sets up a pattern, a rhythmic sequence of images, both positive and negative, horizontal and vertical. Architects and builders must strike a balance between too much order, which may result in visual monotony, as Antoniades warns, and too little order, which presents a chaotic array of built forms—a balance like the one that exists between Islamic courtyard arcades, for example, and the large iwans or other openings that break the wall surface. Most of the monumental and many of the vernacular architectural examples we have chosen have this balance.

The study of formal characteristics can tell us much about historical influences, about affinities and contrasts, and about materials and methods. It can also, if we choose, lead us to the cultural considerations mentioned here. By analyzing how people manipulate form and space in their buildings, we can gain insight into their behavior, values, and desires. People who live in traditional Japanese houses, for example, easily reorganize interior space with movable screens. This reorganization tells us something about their social structure, aesthetics, and architectural philosophy—how they think about what they build. Like most architecture, Japanese houses have both tangible and intangible aspects (see Chapter 15).

A society may let one structure dominate. The "men's houses" of New Guinea, the largest in the villages (see Chapter 4), are built for prestige and suggest a gender bias. The uniformity of size in the cliff dwellings of Mesa Verde (see Chapter 9) appears to reflect a relatively egalitarian social structure. The mosque is the architectural focal point of most Islamic cities. As the largest building, it projects religious and political power. This book is full of examples of how structures reflect the cultural values of their builders. And perhaps, from contemplating the buildings and values of other cultures, we will turn to our own with fresh eyes. What does our built environment say about us?

SOURCES: ABRAMS (1994); ANTONIADES (1992); F. D. CHING (1979); DEWEY (1958), 220; WALDRON (1990).

SUGGESTED READINGS

Antoniades, A. C. 1992. *Architecture and Allied Design*. Dubuque, Iowa: Kendall/Hunt. An influential theoretician addresses the principles of architectural design with clarity and conviction.

Ching, F. D. 1979. *Architecture: Form, Space and Order*. New York: Van Nostrand Reinhold. The hand-lettered text and original illustrations present a comprehensive overview of architectural elements.

Dewey, J. 1958. *Art as Experience*. New York: Capricorn Books, G. P. Putnam's Sons. A dated work but not dated ideas.

⊞ Appendix 1 Maps

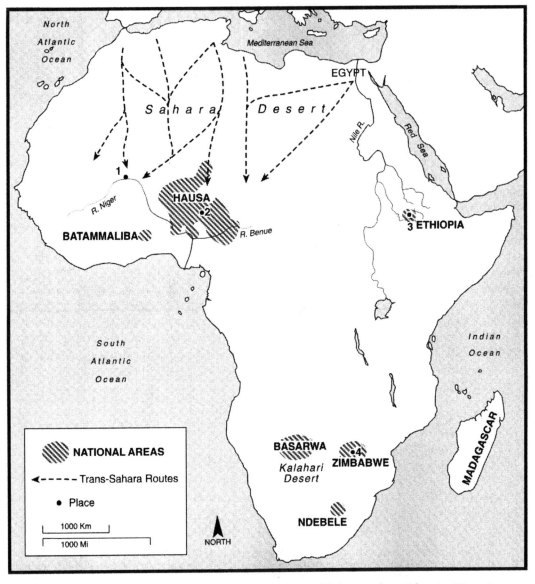

Figure A1. *Map of African Polities: Batammaliba; Hausa; Lalibela Kingdom, Ethiopia; !Kung Basarwa; Kalahari Desert; Ndebele; Zimbabwe; Madagascar (Austronesian language, see Fig. A5). African cities: (1) Timbuktu, Mali; (2) Kano, Nigeria; (3) Lalibela, Ethiopia; (4) Great Zimbabwe, Zimbabwe; →, caravan routes.*

377

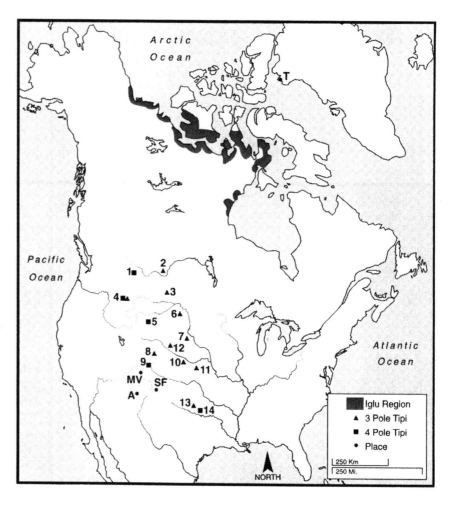

Figure A2. *Map of North American Indian Tribes. (1) Blackfoot; (2) Cree; (3) Assiniboine; (4) Nez Perce; (5) Crow; (6) Mandan; (7) Dakota; (8) Arapaho; (9) Ute; (10) Pawnee; (11) Omaha; (12) Cheyenne; (13) Kiowa; (14) Comanche. Places: Mesa Verde (MV), Acoma (A), Santa Fe (SF).*

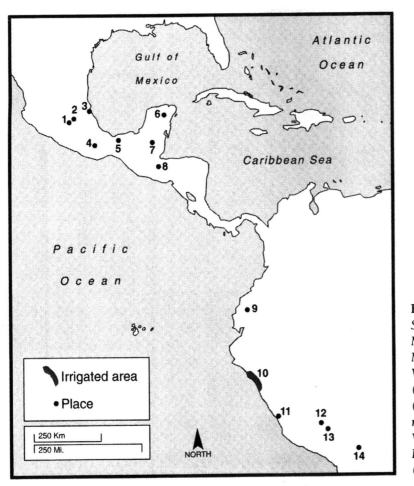

Figure A3. *Map of Central and Northwestern South America. (1) Tenochititlan/Mexico City, Mexico; (2) Teotihuacán, Mexico; (3) El Tajin, Mexico; (4) Monte Alban, Mexico; (5) La Venta, Mexico; (6) Chichen Itzá, Mexico; (7) Tikal, Guatemala; (8) Copan, Honduras; (9) Quito, Ecuador; (10) Irrigated area of northwest coast of Peru, including Chicama Valley; (11) Lima, Peru; (12) Ollantaytambo, Peru; (13) Cuzco, Peru; (14) La Paz, Bolivia (immediately southeast of Lake Titicatia).*

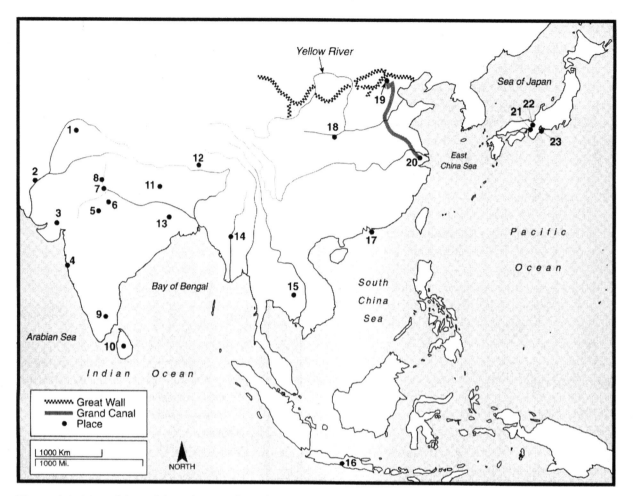

Figure A4. *Map of Asia. (1) Kashmir, India-Pakistan; (2) Mohenjo-Daro, Pakistan; (3) Mount Abu, India; (4) Karli, India; (5) Khajuraho, India; (6) Sanchi, India; (7) Agra, India; (8) Delhi, India; (9) Srirangam, India; (10) Kandy, Sri Lanka (south of Sigiriya); (11) Kathmandu Valley (with Bhaktapur, Kathmandu, and Patan), Nepal; (12) Lhasa, Tibet; (13) Lomas Rishi/Barabar Hills, India; (14) Pagan, Burma/Myanmar; (15) Angkor, Cambodia/Kampuchea; (16) Borobudur, Java; (17) Hong Kong, China; (18) Chang'an/Xian, China; (19) Beijing, China; (20) Suzhou, China; (21) Kyoto, Japan; (22) Nara and Asuka, Japan; (23) Ise, Japan; (∧∧∧) Great Wall of China; heavy bold line, Grand Canal, China.*

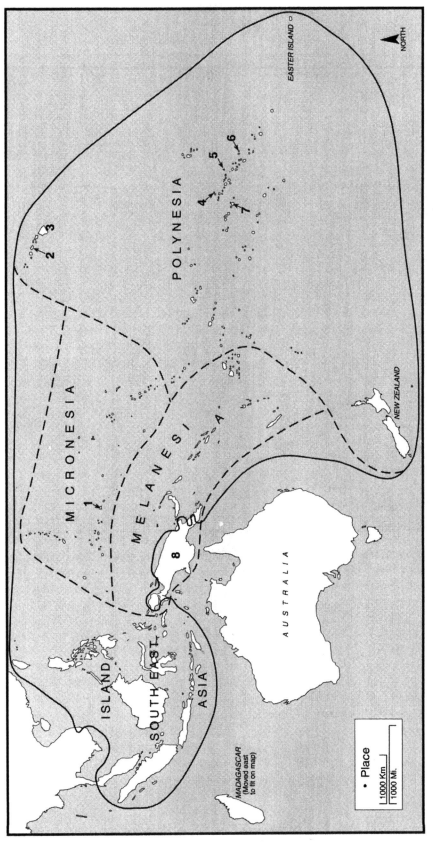

Figure A5. *Map of Oceania.* (1) *Pohmpei (Nan Madol site), Caroline Islands;* (2) *Oahu, Hawaii;* (3) *Hawaii (big island), Hawaii;* (4) *Takaroa, Tuamotu Archipelago;* (5) *Fagatau, Tuamotu;* (6) *Reao, Tuamotu;* (7) *Tahiti, Society Island;* (8) *New Guinea.*

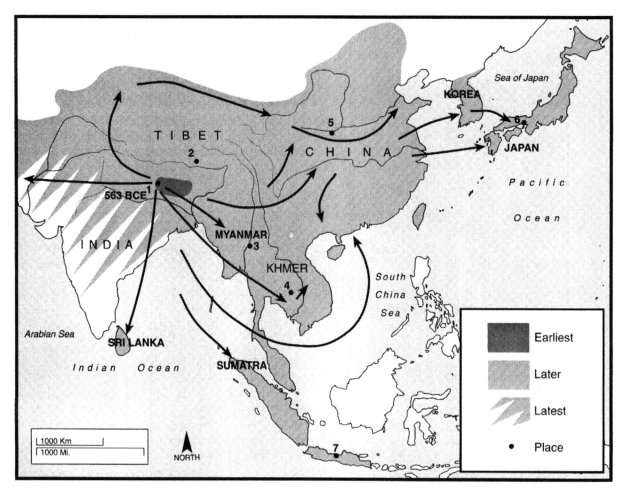

Figure A6. *Spread of Buddhism. (1) Limbini (birthplace of Gautama Buddha), Nepal; (2) Lhasa, Tibet; (3) Pagan, Burma; (4) Angkor, Cambodia; (5) Chang'an/Xian, China; (6) Nara, Japan; (7) Borobudur, Java.*

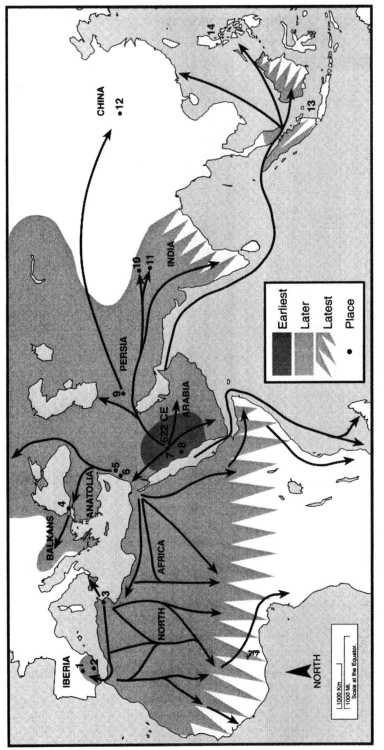

Figure A7. *Spread of Islam.* (1) *Toledo, Spain;* (2) *Granada, Spain;* (3) *Qairawan, Tunisia;* (4) *Istanbul, Turkey;* (5) *Damascus, Syria;* (6) *Jerusalem, Holy Land;* (7) *Medina, Arabia;* (8) *Mecca (birthplace of Mohammed), Arabia;* (9) *Isfahan, Persia;* (10) *Delhi, India;* (11) *Agra, India* (12) *Chang'an/Xian, China,* (13) *Indonesia;* (14) *Philippine Islands.*

⊞ Appendix 2 Materials

Table A1. Materials Used for Wall Building.

	Survival	Insulation	Working	Load-bearing	Stability
Light vegetation	poor, prone to biological attack	moderate	easily cut, carried and manipulated	poor	excellent
Timber	moderate, prone to biological attack	moderate	requires heavy tools	moderate	good
Stone	excellent	poor, allows rising damp	difficult unless rock already fractured; laborious	excellent	poor
Mud	moderate, prone to weathering	good, but allows rising damp	easily shaped and manipulated	moderate	poor

Table A2. Materials Used for Roofing.

	Survival	Insulation	Working	Load-bearing	Stability
Pitched roofs— leaves or thatch	moderate	excellent	easy	moderate	moderate
Pitched roofs— shingle, slates	good	poor	easy	good	poor
Flat roofs— mud or bitumen	poor	good	easy	poor	good

From H. W. M. Hodges (1972), reprinted by permission of Schenkman Publishing Company.

⊞ Glossary

ablution	Cleansing as a religious rite.
aoting yaodong	Underground houses (China).
aperture sluices	Barriers across streams, with openings of a predetermined shape, to regulate the flow of water.
architecture	1. Everything built or constructed or dug out for human occupation.
	2. "The art of building in which human requirements and construction materials are related so as to furnish a practical and aesthetic solution. As an art, architecture . . . involves the manipulation of the relationships of spaces, volumes, planes, masses and voids. Time is also an important factor, since a building is usually comprehended in a succession of experiences rather than all at once." Source: *New Columbia Encyclopedia* (New York: Random House, 1975), 23.
	3. "The art and technique of building as distinguished from the skills associated with construction . . . embrac[ing] both aesthetic and utilitarian ends that may be distinguished but not separated. . . . All but the simplest cultures have evolved characteristic forms of architecture, and the more complex societies command a great variety of styles, techniques, and purposes that shape their buildings." Source: *Encyclopedia Britanica*, 15th ed. Vol. 1 p. 530 "Architecture." Chicago: Encyclopedia Britanica, Inc.
	4. What architects do or make.
avatar	Incarnation of a god (Hindu).
axis mundi	Center of the world (Latin).
badgirs	Wind towers (Iran).
baleen	The elastic, horny material from the mouths of whalebone whales, used by the behemoths to strain their food.
bargeboards	Boards that hang down from the pointed ends of gables.
baulks	Crossbeams.
bath-fountains	*Dharas* or *hitties* in Nepal, which provide both bathing facilities and drinking water.
bay	One of a number of large vertical divisions of an interior wall.

bodhisattvas	Buddhist saints.
brahmans	The highest Hindu social class; includes priests.
canes	Projecting supports made of timbers, found in Peru.
cella	The central sanctuary of a temple.
chac-mool	A statue made in human form, its knees drawn up and leaning back on its elbows with its head turned over its shoulder; its hands are spread out on either side of a "plate" laid flat on its abdomen, between the chac-mool's shoulders and knees, to receive the heart cut from a living victim (Maya).
chaitya	A Buddhist shrine, sometimes only a stupa, sometimes enclosing a stupa. *Chaitya* means "reminder of," and the term is applied to places, symbols, and objects.
char-bagh	A four-part garden, usually divided by water courses (from the Persian).
chigi	Forked finials on a roof at the gable ends over the ridge.
chinampas	Raised planting beds of Mexico.
chowk	A courtyard in an apartment building or palace in Nepal.
clove hitch	A kind of knot.
convergent evolution	The appearance of apparently similar structures in organisms of different lines of descent.
corbelled roofs	Vaults formed of horizontal courses that approach nearer and nearer to one another as they rise toward the apex.
corvee labor	Unpaid labor extracted by a ruler or a government.
cosmic axis	The connection of a particular spot on earth with the unknown depths of earth and with the heavens.
cyclopean wall	A wall of gigantic stones, supposedly built by Cyclops, the giants of Greek mythology.
dado	The lower part of an interior wall with a special finish.
daikoku-bashiras	A thick post in the center of a house, associated with the god of wealth (Japan).
devsirme	A form of taxation levied on Christians by Muslims in the Ottoman Empire.
dhyana	Meditation by priests to invoke a deity.
diwan-i-am	A public audience hall (Middle East).
dotaku	An ancient (first to second century C.E.) ceremonial bell (Asia).
dual opposition	An anthropological term for government by two competing or cooperating divisions of a hierarchy society, personified by their rulers, often two brothers.
emblem glyphs	Symbols inscribed on stelae.
feng-shui	Chinese geomancy.
firdaws	Garden or paradise (see *rawda*).
formally	In terms of their forms.
fusuma	A sliding partition of paper or cloth on a wooden lattice framework (Japan).
Geku	The outer shrine at Ise, Japan.

geomancy	Divination by interpretation of various natural phenomena.
ghats	Places where the dead are burned at a river's edge or at places where two rivers join (Hindu).
ghorfas	Community granaries (North Africa).
golden section	A ratio between two portions of a line or of two sides of a rectangle, in which the lesser of the two is to the greater as the greater is to the sum of both; a ratio of approximately 0.618 to 1.000. Also called the golden mean. Source: *Random House Dictionary*, 1987)
gopura	Towers of gates of an Indian city.
goten	Palace (Japan).
habitus	The set of personally held dispositions around which a person's practical life is structured to become automatic (from the Latin).
hachas	Mesoamerican carved stone objects, possibly used as markers in a ball game.
hadiths	Muslim sayings or writings attributed to the Prophet Mohammed or his followers.
harem	Women's quarters in a Muslim household.
Hisashi	Auxiliary buildings or verandas attached to the main section of a Japanese house.
historiography	The history of the methods and content of historical scholarship.
hogaku	Japanese "direction-angle" orientation, a system similar to Chinese geomancy (*feng-shui*) and to similar astrologically based locational systems of Tibet and India.
horror vaculi	The need to fill all available surfaces, total ornamentation (from the Latin, dread of emptiness).
hortus	Pertaining to horticulture: cultivation of a garden (Latin); or a garden itself.
iconography	The visual images and symbols of a work of art.
iconology	The historical analysis and interpretive study of symbols in their contexts.
iglu (igloo)	A domed house made of blocks of snow.
imam/iman	A Muslim prayer leader.
in situ	Found in the existing, original, or natural place (Latin).
ita-azekura	An ancient joinery method (Japan).
iwan	A vaulted niche or large portal (Middle East).
Jakatas	Stories about the life of Buddha.
jami masjid	A congregational or Friday mosque.
junks	Tall, seagoing ships with square sails, a high stern, and a flat bottom (China).
Kagawa prefecture	A district in Shikoku, Japan.
katsuogi	Horizontal logs placed on the ridge of a roof (Japan).
ken	A unit of measurement about 6 linear feet (2 meters).
Khmer	A Cambodian people who came to dominate most of Indochina.
kiva	An underground circular room used for meetings, rituals, and associated social activities by the Anasazi and other Pueblo cultures.

kotatsu	A covered sunken hearth (or low table). The family gathered around it, keeping their feet warmed by a brazier of charcoal underneath the table (Japan).
Kufi	An angular form of writing developed in Iraq (8th century C.E.).
limes	Frontiers and fortifications of the Roman Empire.
living rock	A stone that is not disconnected from its natural setting.
low relief (bas-relief)	Sculpture in which the figures project slightly from the background.
madrasas	Islamic theological colleges or law schools.
Maghrebi or al-Maghrib	The area occupied by modern Morocco, Algeria, Tunisia, and Libya in North Africa (Arabic).
malqaf	An air-scoop or wind catcher above a building (Iran).
mandalas	Mystical Indian diagrams of the cosmos. Also used in China and Africa.
marae	Sacred enclosures of Polynesia.
martyria	Tombs for martyrs, copying the form of the pagan imperial tomb, which was also copied in the Early Christian baptistry.
masjid	A neighborhood mosque.
mihrab	A niche in a mosque indicating the direction of Mecca.
minbar	A pulpit in a mosque.
mi'ta	A labor force of tributary workers (Peru).
moieties	Tribal units—literally, halves.
monolithic	Literally, made of one stone; all one piece.
monumental architecture	Massive, imposing, great (in quantity or quality), of enduring significance, of heroic (larger than life-size) scale.
moya	The main room of a Japanese house.
Mount Meru	The home of the gods (Hindu, Buddhist).
Mughal (Mogul)	The ruling dynasty in India from the mid-sixteenth to the mid-nineteenth century C.E. (Muslim).
muqarnas	Three-dimensional ornamental vaulting having a stalacite or honeycomb appearance (Islamic architecture).
musalla or *idgah*	Open area for community gatherings (Islamic).
Naiku	The inner (or imperial) shrine at Ise, Japan.
Nashki	An flowing form of calligraphic script (from the 10th century C.E.) (Arabic).
Nestorians	Early Christians of the Middle East and western Asia, who believed that Jesus had two natures and two persons, human and divine.
niwa	A sacred space, garden (Japanese).
okurasho	Ancient Japanese state treasuries.
pairidaeza	A pre-Persian term for enclosure or burial place.
palmas	Part of Mesoamerican ballplayers' equipment—possibly fitted into the yoke at the waist.

paradeisos	The Greek word derived from *pairidaeza*, meaning ideal garden.
party wall	A shared wall between two buildings.
pendentives	Spherical triangles used to transform a square bay into a circular form to support a dome.
piles	Tree trunks (like telephone poles) used as foundations in swampy or muddy terrain.
pokharas	Small artificial lakes or large reservoirs in Nepal.
polders	Low-lying, reclaimed land, protected from the sea by dikes (Dutch term).
Popol Vuh	An ancient Quiche Maya manuscript.
purlin	The longitudinal member of the roof frame, supporting the rafters.
qibla	A mosque wall oriented toward Mecca.
rafters	Upright members of a roof frame.
rathas	A chariot on which the image of a Hindu god is carried in processions.
rawda	A garden or paradise (see *firdaw*).
refrectory	A dining hall, especially of a monastery.
ridgepole	The horizontal timber at the top of a roof frame, to which the rafters are attached.
river training	The term used by Chinese hydraulic engineers for river management.
roof-comb	A lightweight decorated structure placed on top of a building to increase its height (Maya).
safe yield (water)	The minimum flow of a water system in the dry season and the maximum flow during the strongest storms.
sahn	The courtyard of a mosque.
sampans	Small, flat-bottom boats propelled by a single sculling oar or small motor over the stern (China).
sastras	A Hindu architectural treatise (also vastu-sastras).
shakkei	"Borrowed scenery" in Chinese and Japanese garden design.
shinden	An ancient residence having several buildings, a pond, and gardens connected by covered walks (Japan).
shoden	The main building of a Japanese villa.
shogunate	The Japanese military class.
shoin	Originally a writing desk near a window for a priest; the term was later extended to mean a style of residence (Japan).
shoji	Rice-paper-covered wooden-frame sliding screens (Japan).
shuden	The main hall associated with the early shoin style (Japan).
sikhara	A tower-shaft form for temples, developed in India about the sixth century C.E.
sipapu	The hole in a kiva floor or volcano from which Anasazi spirits or first people appeared (Native American).
social distance	The extent to which individuals are excluded from the lives of others (a psychological term).

squinch	Corbeling or bridging the corners of a bay to support a smaller dome or drum.
status	The position of an individual in relation to others, especially with regard to social standing or rank.
stela	Upright slab, usually carved in relief (Latin).
stupa	A monumental pile of earth or other material, commemorating Buddha or a Buddhist saint.
synoikism	The union of several villages into a city, frequently under duress (from the Greek).
tana	A niche near a tokonoma, with one or more shelves (Japan).
tanks	Medium-size water holders, larger than cisterns but smaller than reservoirs.
Taoism	The philosophy and religion of China, based on the writings of Lao-tzu (6th century B.C.E.).
tatami	Straw mats used to cover traditional Japanese floors.
tatar	A porch or colonnade in Islamic buildings.
toko	The shortened version of the word *tokonoma*.
tokobashira	A non-load-bearing post next to a tokonoma.
tokonoma	An alcove for displaying works of art or flower arrangements—a special place in the Japanese home.
tokowaki	An alcove for shelves.
totems	Clan spirits, sometimes depicted on totem poles (Native American).
travois	Two long poles tied together across an animal's back, with a frame between the poles near the ground, to support a load; used for transporting a tipi.
tushahitty	An especially elegant bath or fountain, the focus of a palace courtyard in Nepal.
vara	A Spanish measure of about a yard (.9 meters).
Venus calendar	A Venus-cycle year is 18 months of 20 days, and eight years make a full cycle, equal to five solar years (Maya, Aztec).
vernacular architecture	Buildings using the commonest techniques, decorative features, and materials of a period, region, or group.
viharas	Monasteries of Buddhism in Nepal.
wabi	Rustic refinement aesthetic (Japan).
wall plate	A wooden plate placed flat on the foundation walls, to which is fastened the studs of the walls.
wat	Temple (Kampuchea/Cambodia).
wattle and daub	A method of construction using woven reeds or grasses (wattle) covered with clay or clayey mud (daub).
Zen	A Chinese (sixth century C.E.) and Japanese (twelfth century) religious approach, a form of Mahayana Buddhism.
ziggurat	A Mesopotamian temple-tower made of mud brick.

▦ Selected Bibliography

A. M. H. S. 1996. "Who's Buried in Margarita's Tomb? *Archae-ology* (July–August):17.

Abrams, E. 1994. *How the Maya Built Their World: Energetics and Ancient Architecture.* Austin: University of Texas Press.

Adams, R. E. W. 1982. "Ancient Maya Canals: Grids and lattices in the Maya Jungle." *Archaeology* (November–December): 28–35.

———. 1983. "Ancient Land Use and Cultural History in the Pasion River Region." In *Prehistoric Settlement Patterns: Essays in Honor of G. R. Willey,* 322–38, edited by E. Z. Vogt and R. M. Leventhal. Albuquerque: University of New Mexico Press.

———. 1991. *Prehistoric Mesoamerica.* Rev. ed. Norman: University of Oklahoma Press.

Adams, W. 1991. *Nature Perfected: Gardens Through History.* New York: Abbeville Press.

Adcock, C. 1990. *James Turrell: The Art of Light and Space.* Berkeley: University of California Press.

Al Faruqi, I., and L. Al Faruqi. 1986. *The Cultural Atlas of Islam.* New York: Macmillan.

Al-Azzawi, S. H. 1969. "Oriental Houses in Iraq." In *Shelter and Society,* 91–101, edited by P. Oliver. New York: Praeger.

Alexander, C. 1977. *Pattern Language.* New York: Oxford University Press.

Allchin, F. A. 1980. "A Note on the 'Asokan' Stupas of Patan." In *The Stupa: Its Religious, Historical and Architectural Significance,* 147–56), edited by A. L. Dallapiccola and S. Zingel-Avé Lallemant. Wiesbaden, Germany: F. Steiner Verlag.

Allchin, F. R. 1995. *The Archaeology of Early Historic South Asia.* With contributions from G. Erdoxy, R. A. E. Coningham, D. K. Chakrabarti, and B. Allchin. Cambridge, England: Cambridge University Press.

Alsayyad, N., and G. Boostani. 1988. "Mosques." In *Encyclopedia of Architecture Design, Engineering and Construction,* Vol. 3, 460–76, edited by J. Wilkes and R. Packard. New York: John Wiley & Sons.

Andrews, G. F. 1975. *Maya Cities: Placemaking and Urbanization.* Norman: University of Oklahoma Press.

Andrews, P. A. 1971. "Tents of the Tekna, Southwest Morocco." In *Shelter in Africa,* 124–42, edited by P. Oliver. London: Barrie & Jenkins.

Angelakia, A. N., and A. S. Issar, eds. 1996. *Diacrhonic Climatic Impacts on Water Resources.* Berlin: Springer Verlag. Includes: Davis, O. K. "The Impact of Climatic Change on Available Moisture in Arid Lands: Examples from the American Southwest," 283–300.

"Angkor." 1986. *Encyclopedia Britannica,* 15th ed. Vol. 1, Dubuque, Iowa: 405–06.

Antoniades, A. C. 1992. *Architecture and Allied Design.* Dubuque, Iowa: Kendall/Hunt.

Archer, J. 1994. "Space as Negotiation: Theoretical Considerations in the Historical Analysis of Calcutta, 1690–1850." Paper presented at the meeting of the Society of Architectural Historians, April, Philadelphia. Typescript in the collection of D. P. Crouch.

"Architecture." 1975. *New Columbia Encyclopedia.* New York: Columbia University Press.

Ardeleanu-Jansen, A., U. Franke, and M. Jansen. 1983. "An Approach Towards the Replacement of Artifacts into the Architectural Context of the Great Bath in Mohenjo-Daro." In *Forschungsprojekt DFG Mohenjo-Daro.* Aachen, Germany: Veroffentlichung der Seminarbeitrage.

Arkoun, M. 1994. "The Metamorphosis of the Sacred." In *The Mosque: History, Architectural Development, and Regional Diversity,* 268–72, edited by M. Frishman and H.-U. Khan. London: Thames & Hudson.

Armillas, P. 1971. "Gardens on Swamps." *Science* 174 (November 12): 653–61.

Arnold, D. 1991. *Building in Egypt: Pharonic Stone Masonry.* New York: Oxford University Press.

Ascher, R. 1968. "Time's Arrow." In *Settlement Archaelogy,* 43–52, edited by K. Chang. Palo Alto, Calif.: National Press Books.

Ashby, G. 1983. *Pohnpei: An Island Argosy.* revised 1987. Eugene, OR: Rainy Day Press.

Asher, C. 1992. *The New Cambridge History of India: Architecture of Mughal India.* Cambridge, England: Cambridge University Press.

Ashmore, W. 1992. "Deciphering Maya Architectural Plans." In *New Theories on the Ancient Maya,* 173–84, edited by E. C. Danien and R. J. Sharer. Philadelphia: University Museum, University of Pennsylvania.

Atasoy, N. et al. 1990. *The Art of Islam.* Paris: UNESCO.

Athens, J. S. 1983. "The Megalithic Ruins of Nan Madol." *Natural History* 92 (December):51–60.

Aveni, A. F., ed. 1977. *Archaeoastronomy in Pre-Columbian America.* Austin: University of Texas Press.

———. 1982. "Horizontal Astronomy in Incaic Cuzco" in *Proceedings of the Symposium Space and Time in the Cosmovision of Mesoamerica,* 175–93, edited by F. Tichy. Munich: Wilhelm Finkl Verlag.

———. 1986. "The Nazca Lines: Patterns in the Desert." *Archaeology* (July–August) 32–39.

———. 1989. *Empires of Time: Calendars, Clocks and Cultures.* New York: Basic Books. See especially Chapter 8: "The Incas and Their Orientation Calendar," 278–304.

Azevedo, P. O. D. de. 1982. *Cuzvco Ciudad Historica: Continuidad y Cambio.* Paris: UNESCO.

Babur, 1996. *The Baburnama: Memoires of Babur, Prince and Emperor.* 1996. Thackston, W.M., translator, editor, and annotator. New York and Oxford. Oxford University Press, 1996.

Bacon, Edmund N. 1974. *Design of Cities.* Harmondsworth, England: Penguin Books.

Bacon, Edward, ed. 1963. *Vanished Civilizations of the Ancient World.* New York: McGraw-Hill. Includes:
Pym, C. "Collapse of the Khmers," 105–38. Summers, R., "Zimbabwe," 33–54.

Bacus, E. A. et al., eds. 1993. A Gendered Past: A Critical Bibliography of Gender in Archaeology. Anthropological Technical Report 24. Ann Arbor: University of Michigan.

Badawy, A. 1965. *Ancient Egyptian Architectural Design.* Berkeley: University of California Press.

———. 1986. "Ancient Constructional Diagrams in Egyptian Architecture," *Gazette des Beaux Arts* 107: 51–56.

Badeau, J. S. et al. eds. 1975. *The Genius of Arab Civilization—Sources of Renaissance.* New York: New York University Press.

Bahadori, M. N. 1978. "Passive Cooling Systems in Iranian Architecture." *Scientific American* 238 (February): 144–54.

Baldwin-Smith, E. 1978. *The Dome: A Study in the History of Ideas.* Princeton, N.J.: Princeton University Press.

Bankes, G. H. A. 1972. "Settlement Patterns in the Lower Moche Valley, North Peru." In *Man, Settlement, and Urbanization: Proceedings of the Research Seminar in Archaeology and Related Subjects,* 903–1008, edited by P. J. Ucko, R. Tringham, and G. W. Dimbleby. Cambridge, Mass.: Schenkman.

Bannister Fletcher, A. 1987. *A History of Architecture on the Comparative Method,* 19th ed. London: Butterworths.

Banton, M., ed. 1965. *The Relevance of Models for Social Anthropology,* Vol. 1. London: Association of Anthropology Monographs. Includes:
B. E. Ward, "Varieties of the Conscious Model: The Fishermen of South China," 113–37.

Barba P., L. 1995. "El Impacto Humano en la Paleo-Geograffa de Teotihuacán." Doctoral dissertation, UNAM, Mexico.

Barba P., L. A., L. Mansanilla, R. Chavez, L. Flores, and A. J. Arzate, 1990. "Caves and Tunnels at Teotihuacan, Mexico: A Geological Phenomenon of Archaeological Interest." In *Archaeological Geology of North America: Centennial Special Volume 4, 431–38,* edited by N. P. Lasca and J. Donahue. Geological Society of America, Washington D.C.

Barkindo, B. M., ed. 1989. Kano and Some of Her Neighbors. Kanao, Nigeria: Ahmadu Bello University Press. Includes:
M. T. Sa'ad, "Continuity and Change in Kano Traditional Architecture," 59–77.

Bateson, G. *Naven.* 1958. Stanford, Calif.: Stanford University Press.

Bäumer, B. 1991. "From Guha to Akasa: The Mystical Cave in the Vedic and Saiva Traditions." In *Concepts of Space Ancient and Modern,* 105–07, edited by K. Vatsyayan. New Delhi: Abhinav Publications.

Bawden, G. 1990. "Domestic Space and Social Structure in Pre-Columbian Northern Peru." In *Domestic Architecture and the Use of Space: An Interdisciplinary Study,* 153–71, edited by S. Kent. Cambridge, England: Cambridge University Press. We adopted the term *Euro-American* from this book.

Beach, D. 1993. "Great Zimbabwe." In *The Shona and Their Neighbors,* 74–93. Oxford, England: Blackwell.

Beardsley, R. K., J. W. Hall, and R. E. Ward. 1959. *Village Japan.* Chicago: University of Chicago Press.

Beck, C. M. 1979. "Ancient Roads on the North Coast of Peru". Ph.D. dissertation, University of California, Berkeley.

Becker-Ritterspach, R. O. A. 1995. *Water Conduits in the Kathmandu Valley*. New Delhi: Munshiram Manoharial.

Beckingham, C. F. 1960. *Atlas of the Arab World and the Middle East*. New York: Macmillan.

Beckwith, C., and A. Fisher. 1990. *Africa Ark*. New York: Harry N. Abrams.

Begley, W. E. 1979. "The Myth of the Taj Mahal and a New Theory of Its Symbolic Meaning." *Art Bulletin* (March): 7–37.

———. 1985. *Monumental Islamic Calligraphy from India*. Villa Park, Ill.: Islamic Foundation.

Begley, W. E., and Z. A. Desai, compilers and trans. 1989. *Taj Mahal: The Illumined Tomb, an Anthology of Seventeenth Century Mughal and European Documentary Sources*. Seattle: University of Washington Press.

Beimler, R. R. (text) and Greenleigh, J. (photography). 1991. *The Days of the Dead*. San Francisco: Collins.

Bellwood, P. 1987. *The Polynesians: Prehistory of an Island People.*, rev. ed. London: Thames & Hudson. Original work published 1978.

Belshaw, C. S. 1957. *The Great Village: The Economic and Social Welfare of Hanuabada, an Urban Community in Papua*. London: Routledge & Kegan Paul.

Benjamin, D. J., and D. Stea, eds. 1995. *The Home: Words, Interpretations, Meanings, and Environments*. Aldershot, England: Avebury. Includes:
S. Kent, "Ethnoarchaeology and the Concept of Home: A Cross-Cultural Analysis."

Bent, T. 1893. *Ruined Cities of Mashonaland: Being a Record of Excavations and Exploration in 1891*. London: Longmans, Green.

Berlo, J. C. 1982. Artistic Specialization at Teotihuacan: The Ceramic Incense Burner" In *Pre-Columbian Art History: Selected Readings*, 83–100, edited by A. Crody-Collins. Palo Alto, Calif.: Peek.

———. "Icons and Ideologies at Teotihuacan: The Great Goddess Reconsidered. In *Art, Ideology and the City of Teotihuacan*, 129–68, edited by J. C. Berlo. Washington, D.C.: Dumbarton Oaks Research Library and Collection.

Berlo, J. C., ed. 1992. *Art, Ideology, and the City of Teotihuacan: A Symposium at Dumbarton Oaks*, October 8–9, 1988. Washington, D.C.: Dumbarton Oaks Research Library and Collection. Includes:
J. C. Berlo, "Icons and Ideologies at Teotihuacan: The Great Goddess Reconsidered," 129–168, Introduction.
S. T. Evans and J. C. Berlo, "Teotihuacan: An Introduction," 1–27.
R. Millon, "Teotihuacan Studies: From 1950 to 1990 and Beyond," 339–419.

S. Sugiyama, "Rulership, Warfare, and Human Sacrifice at the Ciudadela: An Iconographic Study of Feathered Serpent Representations," 205–30.
K. A. Taube, "The Iconigraphy of Mirrors at Teotihuacan," 169–204.

Bernstein, J. 1969. *The Wildest Dreams of Kew*. New York: Simon & Schuster.

Bidder, I. 1959. *Lalibela: The Monolithic Churches of Ethiopia*. London: Thames & Hudson.

Blair, K. D. 1983. *4 Villages: Architecture in Nepal*. Los Angeles: Craft and Folk Art Museum.

Blanchard, D. H. 1969. *Ethiopia and Its Culture*. San Antonio, TX: Naylro Co.

Bland, J. O. P. 1909. *Houseboat Days in China*. London, E. Arnold.

Blier, S. P. 1987. *The Anatomy of Architecture: Ontology and Metaphor in Batammaliba Architectural Expression*. New York: Cambridge University Press.

Blunt, W. 1966. *Isfahan, Pearl of Persia*. New York: Stein & Day.

Boas, F. 1888. *The Central Eskimo: Sixth Annual Report*. Washington, D.C.: Bureau of American Ethnology.

Bock, K. E. 1956. *The Acceptance of Histories: Toward a Perspective for Social Sciences*. Berkeley: University of California Press.

Boethius, A. 1960. *The Golden House of Nero*. Ann Arbor: University of Michigan Press.

Bon, R. 1986. "The Role of Construction in the National Economy." *Habitat Internationl*. 10 (No. 4): 93–99.

———. 1988. "Direct and Indirect Resource Utilization by the Construction Sector." *Habitat International* 12 (No. 1): 49–74.

———. 1991. "What Do We Mean by Building Technology?" Lecture presented at University of Reading.

———. 1992. "The Future of International Construction: Secular Patterns of Growth and Decline." *Habitat International* 16 (No. 3): 119–28.

———. 1993. "New Construction versus Maintenance and Repair Construction Technology in the US since World War II. *Construction Management and Economics* 11: 151–62.

———. 1994a. "Whither Global Construction? Part 1." *Building Research and Information* 22 (No. 2): 109–114.

———. 1994b. "Whither Global Construction? Part 2." *Building Research and Information* 22(No. 3): 118–26.

———. 1995. *Building Economics: Bibliography*. Reading, England: University of Reading. Updated periodically.

Bongartz, R. 1976. "Acoma, N(ew) M(exico)—Oldest Town in the U.S.A. *New York Times* (November 28): 7.

Bourdier, J.-P. 1994. "Dwelling with Spirit." *Progressive Architecture* (July): 96–99.

Bourdier, J.-P., and N. Alsayyad, eds. 1989. *Dwellings, Settlements and Tradition: Cross-Cultural Perspectives*. New York: Lanham. Includes Y.-F. Tuan, "Traditional: What Does It Mean?" 27–34. Includes:

B. Bognar, "The Plan of No-Thingness: The Japanese House and the Oriental World Views of the Japanese," 183–212.
R. Waterson, "Migration, Tradition and Change in Some Vernacular Architectures of Indonesia," 477–502.

Bourdier, J.-P., and T. T. Minh-ha. 1997. *Drawn from African Dwellings*. Bloomington: Indiana University Press.

Bourdieu, P. 1973. "The Berber House." In *Rules and Meaning*, 98–110, edited by M. Douglas. New York: Penguin Books.

———. 1977. *Outline of a Theory of Practice*. Cambridge, England: Cambridge University Press.

Bourgeois, J.-L., and C. Pelos. 1983. *Spectacular Vernacular: A New Appreciation of Traditional Desert Architecture*. Salt Lake City, Utah: Peregrine Smith.

Bowden, R. 1984. "Art and Gender Ideology in the Sepik." *Man*, New Series. 19: 445–58.

———. 1990. "The Architecture and Art of Kwoma Ceremonial Houses." In *Sepik Heritage: Tradition and Change in Papua, New Guinea*, 480–90, edited by L. Lutkehaus et al. Durham, N.C.: Wenner-Green Foundation Carolina Press.

Boyd, A. 1962. *Chinese Architecture and Town Planning*. Chicago: University of Chicago Press.

Boyd, R. 1968. *New Directions in Japanese Architecture*. New York: George Braziller.

Brandt, J. H. 1962. "Nan Matol, Ancient Venice of Micronesia." *Archaeology* 25 (No. 2): 99–110.

Brasser, T. J. 1976. "Home, House, and Temple among the Plains Indians." *Canadian Collector* 11 (No. 1): 31–34.

Brasseur de Bourbourg, Abbe. 1866. *Monuments anciens du Mexique. . . .* Paris: A. Bertrand. Includes a section on the Franco-German scholar Waldeck's travels in Mesoamerica.

Bray, W. 1972. "Land-use, Settlement Patterns, and Politics in Prehispanic Middle America: A Review." In *Man, Settlement, and Urbanization*, 909–26, edited by P. J. Ucko, R. Tringham, and G. W. Dimbleby. Cambridge, Mass.: Schenkman.

———. 1983. "Landscape with Figures: Settlement Patterns, Locational Models, and Politics in Mesoamerica." In *Prehistoric Settlement Patterns: Essays in Honor of G. R. Willey*, 167–93, edited by E. Z. Vogt and R. M. Leventhal. Albuquerque: University of New Mexico Press.

Bring, M., and J. Wayembergh. 1981. *Japanese Gardens: Design and Meaning*. New York: McGraw-Hill.

Bristol, H. 1994. "Vanished Japan." *Los Angeles Times Magazine* (March 6). Photographs of Japan at the end of World War II.

Bronson, B. 1978. "Angkor, Anuradhapura, Prambanan, Tikal: Maya Subsistence in an Asian Perspective." In *Pre-Hispanic Maya Agriculture*, 255–300, edited by P. D. Harrison and B. L. Turner II. Albuquerque: University of New Mexico Press.

Brookes, J. 1987. *Gardens of Paradise: The History and Design of the Great Islamic Gardens*. London: Weidenfeld & Nicolson.

Brown, N. W. 1983. "Indonesia Rescues Ancient Borobudur." *National Geographic* 163 (January): 126–42.

Brundage, B. C. 1967. *Lords of Cuzco*. Norman: University of Oklahoma Press.

Bruwer, A. J. 1965. *Zimbabwe: Rhodesia's Ancient Greatness*. Johannesburg, South Africa: Hugh Kertland.

Buck, P. H. (Te Rangi Hiroa). 1964. *Arts and Crafts of Hawaii: II. Houses*. Honolulu: Bishop Museum.

Bulmer, R. 1973. "Why the Caswowary Is Not a Bird." In *Rules and Meaning*, 167–93, edited by M. Douglas. New York: Penguin.

Bunting, B. 1976. *Early Architecture in New Mexico*. Albuquerque: University of New Mexico Press.

Burford, M. A. 1965. "The Economics of Greek Temple Building." *Proceedings of the Cambridge Philological Society* 191: 21–34.

"Bushmen: San." 1986. In *Encyclopedia Britannica*, 15th ed., Vol. 10, 383–84.

Bussagli, M. 1973. *Oriental Architecture*. New York: Harry Abrams.

Bussel, G. W., van, P. L. F. van Dungen, and T. J. J. Leyenaar, eds. 1991. *The Mesoamerican Ballgame 2000 BC–AD 2000*. Leiden: Rijksmuseum vor Volkenkunde. Includes:

M. G. Robertson, "The Ballgame at Chichen Itzá: An Integrating Device of the Polity in the Post-Classic, 91–110.

Butzer, K. W. 1982. "Empires, Capitals and Landscapes of Ancient Ethiopia." *Archaeology* (September–October): 30–37.

Calloway, B. 1987. *Muslim Hausa Women in Nigeria: Tradition and Change*. Syracuse, N.Y.: Syracuse University Press.

Calnek, E. E. 1973. "The Localization of the Sixteenth Century Map Called the Maguey Plan," *American Antiquity* 38: 190–95.

———. 1976. "The Internal Structure of Tenochtitlan." In *The Valley of Mexico: Studies in Pre-Hispanic Ecology and Society*, 287–302, edited by E. R. Wolf.

Canby, T. Y. 1982. "The Anasazi: Riddles in the Ruins." *National Geographic* (November): 562–92.

Carlson, J. B. 1993. "Rise and Fall of the City of the Gods." *Archaeology* (November–December): 58–69.

Carmichael, E., and C. Sayer. 1991. *The Skeleton at the Feast: The Day of the Dead in Mexico*. London: British Museum Press.

Carpenter, E., and M. McLuhan, eds. 1966. *Explorations in Communication*. Boston: Beacon Press. Includes:
D. Lee, "Lineal and Nonlineal Codifications of Reality," 136–54.

Carroll, D., and eds. of the Newsweek Book Division. 1978. *The Taj Mahal*. New York: Newsweek.

Carver, N. 1986. *Silent Cities of Mexico and the Maya*. Kalamazoo, Mich.: Document Press.

———. 1989. *North African Villages: Morocco, Algeria, Tunisia*. Kalamazoo, Mich.: Document Press.

Castedo, L. 1969. *A History of Latin American Art and Architecture*. New York: Praeger.

Caton-Thompson, G. 1931. *The Zimbabwe Culture*. London: Oxford University Press.

———. 1983. *Mixed Memories*. Gateshead, England: Paradigm Press.

Cavalli-Sforza, L. L., P. Monozzi, and A. Piazza. 1994. *The History and Geography of the Human Gene*. Princeton, N.J.: Princeton University Press.

Celik, Z., D. Favro, and R. Ingersoll, eds. 1994. *Streets: Critical Perspectives on Public Space*. Berkeley: University of California Press. Includes:
J. P. Protzen and J. H. Rowe, "Hawkaypota, Terrace of Leisure," 235–46.

Chadwick, D. H. 1987. "At the Crossroads of Kathmandu." *National Geographic* 172 (No. 1): 32–65. Photos by W. Thompson.

Chakrabarti, D. K. 1995. *The Archaeology of Ancient Indian Cities*. New York: Oxford University Press.

Chandra, L. 1980. "Borobudur: A New Interpretation." In *The Stupa: Its Religious, Historical and Architectural Significance*, 301–19, edited by A. L. Dallapiccola and S. Zingel-Avé Lallemant. Wiesbaden, Germany: F. Steiner Verlag.

———. 1991. Life, Space and Structures. In *Concepts of space Ancient and Modern*, 211–18 edited by K. Vatsyayan. New Delhi: Abhlnav Publications.

Chang, A. I. T. 1956. *The Tao of Architecture*. Princeton, N.J.: Princeton University Press.

Chang, K., ed. 1968. *Settlement Archaeology*. Palo Alto, Calif.: National Press Books. Includes:
R. Ascher, "Time's Arrow," 43–52.
J. Rouse, "Prehistory, Typology, and the Study of Society," 10–30.
B. J. Trigger, "The Determination of Settlement Patterns," 53–78.
G. R. Willey, "Settlement Archaeology: An Appraisal," 208–26.

Chang, K.-C. 1962. "A Typology of Settlement and Community Patterns, in Some Circumpolar Societies." *Arctic Anthropology* 1: 28–41.

Chang, S.-D. 1961. "Historical Trends of Chinese Urbanization." *Annals of the Association of American Geographers* 53: 23–45. Rouse, J. 1968. Prehistory, Typology, and the Study of Society." In *Settlement Archaeology*, 10–30, edited by K. Chang, Palo Alto, Calif. National Press Books.

———. 1970. "Some Observations on the Morphology of Chinese Walled Cities." *Annals of the Association of American Geographers* 60 (March): 63–91.

Chapelle, J. 1957. *Nomades Noirs du Sahara: Richerches en Science Humaine, No. 10*. Paris: Librairie Plon.

Chatterjee, A. 1985. "Wage Structures of Artisans and Laborers Engaged in Construction Work in Medieval Rajasthan (AD 1670–1761): A Case Study of Bikaner State. In *Proceedings of the 46th Indian History Congress*, Amritsar, 315–25.

Chejne, A. 1974. *Muslim Spain: Its History and Culture*. Minneapolis: University of Minnesota Press.

Ching, Ch'i-min (Jing Qi Min). 1985. *One Hundred Titles of Traditional Chinese Architecture*. Tianjin, China: Xin Hua Publisher. In Chinese with English subtitles.

Ching, F. D. 1979. *Architecture: Form, Space and Order*. New York: Van Nostrand, Reinhold.

Churchill, W. 1941. Speech to the House Commons on the destruction and possible rebuilding of the House of Commons, May 19.

Cieza de Leon, Pedro de. 1959. *The Incas of Pedro de Cieza de Leon*, ed. with an intro. by V. Von Hagen, trans. H. de Onis. Norman: University of Oklahoma Press.

Clark, J. D. 1972. "Mobility and Settlement Patterns in Sub-Saharan Africa: A Comparison of Late Prehistoric Hunter-Gatherers and Early Agricultural Occupation Units." In *Man, Settlement, and Urbanization*, 127–48, edited by P. J. Ucko, R. Tringham, and G. W. Dimbleby. Cambridge, Mass.: Schenkman.

Clark, J. D., ed. 1957. *Third Pan-African Congress on Prehistory*. London: Chatto & Windus. Includes:
A. Whitty, "The Origins of the Stone Architecture of Zimbabwe," 366–77.

Clark, S., and R. Engelbach. 1930. *Ancient Egyptian Masonry: The Building Craft*. Oxford, England: Oxford University Press.

Clarke, A. C. 1978. *The Fountains of Paradise*. New York: Harcourt, Brace.

Clifford, D. 1983. *A History of Garden Design*. New York: Praeger.

Coaldrake, W. H. 1990. *The Way of the Japanese Carpenter: Tools and Japanese Architecture*. New York: Weatherhill.

Coe, M. D. 1961. "Social Typology and the Tropical Forest Civilizations. *Comparative Studies in Society and History* 4 (November): 65–85.

———. 1964. "The Chinampas of Mexico. *Scientific American* 211 (July): 90–98.

———. 1968. *America's First Civilization: Discovering the Olmecs.* New York: American Heritage.

———. 1996. *The Maya.* 5th ed. London: Thames & Hudson.

Coe, W. 1962. *Mexico.* New York: Praeger.

———. 1967. *Tikal: A Handbook of Ancient Maya Ruins.* Philadelphia: University of Pennsylvania Press.

———. 1982. *Introduction of the Archaeology of Tikal.* Philadelphia: University of Pennsylvania Press.

Coiffier, C. 1990. "Sepik River Architecture: Changes in Cultural Traditions." In *Sepik Heritage: Tradition and Change in Papua, New Guinea,* 491–97, edited by N. Lutkehaus et al. Durham, N.C.: Wenner-Gren Foundation and Carolina Academic Press.

Colcutt, M., et al. 1988. *Cultural Atlas of Japan.* New York: Facts on File.

Colton, H. S. 1936. "The Basaltic Cinder Cones and Lava Flows of the San Francisco Mountain Volcanic Field." *Museum of Northern Arizona Bulletin* 10: 3–49.

Comboz, G. 1932–34. "L'evolution du stupa en Asie." *Melanges Chinois et Bouddhiques* vols. 2,3,4.

Cook, Captain James. 1773–74. *Capt. Cook's Voyage Around the World in 1768, 1769, 1770, and 1771.* London.

Coomaraswamy, A. K., 1992a. "Early Indian Architecture I. Cities and City Gates." *Eastern Art.* Vol. 2. New Delhi: Indira Gandhi National Center for the Arts and Oxford University Press. Original work published 1930.

———. 1992b. *Essays in Early Indian Architecture,* ed. with introduction by M. W. Meister. New Delhi: Indira Gandhi National Center for the Arts and Oxford University Press.

Copplestone, T., ed. 1963. *World Architecture.* New York: Crown Books.

Cordell, L. S., and F. Plog. 1979. "Escaping the Confines of Normative Thought: A Reevaluation of Puebloan Prehistory." *American Antiquity* 44 (No. 3): 405–29.

Cordy, R., and T. John. 1984. *Interpretive Guidebook, Leluh Ruins (Caroline Islands).* Leluh Ruins Landowners Corp., Pohnpei, Caroline Islands.

Courtney-Clarke, M. 1986. *Ndebele: The Art of an African Tribe.* New York: Rizzoli.

Cowell, F. R. 1978. *The Garden as a Fine Art from Antiquity to Modern Times.* Boston: Houghton Mifflin.

Cowgill, G. L. 1974. "Quantitative Studies of Urbanization at Teotihuacan." In *Mesoamerican Archaeology: New Approaches,* 363–96, edited by N. Hammond. Austin: University of Texas Press.

Cragg, K. 1988. *Readings in the Quran.* London: Callen's Liturgical Publications.

Cranstone, B. A. L. 1972. "Environment and Choice in Dwelling and Settlement: an Ethnographical Survey." In *Man, Settlement, and Urbanization,* 487–503, edited by P. J. Ucko, R. Tringham, and G. W. Dimbleby. Cambridge, Mass.: Schenkman.

Creswell, K. 1989. *A Short Account of Muslim Architecture,* rev. and ed. by J. Allan. Aldershot, England: Scolar Press.

Crill, R., J. Guy, and D. Swallow, eds. 1980. *Arts of India: 1500–1900.* London: Victoria and Albert Museum.

Crody-Collins, A., ed. 1982. *Pre-Columbian Art History: Selected Readings.* Palo Alto, CA: Peek. Includes:

J. C. Berlo, "Artistic Specialization at Teotihuacan: The Ceramic Incense Burner," 83–100.

W. J. Cromie, "When Comes El Niño?" *Science* 80 (March–April) 1: 36–43.

Crouch, D. P. 1985. *History of Architecture: Stonehenge to Skyscrapers.* New York: McGraw-Hill.

Crouch, D. P. 1992. "Spanish Water Technology in New Spain: Transfer and Alteration." In *Geschichte der Wucwasserwirtschaft und des Wasserbaus im Mediterranen Raum,* 179–228. Braunschweig, Germany: Technical University, Mitteilungen. Vol. 117.

———. 1993. *Water Management in Ancient Greek Cities.* New York: Oxford University Press.

Crouch, D. P., D. J. Garr, and A. I. Mundigo. 1982. *Spanish City Planning in North America.* Cambridge, Mass.: MIT Press.

Crump, D. J., ed. 1981. *Splendors of the Past.* Washington, D.C.: National Geographic Society. Includes:

L. de la Haba. "Angkor and the Ancient Khmer," 182–219.

C. R. Ramsay, "Land of the Sinhalese Kings," 248–88.

Cunningham, A. 1997. *Mahabodi, or the Great Buddhist Temple Under the Bodhi Tree at Budda-Gaya.* New Delhi: Munshiram Manoharial Publishers.

Dai, W. 1981. "Why the Wall Was Built." in *The Great Wall,* 42–51. New York: McGraw-Hill. Other chapters by Dai: "The Neighbors of the Wall," 158–67.
"Trade Across the Wall," 168–83.

Dales, G. F. 1996. "The Decline of the Harappans. *Scientific American* 214 (May): 93–99.

Dallapiccola, A. L., and S. Zingel-Avé Lallemant, eds. 1980. *The Stupa: Its Religious, Historical and Architectural Significance.* Wiesbaden, Germany: F. Steiner Verlag. Includes:

F. A. Allchin, "A Note on the 'Asokan' Stupas of Patan," 147–56.

L. Chandra, "Borobudur: A New Interpretation," 301–19.

H. G. Franz, "Stupa and Stupa-Temple in the Gandharan Regions and Central Asia," 39–58.

N. Gutschow, "The Urban Context of the Stupa in Bhaktapur/Nepal," 137–46.

J. Irwin, "The Axial Symbolism of the Early Stupa: An Exegesis," 12–38.

L. Ledderose, "Chinese Prototypes of the Pagoda," 238–48.

Danien, E. C., and R. J. Sharer, eds. 1992. *New Theories on the Ancient Maya*. Philadelphia: University Museum, University of Pennsylvania. Includes:

W. Ashmore, "Deciphering Maya Architectural Plans," 173–84.

S. D. Houston, "Classic Maya Politics," 65–69.

W. F. Rust III, "New Ceremonial and Settlement Evidence at La Venta, and its Relation to Preclassic Maya Cultures," 123–39.

Darwin, C. G. 1956. "The Time Scale in Human Affairs." In *Man's Role in Changing the Face of the Earth*," 963–69, edited by W. Thomas et al. Chicago: University of Chicago Press.

Davenport, G. 1981. *The Geography of the Imagination*. San Francisco: North Point Press.

Davidson, B. 1959. *The Lost Cities of Africa*. Boston: Little Brown.

———. 1966. *African Kingdoms*. New York: Time-Life Books.

Davis, O. K. 1996. "The Impact of Climatic Change on Available Moisture in Arid Lands: Examples from the American Southwest." In *Diachronic Climatic Impacts on Water Resources*, 283–300, edited by A. N. Angelakia and A. S. Issar. Dubuque, Iowa: Kendall/Hunt.

de Zevedo, see Azevedo.

de la Haba, see Haba.

de la Hoz, see Sancho de la Hoz

de Montequin, see Montequin.

de Olarte, see Olarte.

de Silva, see Silva.

Denevan, W. M. 1970. "Aboriginal Drained-Field Cultivation in the Americas." *Science* 169:647–54.

Denis, A. J. 1934. *Houseboating in Kashmir*. Los Angeles: Times Mirror Press.

Denyer, S. 1978. *African Traditional Architecture*. New York: Africana Publishing Co.

Desai, D. 1992. "Man and Temple: Architectural and Sculptural Imagery of the Kandariya Mahadeva Temple of Khajuraho." In *Eastern Approaches: Essays on Asian Art and Archaeology*, edited by T. S. Maxwell. Delhi: Oxford University Press.

Dewey, J. 1958. *Art as Experience*. New York: Capricorn Books.

Dickie, J. 1976. "The Islamic Garden in Spain." In *The Islamic Garden*, 89–105, edited by E. MacDougall and R. Ettinghausen. Washington, D.C.: Dumbarton Oaks Colliquium.

———. 1978. "Allah and Eternity: Mosques, Madrasa and Tombs." In *Architecture of the Islamic World: Its History and Social Meaning*, edited by G. Michell. 15–47, New York: William Morrow.

Documentary Sources. 1990. Cambridge, Mass.: Aga Khan Program for Islamic Architecture, Harvard University and MIT.

Domenig, G. 1980. *Tektonik im Primitiven Dachbau [Tectonics in Primitive Roof Construction]*. Zurich: Institut Gaudenz/ETH.

Donley-Reid, L. W. "A Structuring Structure: The Swahili House." In *Domestic Architecture and the Use of Space: An Interdisciplinary Study*, 93–114, edited by S. Kent. Cambridge, England: Cambridge University Press.

Donnan, C. B. 1990. "Masterworks of Art Reveal a Remarkable Pre-Inca World." *National Geographic* 177 (No. 6): 16–33.

Doolittle, W. E. 1990. *Canal Irrigation in Prehistoric Mexico: The Sequence of Technological Change*. Austin: University of Texas Press.

Doresse, J. *Ethiopia*. 1959. London, Elek Books. See Chapter 4: The Zagve Dynasty and the Churches of Lalibela, 93–114.

Doughty, C. M. 1949. *Travels in Arabia Deserta*. London: J. Cape. Reprint of 1888 ed.

Douglas, M. 1972. "Symbolic Orders in the Use of Domestic Space. In *Man, Settlement, and Urbanization*, 513–21, edited by P. J. Ucko, R. Tringham, and G. W. Dimbleby. Cambridge, Mass.: Schenkman.

Douglas, M., ed. 1973. *Rules and Meaning*. New York: Penguin. Includes:

P. Bourdieu, "The Berber House," 98–110.

R. Bulmer, "Why the Caswsowary Is Not a Bird," 167–93.

Durkeim, E., and M. Mauss, "The Social Genesis of Logical Operations," 32–37.

E. Evans-Pritchard, "Time Is Not a Continuum, 75–81.

S. J. Tambiah, "Classification of Animals in Thailand," 127–66, esp. 132–37 about house categories.

Duerden, D. 1968. *African Art*. London: P. Hamlyn.

Dugan, A. 1983. "Wall, Cave, and Pillar Statements, after Asoka." In *New and Collected Poems 1961–1983*. New York: Ecco Press.

Duly, C. 1979. *Houses of Mankind*. London: Thames & Hudson.

Dumerfay, J. 1991. *The Palaces of South-East Asia: Architecture and Customs*, M. Smithies, ed. and trans. New York: Oxford University Press.

Duncann, J. S. 1990. *The City as Text: The Politics of Landscape Interpretation in the Kandyan Kingdom*. Cambridge, England: Cambridge University Press.

Durkeim, E. and M. Mauss. 1973. "The Social Genesis of Logical Operations." In *Rules and Meaning*, 32–37, edited by M. Douglas. New York: Penguin.

Dutton, B. P., ed. 1958. *Indians of the Southwest*. Santa Fe: New Mexico Association on Indian Affairs.

Eddy, F. W. 1984. *Archaeology: A Cultural-Evolutionary Approach*. Englewood Cliffs, N.J.: Prentice Hall.

Eggan, F. 1950. *Social Organization of the Western Pueblos*. Chicago: University of Chicago Press.

Eisner, S., et al. 1992. *Urban Pattern.* 6th ed. New York: Van Nostrand Reinhold.

Eliot, G. 1989. *Ndebele.* 1989. Struik Publishers (Pty) Ltd.

Emory, K. P. 1969. "A Re-examination of East Polynesian Marae: Many Marae Later." In *Studies in Oceanic Culture History,* Vol. 1. 73–92, edited by R. C. Green and M. Kelly. Pacific Anthropological Records No. 11. Honolulu: Department of Anthropology, Bishop Museum. Honolulu.

———. 1971. *Tuamotuan Stone Structures.* Reprint of *Bulletin 118,* Bishop Museum, Honolulu, 1934. New York: Kraus Reprint Co.

Encyclopedia Britannica, 15th ed. 1986. Chicago: Encyclopedia Britanica, Inc. Includes:
 "Angkor," Vol. 1:405–06.
 "Architecture: The History of Western," Vol. 13: 976.
 "Bushmen: San," Vol. 10: 383–84.
 "Hausa," Vol. 5: 752–53.
 "Kampuchea," Vol. 27: 728.
 "Pacific Islands," Vol. 25: 243–92.
 "Pagan (Burma)," Vol. 9: 56–57.
 "Sri Lanka." Vol. 11: 190–92.

Engel H. 1964. *The Japanese House: A Tradition for Contemporary Architecture.* Rutland, Vt.: Charles E. Tuttle.

Erdos, R., and A. Ortiz, eds. 1984. *American Indian Myths and Legends.* New York: Pantheon Books.

"Ethiopian Art." 1972. *Encyclopedia of World Art,* Vol. 5, 80–100. New York: McGraw-Hill.

Ettinghousen, R., and O. Grabar. 1972. *From Byzantium to Sassanian Iran and the Islamic World: Three Modes of Artistic Influence.* Leiden: Brill.

———. 1989. *The Art and Architecture of Islam, 650–1250.* Harmondsworth, England: Penguin.

Evans, S. T., and J. C. Berlo. 1992. "Teotihuacan: An Introduction." In *Art, Ideology, and the City of Teotihugcan,* 1–27, edited by J. C. Berlo. Washington, D.C.: Dumbarton Oaks Research Library and Collection.

Evans-Pritchard, E. 1973. "Time Is Not a Continuum." In *Rules and Meaning,* 75–81, edited by M. Douglas. New York: Penguin.

Fage, J. D., ed., 1978. *The Cambridge History of Africa,* Vol. 2. New York: Cambridge University Press.

Fage, J. D. 1981. "The Development of African Historiography." In *General History of Africa: I. Methodology and African Prehistory,* 25–42, edited by J. Ki-Zerbo. London: Heinemann Educational Books.

Farley, M. 1995. "Human Error Feeds China's Floodwaters." *Los Angeles Times* (July 13).

Farmighetti, R., ed. 1994. *World Almanac.* Mahwah, N.J.: Funk & Wagnalls.

Fathy, H. 1986. *Vernacular Architecture; Principles and Examples with Reference to Hot Arid Climates,* ed. W. Shearer and A. A. Sultan. Chicago: University of Chicago Press.

Feldman, R. A. See Ortloff 1985.

Feng K'o-ts'an. 1673. *Local History of T'an-Ch'eng.* Cited in J. D. Spence, *The Death of Woman Wang.* New York: Viking, 1978.

Fentress, M. 1977–78. "Regional Interaction in Indus Valley Urbanization: The Key Factors of Resource Access and Exchange." In *American Studies in the Anthropology of India,* 389–424, edited by S. Vatuk. New Delhi: Manohar.

———. 1984. "The Indus 'Granaries' Illusion: Illusion, Imagination and Archaeological Reconstruction." In *Studies in the Archaeology and Palaeoanthropology of South Asia* [Delhi], ed. K. A. R. Kennedy and G. L. Passehi: 89–97.

Ferguson, W., and A. Rohn. 1988. *Anasazi Ruins of the Southwest in Color.* Albuquerque: University of New Mexico Press.

———. 1990. *Mesoamerica's Ancient Cities.* Niwot: Colorado University Press.

Feuchtwang, S. D. R. 1974. *An Anthropological Analysis of Chinese Geomancy.* Vieintiane, Laos: Ed. Vithagna.

Findlay, L. 1944. *The Monolithic Churches of Lalibela in Ethopia.* Cairo: Publication de la Societe d'Archaeologie Copte.

Fischer, J. L. 1964. "The Abandonment of Nan Matol, Ancient Capital of Ponape." *Micronesia* 1 (No. 9): 49–54.

Fitch, J. M., and D. P. Branch. 1960. "Primitive Architecture and Climate." *Scientific American* 203 (No. 6): 134–44.

Fitch, R. F. 1927. "Life Afloat in China," *National Geographic* 51 (No. 6): 665–86.

Fitchen, J. 1978. "Building Cheops Pyramid." *Journal of the Society of Architectural Historians* 37 (No. 1): 3–12.

———. 1990. *Building Construction Before Mechanization.* Cambridge, Mass.: MIT Press, 3rd edition.

Fletcher, B.A. see Bannister Fletcher, A.

"Floating Fiesta: On Xochimilco's Canals, Restored to Aztec Spendor, a Place to Go with the Flow." 1995. *Los Angeles Times* (April 9).

"Floods in China Kill 437; Troops Aid in Rescues." 1995. *Los Angeles Times* (July 6).

Fodor's India. 1993. New York: Fodor's Travel Publications.

Fonesca, R. 1986. "The Geometry of Zoser's Step Pyramid at Saqqara." *Journal of the Society of Architectural Historians* 54 (No. 4): 333–38.

Forde, C. D. 1934. *Habitat, Economy and Society: A Geographical Introduction to Ethology.* New York: E. P. Dutton. Includes: "The Ruwala Badawin, Camel Breeders of Northern Africa," 308–27.

"The Blackfoot," 43–68.

"The Bushmen: Hunters in the Kalahari Desert," 24–31.

"The Caribou Hunters [Eskimos]," 107–28.

"The Hopi and Yuma: Flood Farmers in the North American Desert," 220–59.

"Oceanians: People of the East Solomons and the Society Islands," 173–219.

Foresta, R., and M. Livingston. 1991. "Stepwells and the Public Past in Modern India." *Iaste Working Paper Series* 25: 97–110.

Forge, A. 1966. "Art and Environment in the Sepik." *Proceedings of the Royal Anthropological Institute of Great Britain and Ireland.* London, England: The Institute [sic]

———. 1972. "Normative Factors in the Settlement Size of Neolithic Cultivation (New Guinea)". In *Man, Settlement, and Urbanization,* 363–76, edited by P. J. Ucko, R. Tringham, and G. W. Dimbleby. Cambridge, Mass.: Schenkman.

———. 1973. "Style and Meaning in Sepik Art. In *Primitive Art and Society,* 169–92. London: Werner Gren Foundation and Oxford University Press.

Foster, G. M. 1960. "Contemporary Hispanic American Culture: The Product of Acculturation. Chapter 1 of G. M. Foster, *Culture and Conquest: The American Spanish Heritage,* 1–49. New York: Quadrangle Books.

Francotte, H. 1979. *L'Industrie dans la Grece Ancienne: II.* New York: Arno Press. Original work published 1900–01.

Franz, H. G. 1980. "Stupa and Stupa-temple in the Gandharan Regions and Central Asia. In *The Stupa: Its Religious, Historical and Architectural Significance,* 39–58, edited by A. L. Dallapiccola and S. Zingel-Avé Lallemant. Wiesbaden, Germany: F. Steiner Verlag.

Fraser, D. 1968. "Bushmen." In *Village Planning in the Primitive World,* 15–17. New York: G. Braziller.

Frazer, J. G. 1907–15. *The Golden Bough,* 12 vols., 3rd ed. London: Macmillan.

Frazier, I. 1994. *Family.* New York: Farrar, Strauss, & Giroux.

Freidel, D. A. 1983. "Political Systems in Lowland Yucatan: Dynamic Structure in Mayan Settlements." In *Prehistoric Settlement Patterns: Essays in Honor of G. R. Willey,* 374–86, edited by E. Z. Vogt and R. M. Leventhal. Albuquerque: University of New Mexico Press.

Frishman, M. 1994. "Islam and the Form of the Mosque." In *The Mosque: History, Architectural Development and Regional Diversity,* 17–42, edited by M. Frishman and H.-U. Khan. London: Thames & Hudson.

Frishman, M., and H.-U. Khan, eds. 1994. *The Mosque: History, Architectural Development and Regional Diversity.* London: Thames & Hudson. Includes:

M. Arkoun, "The Metamorphosis of the Sacred," 268–72.

M. Frishman, "Islam and the Form of the Mosque," 17–42.

L. Prussin, "Sub-Saharan Africa," 181–94.

W. M. Thackston, "The Role of Calligraphy," 43–54.

Fu, S., et al. 1986. *From Concept to Context: Approaches to Asian and Islamic Calligraphy.* Washington, D.C.: Freer Gallery of Art.

Fuson, R. H. 1969. "The Orientation of Mayan Ceremonial Centers." *Annals of the American Association of Geography.* 59: 494–511.

Futagawa, Y. 1983. See Itoh.

Gallenkamp, C. 1985. *Maya: The Riddle and Rediscovery of a Lost Civilization.* 3rd rev. ed. New York: Viking Press.

Ganesan, S. 1982. *Management of Small Construction Firms: A Case Study of Sri Lanka, Singapore, Hong Kong, Thailand, the Philippines, and Japan.* Tokyo: Asian Productivity Organization.

Garbrecht, G., ed. 1987. *Kolloquium, Wasserbau in der Geschichte.* Braunschweig, Germany: Leichtweiss Inst. für Wasserbau. Includes:

F. Hartung, "Geschichte der Hochwasserfreilung von Alt-Mexico," 157–91.

R. Liang, Z. Zheng, and J. Hu, "River Training Works Throughout the History of China," 191–204.

Garcilaso de la Vega G. S. ("The Inca"). 1961. *The Royal Commentaries of the Inca.* New York: Orion Press.

Gasparini, G., and L. Margolies. 1980. *Inca Architecture,* P. Lyon, trans. Bloomington: Indiana University Press.

Gates, H. L., Jr., ed. 1986. *"Race," Writing, and Difference.* Chicago: University of Chicago: University of Chicago Press. Includes: M. L. Pratt, "Scratches on the Face of the country; or, What Mr. Barrow Saw in the Land of the Bushmen," 136–62.

Gathercole, P. "The Study of Settlement Patterns in Polynesia." In *Man, Settlement, and Urbanization,* 50–60, edited by P. J. Ucko, R. Tringham, and G. W. Dimbleby. Cambridge, Mass.: Schenkman.

Gaur, A. 1994. *A History of Calligraphy.* New York: Cross River Press.

Gelber, M. G. 1986. *Gender and Society in the New Guinea Highlands: An Anthropological Perspective on Antagonism Toward Women.* Boulder, Colo.: Westview Press.

Gernet, J. 1981. Forward. *The Great Wall.* New York: McGraw-Hill.

Gervais, P. 1954. *This Is Kashmir.* London: Cassell.

Ghosh, B., and K. C. Mago. 1974. "Srirangam's Urban From and Pattern in Ancient India." *Ekistics* 38: 377–84.

Gibbs, J. L., ed. 1965. *Peoples of Africa.* New York: Holt, Rinehart & Winston. Includes:

L. Marshall, "The !Kung Bushmen of the Kalahari," 245–67.

M. G. Smith, "The Hausa of Northern Nigeria," 121–43.

Gibbs, P., Y. A. Rahman, and A. Kassim. 1987. *Building a Malay House*. Singapore: Oxford University Press.

Gilmour, D. 1992. *Cities of Spain*. Chicago: I.R. Dee.

Giteau, M. 1976. *The Civilization of Angkor*. New York: Rizzoli.

Glahn, E. 1981. "Chinese Building Standards in the 12th Century." *Scientific American* (May): 162–73.

———. 1984. "Unfolding the Chinese Building Standards: Research on the *Yingzao Fashi*." In *Chinese Traditional Architecture*, 48–57, edited by N. Steinhardt. New York: China House Gallery.

Goetz, H. 1964. *Art of the World*. New York: Crown.

Gonzales, A. R. 1983. "Inca Settlement Patterns in a Marginal Province of the Empire: Sociocultural Implications." In *Prehistoric Settlement Patterns: Essays in Honor of G. R. Willey*, 337–60, edited by E. Z. Vogt and R. M. Leventhal. Albuquerque: University of New Mexico Press.

Goodnow, F. J. 1927. "The Geography of China." *National Geographic* 41 (No. 6): 651–63.

Goodwin, G. 1971. *A History of Ottoman Architecture*. Baltimore: Johns Hopkins University Press.

Grabar, O. 1963. *Islamic Art and Byzantine*. New York: Garland.

———. 1975. "Architecture and Art." In *The Genius of Arab Civilization—Sources of Renaissance*, 77–117, edited by J. S. Badeau et al. New York: New York University Press.

———. 1976. "The Umayyad Dome of the Rock in Jerusalem." *Islamic Art and Architecture*. Vol. 13, 33–62. New York: Garland.

———. 1978a. *The Alhambra*. Cambridge, Mass: Harvard Press.

———. 1978b "The Architecture of Power: Palaces, Citadels, Fortifications." In *Architecture of the Islamic World: Its History and Social Meaning*, 48–79, edited by G. Mitchell.

Grabar, O., and D. Hill. 1964. *Islamic Architecture and Its Decorations*. Chicago: University of Chicago Press.

Grable, D. 1988. *The Egyptian and Inca Gold Traders*. Madera, Reflections Press.

Graburn, N. H. H. 1969. *Eskimos Without Igloos: Social and Economic Development in Sugluk*. Boston: Little, Brown.

The Great Wall. 1981. New York: McGraw-Hill. Includes:
J. Gernet, Forward.
Dai, W.: "Why the Wall Was Built," 42–51. "The Neighbors of the Wall," 158–67. "Trade Across the Wall," 168–83.
Luo, Z.: "How the Wall Was Built," 128–39. "The Great Defense Line," 140–57.

Green, E. L. 1973. "Location Analysis of Prehistoric Maya Sites in Northern British Hondorus [today, Belize]." *American Antiquity* 38 (No. 3): 279–93.

Green, R. C., and M. Kelly, eds., *Studies in Oceanic Culture History*, Vol. 1. Pacific Anthropological Records No. 11. Honolulu: Department of Anthropology, Bishop Museum.

Groslier, B. P., and J. Arthaud. 1968. *Angkor, Art and Civilization*, E. E. Shaw, trans. London: Thames & Hudson.

Grove, A. T. 1989. *The Changing Geography of Africa*. London: Oxford University Press.

Grube, E. 1967. *The World of Islam*. New York: McGraw Hill.

———. 1978. "What Is Islamic Architecture?" In *Architecture of the Islamic World: Its History and Social Meaning*, 10–14, edited by G. Michell. New York William Morrow.

Guidoni, E. 1975. *Primitive Architecture*. New York: Abrams.

———. 1982. *Vicolo E Cortile: Tradizione Islamica e Urbanistica Populare in Sicilia*. Venice: E. Giada.

Gunawardana, R. A. L. H. 1971. "Irrigation and Hydraulic Society in Early Medieval Ceylon." *Past and Present* 53: 3–27.

Gunn, J. M. 1917. *Schat-Chen: Historical Traditions and Narratives of the Queres Indians of Laguna and Acoma*. Albuquerque: Abright & Anderson.

Gutkind, A. E. 1967. *Urban Development in Southern Europe: Spain and Portugal*. Vol. 3 of International History of City Development. New York: Free Press.

Gutschow, N. 1980. "The Urban Context of the Stupa in Bhaktapur/Nepal." In *The Stupa: Its Religious, Historical and Architectural Significance*, 137–46, edited by A. L. Dallapiccola and S. Zingel-Avé Lallemant. Wiesbaden, Germany: F. Steiner Verlag.

———. 1982. *Stadtraum und Ritual der Newarischen Staedte im Kathmand-Tal: Ein Architekturanthropo logische Untersuchung*. Stuttgart, Germany. Verlag W. Kohlhammer.

Gutschow, N., and B. Kölver. 1975. *Ordered Space Concepts and Functions in a Town of Nepal*. Nepal Research Center Publications, W. Voigt, ed.: Leiden: Rijksmuseum vor Volkenkunde.

Haalano, A. n.d. *Bhaktapur—A Town Changing*. Bhaktapur Development Project and GTZ, Frankfurt, Germany, Eschborn.

Haba, L. de la. 1981. "Angkor and the ancient Khmer. In *Splendors of the Past: Lost Cities of the Ancient World*, 182–219. Washington, D.C.: National Geographic Society."
L'habitat rural traditional." 1978. In *Urbanisme et architecture en Chine populaire, 1950–1978*. p. 7, supplement to the *Bulletin D'Information Inter-Etablissement* (No. 35). Paris: Centre D'etudes de Recherches Architecturales.

Hagen, V. W. von. 1961. *The Ancient Sun Kingdoms of the Americas*. Cleveland: World

Hall, J. W., and T. Takeshi, eds. 1977. *Japan in the Muromachi Age*. Berkeley: University of California Press. Includes:
T. Ito, "The Development of Shoin-Style Architecture," 227–239.

Hall, M. 1990a. "A Hidden History: Iron Age Archaeology in Southern Africa. In *A History of African Archaeology*, 59–77, edited by P. Robertshaw. London: J. Currey.

Halloran, R., and G. Rowell. 1994. "Crossroads Kingdom." *Los Angeles Times* (October 9).

Halperin, R., and J. Dow, eds. 1977. *Peasant Livelihood: Studies in Anthropology and Cultural Ecology*. New York: St. Martin's Press. Includes:

W. P. Mitchell, "Irrigation Farming in the Andes," 36–59.

Hambly, G., and W. Swaan. 1968. *Cities of Mughal India: Delhi, Agra, and Fatehpur Sihri*. New York: G. P. Putnam.

Hammond, N. 1972. "The Planning of a Maya Ceremonial Center." *Scientific American* (May): 83–90.

———. 1977. *Social Process in Maya Prehistory: Studies in Memory of Sir Eric Thompson*. London: Academic Press. Includes:

D. E. Puleston, "The Art and Archaeology of Hydraulic Agriculture in the Maya Lowlands," 449–69.

———. 1982. *Ancient Maya Civilization*. Cambridge, England: Cambridge University Press.

———. 1986. "The Emergence of Maya Civilization." *Scientific American* (August): 106–15.

———, ed. 1974. *Mesoamerican Archeology: New Approaches*. Austin: University of Texas Press. Includes:

G. L. Cowgill, "Quantitative Studies of Urbanization at Teotihuacann," 363–96.

Handbook of the American Indian. See F. W. Hodge or W. C. Sturtevant for earlier and later editors.

Harding, S. 1991. *Whose Science? Whose Knowledge?* Ithaca, N.Y.: Cornell University Press.

Hardoy, J. 1973. *Pre-Columbian Cities*, J. Thorne, trans. New York: Walker.

Hardoy, J. E. 1968. *Urban Planning in Pre-Columbian America*. London: Studio Vista.

Harle, B. 1988. *The Art and Architecture of India*. New York: Penguin.

Harris, D. K. 1978. "The Agricultural Foundations of Lowland Maya Civilization: A Critique. In *Pre-Hispanic Maya Agriculture*, 301–23, edited by P. D. Harrison and B. L. Turner II. Albuquerque: University of New Mexico Press.

Harrison, P. D., and B. L. Turner II, eds. 1978. *Pre-Hispanic Maya Agriculture*. Albuquerque: University of New Mexico Press. Includes:

B. Bronson, "Angkor, Anuradhapura, Prambanan, Tikal: Maya Subsistance in an Asian Perspective," 255–300.

D. K. Harris, "The Agricultural Foundations of Lowland Maya Civilization: A Critique," 301–23.

A. H. Siemens, "Karst and the Pre-Hispanic Maya in the Southern Lowlands," 117–43.

B. L. Turner II, "Ancient Agricultural Land Use in the Central Maya Lowlands," 166–210.

Hartung, F. 1987. "Geschichte der Hochwasserfreilung von Alt-Mexico." In *Kolloquium, Wasserbau in der Geschichte*, 157–91, edited by G. Garbrecht. Braunschweig, Germany: Leichtweiss Inst. für Wasserbau.

Harvey, B. 1972. "An Overview of Pueblo Religion." In *New Perspectives on the Puebloes*, 197–217, edited by A. Ortiz. Albuquerque: University of New Mexico Press.

Hashimoto, F. 1981. *Architecture in the Shoin Style: Japanese Feudal Residences*. Tokyo: Kodansha.

Hatipoglu, A. 1993–94. "The Architectural Mystic Suleymaniye." *Cityscope* (December–January): 2–5.

Haury, E. W. 1971. "Speculations on Prehistoric Settlement Patterns in the Southwest. In *Prehistoric Settlement Patterns in the New World*, 3–10, edited by G. Willey. New York: Johnson Reprint Corp. Original work published 1956.

Hauser-Schäublin, B. 1989. *Kultheuser in Nordneuguinea*. Berlin: Akadamie-Verlag.

———. 1990. "In the Swamps and on the Hills: Traditional Patterns and House Structures in the Middle Sepik." In *Sepik Heritage: Tradition and Change in Papua, New Guinea*, 470–79, edited by N. Lutkehaus et al. Durham, N.C.: Wenner-Gren Foundation/Carolina Academic Press.

Havell, E. 1904. *A Handbook to Agra and the Taj, Sikandra, Fatehpur-Sikri*. New York: Longmans, Green.

Haviland, W. A. 1969. "A New Population Estimate for Tikal, Guatamala." *American Antiquity* 34: 429–32.

Hedin, S. 1925. *My Life as an Explorer*. Garden City, N.Y.: Garden City Publishing.

Heldman, M., with S. C. Munro-Hay. 1993. *African Zion: The Sacred Art of Ethiopia*. New Haven, Conn.: Yale University Press.

Henderson, J. 1983. *The World of the Ancient Maya*. Ithaca, N.Y.: Cornell University Press.

Hernandez, J. F., and S. R. Hernandez. 1979. *The Day of the Dead: Tradition and Change in Contemporary Mexico*. Santa Clara: Calif. Triton Museum of Art.

Heyden, D. 1975a. "An Interpretation of the Cave Underneath the Pyramid of the Sun in Teotihuacan, Mexico." *American Antiquity* 40: 131–47.

———. 1975b. *Pre-Columbian Architecture of Mesoamerica*. New York: Abrams.

Hill, D., and L. Golvin. 1976. *Islamic Architecture in North Africa A.D. 800–1500*. Hamden, Conn.: Anchor Books.

Hill, D., and O. Grabar. 1964. *Islamic Architecture and Its Decorations*. Chicago: University of Chicago Press.

Hillerman, T. n.d. *New Mexico, Rio Grande and Other Essays*. Portland, Ore.: Graphic Arts Center Publications.

Historical Relics Unearthed in New China. 1972. Peking: Foreign Language Press.

Hitti, P. K. 1953. "Bedouin Life." In *History of the Arabs*, 23–30. London: Macmillan.

Hla, U. K. (S.S. Ozhegov). 1978. "Traditional Town Planning in Burma." *Journal of the Society of Architectural Historians*, 37 (No. 2): 92–104.

———. 1979. "Ancient Cities in Burma." *Journal of the Society of Architectural Historians* 38 (No. 2): 95–102.

Hoag, J. 1987. *Islamic Architecture.* New York: Electa/Rizzoli.

Hobsbawn, E. J., and T. Ranger, eds. 1983. *The Invention of Tradition.* Cambridge, England: Cambridge University Press. Includes:

T. Ranger, "The Invention of Tradition in Colonial Africa," 211–62.

Hodder, J., ed. 1978. *The Spatial Organization of Culture.* London: Duckworth.

Hodder, J., and C. Orton. 1976. *Spatial Analysis in Archaeology.* Cambridge, England: Cambridge University Press.

Hodge, F. W., ed. 1912. *Handbook of American Indians North of Mexico.* Washington, D.C.: U.S. Government Printing Office. See also W. C. Sturtevant for later editions.

Hodges, H. W. M. 1972. "Domestic Building Materials and Ancient Settlements." In *Man, Settlement, and Urbanization*, 523–30, edited by P. J. Ucko, R. Tringham, and G. W. Dimbleby. Cambridge, Mass.: Schenkman. See the Appendix.

Holt, P., ed. 1979. *Cambridge History of Islam*, Vols. 1A and 2B. Cambridge, England: Cambridge University Press.

Hook, B., ed. 1982. *Cambridge Encyclopedia of China.* New York: Cambridge University Press.

Horton, R. 1967. "African Traditional Thought and Western Science, Parts 1 and 2." *Africa* 37.

Hourani, A. H., and S. M. Stern, eds. 1970. *The Islamic City: A Colloquium.* New York: Oxford University Press.

Houston, G. 1976. "Mandalas: Ritual and Functional." *Tibet Journal* 2 (April–June): 47–58.

Houston, S. D. 1992. "Classic Maya Politics." In *New Theories on the Ancient Maya*, 65–69, edited by E. C. Danien and R. J. Sharer. Philadelphia: University Museum, University of Pennsylvania.

Howard, J. B. 1993. "A Paleohydraulic Approach to Examining Agricultural Intensification in Hohokam Irrigation Systems." In *Research in Economic Anthropology: Economic Aspects of Water Management in the Prehispanic New World, Supplement 7*, 263–326, edited by V. L. Scarborough and B. L. Isaac. Greenwich, Conn.: JAI Press.

Huang Liu-hung. 1694. *A Complete Book Concerning Happiness and Benevolence*, cited in J. D. Spence. *The Death of Woman Wang* (New York: Viking, 1978).

Hungry Wolf, A. 1972. *Tipt Life.* Fort MacCloud, Alberta: Good Medicine [Press].

Huntington, S. L., and J. C. Huntington. 1985. *The Art of Ancient India: Buddhist, Hindu, Jain.* New York: Weatherhill.

Huzayyin, J. 1956. "Changes in Climate, Vegetation, and Human Adjustment in the Saharo-Arab Belt with Special Reference to Africa." In *Man's Role in Changing the Face of the Earth*, 304–19, edited by W. Thomas et al. Chicago: University of Chicago Press.

Hyslop, J. 1984. *The Inca Road System.* Orlando, Fla.: Academic Press.

Ibn Khaldunn. 1958. *The Muqaddimah, An Introduction to History.* New York: Bollingen Series, Pantheon Books. Manuscript written 1377. See especially "Bedouin Civilization," Vol 1, 250–305.

Inn, H. 1946. *Chinese Houses and Gardens*, C. Lee, ed. 18 vols. New York: Crown.

International Association for the Study of Traditional Environments, Traditional Dwellings and Settlements: Working Paper Series in 18 volumes, including:

B.-Z. Liu, "A Chinese Family Village in Hancheng County," Vol. 12.

J. C. Moughtin, "The Work of Dmochowski: Nigerian Traditional Architecture," Vol. 7.

S. Woolard, "Traditional Dwellings of the South Pacific," Vol. 13.

Irwin, G. 1992. *The Prehistoric Exploration and Colonisation of the Pacific.* Cambridge, England: Cambridge University Press.

———. 1980. "The Axial Symbolism of the Early Stupa: An Exegesis." In *The Stupa: Its Religious, Historical and Architectural Significance*, 12–38, edited by A. L. Dallapiccola and S. Zingel-Avé Lallemant. Wiesbaden: Germany: F. Steiner Verlag.

Irwin, J. 1977. "The Stupa and the Cosmic Axis: The Archaeological Evidence." In *South Asian Archaeology 1977*, 12–38, edited by M. Taddei. Naples, Italy: Papers of the Association of South Asian Archaeologists in Western Europe.

Isimoto, Y. (photographs) and K. Tange (text), 1972. *Katsura.* New Haven, CT: Yale University Press.

Isler, M. 1989. "An Ancient Method of Finding and Extending Direction." *Journal of the American Research Center in Egypt* 26: 191–206.

Isozaki, A. 1987. *Katsura Villa*, tr. J. Lamb. New York: Rizzoli.

Itoh, T. 1972. *The Japanese Garden.* New Haven, Conn.: Yale University Press.

———. 1977. "The Development of Shoin-Style Architecture. In

Japan in the Muromachi Age, 227–39, edited by J. W. Hall and T. Takeshi. Berkeley: University of California Press.

Itoh, T. (text), and Y. Futagawa (photos). 1980. *The Traditional Japanese House*. Rev and enlarged ed. New York: Rizzoli.

Itoh, T., and S. Kuzunishi. 1988. *Space and Illusion in the Japanese Garden*. New York: 6th ed. Weatherhill/Tankosha.

Jacobs, J. 1969. *The Ecology of Cities*. New York: Random House.

Jairazbhoy, R. A. 1972. *An Outline of Islamic Architecture*. New York: Asia Publishing House.

James, E. 1822–23. *Account of an Expedition from Pittsburgh to the Rocky Mountains Performed in the Years 1819 and '20, by Order of the Hon. J. C. Calhoun, Sec'y of War: Under the Command of Major Stephen H. Long*. Philadelphia. A slightly different version was published in London.

James, H. L. 1970. *Acoma, the People of the White Rock*. Glorieta, N.M.: Rio Grande Press.

James, V. 1991. *Ancient Sites of O'Ahu*. Honolulu: Bishop Museum Press.

Jansen, M. 1977. "Architectural Problems of Harappa Culture." In *South Asian Archaeology*, 405–31, edited by M. Taddei. Naples, Italy: Papers of the Association of South Asian Archaeologists in Western Europe.

———. 1991. "The Concept of Space in Harappan City Planning—Mohenjo-Daro." In *Concepts of Space Ancient and Modern*, 75–82, edited by K. Vatsyayan. New Delhi: Abhinav Publications.

———. 1993. *Mohenjo-Daro: City of Wells and Drains: Water Splendor 4500 Years Ago*. Bonn: Frontinus Society Publications.

Jansen, M., and G. Urban, eds. 1983. *Interim Reports*, Vol. 1 of *Reports on Field Work Carried Out at Mohenjo-Daro, Pakistan 1982–83*. Aachen, Germany: Forschungsprojekt DFG Mohenjo-Daro.

Jellicoe, G., and S. Jellicoe. 1986. *The Oxford Companion to Gardens*. New York: Oxford University Press.

Jencks, C. 1978. "Meanings of the Chinese Garden." In *The Chinese Garden; History Art and Architecture*, edited by M. Kewsick. with contributions by C. Jencks, New York: Rizzoli.

Joesting, E. 1984. *Kauai, the Separate Kingdom*. Honolulu: University of Hawaii Press and Kauai Museum Association.

Johnson, C. R., comp. n.d. *Village Water Systems: Nepal and Bhutan: Standards and Procedures for the Design of Water Supply Systems in Rural Aral of Nepal and Bhutan*. Paris: UNICEF.

Johnson, K., and T. Ferguson. 1990. *Trusting Ourselves*. New York: Atlantic Monthly Press.

Johnson, W. 1995. "Keeping Cool." *Aramco World* 46 (No. 3): 10–17.

Johnston, S. 1991. *Scholar Gardens of China*. New York: Cambridge University Press.

Jones, D. 1978. "Surface, Pattern and Light." In *Architecture of the Islamic World: Its History and Social Meaning*, 144–75, edited by G. Michell. New York: William Morrow.

Jordan, K. 1982. Khajuraho: Temples Not for Shy. DALLAS MORNING NEWS. June 20. Travel Section: 1.

Jones, O. 1856. *The Grammar of Ornament*, London: Day and Sons.

Juillerat, B. 1990. "Male Ideology and Cultural Fantasy in Yafar Society." In *Sepik Heritage: Tradition and Change in Papua, New Guinea*, 380–84, edited by N. Lutkehaus et al. Durham, N.C.: Wenner-Gren Foundation/Carolina Academic Press.

Jung, C. 1963. *Memories, Dreams, Reflections*. New York: Pantheon Books.

Junsai, S. 1991. "Cave Man Space versus Boat Man Space." In *Concepts of Space Ancient and Modern*, 185–86, edited by K. Vatsyayan. New Delhi: Abhinav Publications.

Kalafatovich, V. C. 1970. "Geologia del Grupo Arqueologico de la Fortaleza de Saccsayhuaman y sus vecindades." *Revista Saccsayhuaman* 1 (July): 61–68.

"Kampuchea." 1986. *Encyclopedia Britannica*, Vol. 27, 798. 15th ed.

Kani, H. 1967. *A General Survey of the Boat People of Hong Kong*. Monograph Series No. 5. Hong Kong: Southeast Asia Studies Section, New Asia Research Institute, Chinese University of Hong Kong.

Kapur, M. 1992. *The History and Culture of Kashmir*. 2nd ed. rev. New Delhi: Anmal Publications.

Kawashima, C. 1986. *Minka: Traditional Houses of Rural Japan*. Tokyo: Kodansha.

Kaye, G. R. 1918. *The Astronomical Observatories of Jai Singh*. Archaeological Survey of India, New Imperial Series, Vol. 40.

Kenko, Y. (1282–1350) 1967. *Tsurezuregusa: Essays on Idleness*. D. Keene, trans. New York: Columbia University Press.

Kent, S. 1991a. Partitioning Space: Cross-Cultural Factors Influencing Domestic Spatial Segmentation. *Environment and Behavior*, 23, 23.4 (July): 438–73, especially 446–49.

Kent, S. 1991b. The Relationship between Mobility Strategies and Site Structure. In *The Interpretation of Spatial Patterning within Stone Age Archaeology*. E. Kroll and T.D. Price, ed. New York: Plurnum Publishing Corporation: 33–60.

Kent, S. 1995a. Ethnoarchaeology and the Concept of Home: A Cross-Cultural Analysis, in *The Home: Words, Interpretations, Meanings, and Environments*. D.J. Benjamin and D. Stea, eds. Aldershot: Avebury, 1995 (read in typescript).

Kent, S. 1995b. Typlolgies: Spatial Relationships, in *Encyclopedia of Vernacular Architecture of the World*. P. Oliver, ed. Cambridge, England.: Cambridge University Press, 1995.

Kent, S. 1995. Unstable Households in a Stable Kalahari Community in Botswana. *American Anthropologist*. 97(2):287–312.

Kent, S., ed. 1990. *Domestic Architecture and the Use of Space: An Interdisciplinary Study*. Cambridge, England: Cambridge University Press. Includes:

G. Bawden, Domestic space and social structure in pre-Columbian northern Peru, 153–71.

S. Kent, Activity areas and architecture, 1–9.

A. Rapoport, Systems of activities and systems of settings, 9–20.

Keswick, M., with contributions by Charles Jencks. 1978. *The Chinese Garden: History, Art and Architecture*. New York: Rizzoli.

Ketchum, R. M. 1957. "Acoma and Santa Fe." In *American Heritage Book of Great Historic Places*, 314–17. New York: American Publishing Co.

Khan, F. A. 1964. *The Indus Valley and Early Iran*. Karachii, Pakistan: Department of Archaeology and Museums.

Ki-Zerbo, J., ed. 1981. *General History of Africa: I. Methodology and African Prehistory*. London: Heinemann Educational Books.

King, E. Viscount of Kingsborough, 1831–1848 9 vol. *Antiquities of Mexico*.

King, G., and R. Lewcock. 1978. "Key Monuments of Islamic Architecture." *Architecture of the Islamic World: Its History and Social Meaning*, 209–80, edited by G. Michell. New York: William Morrow.

Kinross, L. 1977. *The Ottoman Centuries: The Rise and Fall of the Turkish Empire*. New York: William Morrow.

Kirch, P. V. 1985. *Feathered Gods and Fishhooks*. Honolulu: University of Hawaii Press. See especially Figs. 224 and 225: two Hawaiian temples.

———. 1988. "Polynesia's Mystery Islands." *Archaeology* (May–June): 266–31.

Kirch, P. V., and M. Sahlinns, eds. 1992. *Anahulu: Historical Ethnography*, Vol. 1 of *Anthropology of History in the Kingdom of Hawaii*, M. Sahlins with D. B. Barrere, series eds. Chicago: University of Chicago Press.

Kleinbauer, W. E. 1971. *Modern Perspectives in Western Art History*. New York: Holt, Rinehart & Winston. 1971.

Knapp, R. G. 1986. *China's Traditional Rural Architecture: A Cultural Geography of the Common House*. Honolulu: University of Hawaii Press.

———. 1990. *The Chinese House: Craft, Symbol and Folk Tradition*. New York: Oxford University Press.

Knowles, R. L. 1974. *Energy and Form*. Cambridge, Mass.: MIT Press.

———. 1981. *Sun Rhythm Form*. Cambridge, Mass.: MIT Press.

Kobidhvhssnov, Y. M. 1979. *Axum*. State College: Pennsylvania State University Press.

Koch, E. 1991. *Mughal Architecture: Outline of History and Development 1526–1858*. New York: Neues.

Kolata, A. L. 1983. "Chan Chan and Cuzco: On the Nature of the Ancient Andean City." In *Civilization in the Ancient Americas*, 345–71, edited by R. M. Leventhal and A. L. Kolata. Albuquerque: University of New Mexico Press.

Kolota, A. L., ed. 1996. *Tiwanaku and Its Hinterland: Archaeology and Paleoecology of an Andean Civilization*. Washington, D.C.: Smithsonian Institution Press. Includes:

C. R. Ortloff and A. L. Kolata, "Tiwanaku Raised Bed Field Agriculture in the Lake Titicaca Basin of Bolivia." chap. 5.

C. R. Ortloff, "Engineering Aspects of Tiwanaku Groundwater-Controlled Agriculture," chap. 6.

A. L. Kolata and C. R. Ortloff, "Agroecological Perspectives on the Decline of the Tiwanaku State," chap. 8.

Kolata, A. L., and C. Ortloff. 1989. "Thermal Analysis of Twanaku Raised Field System in the Lake Ttiticaca Basin of Bolivia." *Journal of Archaeological Science*, 16: 233–63.

Kolb, M. J. 1992. "Diachronic Design Changes in Heiau Temple Architecture on the Island of Maui, Hawaii," *Asian Perspectives* 31 (No. 1): 9–38.

Konya, A. 1980. *Design Primer for Hot Climates*. London: Architectural Press.

Kosok, P. 1965. *Life, Land and Water in Ancient Peru*. New York: Long Island University Press.

Kostof, S. 1985. *A History of Architecture: Settings and Rituals*. New York: Oxford University Press.

Kowalski, J. K. 1999. *Mesoamerican Architecture as Cultural Symbol*. New York: Oxford University Press.

Krinskey, C. H. 1981. "St. Petersburg-on-the-Hudson: The Albany Mall." In *Art, the Ape of Nature: Essays in Honor of H. W. Janson*, 771–87, edited by L. F. Sandler and M. Barasch. Englewood Cliffs, N.J.: Prentice Hall.

Kristan-Graham, C. B. 1989. "Art, Rulership and the Mesoamerican Body Politic at Tula and Chichen Itzá." Ph.D. dissertation, UCLA.

Kroll, E., and T. D. Price, eds. 1991. *The Interpretation of Spatial Patterning Within Stone Age Archaeology*. New York: Plenum. Includes:

S. Kent, "The Relationship between Mobility Strategies and Site Structure," 33–60.

Kropp, M. 1956. *Cuzco Window on Peru*. New York: Crowell.

Krupp, E. C. 1989. "The Cosmic Temples of Old Beijing." In *World Archaeoastronomy*, 65–75, edited by A. F. Aveni.

Kubler, G. 1975. *The Art and Architecture of Ancient America.* 2nd. ed. Harmondsworth, England: Penguin.

———. 1976. "Methodological Approaches to Pre-Columbian Art." *Actes* 42: Congress International des Americanestes v. VII: 283–90.

Kuhn, T. S. 1986. "The Histories of Science." *Academe* (July–August):

Kuran, A. 1987. *Sinan, the Grand Old Master of Ottoman Architecture.* Washington, D.C.: Institute of Turkish Studies.

Kuznets, S. 1968. *Toward a Theory of Economic Growth.* New York: W. W. Norton.

Landa, Diego de. 1941. "Relacion de las Cosas de Yucatán, A. Tozzer, tr. and ed. In *Papers of the Peabody Museum of Archaeology and Ethnology,* Vol. 18. Cambridge, Mass.: Harvard University.

Landon, P. 1928. *Nepal.* 2 vol. London: Constable.

Lao-tzu, Li Erh. 1972. *Tao-Te Ching* [*Classic of the Way of Power,* ca. sixth century B.C.E.], Trans. G.-F. Feng and J. English. New York: Vintage Books.

Lapidus, I. 1988. *A History of Islamic Societies.* New York: Cambridge University Press.

Lasca, N. P., and J. Donahue, eds. 1990. *Archaeological Geology of North America: Centennial Special Volume 4.* Boulder, Colo: Geological Society of America. Includes:
   Barba P., L. A., L. Mansanilla, R. Chavez, L. Flores, A. J. Arzate, "Caves and Tunnels at Teotihuacan, Mexico: A Geological Phenomenon of Archaeological Interest," 431–38.

Latif, S. 1981. *Agra—Historical and Descriptive with an Account of Akbar and His Court and of the Modern City of Agra.* Calcutta: Oriental Publishers and Booksellers. Reprint of 1896 edition.

Laubin, R., and G. Laubin. 1957. *The Indian Tipi: Its History, Construction, and Use.* Norman, Okla.: University of Oklahoma Press.

Lavin, I. 1980. *Bernini and the Unity of the Visual Arts.* New York: Pierpont Morgan Library and Oxford University Press.

Leach, E. R. 1959. "Hydraulic Society in Ceylon." *Past and Present* 15: 2–26.

Le Bon, G. 1885. *Voyage au Nepal.* Paris: Tour du Monde. Reprint 1981 Bankok White Orchid.

Ledderose, L. 1980. "Chinese Prototypes of the Pagoda." In *The Stupa: Its Religious, Historical and Architectural Significance,* 238–48, edited by A. L. Dallapiccola and S. Zingel-Avé Lallemant. Wiesbaden, Germany: F. Steiner Verlag.

Lee, D. 1966. "Lineal and Nonlineal Codifications of Reality." In *Explorations in Communication,* 136–54, edited by E. Carpenter and M. McLuhan. Boston: Beacon Press.

Lee, R. B. 1972. "!Kung Spatial Organization: An Ecological and Historical perspective." *Human Ecology* 1 (No. 2): 125–47.

———. 1979. *The !Kung San.* Cambridge, England: Cambridge University Press.

Lehmann, P.-H., J. Ullal. 1981. *Tibet: Das Stille Drama auf dem Dach Der Erde.* Hamburg: GEO-Bücher im Verlag Gruner. 1981.

Lehner, E. 1996. *Sudsee-Architektur: Traditionelle Bautypen auf Hawaii, Tonga, Samoa, Neuseeland und den Fidschi-inseln.* Vienna: Phoibos, Verlag.

Lehrman, J. 1980. *Earthly Paradise: Garden and Courtyard in Islam.* Berkeley: University of California Press.

Leluh Ruins, Historical Park. See Cordy and John (1984).

Leonard, J. H., and editors of Time-Life Books. 1967. *Ancient America.* New York: Time.

Leventhal, R. M., and A. L. Kolata, eds. 1983. *Civilization in the Ancient Americas.* Albuquerque: University of New Mexico Press. Includes:
   A. L. Kolata, "Chan Chan and Cuzco: On the Nature of the Ancient Andean City," 345–71.
   J. R. topic, and T. L. Topic," Coast-Highland Relations in Northern Peru: Some Observations on Routes, Networks, and Scales of Interaction," 237–59.

Lewis-Williams, D., and T. Dowson. 1989. *Images of Power: Understanding Bushman Rock Art.* Johannesburg, South Africa: Southern Book Publishing.

L'habitat. See Habitat.

Liang, R., Z. Zheng, and J. Hu. 1987. "River Training Works Throughout the History of China. In *Kolloquium, Wasserbau in der Geschichte,* 191–204, edited by G. Garbrecht. Braunschweig, Germany: Leichtweiss Inst. für Wasserbau.

Liang, S. 1984. *A Pictorial History of Chinese Architecture,* W. Fairbank, ed. Cambridge, MA: MIT Press.

Liu, L. 1989. *Chinese Architecture.* New York: Rizzoli.

Livingston, M., and R. Foresta. 1991. "Stepwells and the Public Past in Modern India." *Iaste Working Paper Series* 25: 97–110.

Losche, D. 1990. "Utopian Visions and the Division of Labor in Abelam Society." In *Sepik Heritage: Tradition and Change in Papua New Guinea,* 395–401, edited by N. Lutkehaus et al. Durham, N.C.: Wenner-Gren Foundation/Carolina Academic Press.

Luo, Z. 1981. "How the Wall Was Built." *The Great Wall,* 128–39. New York: McGraw-Hill. Another chapter by Luo, Z.: "The Great Defense Line," 140–57.

Lutkehaus, N. et al., eds. 1990. *Sepik Heritage: Tradition and Change in Papua New Guinea.* Durham, N.C.: Wenner-Gren Foundation/Carolina Academic Press. Includes:
   R. Bowden, "The Architecture and Art of Kwoma Ceremonial Houses," 480–90.

C. Coiffier, "Sepik River Architecture: Changes in Cultural Traditions," 491–97.

B. Hauser-Schäublin, "In the Swamps and on the Hills: Traditional Patterns and House Structures in the Middle Sepik," 470–79.

B. Juillerat, "Male Ideology and Cultural Fantasy in Yafar Society," 380–84.

D. Losche, "Utopian Visions and the Division of Labor," 395–401.

W. M. Ruff, and R. E. Ruff, "The Village Studies Project for the Recording of Traditional Architecture," 568–86.

P. Swadling, "Sepik Prehistory," 60–76.

P. K. Townsend, "Our Women Are Okay: Aspects of Hiyewe Women's Status," 374–79.

M. H. Williamson, "Gender and the Cosmos in Kwoma Culture," 385–94.

MacCormack, C., and M. Strathern, eds. 1980. *Nature, Culture, and Gender.* Cambridge, England: Cambridge University Press.

MacDougall, E., and R. Ettinghausen, eds. 1976. *The Islamic Garden.* Washington, D.C.: Dumbarton Oaks Colloquium. Includes:

J. Dickie, "The Islamic Garden in Spain," 89–105.

Macmullen, R. 1990. *Changes in the Roman Empire: Essays in the Ordinary.* Princeton, N.J.: Princeton University Press.

Marcus, C. C. 1993. *House as a Mirror of Self: Exploring the Deeper Meaning of Home.* Berkeley, Calif.: Conari Press.

Marcus, J. 1983. "On the Nature of the Mesoamerican City." In *Prehistoric Settlement Patterns: Essays in Honor of G. R. Willey,* 195–242, edited by E. Z. Vogt and R. M. Leventhal. Albuquerque: University of New Mexico Press.

Marinos, P., and G. Koukis, eds. 1988, 1990. *Engineering Geology of Ancient Works, Monuments and Historical Sites.* Vol. 3. Rotterdam, A. A. Balkema. Includes:

Pendergast, D. M. "Engineering Problems in Ancient Maya Architecture: Past, Present, and Future."

G. Veni, "Maya Utilization of Karst Groundwater Resources," 1661–66.

Marinos, P., M. Kavvadas, G. Xiedakis, M. Galos, B. Kleb, and I. Marek. 1994. "Underground Housing and Cellars in Volcanic Tuffs: Variations in Geotechnical Behavior and Experiences from Greece and Hungary." *Proceedings of the 7th International UAEG Congress,* 4415–22. Rotterdam: A. A. Balkema.

Maritan, J. 1953. *Creative Intuition in Art and Poetry.* New York: Pantheon Books.

Marriott, A. 1945. *The Ten Grandmothers.* Normon: University of Oklahoma Press. See esp., "The First Tipi," 64–71.

Marshall, J., and A. Faucher. 1940. *The Monuments of Sanchi.* 3 vols. London: Probsthain.

Marshall, L. 1960. "!Kung Bushmen Bands." *Africa* 30 (No. 4): 325–55.

———. 1965. "The !Kung Bushmen of the Kalahari Desert." In *Peoples of Africa,* 243–67, edited by J. L. Gibbs. New York: Holt, Rinehart & Winston.

Martin, P. S. et al. 1965. *Indians Before Columbus.* Chicago: University of Chicago Press. First published 1947 based on Martin's doctoral dissertation, Dept. of Anthropology, University of Chicago, 1929.

Martin, R. 1973. "Aspects Financiers et sociaux des programes de construction dans villes grecques de Grande Grece." *Economia e Societá Nella Magna Grecia.* Naples, Italy: Arte Tipografica.

Mastyn, T., ed. 1988. *The Cambridge Encyclopedia of the Middle East and North Africa.* New York: Cambridge University Press.

Masuda, T. 1970. *Living Architecture: Japanese.* New York: Grosset & Dunlap.

Masuoka, S. N. "Joking with Death." *Print:* 78–83.

Matienzo. See Regal Matienzo.

Maugh, T. H. II. 1997. "River Tamers." *Los Angeles Times* (May 12).

Maxwell, T. S., ed. 1992. *Eastern Approaches: Essays on Asian Art and Archaeology.* Delhi: Oxford University Press. Includes:

D. Desai, "Man and Temple: Architectural and Sculptural Imagery of the Kandariya Mahadeva Temple of Khajuraho," 141–56.

Mazzolani, S. 1970. *The Idea of the City in Roman Thought: From Walled City to Spiritual Community.* Bloomington: Indiana University Press.

McCullagh, C. B. 1984. *Justifying Historical Descriptions.* Cambridge, Eng.: Cambridge University Press.

McIntosh, R. 1998. "Riddle of Great Zimbabwe." *Archaeology* 51 (No. 4):

McIntyre, L. 1975. *The Incredible Incas and Their Timeless Land.* Washington, D.C.: Special Publications Department, National Geographic Society.

Mead, M. 1949. *Male and Female.* New York: William Morrow.

———. 1956. *New Lives for Old: Cultural Transformation—Manus, 1928–1953.* New York: William Morrow. See esp. chap. 16.

Meisler, S. 1991. "The Golden Age of Andalusia under the Muslim Sultans." *Smithsonian* (August): 42–52.

Meister, M. W. 1991. "The Hindu Temple: Axis of Access." In *Concepts of Space Ancient and Modern* edited by K. Vatsyayan, New Delhi: Abhinav Publications 269–280.

Mendelssohn, K. 1971. "A Scientist Looks at the Pyramids." *American Scientist* 59: 210–20.

Mendelssohn, K. 1974. *The Riddle of the Pyramids*. New York: Praeger.

Mexico's Floating Gardens Restored. 1994. *Los Angeles Times* (April 10).

Michell, G., ed. 1978. *Architecture of the Islamic World: Its History and Social Meaning*. New York: William Morrow. Includes:
J. Dickie, "Allah and Eternity: Mosques, Madrasa and Tombs," 15–47.
O. Grabar, "The Architecture of Power: Palaces, Citadels, Fortifications," 48–79.
E. Grube, "What Is Islamic Architecture?" 10–14.
D. Jones, "Surface, Pattern and Light," 144–75.
King, G., and R. Lewcock, "Key Monuments of Islamic Architecture," 209–80.
G. Petherbridge, "Vernacular Architecture: The House and Society," 176–208.

Michell, G., ed. 1988. *The Hindu Temple*. Chicago: University of Chicago Press.

Michels, J. M., ed. 1979. Introduction. In Y. M. Kobidhvhssnov, *Axum*. State College: Pennsylvania State University Press.

Michener, J. A. 1968. *Iberia*. New York: Random House.

Miksic, J., 1990. *Borobudur: Golden Tales of the Buddha*. Boston: Shambhala.

Miller, A. 1973. *Mural Painting at Teotihuacan*. Washington, D.C.: Dumbarton Oaks.

Miller, D. 1985. "Ideology and the Harappan Civilization." *Journal of Anthropological Archaeology* 4: 34–71.

Miller, M. E. 1990. *The Art of Mesoamerica from Olmec to Aztec*. London: Thames & Hudson.

Miller, W. R. 1965. *Acoma Grammar and Texts*. Berkeley: University of California Press.

Millon, R. 1964. "The Teotihuacan Mapping Project." *American Antiquity* 29 (No. 3): 345–52.

———. 1967. "Teotihuacan." *Scientific American* 216 (No. 6): 38–48.

———. 1970. "Teotihuacan: Completion of Map of Giant Ancient City in the Valley of Mexico." *Science* 170 (October–December): 1077–82.

———. 1973. *The Teotihuacan Map*. Austin: University of Texas Press.

———. 1976. "Social Relations in Ancient Teotihuacan." In *The Valley of Mexico: Studies in Pre-Hispanic Ecology and Society*, 205–48, edited by E. R. Wolf. Albuquerque: University of New Mexico Press.

———. 1992. "Teotihuacan Studies: From 1950 to 1990 and Beyond." In *Art, Ideology, and the City of Teotihuacan*," 339–419, edited by J. C. Berlo. Washington, D.C.: Dumbarton Oaks Research Library and Collection.

Millon, R., B. Drewitt, and J. Bennyhoff. 1966. "The Pyramid of the Sun at Teotihuacan," 1959 Investigations." *Transactions of the American Philosophical Society* 55 (No. 6).

Mindeleff, V. 1886–87. *A Study of Pueblo Architecture: 8th Annual Report*. Washington, D.C.: Bureau of Ethnology.

Minge, W. A. 1991. *Acoma: Pueblo in the Sky*. rev. and expanded ed. Acoma, N. Mex.: Pueblo of Acoma.

Minh-ha, T. T., and Bourdier, J.-P. 1997. *Drawn from African Dwellings*. Bloomington: Indiana University Press.

Mitchell, W. P. 1977. "Irrigation Farming in the Andes., In *Peasant Livelihood: Studies in Economic Anthropology and Cultural Ecology*, 36–59, edited by R. Halperin and J. Dow. New York: St. Martin's Press.

Mizuno, S. 1974. *Asuka Buddhist Art: Horyu-ji*. New York: Weatherhill.

Monsias, C. 1987. " 'Look, Death, Don't Be Inhuman': Notes on a Traditional and Industrial Myth." In *El Dia de los Muertos: The Life of the Dead in Mexican Folk Art*, 9–16, edited by M. T. Pomar. Fort Worth, TX: Fort Worth Art Museum.

Montequin, F. N. A. de. 1978. "The Islamic University and the Classic Plan of the Madrasa." Paper presented at a conference on the Architecture of Colleges, Skidmore College, Saratoga, N.Y. Mont Ê Quin

———. 1979. "The Personality and Morphology of the Islamic City." *Action* 21: 6ff.

———. 1982. *Classicisme et Anti-Classicism Andalous: Les Motifs Decoratifs Vegetaux dans L'Islam Occidental sous les Dynasties Berberes Almaravide et Almohade*. Nauakchott, Mauritania: Institut des Hautes Etudes Islamiques et Arabes.

———. 1983a. *Compendium of Hispano-Islamic Art and Architecture*. 2nd ed. Nauakchott, Mauritania. Institut des Hautes Etudes Islamiques et Arabes.

———. 1983b. "Religious, Social, and Physical Qualities of Islamic Urbanization." *Hamdard Islamicus* 6 (No. 1): 63–86.

———. 1987. *Muslim Architecture of the Iberian Peninsula: Eastern and Western Sources for Hispano-Islamic Building Arts*. West Cornwall, Conn.: Locust Hill Press.

Montiton, A. R. 1874. "Les Paumotous: Les Missions Catholique. *Lyons* 6: 379.

Moore, C. B., ed. 1974. *Reconstructing Complex Societies*, supplement to the *Bulletin of the American School of Oriental Research*, No. 20. Cambridge, MA: Harvard University Press.

Moore, E. 1989. "Water Management in Early Cambodia: Evidence from Aerial Photography." *Geographical Journal*.

———. 1995. "The Waters of Angkor." *Asian Art and Culture*.

Moore, J. D. 1996. *Architecture and Power in the Ancient Andes: The Archaeology of Public Buildings*. New York: Cambridge University Press.

Morgan, W. N. 1989. *Prehistoric Architecture in Micronesia*. Austin: University of Texas Press.

————. 1994. *Ancient Architecture of the Southwest*. Austin: University of Texas Press.

Morley, S. [and G. Brainerd]. 1938+. *The Ancient Maya*. 1st–4th eds. Palo Alto: Stanford University Press. Replaced by the 5th ed., completely rewritten by R. J. Sharer. See Sharer (1994).

Moron, E. 1978. "The Relation between the Pyramid Temple and the City: Angkor Wat." In *Art and Architecture Research Papers*, No. 14: 65–68.

Morris, E. T., 1983. *The Gardens of China: History, Art and Meaning*. New York: Charles Scribner's Sons.

Morse, E. S. 1961. *Japanese Homes and Their Surroundings*. New York: Dover. Original work published 1886.

Morton, W. Brown III. 1983. "Indonesia Rescues Ancient Borobudur." *National Geographic Society* 163 (No. 1): 127–42.

Mosely, M. E. 1983a. "The Good Old Days Were Better: Agrarian Collapse and Tecotnics." *American Anthropologist* 773–99.

————. 1983b. "Patterns of Settlement and Preservation in the Viru and Moche Valleys. In *Prehistoric Settlement Patterns: Essays in Honor of G. R. Willey*, 423–42, edited by E. Z. Vogt and R. M. Leventhal, Albuquerque: University of New Mexico Press.

Mosely, M. E., R. A. Feldman, C. R. Ortloff, and A. Navarez. 1983. "Principles of Agrarian Collapse in the Cordillera Niugra, Peru." *Annals of the Carnegie Museum* 52 (No. 16), article 13.

Moss, L. 1965. "Space and Direction in the Chinese Garden." *Landscape* 14 (Spring): 29–33.

Moughtin, J. C. 1964. "The Traditional Settlements of the Hausa People." *Town Planning Review* (April): 21–34.

————. 1985. *Hausa Architecture*. London: Ethnographic.

Moynihan, E. 1979. *Paradise as a Garden in Persia and Mughal India*. New York: George Braziller.

Mumford, L. 1961. *The City in History*. New York: Harcourt, Brace & World.

Munsterberg, H. 1970. *Art and Architecture of India and Southeast Asia*. New York: Harry Abrams.

————. 1989. *Art of India and Southeast Asia*. New York: Oxford University Press.

————. 1973. *The Arts of Japan*. Rutland, Vt.: Charles E. Tuttle.

Murasaki Shikibu. 1988. *The Tale of the Genji*. Edited by R. Bowing. New York: Cambridge University Press. Orginally written in the 11th century.

Murphy, M. G. 1973. *Our Knowledge of the Historical Past*. Indianapolis: Bobbs-Merrill.

Musil, A. 1928. "Manners and Customs of the Rulawa Bedoin." *Oriental Explorations and Studies* 6. New York: American Geographic Society.

Myrdal, G. 1962. *An American Dilemma*. Rev. ed. New York: Harper & Row.

Nabokov, P. 1981. *Adobe: Pueblo and Hispanic Folk Traditions of the Southwest*. Washington, D.C.: Smithsonian Institution Press.

————. 1986. *Architecture of Acoma Pueblo: The 1934 Historic American Buildings Survey Project*. Santa Fe, N. Mex.: Ancient City Press.

Nabokov, P., and R. Easton. 1989. *Native American Architecture*. new York: Oxford University Press.

Nan Madol: Venice of the Pacific [Poster]. n.d. Ponape, Micronesia.

Nast, H. 1993. "Engendering 'Space': State Formation and the Restructuring of the Kano Palace Following the Islamic Holy War in Northern Nigeria, 1807–1903." *Historical Geography* 2 (Nos. 1–2): 62–75.

Nebel, C. 1963. *Viaje Pintoresco y Arqueologico Sobre La Parte Mas Interesante de la Republicana Mexicana*. Mexico City: Liberia de M. Porrua. Reprint of 1829–34 work.

Necipoglu, G. 1995. *The Topkapi Scroll—Geometry and Ornament in Islamic Architecture*. Santa Monica, Calif.: Getty Trust Publications.

Needham, J. 1971. *Science and Civilization in China*. Cambridge, England: Cambridge University Press. Includes:
Vol. III.I: *Mathematics and the Sciences of the Heavens and the Earth*.
Vol. IV.I: *Physics and Physical Technology*
Vol. IV.II: *Mechanical Engineering*. Includes "Hydraulic Engineering," 330–61; "Power Sources (Water)," 362–434.
Vol. IV.III: *Civil Engineering and Nautics*.

Netherly, P. J. 1984. "The Management of Late Andean Irrigation Systems on the North Coast of Peru." *American Antiquity* 49: (No. 2) 227–54.

Neuerburg, N. 1977. "Painting in the California Missions." *American Art Review* 4 (No. 1): 72–88.

New Columbia Encyclopedia. 1975. New York: Random House.

Nials, F. L., E. E. Deeds, M. E. Moseley, S. G. Pozorski, T. G. Pozorski, and R. Feldman. 1979. "El Niño: The Catastrophic Flooding of Coastal Peru." *Field Museum of Natural History Bulletin*. I (July–August): 4–14 and 2 (September): 4–10.

Nicolais, J. 1971. "Nepal: Water as Element in Urban Architecture. *Architecture & Urbanism* 1 (No. 7): n.p.

Nicholson, H. B. 1983. "Mesoamerican Ethnohistorical Sources and Their Relevance to Pre-Hispanic Settlement Pattern Studies," in Prehistoric Settlement Patterns: Essays in Honor of G. R. Willey. E. Z. Vogt and R. M. Leventhal, ed. Albuquerque: University of New Mexico Press.

Niles, S. 1987. "Niched Walls in Inca Design." *Journal of the Society of Architectural Historians*. 46 (No. 3): 277–85.

Niles, S. A. 1982. "Style and Function in Inca Agricultural Works near Cuzco." *Nawpa Pacha* 20: 163–77.

Nishi, S., and K. Hozumi. 1985. *What is Japanese Architecture?* M. Horton, trans. New York: Kodansha.

Nishihara, K. 1968. *Japanese Houses: Patterns for Living*, R. Gage, trans. Tokyo: Japan Publications.

Nooter, M. H., ed. 1993. *Secrecy: African Art that Conceals and Reveals*. New York: Museum for African Art.

Nuseibeh, S., and O. Grabar. 1996. *The Dome of the Rock*. New York: Rizzoli.

O'Brien, D., and S. W. Tiffany, eds. 1984. *Rethinking Women's Roles: Perspectives from the Pacific*. Berkeley: University of California Press. Includes: M. Strathern, "Domesticity and the Denigration of Women," 13–31.

O'Brien, M. J., D. E. Lewarch, R. D. Mason, and J. A. Neely. 1980. "Functional Analysis of Water Control Features at Monte Alban, Oaxaxa, Mexico." *World Archaeology* 11: 342–55.

Okawa, N. 1975. *Edo Architecture: Katsura and Nikko*. New York: Weatherhill-Heibonsha.

Olarte E., J. de 1970. "Marco Geográfico de Saccsayhuaman." *Revista Saqsaywaman* 1 (July): 43–59.

Oliver, D. L. 1989. "Domicile." Chapter 9 in *Oceania: The Native Cultures of Australia and the Pacific Islands*. Honolulu: University of Hawaii Press.

Olivier, P. 1975. *African Shelter*. London: Arts Council of Great Britain.

———. 1987. *Dwellings: The House Across the World*. Austin: University of Texas Press.

Oliver, P., ed. 1969. *Shelter and Society*. New York: Praeger.

———. 1971. *Shelter in Africa*. New York: Praeger.

———. 1975. *Shelter, Sign and Symbol*. London: Barrie & Jenkins.

———. 1995. *Encyclopedia of Vernacular Architecture of the World*. Cambridge, England: Cambridge University Press. Includes:
S. Kent, "Typologies: Spatial Relations,"

Opie, J. 1970. *Island Ceylon*. New York: Viking.

Ortiz, A. 1969. *The Tewa World*. Chicago: University of Chicago Press.

Ortiz, A. 1972. "Ritual Drama and the Pueblo World View." In *New Perspectives on the Puebloes*, 135–61 and 296–300, edited by A. Ortiz. Albuquerque: University of New Mexico Press.

Ortiz, A., ed. 1972. *New Perspectives on the Puebloes*. Albuquerque: University of New Mexico Press. Includes:

A. Ortiz, "Ritual Drama and the Pueblo World View," 135–61 and 296–300.

Ortiz, A., and R. Erdos, eds. 1984. *American Indian Myths and Legends*. New York: Pantheon. Includes:
B. Harvey III, "An Overview of Pueblo Religion," 197–217.

Ortloff, C. R. 1988. "Canal Builders of Pre-Inka Peru." *Scientific American* (Dec.): 100–107.

Ortloff, C. R. 1996. "Engineering Aspects of Tiwanaku Groundwater-Controlled Agriculture," Chapter 6 in *Tiwanaku and Its Hinterland: Archaeology and Paleoecology of an Andean Civilization*. A. L. Kolota, ed. Washington: Smithsonian Institution Press.

Ortloff, C. R. and A. L. Kolata. 1996. "Tiwanaku Raised Bed Field Agriculture in the Lake Titicaca Basin of Bolivia," Chapter 5 in *Tiwanaku and Its Hinterland: Archaeology and Paleoecology of an Andean Civilization*. A. L. Kolota, ed. Washington: Smithsonian Institution Press.

Ortloff, C. R. and A. L. Kolata. 1996. "Agroecological Perspectives on the Decline of the Tiwanaku State," Chapter 8 in *Tiwanaku and Its Hinterland: Archaeology and Paleoecology of an Andean Civilization*. A. L. Kolota, ed. Washington: Smithsonian Institution Press.

Ortloff, C. R., R. A. Feldman, M. E. Moseley. 1985. "Hydraulic Engineering and Historical Aspects of the Pre-Columbiean Intravalley Canal Systems of the Moche Valley, Peru." *Journal of Field Archaeology*. 12: 77–98.

Özdural, A. 1995. "Omar Khayam, Mathematicians, and Conversazioni with Artisans." *Journal of the Society of Architectural Historians* 54 (No. 1): 54–71.

Ozhegov. See Hla.

Öziş, Ü. 1991. Mimar Sinan'in köprüleri (Bridges of Sinnan, the Architect). Ismir (Turkey): Mimarlar Odasi, "Egemimarlik". y.1, n.2 (Temmuz 1991): 38–41.

Öziş, Ü. and Y. Arisoy. 1991. Mimar Sinan' in su yapilari (Hydraulic works of Sinan, the Architect). Izmir (Turkey): Mimarlar Odasi. "Egemimarlik". y.1, n.2 (Temmuz 1991): 34–37.

"Pacific Islands." 1986. *Encyclopedia Britannica*. 15th ed. Vol. 25, 243–92.

"Pagan (Burma)." 1986. *Encyclopedia Britannica*. 15th ed. Vol. 9, 56–57.

Paine, R. T., and A. Soper. 1969. *The Art and Architecture of Japan*. Baltimore: Penguin.

Pal, P. 1985. *Art of Nepal*. Los Angeles: Los Angeles County Museum of Art and University of California Press.

Pal, P., J. Leoshko, J. Dye III, and S. Markel. 1989. *Romance of the Taj Mahal*. New York: Thames & Hudson.

Panofsky, E. 1972. *Studies in Iconology*. New York: Harper & Row.

Pardo, L. A. 1970. "La Fortaleza de Saccsayhuaman." *Revista Saqsaywaman*, 1 (July): 89–135.

Pardo, L. A., and O. L. de Guevara Aviles. 1970. "Plan de Trabajo." *Revista Saqsaywaman*, 1 (July): 17–18 and fold-out plans.

Parent, M. N. 1983. *The Roof in Japanese Buddhist Architecture*. New York: Weatherhill.

Parfitt, T. 1993. *Journey to the Vanished City: The Search for the Lost Tribes of Israel*. New York: St. Martin's Press.

Parsons, J. R. 1968. "Teotihuacan, Mexico, and Its Impact on Regional Demography." *Science* 162 (November) 872–77.

Paz, O. 1985. *Labyrinth of Solitude*. New York: Grove Press.

Pendergast, D. M. 1988. "Engineering Problems in Ancient Maya Architecture: Past, Present, and Future." In *Engineering Geology of Ancient Works, Monuments and Historical Sites*, Vol. 3, 1653–60, edited by P. Marinos and G. Koukis. Rotterdam: A. A. Balkema.

Peoples of the Artic (map). 1983. National Geographic Society.

Perry, F. V., W. S. Baldridge, D. J. De Paolo, and M. Shafiqallah. 1990. "Evolution of a Magmatic System During Continental Extension: The Mt. Taylor Volcanic Field." *Journal of Geophysical Research* 95 (November 10): 327–48.

Petherbridge, G. 1978. "Vernacular Architecture: The House and Society." In *Architecture of the Islamic World: Its History and Social Meaning*, 176–208, edited by G. Michel. New York: William Morrow.

Petruccioli, A. 1985. *Dar Al Islam*. Rome: Cariucci Editore.

Pieper, J. 1975. "Three Cities of Nepal." *Shelter, Sign and Symbol*, 52–69, edited by P. Oliver. London: Barrie & Jenkins.

———. 1983. "Festivals as a Matter of Course in the Public Life of Traditional India. In *Forschung Sprojekt DFG Mohenjo-Daro*, edited by G. Urban and M. Jansen, Aachen, Germany: Veröffentlicheung des Geodotischen Instituts der Rheinisch-Westfalischen Technischen Hoch Schule. Nr.34.

———. 1991. "Arboreal Art and Architecture in India." In *Concepts of Space Ancient and Modern*, 333–42, edited by K. Vatsayan. New Delhi: Abhinav Publications.

Pomar, M. T. 1987. *El Dia de los Muertos: The Life of the Dead in Mexican Folk Art*. Fort Worth Art Museum. Includes: C. Monsias, " 'Look, Death, Don't Be Inhuman': Notes on a Traditional and Industrial Myth," 9–16.

Powell, J. W. 1972. *The Hopi Villages*. Palmer Lake, Colo.: Filter Press. Reprint, with additional illustrations, of *The Ancient Province of Tusayan*, 1875.

Pradhan, R. 1991. "The Theater-Architecture of Nepal." In *Concepts of Space Ancient and Modern*, 429–36, edited by K. Vatsyayan. New Delhi: Abhinav Publications.

Pratt, M. L. 1986. "Scratches on the Face of the Country; or, What Mr. Barrow Saw in the Land of the Bushmen." In *"Race," Writing, and Difference*, 138–62, edited by H. L. Gates, Jr. Chicago: University of Chicago Press.

Prescott, W. H. n.d. *History of the Conquest of Mexico*. New York: Modern Library Original work published 1856.

Prescott, W. H. n.d. *History of the Conquest of Peru*. New York: Modern Library. Original work published 1856. Also published as *The Incas*. New York: Crescent Books, 1981.

Preziosi, D. 1989a. Letter regarding "Some Observations on Recent Architectural History." *Art Bulletin* (June): 310–11.

Preziosi, D. 1989b. *Rethinking Art History: Observations on a Coy Science*. New Haven, Conn.: Yale University Press.

Proskouriakoff, T. 1963. *An Album of Maya Architecture*. Norman: University of Oklahoma Press.

Protzen, J. 1993. *Inca Architecture and Construction at Ollantaytambo*. New York: Oxford University Press.

Protzen, J. P. 1986. "Inca Stone Masonry." *Scientific America* (February): 94–105.

Protzen, J. P., and J. H. Rowe. 1994. "Hawkaypota, Terrace of Leisure. In *Streets: Critical Perspectives on Public Space*, 235–45, edited by Z. Celik, D. Favro, and R. Ingersoll. Berkeley: University of California Press.

Prussin, L. 1969. *Architecture in Northern Ghana*. Berkeley: University of California Press.

———. 1974. "An Introduction to Indigenous African Architecture." *Journal of the Society of Architectural Historians*. 33 (No. 3): 183–205.

———. 1986. *Hatumere: Islamic Design in West Africa*. Berkeley: University of California Press.

Prussin, L. 1994. "Sub-Saharan African." In *The Mosque: History, Architectural Development and Regional Diversity*, 181–94, edited by M. Frishman and H.-U. Khan. London: Thames & Hudson.

———. 1995. *African Nomadic Architecture*. Washington, D.C.: Smithsonian Institution Press.

Puleston, D. E. 1977. "The Art and Archaeology of Hydraulic Agriculture in the Maya Lowlands." In *Social Process in Maya Prehistory: Studies in Memory of Sir Eric Thompson*, 449–69, edited by N. Hammond. London: Academic Press.

Pyatt, G., and A. Roe. 1977. *Social Accounting for Development Planning with Special Reference to Sri Lanka*. New York: Cambridge University Press.

Pym, C. 1963. "Collapse of the Khmers." In *Vanished Civilizations of the Ancient World*, 105–38, edited by Edward Bacon. New York: McGraw-Hill.

Ramsay, C. R. 1981. "Land of the Sinhalese Kings." In *Splendors of the Past: Lost Cities of the Ancient World*, 248–88. Washington, D.C.: National Geographic Society.

Random House Atlas of the Oceans. 1991. New York: Mitchell Beazley Publishers.

Ranger, T. 1983. "The Invention of Tradition in Colonial Africa." In *The Invention of Tradition,* 211–62, edited by E. J. Hobsbawn and T. Ranger. Cambridge, England: Cambridge University Press.

Rappaport, R. A. 1968. *Pigs for the Ancestors: Ritual in the Ecology of a New Guinea People.* New Haven, Conn.: Yale University Press.

Rapoport, A. 1969. *House Form and Culture.* Englewood Cliffs, N.J.: Prentice Hall.

———. 1982. *The Meaning of the Built Environment: A Non-Verbal Communication Approach.* Beverly Hills, Calif.: Sage.

———. 1990. "Systems of Activities and Systems of Settings. In *Domestic Architecture and the Use of Space: An Interdisciplinary Study,* 9–20, edited by S. Kent. Cambridge, England: Cambridge University Press.

Raschka, M. 1996. "Beirut Digs Out." *Archaeology* 49 (No. 4): 44–50.

Rasmussen, S. E. 1969. *Towns and Buildings: Described in Drawings and Words.* Cambridge, Mass.: MIT Press.

Rayner, W. 1962. *The Tribe and Its Successors.* New York: Praeger.

Reed, E. K. 1971. "Types of Village Planning Layouts in the Southwest." In *Prehistoric Settlement Patterns in the New World,* 11–17, edited by G. Willey. New York: Johnson Reprint Corp. Reprint of 1956 edition.

Regal Matienzo, A. 1972. *Los Puentes des Inca en el Antiguo Peru.* Lima: no publisher.

Regmi, D. R. 1983. *Inscriptions of Ancient Nepal.* New Delhi: Abhinav Publications.

Reich, K. 1994. "Fears in Mexico Heating Up as Volcano Stirs." *Los Angeles Times* (July 16).

Richards, P. 1978. "The Spatial Organization of Culture." In *The Spatial Organization of Culture,* edited by J. Hodder. London: Duckworth.

Rivera Serna, R. 1966. Libro primero de cabildas dela ciudad del Cuzco [1534]. Documenta, No. 4, 1965: 441–480, especially 468–473. Lima.

Robertshaw, P., ed. 1990. *A History of African Archaeology.* London: J. Currey. Includes:
M. Hall, "A 'Hidden History': Iron Age Archaeology in Southern Africa," 59–77.

Robertson, M. G. 1991. "The Ballgame at Chichen Itzá: An Integrating Device of the Polity in the Post-Classic." In *The Mesoamerican Ballgame,* 91–110, edited by G. W. van Bussel, P. L. F. van Dungen, and T. J. J. Leyenaar. Leiden: Rijksmuseum vor Volkenkunde.

Robinson, F. 1982. *Atlas of the Islamic World Since 1500.* New York: Facts on File.

———. 1989. *Cambridge Encyclopedia of India, Pakistan, Bangladesh, Sri Lanka, Nepal, Bhutan and the Maldives.* Cambridge, England: Cambridge University Press.

Rogers, M. 1976. *The Making of the Past: The Spread of Islam.* Oxford, England: El Sevier Phaidon.

Roth, G. 1980. "Symbolism of the Buddhist Stupa." In *The Stupa: Its Religious, Historical and Architectural Significance,* 183–209, edited by A. L. Dallapiccola and S. Zingel-Avé Lallemant. Wiesbaden, Germany: F. Steiner Verlag.

Rowe, J. H. 1944. "Introduction to the Archaeology of Cuzco." Reprint 1969 by NY: Kraus Reprint Co. *Papers of the Peabody Museum* [Harvard University] 27 (No. 2): 1943–47.

Rowe, J. H. 1967. "Urban Settlements in Ancient Peru." In *Peruvian Archaeology: Selected Readings,* 293–320, edited by J. H. Rowe and D. Menzel. Palo Alto, Calif.: Peek.

Rowe, J. H., and D. Menzel. 1967. *Peruvian Archaeology: Selected Readings.* Palo Alto, Calif.: Peek. Includes:
J. H. Rowe, "Urban Settlements in Ancient Peru," 293–320.
D. E. Thompson and J. V. Murra, "The Inca Bridges in the Huanuco Area," 235–42.

Rowe, J. H. and J. P. "Protzen, Hawkaypota, Terrace of Leisure," in Celik et al, eds., 1994: 235–46.

Rowland, B. 1977. *The Art and Architecture of India: Buddhist Hindu Jain.* 3rd rev. ed. New York: Penguin.

Rudofsky, B. 1964. *Architecture Without Architects.* New York: Museum of Modern Art.

———. 1977. *The Prodigious Builders.* New York: Harcourt, Brace & World.

Ruff, W. M., and R. E. Ruff. 1990. "The Village Studies Project for the Recording of Traditional Architecture. In *Sepik Heritage: Tradition and Change in Papua New Guinea,* 568–86, edited by N. Lutkehaus et al. Durham, N.C.: Wenner-Gren Foundation/Carolina Academic Press.

Ruitenbeek, K. 1986. "Craft and Ritual in Traditional Chinese Carpentry: With a Bibliographical Note on the *Lu Ban Jing.*" *Chinese Science* Vol. 7, 1–23.

———. 1993. *Carpentry and Building in Later Imperial China: A Study of the 15th Century Carpenter's Manual La Ban Jing.* New York: E. J. Brill.

Rushing, W. J. 1992. Review of exhibit "La Noche de los Muertos" at Laumeier Sculpture Park, St. Louis, in *New Art Examiner* (January).

Rust III, W. F. 1992. "New Ceremonial and Settlement Evidence at La Venta, and its Relation to Preclassic Maya Cultures." In *New Theories on the Ancient Maya,* 123–39, edited by E. C. Danien and R. J. Sharer. Philadelphia: University Museum, University of Pennsylvania.

Rust, W. F., and R. J. Sharer. 1988. "Olmec Settlement Data from La Venta, Tabasco, Mexico." *Science* 242: 102–04.

Rkywert, J. H. 1984. *On Adam's House in Paradise*. 2nd ed. Cambridge, Mass.: MIT Press.

Sa'ad, M. T. 1989. "Continuity and Change in Kano Traditional Architecture." In *Kano and Some of Her Neighbors*, 59–77, edited by B. M. Barkindo. Kano, Nigeria: Ahmadu Bello University Press.

Sahlins, M., and D. B. Barrére. 1992. *The Archaeology of History*, Vol. 2 of *Anahulu: Historical Ethnology*, Kirch, P. V. and M. Sahlins, series eds. Chicago: University of Chicago Press.

Saile, D. G. 1977. "Making a House in the Pueblo Indian World." *Architectural Association Quarterly* 9 (Nos. 2–3): 72–81.

———. 1978. "Understanding Prehistoric Pueblo Architecture." *ERDA (Environmental Design Research Association) Proceedings* 8: 52–69.

Sancho de la Hoz, P. 1534. *Relacions*.

Sanday, J. 1974. "The Hanuman Dhoka Royal Palace Kathmandu: Building Conservation and Local Traditional Crafts." London: *Art and Archaeological Research Papers*.

———. 1978. *Building Conservation in Nepal*. Paris: UNESCO.

———. 1979. *Monuments of the Kathmandu Valley*. Paris: UNESCO.

Sanders, W. T. 1971. "The Central Mexican Symbiotic Region: A Study in Prehistoric Settlement Patterns." In *Prehistoric Settlement Patterns in the New World*, 115–27, edited by G. R. Willey. New York: Johnson Reprint Corp. Original work published 1956.

Sanders, W. T., J. R. Parsons, and R. S. Stanley. 1979. *The Basin of Mexico: Ecological Processes in the Evolution of a Civilization*. New York: Academic Press.

Sanders, W. T., and R. S. Stanley. 1983. "A Tale of Three Cities: Energetics and Urbanism in Pre-Hispanic Central Mexico." In *Prehistoric Settlement Patterns: Essays in Honor of G. R. Willey*, 243–91, edited by E. Z. Vogt and R. M. Leventhal. Albuquerque: University of New Mexico Press.

Sandler, L. F., and M. Barasch, eds. 1981. *Art, the Ape of Nature: Essays in Honor of H. W. Janson*. Englewood Cliffs, N.J.: Prentice Hall. Includes:
C. H. Krinskey, "St. Petersburg-on-the-Hudson: The Albany Mall," 771–87.

Sanyal, S. 1979. *The Boats and Boatmen of Kashmir*. New Delhi: Sagar.

Scarborough, V. L., and G. Gallopin. 1991. "A Water Storage Adaptation in the Maya Lowlands." *Science* 251 (February 8): 658–62.

Scarborough, V. L., and B. L. Isaac, eds. 1993. *Research in Economic Anthropology: Economic Aspects of Water Management in the Prehispanic New World*, Supplement 7. Greenwich, Conn.: JAI Press. Includes:

J. B. Howard, "A Paleohydraulic Approach to Examining Agricultural Intensification in Hohokam Irrigation Systems," 263–326.

Scarborough, V. L., and D. Wilcox, eds. 1991. *The Mesoamerican Ballgame*. Tucson: University of Arizona Press.

Scerrato, U. 1976. *Monuments of Civilization: Islam*. New York: Grosset & Dunlap.

Schafer, E. 1967. *Ancient China*. New York: Time Life Books.

Schaller, G. B. 1993. "Tibet's Remote Chang Tang." *National Geographic* 184 (No. 2): 62–87.

Schele, L., and D. Friedel. 1990. *A Forest of Kings*. New York: William Morrow.

Schele, L., and M. E. Miller. 1986. *The Blood of Kings*. New York: Geroge Braziller.

Schimmel, A. 1984. *Calligraphy and Islamic Culture*. New York: New York University Press.

Schmertz, M. F. 1980. "Search for Meanings in the Architecture of Islam." *Architectural Record* 168 (August): 86–89.

Schoenauer, N., and S. Seeman. 1962. *The Court-Garden House*. Montreal: McGill University Press.

Schuster, A. M. H. 1994. "Hidden Sanctuaries of Ethiopia." *Archaeology* (January–February): 28–35.

Schwerdtfeger, F. W. 1978. "Urban Settlement Patterns in Northern Nigeria." *Scientific American* v. 238 (No. 2): 144–54.

Scully, V. 1975. *Pueblo, Mountain, Village, Dance*. 2nd ed. New York: Viking.

Sebag, P. 1965. *Great Mosque of Kairouan*. New York: Macmillan.

Sedgwick, Mrs. W. 1926. *Acoma, the Sky City*. Cambridge, Mass.: Harvard University Press.

Segal, A. 1981. "Roman Cities in the Province of Arabia." *Journal of the Society of Architectural Historians* 40 (No. 1): 108–21.

Sekel, D. 1964. *The Art of Buddhism*. London: Methuen.

Sekler, E. F. 1980. *Proposal for the Urbanistic Conservation of Patan (Lalitpur) Durbar Square as a Monument Zone*. Cambridge, Mass.: Harvard Graduate School of Design, Publication Series in Architecture.

Sekler, E. F. 1997. *Summary of the Master Plan for the Conservation of the Cultural Heritage in the Kathmandu Valley*. Cambridge, Mass.: Harvard Graduate School of Design, Publication Series in Architecture.

Serna, see Rivera Serna, R.

Sharer, R. J. 1994. *The Ancient Maya*. 5th ed. Stanford, CA: Stanford University Press.

Shearer, A. 1983. *Traveler's Guide to Northern India*. New York: Alfred A. Knopf.

Sherratt, A., ed. 1980. "Zimbabwe." *The Cambridge Encyclopedia of Archaeology*. New York: Cambridge University Press, 1980.

Shetty, R. ca 1988. Lecture on the formal patterns of Indian cities, given at Rensselaer Polytechnic Institute School of Architecture.

Shih Lei. 1964. "The Family System of the Paiwan at SuPaiwan Village." *Bulletin of the Institute of Ethnology* (Academia Sinica). Quoted by Waterson (1990).

Shimizu, B. A. 1980. *An Architectural Analysis of Hawaiian Heiau Focusing on the Island of Oahu.* M.A. thesis, Department of Architecture, University of Hawaii, Honolulu.

Shomaker, J. 1967. "The Mt. Taylor Volcanic Field,: A Digest of the Literature." In *Guidebook of Defiance—Zuni—Mt. Taylor Region, Arizona and New Mexico,* 195–201, edited by F. D. Trauger. Socorro, NM: New Mexico Geological Society.

Sickman, L. 1968. *The Art and Architecture of China.* 3rd ed. Baltimore: Penguin.

Siemens, A. H. 1978. "Karst and the Pre-Hispanic Maya in the Southern Lowlands." In *Pre-Hispanic Maya Agriculture,* 117–43, edited by P. D. Harrison and B. L. Turner II. Albuquerque: University of New Mexico Press.

Siemens, A. H., and D. E. Puleston. 1972. "Ridged Fields and Associated Features in Southern Campeche: New Perspectives on the Lowland Maya." *American Antiquity* 37 (No. 2): 228–39.

Silberbauer, G. 1981. *Hunters and Habitat in the Central Kalahari Desert.* Cambridge, England: Cambridge University Press.

Silva, K. M., de. 1981. *A History of Sri Lanka.* Delhi: Oxford University Press.

Singh, P. 1978. *Stone Observatories in India.* Jaipur, India: Bharata Manisha.

Sis, V., and J. Vanis. 1957. *On the Road Through Tibet.* London: Spring Books.

Skinner, G. W., ed. 1977. *The City in Late Imperial China.* Stanford, Calif.: Stanford University Press. Includes:
Skinner, G. W. 1977. "Cities and the Hierarchy of Local Systems." 275–351.

Slusser, M. S. 1982. *Nepal Mandala: A Cultural Study of the Katmandu Valley.* Princeton, N.J.: Princeton University Press.

Slusser, M. S., and G. Vajracarya. 1974. "Two Medieval Nepalese Buildings: An Architectural and Cultural Study." *Artibus Asiae* 36 (No. 3): 169–237.

Smith, E. Baldwin, see Baldwin Smith, E.

Smith, M. E. 1979. "The Aztec Marketing System and Settlement Patterns in the Valley of Mexico: A Central Place Analysis." *American Antiquity* 110–125.

Smith, M. G. 1955. *The Economy of Hausa Communities of Zaria.* London: Her Majesty's Stationery Office.

———. 1965. The Hausa of Northern Nigeria. In *Peoples of Africa,* 119–56, edited by J. L. Gibbs. New York: Holt, Rinehart & Winston.

———. 1972. "Complexity, Size, and Urbanization." In *Man, Settlement, and Urbanization,* 567–74, edited by P. J. Ucko, R. Tringham, and G. W. Dimbleby. Cambridge, Mass.: Schenkman.

Smith, P. E. L. 1972. "Land Use, Settlement Patterns and Subsistence Agriculture: A Demographic Perspective." In *Man, Settlement, and Urbanization,* 409–25, edited by P. J. Ucko, R. Tringham, and G. W. Dimbleby. Cambridge, Mass.: Schenkman.

Snellgrove, D. L. 1961. "Shrines and Temples of Nepal." *Arts Asiatiques* 8 (No. 1): 3–10.; 8.2: 93–120.

Snellgrove, D. L., and H. Richardson. 1980. *A Cultural History of Tibet.* Boulder, Colo.: Prajna Press. Reprint of the 1968 book published by G. Weidenfeld Nicolson, London, which had much better illustrations.

Snodgrass, A. 1985. *The Symbolism of the Stupa.* Ithaca, N.Y.: Cornell University, Institute of Southeast Asian Studies.

Snouck Hurgronje, C. 1906. *The Acehnese,* 2 vols. Leidew Brill.

Soper, A. 1942. *The Evolution of Buddhist Architecture in Japan.* Princeton N.J.: Princeton University Press.

Soruco Saenz, E. 1989. "Una Cueva Ceremonial en Teotihuacan y Sus Implicaciones Astronmicas Religiousas." In *Memorias del Simposio Sobre Arqueostronomia y Etnoastronomia.* Mexico City: UNAM, Instituto de Investigaciones Historicas.

Spence, J. D. 1978. *The Death of Woman Wang.* New York: Viking. Cites Feng K'o-ts'an, *Local History of T'an-Ch'eng* (1673) and Huang Liu-hung, *A Complete Book Concerning Happiness and Benevolence,* (1694).

Spicer, E. H. 1971. "Persistent Cultural Systems." *Science* 174 (November): 795–800.

Splendors of the Past: Lost Cities of the Ancient World. 1981. Washington, D.C.: National Geographic Society. Includes:
L. de la Haba, "Angkor and the Ancient Khmer," 182–219.
C. R. Ramsay, "Land of the Sinhalese Kings," 248–88.

Squier, E. 1973. Peru: *Incidents of Travel and Exploration in the Land of the Incas.* New York: AMS Press. Reprint of 1877 ed.

"Sri Lanka." 1986. *Encyclopedia Britannica.* 15th ed., Vol. 11: 190–92.

Stanier, R. S. 1953. "The Cost of the Parthenon." *Journal of Hellenic Studies* 73: 68–76.

Stefansson, V. 1943. *The Friendly Artic.* New York: Macmillan.

Steinhardt, N. S. 1984. "Bracketing System of the Song Dynasty." *Chinese Traditional Architecture,* 122–25. New York: China House Gallery. Includes:
N. S. Steinhardt, "Bracketing System of the Song Dynasty," 122–25.
E. Glahn, "Unfolding the Chinese Building Standards." Research on the *Yingzao Fashi,*" 48–57.

———. 1986. "Why Were Chang'an and Beijing So Different?

Journal of the Society of Architectural Historians (December): 342ff.

———— 1990. *The Chinese Imperial City.* Honolulu: University of Hawaii Press.

Stephens, J. L. 1949. *Incidents of Travel in Central America, Chiapas and Yucatan 1841.* 2 vols., R. Predmore ed. New Brunswick, N.J.: Rutgers University Press. Reprint of 1846 ed.

Stephens, J. L. *Incidents of Travel in Yucatan, 1843.* New York: Harper and Brothers.

Stern, T. 1950. *The Rubber-Ball Games of the Americas.* Monograph 17. New York: American Ethnological Society.

Stewart, D., and editors of Newsweek Book Division. 1974. *The Alhambra.* New York: Newsweek.

Stiehm, J., ed. 1984. *Women's Views of the Political World of Men.* Dobbs Ferry, N.Y.: Transnational Publishers.

Stierlin, H. 1964. *Living Architecture: Mayan.* New York: Grosset & Dunlap.

————. 1981. *Art of the Maya: From the Olmecs to the Toltec-Maya.* New York: Rizzoli.

————. 1991. *Alhambra.* Paris: Imprime Nationale.

Stinchecum, A. 1994. "A World Away: Little Lamma Island, a 40-Minute Ferry Ride from Hong Kong, Offers a Rural Respite from the Crowds." *Los Angeles Times* (May 22).

Stirling, M. W. 1942. *Origin Myth of Acoma and Other Records.* Washington, D.C.: U.S. Government Printing Office.

Strachan, P. 1989. *Pagan: Art and Architecture of Old Burma.* Whiting Bay, Arran, Scotland: Kiscadale Publications.

Strathern, M. 1984. "Domesticity and the Denigration of Women." In *Rethinking Women's Roles: Perspectives from the Pacific,* 13–31, edited by D. O'Brien and S. W. Tiffany. Berkeley: University of California Press.

Stratton, A. 1972. *Sinan.* New York: Charles Scribner's Sons.

Stubbs, S. A. 1950. *Bird's-Eye View of the Puebloes.* Norman: University of Oklahoma Press.

Sturtevant, W., ed. 1978. *Handbook of North American Indians.* Washington, D.C.: Smithsonian Institution. See also F. W. Hodge's book of the same title and publisher, 1912.

Sufi, G. 1948. *Kashmir, Being a History of Kashmir from the Earliest Times to Our Own.* Lahore: University of the Punjab.

Sugiyama, S. 1992. "Rulership, Warfare, and Human Sacrifice at the Ciudadela: An Iconographic Study of Feathered Serpent Representations." In *Art, Ideology, and the City of Teotihuacan,* 203–30, edited by J. C. Berlo. Washington, D.C. Dumbarton Oaks Research Library.

Summers, R. 1963. "Zimbabwe." In *Vanished Civilizations of the Ancient World,* 33–54, edited by Edward Bacon. New York: McGraw-Hill.

Suzuki, K. 1980. *Early Buddhist Architecture in Japan.* Tokyo: Kodansha.

Swaan, W. 1966. "Pagan." In *The Lost Cities of Asia,* 90–120. New York: G. P. Putnam's Sons.

Swadling, P. 1990. "Sepik Prehistory." In *Sepik Heritage: Tradition and Change in Papua New Guinea,* 60–76, edited by N. Lutkenhaus et al. Durham, N.C.: Wenner-Gren Foundation/Carolina Academic Press.

Taddei, M. ed. 1977. *South Asian Archaeology.* Naples, Italy: Papers of the Association of South Asian Archaeologists in Western Europe. Includes:
J. Irwin, "The Stupa and the Cosmic Axis: The Archaeological Evidence," 12–38

Tainter, J. A. 1988. *The Collapse of Complex Societies.* Cambridge, England: Cambridge University Press.

Tainter, J. A., and D. A. Gillio. 1980. *Cultural Resources Overview: Mt. Taylor Area, New Mexico.* Santa Fe, N.M.: Bureau of Land Management.

Talay, L. E. 1994. "Indiana Joans." *Archaeology* (May–June): 60–63.

Tambiah, S. J. 1973. "Classification of Animals in Thailand." In *Rules and Meaning,* 127–66, edited by M. Douglas. New York: Penguin. See esp. 132–37 about house categories.

Tange, K. 1965. *Ise: Prototype of Japanese Architecture.* Cambridge, Mass.: MIT Press.

Tange, K. (text) and Y. Isimoto (photographs). *Katsura.* 1972. New Haven, Conn.: Yale University Press.

Taube, K. A. 1992a. "The Iconography of Mirrors at Teotihuacan." In *Art, Ideology, and the City of Teotihuacan,* 169–204, edited by J. C. Berlo. Washington, D.C. Dumbarton Oaks Research Library and collection.

Taube, K. A. 1992b. "The Temple of Quetzalcoatl and the Cult of Sacred War at Teotihuacan." *RES.* 21.

Taut, B. 1958. *Houses and People of Japan.* 2nd ed. Tokyo: Sanseido.

Tempest, R. 1995. "Program in Barren Region of China Offers Villagers Chance to Start Over Elsewhere." *Los Angeles Times* (July 16).

————. 1996. "Bulldozing the Heart of Old Peking." *Los Angeles Times* (January 10).

Thackston, W. M. 1994. "The Role of Calligraphy." In *The Mosque: History, Architectural Development and Regional Diversity,* 43–54, edited by M. Frishman and H.-U. Khan. London: Thames & Hudson.

Thackston, W. M., trans., ed., and annotator. 1996. *The Baburnama: Memoirs of Babur, Prince and Emperor.* New York: Oxford University Press.

Thapa, J. 1988. "How Space Is Conceived and Land Used in Nepal" Lecture given at Rensselaer Polytechnic Institute.

Thapar, R. 1966. *A History of India*. Harmondsworth, England: Penguin.

Thomas, W., C. O. Sauer, M. Bates, and L. Mumford, eds. 1956. *Man's Role in Changing the Face of the Earth*. Chicago: University of Chicago Press. Includes:
C. G. Darwin, "The Time Scale in Human Affairs," 963–69.
Huzayyin, J. "Changes in Climate, Vegetation, and Human Adjustment in the Saharo-Arab Belt with Special Reference to Africa," 304–19.

Thompkins, P. 1976. *Mysteries of the Mexican Pyramids*. New York: Harper & Row.

Thompson, D. E., and J. V. Murra. 1966. "The Inca Bridges in the Huanuco Region." *American Antiquity* 31 (No. 5): 632–39.

Thompson, G. C. See Caton-Thompson.

Thorp, R. L. 1986. "Architectural Principles in Early Imperial China: Structural Problems and Their Solution." *Art Bulletin*. (September): 360–78.

Tichy, F. ed. 1982. *Proceedings of the Symposium: Space and Time in the Cosmovision of Mesoamerica*. Munich: Wilhelm Fink Verlag. Includes:
A. F. Aveni, "Horizontal Astronomy in Incaic Cuzco," 175–93.

Tiwari, S. R. *"The Urban Spaces of Kathmandu Valley Towns: A Historical Perspective*. Typescript supplied by the author, a professor of architecture at Tiburon University in Kathmandu.

Tobias, P. V., ed. 1978. *The Bushmen: San Hunters and Herders of Southern Africa*. Cape Town, South Africa: Ruman & Rousseau.

Tobriner, S. 1972. "The Fertile Mountain: An Investigation of Cerro Gordo's Importance to the Town Plan and Iconography of Teotihuacan." *Teotihuacan*. 11: 103–15. Published by Sociedad Mexicana de Anthropologia, Mesa Radendo, Mexico.

Topic, J. R., and T. L. Topic. 1983. "Coast-Highland Relations in Northern Peru: Some Observations on Routes, Networks, and Scales of Interaction." In *Civilization in the Ancient Americas*, 237–59, edited by R. M. Leventhal and A. L. Kolata. Albuquerque: University of New Mexico Press.

Topping, A. (text and photos). 1979. "Journey to Tibet: Hidden Splendors of an Exiled Deity." *New York Times Magazine* (December 9): 68–82.

Townsend, P. K. 1990. "Our Women Are Okay: Aspects of Hiyewe Women's Status." In *Sepik Heritage: Tradition and Change in Papua New Guinea*, 374–79, edited by N. Lutkehaus et al. Durham, N.C. Wenner-Gren Foundation/ Carolina Academic Press.

Trauger, F. D. 1967. *Guidebook of Defiance—Zuni—Mt. Taylor Region, Arizona and New Mexico*. Socorro, New Mexico Geological Society. Includes:

J. Shomaker, "The Mt. Taylor Volcanic Field: A Digest of the Literature," 195–201.

Tremearne, A. J. N. 1910. "Hausa Houses." *Man* (No. 99): 177–180.

Trigger, B. J. 1968. "The Determination of Settlement Patterns." In *Settlement Archaeology*, 53–78, edited by K. Chang. Palo Alto, Calif.: National Press Books.

———. 1972. "The Determinants of Urban Growth in Pre-industrial Societies." In *Man, Settlement, and Urbanization*, 98–106, edited by P. J. Ucko, R. Tringham, and G. W. Dimbleby. Cambridge, Mass.: Schenkman.

———. 1984. "Alternative Archaeologies: Nationalist, Colonialist, Imperialist." *Man* New Series 19: 355–70.

Tuan, Y.-F. 1974. *Topophiliia*. Englewood Cliffs, N.J.: Prentice Hall.

Tucci, G. 1988–89. *Indo-Tibetica*. New Delhi: Aditya Prakashan. Reprint. Vol. 1 on the stupa: Vols. 3 and 4 on Tibetan architecture.

Turner, B. L. II. 1978. "Ancient Agricultural Land Use in the Central Maya Lowlands. In *Pre-Hispanic Maya Architecture*, 166–210, edited by P. D. Harrison and B. L. Turner. Albuquerque: University of New Mexico Press.

Tyler, H. A. 1964. *Pueblo Gods and Myths*. Norman: University of Oklahoma Press.

U Kan Hla. See Hla.

Ucko, P. J., R. Tringham, G. W. Dimbleby, eds. 1972. *Man, Settlement, and Urbanization*. Proceedings of the Research Seminar in Archaeology and Related Subjects. Cambridge, Mass.: Schenkman. Includes:
G. H. A. Bankes, "Settlement Patterns in the Lower Moche Valley, North Peru," 903–1008.
W. Bray, "Land-use, Settlement Patterns, and Politics in Prehispanic Middle America: A Review," 909–26.
J. D. Clark, "Mobility and Settlement Patterns in Sub-Saharan Africa: A Comparison of Late Prehistoric Hunter-Gatherers and Early Agricultural Occupation Units," 127–48.
B. A. L. Cranstone, "Environment and Choice in Dwelling and Settlement: An Ethnographical Survey," 487–503.
M. Douglas, "Symbolic Orders in the Use of Domestic Space," 513–21.
A. Forge, "Normative Factors in the Settlement Size of Neolithic Cultivation (New Guinea)," 363–76.
P. Gathercole, "The Study of Settlement Patterns in Polynesia," 50–60.
H. W. M. Hodges, "Domestic Building Materials and Ancient Settlements," 523–30. Table 1: Materials used for wall building and roofs, 524. See Appendix here.

M. G. Smith, "Complexity, Size, and Urbanization," 567–74.

P. E. L. Smith, "Land-Use, Settlement Patterns, and Subsistence Agriculture: A Demographic Perspective," 409–25.

B. Trigger, "The Determinants of Urban Growth in Pre-Industrial Societies, 98–106.

A. Whitty, "Ziimbabwe and Inyanga," 899–902.

United Nations Economic Commission for Asia and the Far East. 1961. *Study on Building Costs in Asia and the Far East*. Bangkok: United Nations Economic Commission for Asia and the Far East.

Urban, G., and M. Jansen, eds. 1983. *Dokumentation in der Archaeologie, Techniken, Methoden, Analysen. Veröffentlichungen der Seminarberichte vom 5. bis 6 December, 1981, Aachen*. Aachen, Germany: Nr. 34. Forschungsprojekt "Mohenjo-Daro."

Valcarel, "Sajsawaman redescubierto." 1934–35. *Revistsa del Museo Nacional* (Limia). Vol. 3 (1934): 3–36 and 211–33; Vol. 4 (1935) 1:1–24; 2:163–204, with plans and data from the 1934 excavations.

Vale, E. 1985. "Life in Dollop Reflects Rugged Simplicity—As It Has for Centuries." *Smithsonian* (November): 128–43.

Van Beek, G. W. 1987. "Arches and Vaults in the Ancient Near East." *Scientific American* 257 (No. 1): 96–103.

Van Bussel. See Bussel.

Vance Bibliographies 1985. *Building Estimates and Costs*. Monticello, Ill. (Feb.)

Van der Post, L. 1958. *The Lost World of the Kalahari*. New York: William W. Morrow.

Vann, L. 1987. "Tank and Canals: Irrigation Systems in Ancient Sri Lanka." In *Water for the Future: Water Resources Developments in Perspective*, 163–76, edited by W. O. Wunderlich and J. E. Prins. Rotterdam: A. A. Balkema.

Van Wyk. See Wyk.

Vatsyayan, K., ed. 1991. *Concepts of Space Ancient and Modern*. New Delhi: Abhinav Publications. Includes:

B. Bäumer, "From Guha to Akosa: The Mystical Cave in the Vedic and Siava Traditions," 105–121

L. Chandra, "Life, Space and Structures," 211–18.

M. Jansen, "The Concept of Space in Harappan City Planning—Mohenjo-Daro," 75–82.

S. Junsai, "Cave Man Space versus Boat Man Space," 185–88.

M. W. Meister, The Hindu Temple: Axis of Access." 269–280.

J. Pieper, "Arboreal Art and Architecture in India," 333–42.

R. Pradhan, "The Theater-Architecture of Nepal," 429–36.

G. Wijesuriya, "Concepts of Buddhist Metaphysics and Their Application through Physical Spaces with Special Reference to the Forest Monasteries in Sri Lanka," 231–38.

Vatuk, S., ed. 1978. *American Studies in the Anthropology of India*. New Delhi: Manohar. Includes:

M. Fentress, "Regional Interaction in Indus Valley Urbanization: The Key Factors of Resource Access and Exchange," 389–424.

Veblen, T. 1934. *The Theory of the Leisure Class*. New York: Modern Library.

Veni, G. 1990. "Maya Utilization of Karst Groundwater Resources." In *Engineering Geology of Ancient Works, Monuments and Historical Sites*, Vol. 3, 1661–66, edited by P. Marinos and G. Koukis. Rotterdam: A. A. Balkema.

Vogt, E. Z. 1971. An Appraisal of *Prehistoric Settlement Patterns in the New World*. In *Prehistoric Settlement Patterns in the New World*, 180ff., edited by G. Willey. New York: Johnson Reprint Corp. Original work published 1956.

Vogt, E. Z. and R. M. Leventhal, eds. 1983. *Prehistoric Settlement Patterns: Essays in Honor of G. R. Willey*. Albuquerque: University of New Mexico Press. Includes:

W. Bray, "Landscape with Figures: Settlement Patterns, Locational Models, and Politics in Mesoamerica," 167–93.

D. A. Freidel, "Political Systems in Lowland Yucatan: Dynamic Structure in Mayan Settlements," 375–86.

A. R. Gonzales, "Inca Settlement Patterns in a Marginal Province of the Empire: Sociocultural Implications," 337–60.

J. Marcus, "On the Nature of the Mesoamerican City," 195–242.

M. E. Moseley, "Patterns of Settlement and Preservation in the Viru and Moche Valleys," 423–42.

H. B. Nicholson, "Mesoamerican Ethnohistorical Sources and Their Relevance to Pre-Hispanic Settlement Pattern Studies," 399–412.

Sanders, W. T., and R. S. Stanley," A Tale of Three Cities: Energetics and Urbanism in Pre-Hispanic Central Mexico," 243–91.

P. Wheatley, "The Concept of Urbanism," 601–37.

Volwahsen, A. 1969. *Living Architecture: Indian*. New York: Grosset & Dunlap. von Hagen. See Hagen.

———. 1978. "Sacred Space, Architectural Tradition, and the Contemporary Designer." In *EDRA [Environmental Design Research Association]* Proceedings 8: 47–53.

Waldeck, F. [J.] 1838. *Voyage Pittoresque et Archaeologie dans la Provence D'Yucatan*. Paris: B. Dufour etc.

Waldron, A. 1990. *The Great Wall of China: From History to Myth*. New York: Cambridge University Press.

Wallace, W. 1994. *Michelangelo at San Lorenzo: The Genius as Entrepreneur*. New York: Cambridge University Press. Includes:
What Was the Cost of the Laurentian Library?

Waln, N. 1933. *The House of Exile*. Boston; Little, Brown.

Wang, J. 1988. *The Chinese Garden*. New York: Oxford University Press.

Ward, B. E. 1965. "Varieties of the Conscious Model: The Fishermen of South China." In *The Relevance of Models for Social Anthropology*, Vol. 1, 113–37, edited by M. Banton. London: Association of Anthropology Monographs.

Watanabe, Y. 1974. *Shinto Art: Ise and Izumo Shrines*, Vol. 3, R. Ricketts, trans. New York: Weatherhill/Heibonsha.

Water Problems in the Development of Beijing as a City. 1955. Bejing: Planning Department.

Waterson, R. 1990. *The Living House: An Anthropology of Architecture in Southeast Asia*. Singapore: Oxford University Press.

———. 1998. *The Architecture of South-East Asia Through Travellers' Eyes*. Kuala Lumpur, Malaysia: Oxford University Press.

Watson, F. 1975. *A Concise History of India*. New York: Charles Scribner's Sons.

Wauchope, R. 1962. *Lost Tribes and Sunken Continents: Myth and Method in the Study of American Indians*. Chicago: University of Chicago Press.

Weaver, M. P. 1993. *The Aztecs, Mayas, and Their Predecessors*. 3rd ed. San Diego: Academic Press.

Welch, A. 1979. *Calligraphy in the Arts of the Muslim World*. Austin: University of Texas Press.

Wells, C. 1952. *The Road to Shalimar*. Garden City, N.Y.: Doubleday.

Wescoat, J., and J. Wolschke-Bulmahen, eds. 1996. *Mughal Gardens: Sources, Places, Representations, and Prospects*. Washington, D.C.: Dumbarton Oaks Research Library and Collection.

Westwood, J., ed. 1987. *The Atlas of Mysterious Places: The World's Unexplained Sacred Sites, Symbols Landscapes Ancient Cities and Lost Lands*. New York: Weidenfeld & Nicholson.

Wheatley, P. 1972. "The Concept of Urbanism, In *Man, Settlement, and Urbanization*, 601–37, edited by P. J. Ucko, R. Tringham, and G. W. Dimbleby. Cambridge, Mass.: Schenkman.

Wheeler, K. 1997. "Road to Ruins." *Escape* (January): 56–63 and 100–102.

Wheeler, R. E. M. 1966. *Civilization of the Indus Valley and Beyond*. New York: McGraw Hill.

White, L. 1928. "A Comparative Study of Keresan Medicine Societies." *Proceedings of the International Congress of Americanists*, 23rd sess. New York: 1928:604–19.

———. 1942. "The Pueblo of Santa Ana, New Mexico." *American Anthropological Association*. Mervasha, Wisc.

———. 1973. *The Acoma Indians: 47th Annual Report of the Bureau of Ethnology*. Glorieta, N. Mex.: Rio Grande Press. Reprint of 1929–30 ed.

White, L. A. 1962. "Cosmology and Pueblo Life." In *The Pueblo of Sia, New Mexico*, 110–22. Washington, D.C.: U.S. Government Printing Office. American Ethnology, Bulletin 184.

Whitty, A. 1957. "The Origins of the Stone Architecture of Zimbabwe." In *Third Pan-African Congress on Prehistory*, 366–77, edited by J. Clark. London: Chatto & Windus.

———. 1972. ""Zimbabwe and Inyanga." In *Man, Settlement, and Urbanization*, 899–902, edited by P. J. Ucko, R. Tringham, and G. W. Dimbleby. Cambridge, Mass.: Schenkman.

Wijesuriya, G. 1991. "Concepts of Buddhist Metaphysics and Their Application through Physical Spaces with Special Reference to the Forest Monasteries in Sri Lanka." In *Concepts of Space Ancient and Modern*, 231–38, edited by K. Vatsyayan. New Delhi: Abhinav Publications.

Wilber, D. N. 1979. *Persian Gardens and Garden Pavilions*. Washington, D.C.: Dumbarton Oaks Research Library and Collection.

Wilder, T. 1929. *The Bridge of San Luis Rey*. New York: A. and C. Boni.

Wilford, J. N. 1980. "Maya Canals Found by Radar." *New York Times* (May 13).

———. 1993. "Place of the Gods' Slowly Yielding Its Secrets." *Daily News* (July 4).

———. 1994. "Sexes Equal on South Sea Isle." *New York Times* (March 29).

Wilkes, J., and R. Packard, eds. 1988–89. *Encyclopedia of Architecture, Design, Engineering and Construction*. Vol. 1. New York: John Wiley & Sons. Includes:
N. Alsayyad, and G. Boostani, "Mosques," 460–76.

Wilkin, G. C. 1971. "Food-Producing Systems Available to the Ancient Maya." *American Antiquity*, 36 (No. 4): 432–48.

Willey, G. R. ed. 1965. *Handbook of Middle American Indians*. Vol. 2. Austin: University of Texas Press.

Willey, G. R. 1968. "Settlement Archaeology: An Appraisal." In *Settlement Archaeology*, 208–26, edited by K. Chang. Palo Alto, Calif.: National Press Books.

———. 1971. *Prehistoric Settlement Patterns in the New World*. New York: Johnson Reprint Corp. Reprint of 1956 ed. Includes:
E. W. Haury, "Speculations on Prehistoric Settlement Patterns in the Southwest," 3–10.

E. K. Reed, "Types of Village Planning Layouts in the Southwest," 11–17.

W. T. Sanders, "The Central Mexican Symbiotic Region: A Study," 115–27.

E. Z. Vogt, "An Appraisal of *Prehistoric Settlement Patterns in the New World*," 180 ff.

Willey, G. R., and W. R. Bullard. 1965. "Prehistoric Settlement Patterns in the Maya Lowlands." *Handbook of Middle American Indians*, Vol. 2, 360–77, edited by G. R. Willey. Austin: University of Texas Press.

Williamson, M. H. 1989. "Sex Relations and Gender Relations: Understanding Kwona Conception." *Mankind* 14: 13–23.

———. 1990. "Gender and the Cosmos in Kwoma Culture." Lutkehaus et al.: 385–94.

Wilson, C. 1992. *Notes for the 1992 tour of Acoma-Laguna by the Society of Architectural Historians*. Philadelphia: Society of Architectural Historians.

Wilson, R. A. 1885. *Mexico and Its Religion*. New York: Harper & Bros.

Winter, M. 1989. *Oaxaca: The Archaeological Record*. Mexico City: Edicion. Minutiae Mexicana.

Wiredu, J. E. 1984. "How Not to Compare African Thought With Western Thought. In *African Philosophy: An Introduction*, edited by R. A. Wright. Lanham, MD: University Press of America.

Wittfogel, K. A. 1972. "The Hydraulic Approach in Pre-Spanish Mesoamerica." In *The Pre-History of the Tehuacan Valley*, Vol. 4, 59–80. Austin: University of Texas Press.

Wittfogel, K. A. 1957. *Oriental Despotism*. New Haven, Conn.: Yale University Press.

Wolf, E. R., ed. 1976. *The Valley of Mexico: Studies in Pre-Hispanic Ecology and Society*. Albuquerque: University of New Mexico Press. Includes:

E. E. Calnek, "The Internal Structure of Tenochtitlan," 287–302.

R. Millon, "Social Relations in Ancient Teotihuacan," 205–48.

World Health Organization, Community Water Supply Unit. n.d. *Community Water Supply: The Village Tank as a Source of Drinking Water*. Rome: World Health Organization.

Wright, R. A., ed. 1984. *African Philosophy: An Introduction*. Lanham, MD: University Press of America. Includes:

J. E. Wiredu, "How Not to Compare African Thought with Western Thought."

Wu, N. 1963. *Chinese and Indian Architecture*. New York: George Braziller.

Wunderlich, W. O., and J. E. Prins, eds. 1987. *Water for the Future: Water Resources Developments in Perspective. Proceedings of the International Symposium on Water for the Future, Rome, 6–11 April, 1987*. Boston: A. A. Balkema. Includes: L. Vann, "Tank and Canals: Irrigation Systems in Ancient Sri Lanka," 163–76.

Wyk, G. van. 1993. "Secret Resistance in the Murals of Sotho-Tswana Women." In *Secrecy: African Art that Conceals and Reveals*, edited by M. H. Nooter, New York: Museum for African Art. See 93–97 on Ndebele art.

The Yingxian Timber Pagoda. Illustrated booklet in Chinese with an English summary, purchased at the site in China in 1987.

Yule, H. 1858. *A Narrative of the Mission Sent by the Governor-General of India to the Court of Ave in 1855*. London: Smith, Elder.

Yule, H., ed. 1855, 2nd ed. 1876. *The Book of Marco Polo*. London: J. M. Murray.

Yusaf, Muhhamad Kamel al-Din'Ali 1977. *The Holy Qur'an*, Translation and commentary. Muslim Students' Association of the US and Canada: American Trust Publications.

Ziudema, R. T. 1964. *The Ceque System of Cuzco*. Leiden: E. J. Brill.

VISUAL AND AUDIO RESOURCES

Audio-Forum Languages, Guilford, Conn. *Native American Indian Programs: Apache, Cherokee, Chickasaw, Choctaw, Kiowa, Lakota, Lenape, Mohawk, Navajo, Ojibwe, Passamaquoddy, Salish, Tlingit*.

CD-ROMs offered by the Metropolitan Museum of Art, New York City (and other museums) include "Splendors of Imperial China."

Educational Film and Video Locator, R. R. Bowker Co, 121 Chanlon Road, New Providence, NJ 07974.

Ovation, a fine arts cable television network (since 1996), with such offerings as *Distant Echoes: Yo-Yo Ma and the Kalahari Bushmen*, a documentary of the cellist's exploration of the oldest South African music.

Program for Art on Film, 980 Madison Avenue, New York, NY 10021, offering, for instance, five films on the Hausa (in 1995–96).

Prussin, L. *Negayati*, a film on the Gabra of north Kenya, available in 16 mm and video from the Smithsonian National Museum of African Art.

Yano Electric Co. games on CD, such as "Cosmology of Kyoto," which deals with the ancient city and its myths.

⊞ Credit List

1.1 a: Photo courtesy R. Brown; b: Photo courtesy R. Arnett, from *India Unveiled* (Columbus, GA: Atman Press, 1996).
1.2 From A. Volwahsen (1969).
1.3 Photo courtesy R. Arnett, from *India Unveiled* (Columbus, GA: Atman Press, 1996).
1.4 Photo courtesy G. Weill.
1.5 From A. Volwahsen (1969).
1.6 a and b: From K. Vatsyayan (1991), reprinted by permission of the Archaeological Survey of India.
1.7 From A. Volwahsen, 1969.
1.8 Photo courtesy A. F. Kersting, by permission.
1.9 Drawings a, b, and c: From H. Yule (1858); d redrawn by C. Langford from R. T. Paine and A. Soper (1969), by permission of Penguin Books/Yale University Press.
1.10 Photo courtesy H. Davis.
1.11 Drawings a, b, and c: From H. Yule (1858).

2.1 Photo courtesy A. T. Grove.
2.2 Photo courtesy N. Macindoe.
2.3 Drawn by R. O. Sweeney (1852). Reprinted by permission of the Trustees of the British Museum.
2.4 Reprinted from Hungary Wolf (1972), by permission of Good Medicine Press.
2.5 Redrawn by C. Langford from A. Badawy (1965), by permission of the Department of Near Eastern Studies, Johns Hopkins University.
2.6 Redrawn by C. Langford from M. Isler (1989), by permission of the *Journal of the American Research Center in Egypt.*
2.7 The Victoria and Albert Museum, London, by permission.
2.8 Photo courtesy F. Sahba, construction manager of the Baha'i Project.
2.9 Reprinted from P. Pal (1985), by permission of the Los Angeles County Museum of Art.
2.10 Redrawn by C. Langford from G. Michell (1988), by permission of G. Michell.
2.11 a and b: Reprinted courtesy of N. S. Steinhardt.
2.12 Drawing by E. Glahn (1984), by permission of N. S. Steinhardt, from *Chinese Traditional Architecture* (New York: China Institute in American, 1984).

3.1 Photo©M. Livingston, by permission.
3.2 Photo courtesy D. P. Crouch.
3.3 Plans a and b: Redrawn by C. Langford by permission J. Nicolais (1971). *Architecture Urbanism.*
3.4 Redrawn by C. Langford from P. Netherly (1984), by permission of *American Archaeology* and A. A. Balkema.
3.5 Diagram, C. Ortloff (1983), by permission.
3.6 a: Redrawn by C. Langford from R. Liang, Z. Zheng, and J. Hu (1987), by permission of A. A. Balkema; b: As reprinted in J. Needham (1971), by permission of Cambridge University Press.
3.7 Redrawn by C. Langford from R. Liang et al. (1987), by permission of A. A. Balkema.
3.8 a: Photo courtesy Mrs. DeVore/Anthro Photographs; b: Reprinted by permission from N. M. England, *Music Among the Zu'l'wa-si and Related Peoples of Nambia, Botswana, and Angola* (New York: Garland Publishing, 1995), 253, fig. 37, with English translations added by R. Y. D. Tan.
3.9 Original map by A. Musil, with data added by C. D. Forde (1934), from Doughty and Raswan (cited in Forde). Redrawn by C. Langford, by permission of the American Geographic Society.
3.10 a: Photo courtesy M. E. Sigmond; b: Diagram, A. Rapoport (1969), reprinted by permission of Prentice Hall.
3.11 Photo courtesy J. Roorda.
3.12 From T. Itoh and Y. Futagawa (1963) courtesy of Harper-Collins.
3.13 From E. S. Morse (1886).
3.14 From M. G. Smith (1955), courtesy of Mrs. Smith.
3.15 From Ching, Ch'i-min (Jing Qi Min) (1985).
3.16 From B. Rudofsky (1977), by permission of Harcourt, Brace and Company.

3.17 Photo courtesy D. P. Crouch.

3.18 Photo courtesy N. F. Carver, Jr., by permission.

3.19 Photo courtesy R. Lowey-Ball, by permission.

3.20 Photo courtesy A. T. Grove, by permission.

3.21 Reproduced from D. K. Chakrabarti (1995), after R. E. M. Wheeler (1966).

3.22 Courtesy M. Jansen (1993).

3.23 Photo courtesy J. Roorda.

3.24 From W. H. Coaldrake (1990), by courtesy Weatherhill, Inc.

3.25 From M. D. Coe (1964), by permission of *Scientific American.*

3.26 a: Reproduced from A. P. Maudslay, *The True History of the Conquest of New Spain by Bernal Diaz del Castillo, One of Its Conquerors* (London: Hakluyt Socity, 1910), from a map in the Archives of Mexico City; b: Reprinted from M. D. Coe (1964), by permission of *Scientific American.*

4.1 From F. Boas (1888).

4.2 Photo courtesy G. Hirsh.

4.3 Drawings by K. Blair, from *4 Villages: Architecture in Nepal* (Los Angeles: Craft and Folk Art Museum, 1983), by permission of the publisher.

4.4 Reprinted from H. Yule (1875).

4.5 Photo courtesy B. Lipton.

4.6 Redrawn by C. Langford from S. H. Al-Azzawi (1969). By permission of Barrie/Jenkins.

4.7 Photo courtesy N. Macindoe.

4.8 Photo courtesy N. Macindoe.

4.9 Photo by F. Hurley, permission courtesy the Australian Museum in Sydney.

4.10 From P. Gibbs, Y. A. Rahman, and A. Kassim (1987).

5.1 Redrawn by C. Langford from I. Bidder (1959), adapted from Monti della Corte. By permission of Thames & Hudson.

5.2 a: Redrawn by C. Langford from I. Bidder (1959) by permission of Thames & Hudson. Adapted from Monti della Corte; b: Photo H. Stump, courtesy the Harold Stump Architectural Foundation, Berkeley, California.

5.3 a: From Raffles, *History of Java* (1817), reprinted from R. Waterson (1969); b: From Dumarçay and Smithies, *Cultural Sites of Malaysia, Singapore, and Indonesia* (New York: Oxford University Press, 1998).

5.4 a: Photo courtesy J. Kavelin. b: Photo courtesy G. Weill.

5.5 From A. Snodgrass (1985), by permission of Cornell University Institute for Southeast Asian Studies.

5.6 Photo courtesy L. Polk.

5.7 Photo courtesy L. Polk.

5.8 Reprinted from H. Engle (1964), by permission of Charles E. Tuttle Company, Publishers.

5.9 Reprinted from H. Engel (1964), by permission of Charles E. Tuttle Company, Publishers.

5.10 Photo courtesy J. Rice.

5.11 From J. Protzen (1993), by permission.

5.12 a: Drawing by E. S. Squier (1877), by permission of Harvard University Press and the Peabody Museum; b: Drawing by P. von Hagen, after a photo by E. Squier.

5.13 Photo courtesy J. Maquet.

6.1 Photo from J. Needham (1971), by permission of Cambridge University Press.

6.2 From H. Kani (1967), by permission of the New Asia Research Institute of the University of Hong Kong.

6.3 Photo copyright Georg Gerster.

6.4 Photo courtesy R. Arnett, from *India Unveiled* (Columbus, GA: Atman Press, 1996).

6.5 Photo courtesy J. Thapa.

6.6 Sketch, A. Rapoport (1969), reprinted by permission of Prentice Hall.

6.7 Photo courtesy W. Scherlis, reprinted by permission of the *New York Times.*

6.8 Redrawn by C. Langford from H. Nast (1993), by permission of *Historical Geography.*

6.9 Drawings from M. T. Sa'ad (1989), cited from Montell (1895) and Raphael (1915).

7.1 From E. S. Morse, *Japanese Homes and Their Surroundings* (New York: Dover Publications, 1961, reprint of 1886 edition).

7.2 Drawing by Diego Rivera, reprinted by permission of the Museum of Modern Art, New York.

7.3 Photo by Juan Carlo, courtesy the *Ventura* (California) *County Star.*

7.4 Map courtesy N. Gutschow (1982).

7.5 Photo copyright M. Livingston, by permission.

7.6 Photo courtesy N. Gutschow.

7.7 Photo courtesy R. Brown.

7.8 Redrawn by C. Langford courtesy F.-A. de Montequin (1982).

7.9 a and b: After Bacon (1963), from Vanished Civilizations of the Ancient World.

7.10 Redrawn by C. Langford from R. Millon (1992).

7.11 Photo courtesy L. Williams and J. Carlson.

7.12 Map by C. Langford, after maps by F. Eggan (1950), University of Chicago Press, and J. A. Tainter, courtesy the U.S. Forest Service.

7.13 Redrawn by C. Langford from L. White (1962).

7.14 Redrawn by C. Langford from a drawing by a Native American, published in C. D. Forde (1934).

7.15 Redrawn by C. Langford from D. G. Saile (1977), by permission of the *Architectural Association Quarterly.*

7.16 Photo by Edward Curtis, courtesy the Washington State Historical Society, Tacoma.

8.1 Drawings courtesy W. N. Morgan (1989), by permission of University of Texas Press.

8.2   Photo from a poster sold on Pohnpei.

8.3   Photo by B. Seitz/Art Resource, New York.

8.4   Engraving by T. Bent (1893).

8.5   Redrawn by C. Langford from A. Whitty (1957), by permission of Chatto and Windus.

8.6   Photo courtesy M. B. Matter.

8.7   Engraving from J. Kurschner, *China* (Leipzig: 1901), reprinted in J. Gernet (1981).

8.8   From G. Gasparini and L. Margolies (1980), by permission of Indiana University Press.

8.9   Photo courtesy Oxford University Press.

8.10 and 8.11 Redrawn by C. Langford, from maps in E. Squier (1877), B. C. Brundage (1967), and P. Gasparini and Margolies, 1980, collated by D. P. Crouch. By permission of University of Oklahoma Press and Indiana University Press.

8.12 From Huaman Pomo, *Nueva Cronica Buen Gobierno* (Paris, 1936), reprinted in B. C. Brundage (1967), by permission of University of Oklahoma Press.

8.13 Redrawn by C. Langford from I. Lapidus (1988), by permission of Cambridge University Press.

8.14 Plan from E. Havell (1904).

8.15 Photo courtesy J. Thapa.

8.16 Reproduced by permission of the India Office Records, British Library.

9.1   Reprinted from Gutkind (1967), by permission of Macmillan/Simon and Schuster.

9.2   Photo courtesy D. P. Crouch.

9.3   From A. Volwahsen (1969).

9.4   From N. Gutschow (1982), by permission.

9.5   From N. Steinhardt (1986): 342, by permission of the *Journal of the Society of Architectural Historians*.

9.6   From T. Masuda (1970).

9.7   Courtesy S. Nishi and K. Hozumi (1986).

9.8   From P. S. Martin, et al. (1957), by permission of University of Chicago Press.

9.9   Photo by J. Nusbaum, courtesy Denver Public Library/Western History Department.

9.10 From J. C. Berlo and R. B. Phillips (eds.), *Native North American Art* (Oxford, England: Oxford University Press, 1998).

9.11 Photo courtesy U.S. National Archives, Photo No. 77-WA-11.

9.12 Photo courtesy S. Harby.

9.13 Redrawn by C. Langford from W. E. Begley (1979), by permission of the *Art Bulletin*.

9.14 Photo courtesy S. Harby.

9.15 From T. Masuda (1970).

9.16 Photo courtesy N. F. Carver, Jr.

9.17 Photo permission of the Art Museum of the University of Michigan.

9.18 Nineteenth-century print from L. Kuch, *The Art of Japanese Gardens* (New York: Johnd Day Co., 1940).

10.1 Photo courtesy D. Bryant/Art Resource, New York.

10.2 Photo courtesy the Proctor Stafford Collection, museum purchase with funds provided by Mr. and Mrs. Allan C. Balch. By permission of the Los Angeles County Museum of Art.

10.3 Redrawn by C. Langford, from a drawing by F.-A. de Montêquin (lecture at Skidmore College, 1978), by permission.

10.4 Photo courtesy S. Harby.

10.5 Photo courtesy Oxford University Press.

10.6 a: Reconstruction view by Heizer and Graham; b: Plan by Heizer and Graham. Both from *Contributions of the University of California Archaeological Research Facility* 5 (July 1968). Reprinted by permission of the Archaeological Research Facility, University of California, Berkeley.

10.7 Reprinted from J. Marcus (1983), courtesy of University of New Mexico Press.

10.8 Photo courtesy B. Paltridge.

10.9 Photo courtesy L. Williams.

10.10 Plan from R. J. Sharer (1994), by permission of Stanford University Press.

10.11 Photo courtesy N. F. Carver, Jr.

10.12 Drawing from K. P. Emory (1934 and 1971), by permission of Bishop Museum, Honolulu.

10.13 Photo courtesy L. Polk.

10.14 Photo courtesy R. F. Gatje, by permission.

10.15 Courtesy P. Oliver (1987).

10.16 Photo courtesy J. Berry.

10.17 Drawing from H. L. Roth, *The Natives of Sarawak and British North Borneo, II* (London: Truslove and Hudson, 1896), reprinted in R. Waterson (1998).

10.18 Drawings from P. Gibbs et al. (1987).

10.19 From Vroklage (1936), reprinted in R. Waterson (1990).

10.20 Photo courtesy N. Smith.

10.21 Photo courtesy F. Haar (1989), by permission.

10.22 Photo courtesy N. F. Carver, Jr.

10.23 Redrawn by C. Langford after H. Engle's photo of the scroll (1964), by permission of Charles E. Tuttle Company, Publishers.

10.24 Drawing from P. Gibbs et al. (1987).

11.1 Drawing from W. Johnson (1995), by permission of Aramco World.

11.2 Drawing from J. Needham (1971), by permission of Cambridge University Press.

11.3 Courtesy U.S. National Archives: Record Group 77: Fortification File, Dr. 142

11.4 From S. A. Stubbs (1950), by permission of University of Oklahoma Press.

11.5 a: Photo courtesy J. H. Stubbs; b: View by L. Delaporte (1880).

11.6 Photo courtesy G. Weill.

11.7 Plan courtesy J. Dumarçay, *The Site of Angkor* (Oxford, England: Oxford University Press, 1998).

11.8 From Edmund N. Bacon (1969), by permission of Penguin Books.

11.9 Photo courtesy R. Krupp, Griffith Observatory, Los Angeles.

11.10 Redrawn by C. Langford from J. Needham (1971), by permission of Cambridge University Press.

11.11 Redrawn by C. Langford after maps of R. Millon (1967 and 1973), S. Tobriner (1978), and Barba et al. (1990), compiled by D. P. Crouch, by permission.

11.12 Photo courtesy Carlos Blanco.

12.1 Redrawn by C. Langford from L. Vann (1987), by permission of A. A. Balkema.

12.2 Drawing from J. Needham (1971), by permission of Cambridge University Press.

12.3 a: Drawings by Gonzales; b: Drawings by Linkens. Kindly supplied by L. Vaunn, by permission of A. A. Balkema.

12.4 a: Photo courtesy S. Goldenberg; b: Photo courtesy D. Hisar.

12.5 Redrawn by C. Langford and adapted by D. P. Crouch from M. S. Slusser (1982), by permission of Princeton University Press.

12.6 a: Engraving made for G. le Bon (1885); b: From E. Sekler (1980), by permission.

13.1 Photo courtesy J. Wang.

13.2 The Victoria and Albert Museum, London, by permission.

13.3 From W. M. Thackston (1994). Photo by permission of the Courtauld Institute of Art of the University of London.

13.4 From the manuscript, Diwan of Amir Hassan Dihlawi, accession no. W650 f. 187, by permission of the Walters Art Gallery, Baltimore.

13.5 From A. Gaur (1994). Photos by permission of the British Library, Oriental and India Office Collections.

13.6 Photos courtesy A. Elliott, from The Ndebele (Capetown, South Africa: Struik Publishers Ltd., 1995), by permission of Mrs. Elliott.

13.7 Photo courtesy N. Macindoe.

14.1 Photo courtesy N. F. Carver, Jr.

14.2 Photo courtesy J. Wang.

14.3 Drawn by C. Langford from maps by W. A. Minge (1976), R. L. Knowles (1974), and M. W. Stirling (1942), compiled by D. P. Crouch, by permission.

14.4 Redrawn by C. Langford from R. L. Knowles (1974), by permission.

14.5 Photo courtesy A. C. Vroman, University Print Collection, UCR/California Museum of Photography, University of California at Riverside.

14.6 Reprinted from an engraving from a painting by Titian Ramsey (Peale) in E. James (1820), courtesy the New York Public Library.

14.7 Reprinted from Hungry Wolf (1972), by permission of Good Medicine Press.

14.8 From E. C. Danien and R. J. Sharer (1992), Tikal project, the University Museum, University of Pennsylvania, by permission.

14.9 Photo courtesy Tikal Project, the University Museum, University of Pennsylvania.

15.1 From A. I. T. Chang (1956), by permission of Princeton University Press.

15.2 Redrawn by C. Langford from S. Blier (1987), by permission of Cambridge University Press.

15.3 From C. Nebel (1829–34), courtesy Special Collections, University of California, Los Angeles.

16.1 Photo courtesy J. Rice.

16.2 Photo courtesy J. Thapa.

16.3 Redrawn by C. Langford after H. de al Croix and R. Tansey, Gardner's Art through the Ages, 8th ed. (New York: Harcourt Brace Jovanovich, 1986), by permission of Harcourt Brace Jovanovich.

16.4 Photo courtesy Oxford University Press.

16.5 and 16.6 Photos courtesy N. F. Carver, Jr.

16.7 Reprinted from Gutkind (1967), by permission of Macmillan/Simon and Schuster.

16.8 Drawing from D. Angulo, Historia del Arte Hispano-Americana, I. Barcelona (1945), reprinted by permission.

16.9 The Archivo General de Indias, Sevilla, Spain, reprinted by permission.

16.10 a: From E. F. Sekel (1964), by permission of Methuen; b: From A. Snodgrass (1985), by permission of Cornell University Institute for Southeast Asian Studies.

16.11 From N. S. Steinhardt (1984), by permission.

16.12 Photo courtesy the University Museum, University of Oregon.

16.13 Photo courtesy D. P. Crouch.

16.14 and 16.15 Photos courtesy the Aga Khan Program for Islamic Architecture at Harvard University and the Massachusetts Institute of Technology, by permission.

16.16 The Aga Khan Visual Archives, MIT/Walter Denny (1984), by permission.

17.1 Courtesy S. Nishi and K. Hozumi (1985).

17.2 Architecture student's model of Inner Shrine (Naiku), Rensselaer Polytechnic Institute, collection D. P. Crouch.

17.3 Photo courtesy N. F. Carver, Jr.

17.4 Adapted and simplified from R. Bon (1986 and 1992).

17.5 From Sharer (1994), by permission of Stanford University Press.

17.6 From E. Abrams (1994), by permission of University of Texas Press.

⊞ Index